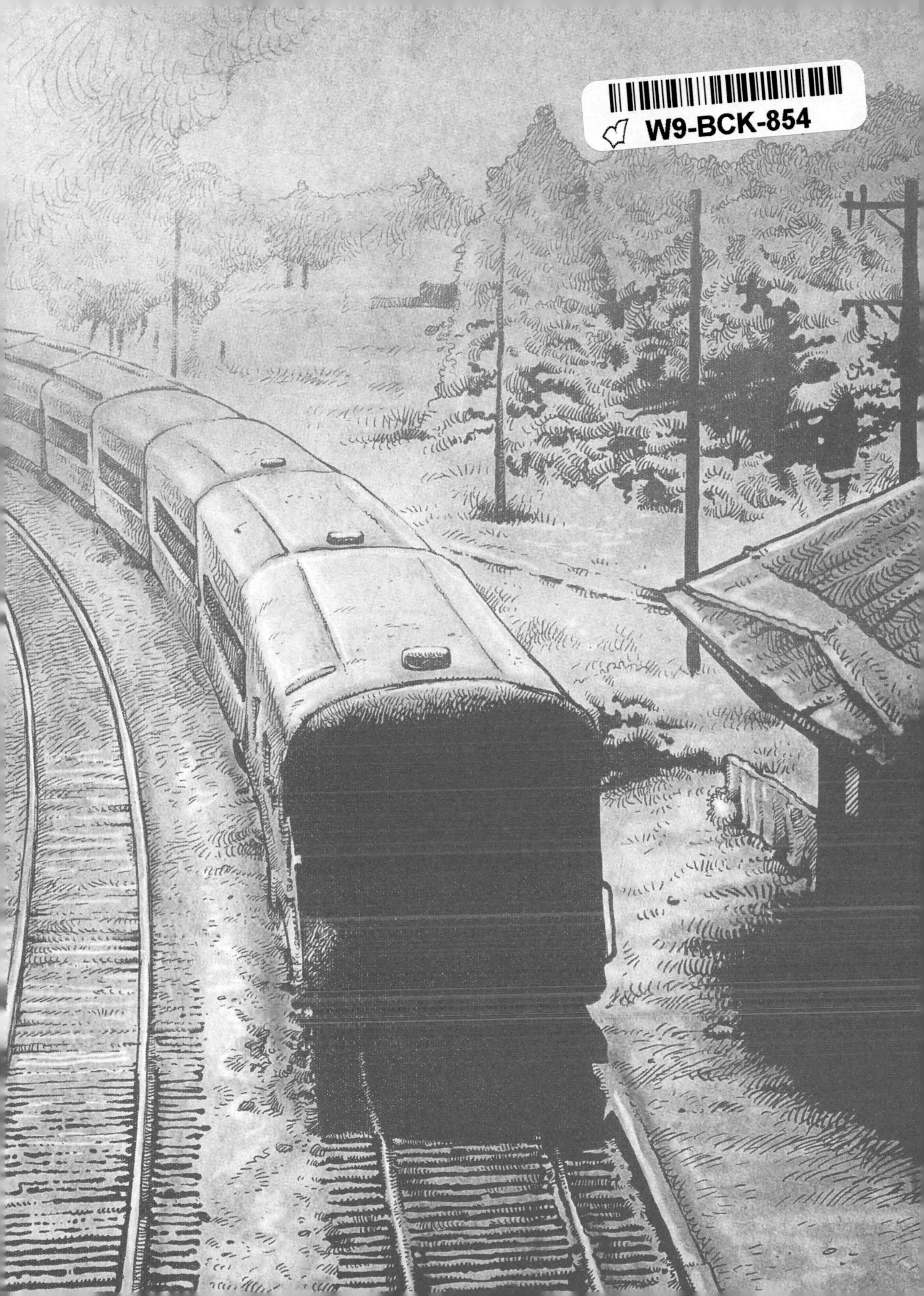

A REVOLUTIONARY LIFE

DISCARDED

Jon Lee Anderson and José Hernández

Translated by Megan McDowell

PENGUIN PRESS

NEW YORK

2018

PENGUIN PRESS

An imprint of Penguin Random House LLC
375 Hudson Street
New York, New York 10014
penguinrandomhouse.com

Originally published in Spanish as *Che: Una vida revolucionaria*
by Sexto Piso, Mexico City, 2016.

Adapted from *Che Guevara: A Revolutionary Life* by Jon Lee Anderson (Grove Press, 1997).

ISBN: 9780735221772 (hardcover)

Printed in China
1 3 5 7 9 10 8 6 4 2

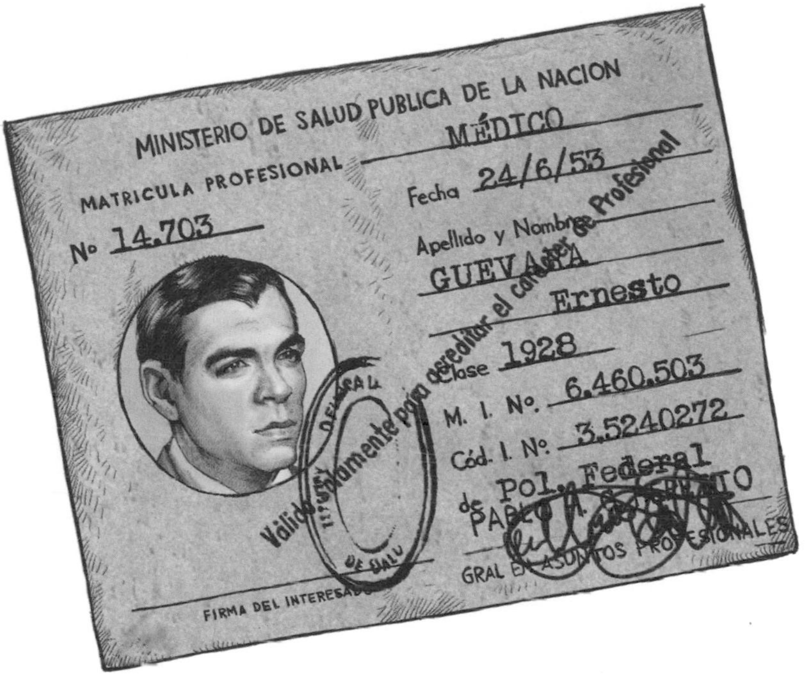

MINISTERIO DE SALUD PUBLICA DE LA NACION
MATRICULA PROFESIONAL
MÉDICO
Fecha 24/6/53
Nº 14.703
Apellido y Nombre
GUEVARA
Ernesto
Clase 1928
M. I. Nº. 6.460.503
Cód. I. Nº. 3.5240272
de Pol. Federal
Válido solamente para acreditar el carácter de Profesional
GRAL EN ASUNTOS PROFESIONALES
FIRMA DEL INTERESADO

INTRODUCTION

Jon Lee Anderson

The figure of Che Guevara is unmatched in the modern world. Since his death in 1967 at the age of thirty-nine, the Argentine revolutionary's posthumous legacy around the world has acquired a status that is at once crassly commercial and authentically mythological.

More than any other contemporary cult figure, more than Elvis, Messi, or Lady Gaga, more than Mao or any of Warhol's other pop portraits, the image of Che—especially his implacable face as depicted by Korda—has become the most recognized human image in the world. Che's face appears on bumper stickers on Pakistani buses, tattooed on the bodies of Mike Tyson and Diego Maradona, on canned energy drinks in Austria—"Che: The Energy of Freedom"—and he is venerated as Saint Che's face of La Higuera in the Bolivian village where he was assassinated. One English academic has dedicated years to amassing an endless collection of pictorial interpretations of Che as the reincarnation of Christ. For many, the image of his half-naked cadaver stretched out in the laundry room of the Nuestro Señor de Malta Hospital in Vallegrande, Bolivia, evoked Christ in his final agony. There are also documentaries, songs, poetry books, and plays inspired by Che, as well as feature films, novels, and biographies—including the one I wrote.

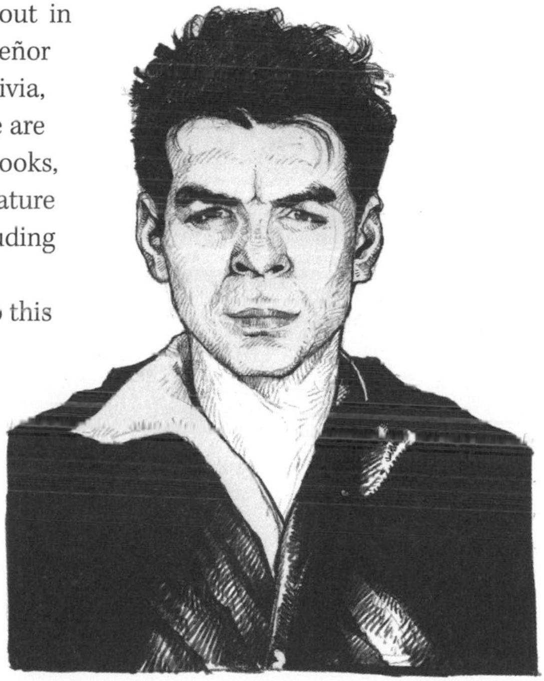

Of course, there is another side to this adoration. One Cuban-born man living in exile in Miami has tasked himself with undermining what he sees as Che's undeserved positive image, denouncing him as a sadistic murderer, even a psychopath, and he spends a great deal of his time on social

media attacking celebrities seen wearing Che T-shirts. Another Cuban exile, the ex-CIA agent Félix Rodríguez—who ordered Che's execution—has his own fixation on the man whose death made him famous. Among his claims is that when Che died, he transferred to Rodríguez the asthma that had afflicted him throughout his life: Rodríguez claims to still suffer from it today.

Some years ago, Che's diverse legacy piqued my curiosity and inspired me to write about him. I was interested in understanding who this man truly was beyond the iconography and the polemics. That was, more or less, the guiding idea of my investigation, and in my biography I tried above all to convey an impartial idea of who Che had really been in life.

To be sure, the reputations of public figures do not remain the same forever. New generations go back over the legacies of historic personalities and judge them with fresh eyes. During the nineties, when my biography first appeared, it didn't seem especially noteworthy to readers that Che had served as the fledgling Cuban revolution's supreme prosecutor, presiding over the summary convictions and executions by firing squad of more than three hundred war criminals of the ancien régime—murderers and torturers, mostly. Two decades on, however, this facet of Che provokes unease in young readers who seem surprised to discover that Che was a flesh-and-blood revolutionary, and that, ergo, he killed people. Similar concerns exist about Che's supposed homophobia; this worry is characteristic of a generation whose political and social perceptions have been formed in an age in which questions of personal identity have taken precedence over traditional forms of ideological commitment. As the eternalized paragon of youthful rebellion that he is, perhaps it is necessary, after all, to reevaluate Che Guevara through the prism of each new generation. This presents a challenge and poses a question: How do we explain Che to youngsters who, unlike those of us who lived through the sixties and seventies, can't imagine picking up a gun to fight for their ideals? For a generation more used to expressing resistance with a click on their iPhones than taking to the streets, the life of Che Guevara—a well-born young man from Argentina who studied medicine but then took up arms to change a world he considered unjust—can be unexpectedly revelatory. It is my feeling that the key lies in telling Che's story in such a way that may provoke disquiet but also, perhaps, some reflection. This book, a collaboration with the Mexican graphic artist José Hernández, is an attempt to achieve that. I hope we have succeeded.

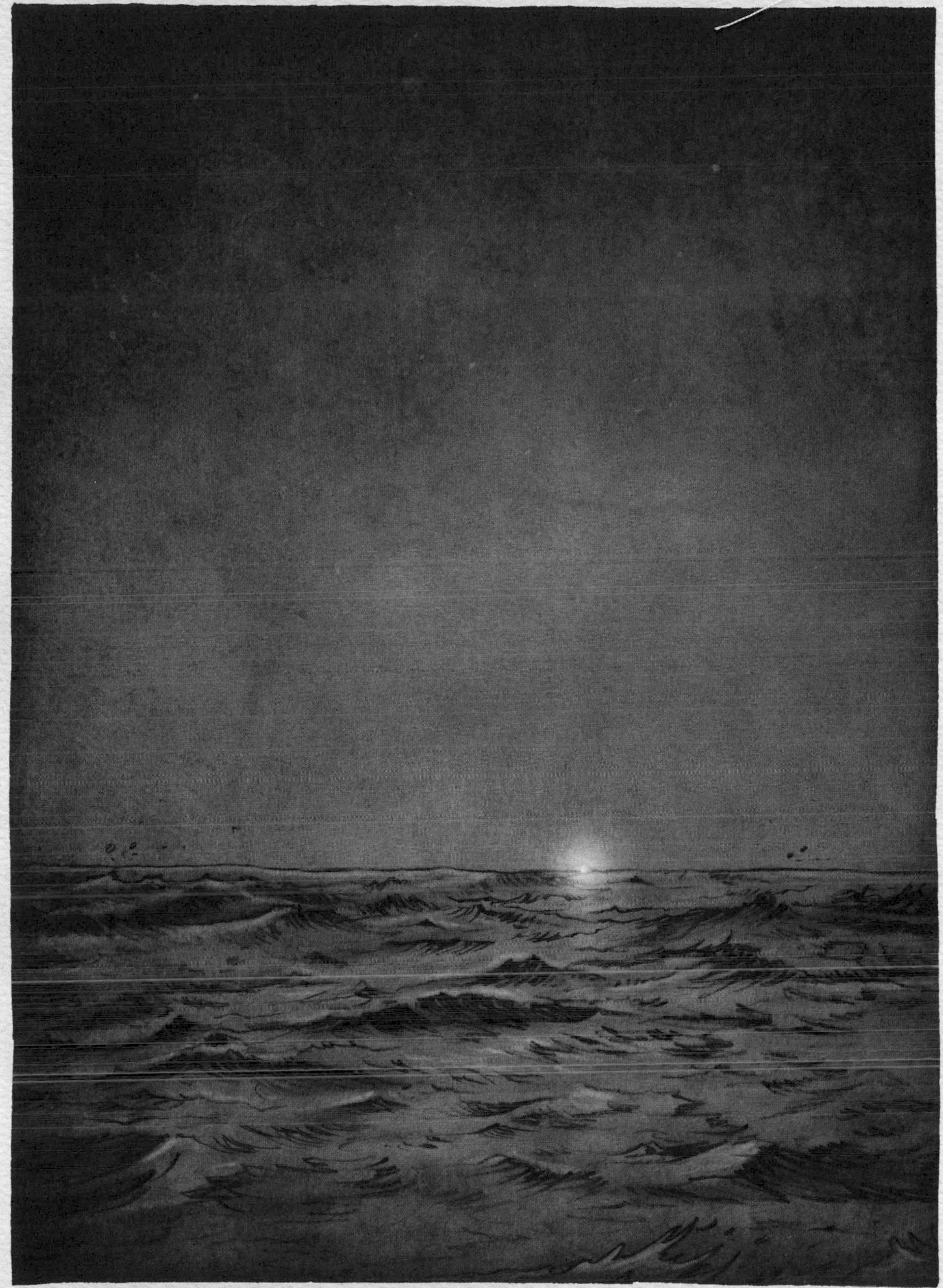

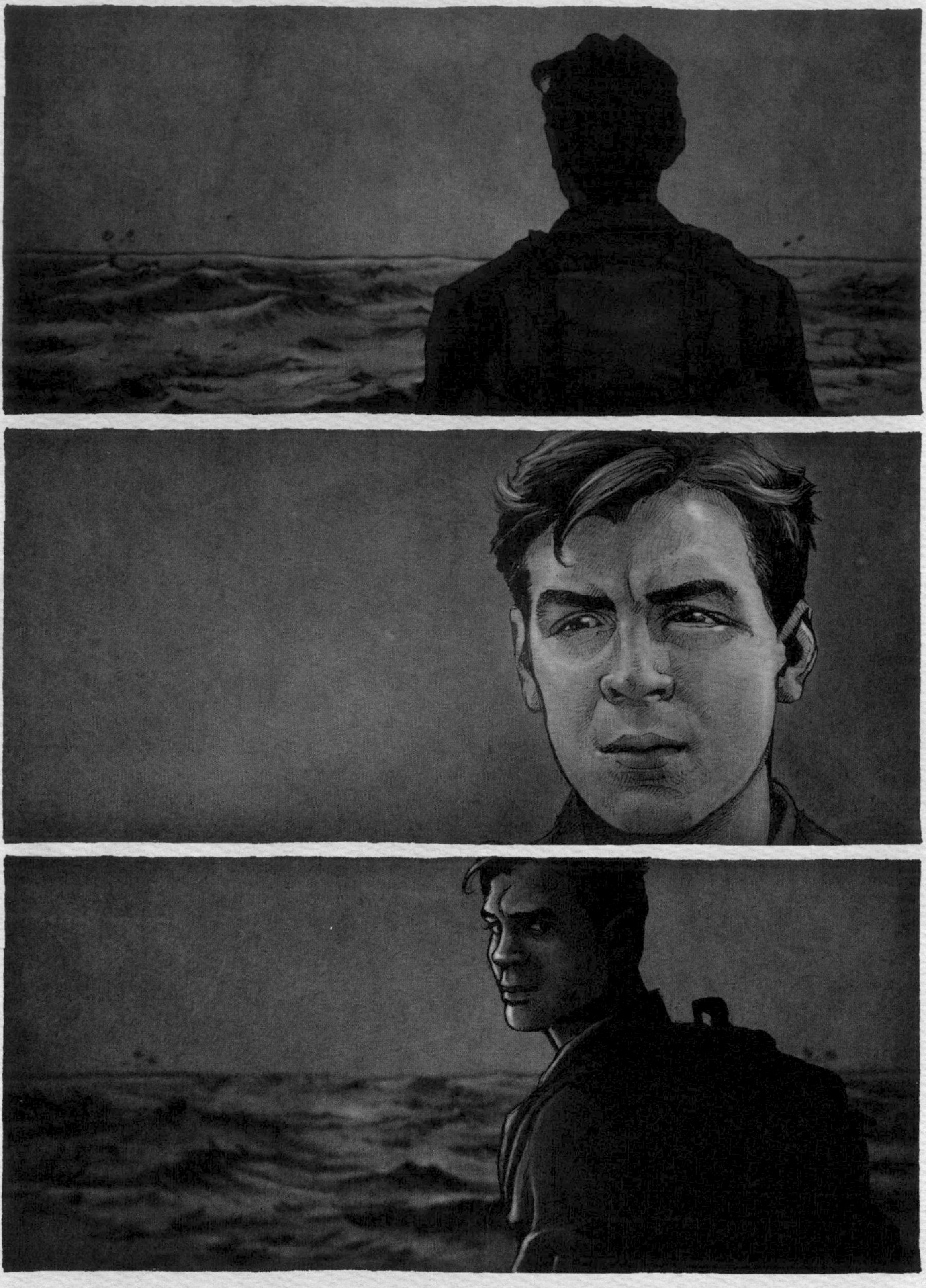

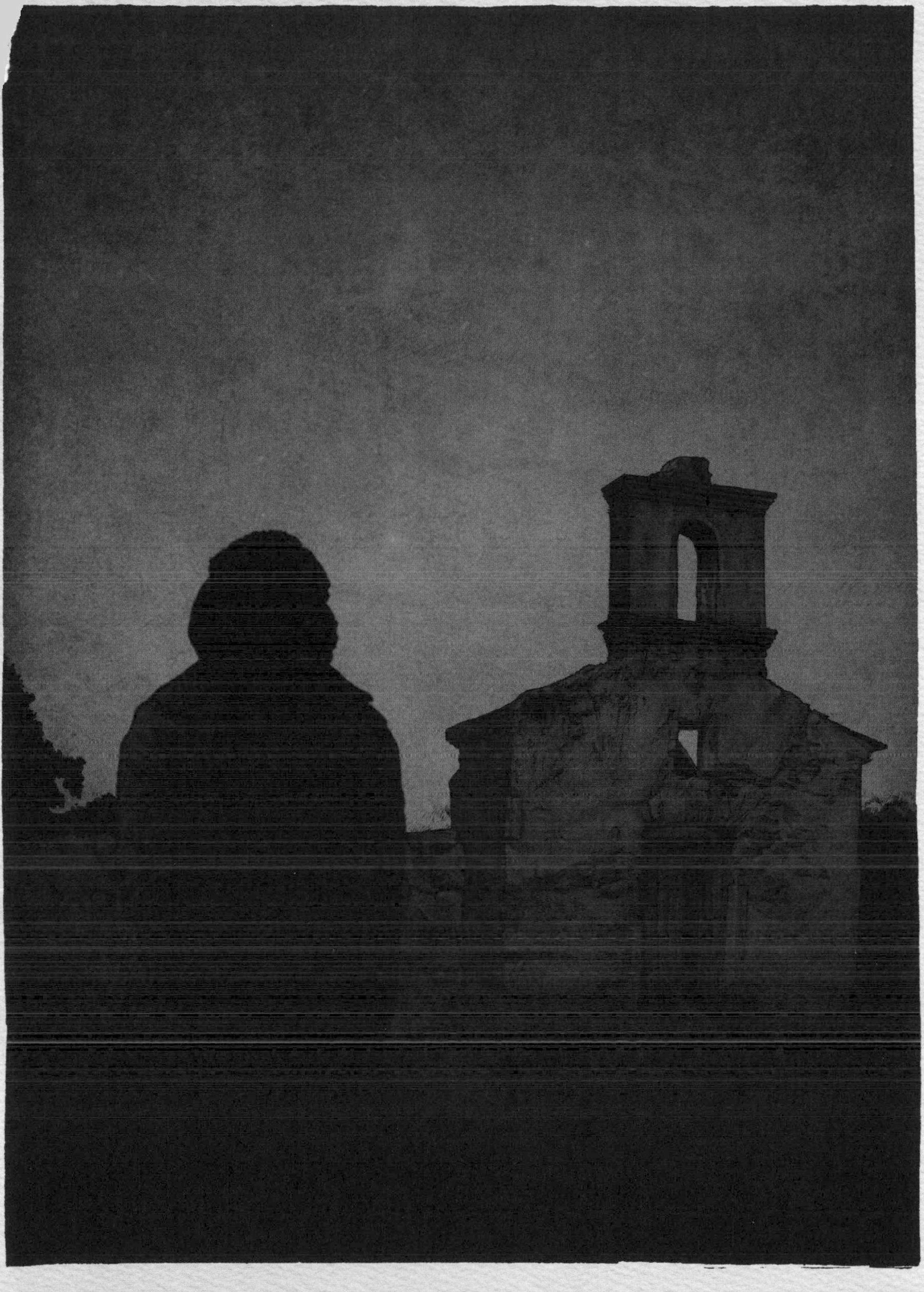

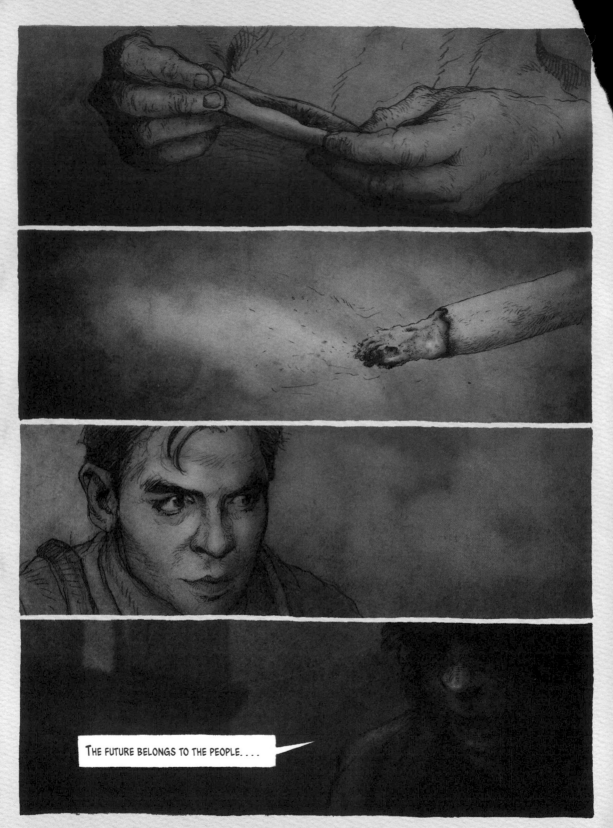

THE FUTURE BELONGS TO THE PEOPLE. . . .

4

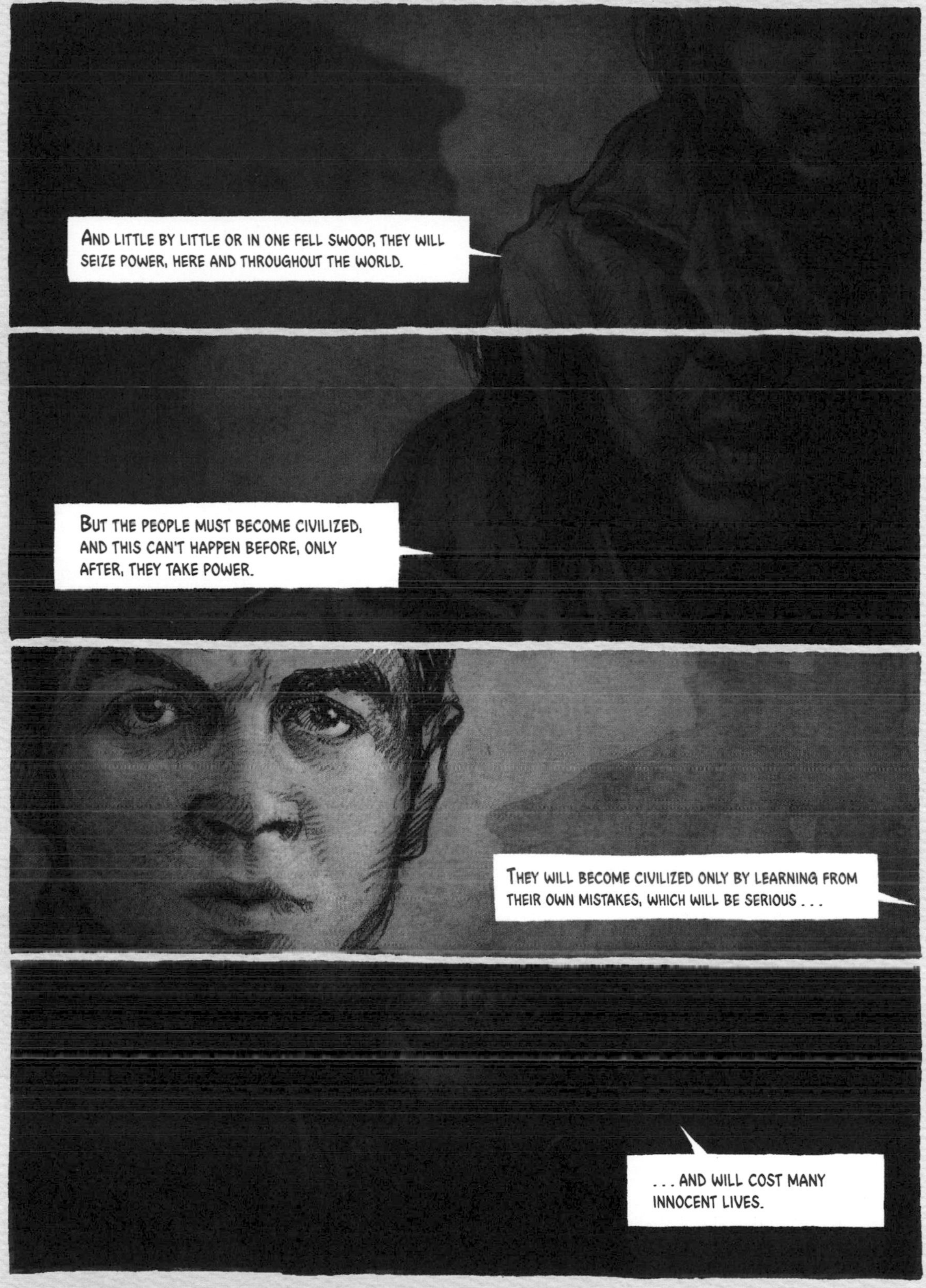
AND LITTLE BY LITTLE OR IN ONE FELL SWOOP, THEY WILL SEIZE POWER, HERE AND THROUGHOUT THE WORLD.
BUT THE PEOPLE MUST BECOME CIVILIZED, AND THIS CAN'T HAPPEN BEFORE, ONLY AFTER, THEY TAKE POWER.
THEY WILL BECOME CIVILIZED ONLY BY LEARNING FROM THEIR OWN MISTAKES, WHICH WILL BE SERIOUS . . .
. . . AND WILL COST MANY INNOCENT LIVES.

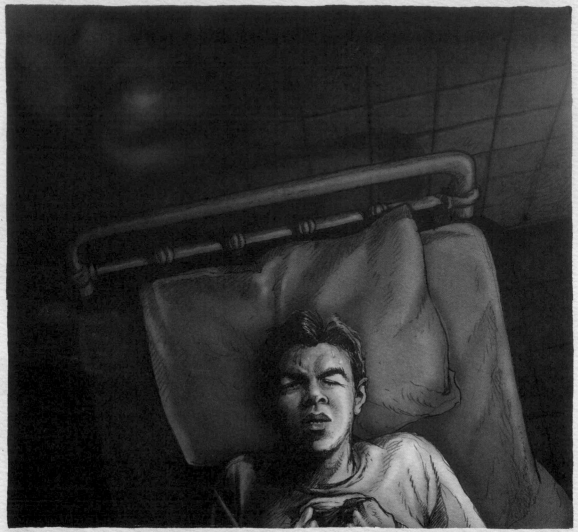

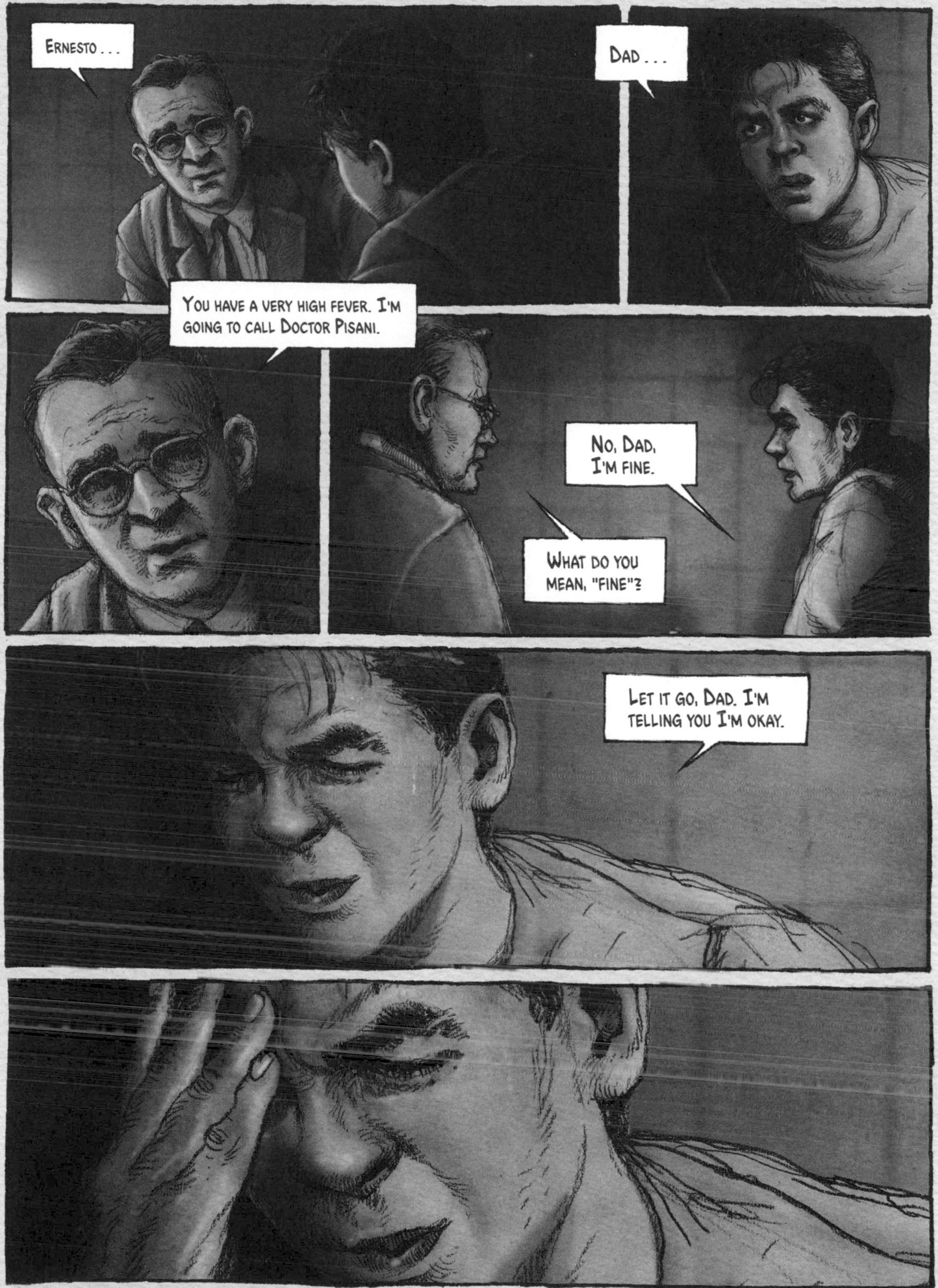
ERNESTO . . .
DAD . . .
YOU HAVE A VERY HIGH FEVER. I'M GOING TO CALL DOCTOR PISANI.
NO, DAD, I'M FINE.
WHAT DO YOU MEAN, "FINE"?
LET IT GO, DAD. I'M TELLING YOU I'M OKAY.

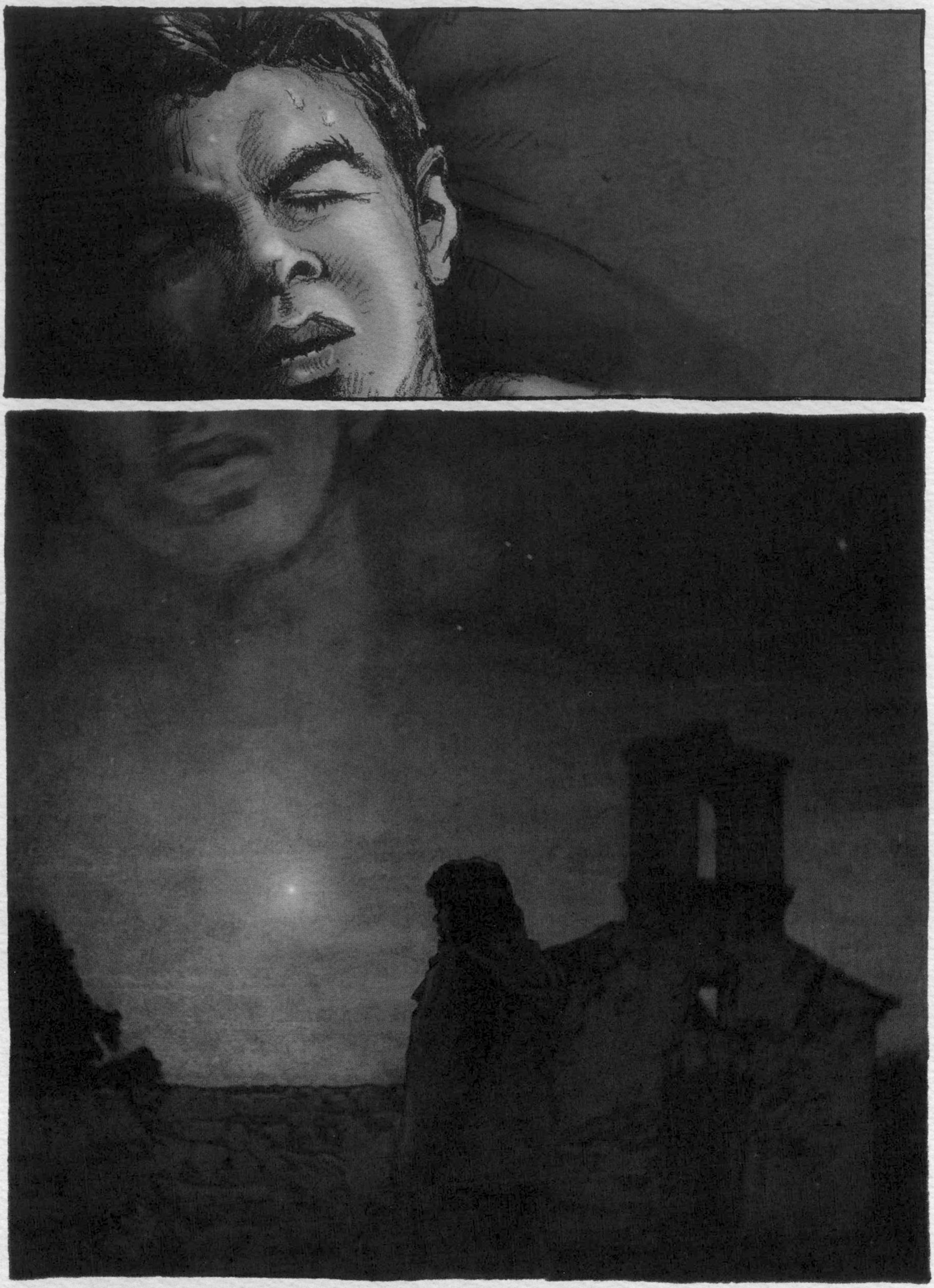

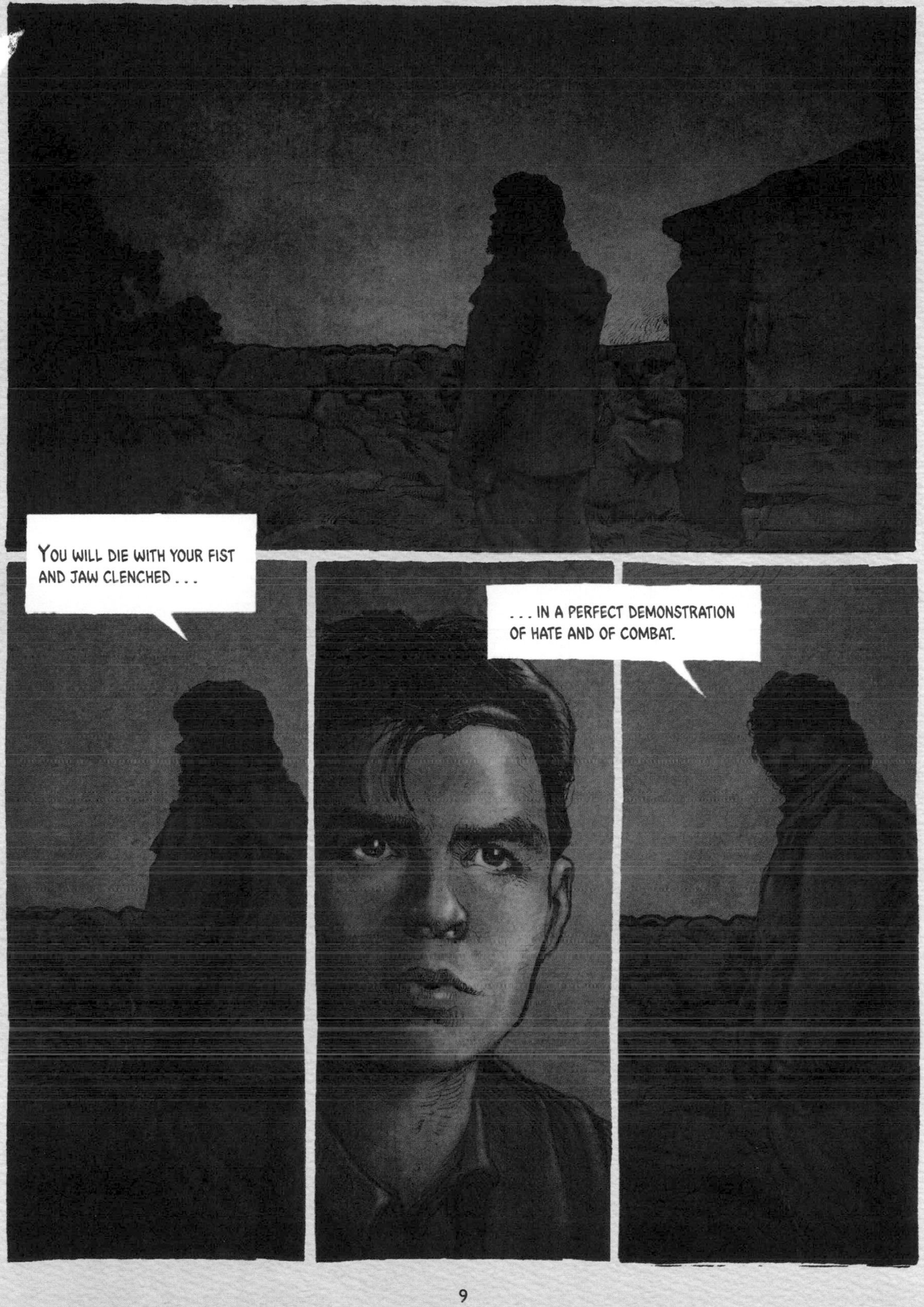
YOU WILL DIE WITH YOUR FIST AND JAW CLENCHED . . .
. . . IN A PERFECT DEMONSTRATION OF HATE AND OF COMBAT.

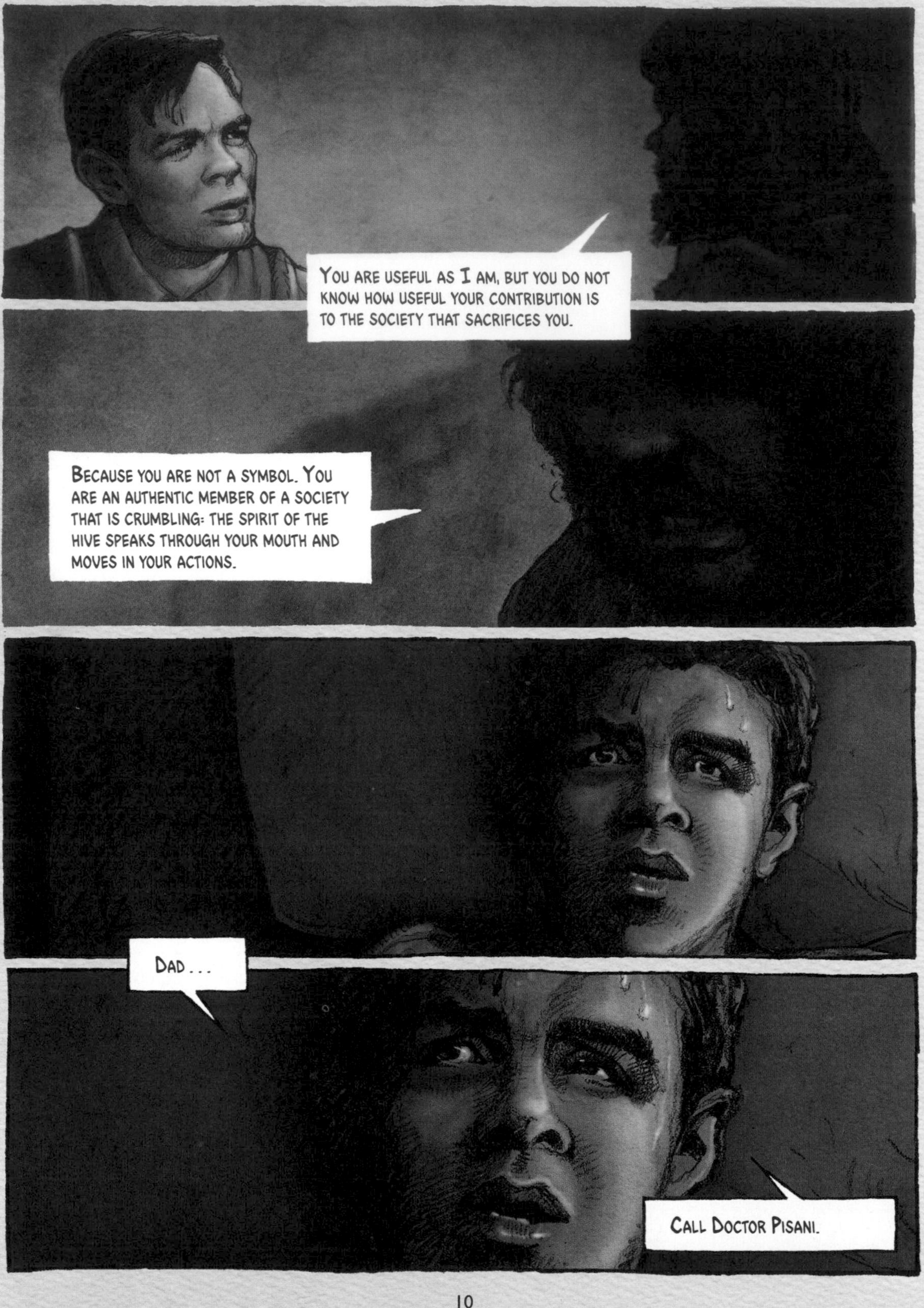
You are useful as I am, but you do not know how useful your contribution is to the society that sacrifices you.
Because you are not a symbol. You are an authentic member of a society that is crumbling: the spirit of the hive speaks through your mouth and moves in your actions.
Dad . . .
Call Doctor Pisani.

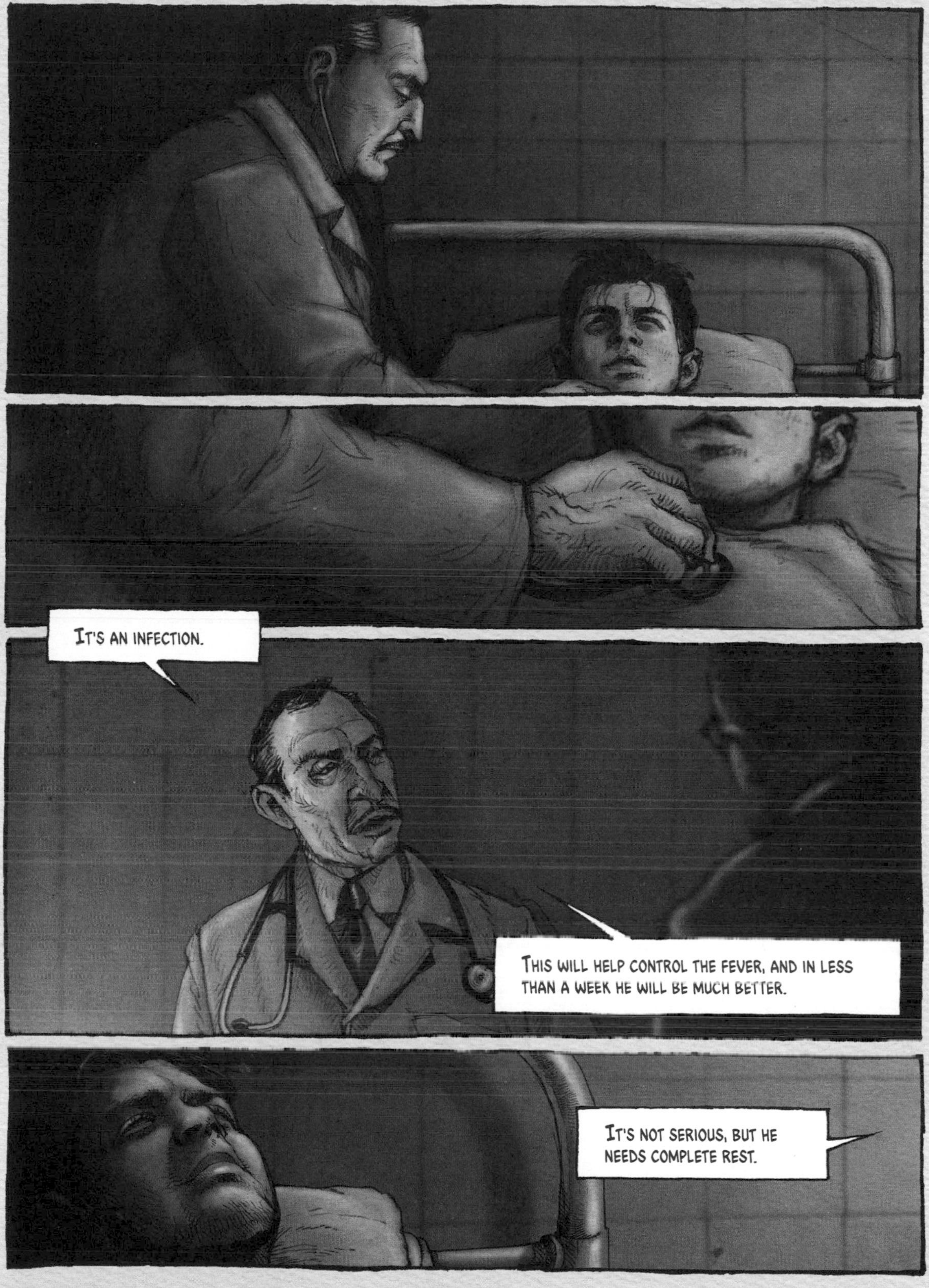
It's an infection.
This will help control the fever, and in less than a week he will be much better.
It's not serious, but he needs complete rest.

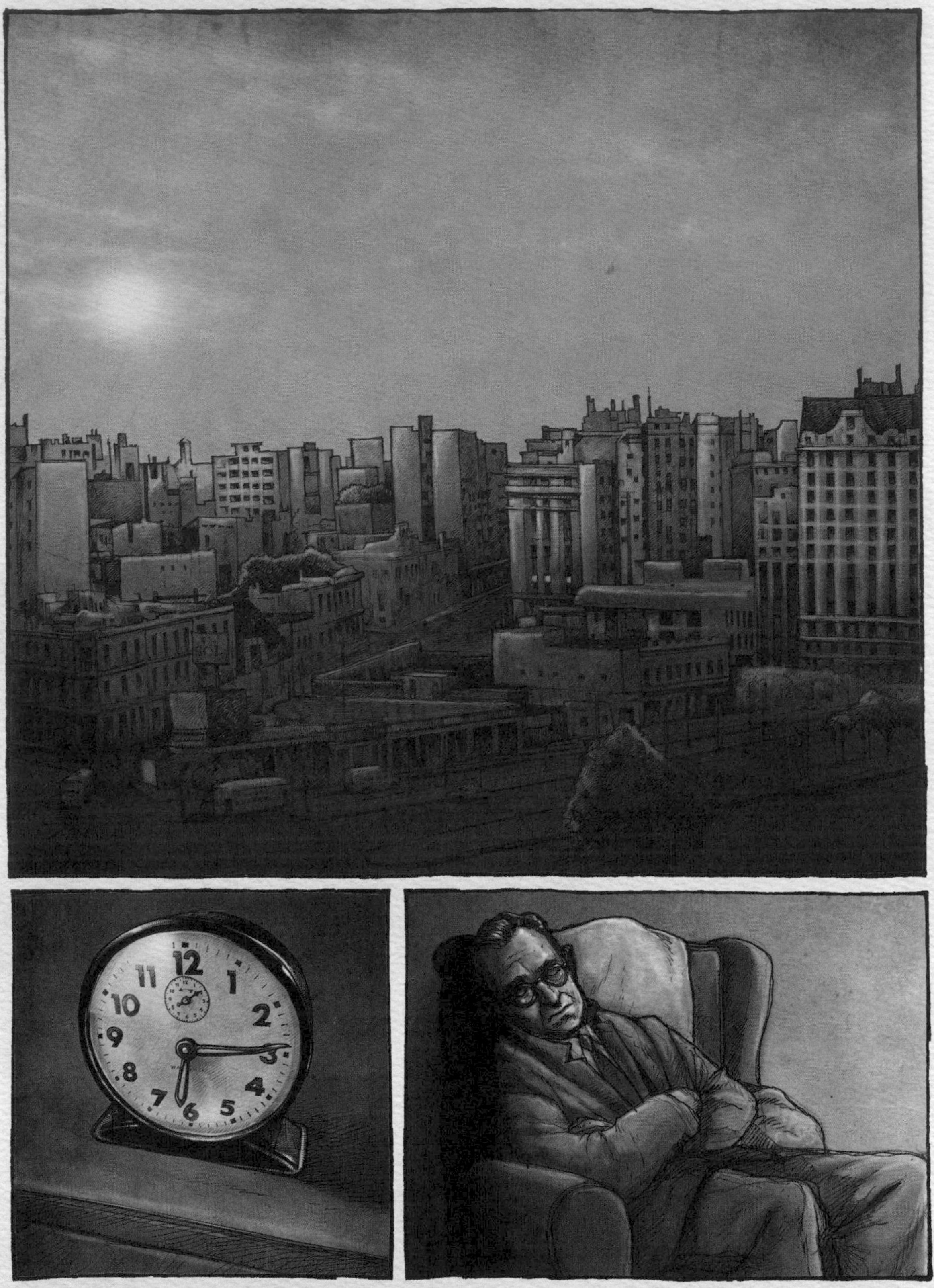

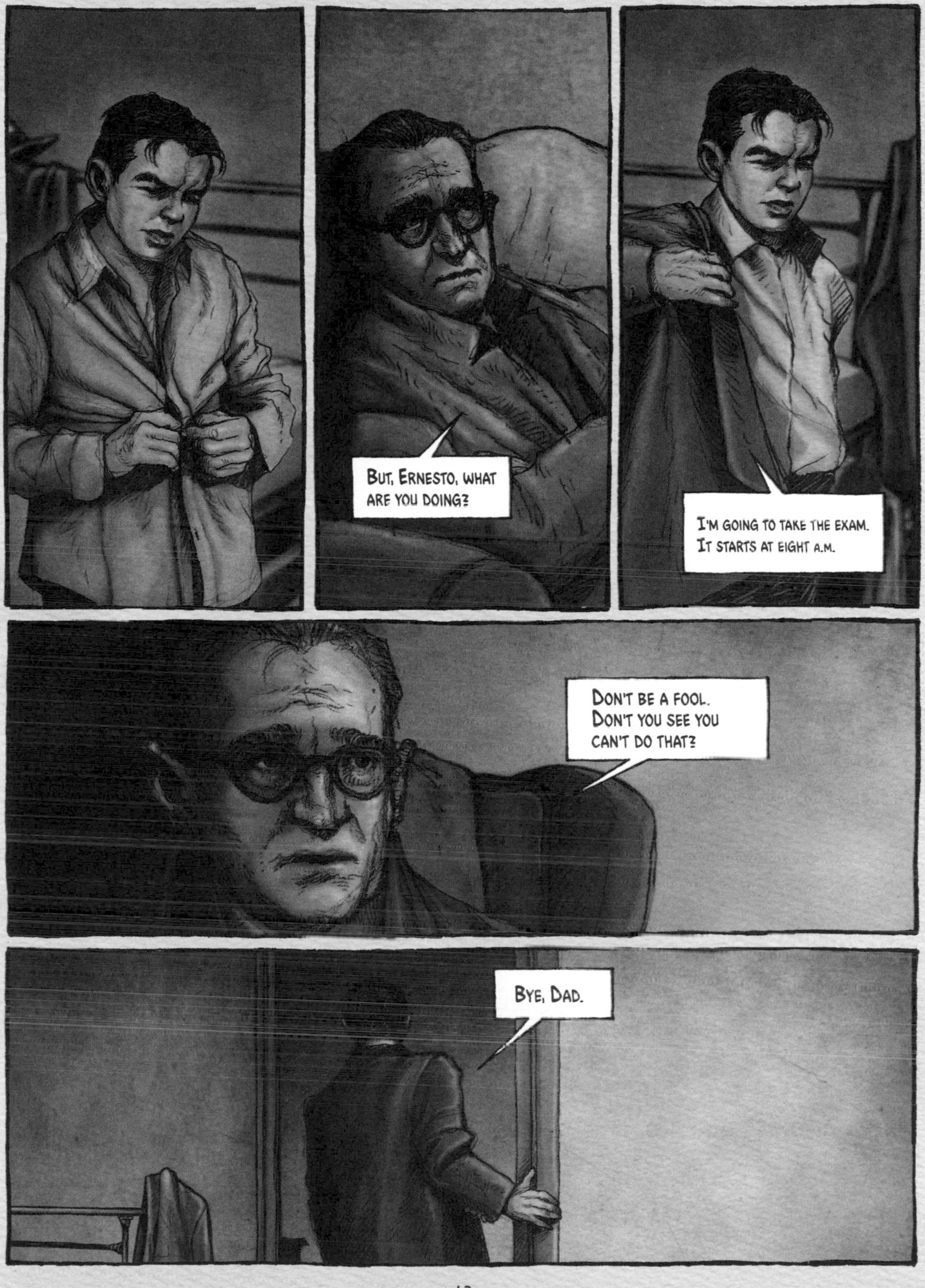
But, Ernesto, what are you doing?
I'm going to take the exam. It starts at eight a.m.
Don't be a fool. Don't you see you can't do that?
Bye, Dad.

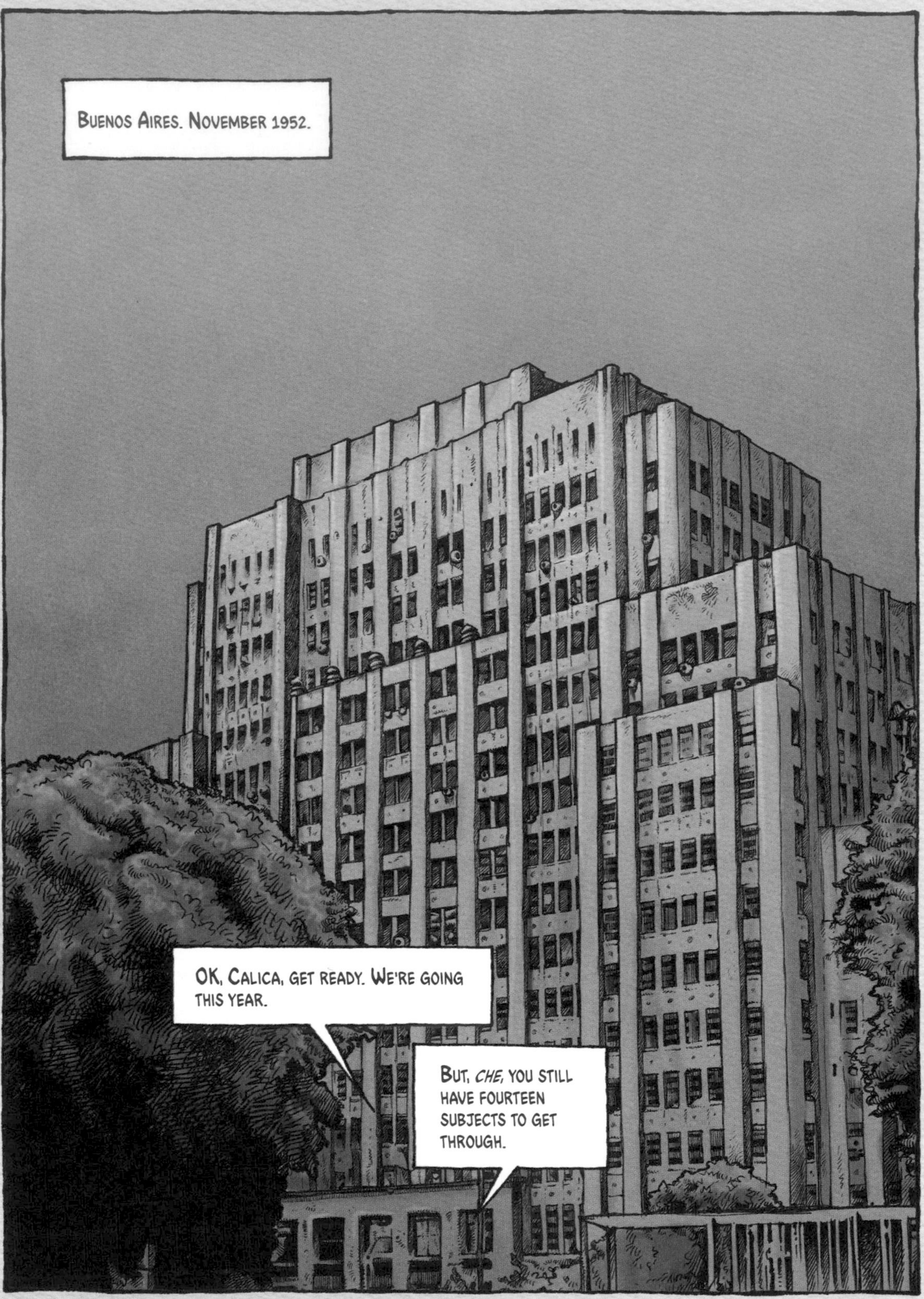
BUENOS AIRES. NOVEMBER 1952.
OK, CALICA, GET READY. WE'RE GOING THIS YEAR.
BUT, *CHE*, YOU STILL HAVE FOURTEEN SUBJECTS TO GET THROUGH.

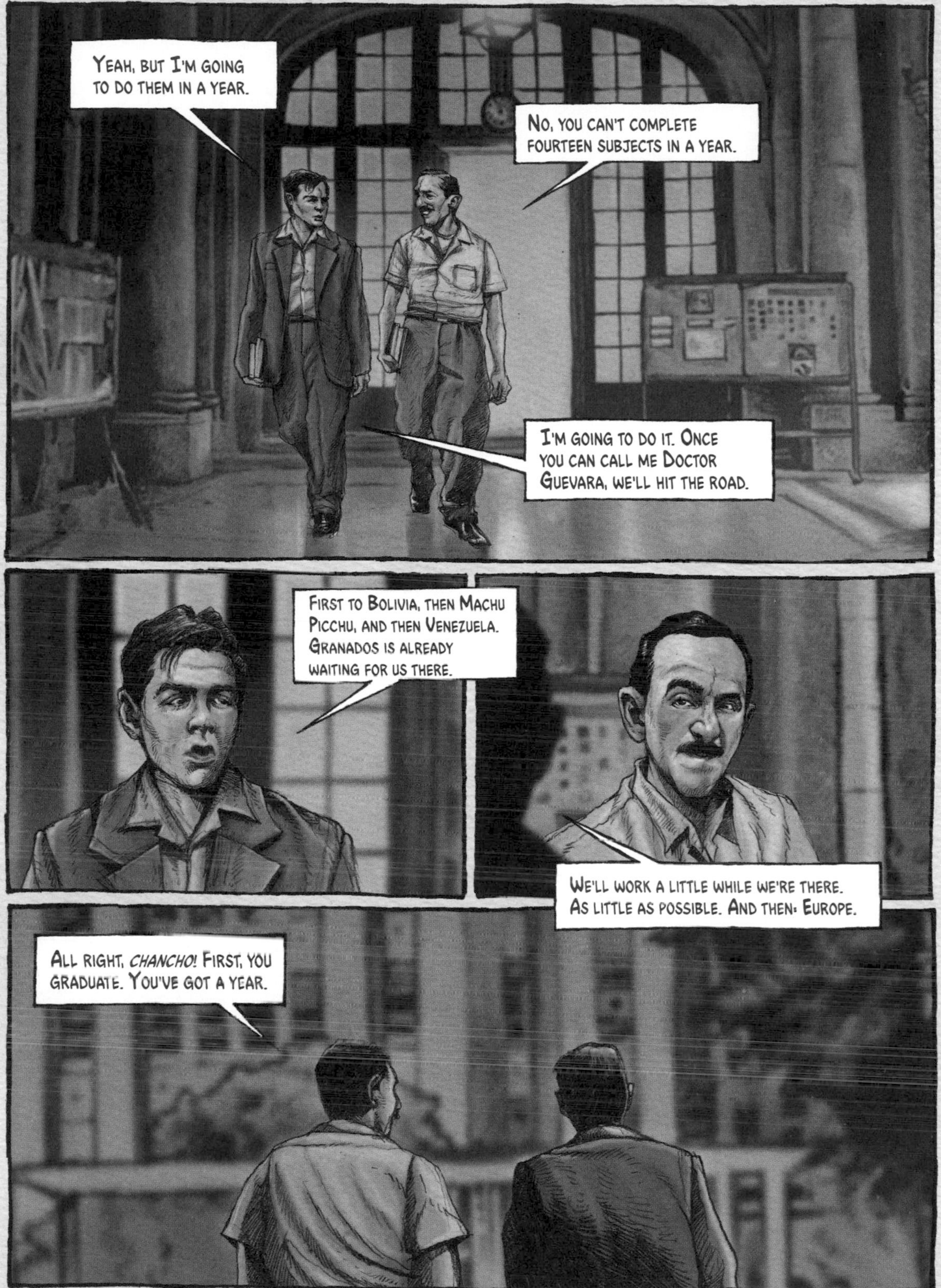
YEAH, BUT I'M GOING TO DO THEM IN A YEAR.
NO, YOU CAN'T COMPLETE FOURTEEN SUBJECTS IN A YEAR.
I'M GOING TO DO IT. ONCE YOU CAN CALL ME DOCTOR GUEVARA, WE'LL HIT THE ROAD.
FIRST TO BOLIVIA, THEN MACHU PICCHU, AND THEN VENEZUELA. GRANADOS IS ALREADY WAITING FOR US THERE.
WE'LL WORK A LITTLE WHILE WE'RE THERE. AS LITTLE AS POSSIBLE. AND THEN: EUROPE.
ALL RIGHT, *CHANCHO*! FIRST, YOU GRADUATE. YOU'VE GOT A YEAR.

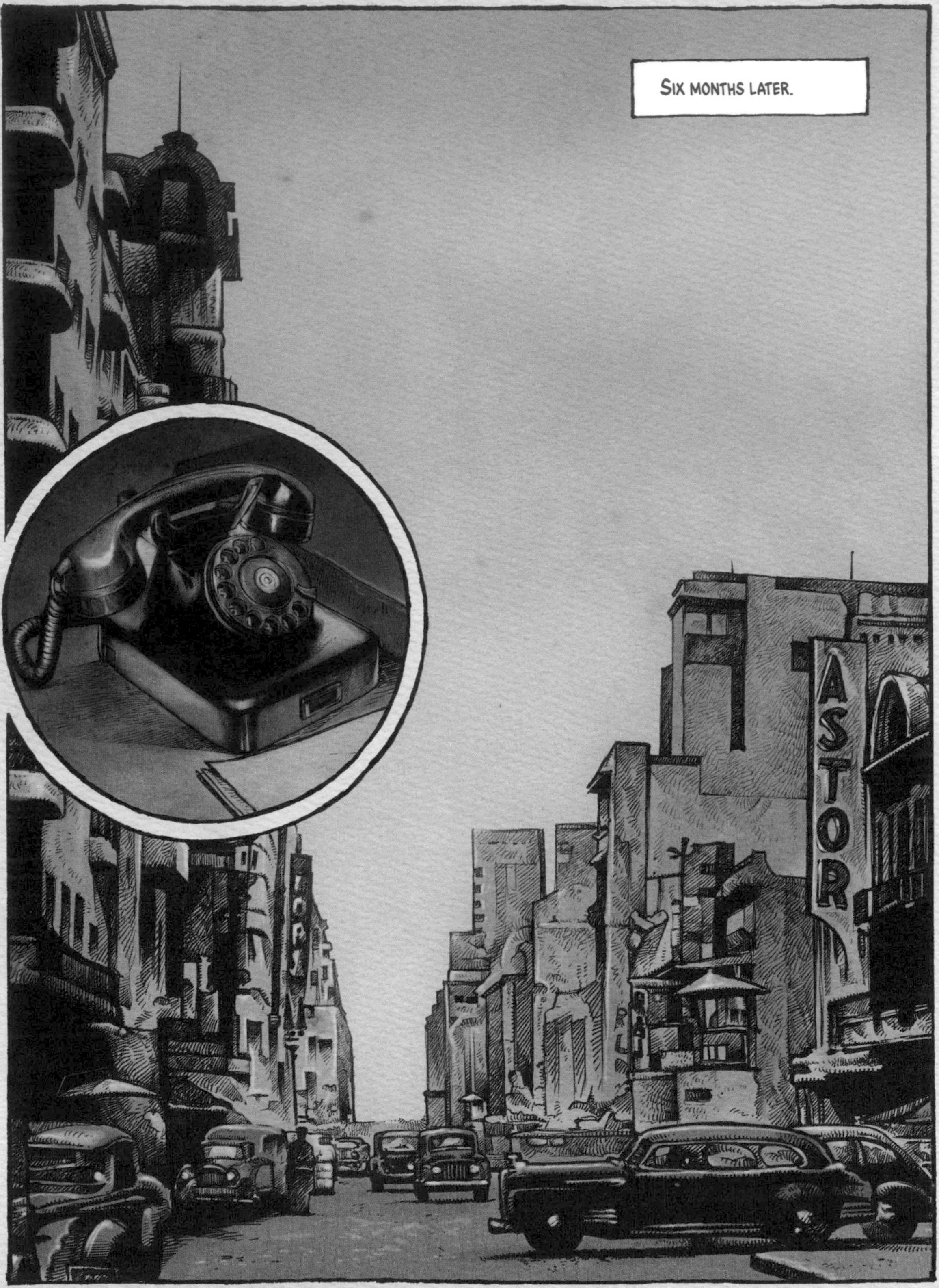
SIX MONTHS LATER.
ASTOR

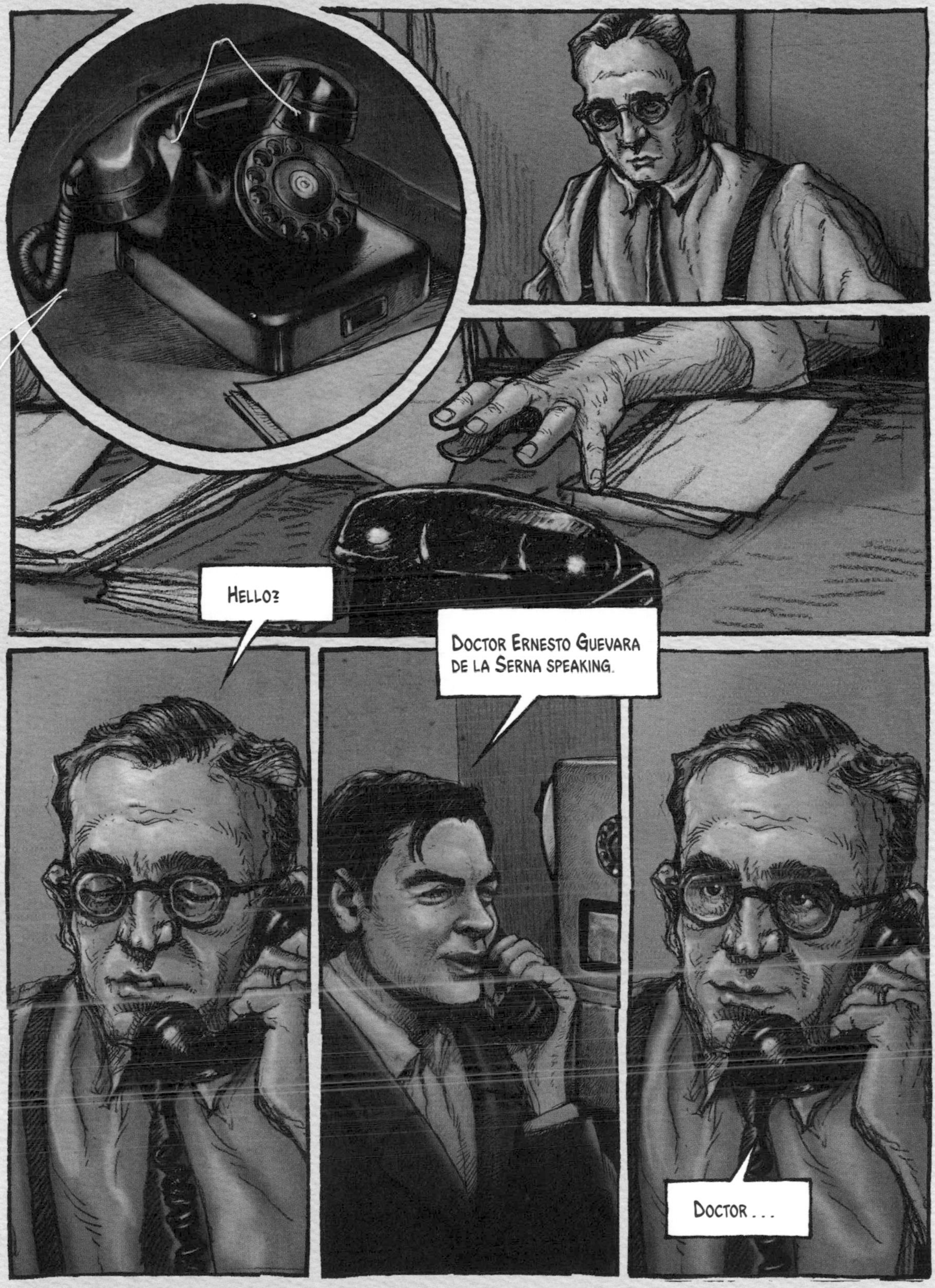
HELLO?
DOCTOR ERNESTO GUEVARA DE LA SERNA SPEAKING.
DOCTOR . . .

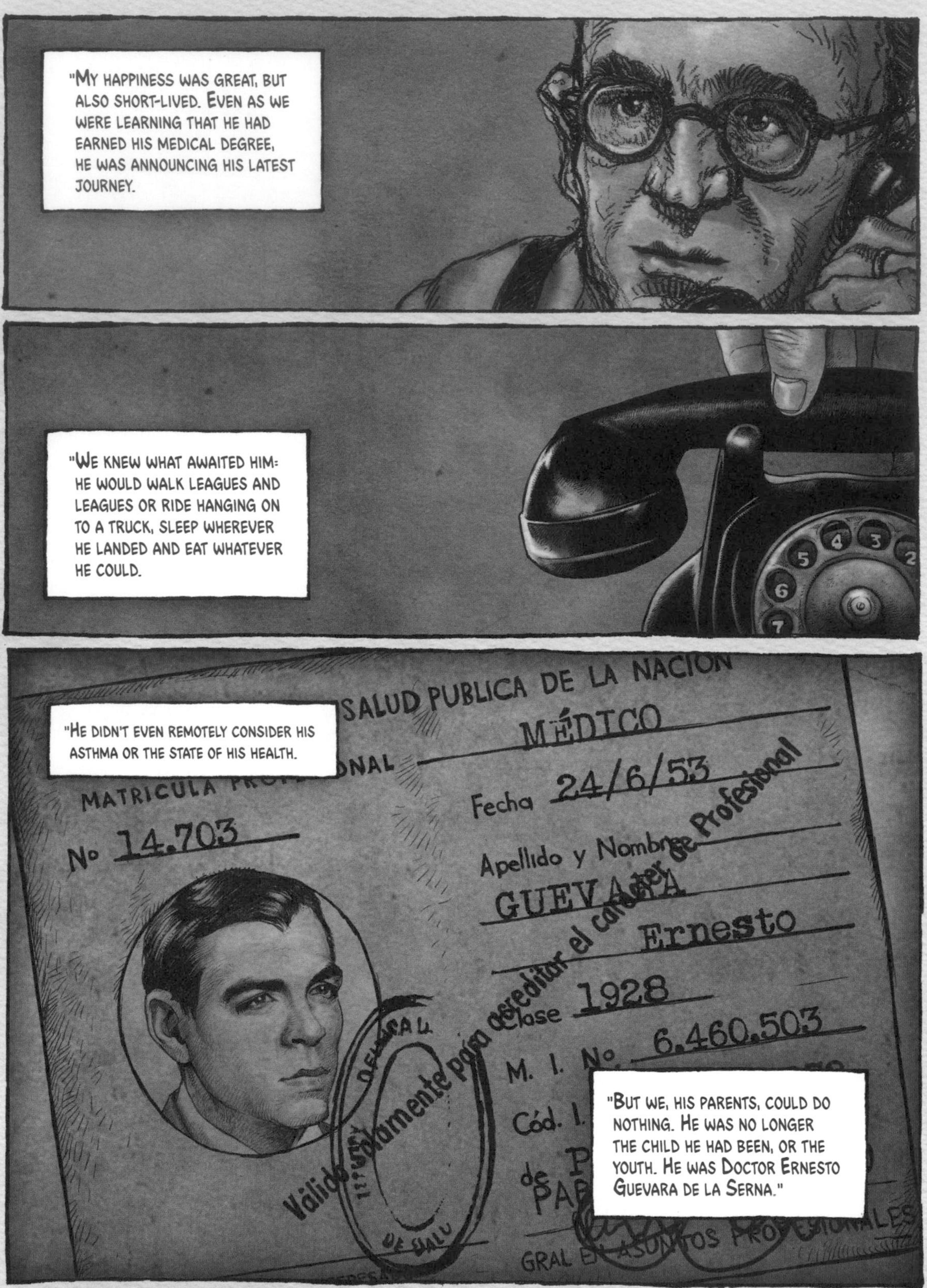
"MY HAPPINESS WAS GREAT, BUT ALSO SHORT-LIVED. EVEN AS WE WERE LEARNING THAT HE HAD EARNED HIS MEDICAL DEGREE, HE WAS ANNOUNCING HIS LATEST JOURNEY.
"WE KNEW WHAT AWAITED HIM: HE WOULD WALK LEAGUES AND LEAGUES OR RIDE HANGING ON TO A TRUCK, SLEEP WHEREVER HE LANDED AND EAT WHATEVER HE COULD.
SALUD PUBLICA DE LA NACION
"HE DIDN'T EVEN REMOTELY CONSIDER HIS ASTHMA OR THE STATE OF HIS HEALTH.
MÉDICO
MATRICULA PRO
NAL
Fecha 24/6/53
No 14.703
Apellido y Nombre
GUEVARA
Ernesto
Clase 1928
M. I. No 6.460.503
Cód. I.
Válido solamente para acreditar el carácter de Profesional
"BUT WE, HIS PARENTS, COULD DO NOTHING. HE WAS NO LONGER THE CHILD HE HAD BEEN, OR THE YOUTH. HE WAS DOCTOR ERNESTO GUEVARA DE LA SERNA."
GRAL EN ASUNTOS PROFESIONALES

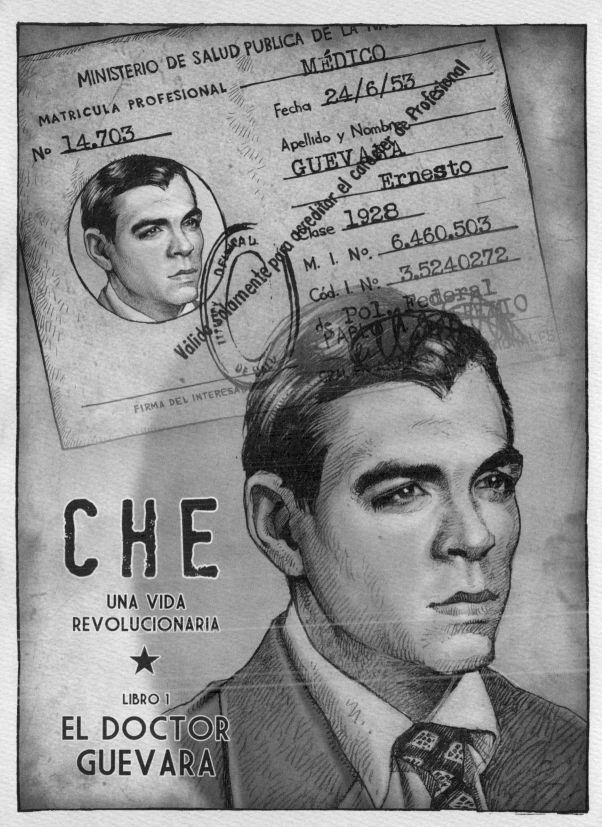

MINISTERIO DE SALUD PUBLICA DE LA NAC...

MÉDICO

MATRICULA PROFESIONAL

Nº 14.703

Fecha 24/6/53

Apellido y Nombre Profesional

GUEVARA

Ernesto

Válido únicamente para acreditar el carácter

Clase 1928

M. I. Nº 6.460.503

Cód. I. Nº 3.5240272

de Pol. Federal

PABLO N. SANTO

FIRMA DEL INTERESADO

CHE

UNA VIDA
REVOLUCIONARIA

★

LIBRO 1
EL DOCTOR
GUEVARA

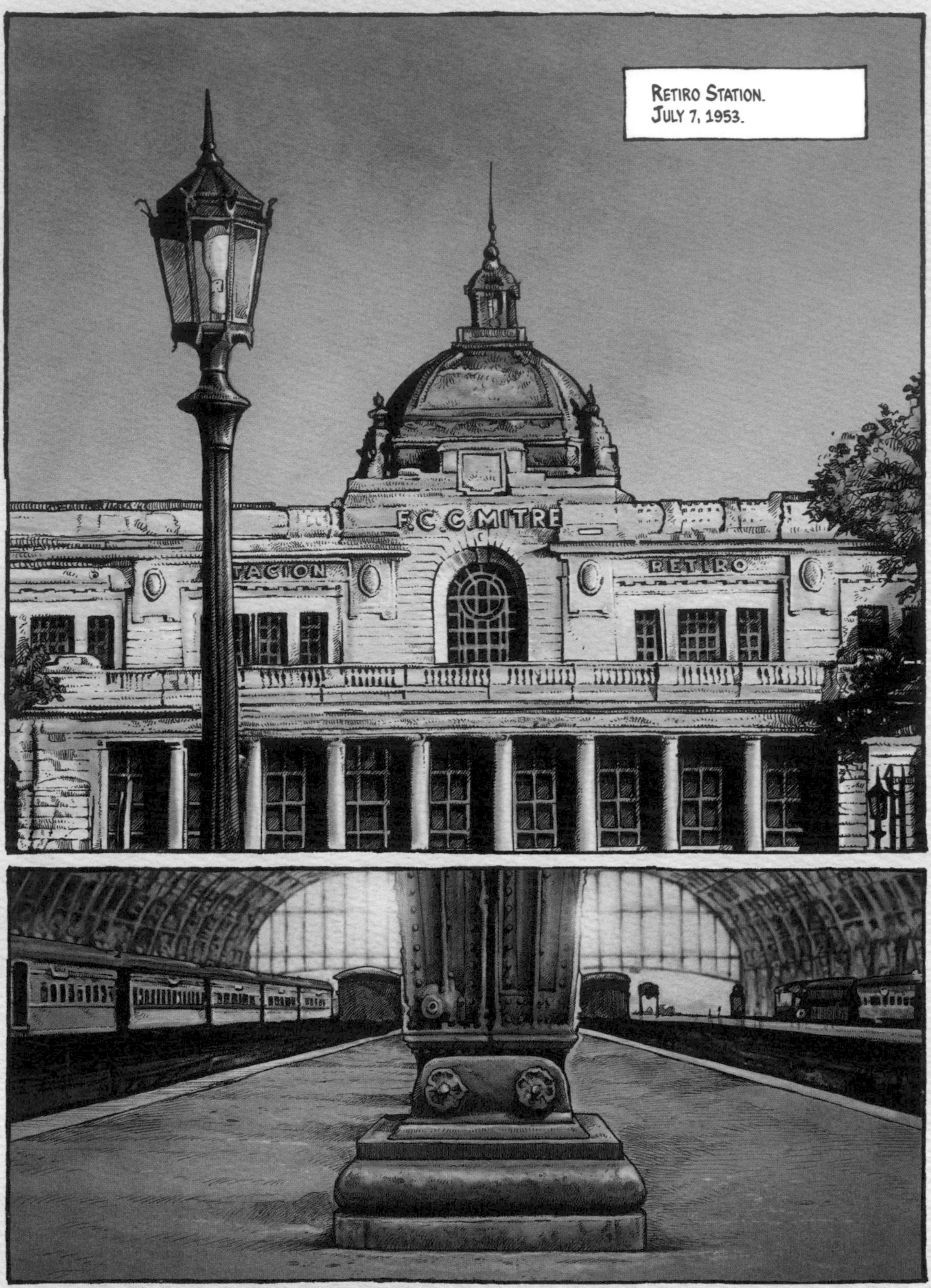
RETIRO STATION.
JULY 7, 1953.
F C C MITRE
TACION
RETIRO

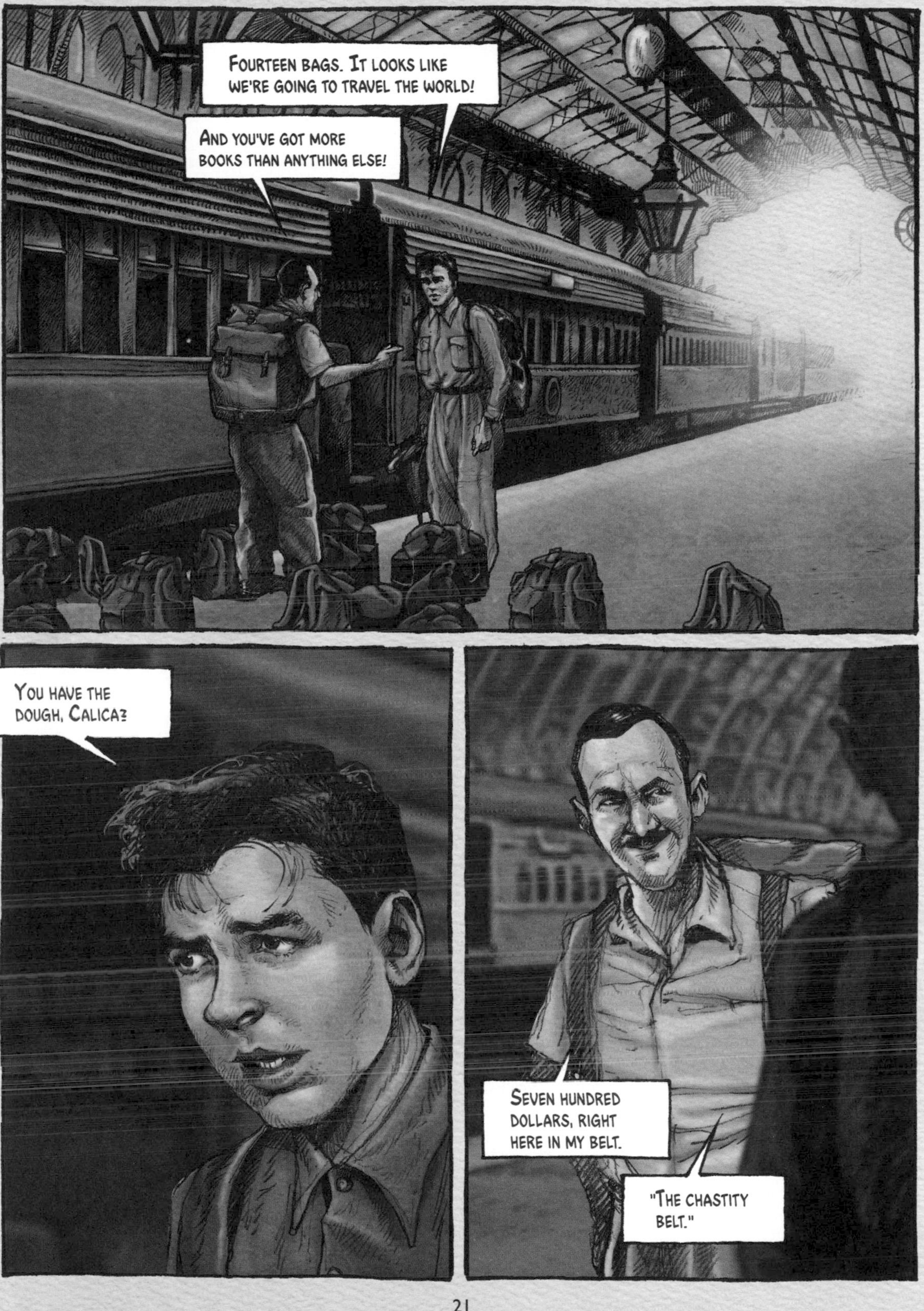
FOURTEEN BAGS. IT LOOKS LIKE WE'RE GOING TO TRAVEL THE WORLD!
AND YOU'VE GOT MORE BOOKS THAN ANYTHING ELSE!
YOU HAVE THE DOUGH, CALICA?
SEVEN HUNDRED DOLLARS, RIGHT HERE IN MY BELT.
"THE CHASTITY BELT."

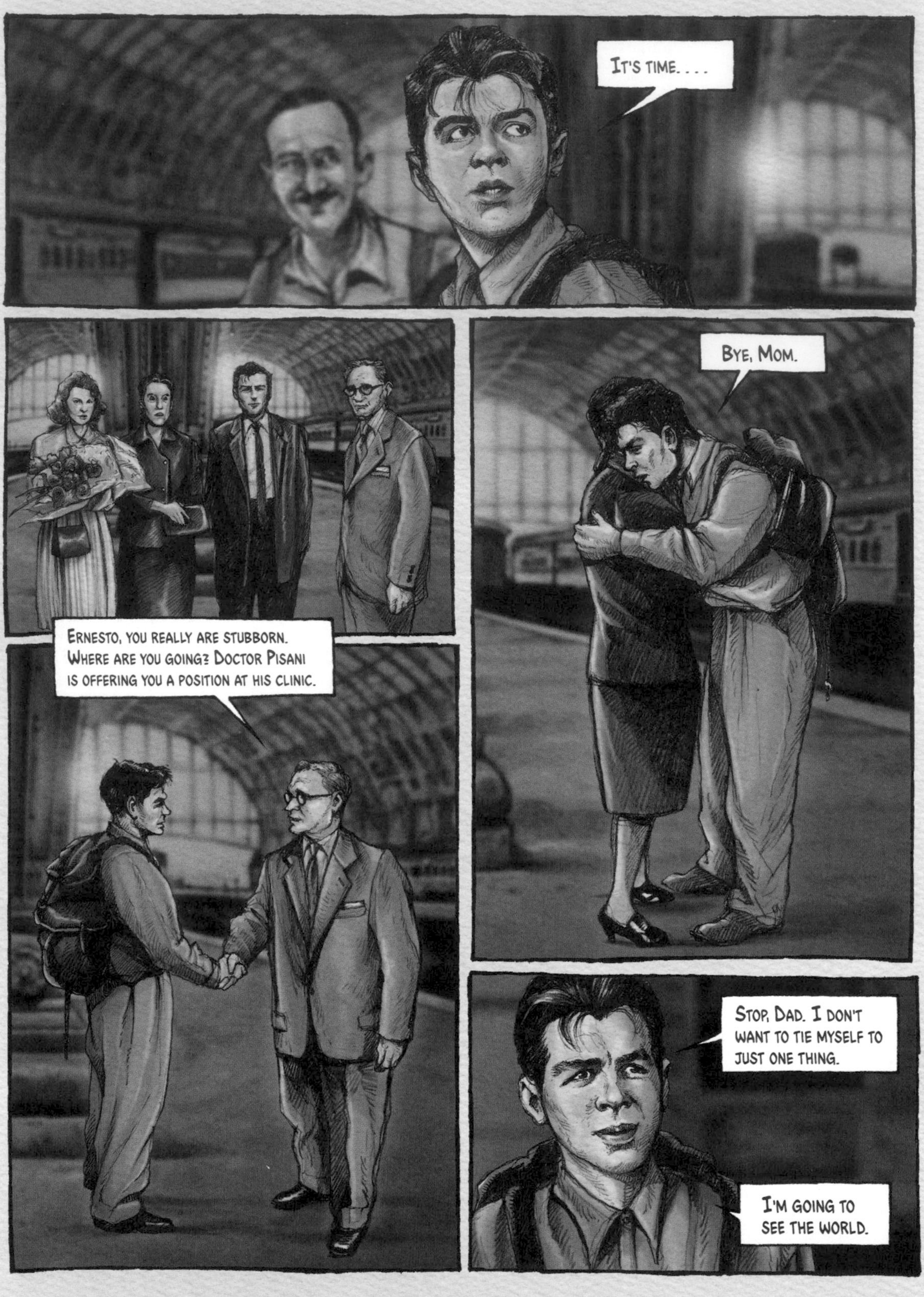
It's time. . . .
Ernesto, you really are stubborn. Where are you going? Doctor Pisani is offering you a position at his clinic.
Bye, Mom.
Stop, Dad. I don't want to tie myself to just one thing.
I'm going to see the world.

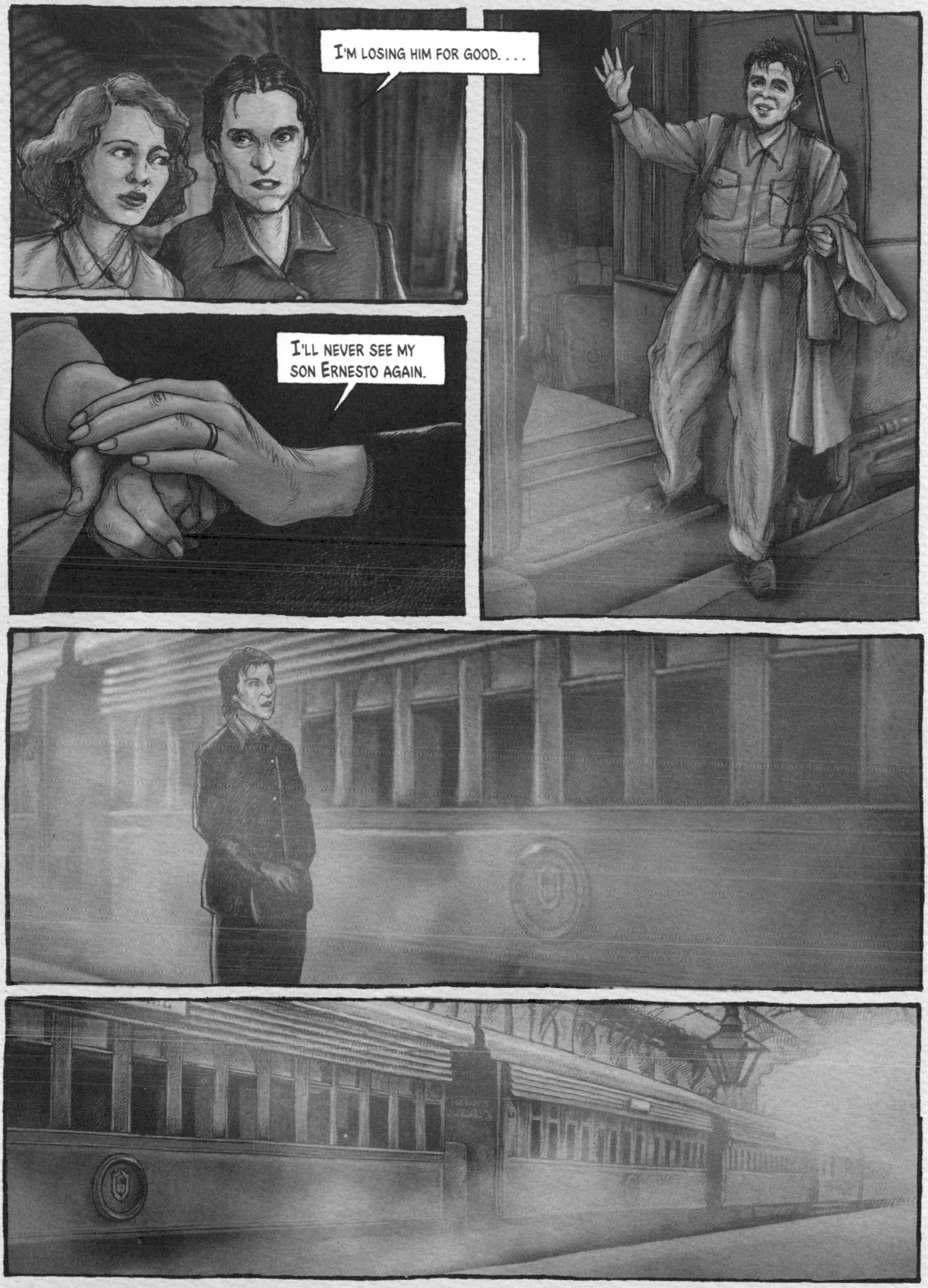
I'M LOSING HIM FOR GOOD. . . .
I'LL NEVER SEE MY SON ERNESTO AGAIN.

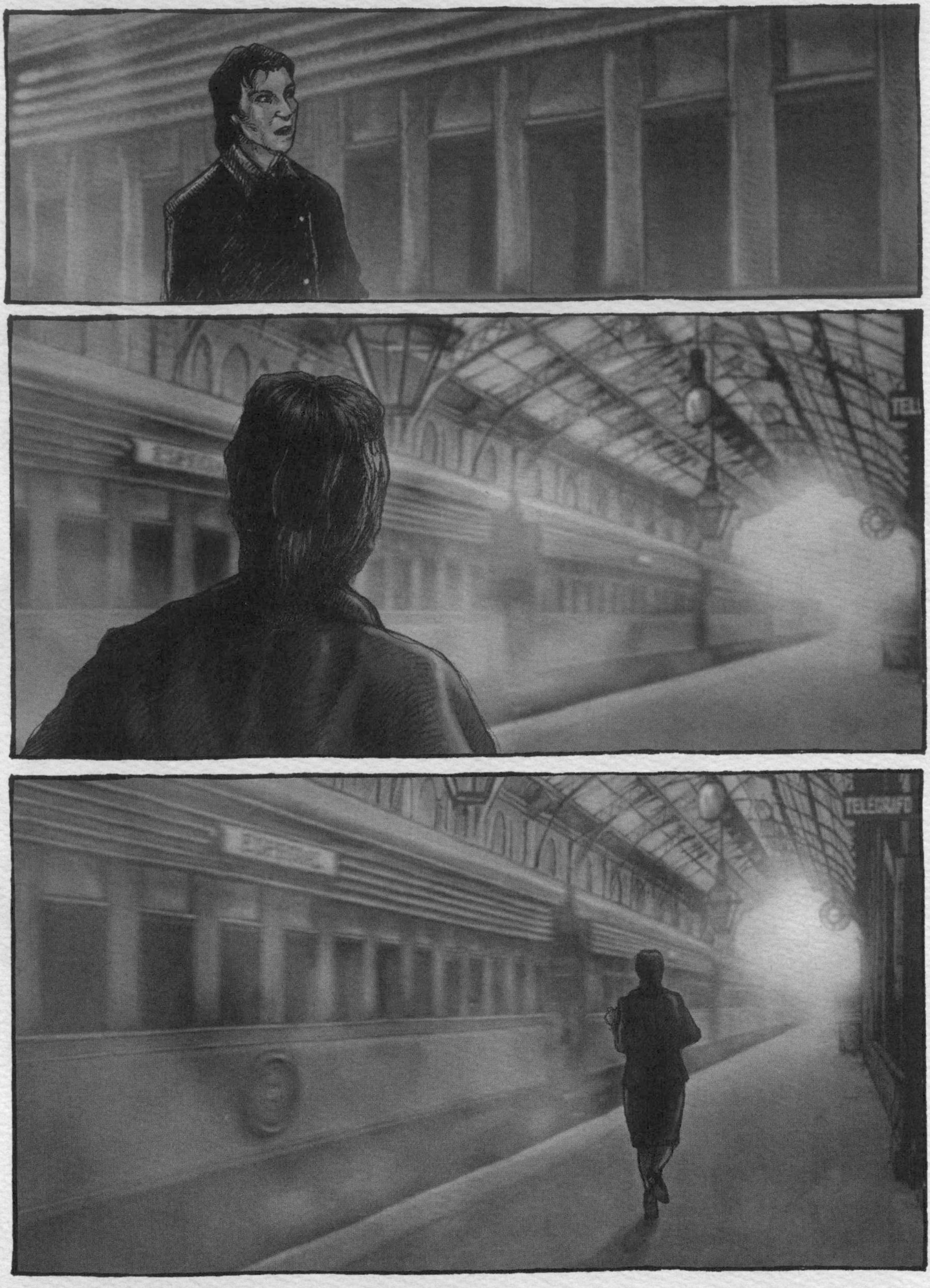
TELEGRAFO

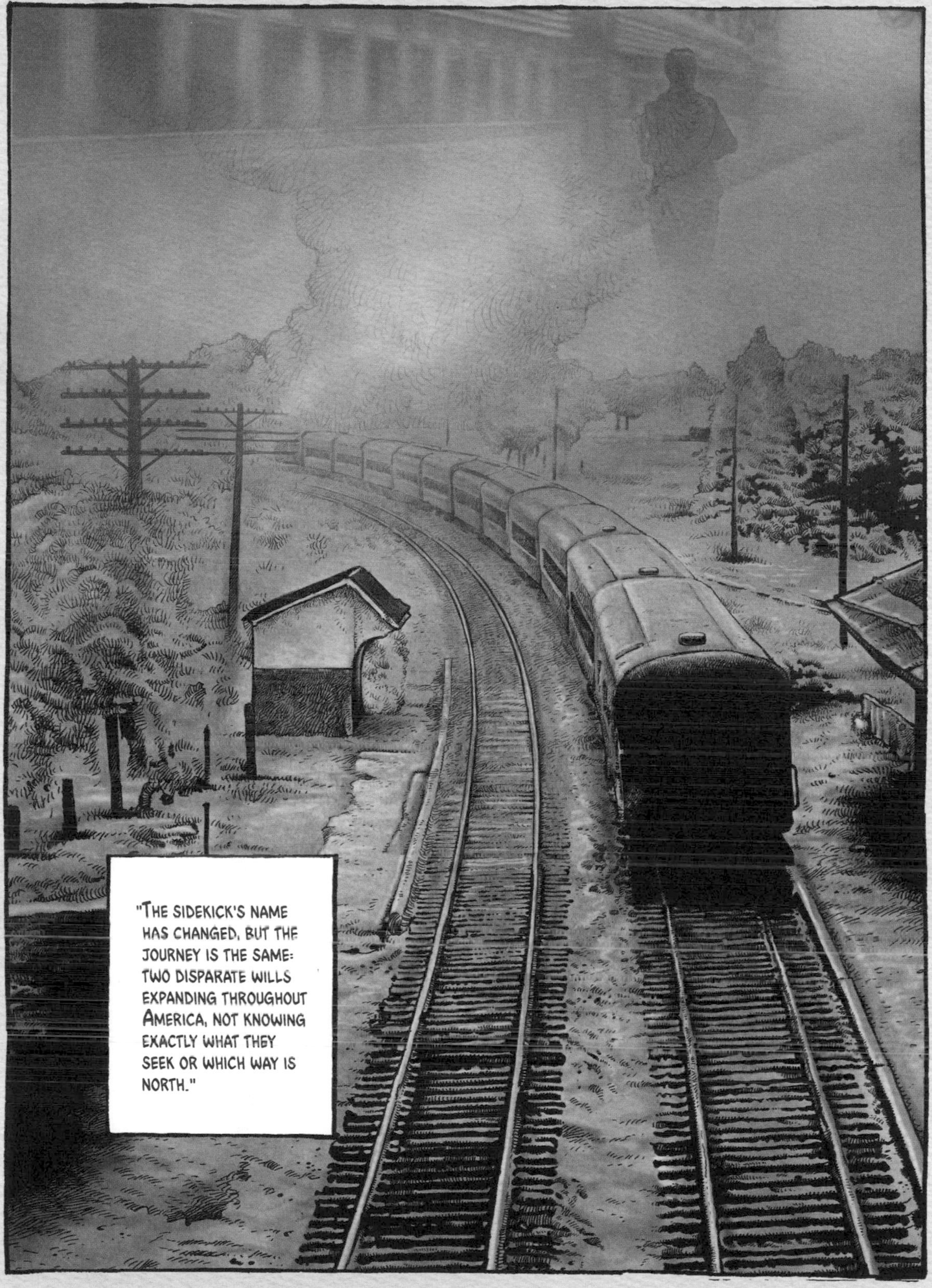
"THE SIDEKICK'S NAME HAS CHANGED, BUT THE JOURNEY IS THE SAME: TWO DISPARATE WILLS EXPANDING THROUGHOUT AMERICA, NOT KNOWING EXACTLY WHAT THEY SEEK OR WHICH WAY IS NORTH."

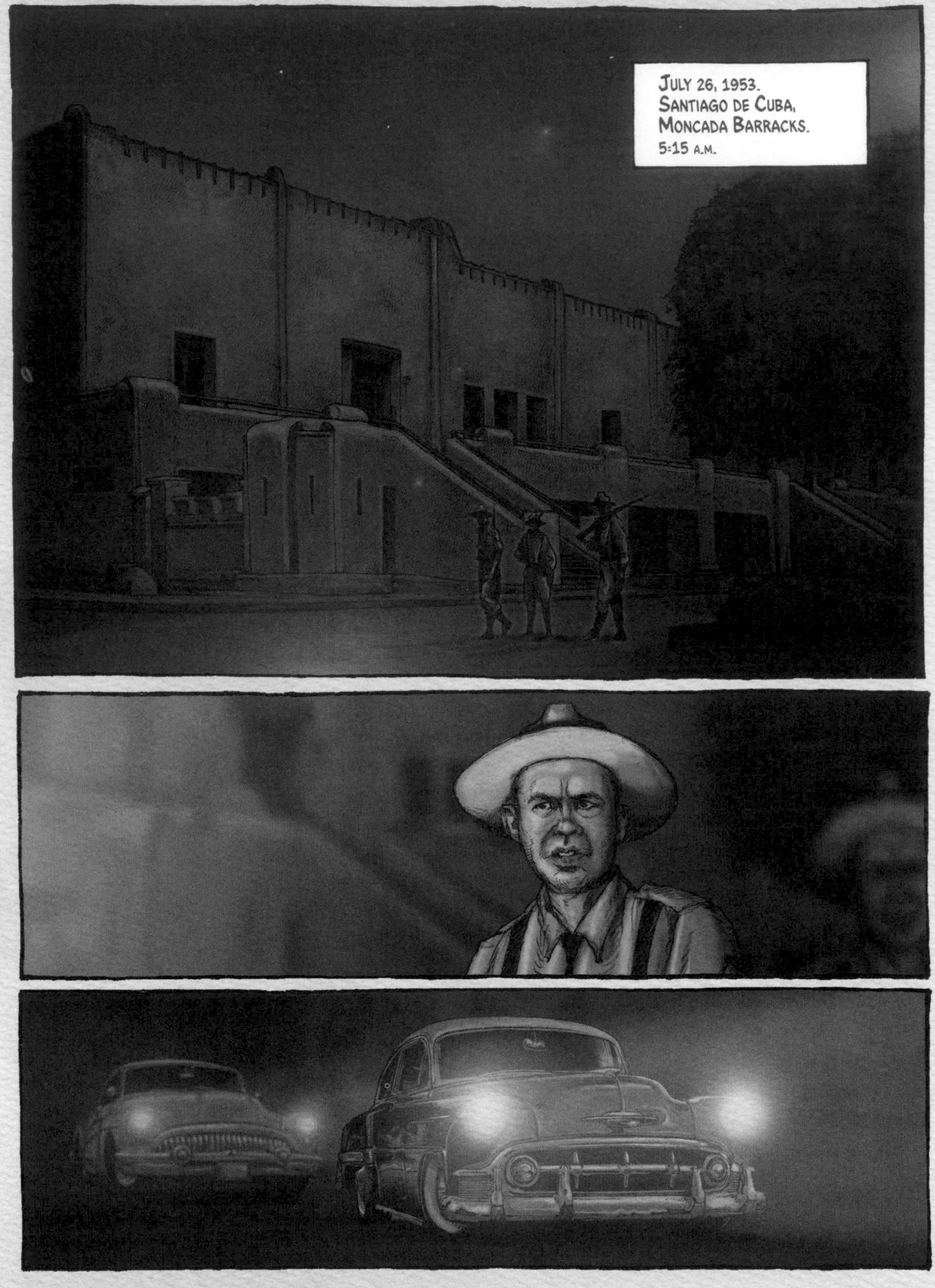
July 26, 1953.
Santiago de Cuba,
Moncada Barracks.
5:15 a.m.

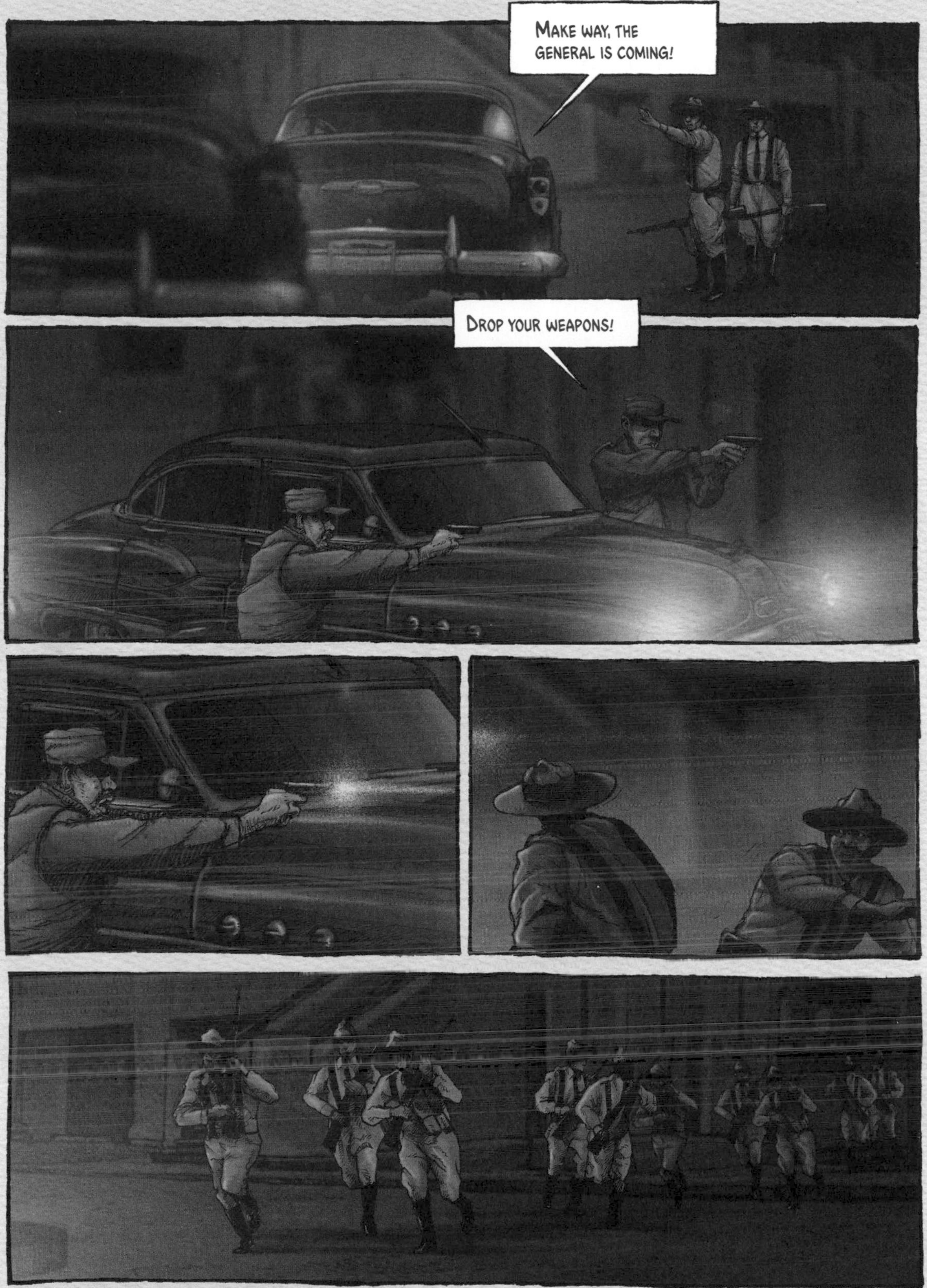
MAKE WAY, THE GENERAL IS COMING!
DROP YOUR WEAPONS!

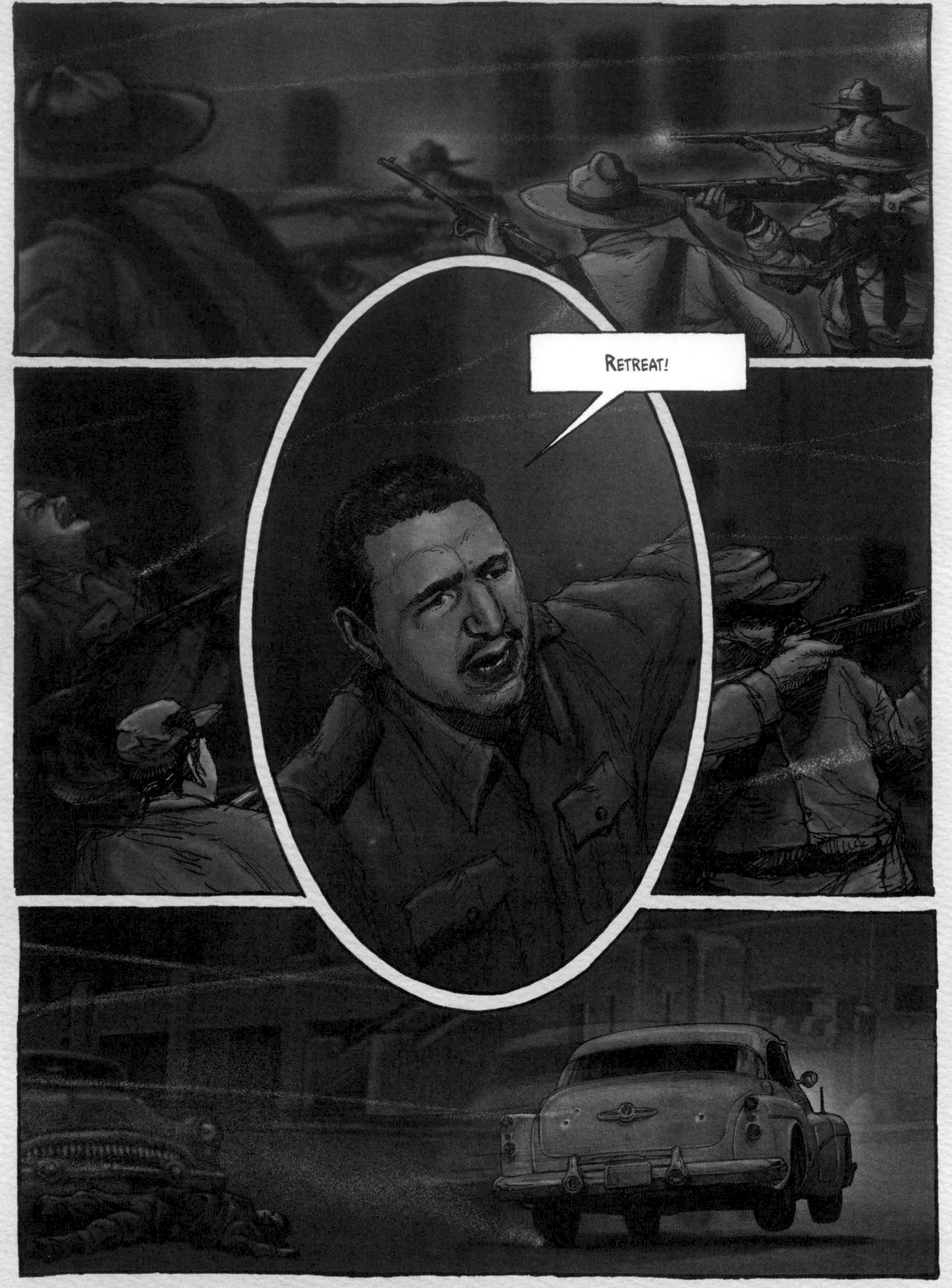
RETREAT!

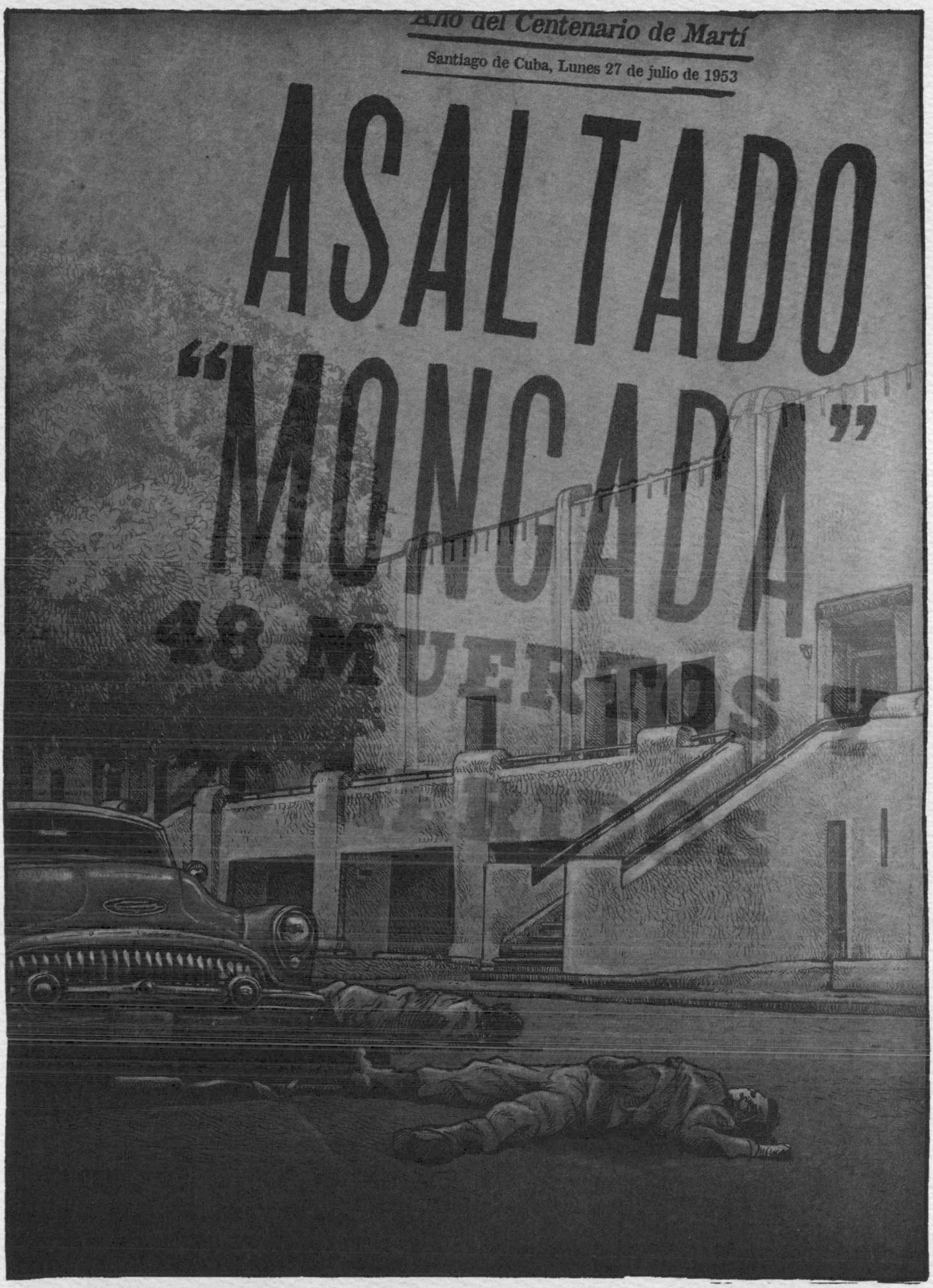
Año del Centenario de Martí
Santiago de Cuba, Lunes 27 de julio de 1953
ASALTADO "MONCADA"

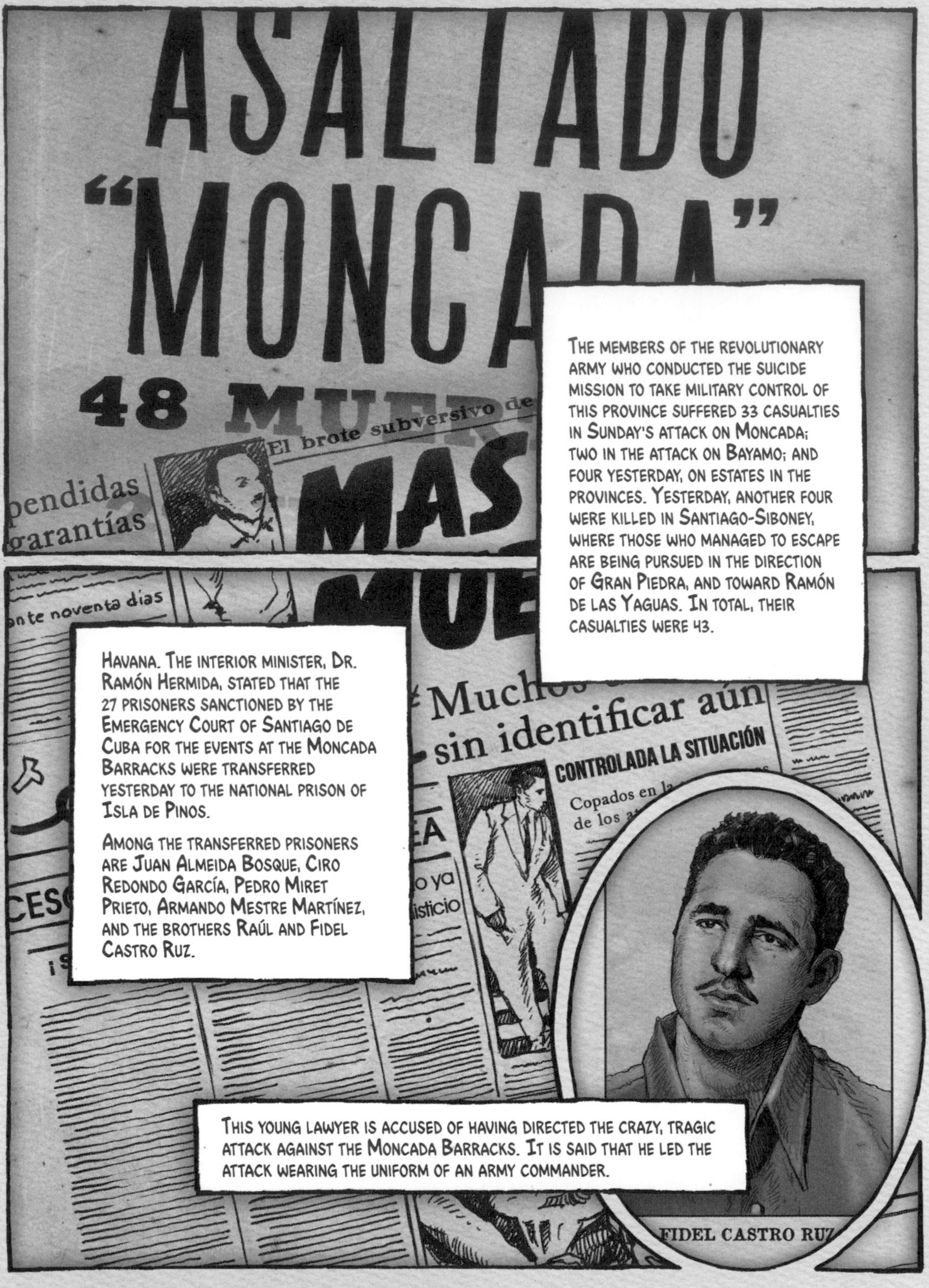
ASALTADO "MONCADA"
48 MUER
El brote subversivo de
pendidas garantías
MAS
MUE
nte noventa dias
THE MEMBERS OF THE REVOLUTIONARY ARMY WHO CONDUCTED THE SUICIDE MISSION TO TAKE MILITARY CONTROL OF THIS PROVINCE SUFFERED 33 CASUALTIES IN SUNDAY'S ATTACK ON MONCADA; TWO IN THE ATTACK ON BAYAMO; AND FOUR YESTERDAY, ON ESTATES IN THE PROVINCES. YESTERDAY, ANOTHER FOUR WERE KILLED IN SANTIAGO-SIBONEY, WHERE THOSE WHO MANAGED TO ESCAPE ARE BEING PURSUED IN THE DIRECTION OF GRAN PIEDRA, AND TOWARD RAMÓN DE LAS YAGUAS. IN TOTAL, THEIR CASUALTIES WERE 43.
HAVANA. THE INTERIOR MINISTER, DR. RAMÓN HERMIDA, STATED THAT THE 27 PRISONERS SANCTIONED BY THE EMERGENCY COURT OF SANTIAGO DE CUBA FOR THE EVENTS AT THE MONCADA BARRACKS WERE TRANSFERRED YESTERDAY TO THE NATIONAL PRISON OF ISLA DE PINOS.
AMONG THE TRANSFERRED PRISONERS ARE JUAN ALMEIDA BOSQUE, CIRO REDONDO GARCÍA, PEDRO MIRET PRIETO, ARMANDO MESTRE MARTÍNEZ, AND THE BROTHERS RAÚL AND FIDEL CASTRO RUZ.
Muchos
sin identificar aún
CONTROLADA LA SITUACIÓN
Copados en la
de los a
FIDEL CASTRO RUZ
THIS YOUNG LAWYER IS ACCUSED OF HAVING DIRECTED THE CRAZY, TRAGIC ATTACK AGAINST THE MONCADA BARRACKS. IT IS SAID THAT HE LED THE ATTACK WEARING THE UNIFORM OF AN ARMY COMMANDER.

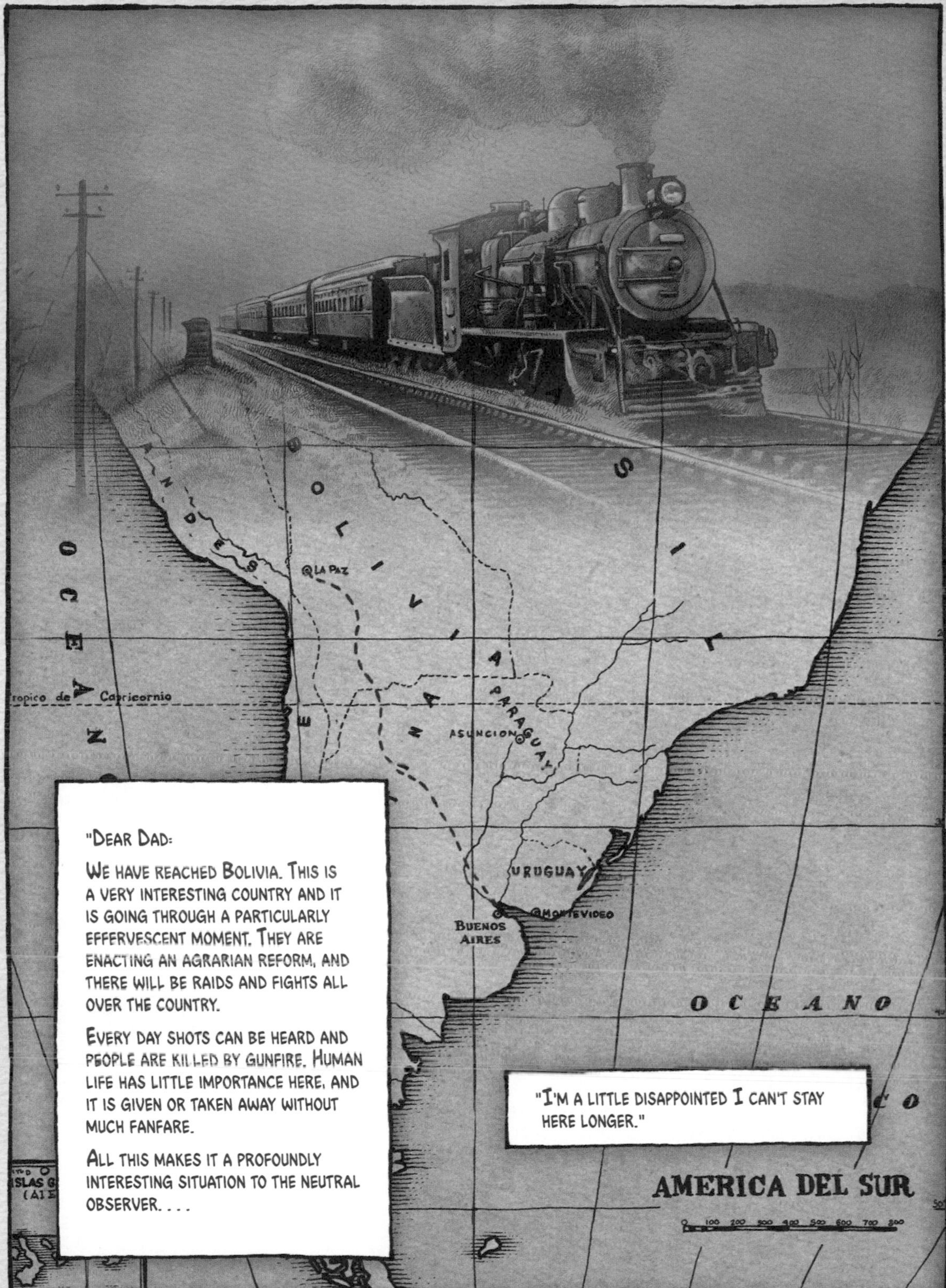
"DEAR DAD:
WE HAVE REACHED BOLIVIA. THIS IS A VERY INTERESTING COUNTRY AND IT IS GOING THROUGH A PARTICULARLY EFFERVESCENT MOMENT. THEY ARE ENACTING AN AGRARIAN REFORM, AND THERE WILL BE RAIDS AND FIGHTS ALL OVER THE COUNTRY.
EVERY DAY SHOTS CAN BE HEARD AND PEOPLE ARE KILLED BY GUNFIRE. HUMAN LIFE HAS LITTLE IMPORTANCE HERE, AND IT IS GIVEN OR TAKEN AWAY WITHOUT MUCH FANFARE.
ALL THIS MAKES IT A PROFOUNDLY INTERESTING SITUATION TO THE NEUTRAL OBSERVER. . . .
"I'M A LITTLE DISAPPOINTED I CAN'T STAY HERE LONGER."
BOLIVIA
ANDES
LA PAZ
PARAGUAY
ASUNCION
URUGUAY
MONTEVIDEO
BUENOS AIRES
Tropico de Capricornio
OCEANO
AMERICA DEL SUR

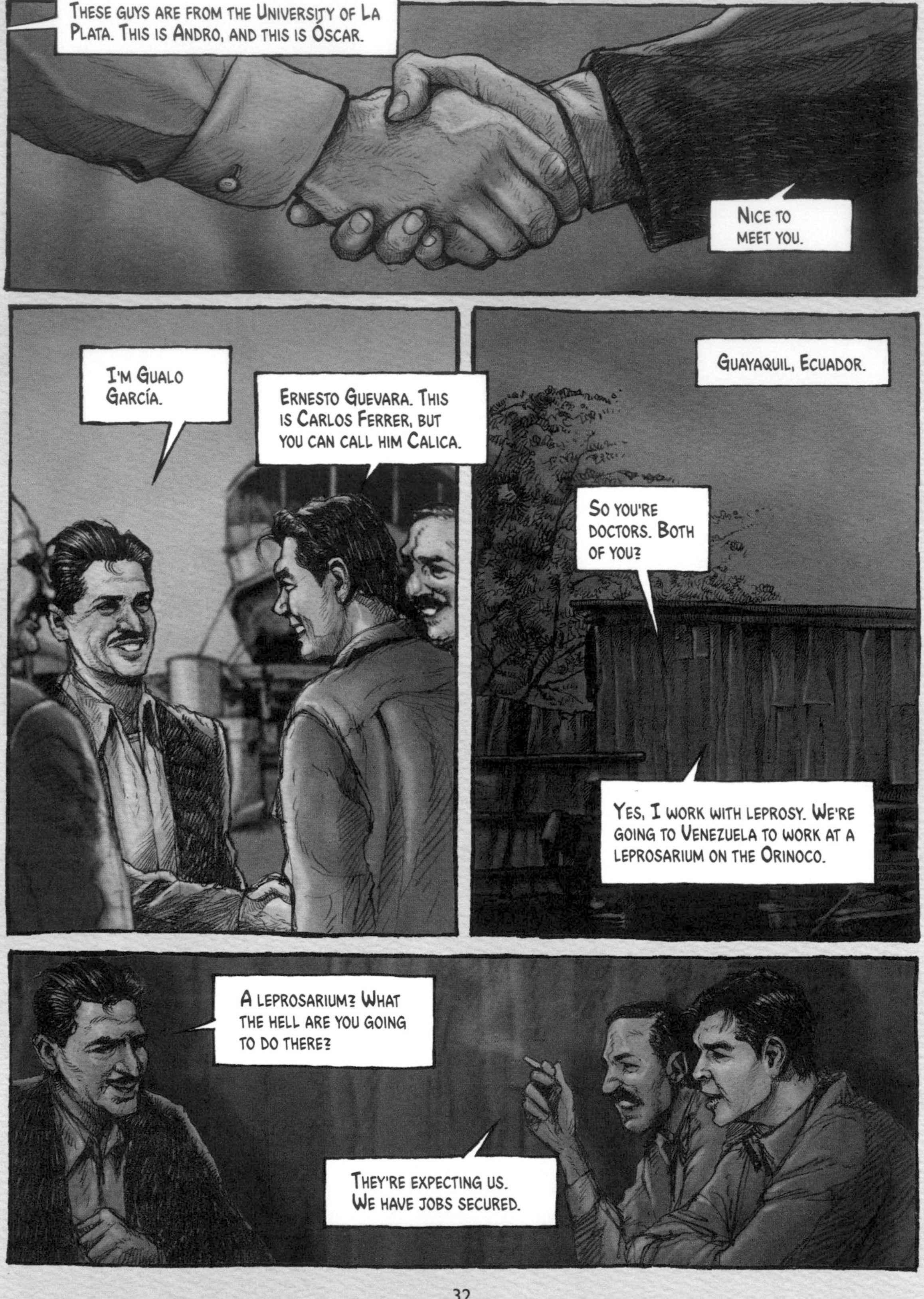
These guys are from the University of La Plata. This is Andro, and this is Óscar.
Nice to meet you.
I'm Gualo García.
Ernesto Guevara. This is Carlos Ferrer, but you can call him Calica.
Guayaquil, Ecuador.
So you're doctors. Both of you?
Yes, I work with leprosy. We're going to Venezuela to work at a leprosarium on the Orinoco.
A leprosarium? What the hell are you going to do there?
They're expecting us. We have jobs secured.

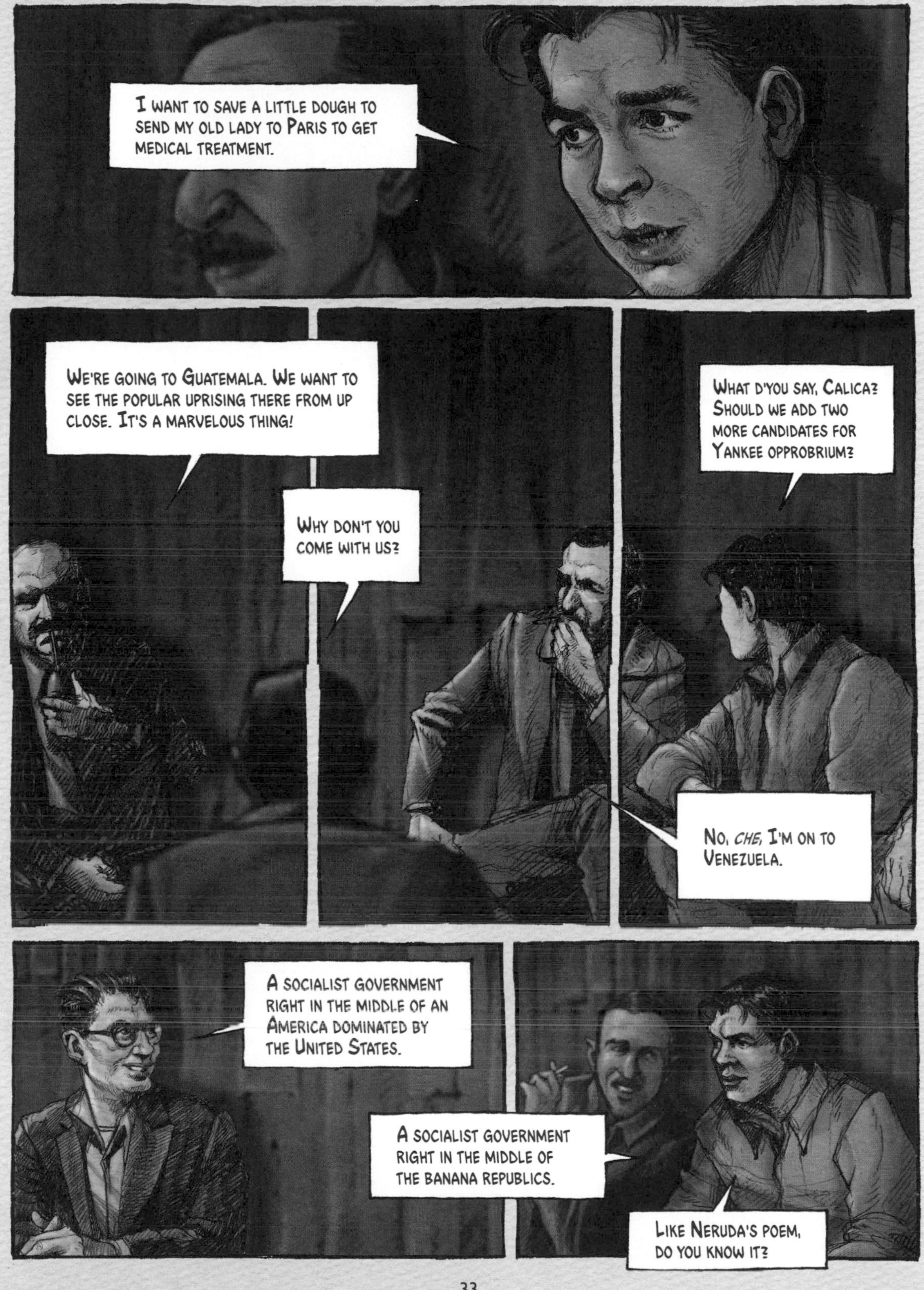
I WANT TO SAVE A LITTLE DOUGH TO SEND MY OLD LADY TO PARIS TO GET MEDICAL TREATMENT.
WE'RE GOING TO GUATEMALA. WE WANT TO SEE THE POPULAR UPRISING THERE FROM UP CLOSE. IT'S A MARVELOUS THING!
WHY DON'T YOU COME WITH US?
WHAT D'YOU SAY, CALICA? SHOULD WE ADD TWO MORE CANDIDATES FOR YANKEE OPPROBRIUM?
NO, *CHE*, I'M ON TO VENEZUELA.
A SOCIALIST GOVERNMENT RIGHT IN THE MIDDLE OF AN AMERICA DOMINATED BY THE UNITED STATES.
A SOCIALIST GOVERNMENT RIGHT IN THE MIDDLE OF THE BANANA REPUBLICS.
LIKE NERUDA'S POEM, DO YOU KNOW IT?

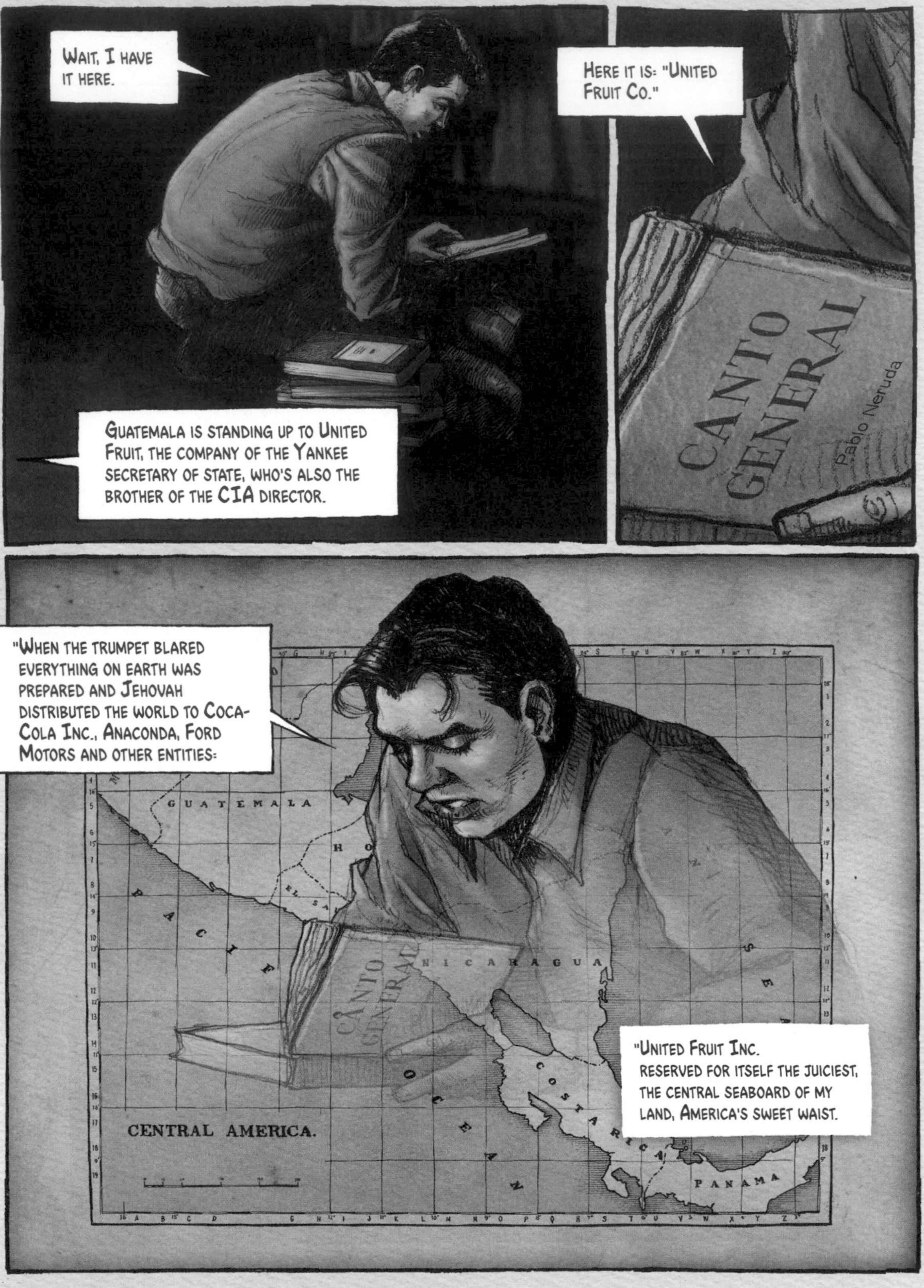
WAIT, I HAVE IT HERE.
GUATEMALA IS STANDING UP TO UNITED FRUIT, THE COMPANY OF THE YANKEE SECRETARY OF STATE, WHO'S ALSO THE BROTHER OF THE CIA DIRECTOR.
HERE IT IS: "UNITED FRUIT CO."
CANTO GENERAL
Pablo Neruda
"WHEN THE TRUMPET BLARED EVERYTHING ON EARTH WAS PREPARED AND JEHOVAH DISTRIBUTED THE WORLD TO COCA-COLA INC., ANACONDA, FORD MOTORS AND OTHER ENTITIES:
GUATEMALA
NICARAGUA
CANTO GENERAL
COSTA RICA
PANAMA
CENTRAL AMERICA.
"UNITED FRUIT INC.
RESERVED FOR ITSELF THE JUICIEST, THE CENTRAL SEABOARD OF MY LAND, AMERICA'S SWEET WAIST.

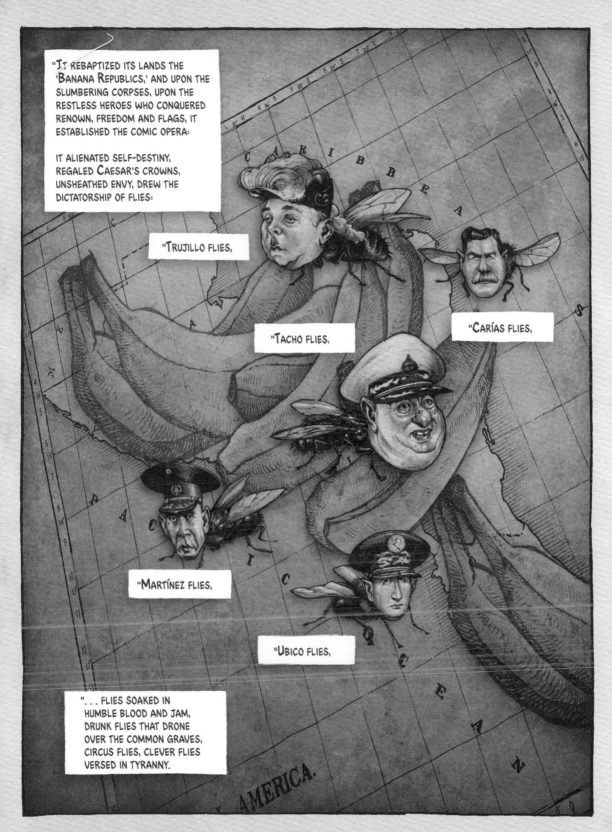

"It rebaptized its lands the 'Banana Republics,' and upon the slumbering corpses, upon the restless heroes who conquered renown, freedom and flags, it established the comic opera:

It alienated self-destiny, regaled Caesar's crowns, unsheathed envy, drew the dictatorship of flies:

"Trujillo flies,

"Carías flies,

"Tacho flies,

"Martínez flies,

"Ubico flies,

". . . flies soaked in humble blood and jam, drunk flies that drone over the common graves, circus flies, clever flies versed in tyranny.

AMERICA.

35

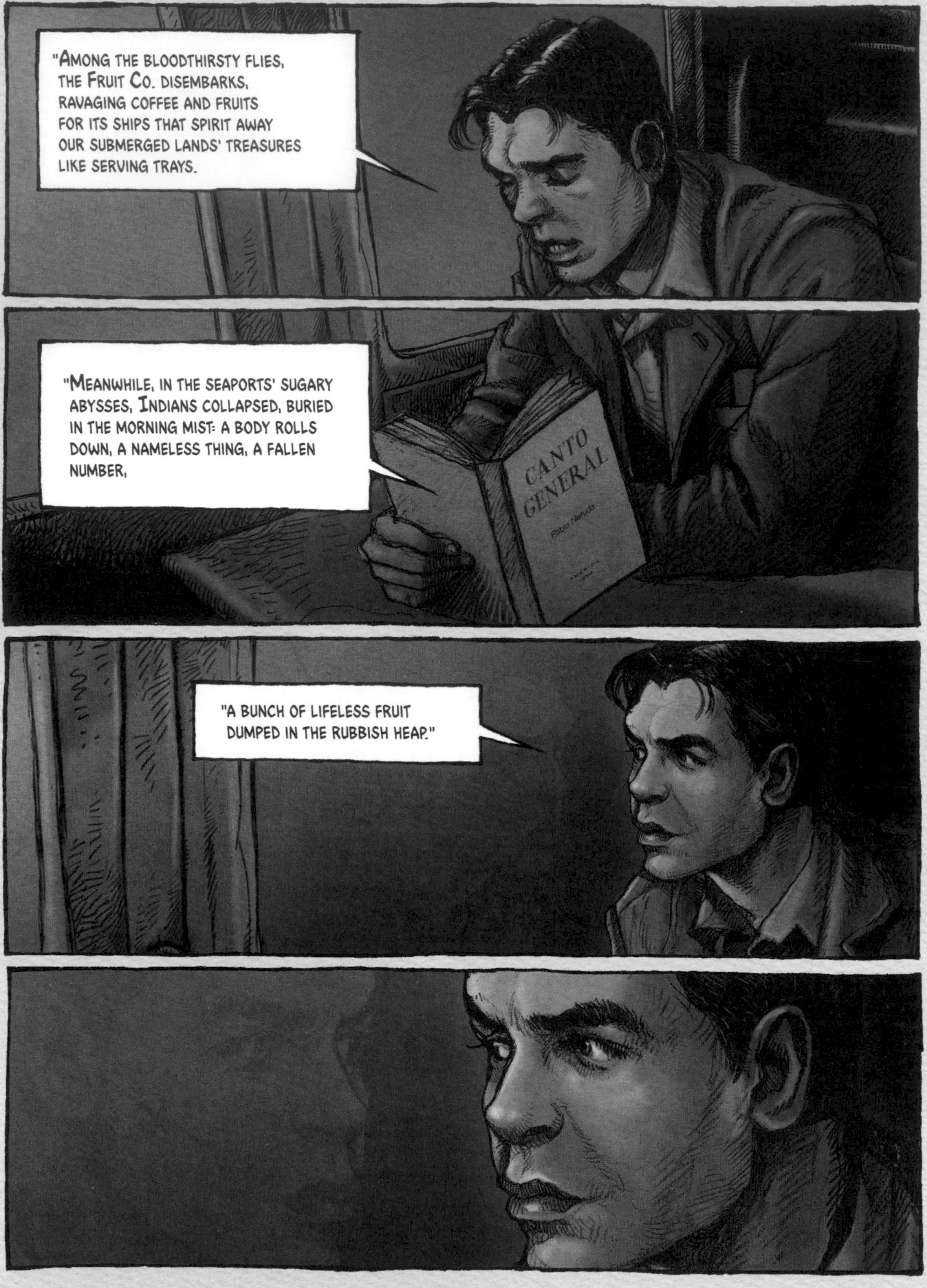
"AMONG THE BLOODTHIRSTY FLIES, THE FRUIT CO. DISEMBARKS, RAVAGING COFFEE AND FRUITS FOR ITS SHIPS THAT SPIRIT AWAY OUR SUBMERGED LANDS' TREASURES LIKE SERVING TRAYS.
"MEANWHILE, IN THE SEAPORTS' SUGARY ABYSSES, INDIANS COLLAPSED, BURIED IN THE MORNING MIST: A BODY ROLLS DOWN, A NAMELESS THING, A FALLEN NUMBER,
CANTO GENERAL
Pablo Neruda
"A BUNCH OF LIFELESS FRUIT DUMPED IN THE RUBBISH HEAP."

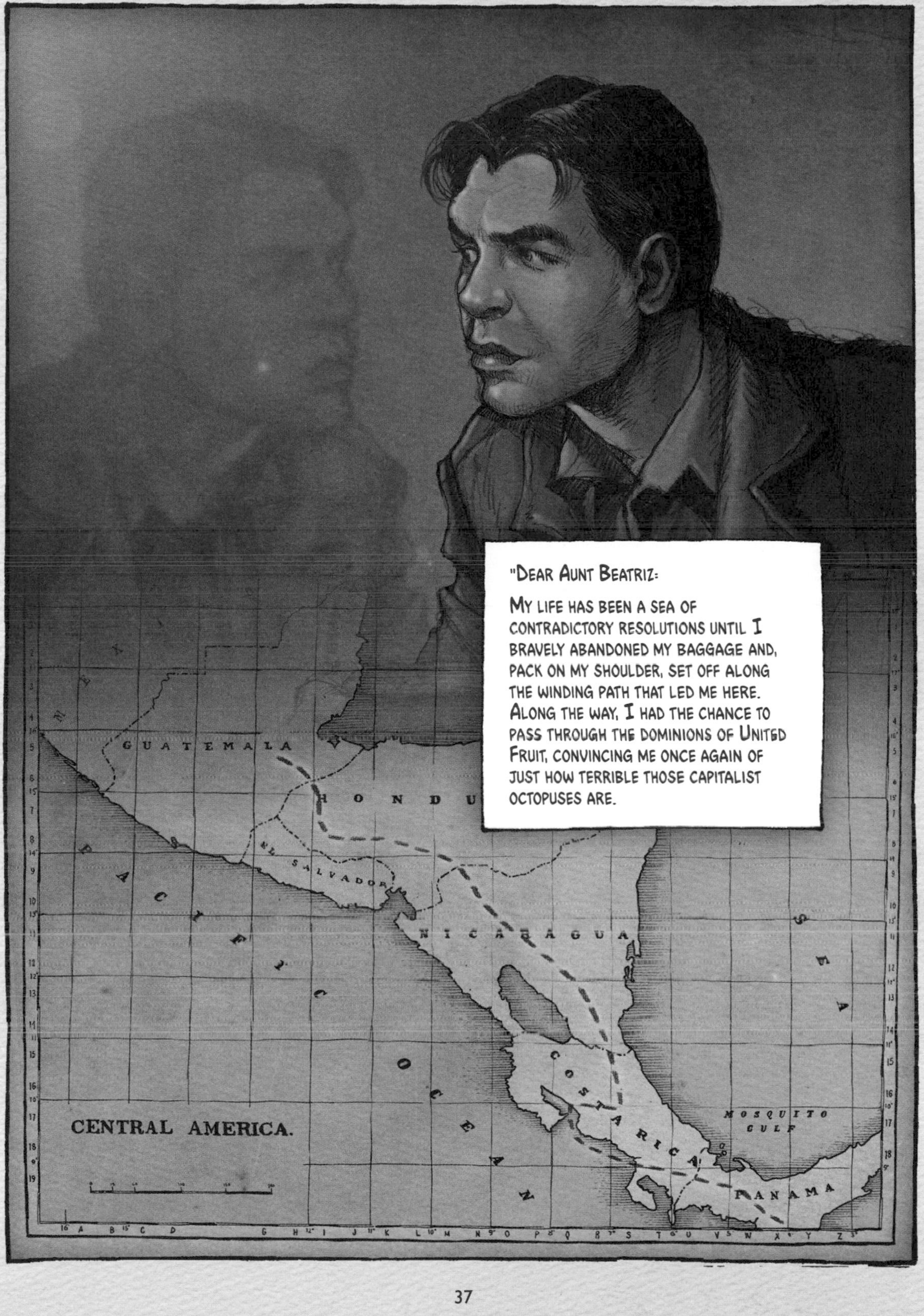
"Dear Aunt Beatriz:
My life has been a sea of contradictory resolutions until I bravely abandoned my baggage and, pack on my shoulder, set off along the winding path that led me here. Along the way, I had the chance to pass through the dominions of United Fruit, convincing me once again of just how terrible those capitalist octopuses are.
GUATEMALA
HONDU
EL SALVADOR
NICARAGUA
PACIFIC OCEAN
COSTA RICA
MOSQUITO GULF
PANAMA
CENTRAL AMERICA.

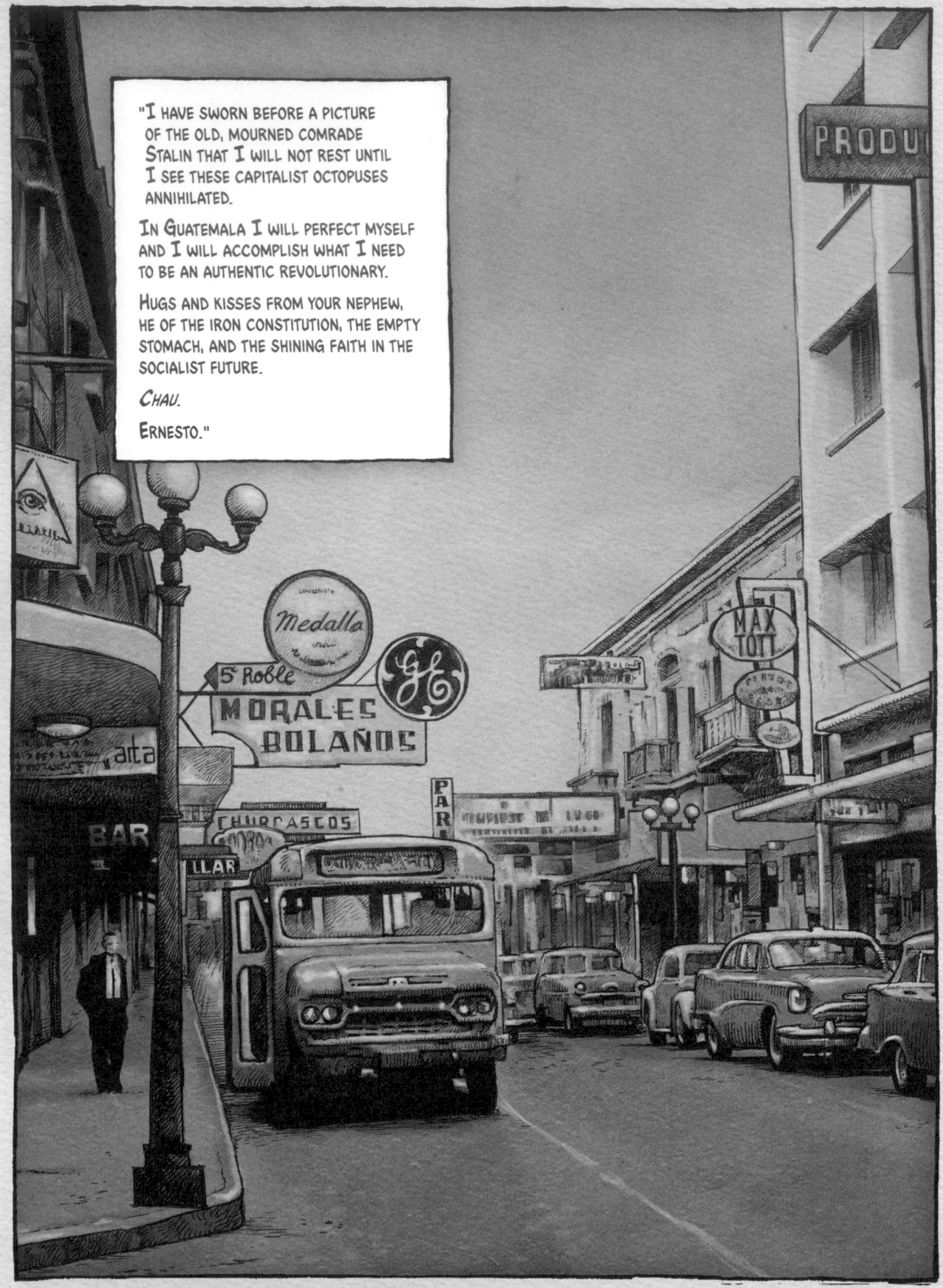
"I HAVE SWORN BEFORE A PICTURE OF THE OLD, MOURNED COMRADE STALIN THAT I WILL NOT REST UNTIL I SEE THESE CAPITALIST OCTOPUSES ANNIHILATED.
IN GUATEMALA I WILL PERFECT MYSELF AND I WILL ACCOMPLISH WHAT I NEED TO BE AN AUTHENTIC REVOLUTIONARY.
HUGS AND KISSES FROM YOUR NEPHEW, HE OF THE IRON CONSTITUTION, THE EMPTY STOMACH, AND THE SHINING FAITH IN THE SOCIALIST FUTURE.
CHAU.
ERNESTO."
PRODU
Medalla
5a Roble
MORALES BOLAÑOS
MAX TOTT
CHURRASCOS
BAR
LLAR
PAR

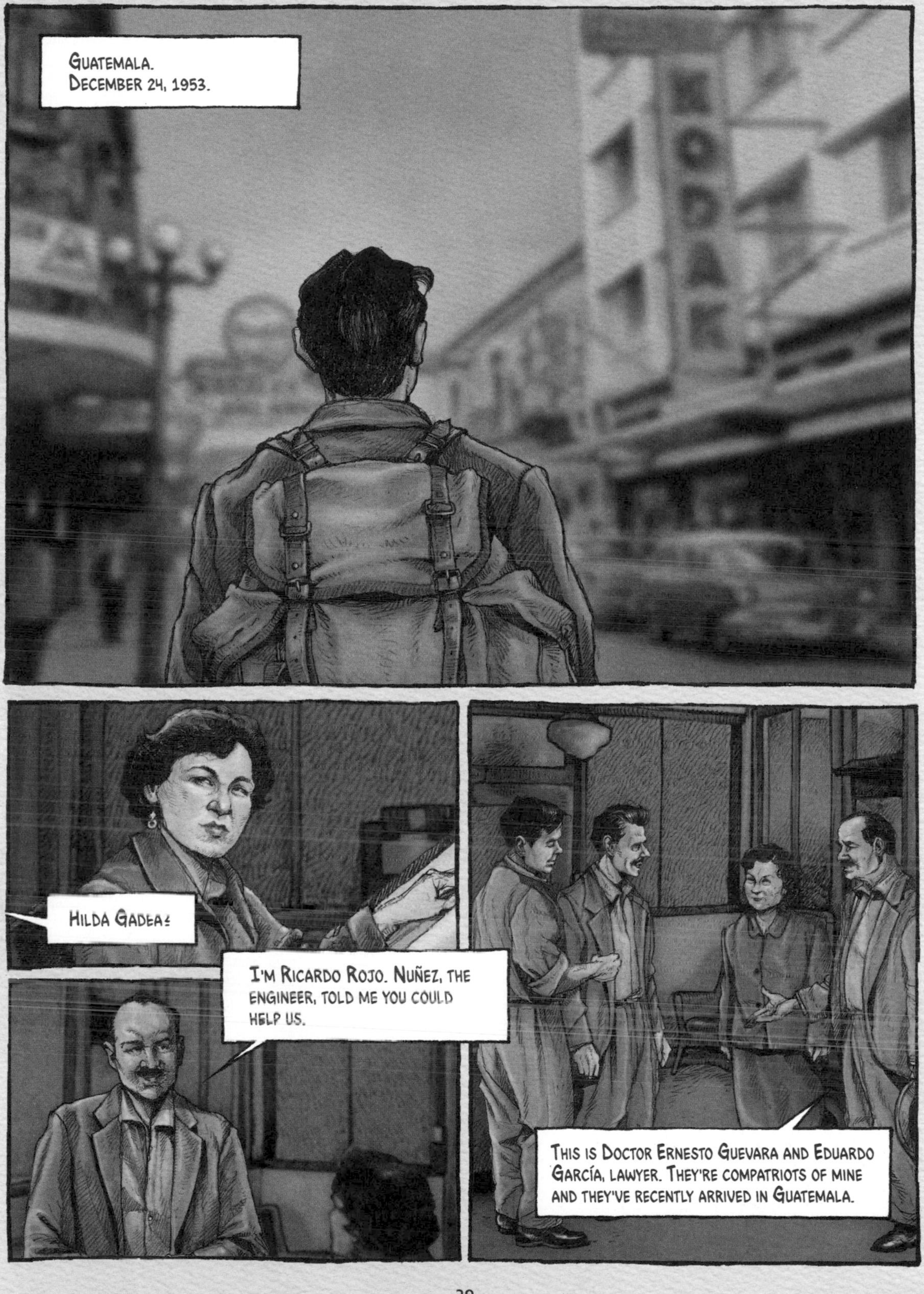
GUATEMALA.
DECEMBER 24, 1953.
HILDA GADEA?
I'M RICARDO ROJO. NUÑEZ, THE ENGINEER, TOLD ME YOU COULD HELP US.
THIS IS DOCTOR ERNESTO GUEVARA AND EDUARDO GARCÍA, LAWYER. THEY'RE COMPATRIOTS OF MINE AND THEY'VE RECENTLY ARRIVED IN GUATEMALA.

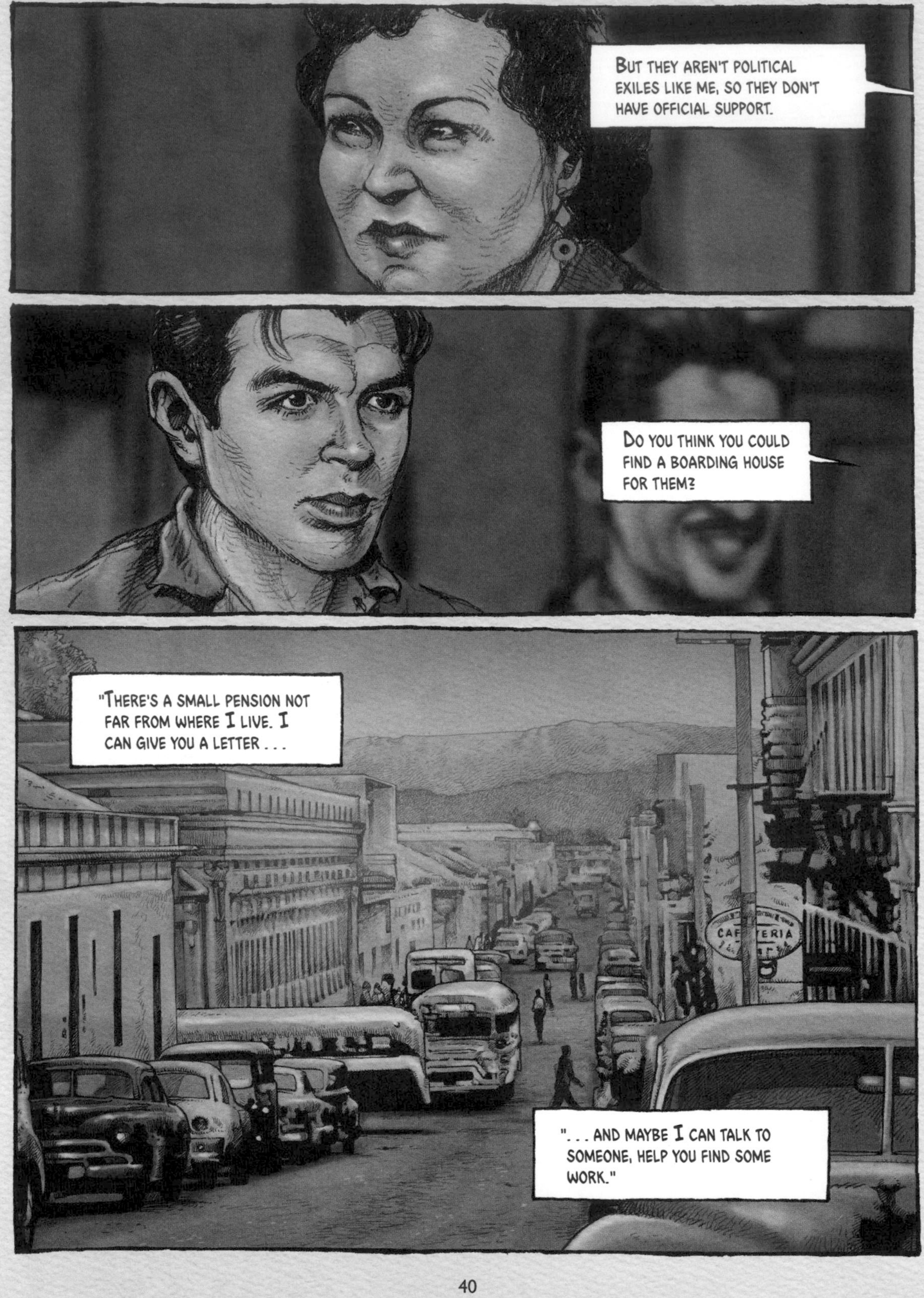
But they aren't political exiles like me, so they don't have official support.
Do you think you could find a boarding house for them?
"There's a small pension not far from where I live. I can give you a letter . . .
Caf eteria
". . . and maybe I can talk to someone, help you find some work."

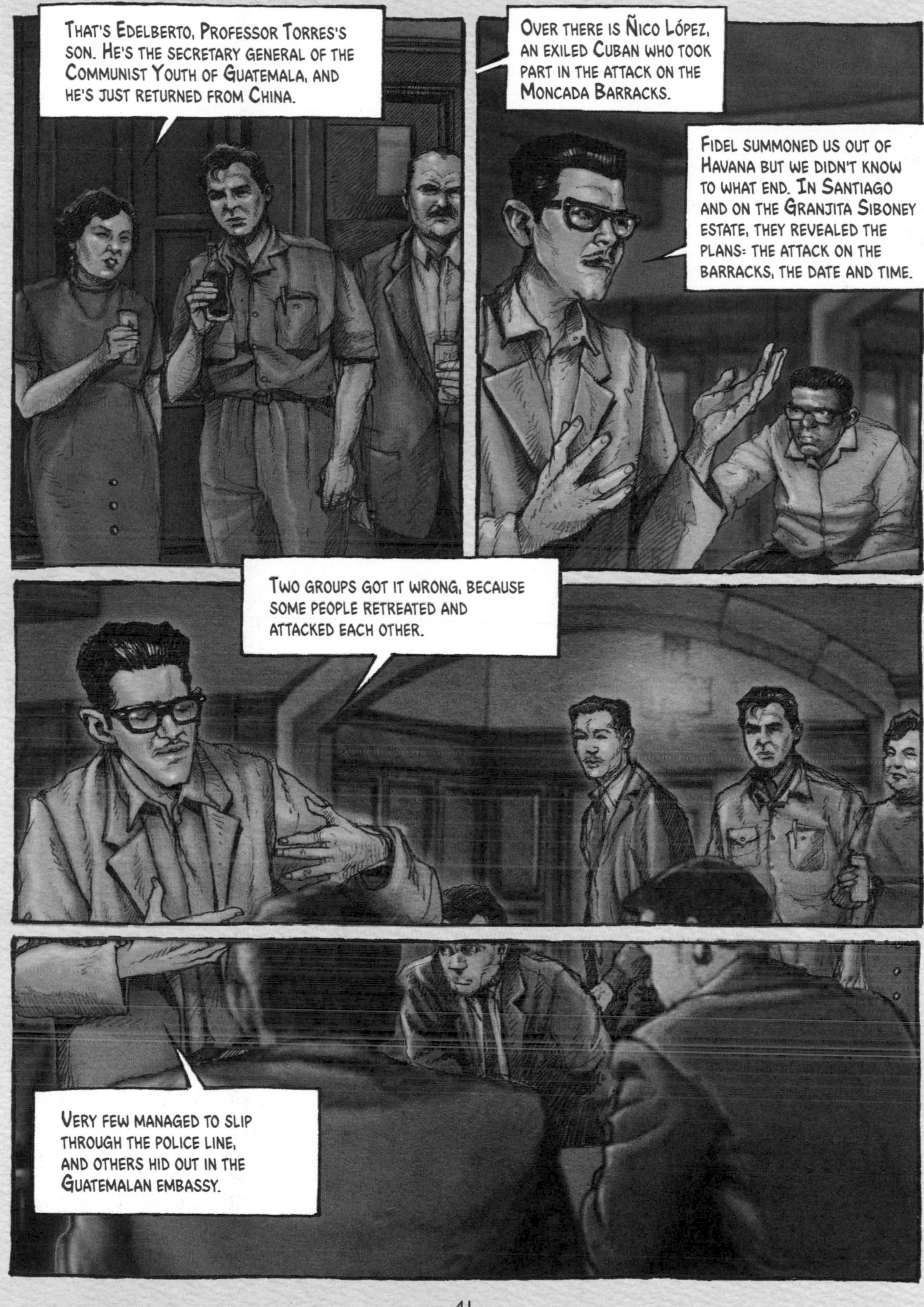
That's Edelberto, Professor Torres's son. He's the secretary general of the Communist Youth of Guatemala, and he's just returned from China.
Over there is Ñico López, an exiled Cuban who took part in the attack on the Moncada Barracks.
Fidel summoned us out of Havana but we didn't know to what end. In Santiago and on the Granjita Siboney estate, they revealed the plans: the attack on the barracks, the date and time.
Two groups got it wrong, because some people retreated and attacked each other.
Very few managed to slip through the police line, and others hid out in the Guatemalan embassy.

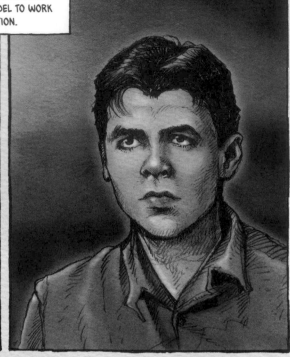

I KNOW I'M NOT GOING TO BE HERE LONG. SOON WE'LL MEET UP WITH FIDEL TO WORK FOR THE REVOLUTION.

FIDEL IS THE GREATEST AND MOST HONEST MAN CUBA HAS HAD SINCE MARTÍ.

HE WILL MAKE THE REVOLUTION.

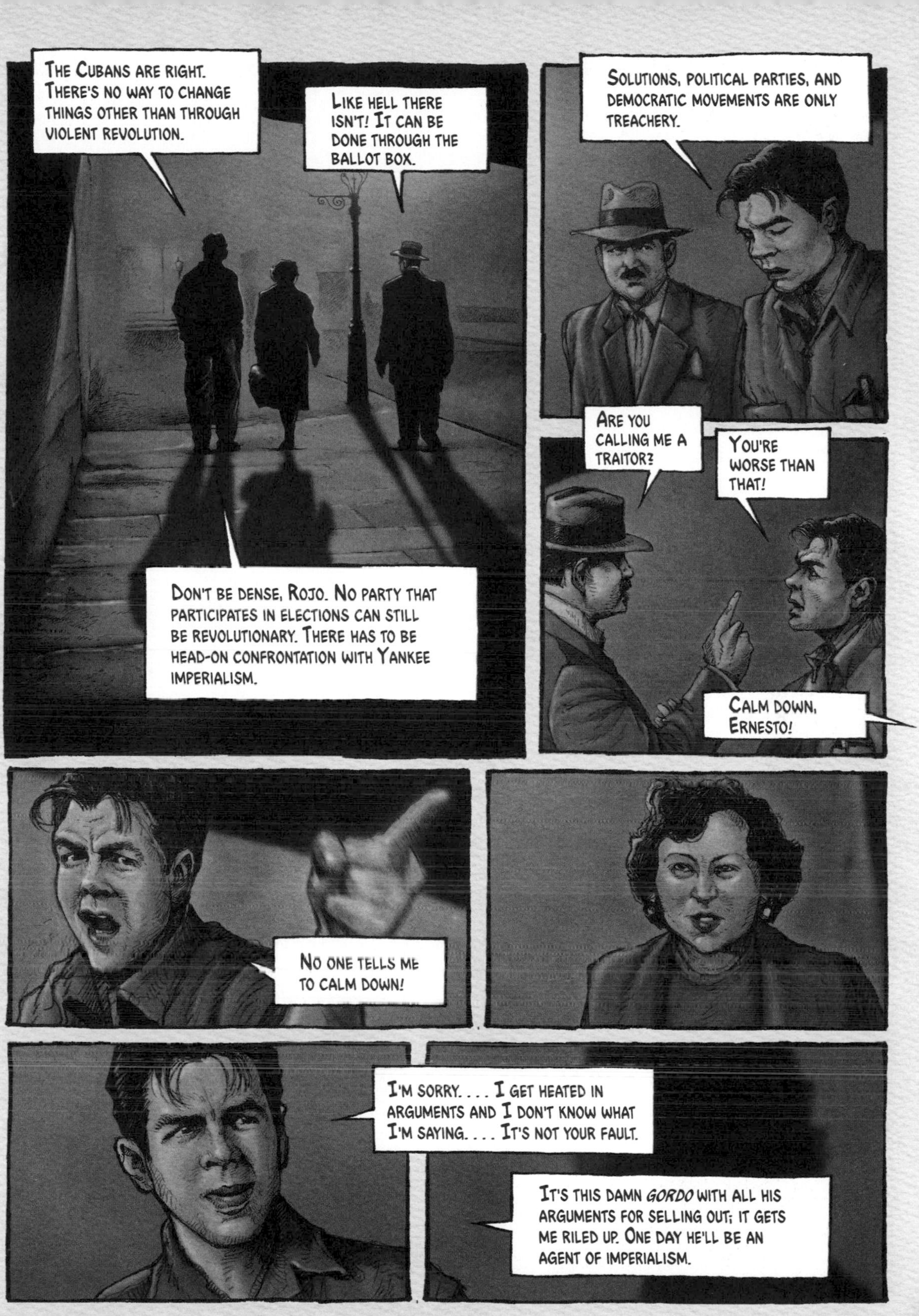
THE CUBANS ARE RIGHT. THERE'S NO WAY TO CHANGE THINGS OTHER THAN THROUGH VIOLENT REVOLUTION.
LIKE HELL THERE ISN'T! IT CAN BE DONE THROUGH THE BALLOT BOX.
DON'T BE DENSE, ROJO. NO PARTY THAT PARTICIPATES IN ELECTIONS CAN STILL BE REVOLUTIONARY. THERE HAS TO BE HEAD-ON CONFRONTATION WITH YANKEE IMPERIALISM.
SOLUTIONS, POLITICAL PARTIES, AND DEMOCRATIC MOVEMENTS ARE ONLY TREACHERY.
ARE YOU CALLING ME A TRAITOR?
YOU'RE WORSE THAN THAT!
CALM DOWN, ERNESTO!
NO ONE TELLS ME TO CALM DOWN!
I'M SORRY. . . . I GET HEATED IN ARGUMENTS AND I DON'T KNOW WHAT I'M SAYING. . . . IT'S NOT YOUR FAULT.
IT'S THIS DAMN *GORDO* WITH ALL HIS ARGUMENTS FOR SELLING OUT; IT GETS ME RILED UP. ONE DAY HE'LL BE AN AGENT OF IMPERIALISM.

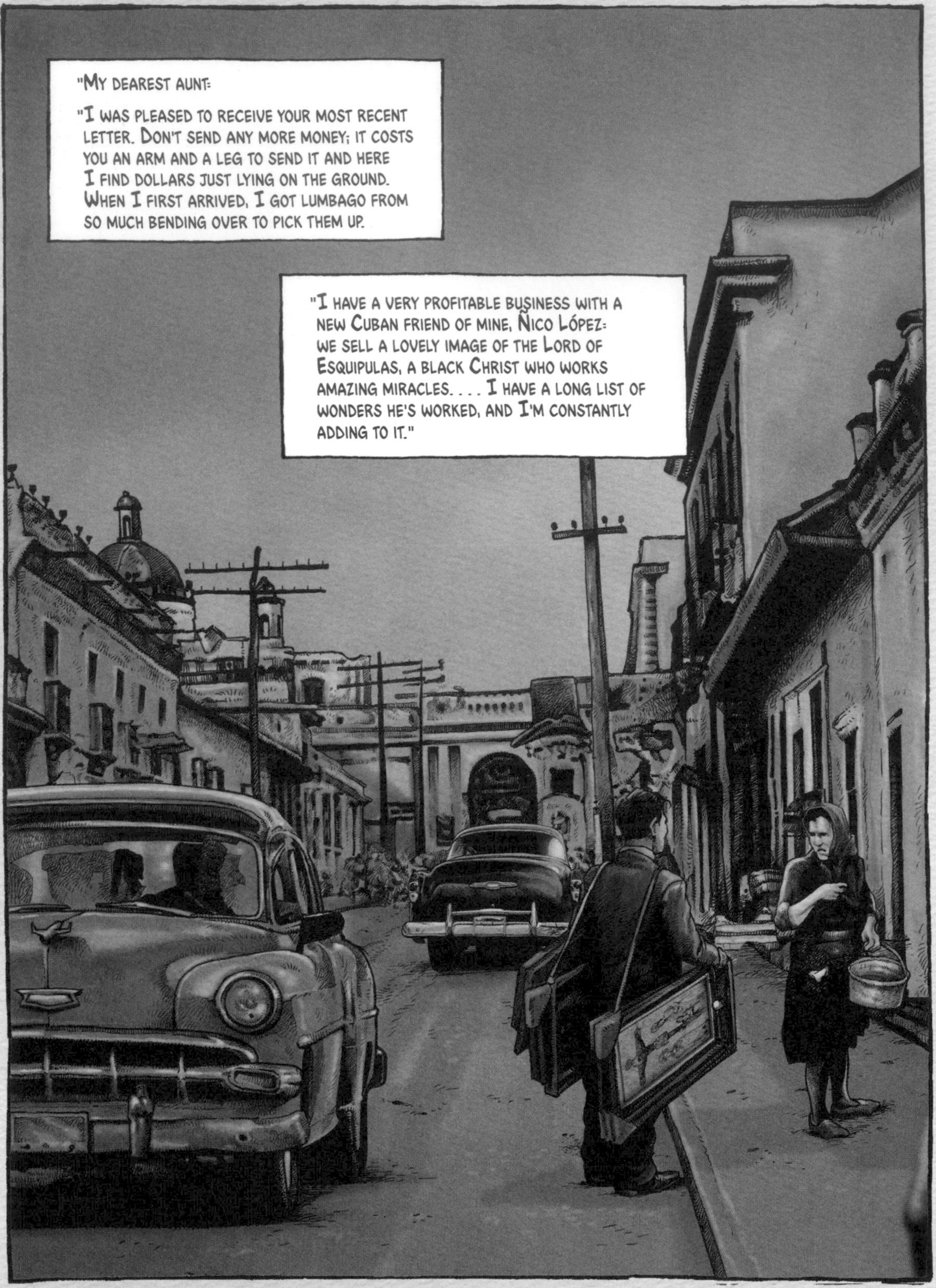
"MY DEAREST AUNT:
"I WAS PLEASED TO RECEIVE YOUR MOST RECENT LETTER. DON'T SEND ANY MORE MONEY; IT COSTS YOU AN ARM AND A LEG TO SEND IT AND HERE I FIND DOLLARS JUST LYING ON THE GROUND. WHEN I FIRST ARRIVED, I GOT LUMBAGO FROM SO MUCH BENDING OVER TO PICK THEM UP.
"I HAVE A VERY PROFITABLE BUSINESS WITH A NEW CUBAN FRIEND OF MINE, ÑICO LÓPEZ: WE SELL A LOVELY IMAGE OF THE LORD OF ESQUIPULAS, A BLACK CHRIST WHO WORKS AMAZING MIRACLES. . . . I HAVE A LONG LIST OF WONDERS HE'S WORKED, AND I'M CONSTANTLY ADDING TO IT."

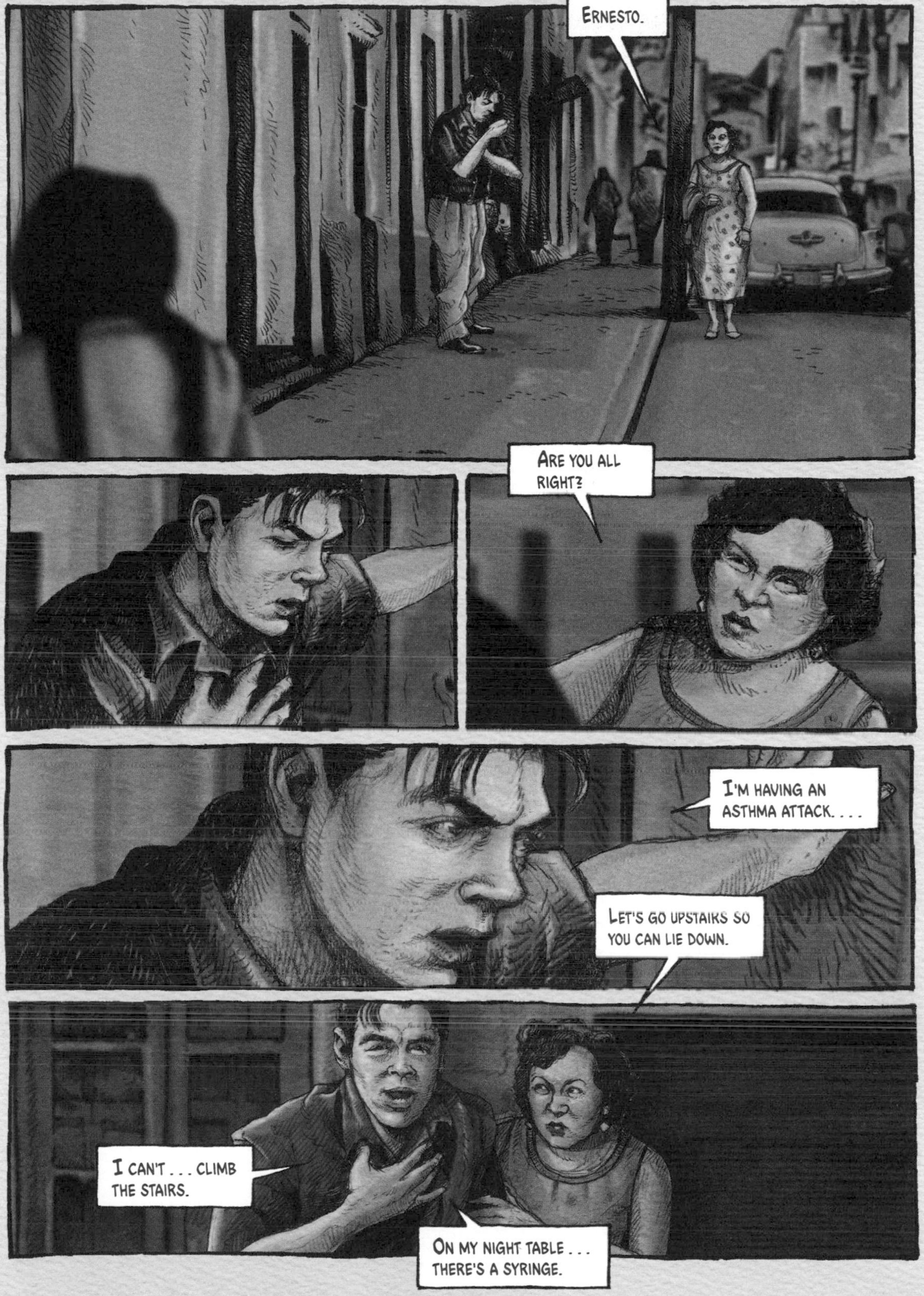
ERNESTO.
ARE YOU ALL RIGHT?
I'M HAVING AN ASTHMA ATTACK. . . .
LET'S GO UPSTAIRS SO YOU CAN LIE DOWN.
I CAN'T . . . CLIMB THE STAIRS.
ON MY NIGHT TABLE . . . THERE'S A SYRINGE.

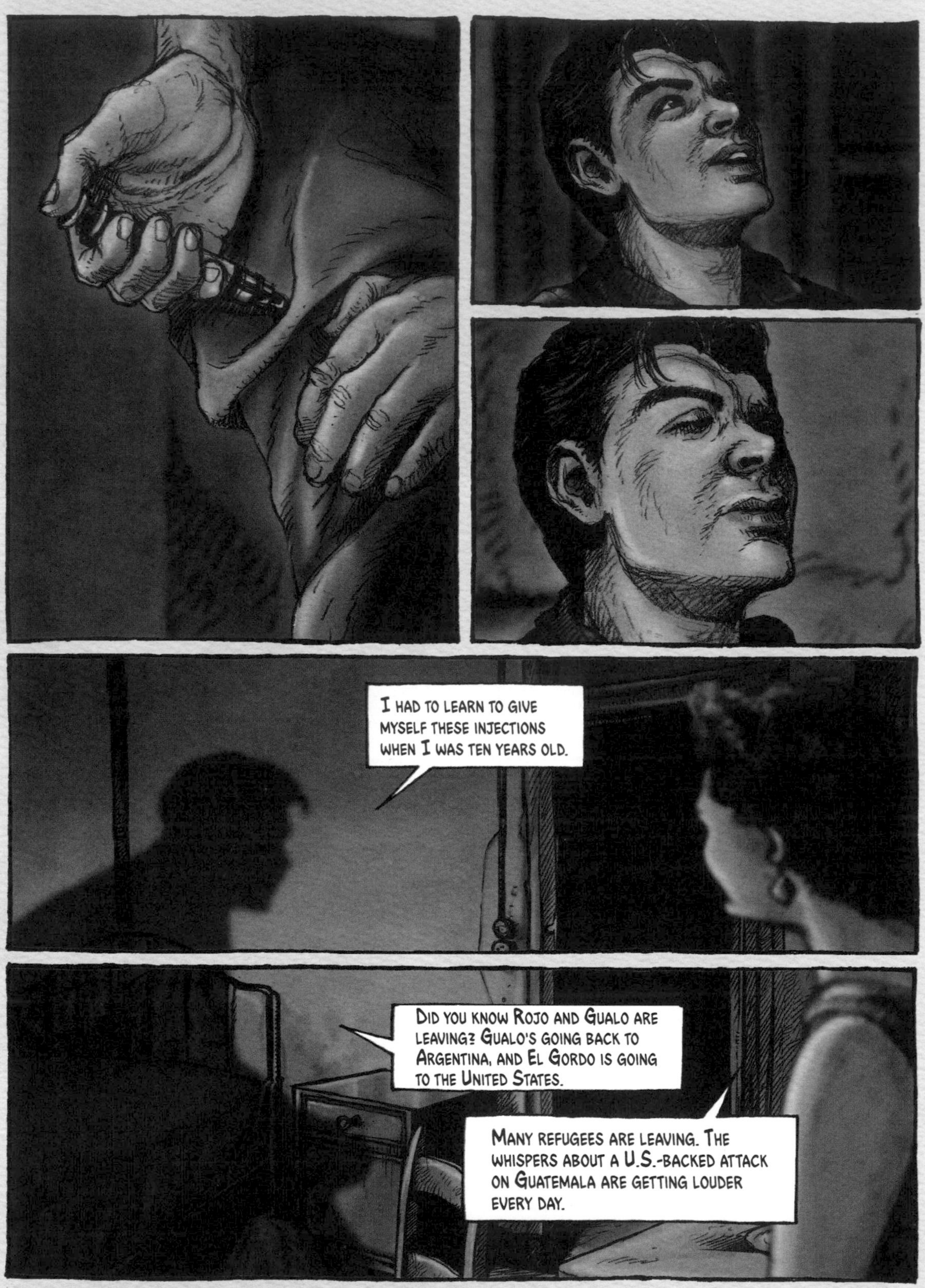
I HAD TO LEARN TO GIVE MYSELF THESE INJECTIONS WHEN I WAS TEN YEARS OLD.
DID YOU KNOW ROJO AND GUALO ARE LEAVING? GUALO'S GOING BACK TO ARGENTINA, AND EL GORDO IS GOING TO THE UNITED STATES.
MANY REFUGEES ARE LEAVING. THE WHISPERS ABOUT A U.S.-BACKED ATTACK ON GUATEMALA ARE GETTING LOUDER EVERY DAY.

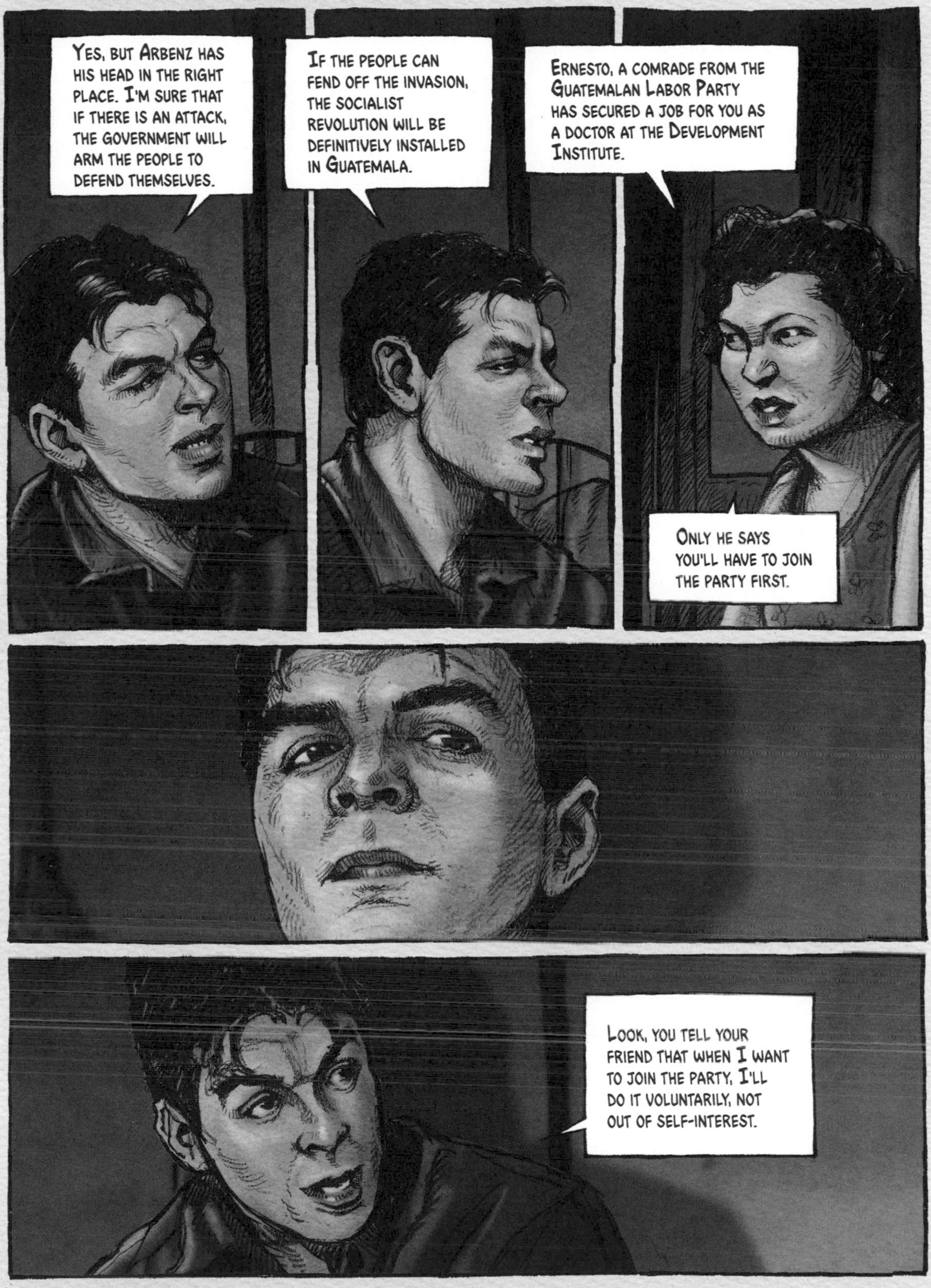
YES, BUT ARBENZ HAS HIS HEAD IN THE RIGHT PLACE. I'M SURE THAT IF THERE IS AN ATTACK, THE GOVERNMENT WILL ARM THE PEOPLE TO DEFEND THEMSELVES.
IF THE PEOPLE CAN FEND OFF THE INVASION, THE SOCIALIST REVOLUTION WILL BE DEFINITIVELY INSTALLED IN GUATEMALA.
ERNESTO, A COMRADE FROM THE GUATEMALAN LABOR PARTY HAS SECURED A JOB FOR YOU AS A DOCTOR AT THE DEVELOPMENT INSTITUTE.
ONLY HE SAYS YOU'LL HAVE TO JOIN THE PARTY FIRST.
LOOK, YOU TELL YOUR FRIEND THAT WHEN I WANT TO JOIN THE PARTY, I'LL DO IT VOLUNTARILY, NOT OUT OF SELF-INTEREST.

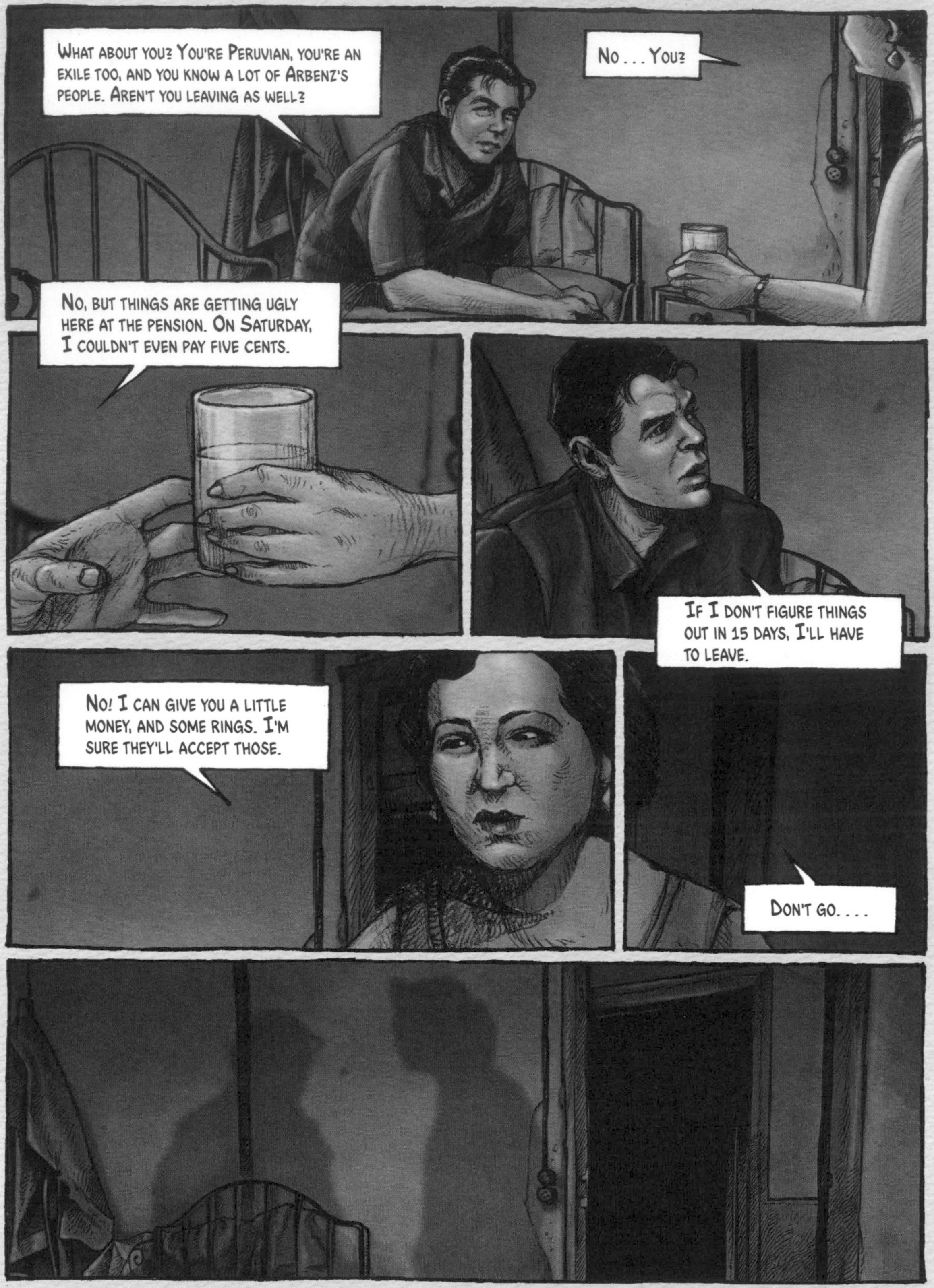
WHAT ABOUT YOU? YOU'RE PERUVIAN, YOU'RE AN EXILE TOO, AND YOU KNOW A LOT OF ARBENZ'S PEOPLE. AREN'T YOU LEAVING AS WELL?
NO . . . YOU?
NO, BUT THINGS ARE GETTING UGLY HERE AT THE PENSION. ON SATURDAY, I COULDN'T EVEN PAY FIVE CENTS.
IF I DON'T FIGURE THINGS OUT IN 15 DAYS, I'LL HAVE TO LEAVE.
NO! I CAN GIVE YOU A LITTLE MONEY, AND SOME RINGS. I'M SURE THEY'LL ACCEPT THOSE.
DON'T GO. . . .

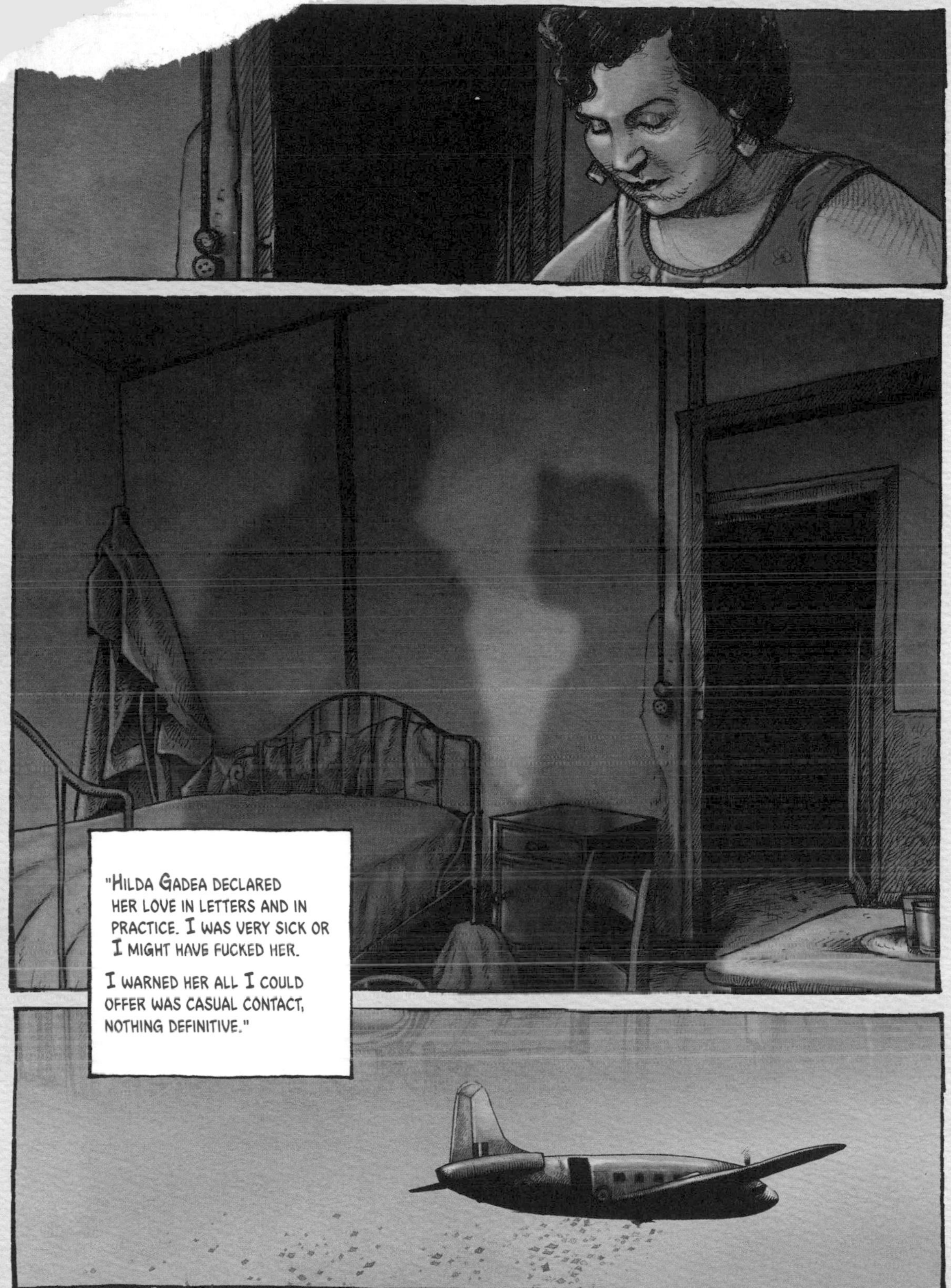
"Hilda Gadea declared her love in letters and in practice. I was very sick or I might have fucked her.
I warned her all I could offer was casual contact, nothing definitive."

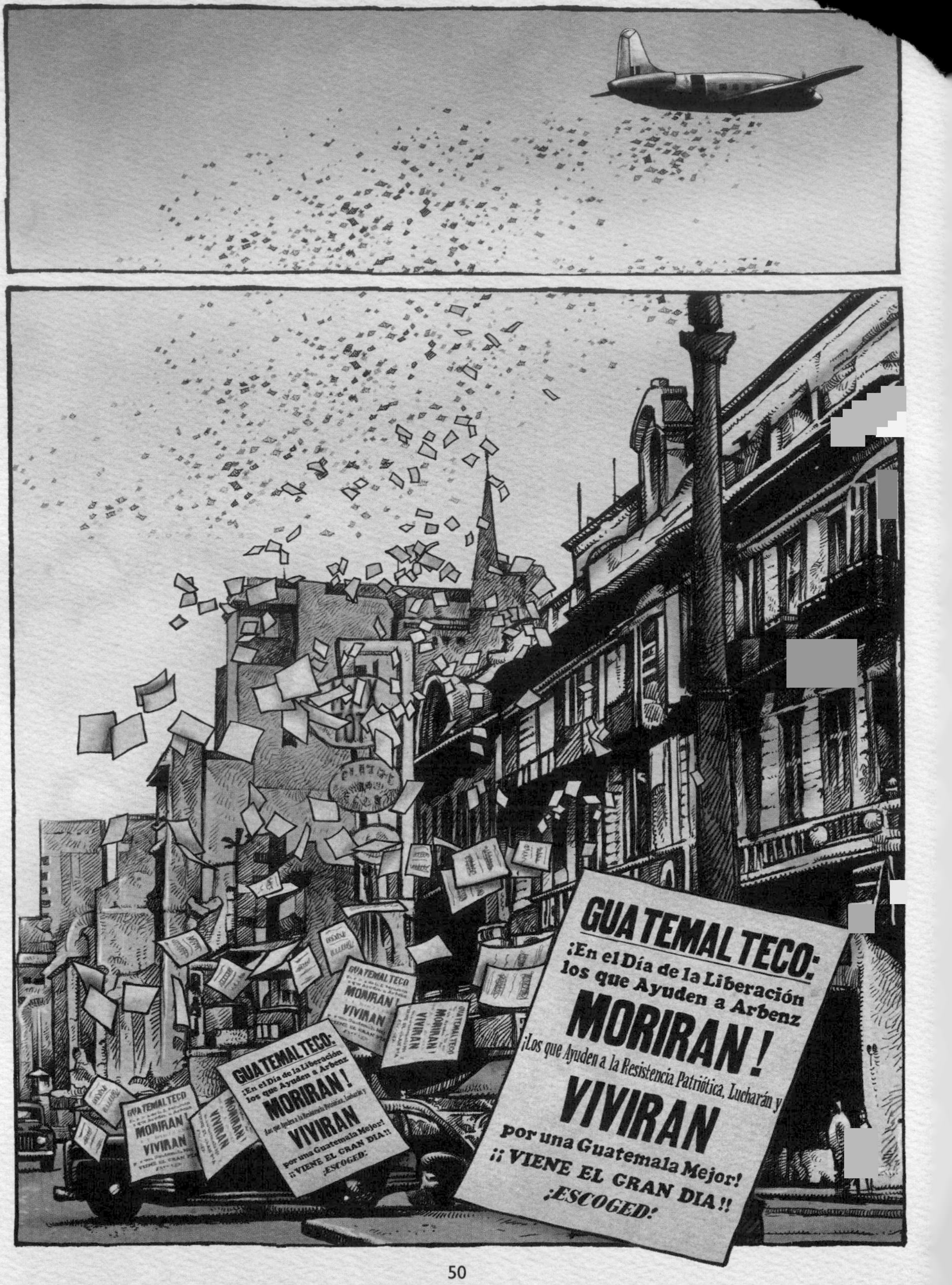
GUA TEMAL TECO:
¡En el Día de la Liberación
los que Ayuden a Arbenz
MORIRAN!
¡Los que Ayuden a la Resistencia Patriótica, Lucharán y
VIVIRAN
por una Guatemala Mejor!
¡¡ VIENE EL GRAN DIA!!
¡ESCOGED!

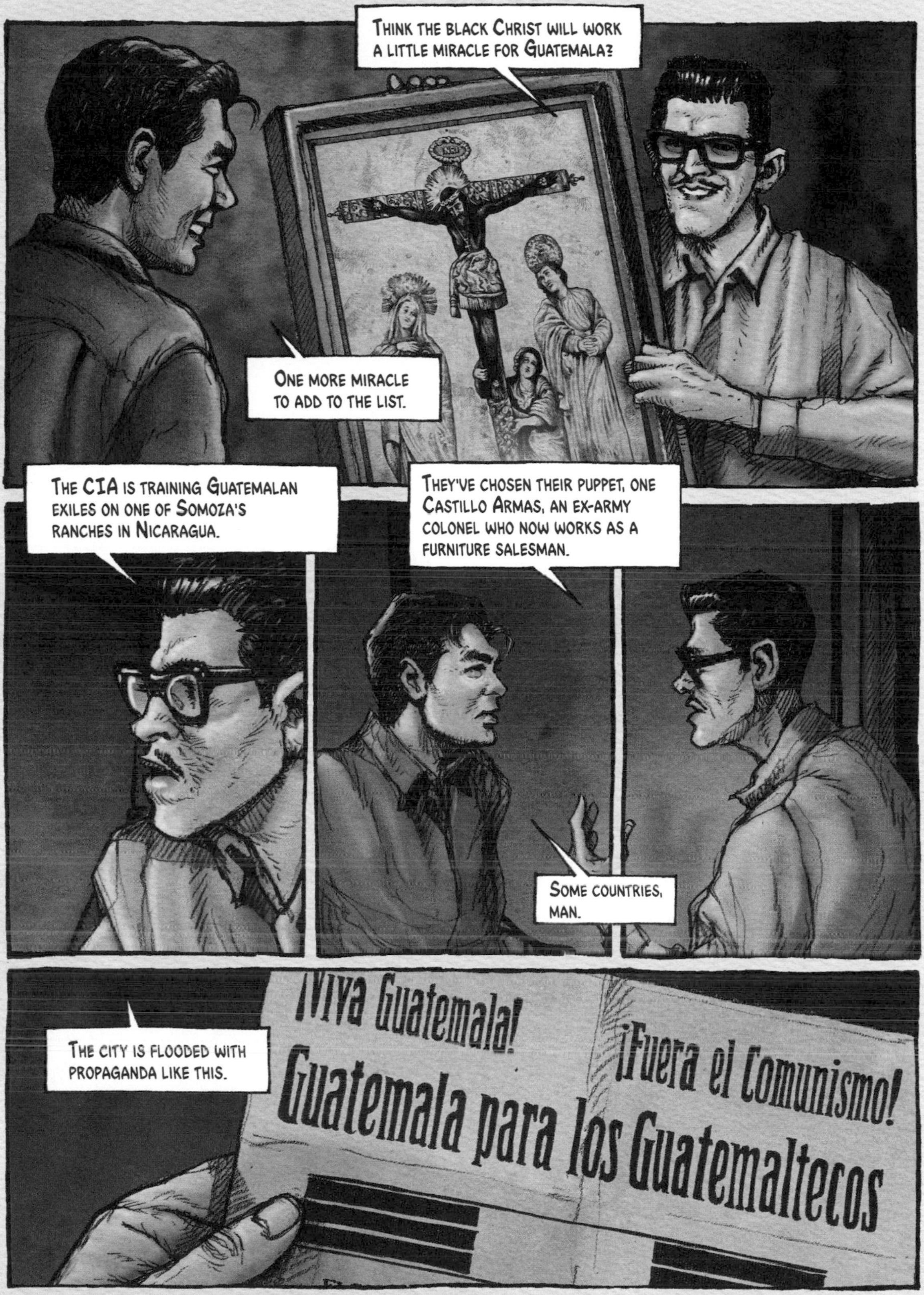
Think the black Christ will work a little miracle for Guatemala?
One more miracle to add to the list.
The CIA is training Guatemalan exiles on one of Somoza's ranches in Nicaragua.
They've chosen their puppet, one Castillo Armas, an ex-army colonel who now works as a furniture salesman.
Some countries, man.
The city is flooded with propaganda like this.
¡Viva Guatemala!
¡Fuera el Comunismo!
Guatemala para los Guatemaltecos

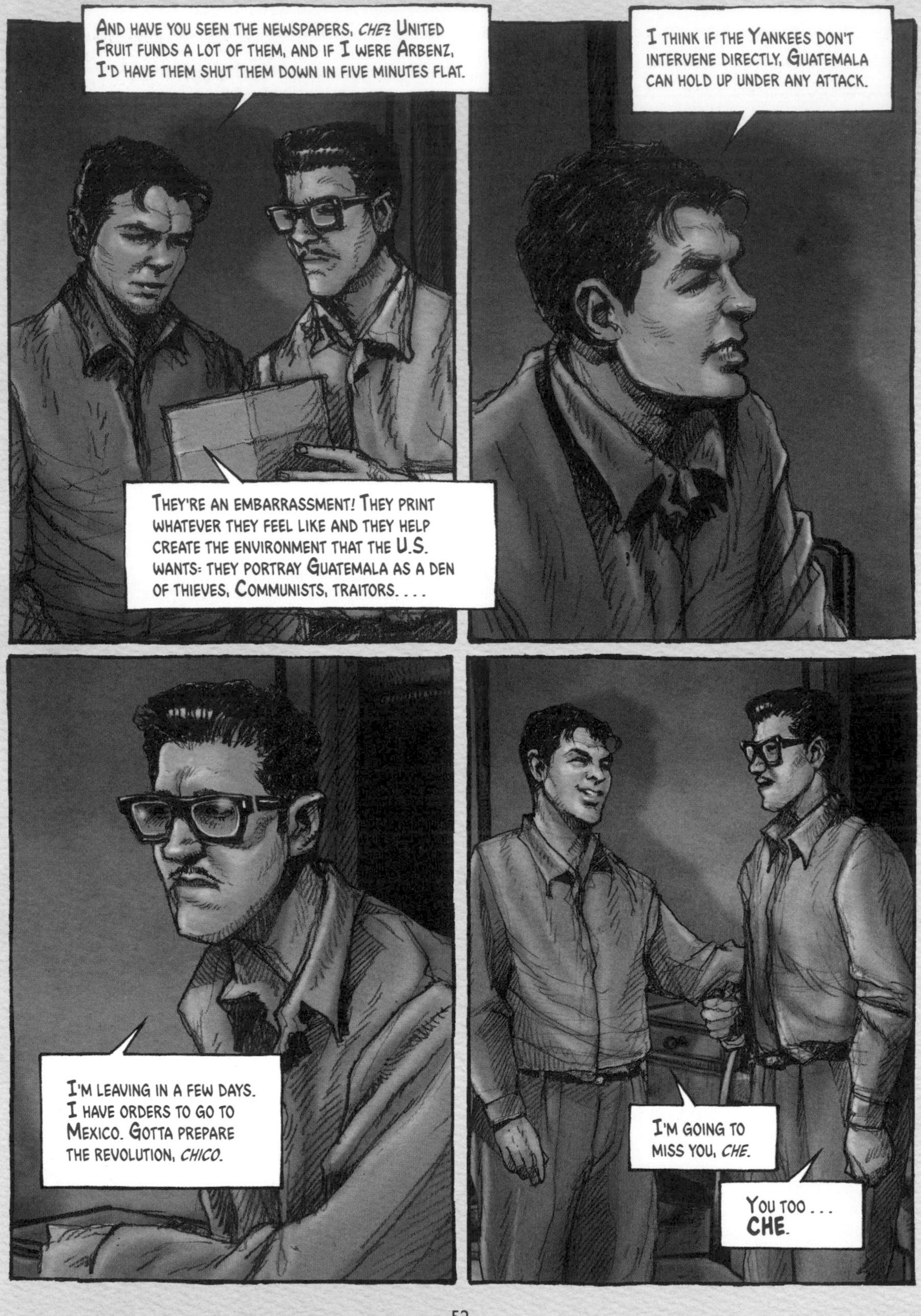
AND HAVE YOU SEEN THE NEWSPAPERS, CHE? UNITED FRUIT FUNDS A LOT OF THEM, AND IF I WERE ARBENZ, I'D HAVE THEM SHUT THEM DOWN IN FIVE MINUTES FLAT.
THEY'RE AN EMBARRASSMENT! THEY PRINT WHATEVER THEY FEEL LIKE AND THEY HELP CREATE THE ENVIRONMENT THAT THE U.S. WANTS: THEY PORTRAY GUATEMALA AS A DEN OF THIEVES, COMMUNISTS, TRAITORS. . . .
I THINK IF THE YANKEES DON'T INTERVENE DIRECTLY, GUATEMALA CAN HOLD UP UNDER ANY ATTACK.
I'M LEAVING IN A FEW DAYS. I HAVE ORDERS TO GO TO MEXICO. GOTTA PREPARE THE REVOLUTION, CHICO.
I'M GOING TO MISS YOU, CHE.
YOU TOO . . . CHE.

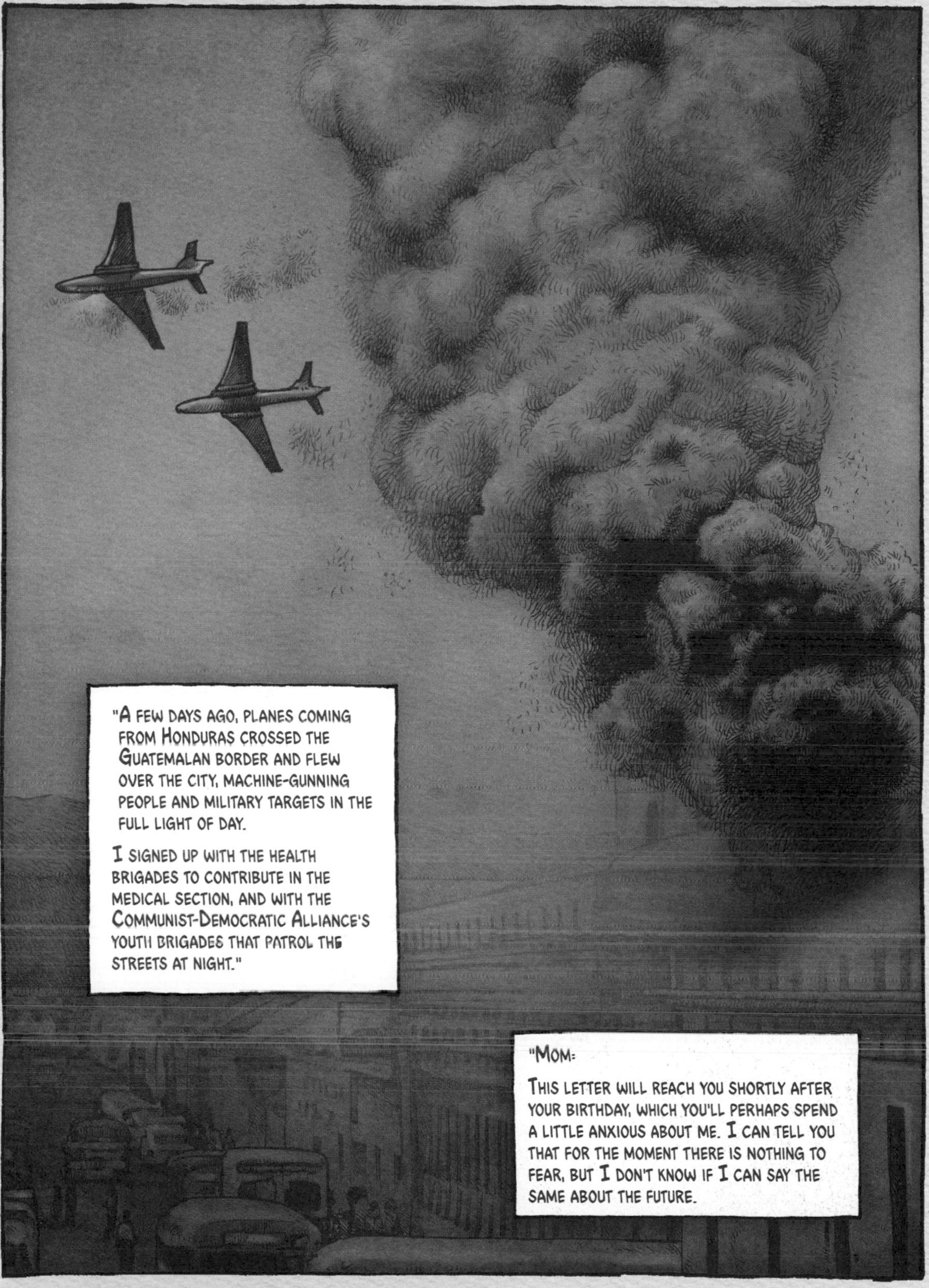
"A FEW DAYS AGO, PLANES COMING FROM HONDURAS CROSSED THE GUATEMALAN BORDER AND FLEW OVER THE CITY, MACHINE-GUNNING PEOPLE AND MILITARY TARGETS IN THE FULL LIGHT OF DAY.
I SIGNED UP WITH THE HEALTH BRIGADES TO CONTRIBUTE IN THE MEDICAL SECTION, AND WITH THE COMMUNIST-DEMOCRATIC ALLIANCE'S YOUTH BRIGADES THAT PATROL THE STREETS AT NIGHT."
"MOM:
THIS LETTER WILL REACH YOU SHORTLY AFTER YOUR BIRTHDAY, WHICH YOU'LL PERHAPS SPEND A LITTLE ANXIOUS ABOUT ME. I CAN TELL YOU THAT FOR THE MOMENT THERE IS NOTHING TO FEAR, BUT I DON'T KNOW IF I CAN SAY THE SAME ABOUT THE FUTURE.

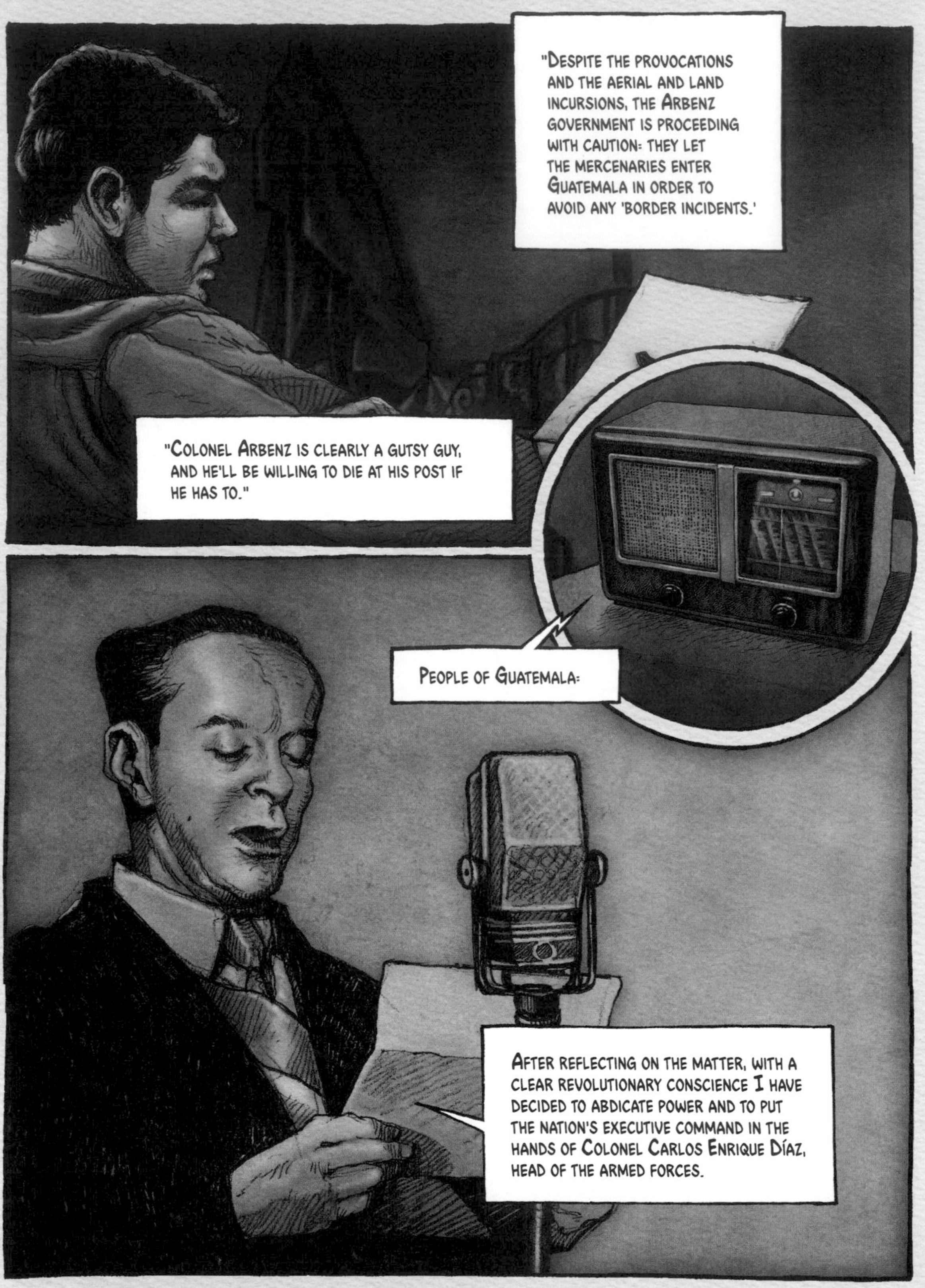
"DESPITE THE PROVOCATIONS AND THE AERIAL AND LAND INCURSIONS, THE ARBENZ GOVERNMENT IS PROCEEDING WITH CAUTION: THEY LET THE MERCENARIES ENTER GUATEMALA IN ORDER TO AVOID ANY 'BORDER INCIDENTS.'
"COLONEL ARBENZ IS CLEARLY A GUTSY GUY, AND HE'LL BE WILLING TO DIE AT HIS POST IF HE HAS TO."
PEOPLE OF GUATEMALA:
AFTER REFLECTING ON THE MATTER, WITH A CLEAR REVOLUTIONARY CONSCIENCE I HAVE DECIDED TO ABDICATE POWER AND TO PUT THE NATION'S EXECUTIVE COMMAND IN THE HANDS OF COLONEL CARLOS ENRIQUE DÍAZ, HEAD OF THE ARMED FORCES.

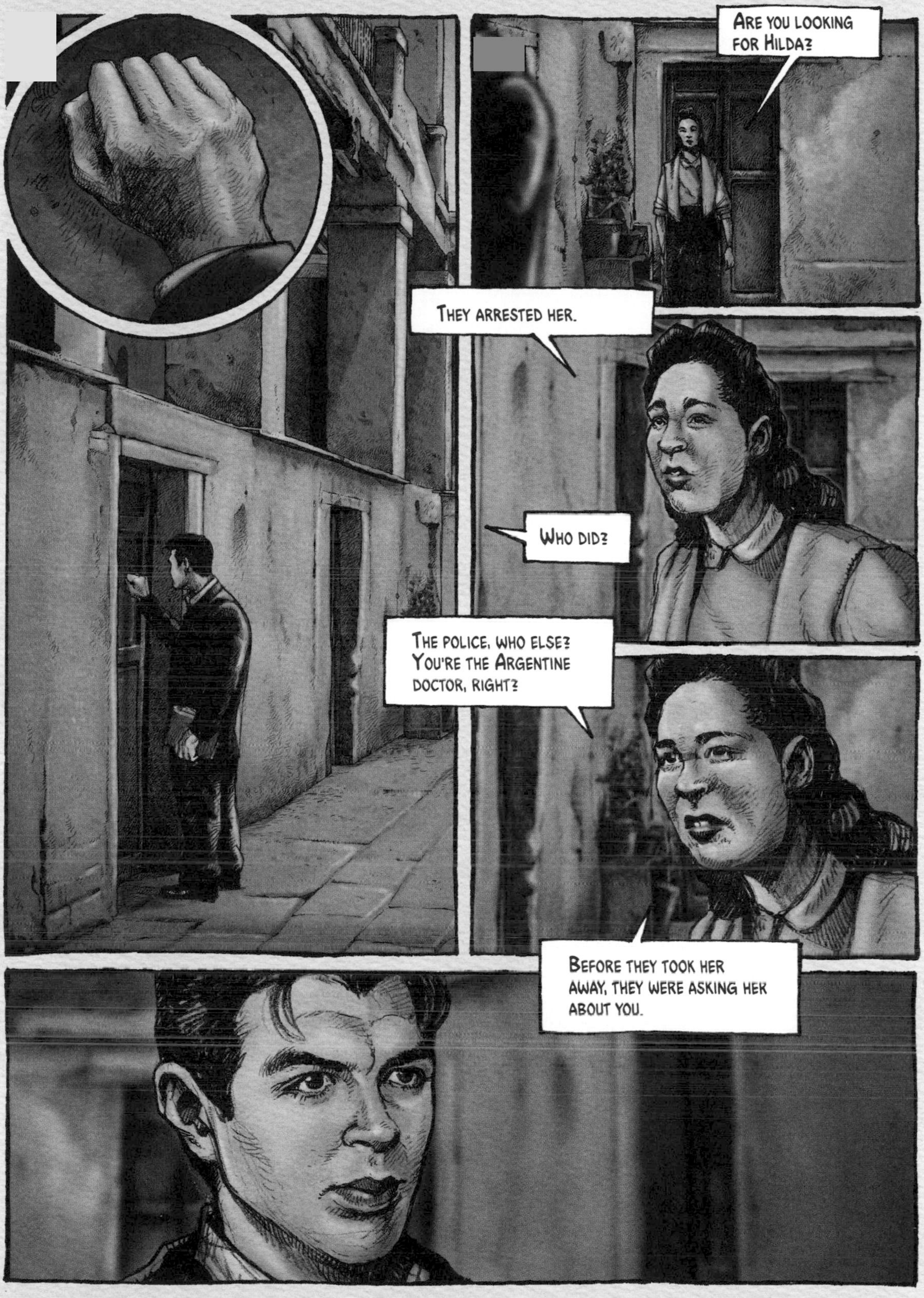
Are you looking for Hilda?
They arrested her.
Who did?
The police, who else? You're the Argentine doctor, right?
Before they took her away, they were asking her about you.

ARGENTINE DOCTOR, 25 YEARS OLD, CAME TO GUATEMALA TO STUDY "MEDICAL CARE AMID SOCIAL REVOLUTION . . . "

SHOULD WE OPEN A FILE ON THIS ONE, MR. PHILLIPS?

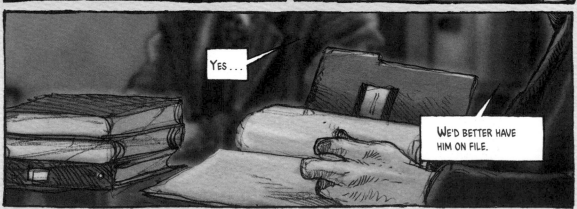

YES . . .

WE'D BETTER HAVE HIM ON FILE.

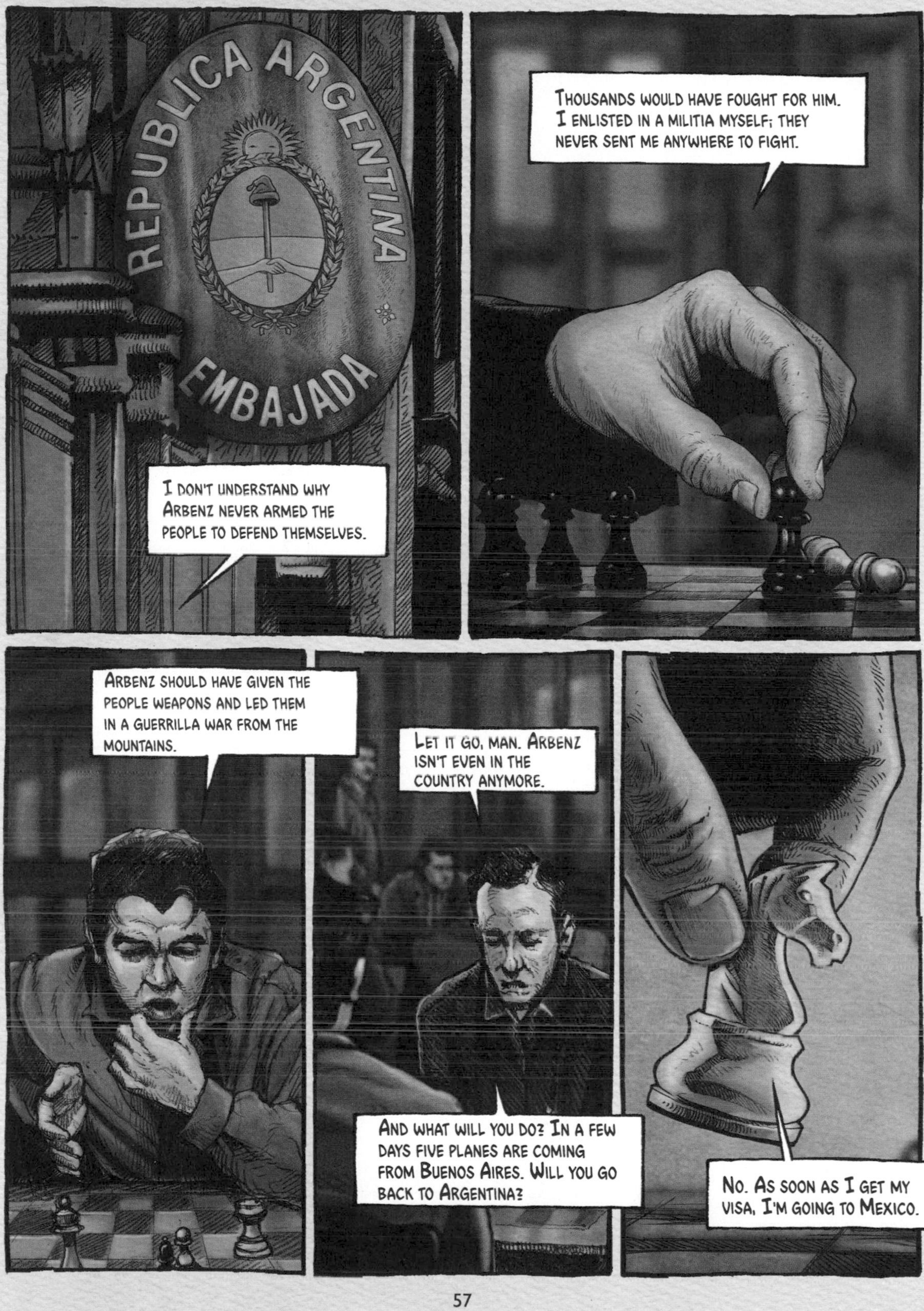
REPUBLICA ARGENTINA
EMBAJADA
I DON'T UNDERSTAND WHY ARBENZ NEVER ARMED THE PEOPLE TO DEFEND THEMSELVES.
THOUSANDS WOULD HAVE FOUGHT FOR HIM. I ENLISTED IN A MILITIA MYSELF; THEY NEVER SENT ME ANYWHERE TO FIGHT.
ARBENZ SHOULD HAVE GIVEN THE PEOPLE WEAPONS AND LED THEM IN A GUERRILLA WAR FROM THE MOUNTAINS.
LET IT GO, MAN. ARBENZ ISN'T EVEN IN THE COUNTRY ANYMORE.
AND WHAT WILL YOU DO? IN A FEW DAYS FIVE PLANES ARE COMING FROM BUENOS AIRES. WILL YOU GO BACK TO ARGENTINA?
NO. AS SOON AS I GET MY VISA, I'M GOING TO MEXICO.

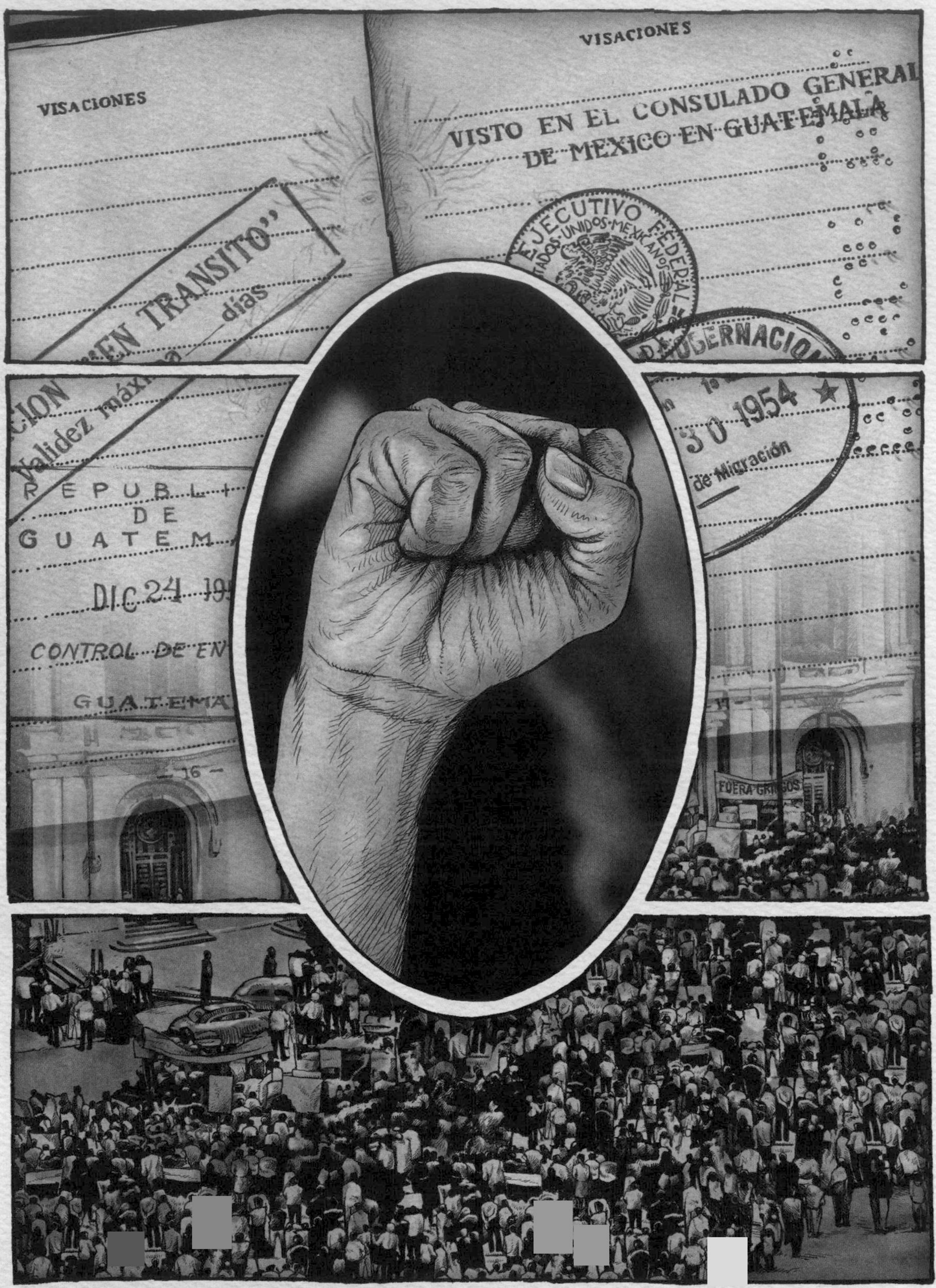
VISACIONES
VISACIONES
VISTO EN EL CONSULADO GENERAL
DE MEXICO EN GUATEMALA
EJECUTIVO FEDERAL
"EN TRANSITO"
días
R E P U B L I
D E
G U A T E M
DIC 24 19
CONTROL DE EN
GUATEMA
— 16 —
30 1954
de Migración
FUERA GRINGOS

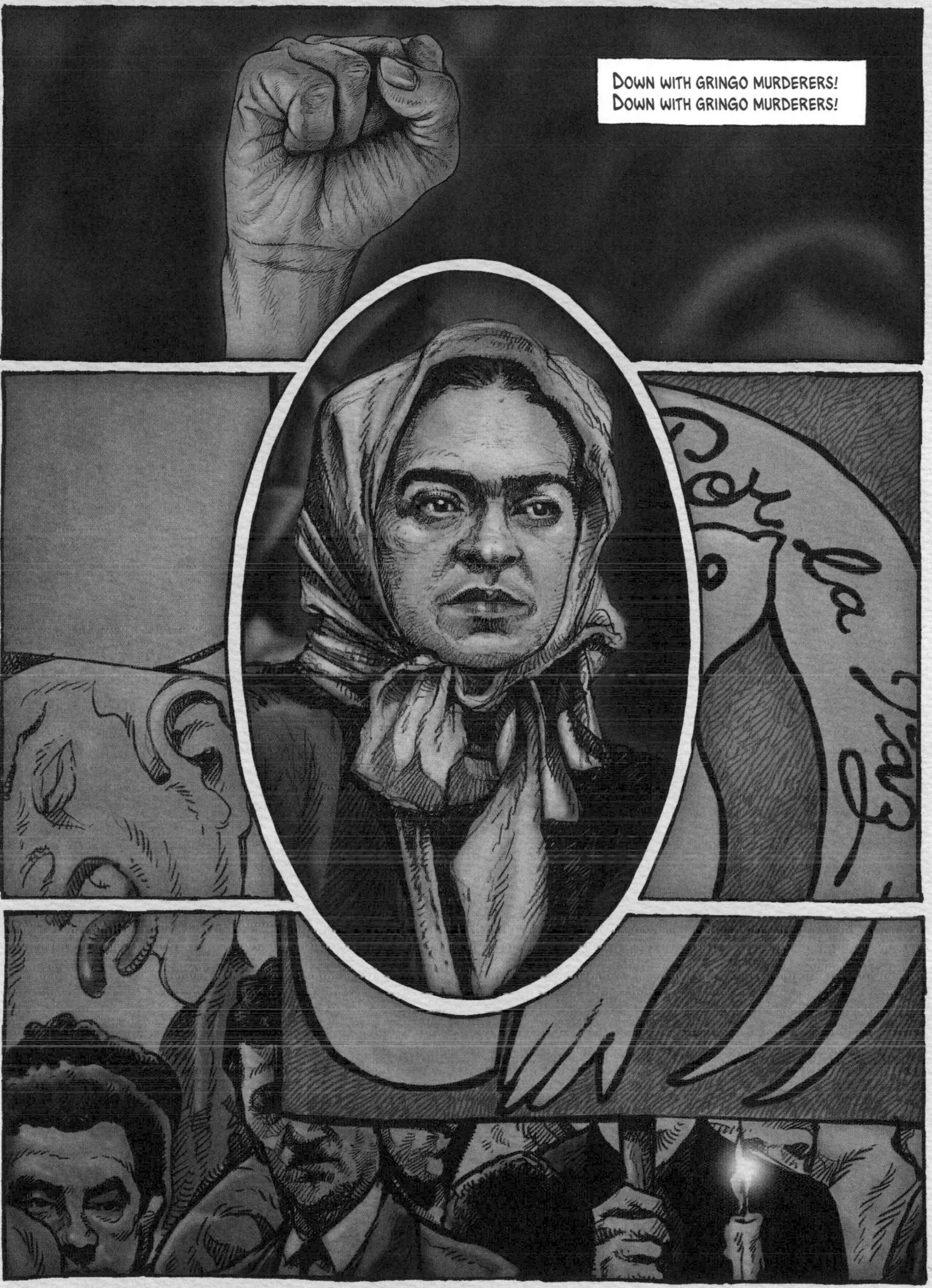
DOWN WITH GRINGO MURDERERS!
DOWN WITH GRINGO MURDERERS!

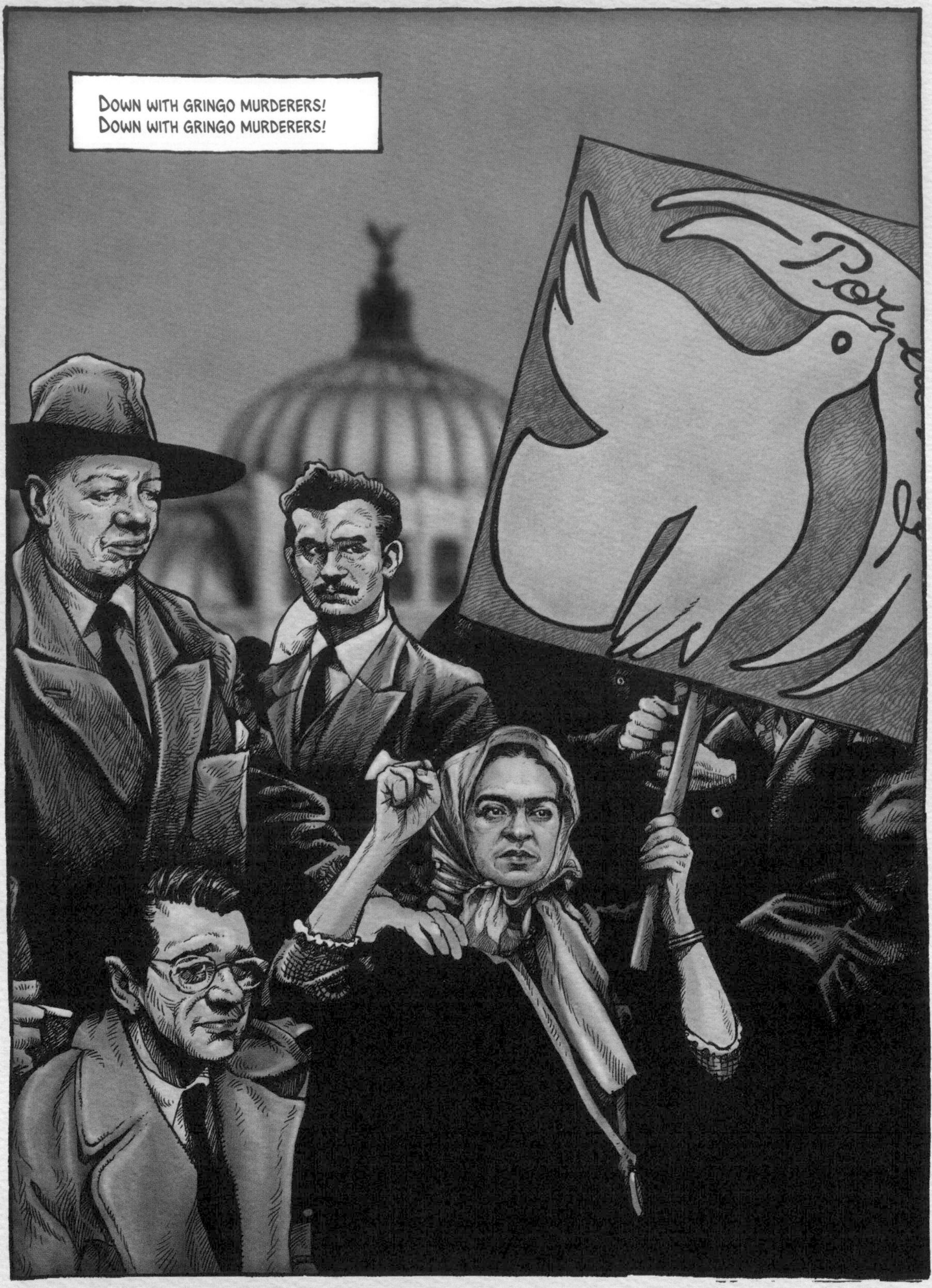
DOWN WITH GRINGO MURDERERS!
DOWN WITH GRINGO MURDERERS!

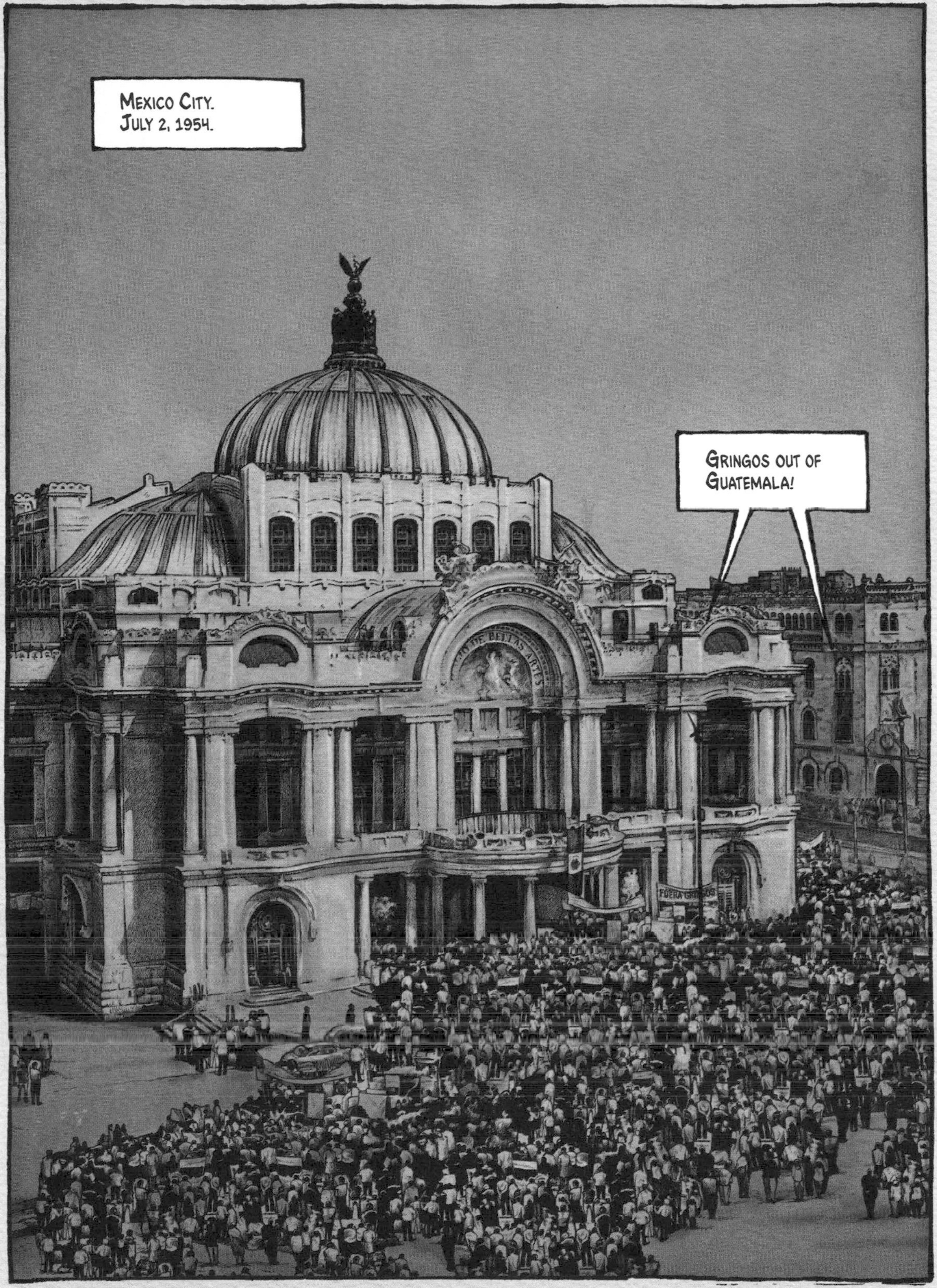
Mexico City.
July 2, 1954.
Gringos out of Guatemala!

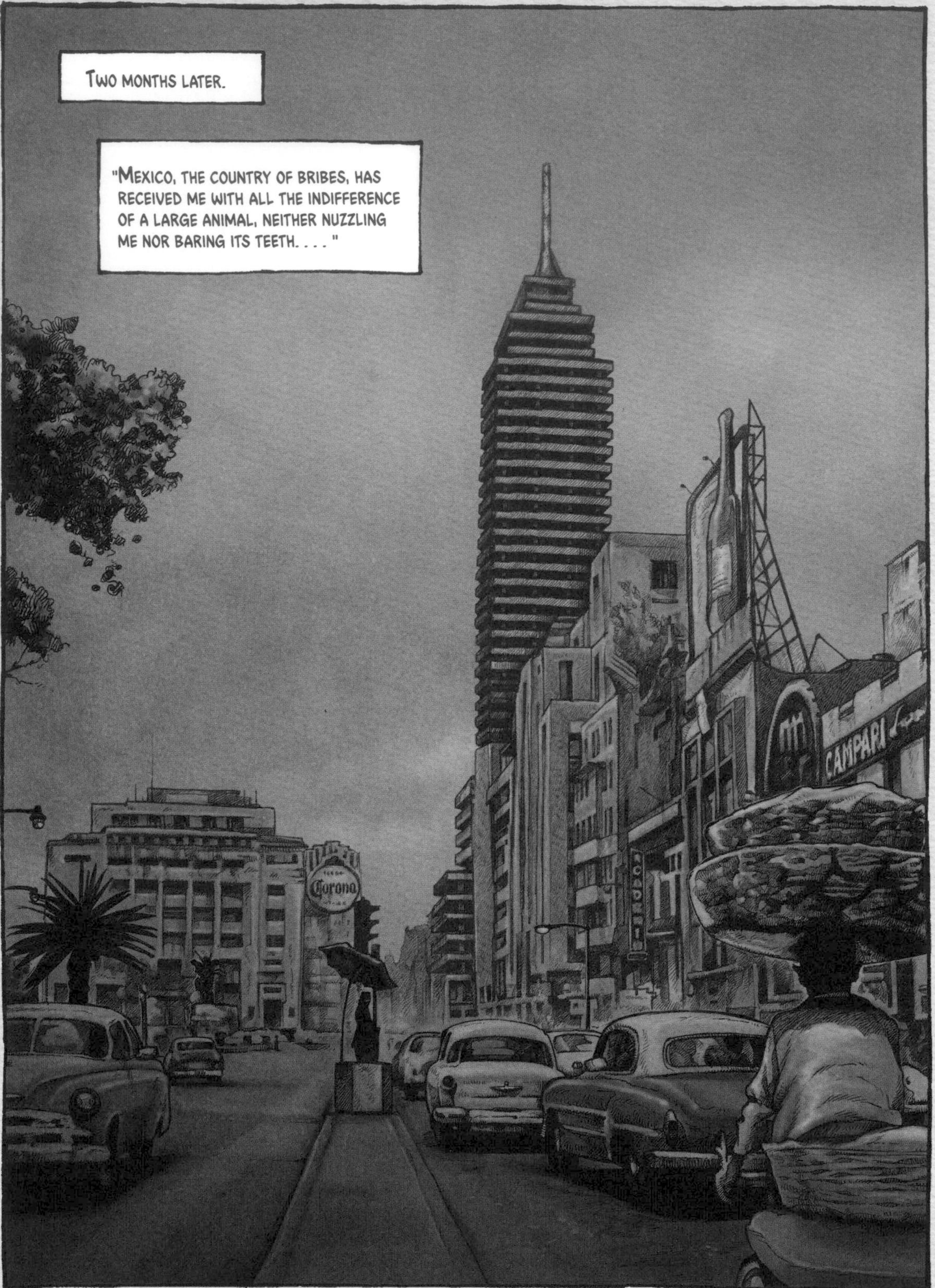
Two months later.
"Mexico, the country of bribes, has received me with all the indifference of a large animal, neither nuzzling me nor baring its teeth. . . ."
Corona
Campari

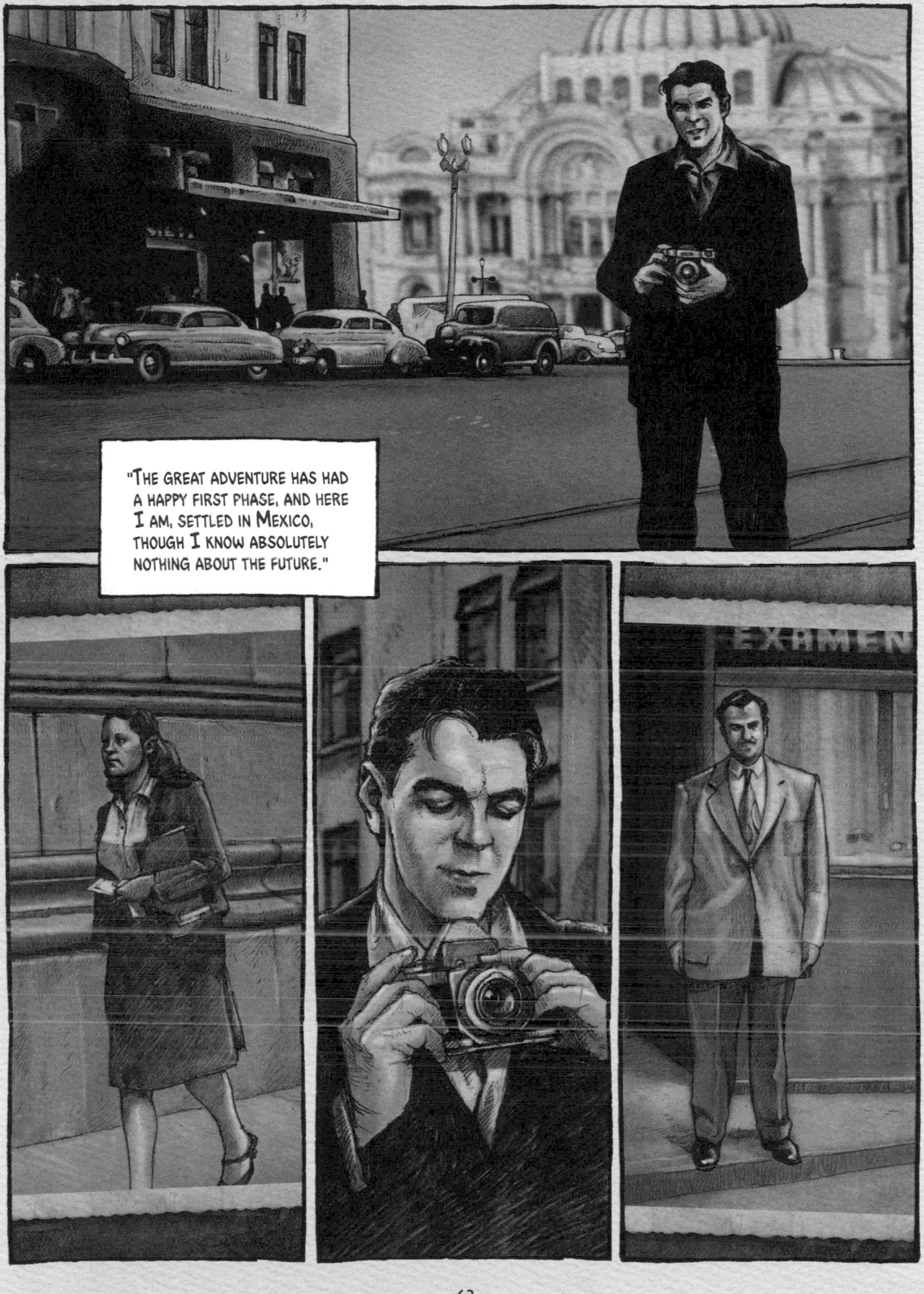
"THE GREAT ADVENTURE HAS HAD A HAPPY FIRST PHASE, AND HERE I AM, SETTLED IN MEXICO, THOUGH I KNOW ABSOLUTELY NOTHING ABOUT THE FUTURE."
EXAMEN

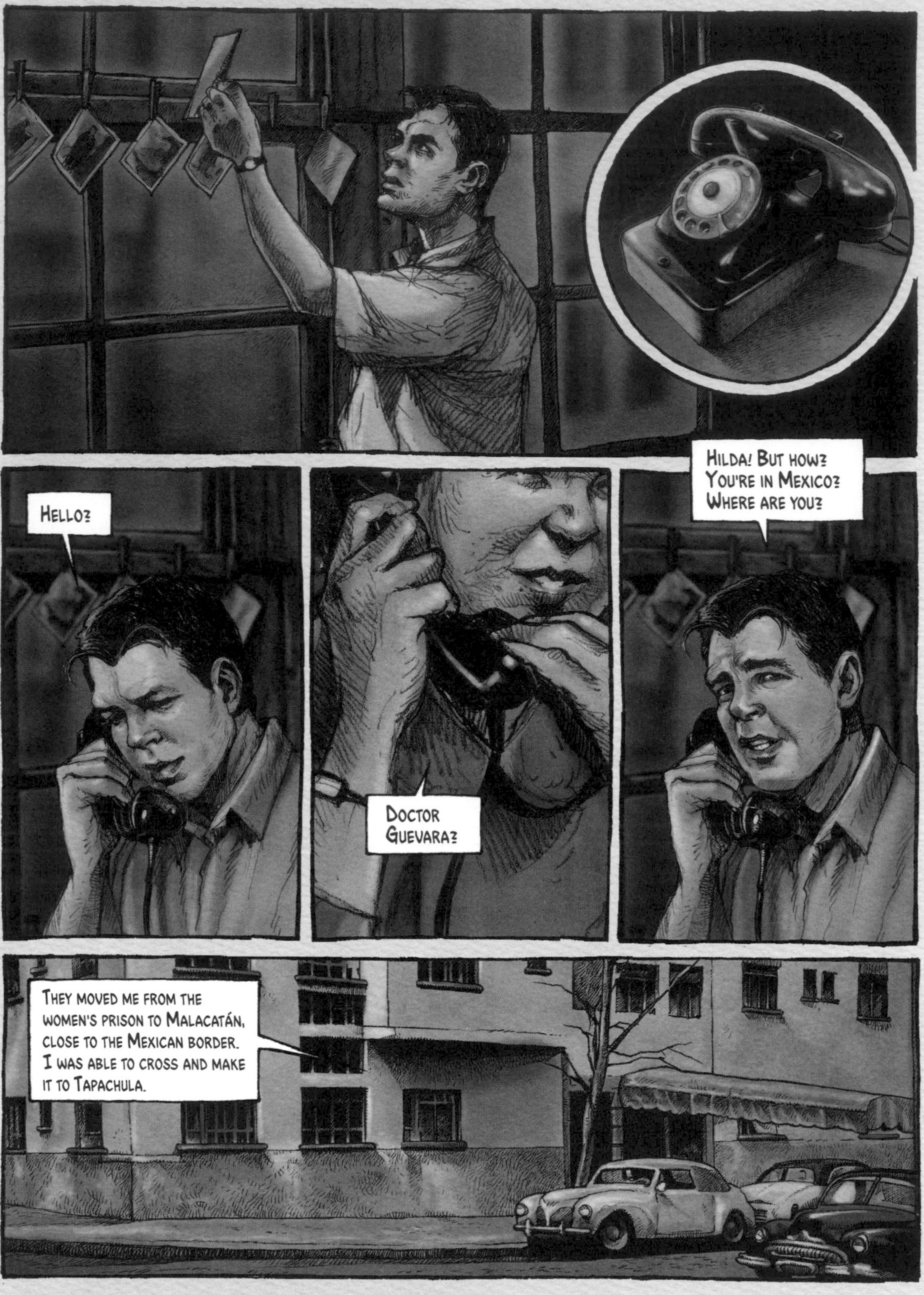
HELLO?
DOCTOR GUEVARA?
HILDA! BUT HOW? YOU'RE IN MEXICO? WHERE ARE YOU?
THEY MOVED ME FROM THE WOMEN'S PRISON TO MALACATÁN, CLOSE TO THE MEXICAN BORDER. I WAS ABLE TO CROSS AND MAKE IT TO TAPACHULA.

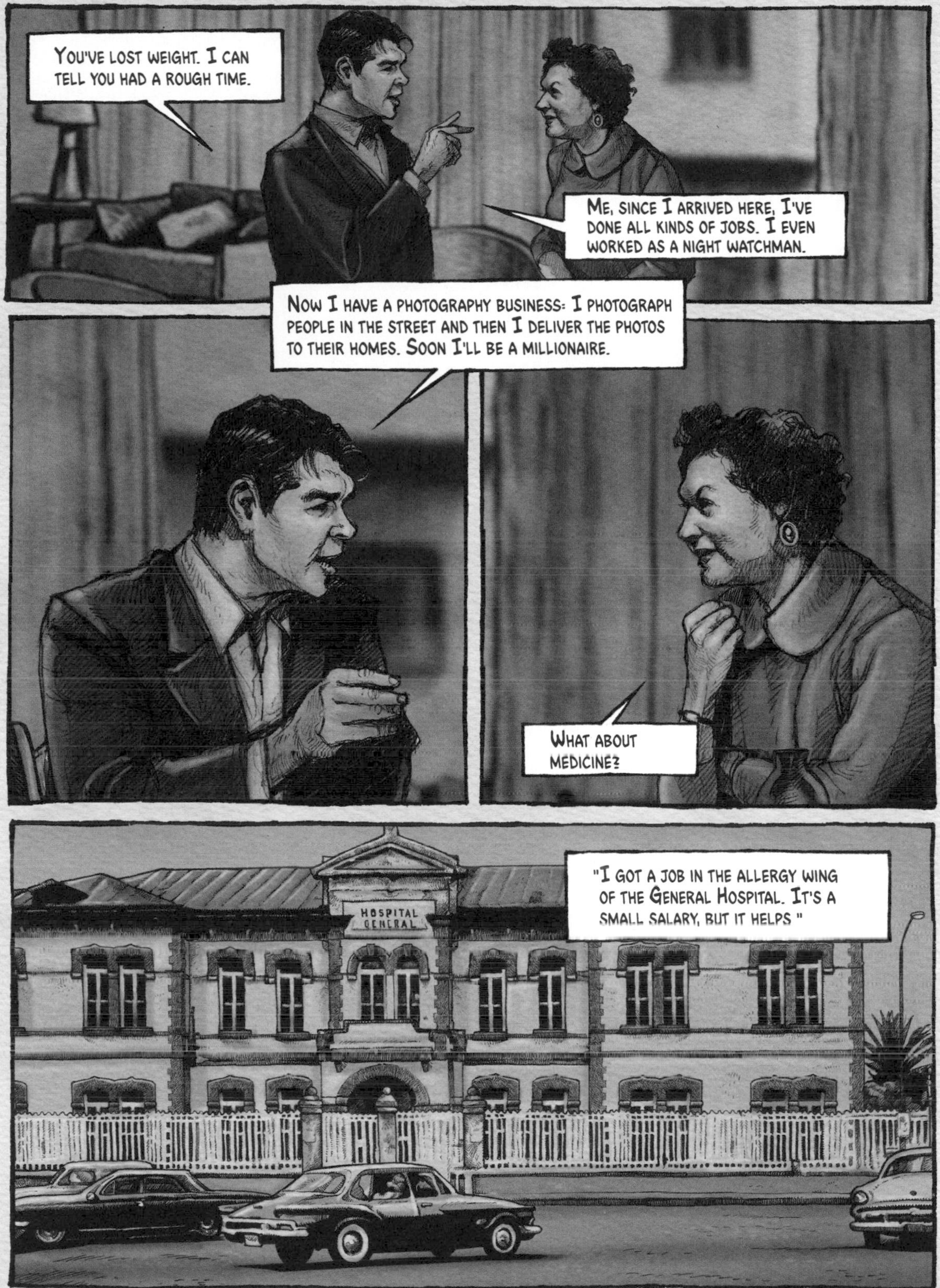
YOU'VE LOST WEIGHT. I CAN TELL YOU HAD A ROUGH TIME.
ME, SINCE I ARRIVED HERE, I'VE DONE ALL KINDS OF JOBS. I EVEN WORKED AS A NIGHT WATCHMAN.
NOW I HAVE A PHOTOGRAPHY BUSINESS: I PHOTOGRAPH PEOPLE IN THE STREET AND THEN I DELIVER THE PHOTOS TO THEIR HOMES. SOON I'LL BE A MILLIONAIRE.
WHAT ABOUT MEDICINE?
HOSPITAL GENERAL
"I GOT A JOB IN THE ALLERGY WING OF THE GENERAL HOSPITAL. IT'S A SMALL SALARY, BUT IT HELPS"

María, how are you?
Oh, Doctor. I'm here, which is already something.
I slept real bad, Doctor, I felt like I was suffocating.
Your daughter isn't coming today?
No, Doctor, she has to take care of my grandchildren. . . .
And wash all the clothes I can't wash because I'm here.
What are you doing there, María?
Praying, Doctor, what else? Asking God to remember me.

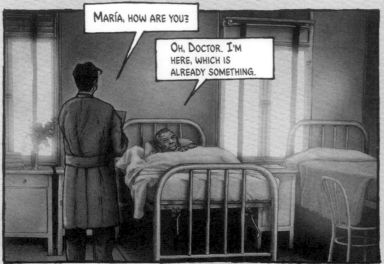

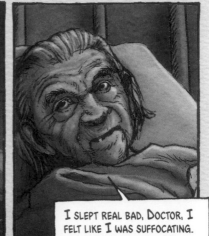

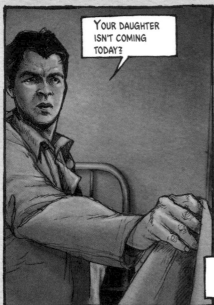

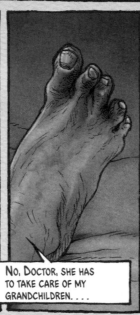

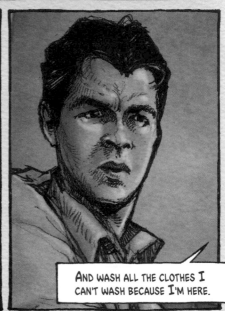

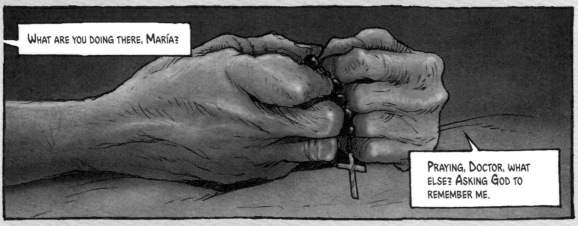

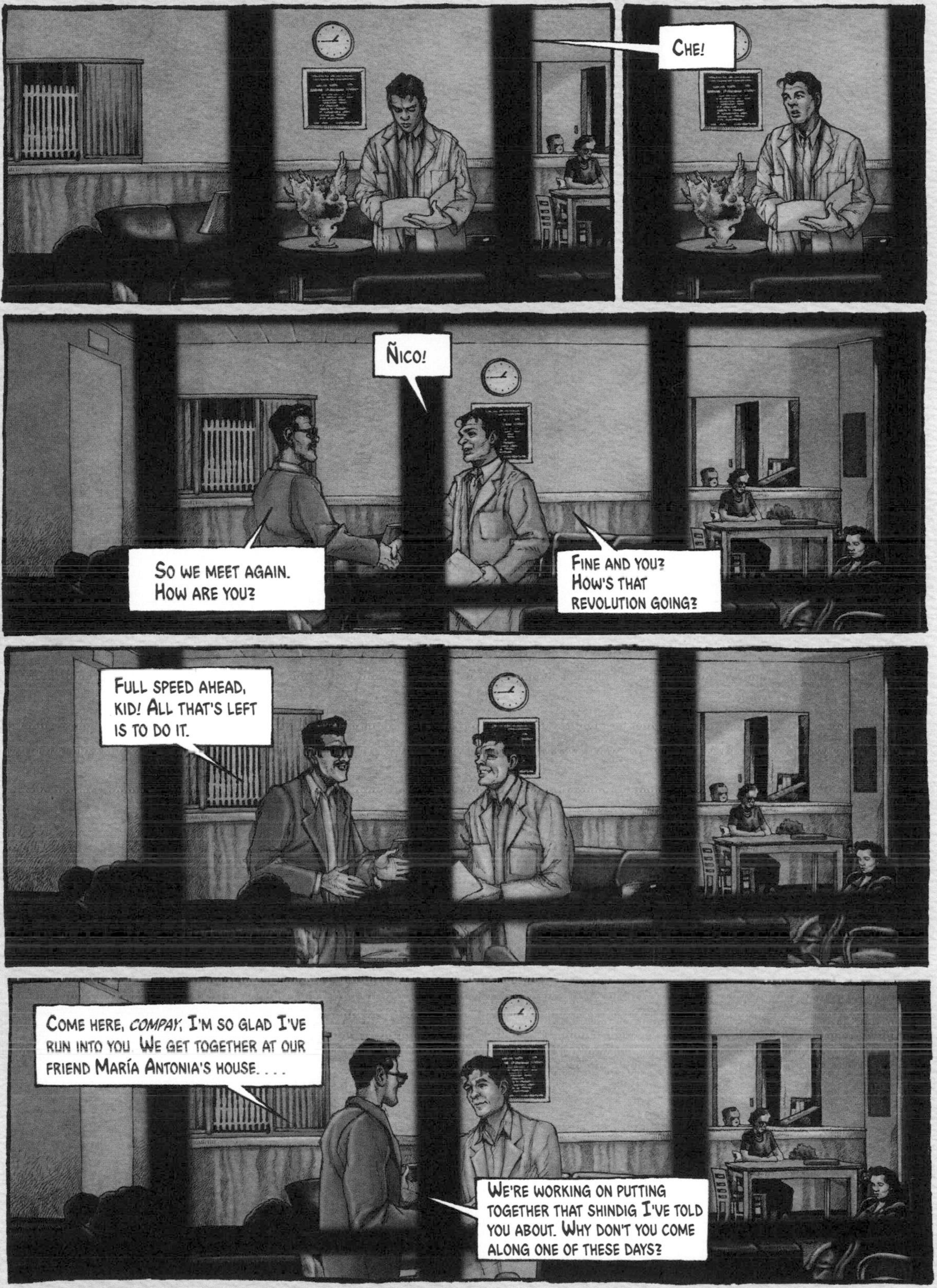
CHE!
ÑICO!
SO WE MEET AGAIN. HOW ARE YOU?
FINE AND YOU? HOW'S THAT REVOLUTION GOING?
FULL SPEED AHEAD, KID! ALL THAT'S LEFT IS TO DO IT.
COME HERE, *COMPAY*. I'M SO GLAD I'VE RUN INTO YOU. WE GET TOGETHER AT OUR FRIEND MARÍA ANTONIA'S HOUSE. . . .
WE'RE WORKING ON PUTTING TOGETHER THAT SHINDIG I'VE TOLD YOU ABOUT. WHY DON'T YOU COME ALONG ONE OF THESE DAYS?

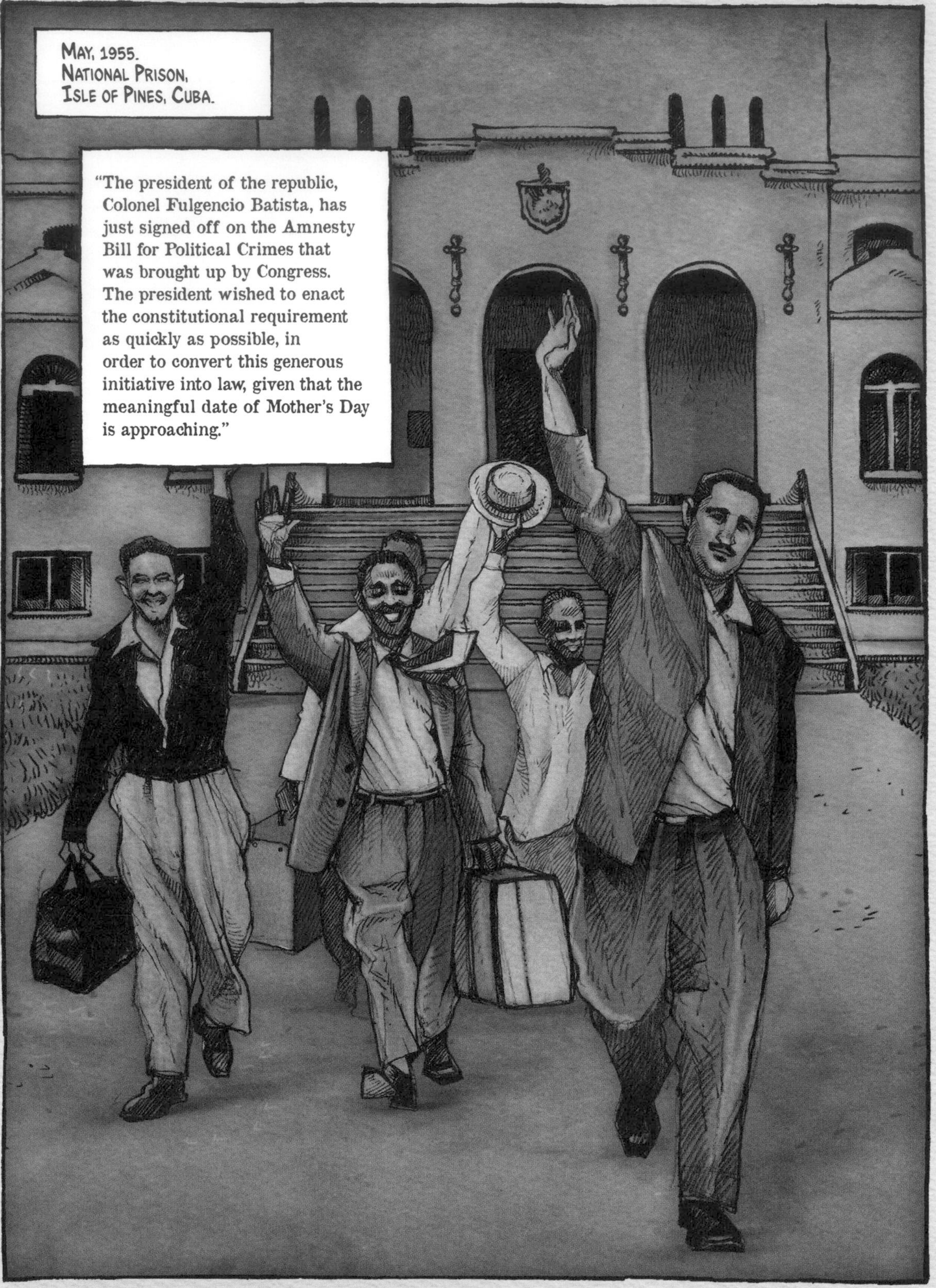
MAY, 1955.
NATIONAL PRISON,
ISLE OF PINES, CUBA.
"The president of the republic, Colonel Fulgencio Batista, has just signed off on the Amnesty Bill for Political Crimes that was brought up by Congress. The president wished to enact the constitutional requirement as quickly as possible, in order to convert this generous initiative into law, given that the meaningful date of Mother's Day is approaching."

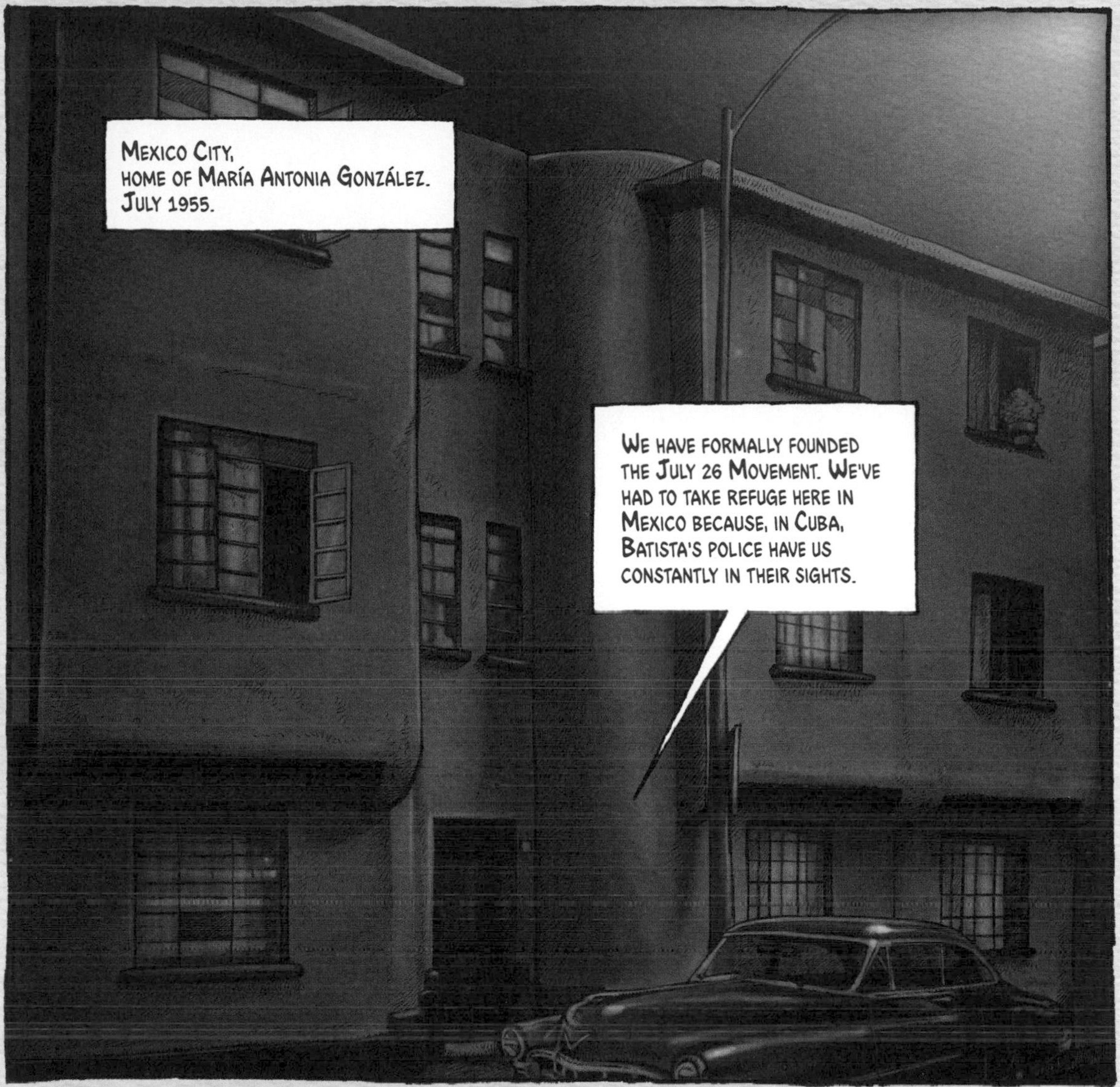
MEXICO CITY, HOME OF MARÍA ANTONIA GONZÁLEZ. JULY 1955.
WE HAVE FORMALLY FOUNDED THE JULY 26 MOVEMENT. WE'VE HAD TO TAKE REFUGE HERE IN MEXICO BECAUSE, IN CUBA, BATISTA'S POLICE HAVE US CONSTANTLY IN THEIR SIGHTS.

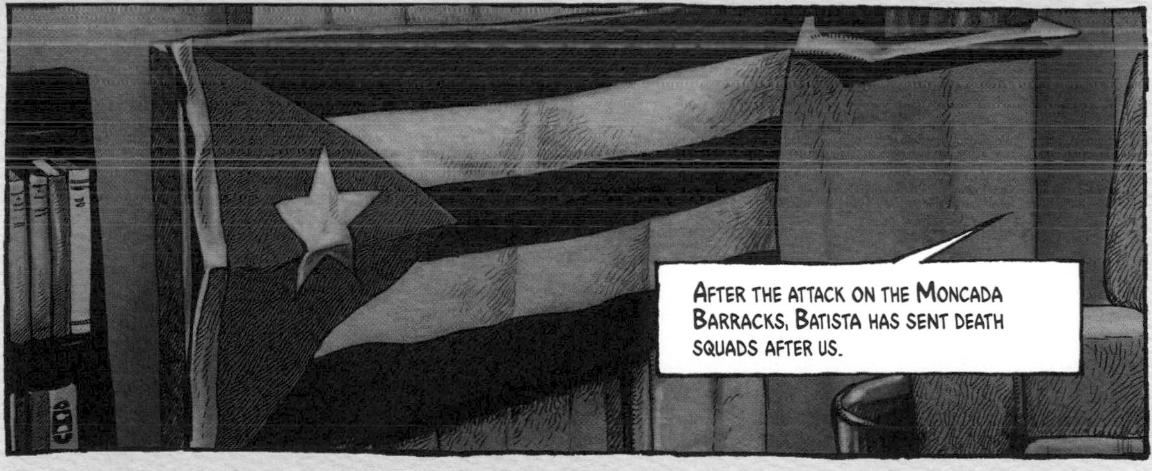
AFTER THE ATTACK ON THE MONCADA BARRACKS, BATISTA HAS SENT DEATH SQUADS AFTER US.

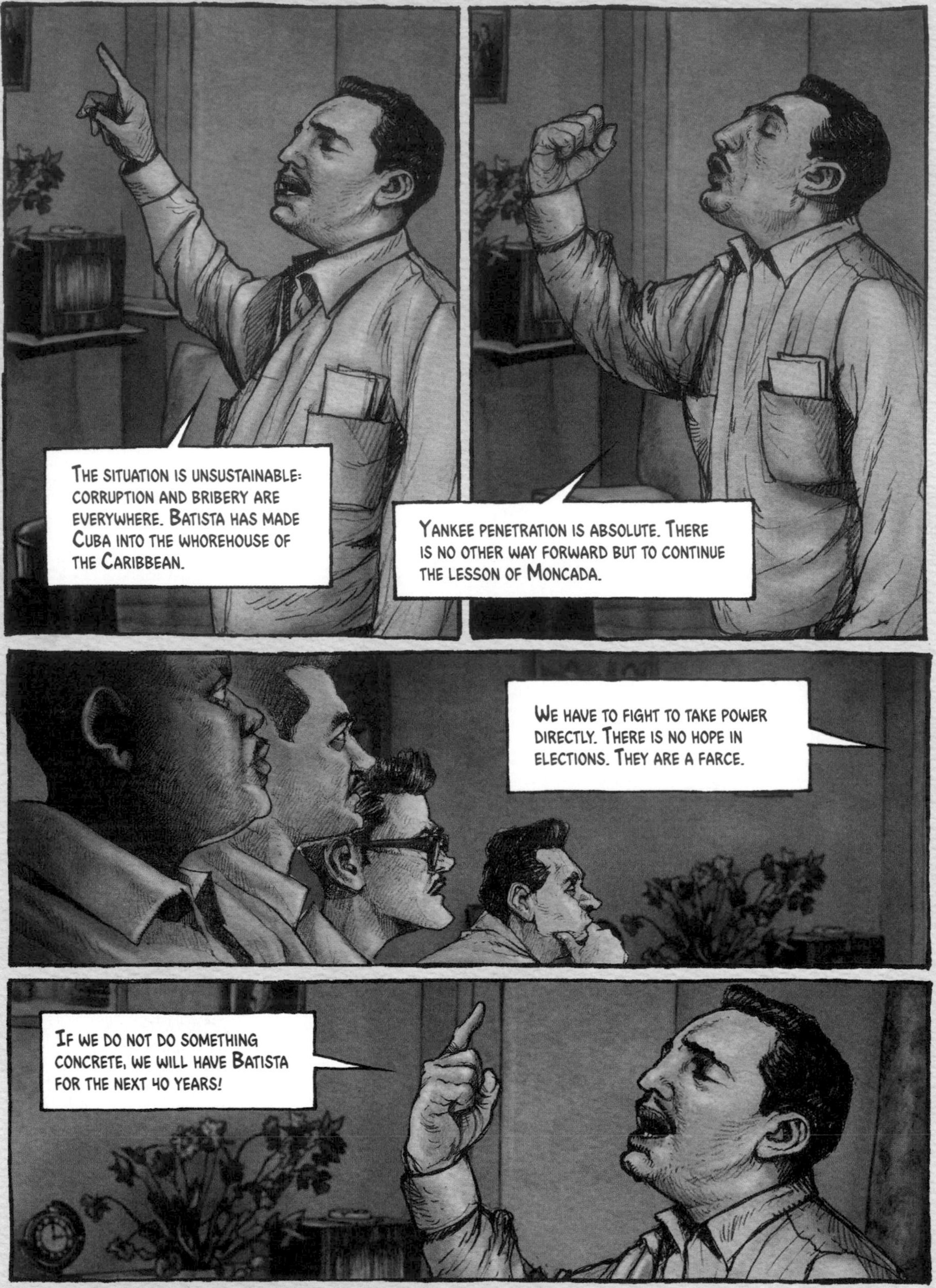
THE SITUATION IS UNSUSTAINABLE: CORRUPTION AND BRIBERY ARE EVERYWHERE. BATISTA HAS MADE CUBA INTO THE WHOREHOUSE OF THE CARIBBEAN.
YANKEE PENETRATION IS ABSOLUTE. THERE IS NO OTHER WAY FORWARD BUT TO CONTINUE THE LESSON OF MONCADA.
WE HAVE TO FIGHT TO TAKE POWER DIRECTLY. THERE IS NO HOPE IN ELECTIONS. THEY ARE A FARCE.
IF WE DO NOT DO SOMETHING CONCRETE, WE WILL HAVE BATISTA FOR THE NEXT 40 YEARS!

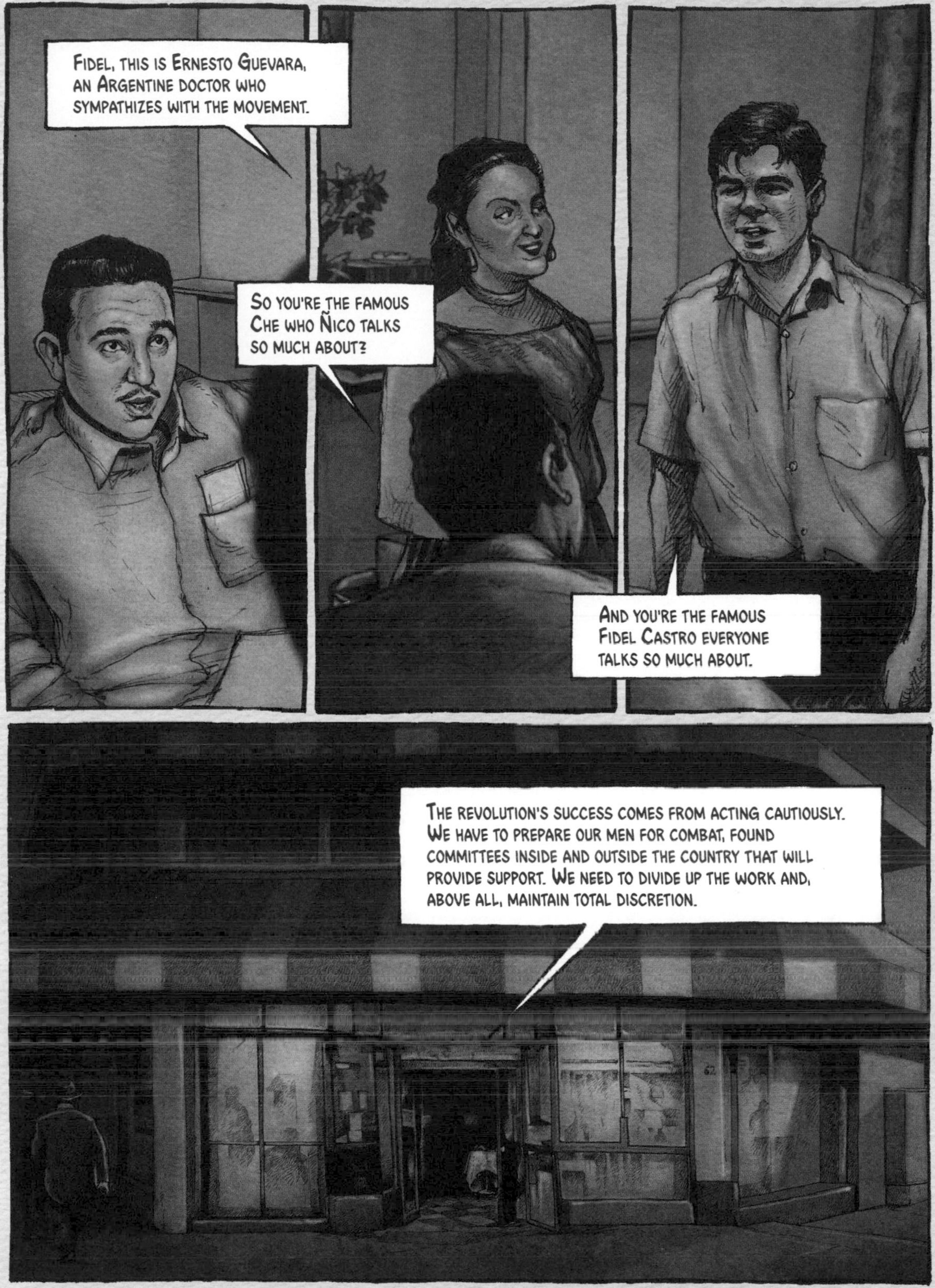

FIDEL, THIS IS ERNESTO GUEVARA, AN ARGENTINE DOCTOR WHO SYMPATHIZES WITH THE MOVEMENT.
SO YOU'RE THE FAMOUS CHE WHO ÑICO TALKS SO MUCH ABOUT?
AND YOU'RE THE FAMOUS FIDEL CASTRO EVERYONE TALKS SO MUCH ABOUT.
THE REVOLUTION'S SUCCESS COMES FROM ACTING CAUTIOUSLY. WE HAVE TO PREPARE OUR MEN FOR COMBAT, FOUND COMMITTEES INSIDE AND OUTSIDE THE COUNTRY THAT WILL PROVIDE SUPPORT. WE NEED TO DIVIDE UP THE WORK AND, ABOVE ALL, MAINTAIN TOTAL DISCRETION.

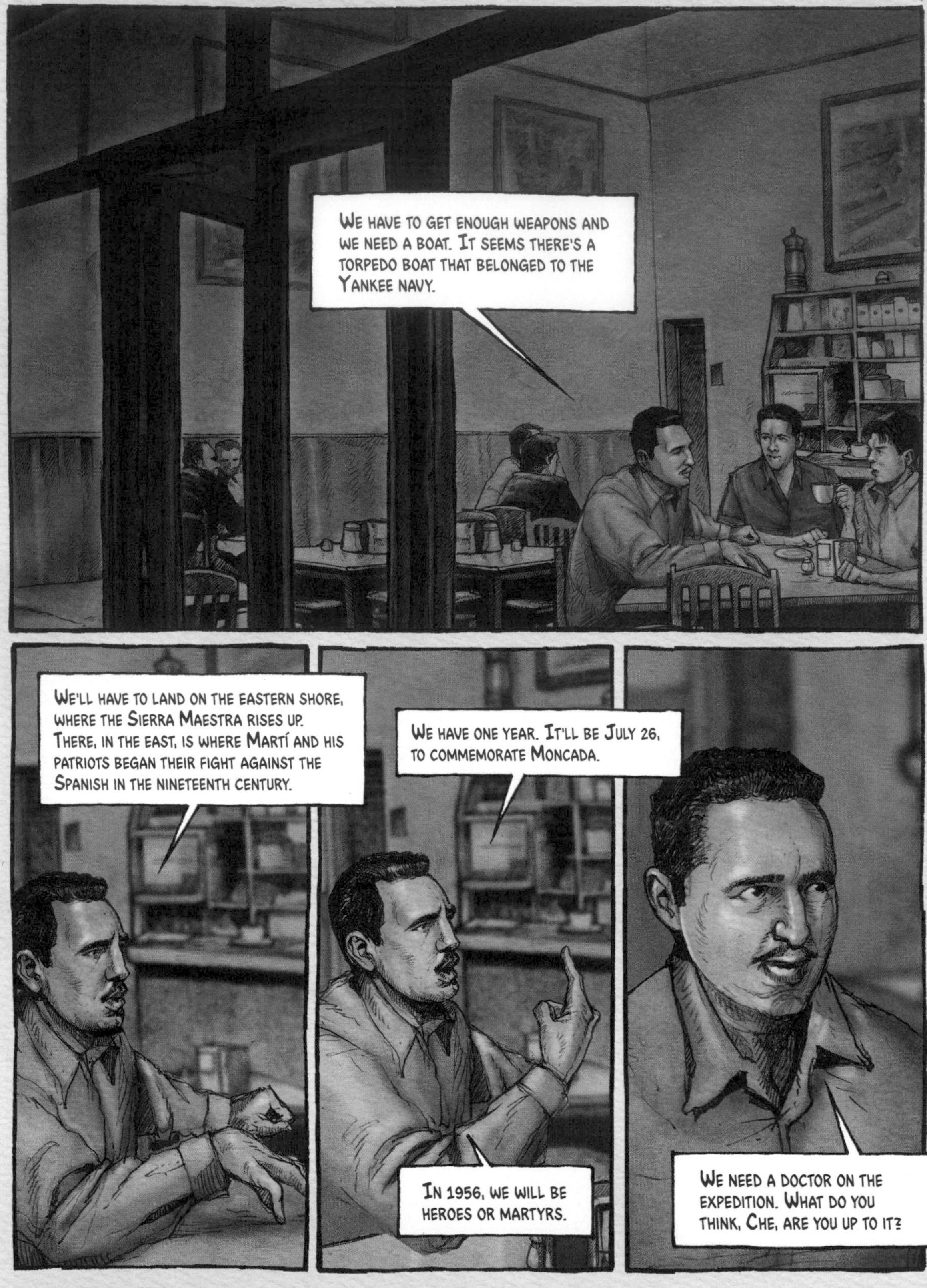
We have to get enough weapons and we need a boat. It seems there's a torpedo boat that belonged to the Yankee navy.
We'll have to land on the eastern shore, where the Sierra Maestra rises up. There, in the east, is where Martí and his patriots began their fight against the Spanish in the nineteenth century.
We have one year. It'll be July 26, to commemorate Moncada.
In 1956, we will be heroes or martyrs.
We need a doctor on the expedition. What do you think, Che, are you up to it?

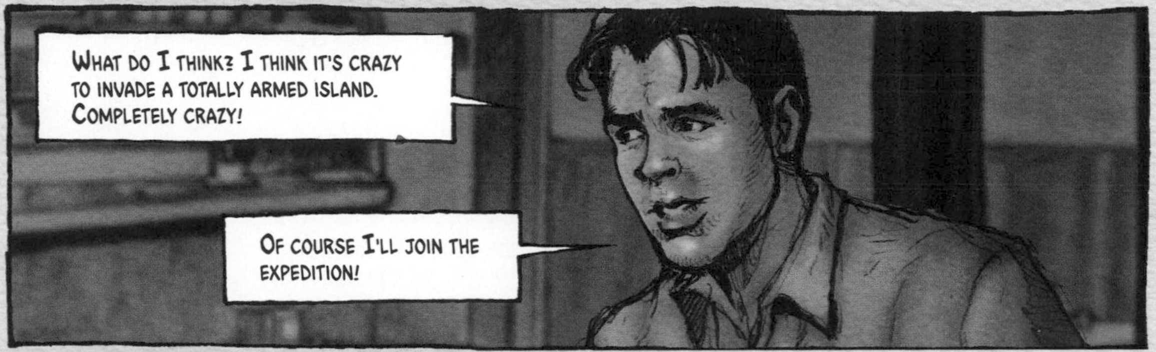
What do I think? I think it's crazy to invade a totally armed island. Completely crazy!
Of course I'll join the expedition!
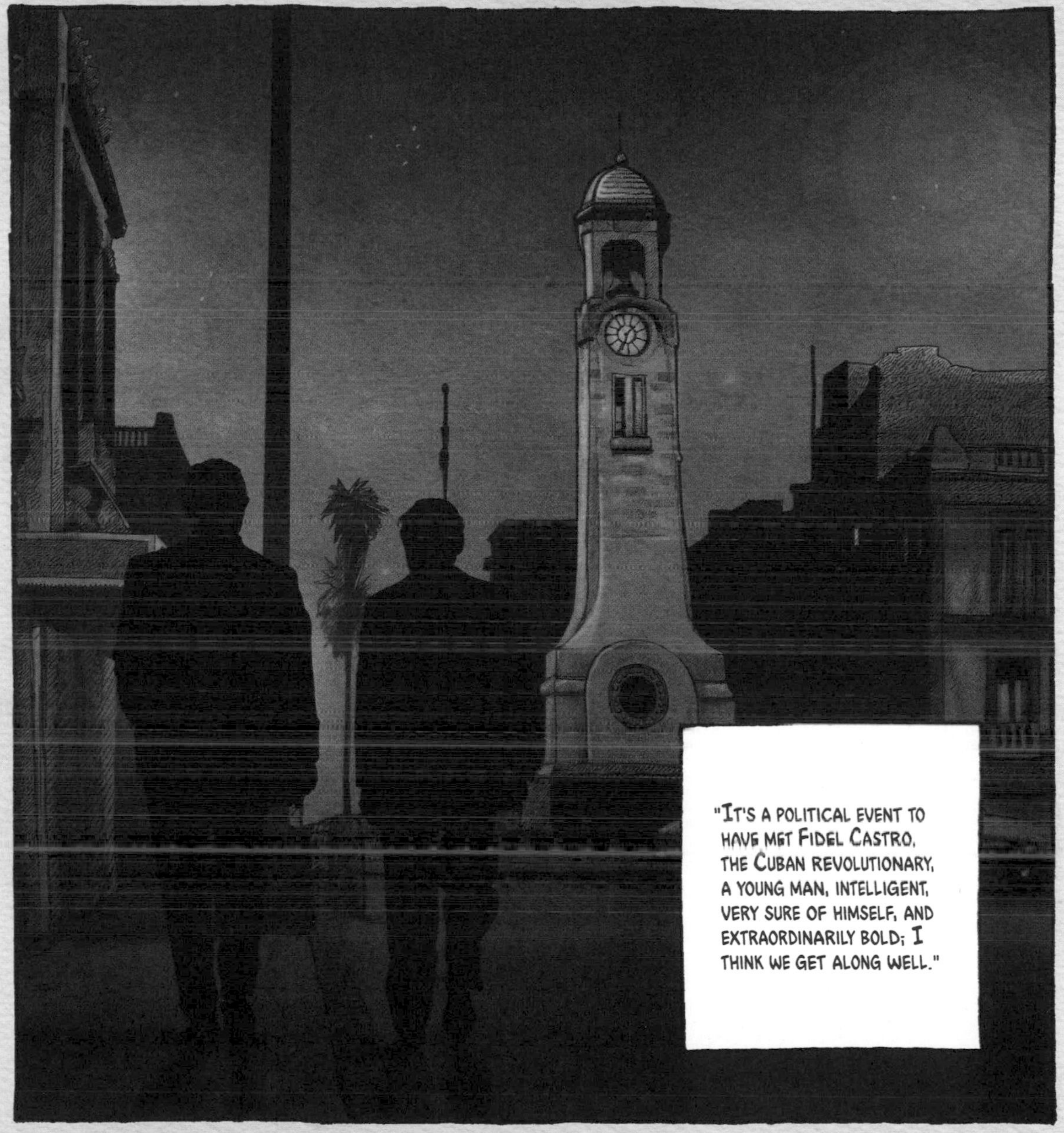
"It's a political event to have met Fidel Castro, the Cuban revolutionary, a young man, intelligent, very sure of himself, and extraordinarily bold; I think we get along well."

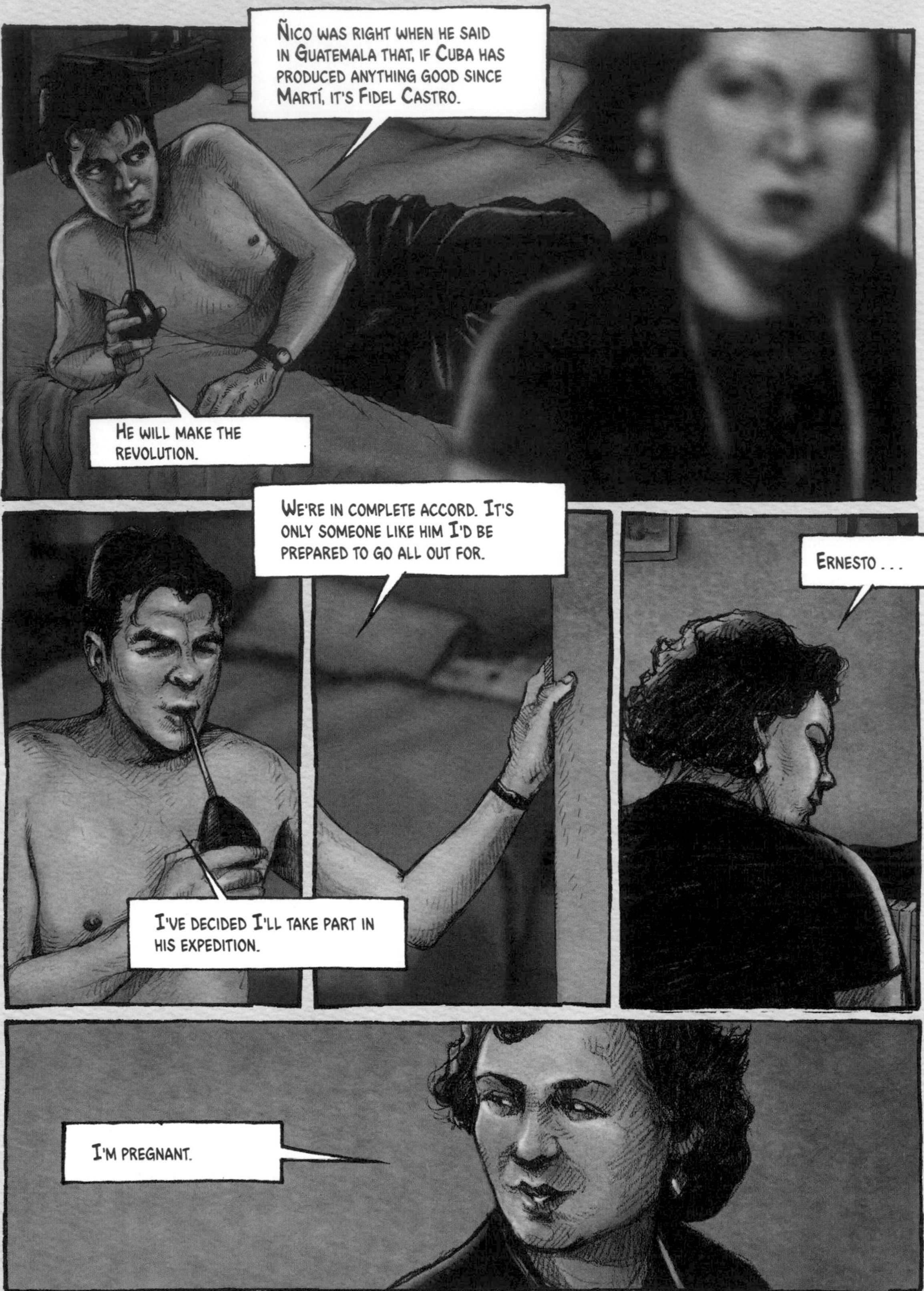
Ñico was right when he said in Guatemala that, if Cuba has produced anything good since Martí, it's Fidel Castro.
He will make the revolution.
We're in complete accord. It's only someone like him I'd be prepared to go all out for.
I've decided I'll take part in his expedition.
Ernesto . . .
I'm pregnant.

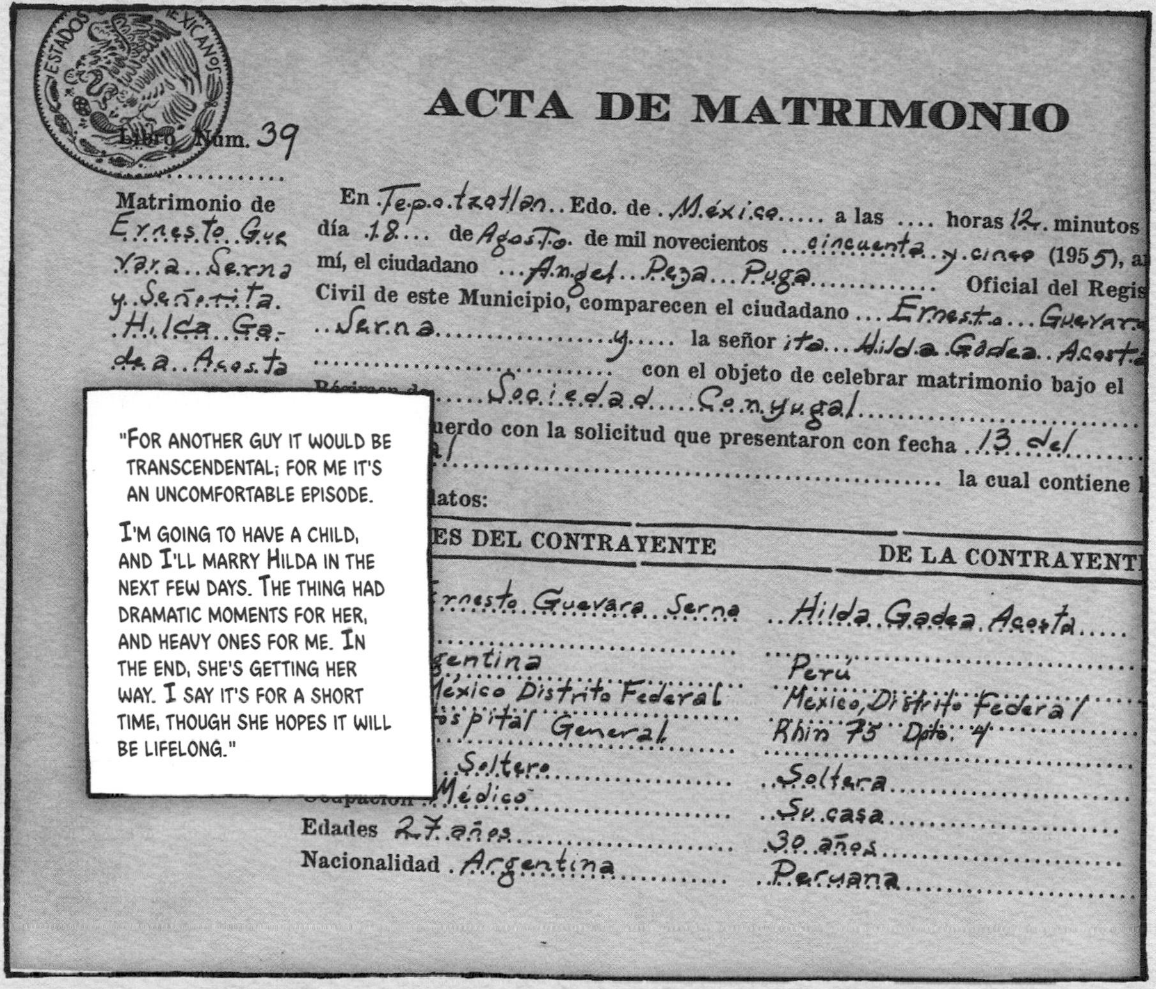

ACTA DE MATRIMONIO

Libro Núm. 39

Matrimonio de
Ernesto Gue
vara Serna
y Señorita
Hilda Ga
dea Acosta

En Tepotzotlan. Edo. de México. a las .... horas 12. minutos
día 18... de Agosto. de mil novecientos cincuenta y cinco (1955), a.
mí, el ciudadano ...Angel Reza Puga............ Oficial del Regis
Civil de este Municipio, comparecen el ciudadano ...Ernesto Guevara
Serna..................y.... la señor ita...Hilda Gadea Acosta
.... con el objeto de celebrar matrimonio bajo el
Régimen de ...Sociedad Conyugal.......
...uerdo con la solicitud que presentaron con fecha .13. del
.... la cual contiene l
...atos:

> "FOR ANOTHER GUY IT WOULD BE TRANSCENDENTAL; FOR ME IT'S AN UNCOMFORTABLE EPISODE.
>
> I'M GOING TO HAVE A CHILD, AND I'LL MARRY HILDA IN THE NEXT FEW DAYS. THE THING HAD DRAMATIC MOMENTS FOR HER, AND HEAVY ONES FOR ME. IN THE END, SHE'S GETTING HER WAY. I SAY IT'S FOR A SHORT TIME, THOUGH SHE HOPES IT WILL BE LIFELONG."

...ES DEL CONTRAYENTE	DE LA CONTRAYENT
...rnesto Guevara Serna	Hilda Gadea Acosta
...entina	Perú
México Distrito Federal	México, Distrito Federal
...spital General	Rhin 75 Dpto. 4
...Soltero	Soltera
Ocupación Médico	Su casa
Edades 27 años	30 años
Nacionalidad Argentina	Peruana

...cer a los contrayentes y que éstos son las mismas personas a que se refiere
...solicitud matrimonial, la cual obra en el expediente número .39. del apén-
...e de matrimonio del año en curso.

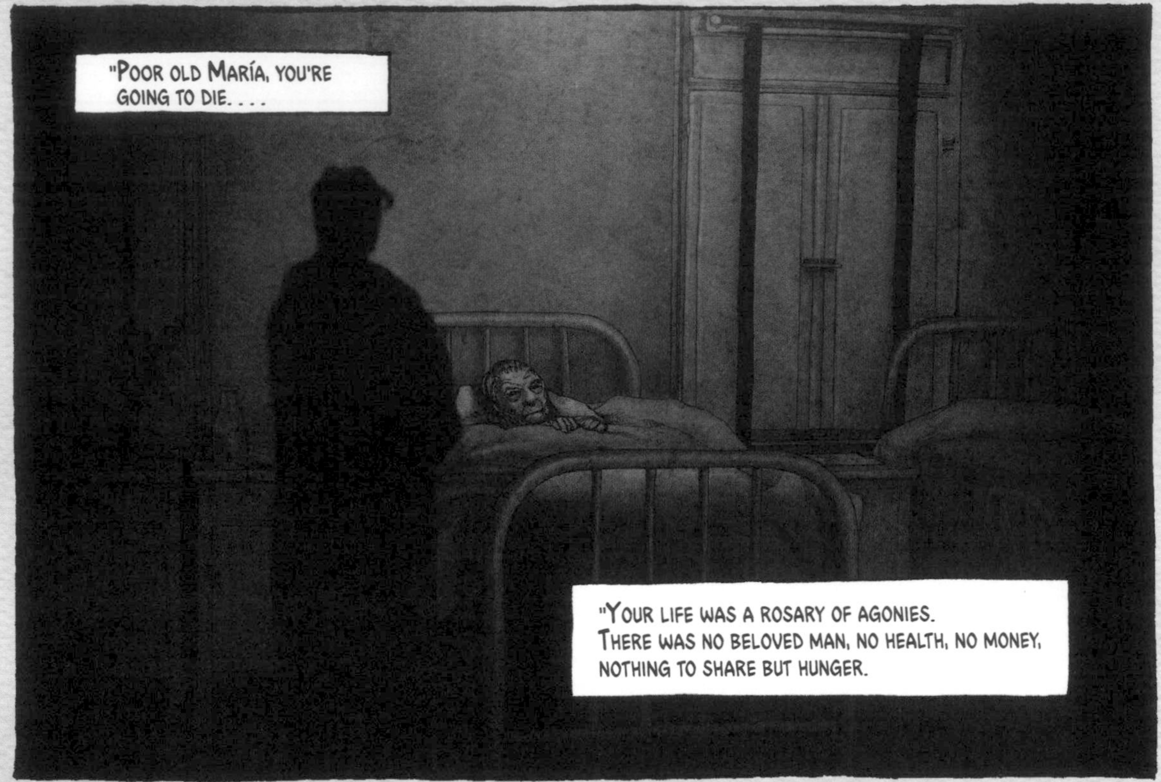
"POOR OLD MARÍA, YOU'RE GOING TO DIE. . . .
"YOUR LIFE WAS A ROSARY OF AGONIES. THERE WAS NO BELOVED MAN, NO HEALTH, NO MONEY, NOTHING TO SHARE BUT HUNGER.

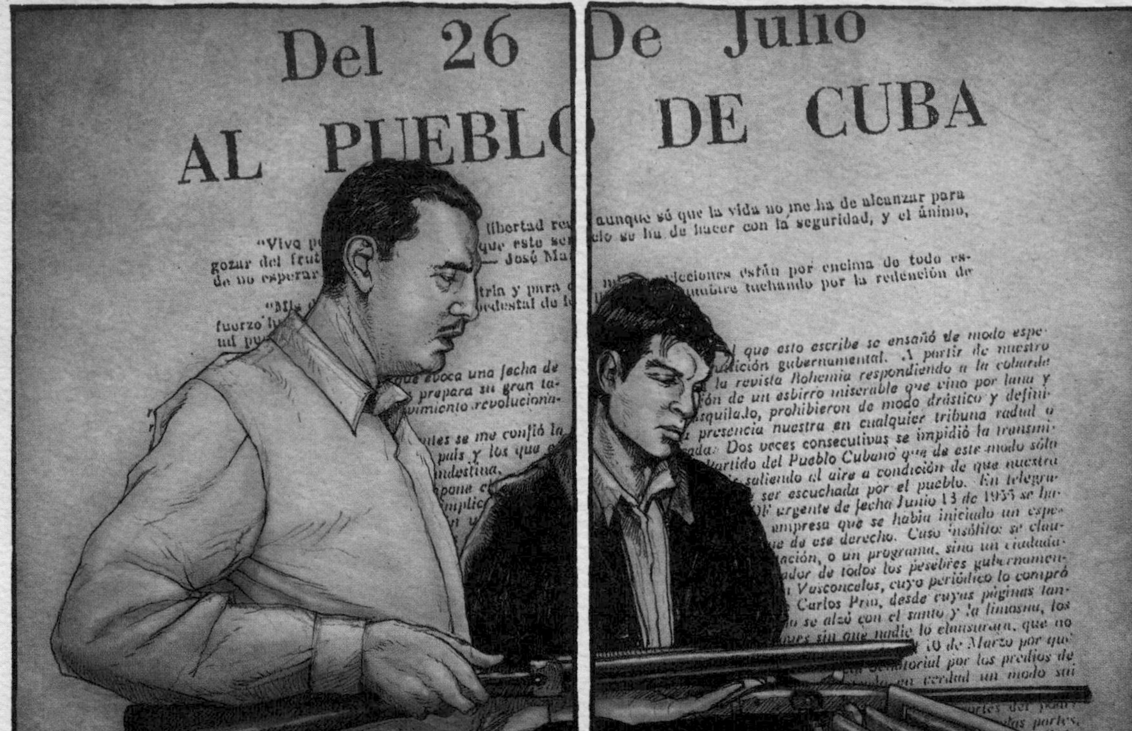
Del 26 De Julio
AL PUEBL DE CUBA

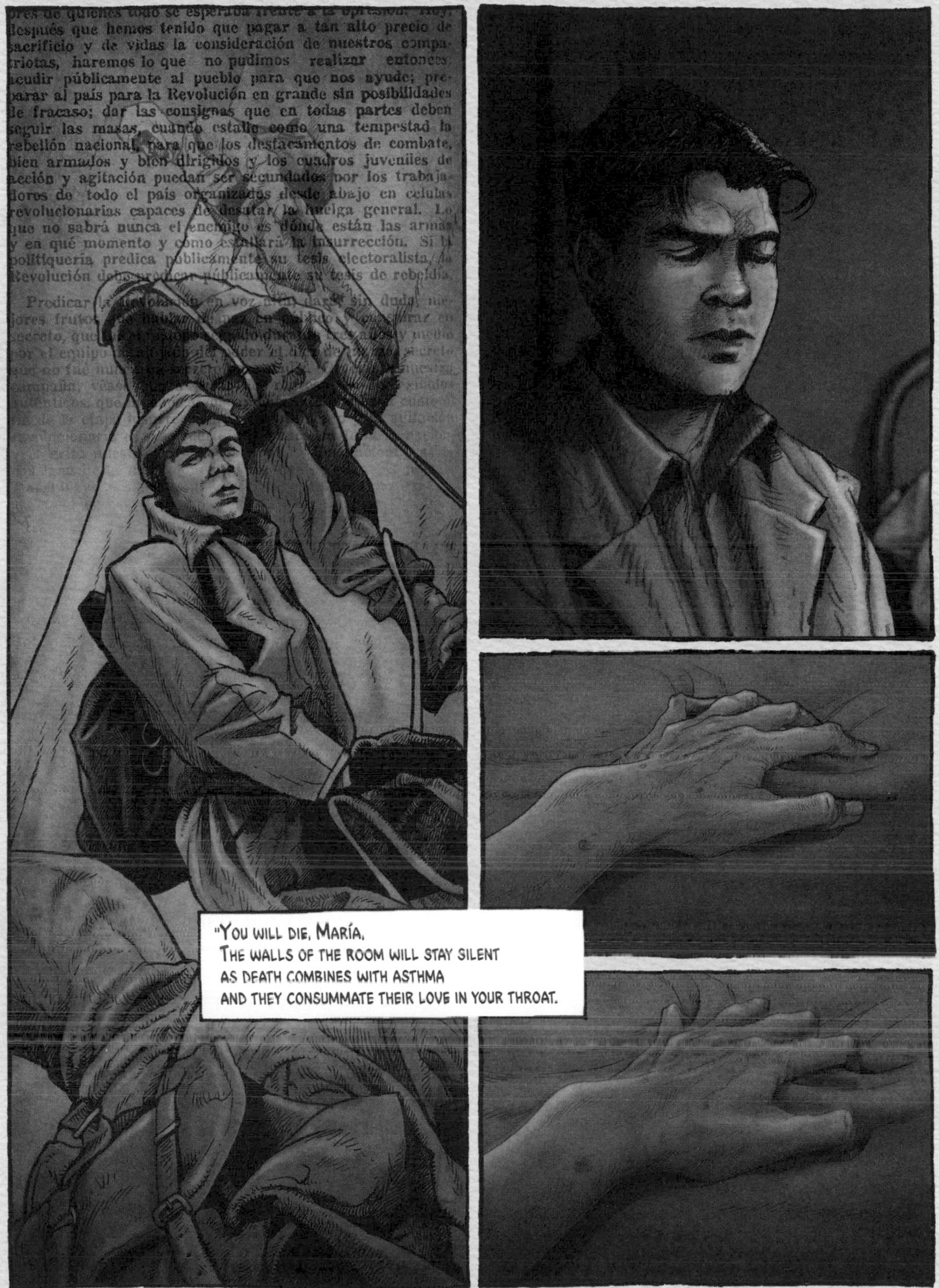
lespués que hemos tenido que pagar a tan alto precio de
sacrificio y de vidas la consideración de nuestros compa-
triotas, haremos lo que no pudimos realizar entonces:
acudir públicamente al pueblo para que nos ayude; pre-
parar al país para la Revolución en grande sin posibilidades
le fracaso; dar las consignas que en todas partes deben
seguir las masas, cuando estalle como una tempestad la
rebelión nacional, para que los destacamentos de combate,
bien armados y bien dirigidos y los cuadros juveniles de
acción y agitación puedan ser secundados por los trabaja-
dores de todo el país organizados desde abajo en células
revolucionarias capaces de desatar la huelga general. Lo
que no sabrá nunca el enemigo es dónde están las armas
y en qué momento y cómo estallará la insurrección. Si la
politiquería predica públicamente su tesis electoralista, la
Revolución debe predicar públicamente su tesis de rebeldía.
"You will die, María.
The walls of the room will stay silent
as death combines with asthma
and they consummate their love in your throat.

"TAKE THIS HAND OF A MAN THAT SEEMS LIKE A BOY'S
BETWEEN YOURS POLISHED BY YELLOW SOAP.
SCRUB YOUR HARD CALLUSES AND PURE KNUCKLES
IN THE SMOOTH SHAME OF MY DOCTOR'S HANDS."

"NO! DON'T DO IT!
DO NOT PRAY TO THE INDOLENT GOD
WHO FOR ALL YOUR LIFE DENIED YOUR HOPE.
DO NOT ASK DEATH FOR CLEMENCY.
YOUR LIFE WAS HORRIBLY CLOTHED IN HUNGER
AND ENDS DRESSED IN ASTHMA."

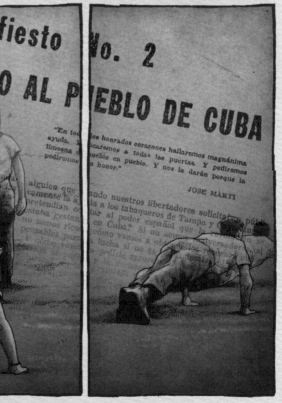

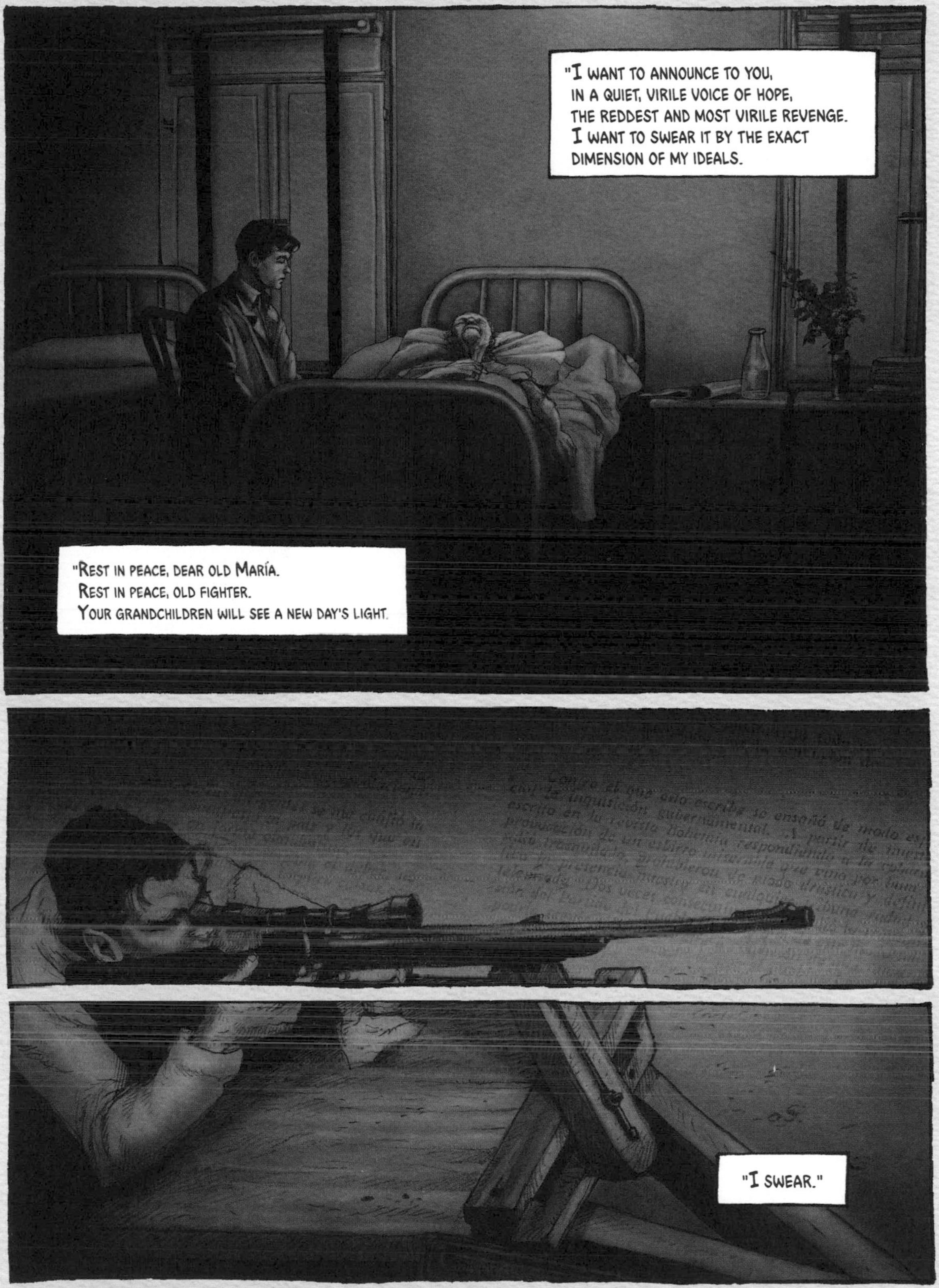
"I WANT TO ANNOUNCE TO YOU, IN A QUIET, VIRILE VOICE OF HOPE, THE REDDEST AND MOST VIRILE REVENGE. I WANT TO SWEAR IT BY THE EXACT DIMENSION OF MY IDEALS.
"REST IN PEACE, DEAR OLD MARÍA. REST IN PEACE, OLD FIGHTER. YOUR GRANDCHILDREN WILL SEE A NEW DAY'S LIGHT.
"I SWEAR."

HOW'S THE ARGENTINE LOOK TO YOU?

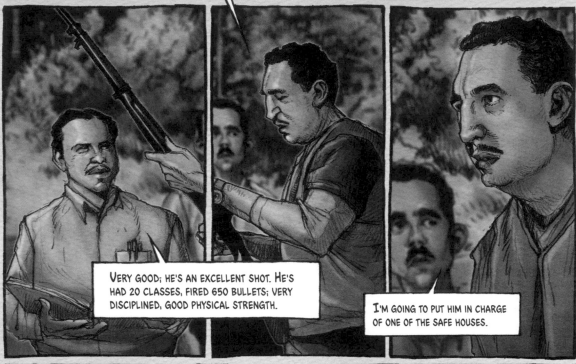

VERY GOOD; HE'S AN EXCELLENT SHOT. HE'S HAD 20 CLASSES, FIRED 650 BULLETS; VERY DISCIPLINED, GOOD PHYSICAL STRENGTH.

I'M GOING TO PUT HIM IN CHARGE OF ONE OF THE SAFE HOUSES.

BUT, FIDEL, YOU CAN'T DO THAT. THE ARGENTINE ISN'T CUBAN.

OF COURSE HE ISN'T, JACKASS! AND EVEN THOUGH HE WASN'T BORN ON THE ISLAND, HE IS WILLING TO SHED HIS BLOOD FOR HER.

80

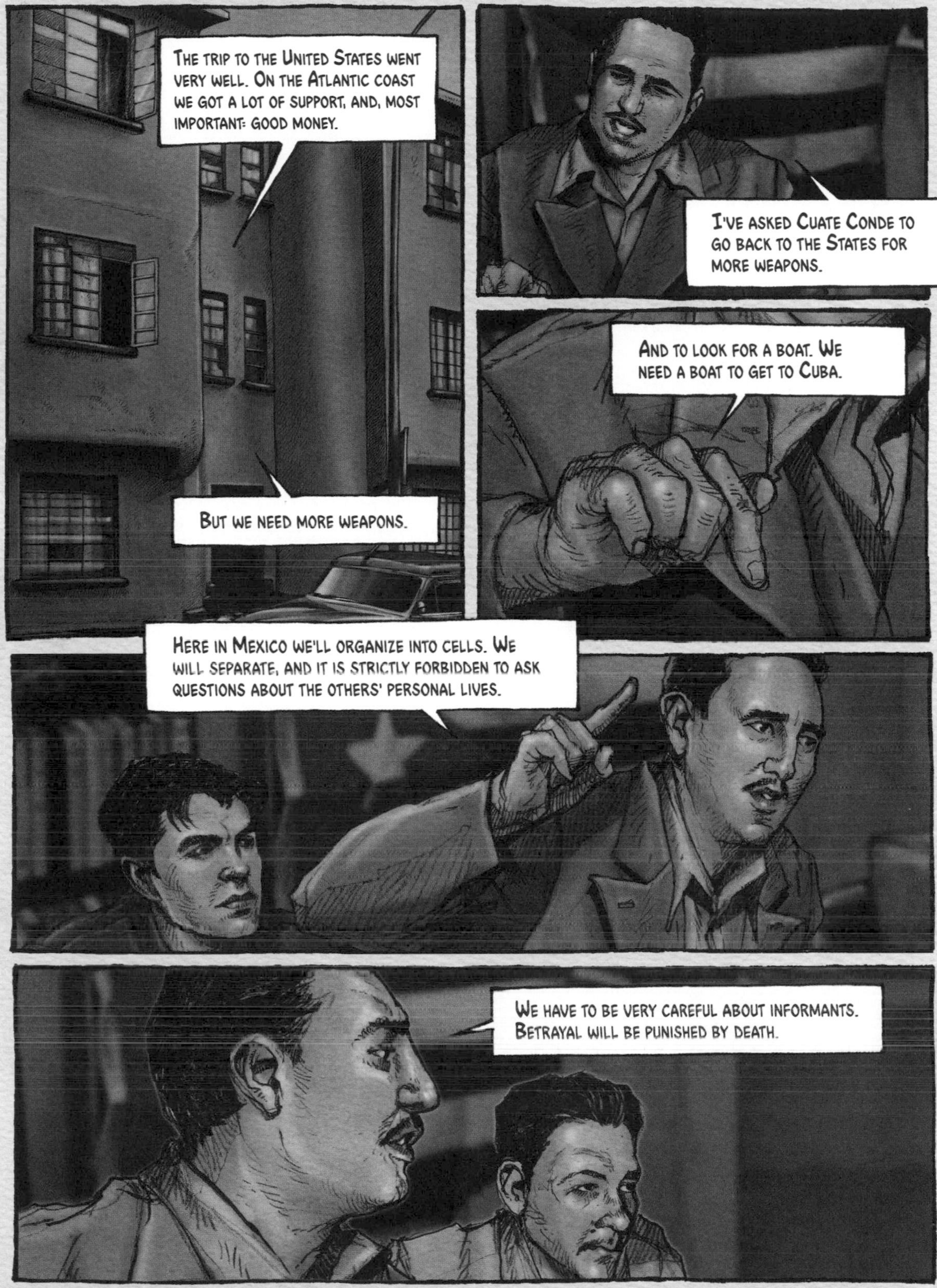
THE TRIP TO THE UNITED STATES WENT VERY WELL. ON THE ATLANTIC COAST WE GOT A LOT OF SUPPORT, AND, MOST IMPORTANT: GOOD MONEY.
BUT WE NEED MORE WEAPONS.
I'VE ASKED CUATE CONDE TO GO BACK TO THE STATES FOR MORE WEAPONS.
AND TO LOOK FOR A BOAT. WE NEED A BOAT TO GET TO CUBA.
HERE IN MEXICO WE'LL ORGANIZE INTO CELLS. WE WILL SEPARATE, AND IT IS STRICTLY FORBIDDEN TO ASK QUESTIONS ABOUT THE OTHERS' PERSONAL LIVES.
WE HAVE TO BE VERY CAREFUL ABOUT INFORMANTS. BETRAYAL WILL BE PUNISHED BY DEATH.

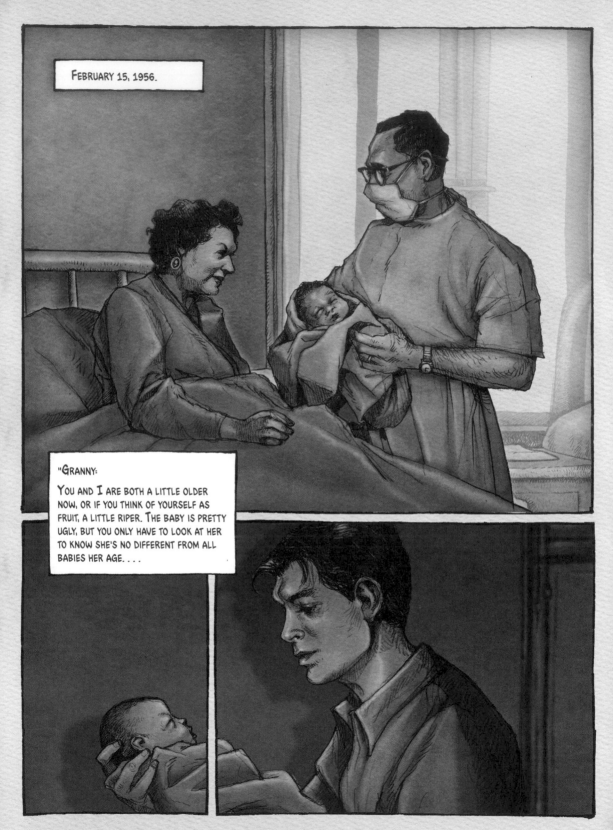

FEBRUARY 15, 1956.

"GRANNY:

YOU AND I ARE BOTH A LITTLE OLDER NOW, OR IF YOU THINK OF YOURSELF AS FRUIT, A LITTLE RIPER. THE BABY IS PRETTY UGLY, BUT YOU ONLY HAVE TO LOOK AT HER TO KNOW SHE'S NO DIFFERENT FROM ALL BABIES HER AGE. . . .

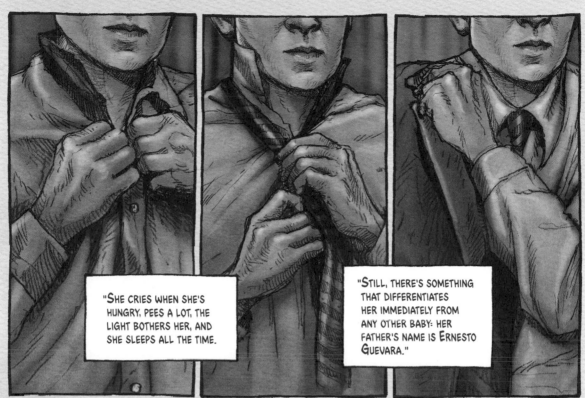

"SHE CRIES WHEN SHE'S HUNGRY, PEES A LOT, THE LIGHT BOTHERS HER, AND SHE SLEEPS ALL THE TIME.

"STILL, THERE'S SOMETHING THAT DIFFERENTIATES HER IMMEDIATELY FROM ANY OTHER BABY: HER FATHER'S NAME IS ERNESTO GUEVARA."

DON ERASMO, THIS IS MR. ERNESTO GONZÁLEZ, THE MAN I TOLD YOU ABOUT. HE'S FROM EL SALVADOR AND HE'S VERY INTERESTED IN RENTING YOUR RANCH, MAYBE BUYING IT.

RANCHO SAN MIGUEL, CHALCO, STATE OF MEXICO.

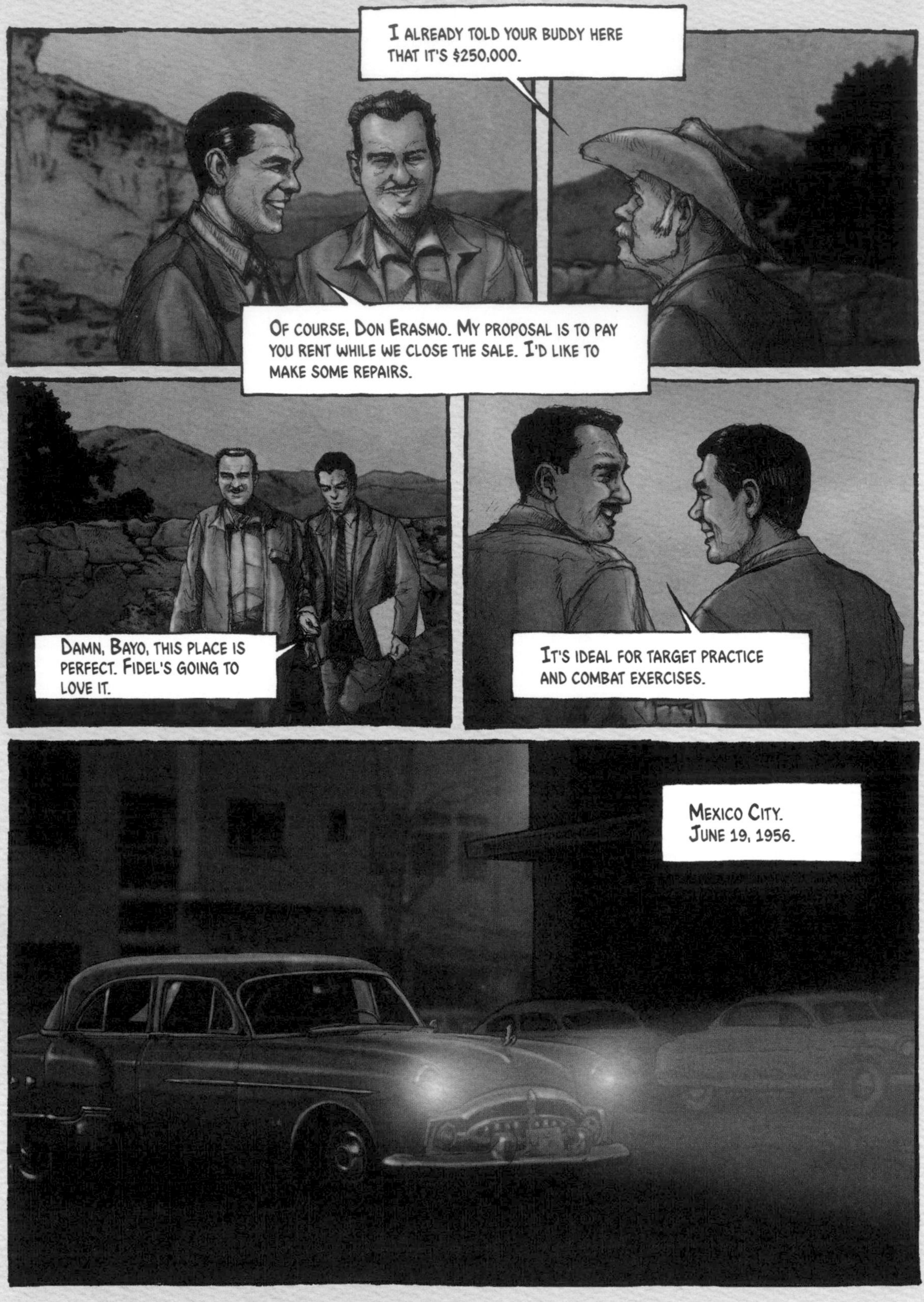
I ALREADY TOLD YOUR BUDDY HERE THAT IT'S $250,000.
OF COURSE, DON ERASMO. MY PROPOSAL IS TO PAY YOU RENT WHILE WE CLOSE THE SALE. I'D LIKE TO MAKE SOME REPAIRS.
DAMN, BAYO, THIS PLACE IS PERFECT. FIDEL'S GOING TO LOVE IT.
IT'S IDEAL FOR TARGET PRACTICE AND COMBAT EXERCISES.
MEXICO CITY. JUNE 19, 1956.

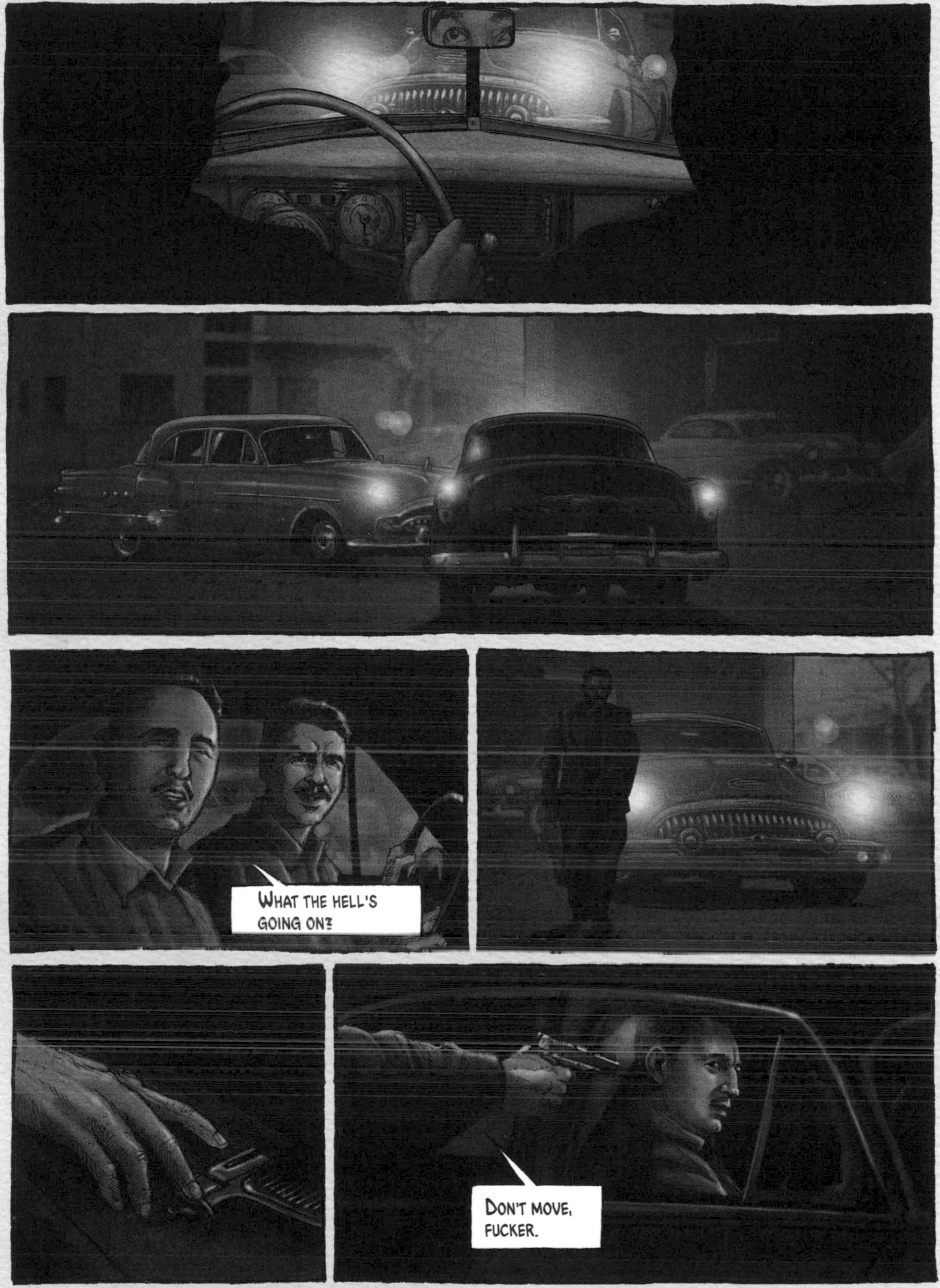
WHAT THE HELL'S GOING ON?
DON'T MOVE, FUCKER.

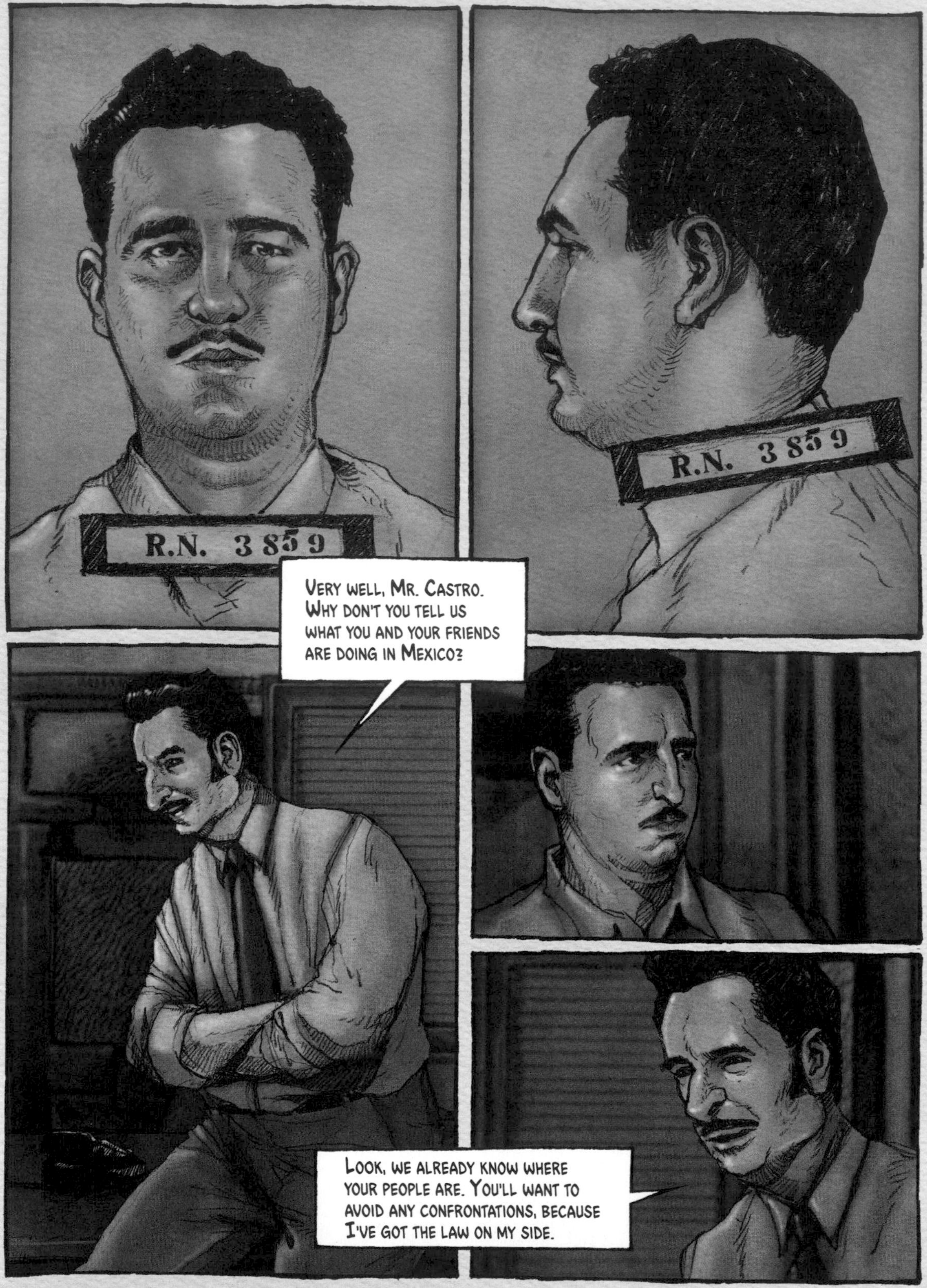
R.N. 3859
R.N. 3859
Very well, Mr. Castro. Why don't you tell us what you and your friends are doing in Mexico?
Look, we already know where your people are. You'll want to avoid any confrontations, because I've got the law on my side.

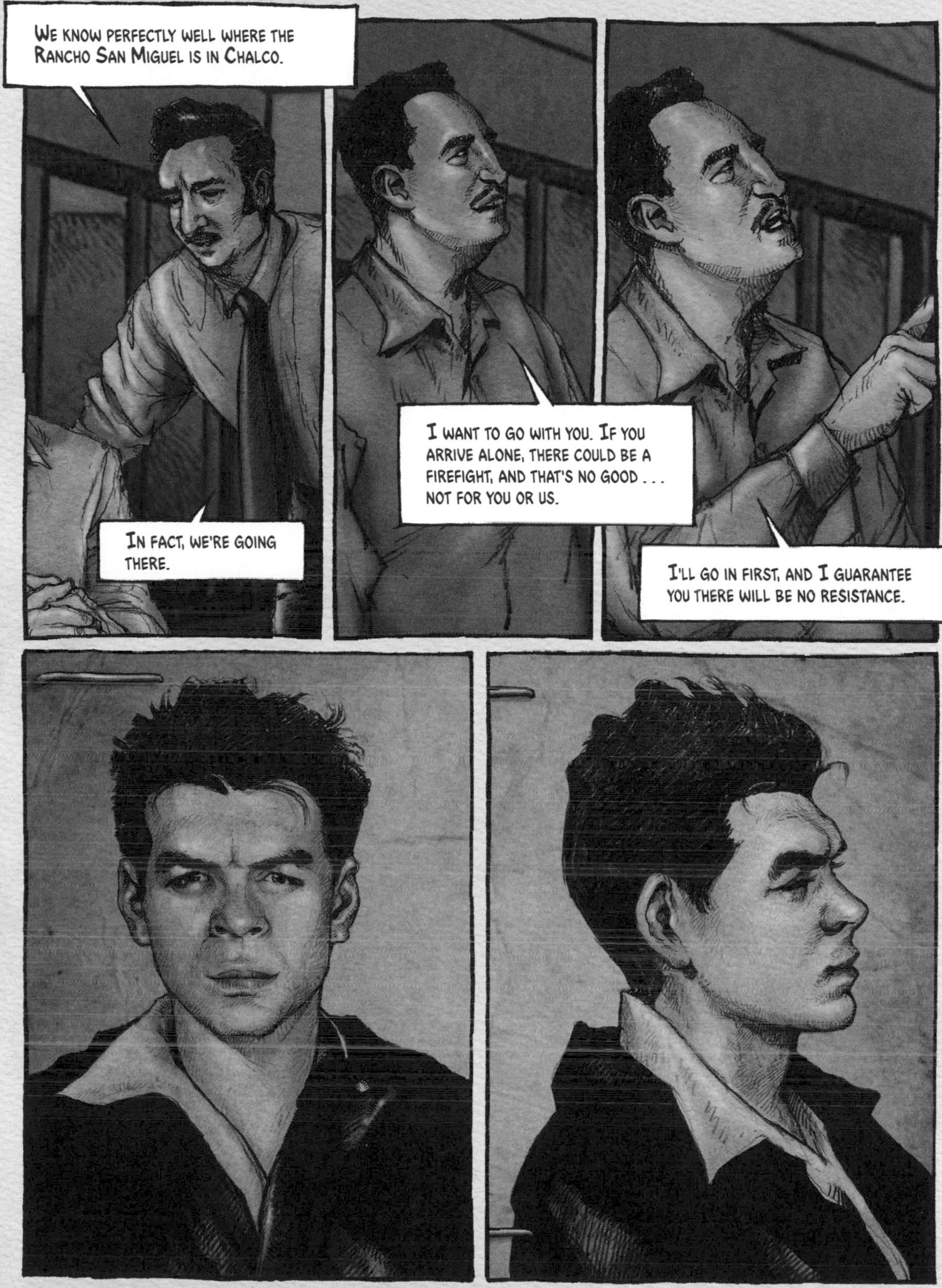
WE KNOW PERFECTLY WELL WHERE THE RANCHO SAN MIGUEL IS IN CHALCO.
IN FACT, WE'RE GOING THERE.
I WANT TO GO WITH YOU. IF YOU ARRIVE ALONE, THERE COULD BE A FIREFIGHT, AND THAT'S NO GOOD . . . NOT FOR YOU OR US.
I'LL GO IN FIRST, AND I GUARANTEE YOU THERE WILL BE NO RESISTANCE.

DIRECCIÓN FEDERAL DE SEGURIDAD
DEPARTAMENTO NACIONAL DE IDENTIFICACION
MEXICO, D.F.

25 de Junio de 1956

FILIACION

............ERNESTO GUEVARA SERNA....
Nombre completo

Fecha de Nacimiento 14 de Junio de 1928............
Lugar de Nacimiento ROSARIO, ARGENTINA............
Nombre de los Padres ERNESTO GUEVARA LINCHI y SERGIO DE LA SERNA
Esposa HILDA GADEE ACOSTA........................
Estado Civil casado............ Estatura 1.73 mts....
Color.....blanco.............. Pelo cast. cl.........
Frente vertc............... Nariz recta........
Ojos cafes. cl.............. Cejas pobl......
Boca grande............. Mentón .
Ocupación MEDICO. UNIVERSIDAD de BUE
Dirección NAPOLES 40.................
Señas particulares .....ninguna a la vista
....
....INMIGRANTE - pasado el tiempo de MIGRACION.....
....dice ser TURISTA-
....AD HONORE en la UNIVERSIDAD DE MEXICO

"DEAR PARENTS:

I RECEIVED YOUR LETTER HERE IN MY NEW, DELICATE MANSION: IMMIGRATION PRISON. I'LL PAINT YOU A PICTURE OF THE CASE, TO GIVE YOU AN IDEA.

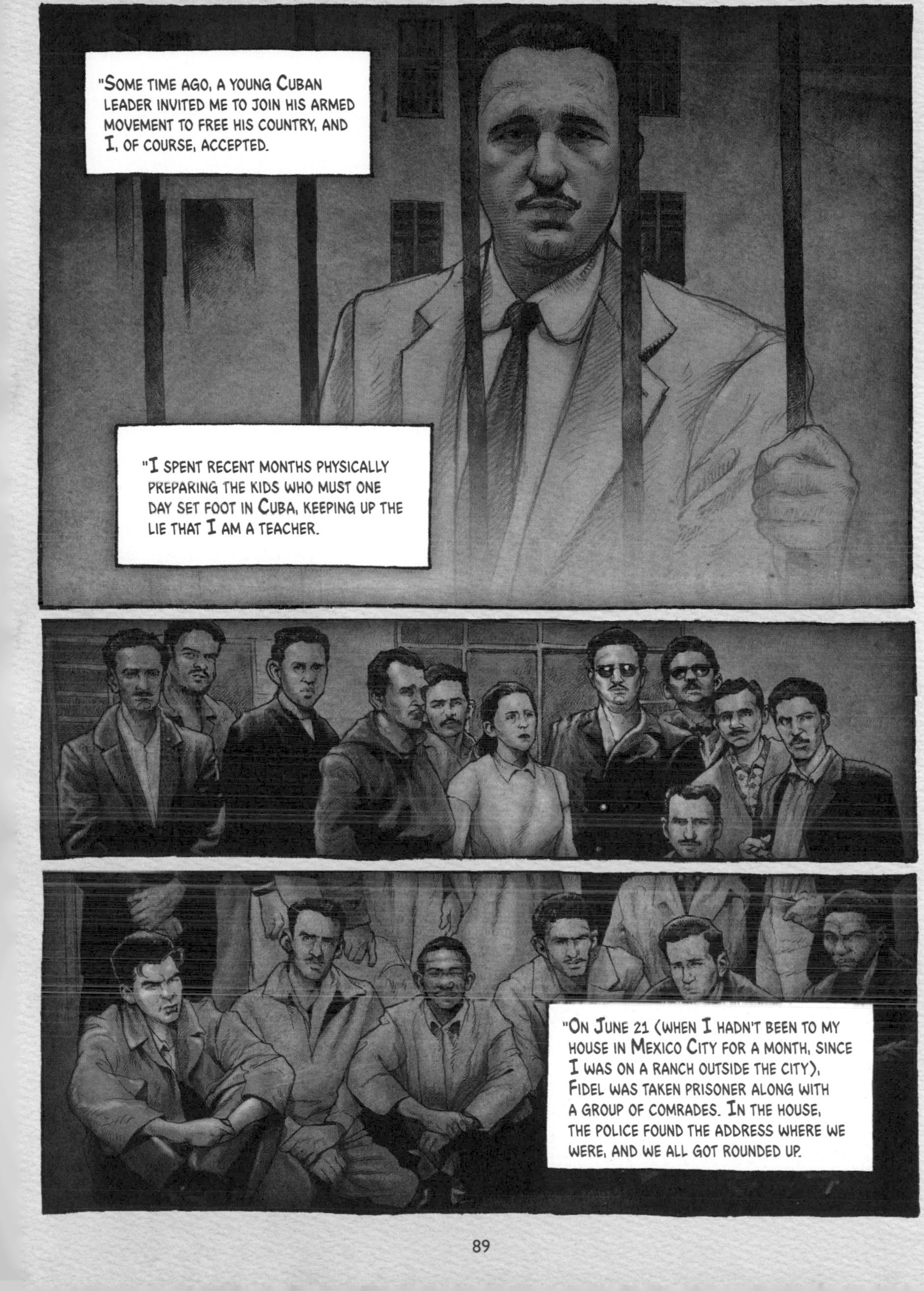
"Some time ago, a young Cuban leader invited me to join his armed movement to free his country, and I, of course, accepted.
"I spent recent months physically preparing the kids who must one day set foot in Cuba, keeping up the lie that I am a teacher.
"On June 21 (when I hadn't been to my house in Mexico City for a month, since I was on a ranch outside the city), Fidel was taken prisoner along with a group of comrades. In the house, the police found the address where we were, and we all got rounded up.

"THIS IS A SYNTHESIS OF PAST EVENTS; OF WHAT IS TO COME, I WILL ONLY SAY THAT MY FUTURE IS TIED TO THE CUBAN REVOLUTION. I EITHER TRIUMPH WITH IT OR DIE THERE.

"I'VE SPENT MY LIFE STUMBLING AROUND IN SEARCH OF TRUTH, AND NOW I'M ON THE RIGHT PATH AND HAVE A DAUGHTER WHO WILL SURVIVE ME. I HAVE CLOSED THE CYCLE.

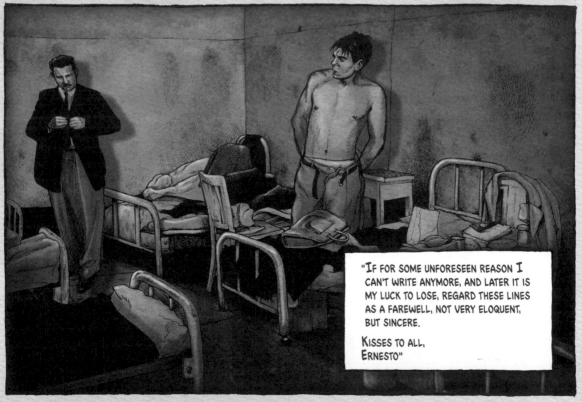

"IF FOR SOME UNFORESEEN REASON I CAN'T WRITE ANYMORE, AND LATER IT IS MY LUCK TO LOSE, REGARD THESE LINES AS A FAREWELL, NOT VERY ELOQUENT, BUT SINCERE.

KISSES TO ALL,
ERNESTO"

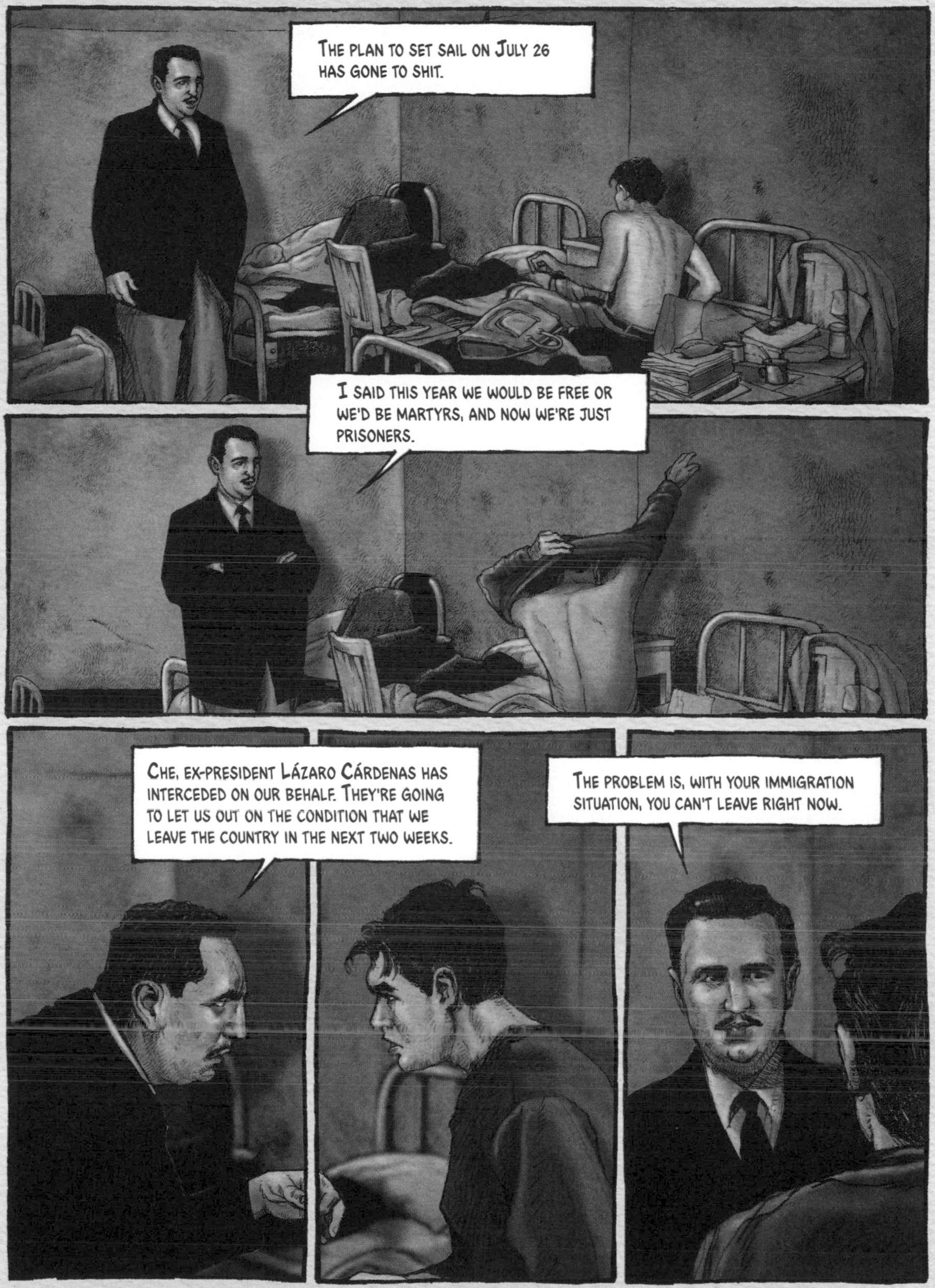
The plan to set sail on July 26 has gone to shit.
I said this year we would be free or we'd be martyrs, and now we're just prisoners.
Che, ex-president Lázaro Cárdenas has interceded on our behalf. They're going to let us out on the condition that we leave the country in the next two weeks.
The problem is, with your immigration situation, you can't leave right now.

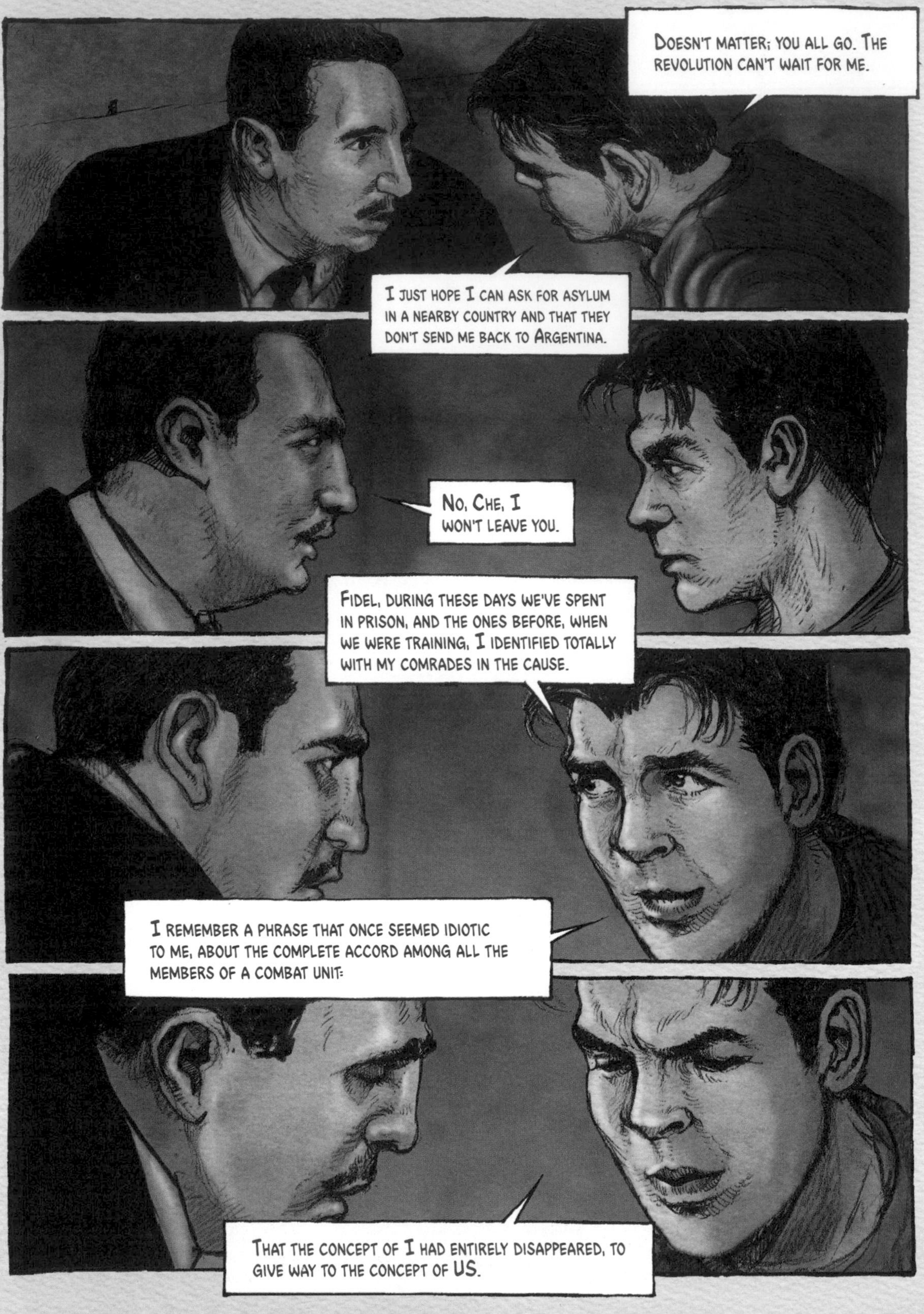

DOESN'T MATTER; YOU ALL GO. THE REVOLUTION CAN'T WAIT FOR ME.
I JUST HOPE I CAN ASK FOR ASYLUM IN A NEARBY COUNTRY AND THAT THEY DON'T SEND ME BACK TO ARGENTINA.
NO, CHE, I WON'T LEAVE YOU.
FIDEL, DURING THESE DAYS WE'VE SPENT IN PRISON, AND THE ONES BEFORE, WHEN WE WERE TRAINING, I IDENTIFIED TOTALLY WITH MY COMRADES IN THE CAUSE.
I REMEMBER A PHRASE THAT ONCE SEEMED IDIOTIC TO ME, ABOUT THE COMPLETE ACCORD AMONG ALL THE MEMBERS OF A COMBAT UNIT:
THAT THE CONCEPT OF I HAD ENTIRELY DISAPPEARED, TO GIVE WAY TO THE CONCEPT OF US.

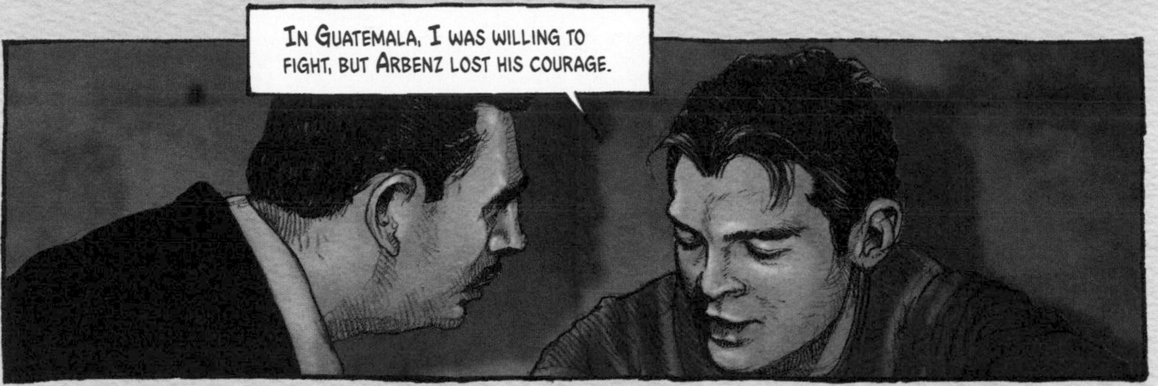
IN GUATEMALA, I WAS WILLING TO FIGHT, BUT ARBENZ LOST HIS COURAGE.

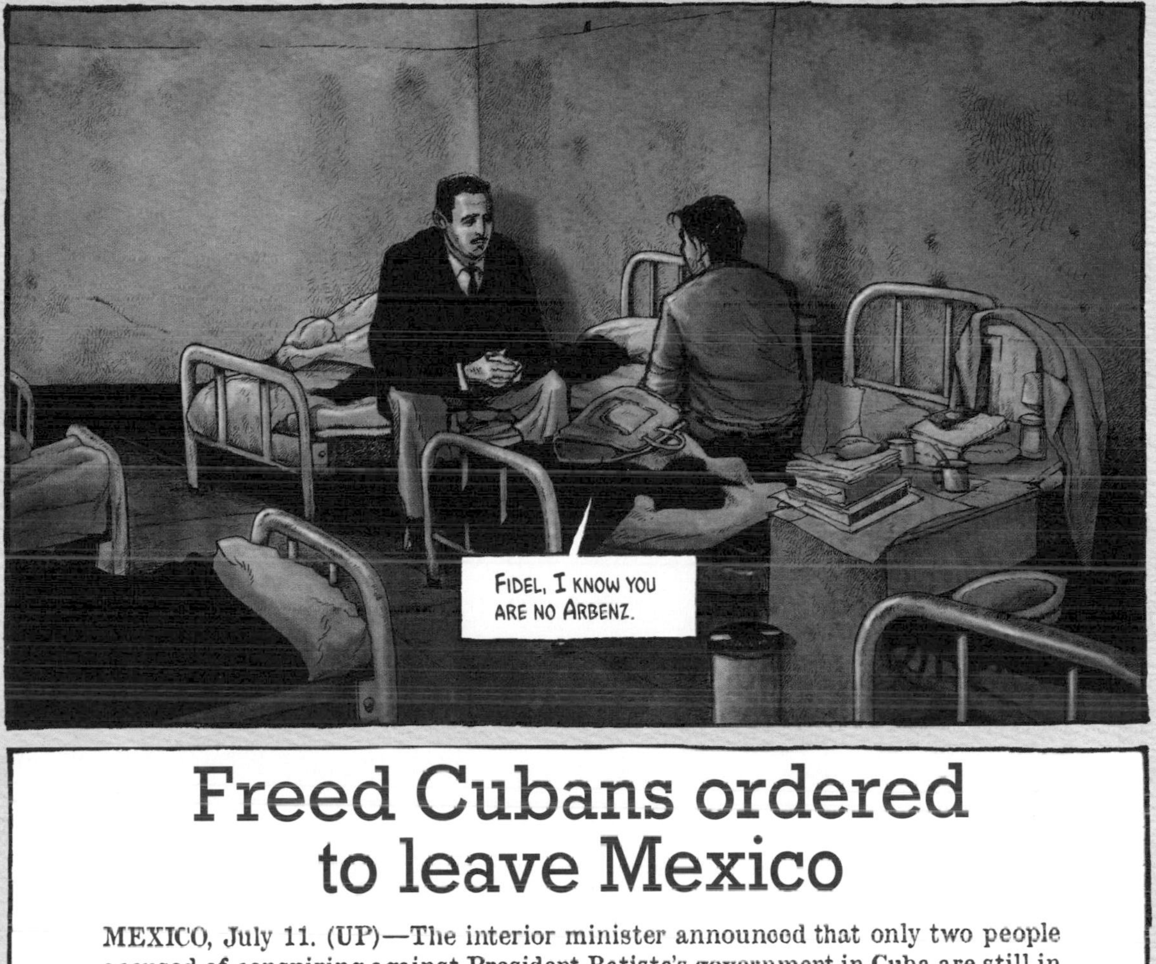
FIDEL, I KNOW YOU ARE NO ARBENZ.

Freed Cubans ordered to leave Mexico

MEXICO, July 11. (UP)—The interior minister announced that only two people accused of conspiring against President Batista's government in Cuba are still in custody. Those detained are Argentine doctor Guevara Serna and Cuban Calixto García Martínez.

He said they will not be freed until Judge Lavalle, in a hearing set for the 19th, orders their release or brings charges.

Cuban Santiago Hitzel was set free last night, and he and the other 19 who had already been released have been invited to leave Mexican territory "as soon as possible."

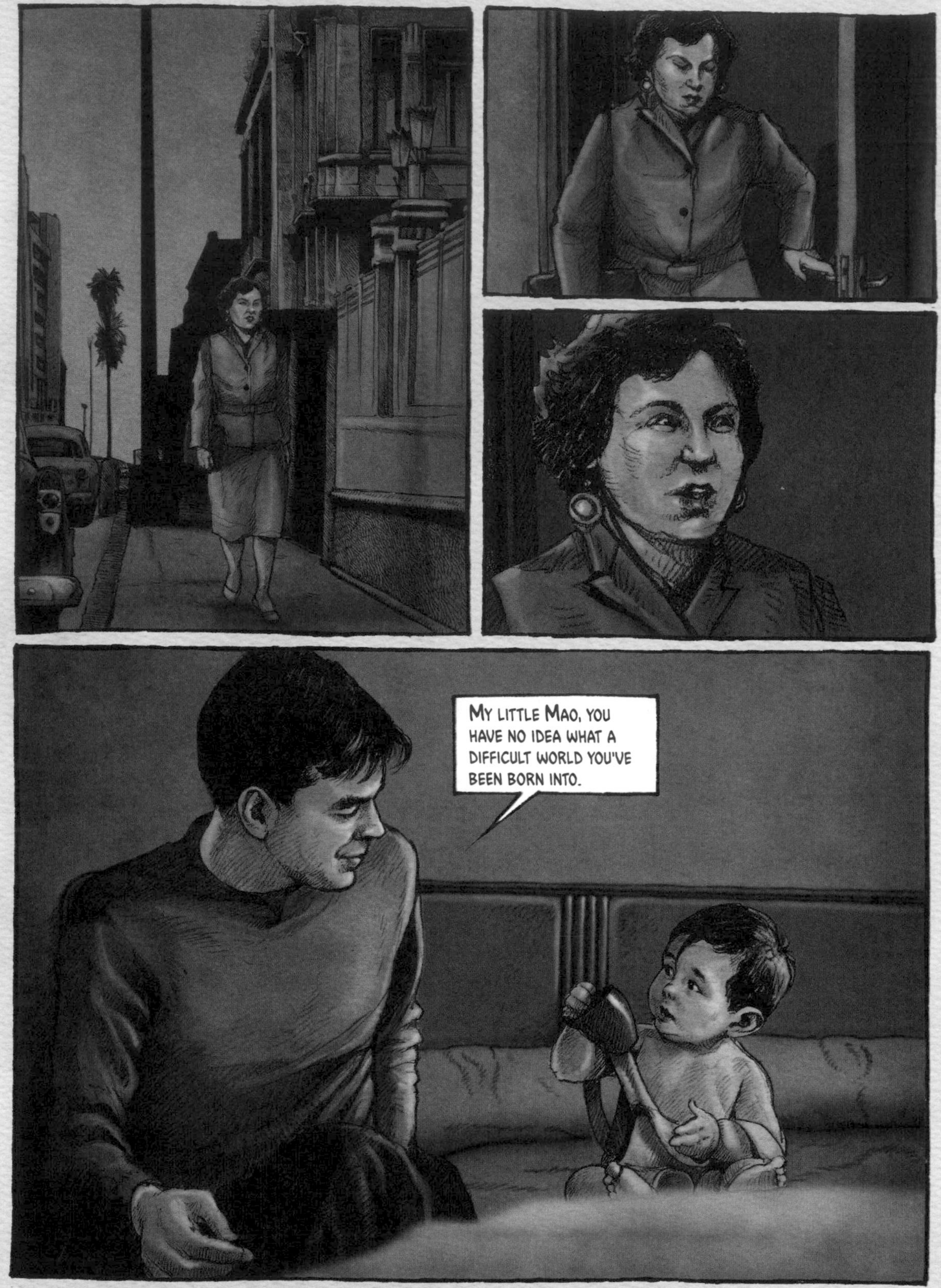
My little Mao, you have no idea what a difficult world you've been born into.

WHEN YOU GROW UP, THIS WHOLE CONTINENT WILL BE BATTLING THE GREAT ENEMY: YANKEE IMPERIALISM.

AND MAYBE THE WHOLE WORLD WILL BE TOO. YOU WILL ALSO HAVE TO FIGHT.

AND IT'S POSSIBLE I WON'T BE HERE, BUT THE FLAMES OF THE STRUGGLE WILL COVER THE CONTINENT.

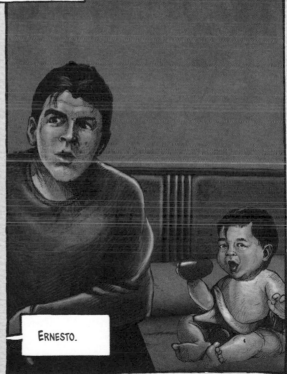

ERNESTO.

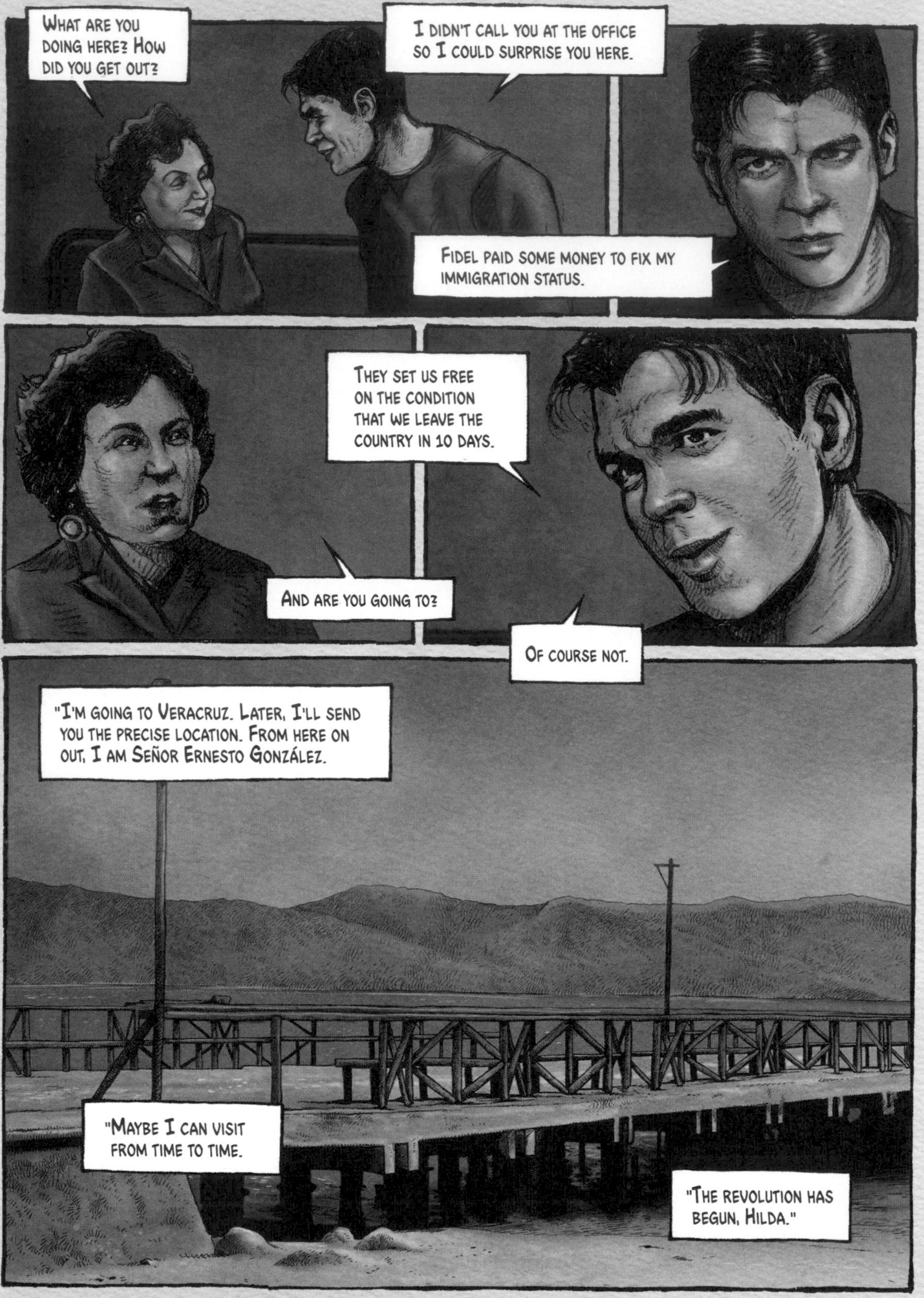
WHAT ARE YOU DOING HERE? HOW DID YOU GET OUT?
I DIDN'T CALL YOU AT THE OFFICE SO I COULD SURPRISE YOU HERE.
FIDEL PAID SOME MONEY TO FIX MY IMMIGRATION STATUS.
THEY SET US FREE ON THE CONDITION THAT WE LEAVE THE COUNTRY IN 10 DAYS.
AND ARE YOU GOING TO?
OF COURSE NOT.
"I'M GOING TO VERACRUZ. LATER, I'LL SEND YOU THE PRECISE LOCATION. FROM HERE ON OUT, I AM SEÑOR ERNESTO GONZÁLEZ.
"MAYBE I CAN VISIT FROM TIME TO TIME.
"THE REVOLUTION HAS BEGUN, HILDA."

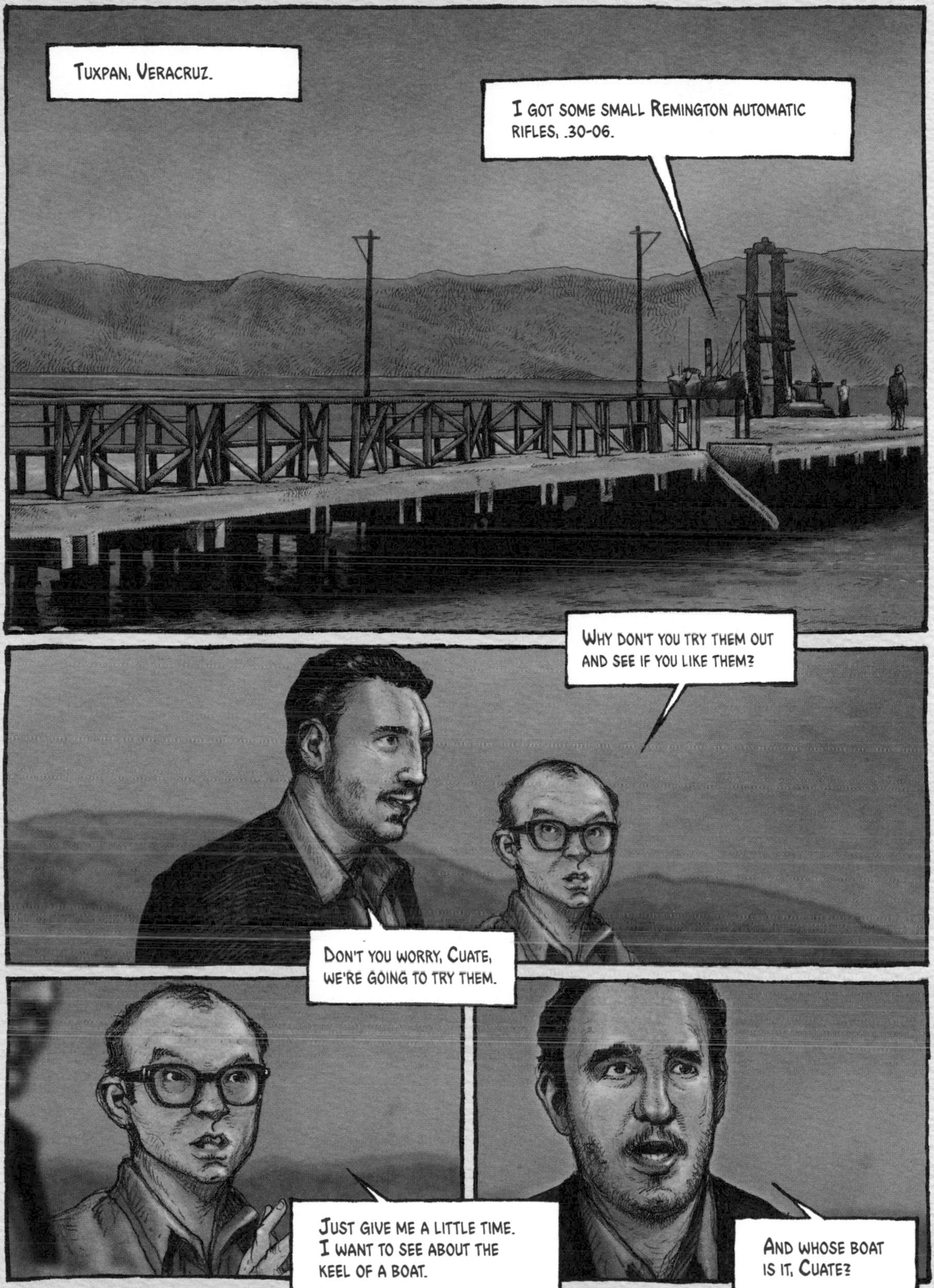
Tuxpan, Veracruz.
I got some small Remington automatic rifles, .30-06.
Why don't you try them out and see if you like them?
Don't you worry, Cuate, we're going to try them.
Just give me a little time. I want to see about the keel of a boat.
And whose boat is it, Cuate?

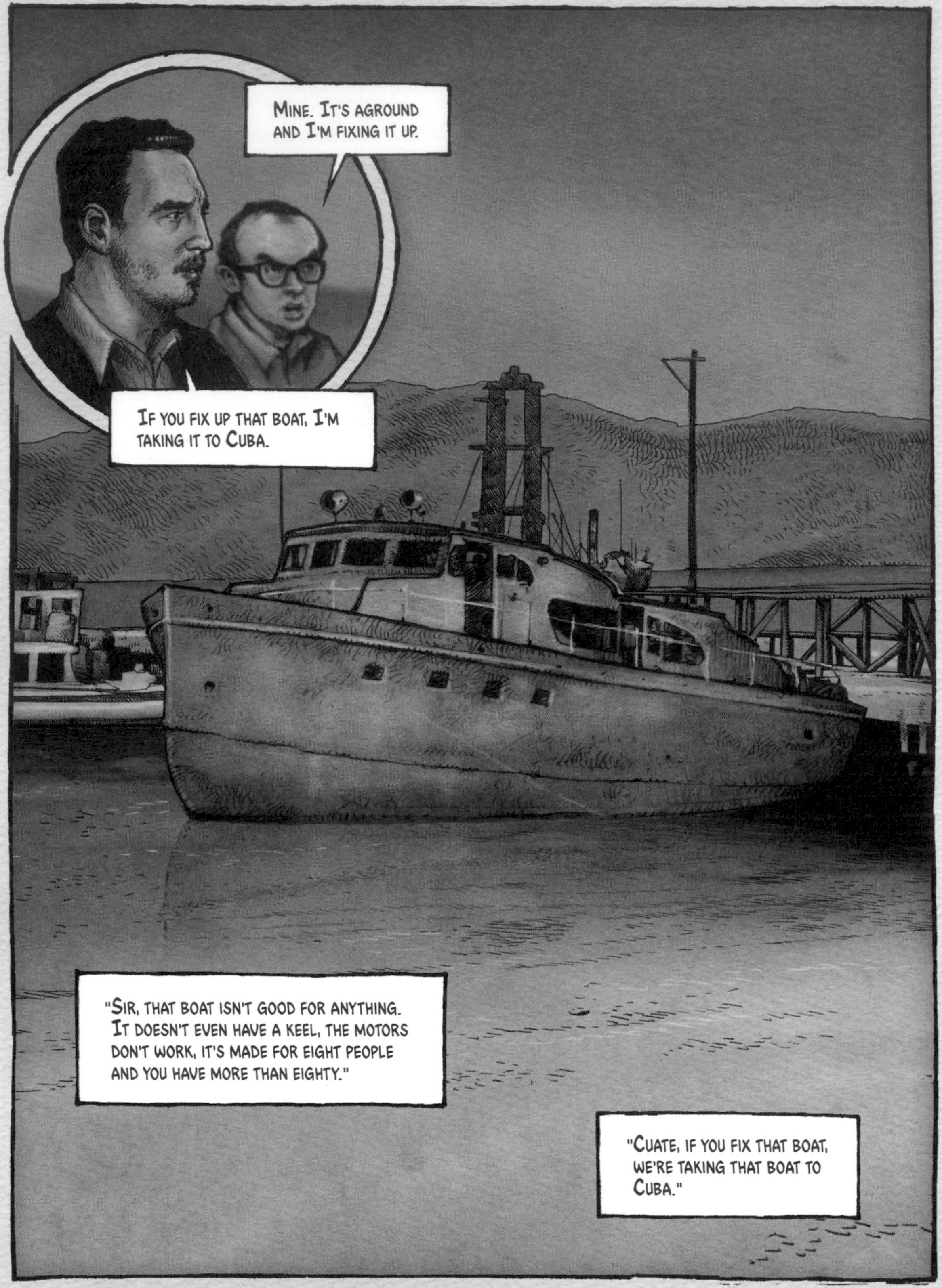
Mine. It's aground and I'm fixing it up.
If you fix up that boat, I'm taking it to Cuba.
"Sir, that boat isn't good for anything. It doesn't even have a keel, the motors don't work, it's made for eight people and you have more than eighty."
"Cuate, if you fix that boat, we're taking that boat to Cuba."

It's time.

Tomorrow, everyone in safe houses in Mexico City, Veracruz, and Tamaulipas is to go to Poza Rica.

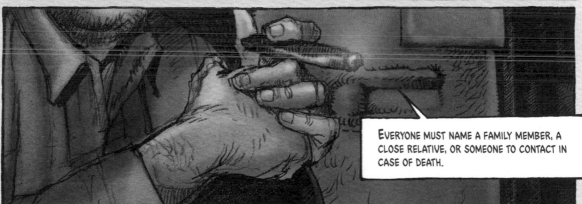

Everyone must name a family member, a close relative, or someone to contact in case of death.

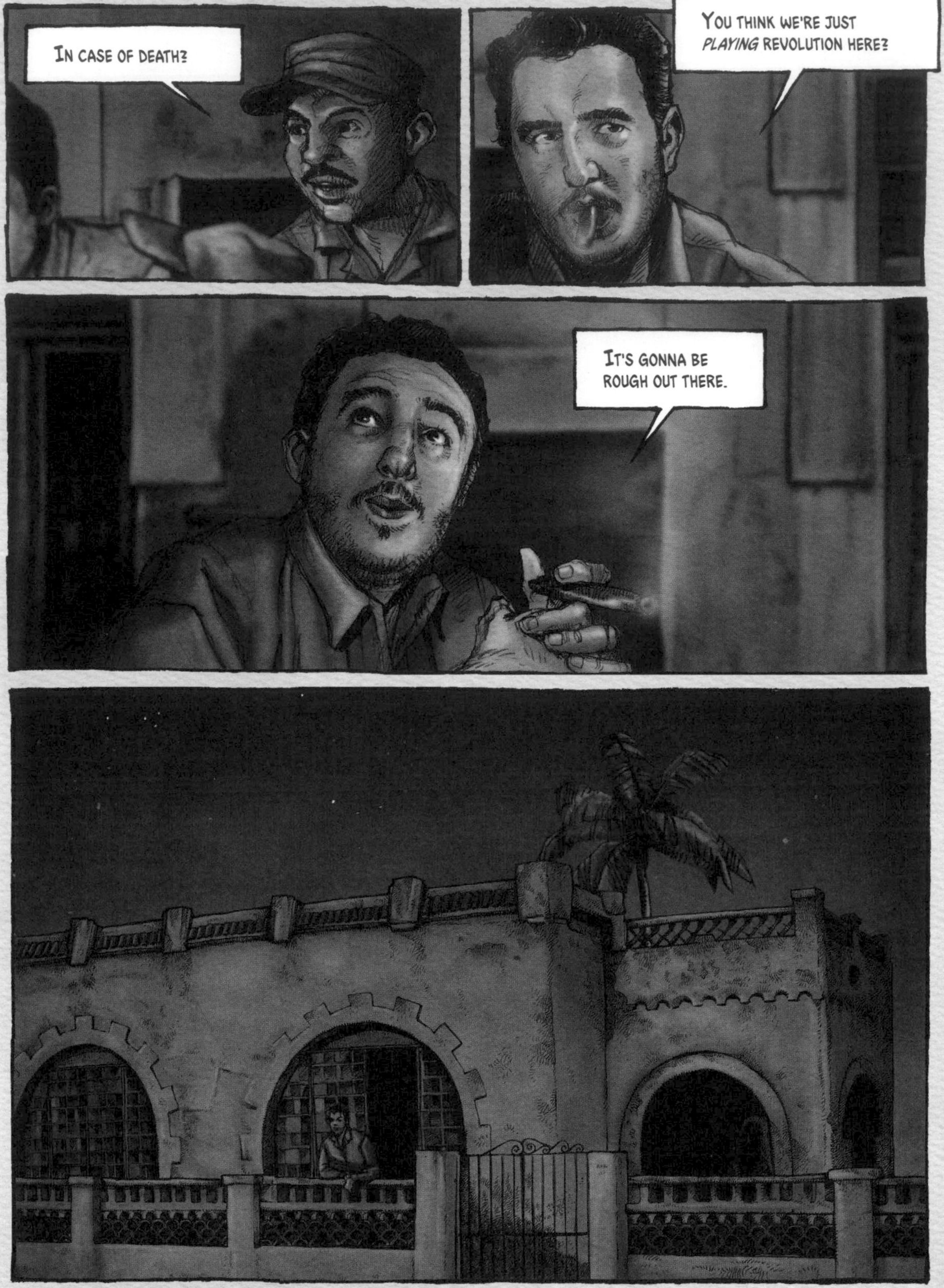

IN CASE OF DEATH?
YOU THINK WE'RE JUST *PLAYING* REVOLUTION HERE?
IT'S GONNA BE ROUGH OUT THERE.

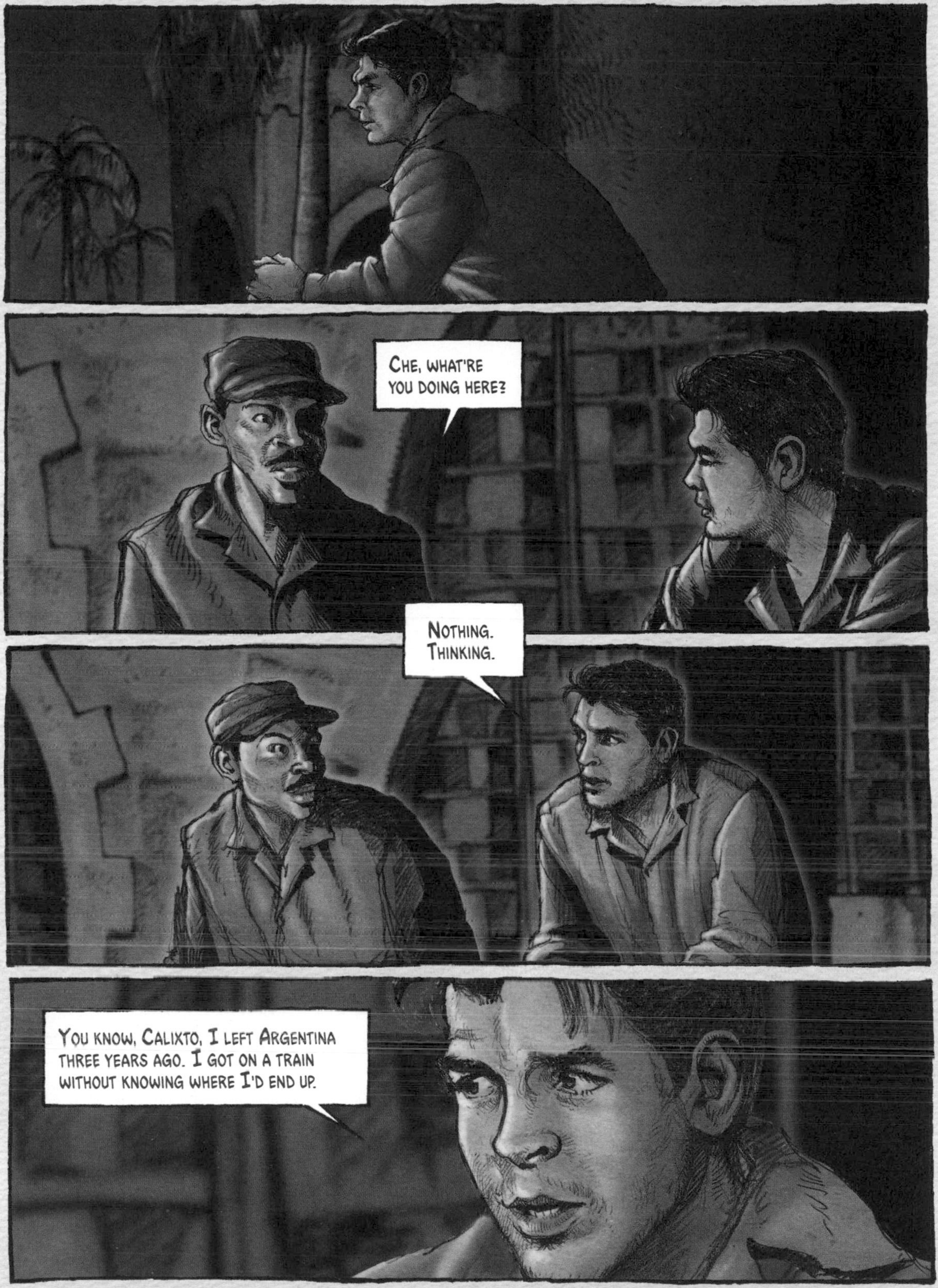
CHE, WHAT'RE YOU DOING HERE?
NOTHING. THINKING.
YOU KNOW, CALIXTO, I LEFT ARGENTINA THREE YEARS AGO. I GOT ON A TRAIN WITHOUT KNOWING WHERE I'D END UP.

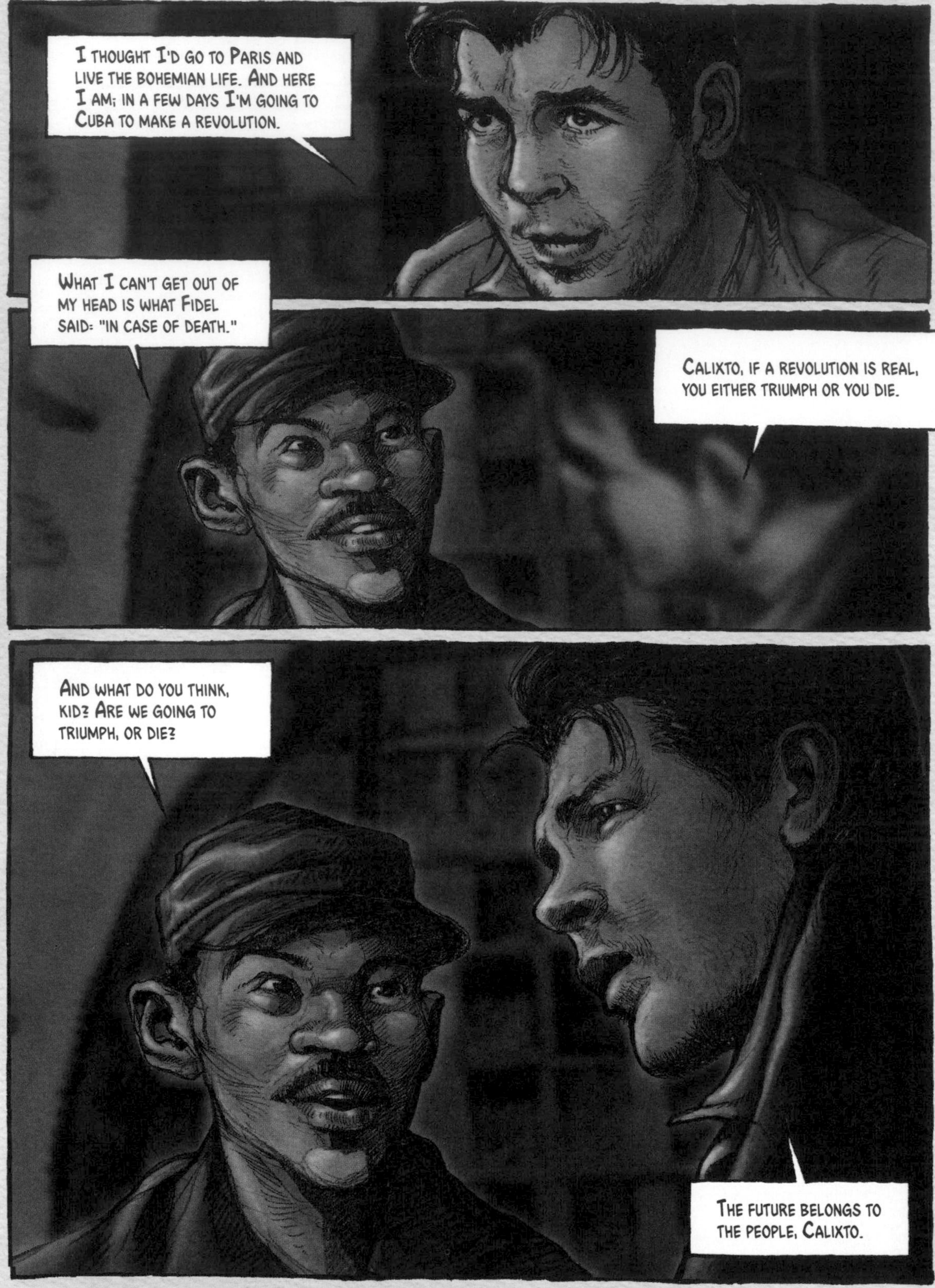
I THOUGHT I'D GO TO PARIS AND LIVE THE BOHEMIAN LIFE. AND HERE I AM; IN A FEW DAYS I'M GOING TO CUBA TO MAKE A REVOLUTION.
WHAT I CAN'T GET OUT OF MY HEAD IS WHAT FIDEL SAID: "IN CASE OF DEATH."
CALIXTO, IF A REVOLUTION IS REAL, YOU EITHER TRIUMPH OR YOU DIE.
AND WHAT DO YOU THINK, KID? ARE WE GOING TO TRIUMPH, OR DIE?
THE FUTURE BELONGS TO THE PEOPLE, CALIXTO.

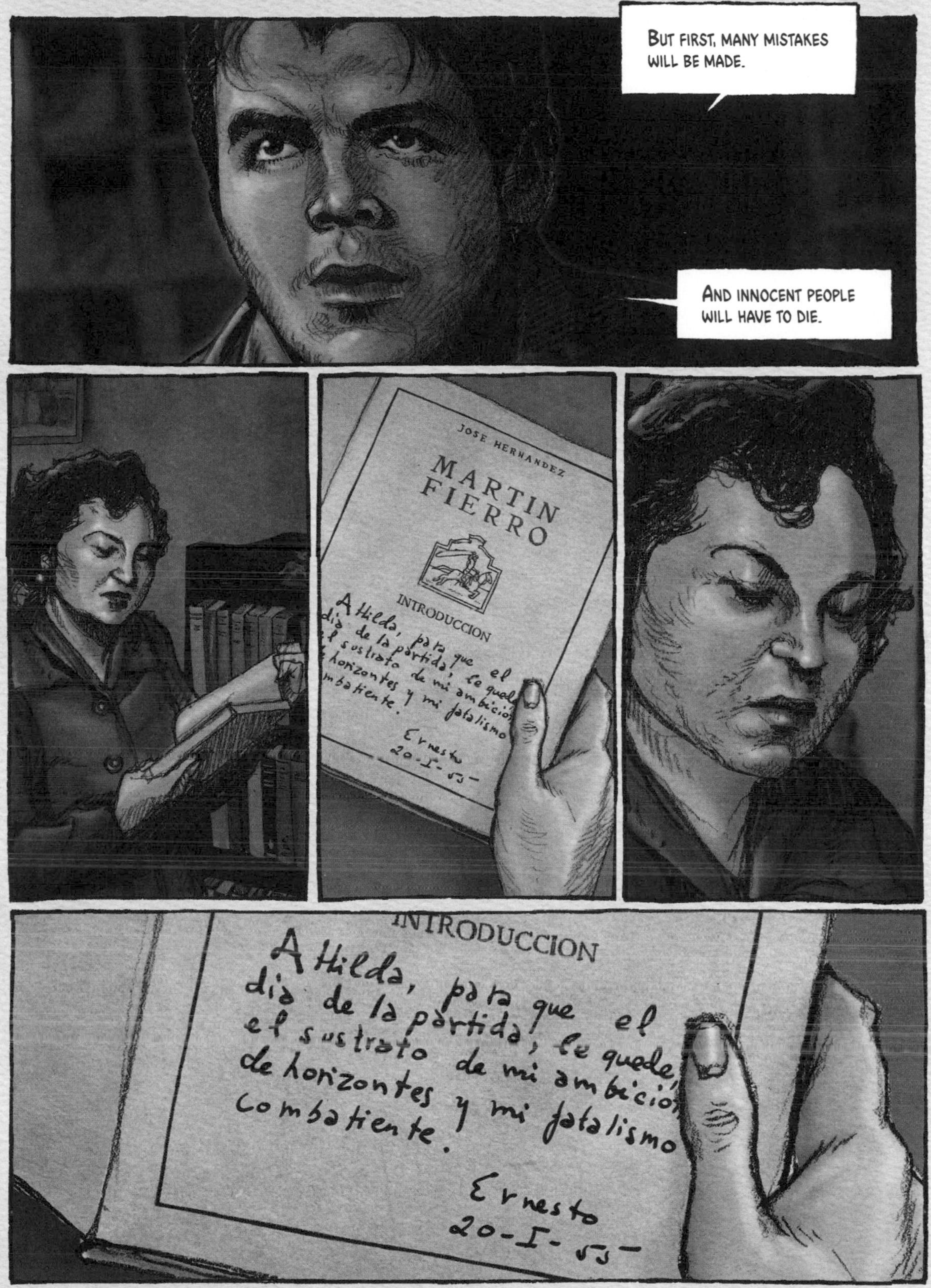
BUT FIRST, MANY MISTAKES WILL BE MADE.
AND INNOCENT PEOPLE WILL HAVE TO DIE.
JOSE HERNANDEZ
MARTIN FIERRO
INTRODUCCION
A Hilda, para que el dia de la partida, te quede el sustrato de mi ambición de horizontes y mi fatalismo combatiente.
Ernesto
20-I-55-

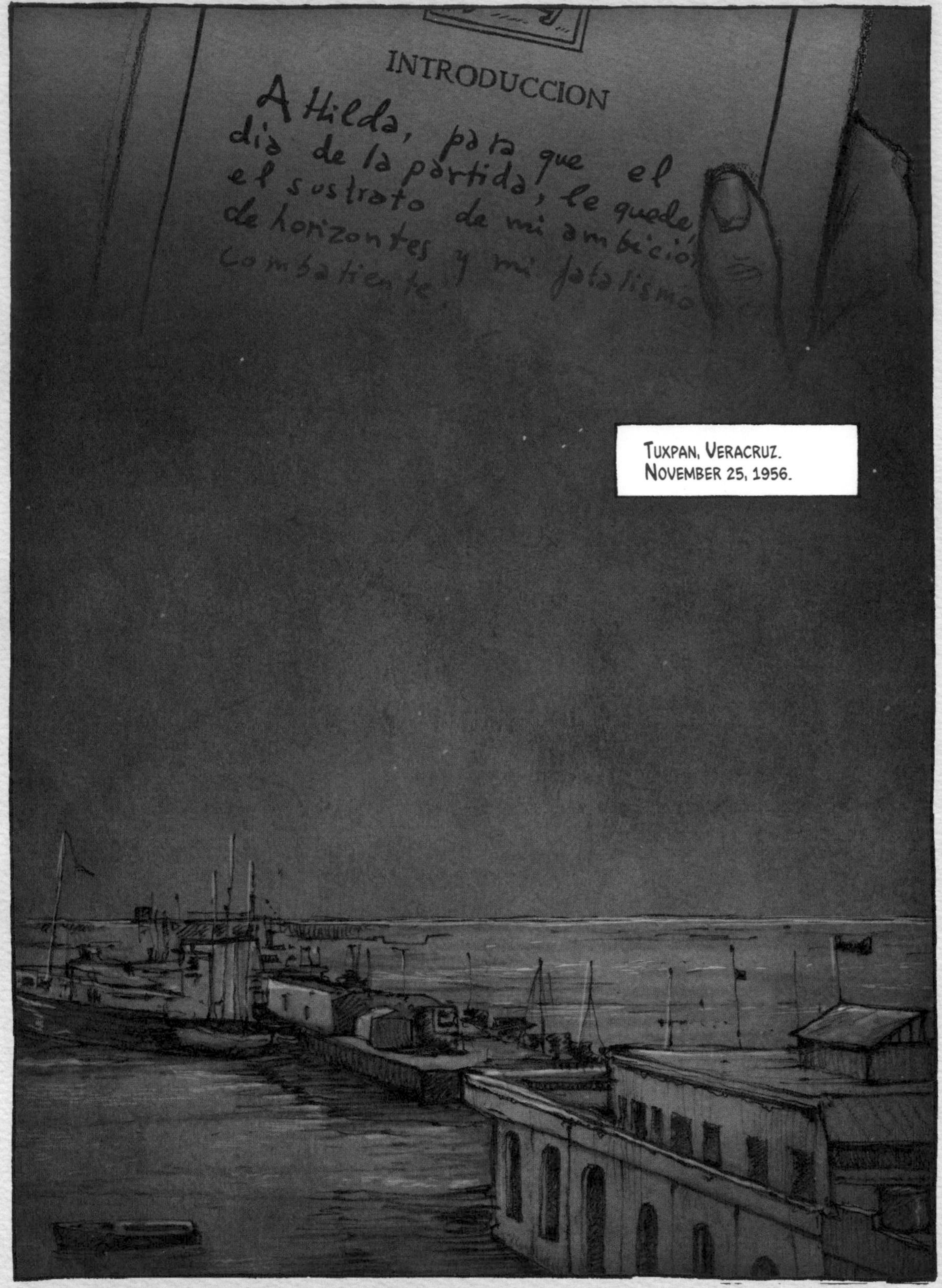
INTRODUCCION
A Hilda, para que el día de la partida, le quede el sustrato de mi ambición de horizontes y mi fatalismo combatiente.
TUXPAN, VERACRUZ.
NOVEMBER 25, 1956.

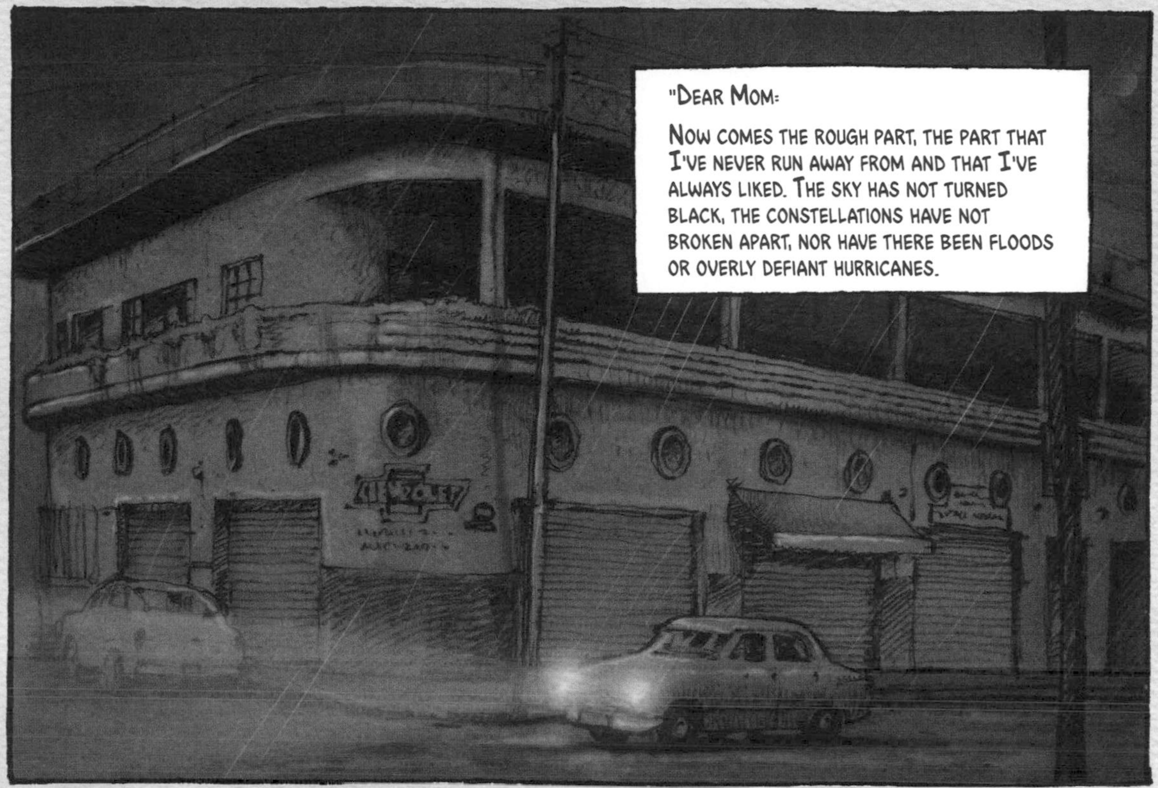
"Dear Mom:
Now comes the rough part, the part that I've never run away from and that I've always liked. The sky has not turned black, the constellations have not broken apart, nor have there been floods or overly defiant hurricanes.

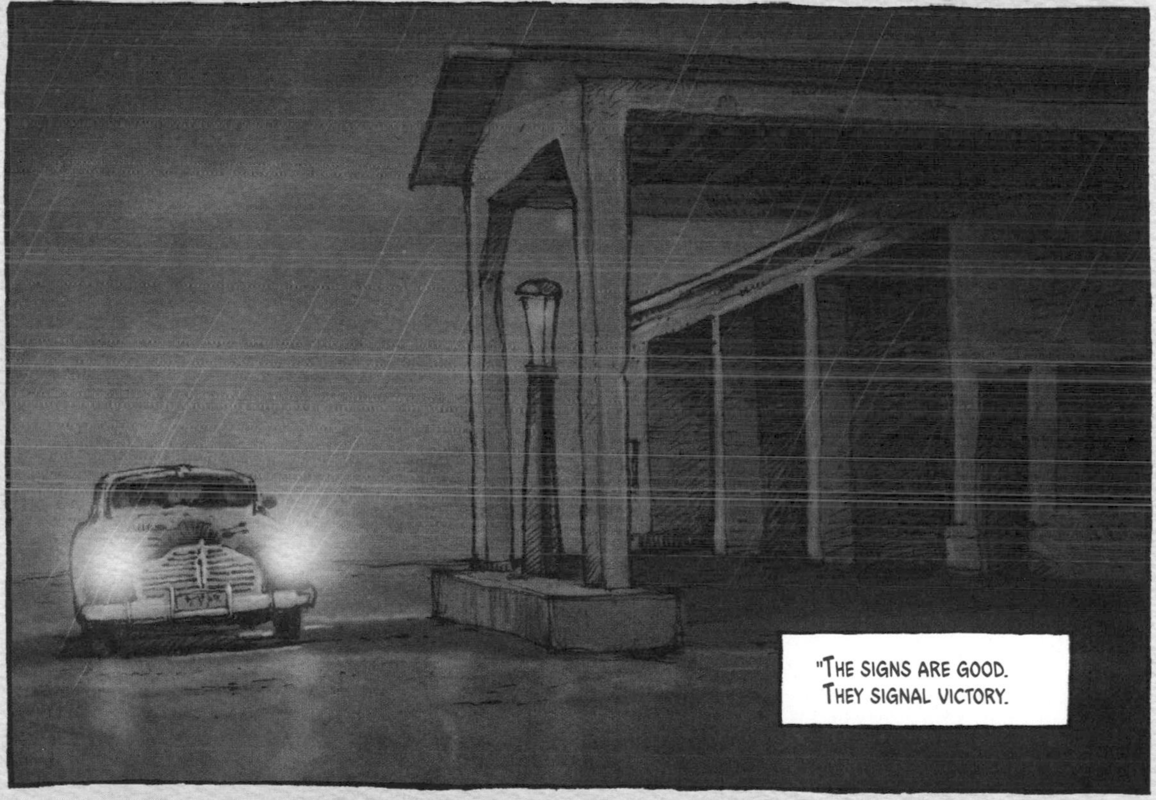
"The signs are good. They signal victory.

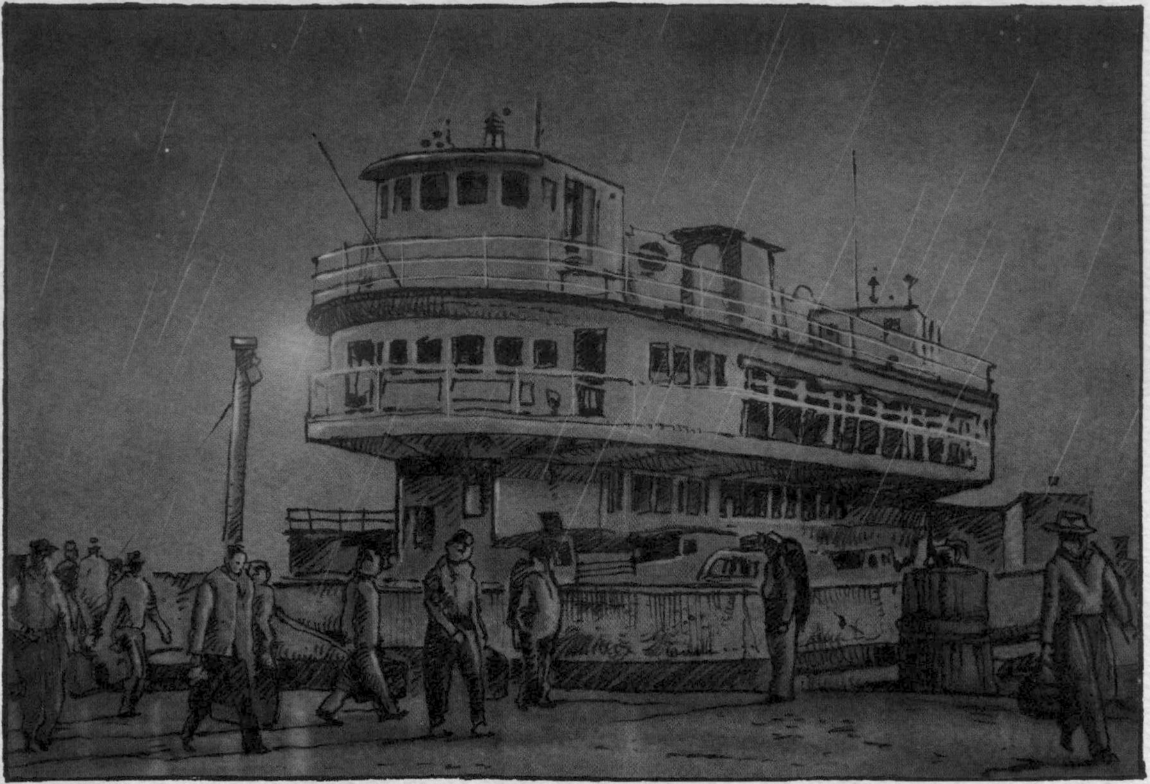

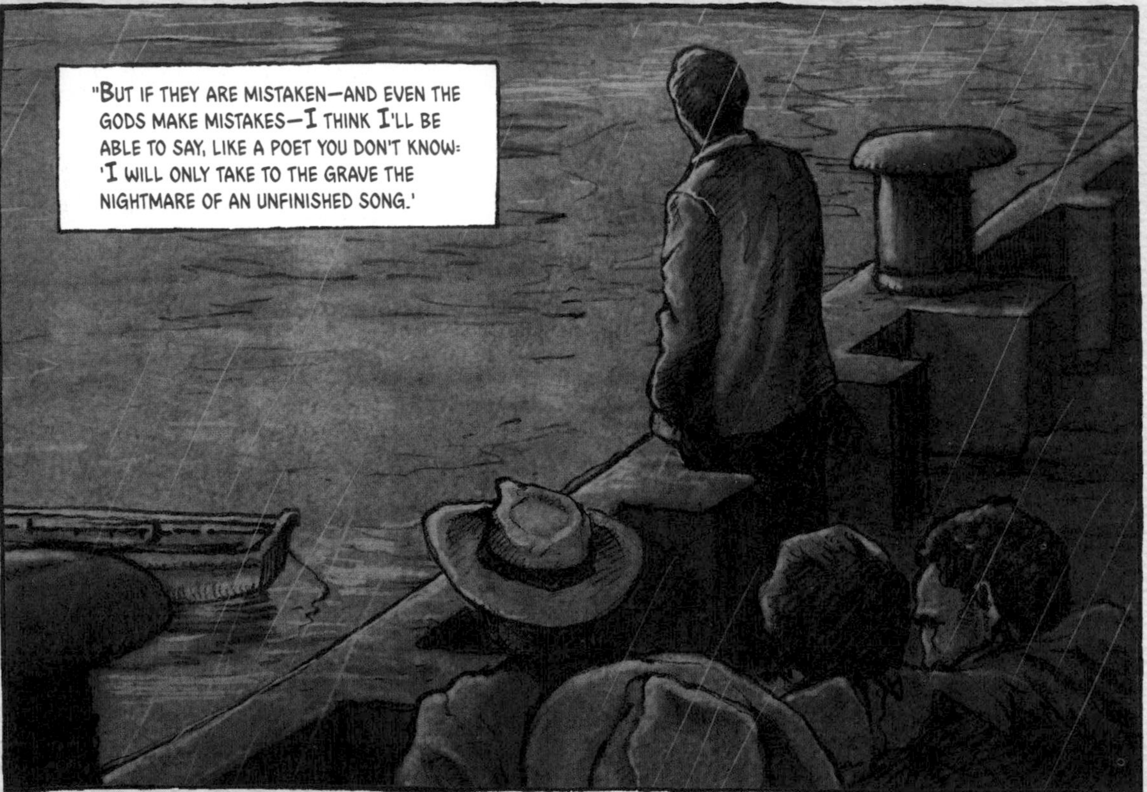
"BUT IF THEY ARE MISTAKEN—AND EVEN THE GODS MAKE MISTAKES—I THINK I'LL BE ABLE TO SAY, LIKE A POET YOU DON'T KNOW: 'I WILL ONLY TAKE TO THE GRAVE THE NIGHTMARE OF AN UNFINISHED SONG.'

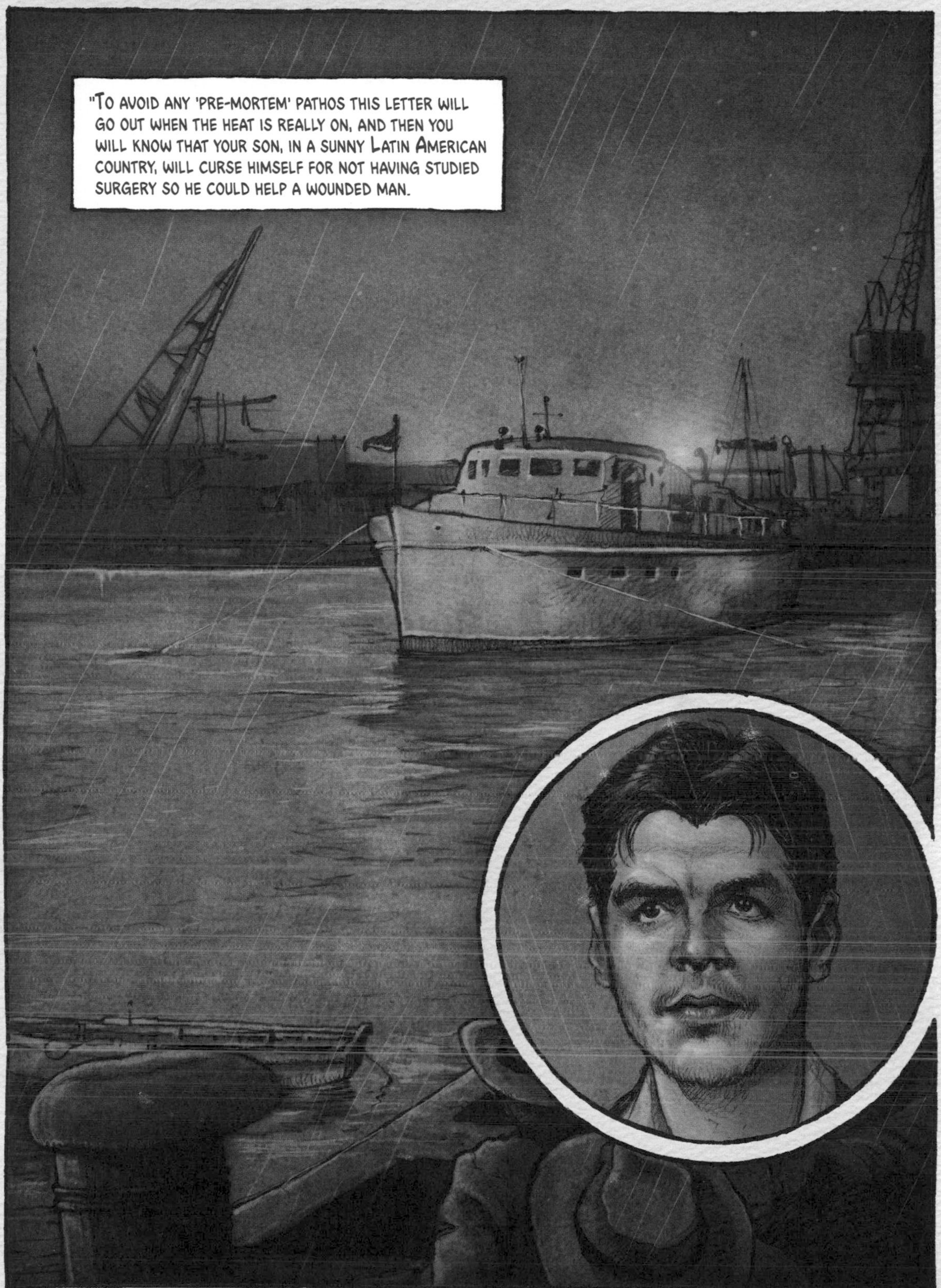
"TO AVOID ANY 'PRE-MORTEM' PATHOS THIS LETTER WILL GO OUT WHEN THE HEAT IS REALLY ON, AND THEN YOU WILL KNOW THAT YOUR SON, IN A SUNNY LATIN AMERICAN COUNTRY, WILL CURSE HIMSELF FOR NOT HAVING STUDIED SURGERY SO HE COULD HELP A WOUNDED MAN.

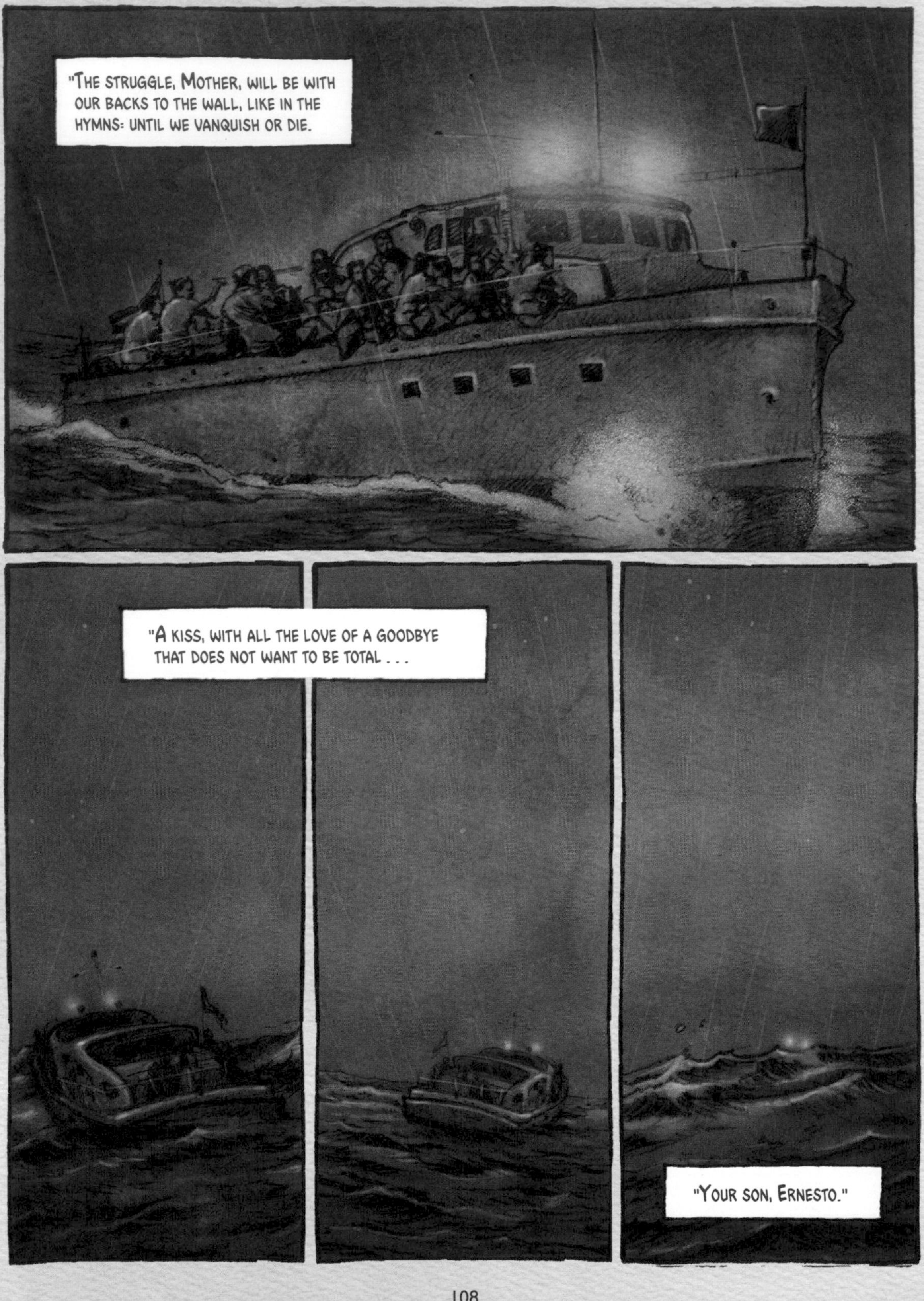
"The struggle, Mother, will be with our backs to the wall, like in the hymns: until we vanquish or die.
"A kiss, with all the love of a goodbye that does not want to be total . . .
"Your son, Ernesto."

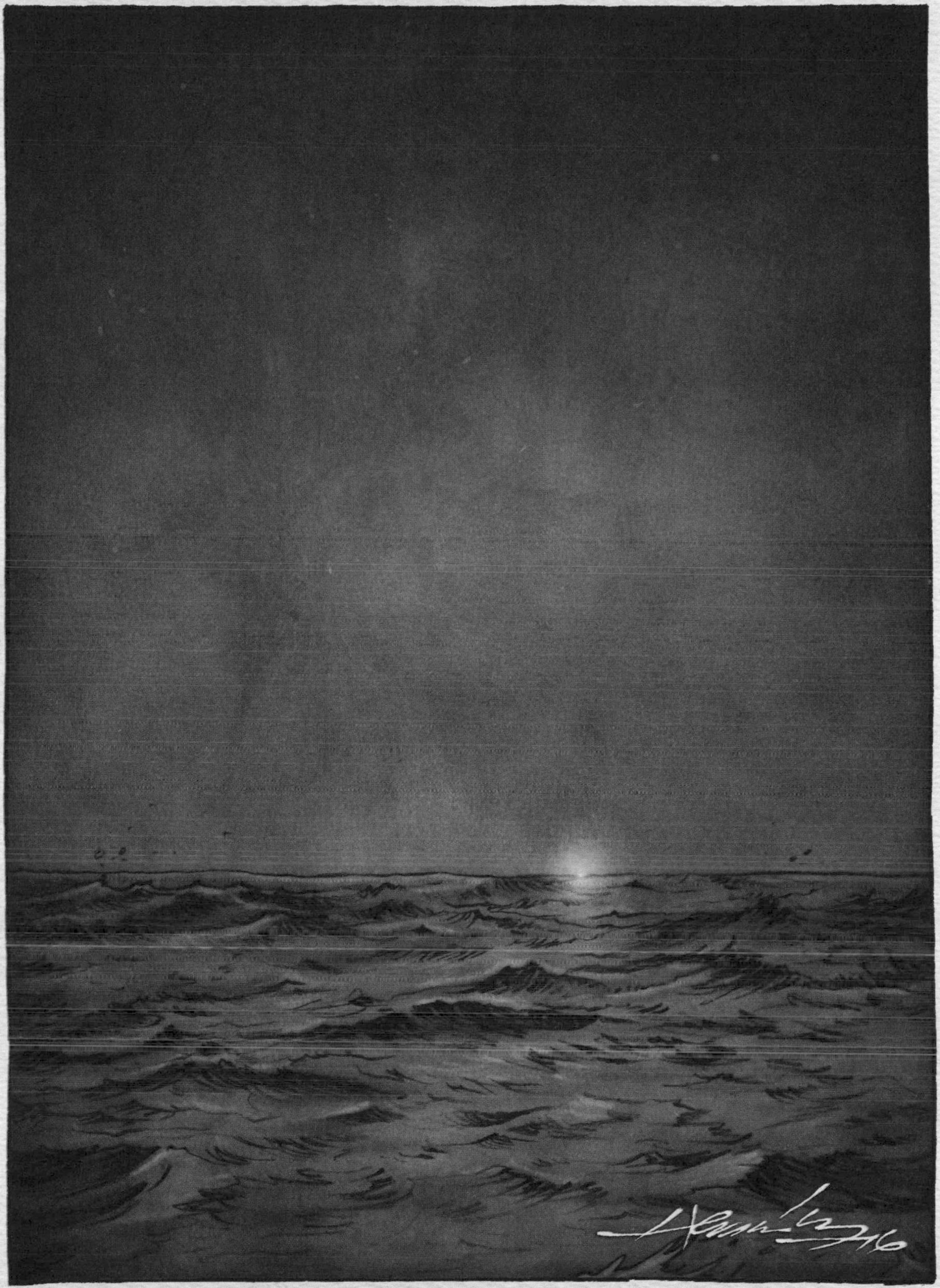

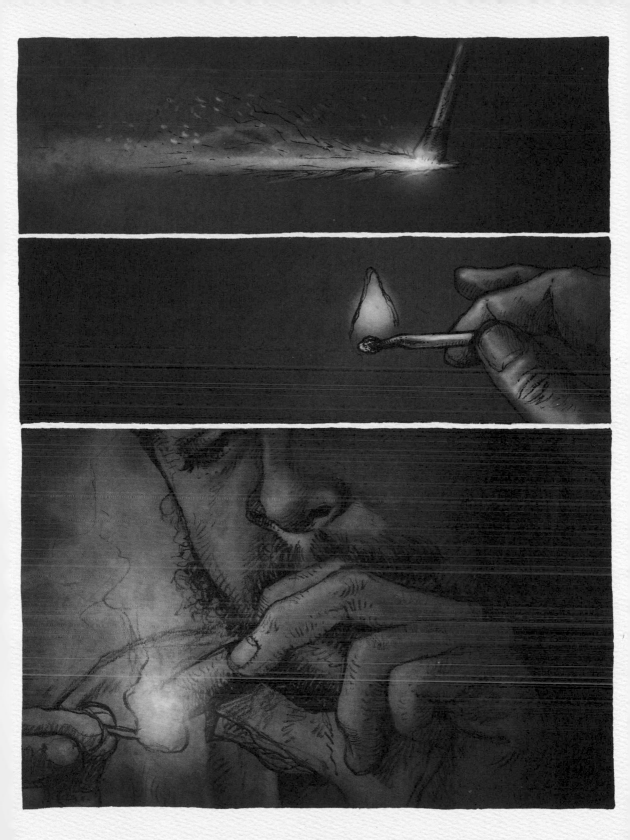

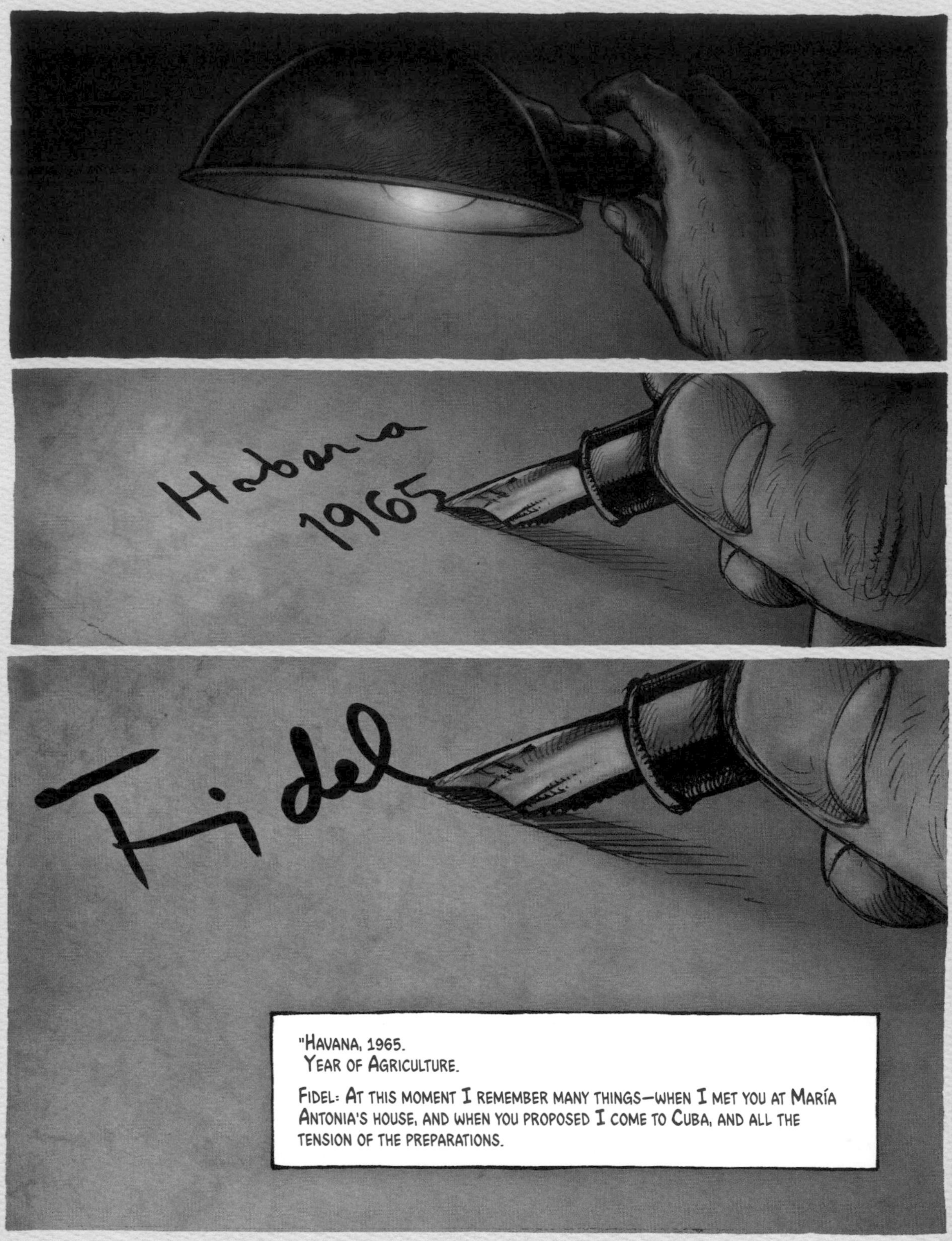
Habana
1965
Fidel
"HAVANA, 1965.
YEAR OF AGRICULTURE.
FIDEL: AT THIS MOMENT I REMEMBER MANY THINGS—WHEN I MET YOU AT MARÍA ANTONIA'S HOUSE, AND WHEN YOU PROPOSED I COME TO CUBA, AND ALL THE TENSION OF THE PREPARATIONS.

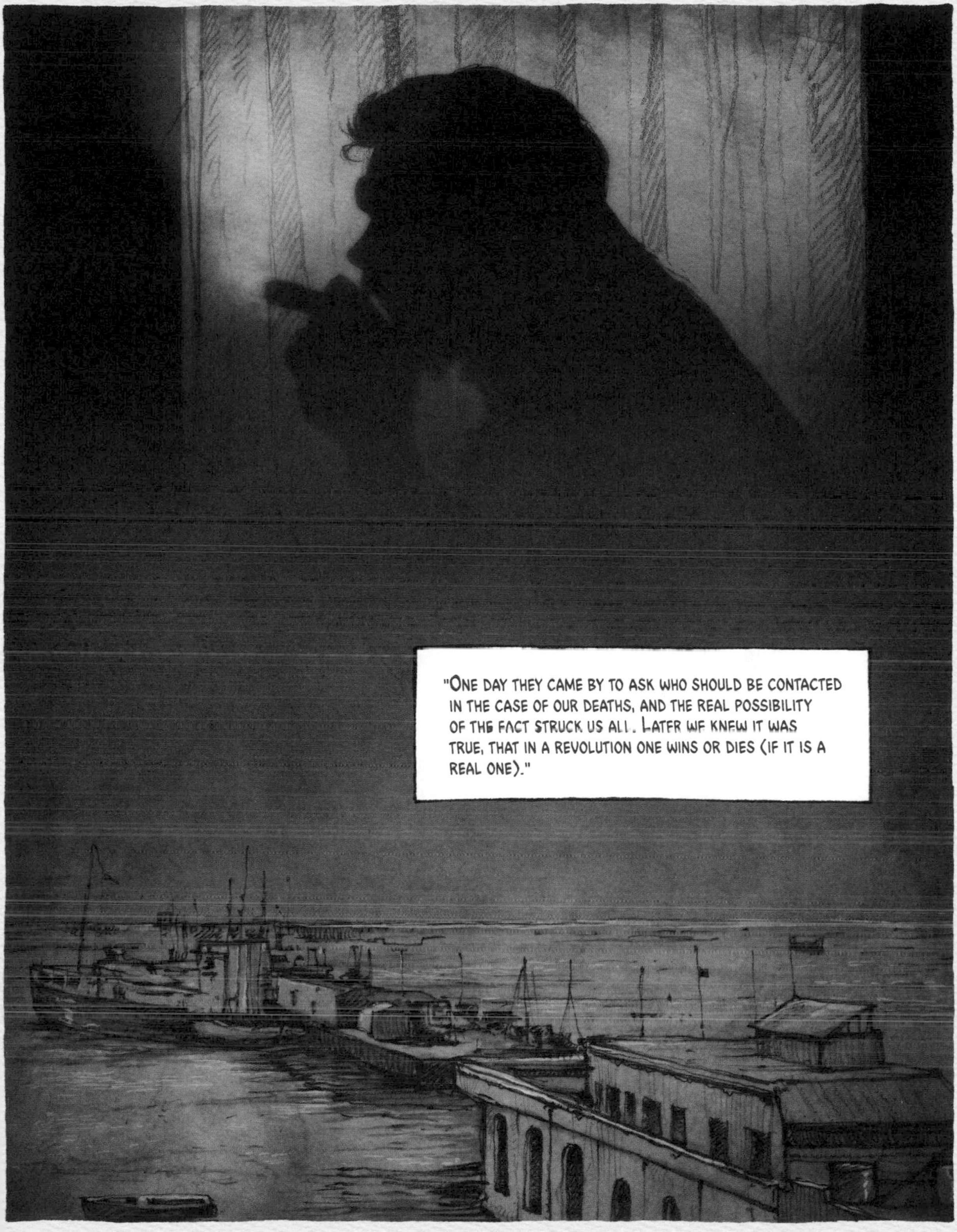
"ONE DAY THEY CAME BY TO ASK WHO SHOULD BE CONTACTED IN THE CASE OF OUR DEATHS, AND THE REAL POSSIBILITY OF THE FACT STRUCK US ALL. LATER WE KNEW IT WAS TRUE, THAT IN A REVOLUTION ONE WINS OR DIES (IF IT IS A REAL ONE)."

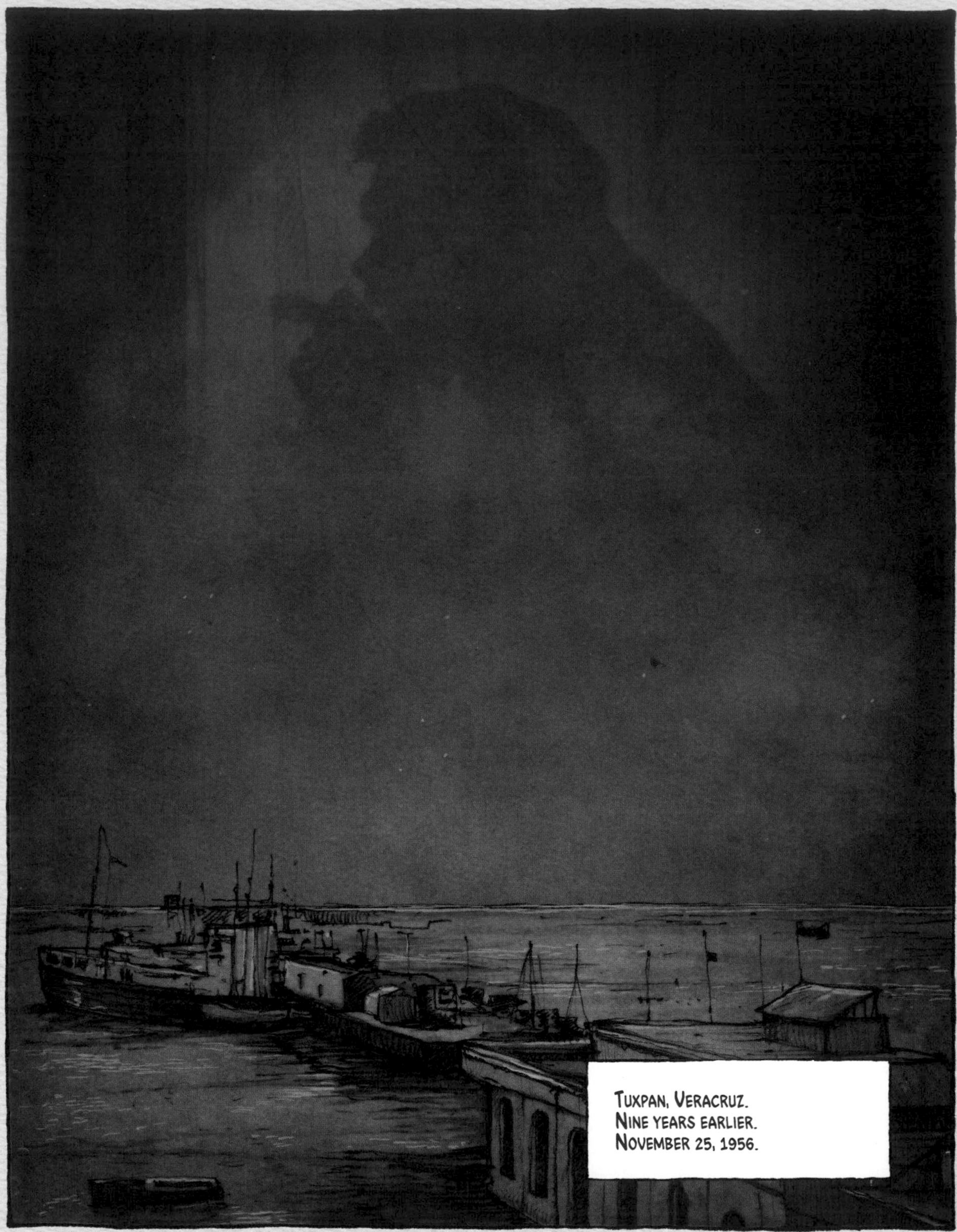
TUXPAN, VERACRUZ.
NINE YEARS EARLIER.
NOVEMBER 25, 1956.

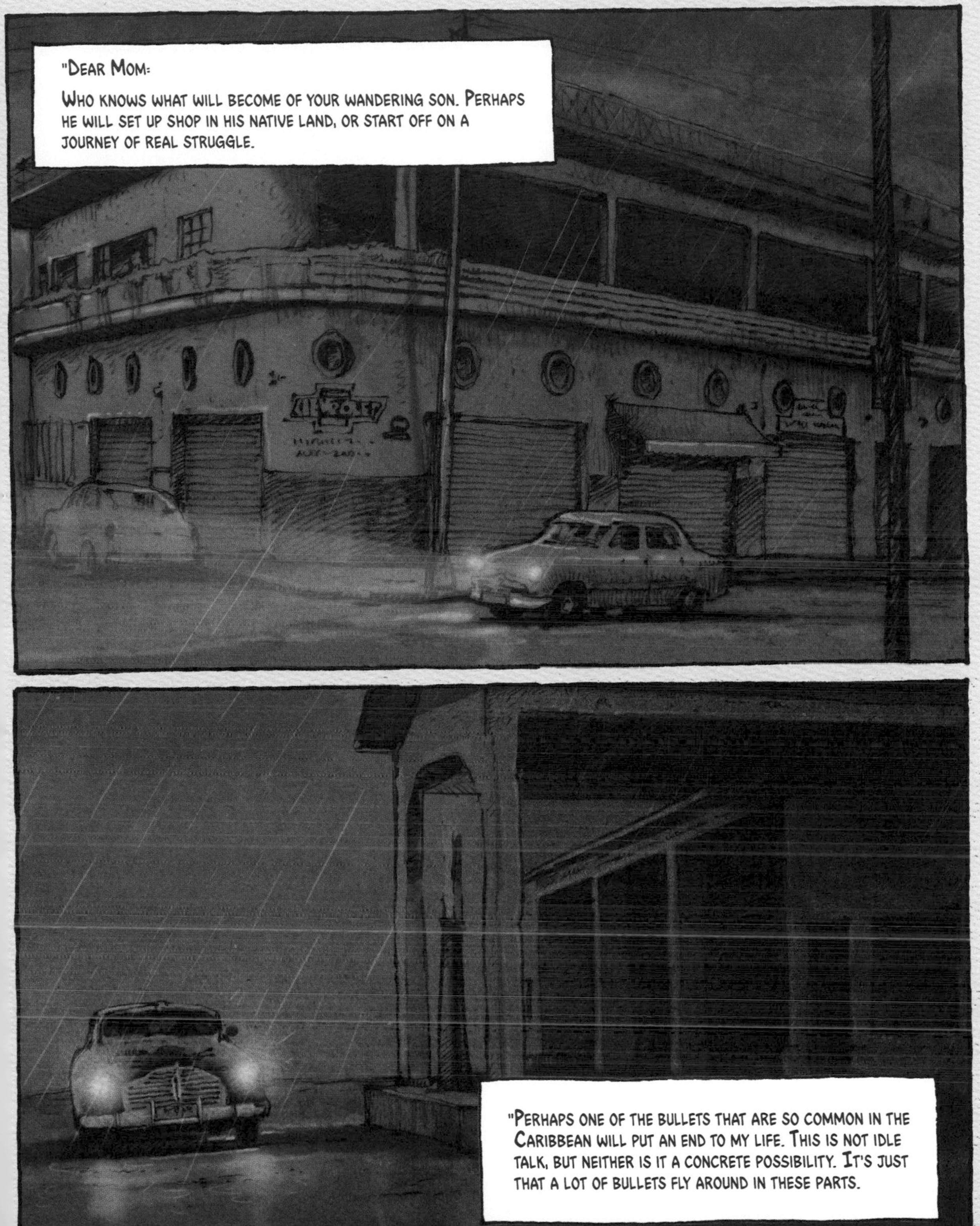
"DEAR MOM:
WHO KNOWS WHAT WILL BECOME OF YOUR WANDERING SON. PERHAPS HE WILL SET UP SHOP IN HIS NATIVE LAND, OR START OFF ON A JOURNEY OF REAL STRUGGLE.
"PERHAPS ONE OF THE BULLETS THAT ARE SO COMMON IN THE CARIBBEAN WILL PUT AN END TO MY LIFE. THIS IS NOT IDLE TALK, BUT NEITHER IS IT A CONCRETE POSSIBILITY. IT'S JUST THAT A LOT OF BULLETS FLY AROUND IN THESE PARTS.

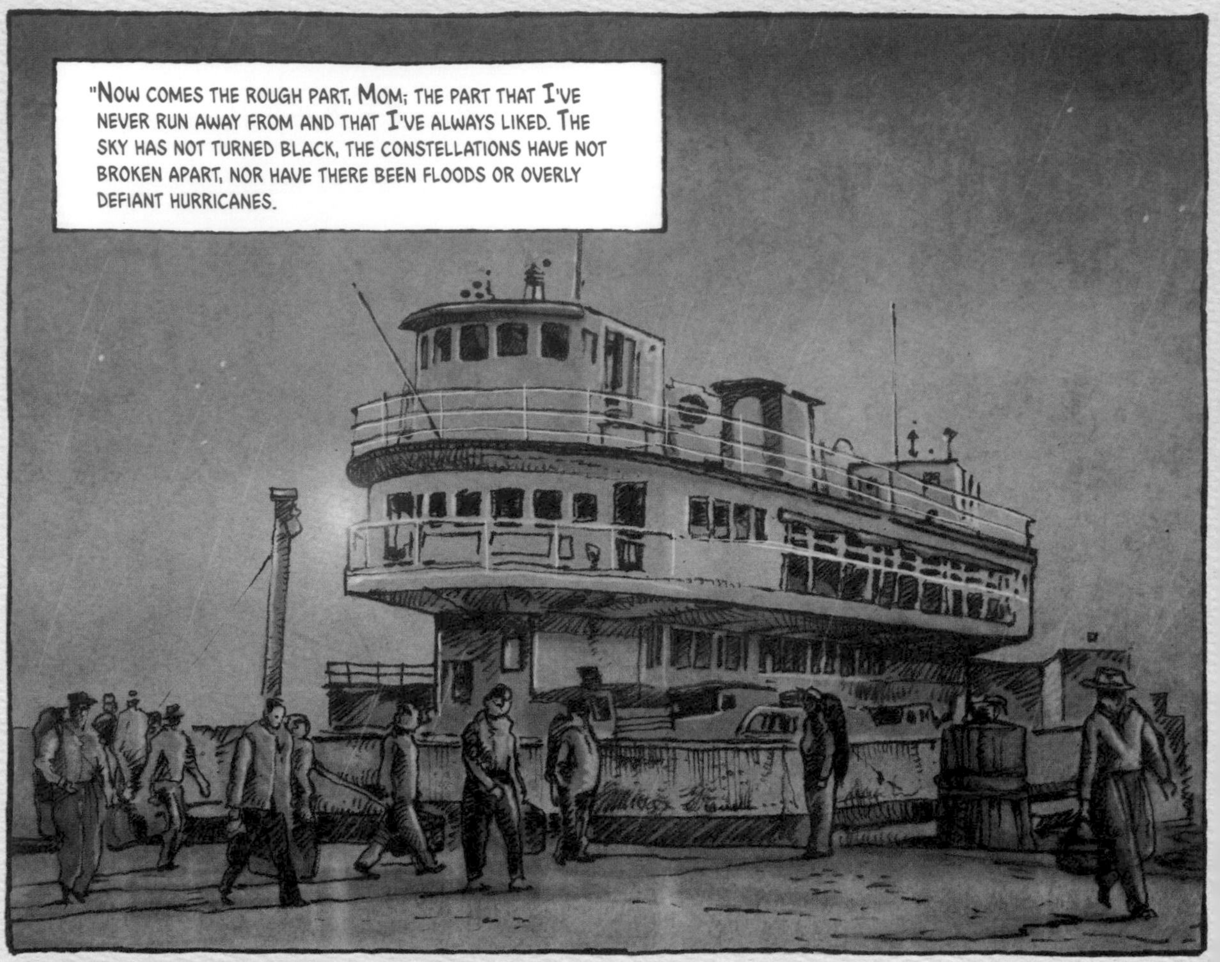
"NOW COMES THE ROUGH PART, MOM; THE PART THAT I'VE NEVER RUN AWAY FROM AND THAT I'VE ALWAYS LIKED. THE SKY HAS NOT TURNED BLACK, THE CONSTELLATIONS HAVE NOT BROKEN APART, NOR HAVE THERE BEEN FLOODS OR OVERLY DEFIANT HURRICANES.

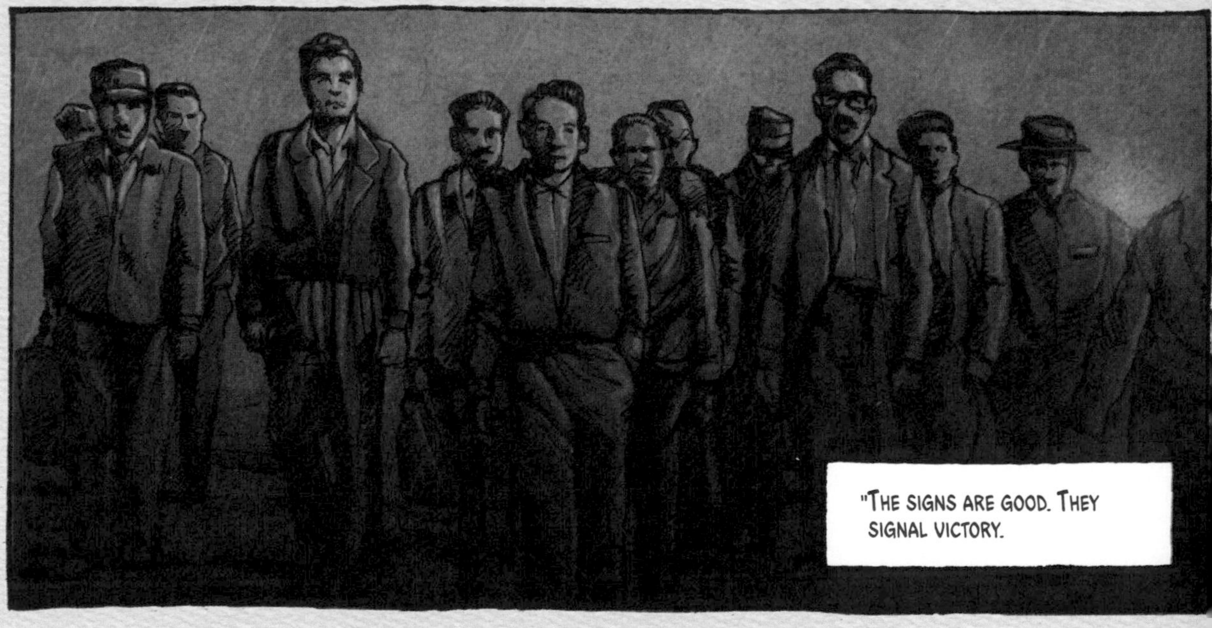
"THE SIGNS ARE GOOD. THEY SIGNAL VICTORY.

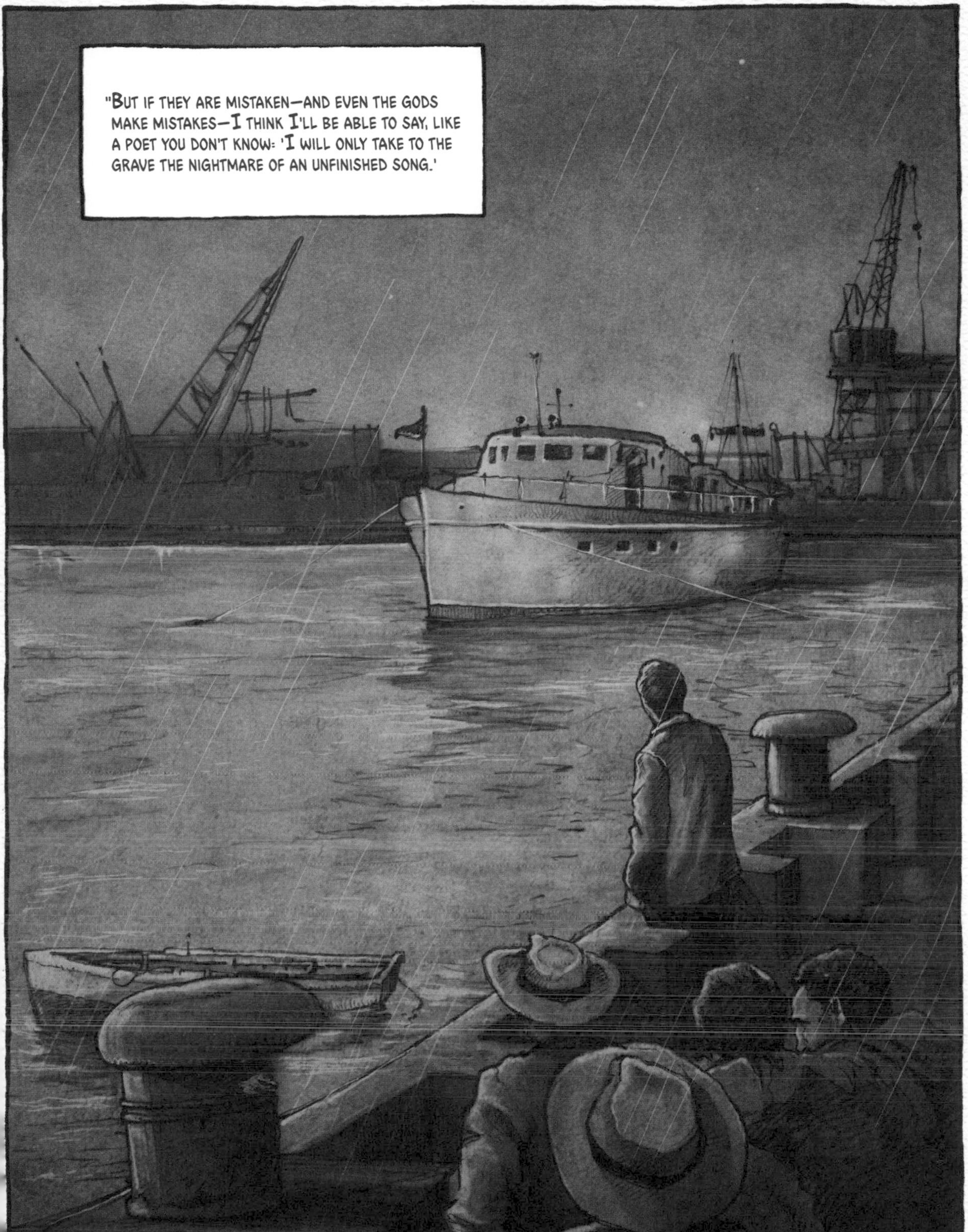
"BUT IF THEY ARE MISTAKEN—AND EVEN THE GODS MAKE MISTAKES—I THINK I'LL BE ABLE TO SAY, LIKE A POET YOU DON'T KNOW: 'I WILL ONLY TAKE TO THE GRAVE THE NIGHTMARE OF AN UNFINISHED SONG.'

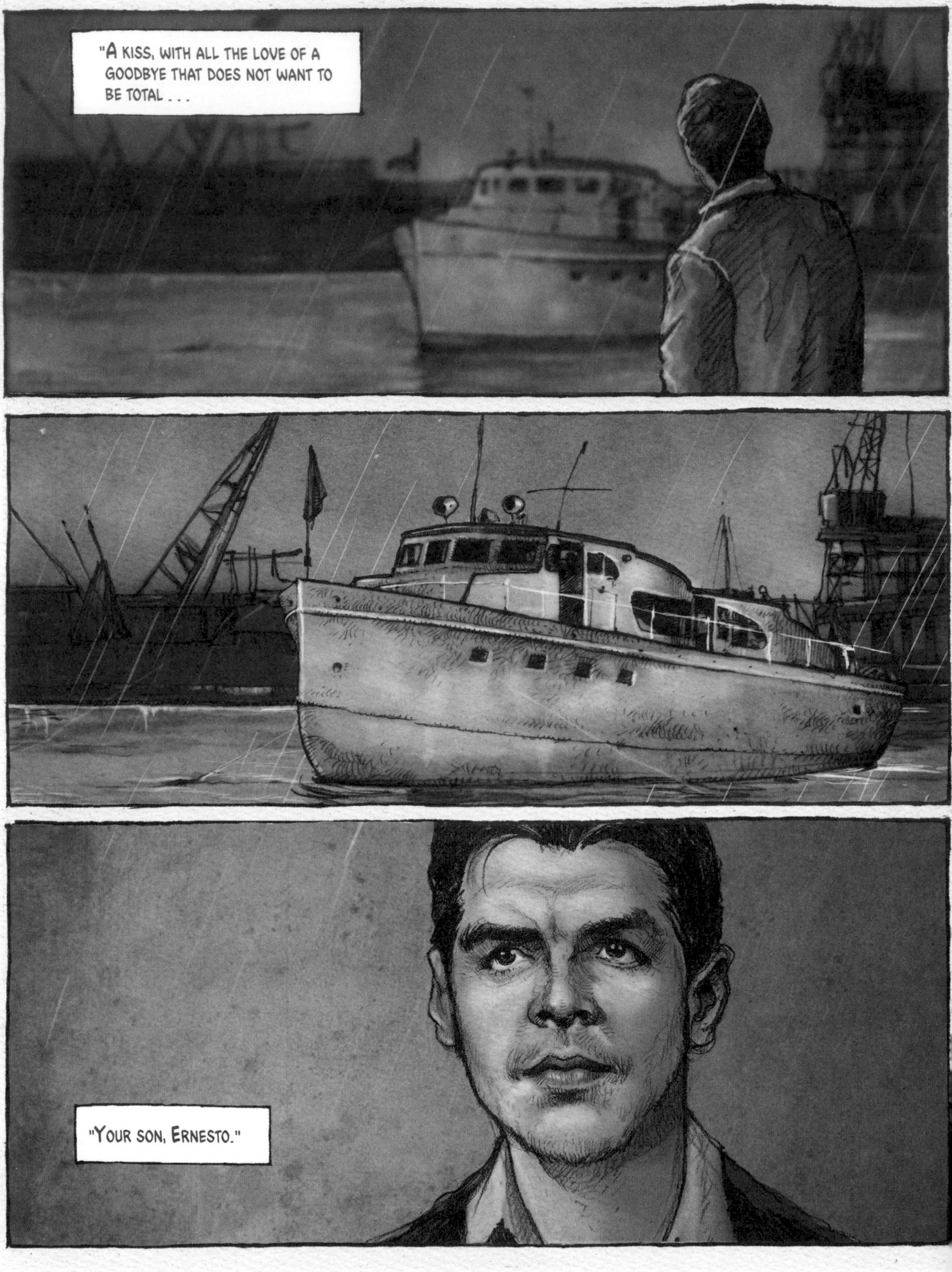
"A KISS, WITH ALL THE LOVE OF A GOODBYE THAT DOES NOT WANT TO BE TOTAL . . .
"YOUR SON, ERNESTO."

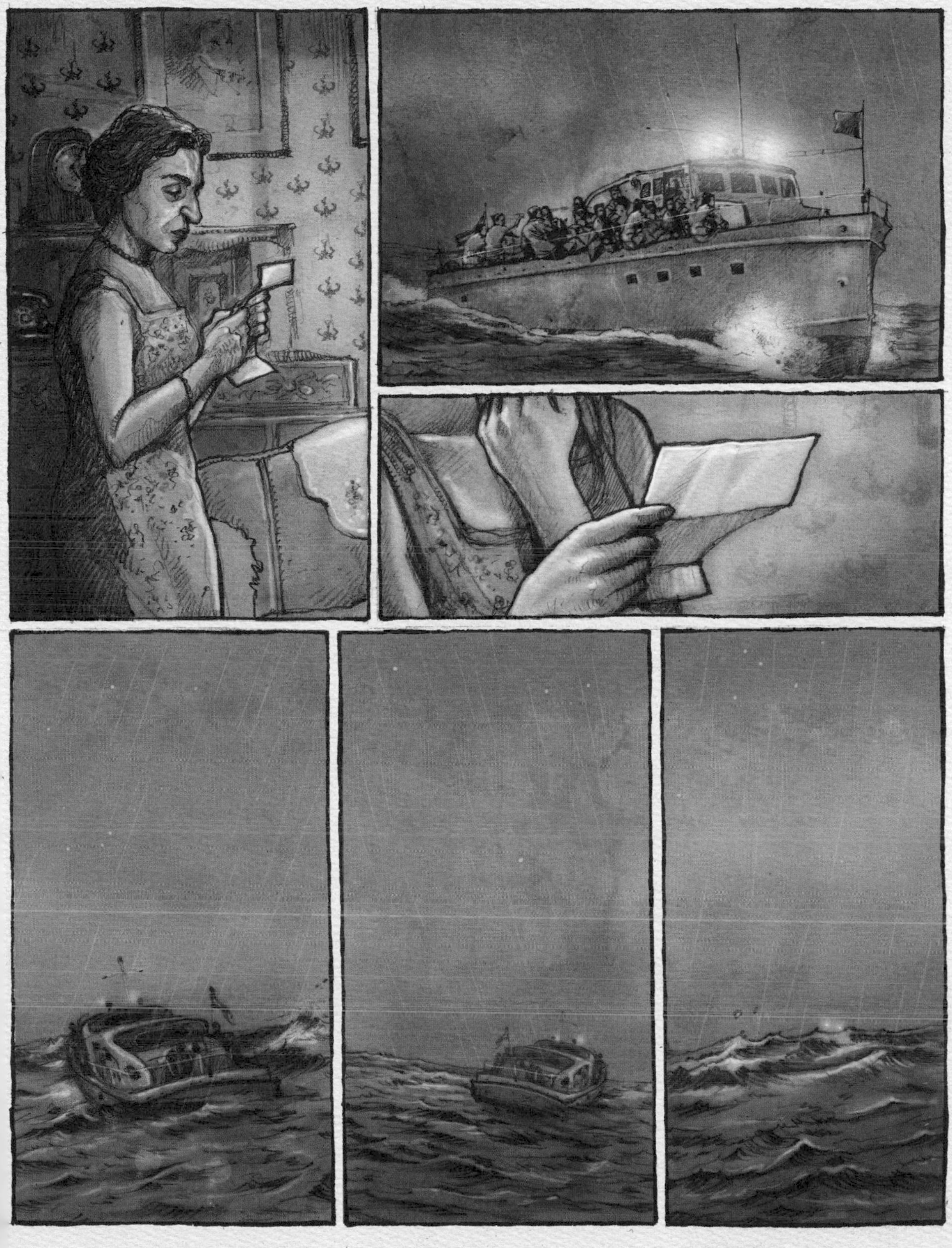

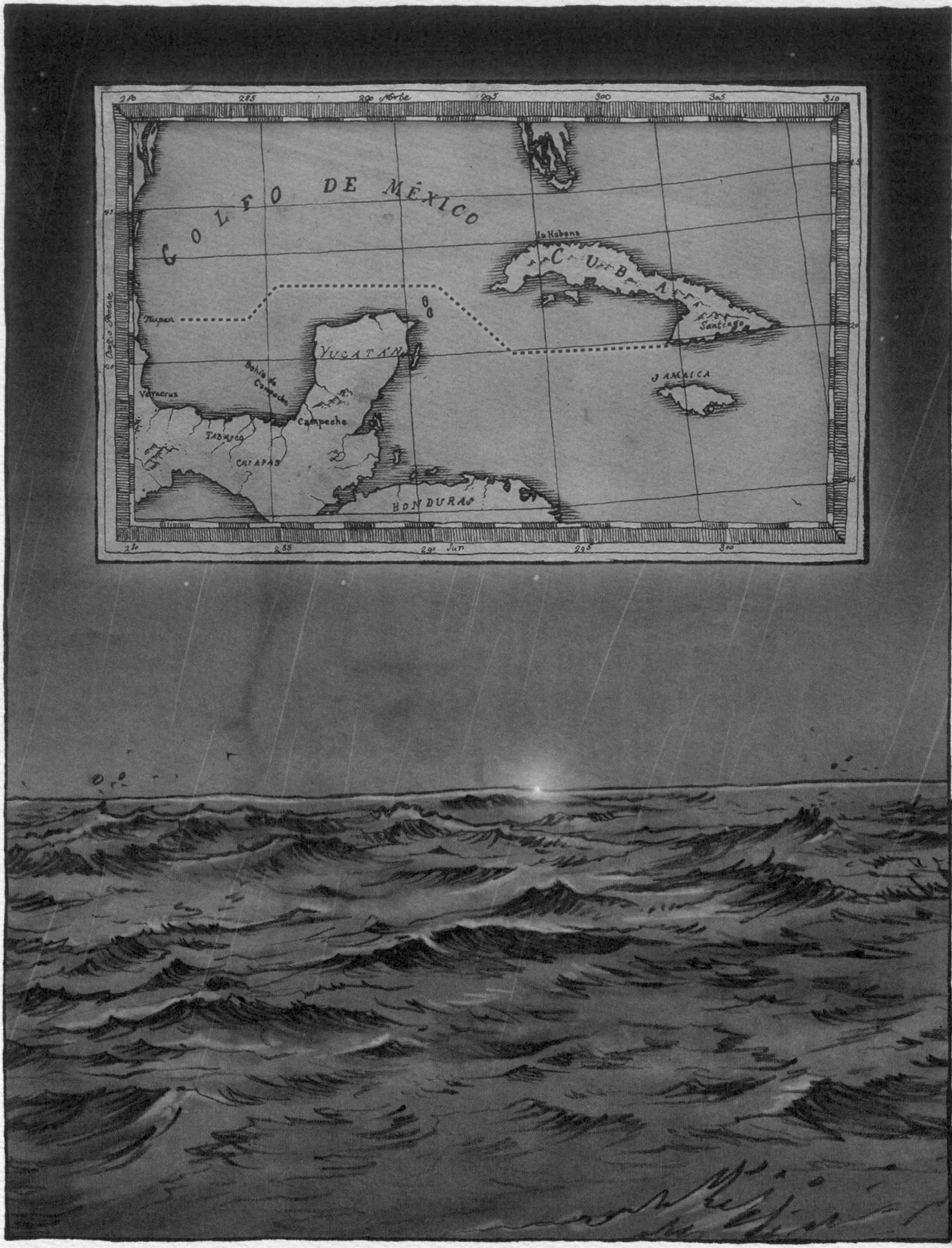
GOLFO DE MÉXICO
La Habana
CUBA
Santiago
JAMAICA
Tuxpan
YUCATÁN
Bahía de Campeche
Veracruz
Campeche
Tabasco
CHIAPAS
HONDURAS

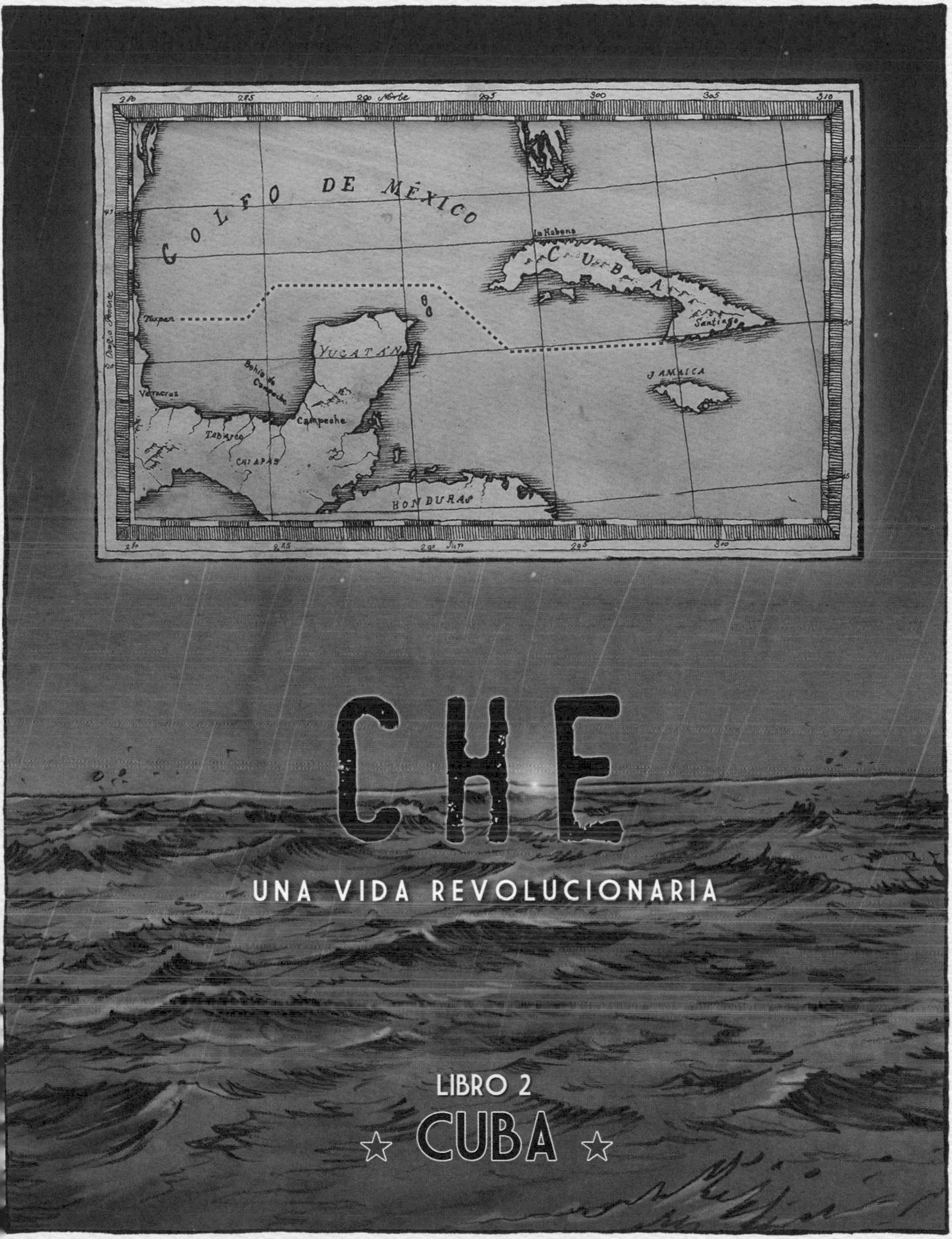
GOLFO DE MÉXICO
La Habana
CUBA
Santiago
JAMAICA
YUCATÁN
Tuxpan
Veracruz
Campeche
Tabasco
CHIAPAS
HONDURAS
CHE
UNA VIDA REVOLUCIONARIA
LIBRO 2
CUBA

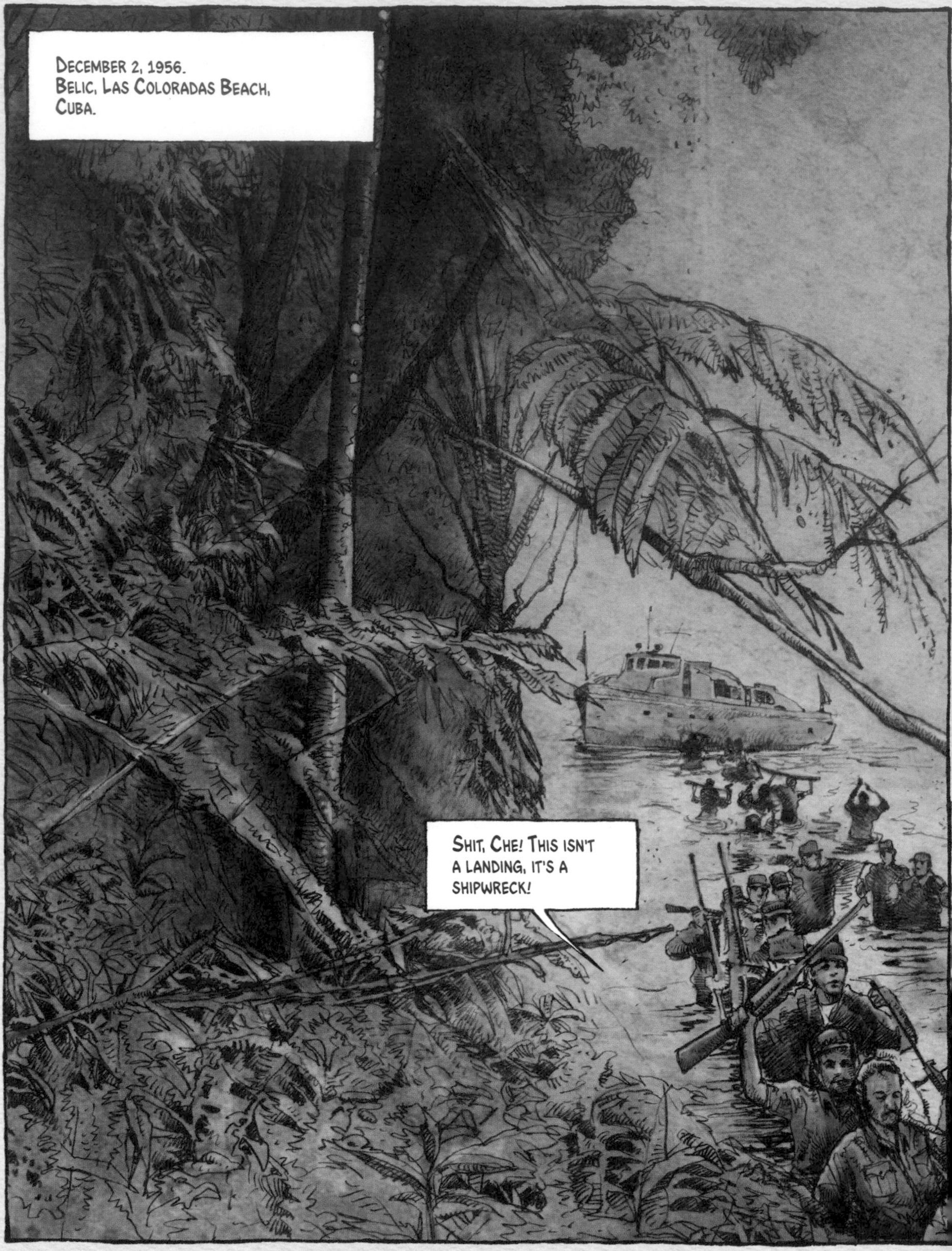
DECEMBER 2, 1956.
BELIC, LAS COLORADAS BEACH,
CUBA.
SHIT, CHE! THIS ISN'T A LANDING, IT'S A SHIPWRECK!

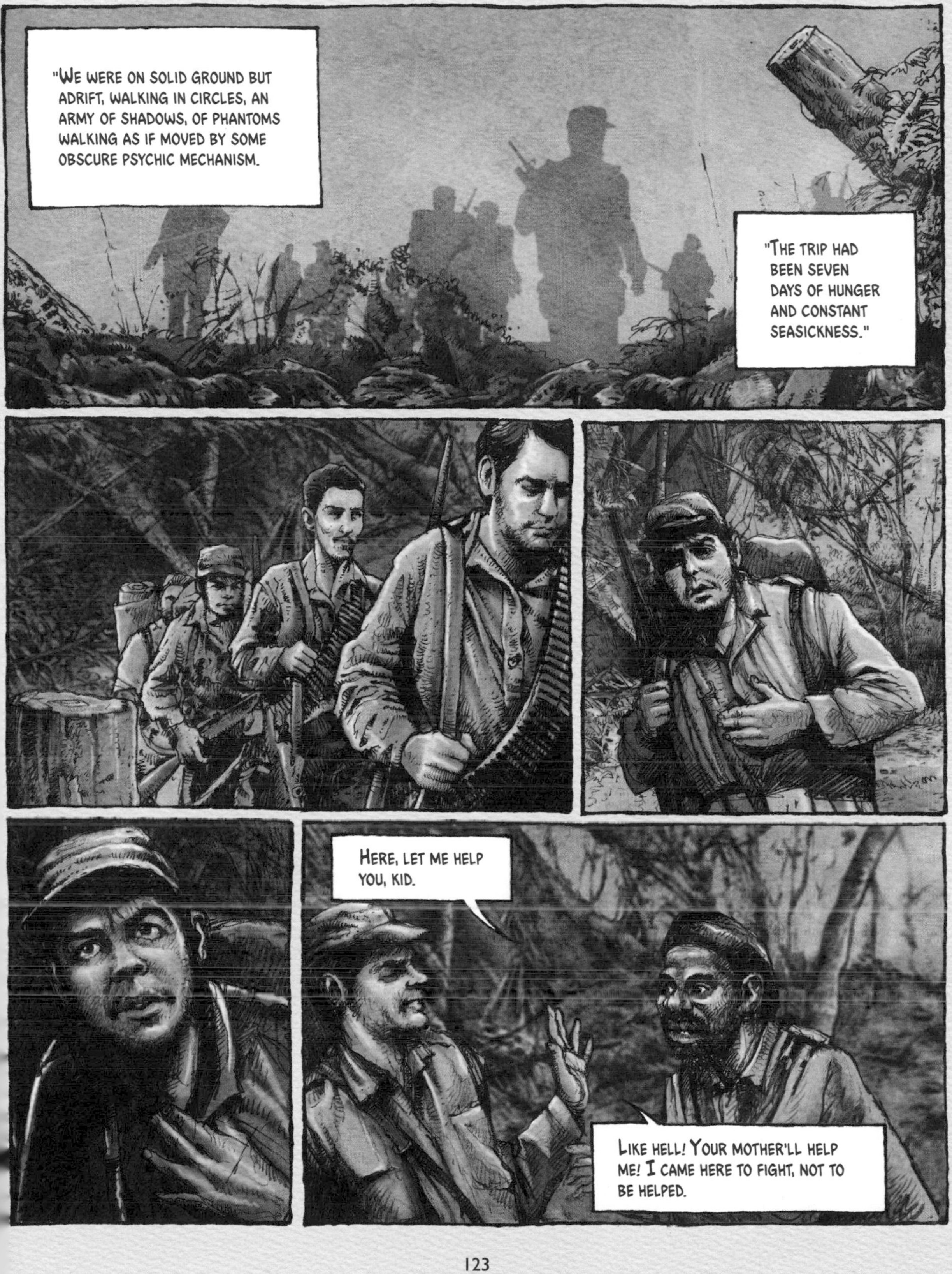
"We were on solid ground but adrift, walking in circles, an army of shadows, of phantoms walking as if moved by some obscure psychic mechanism.
"The trip had been seven days of hunger and constant seasickness."
Here, let me help you, kid.
Like hell! Your mother'll help me! I came here to fight, not to be helped.

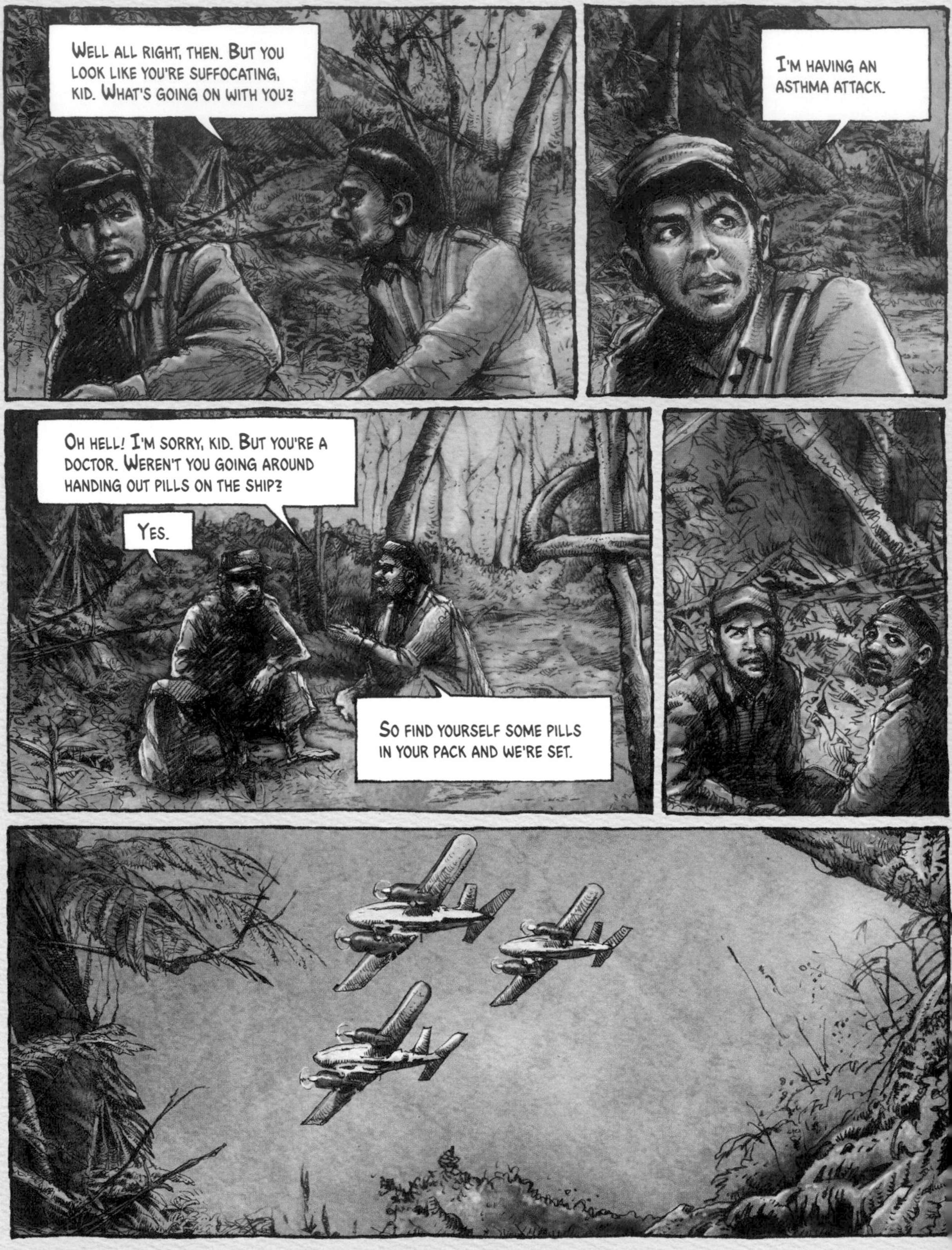
WELL ALL RIGHT, THEN. BUT YOU LOOK LIKE YOU'RE SUFFOCATING, KID. WHAT'S GOING ON WITH YOU?
I'M HAVING AN ASTHMA ATTACK.
OH HELL! I'M SORRY, KID. BUT YOU'RE A DOCTOR. WEREN'T YOU GOING AROUND HANDING OUT PILLS ON THE SHIP?
YES.
SO FIND YOURSELF SOME PILLS IN YOUR PACK AND WE'RE SET.

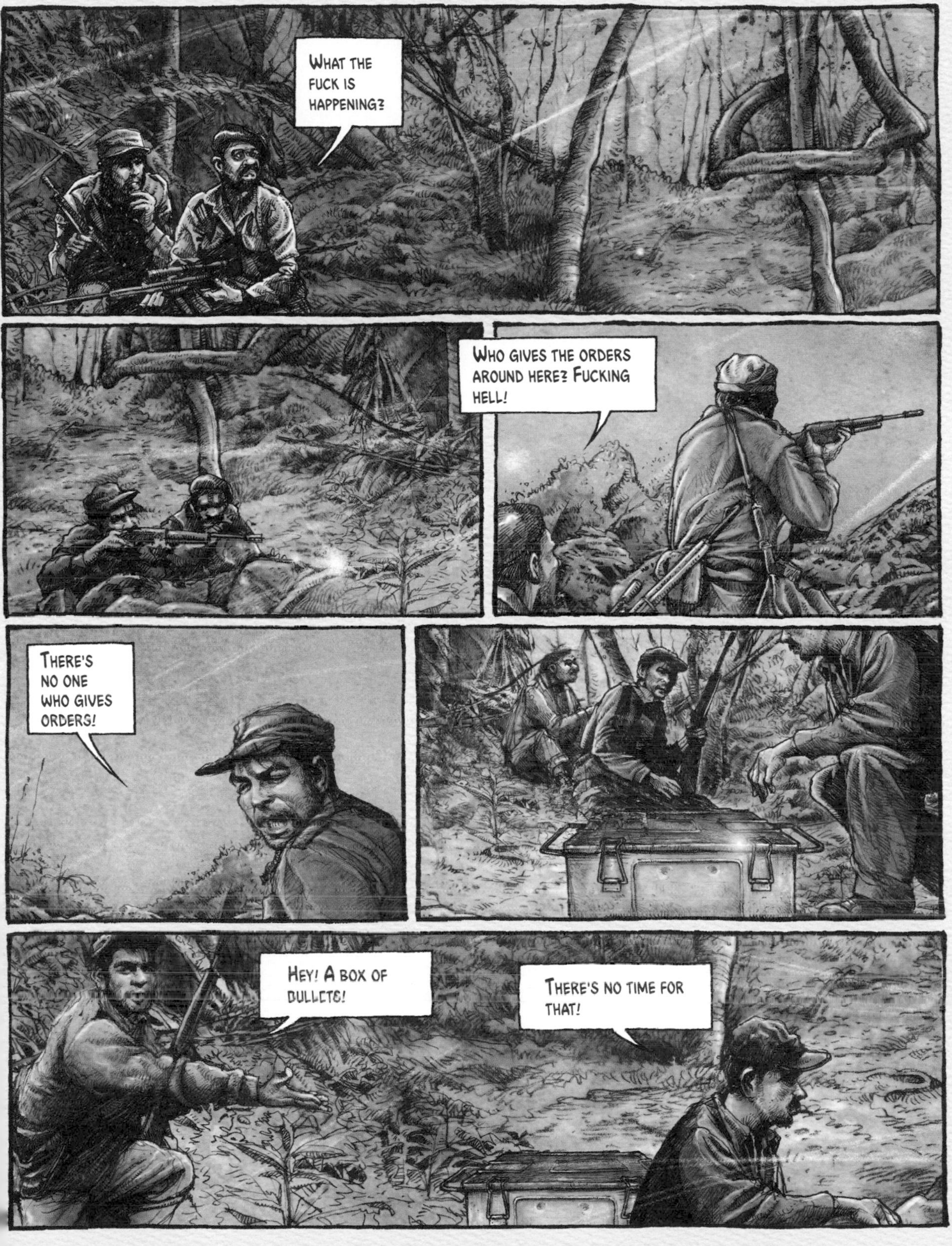
WHAT THE FUCK IS HAPPENING?
WHO GIVES THE ORDERS AROUND HERE? FUCKING HELL!
THERE'S NO ONE WHO GIVES ORDERS!
HEY! A BOX OF BULLETS!
THERE'S NO TIME FOR THAT!

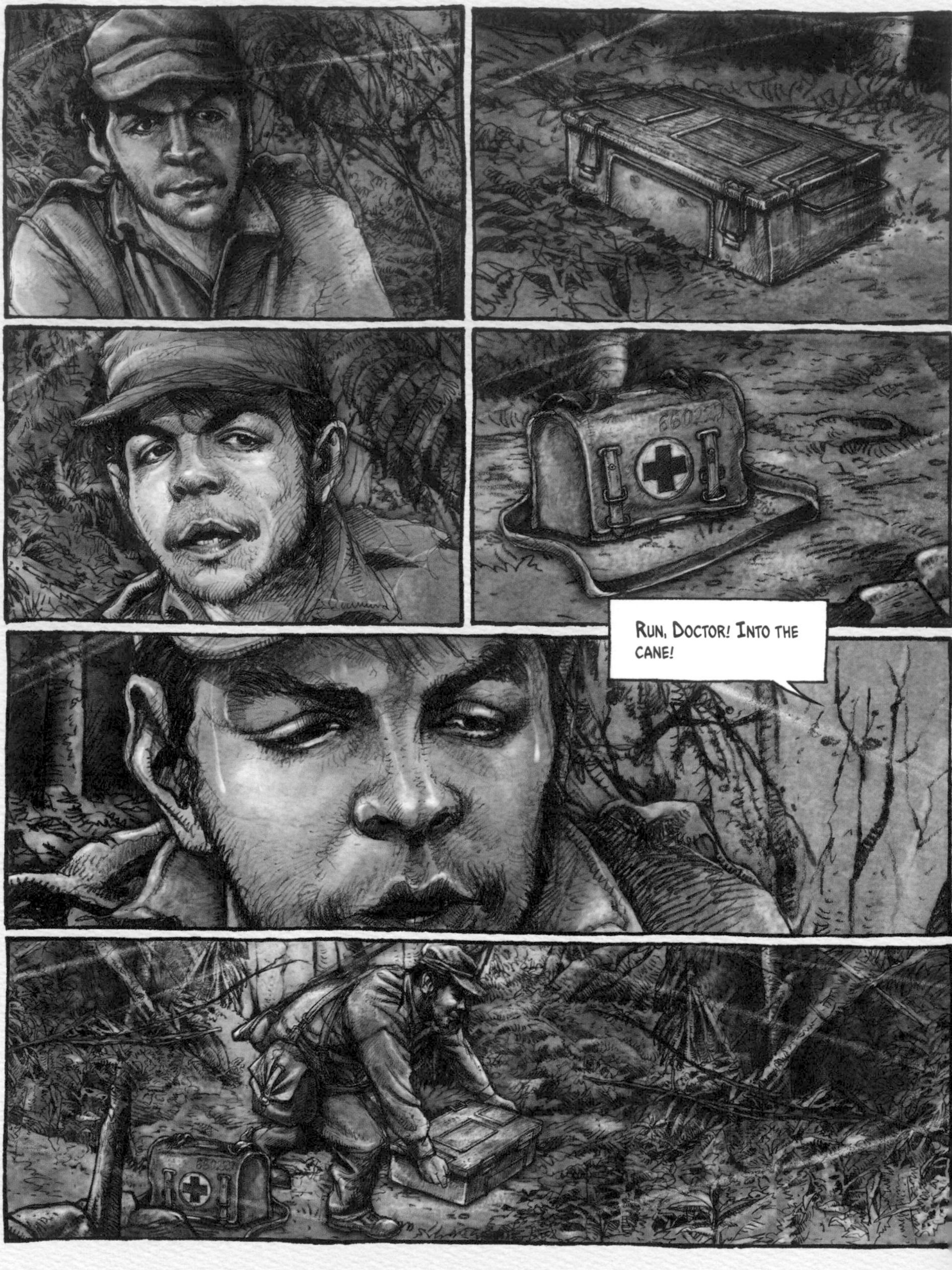
RUN, DOCTOR! INTO THE CANE!

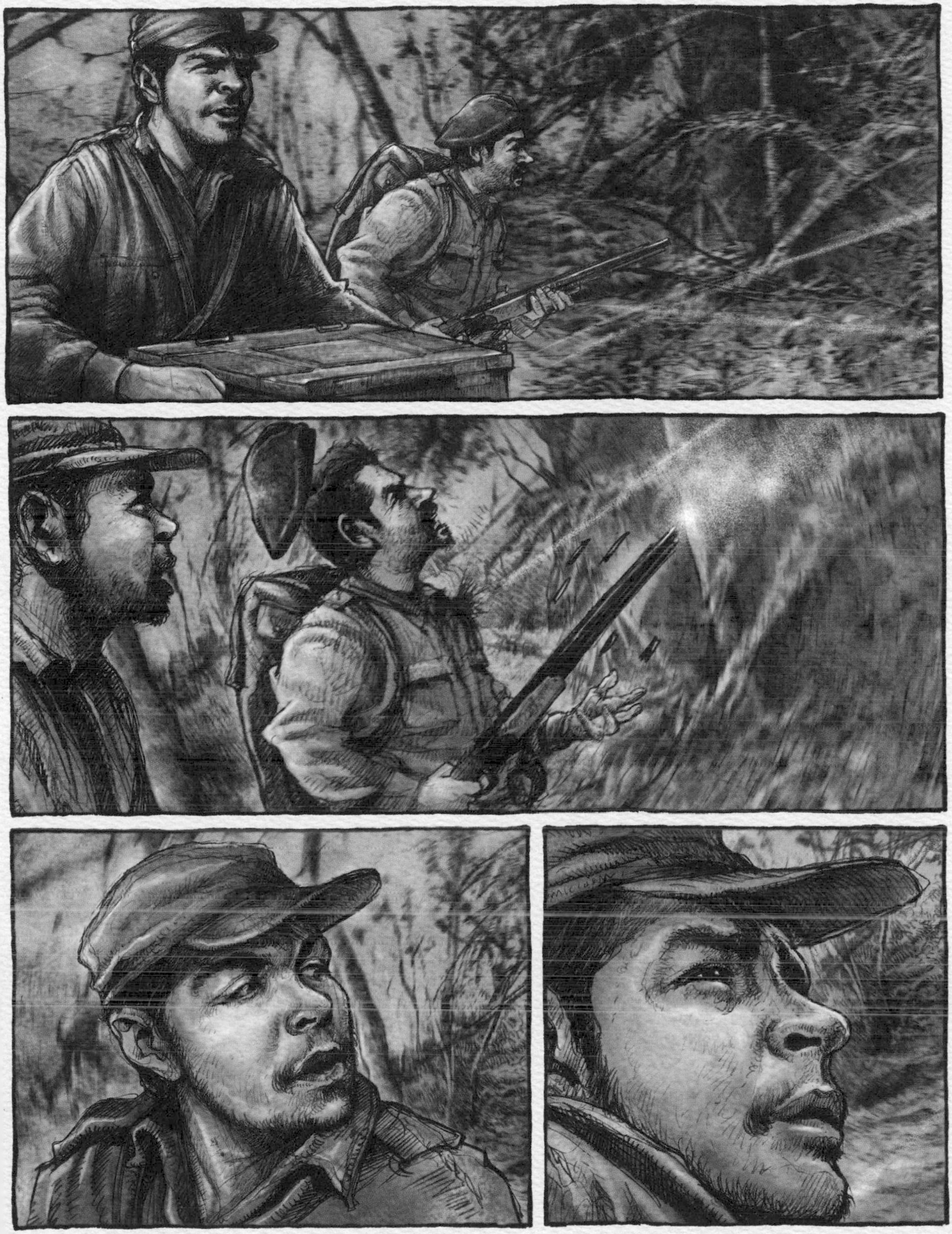

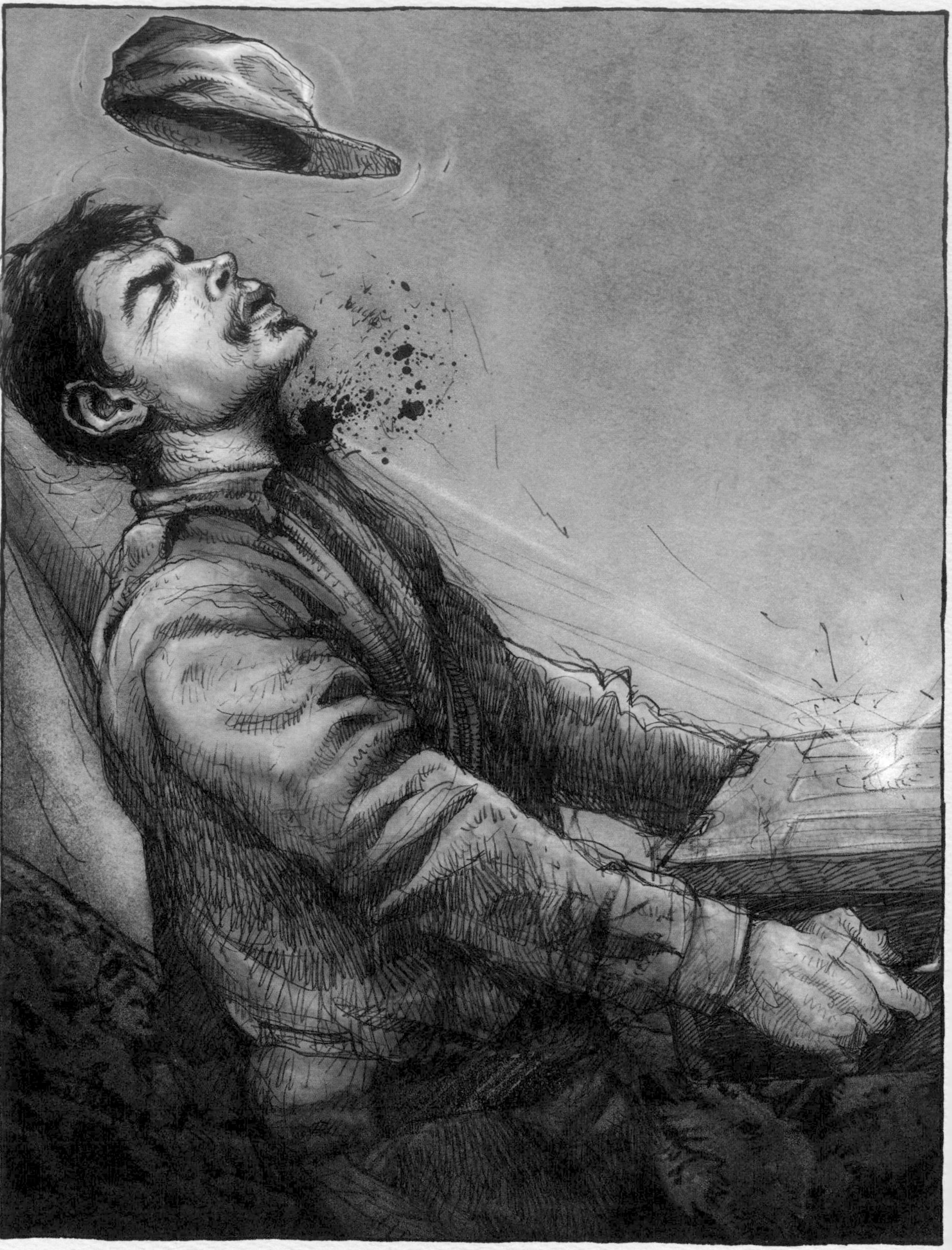

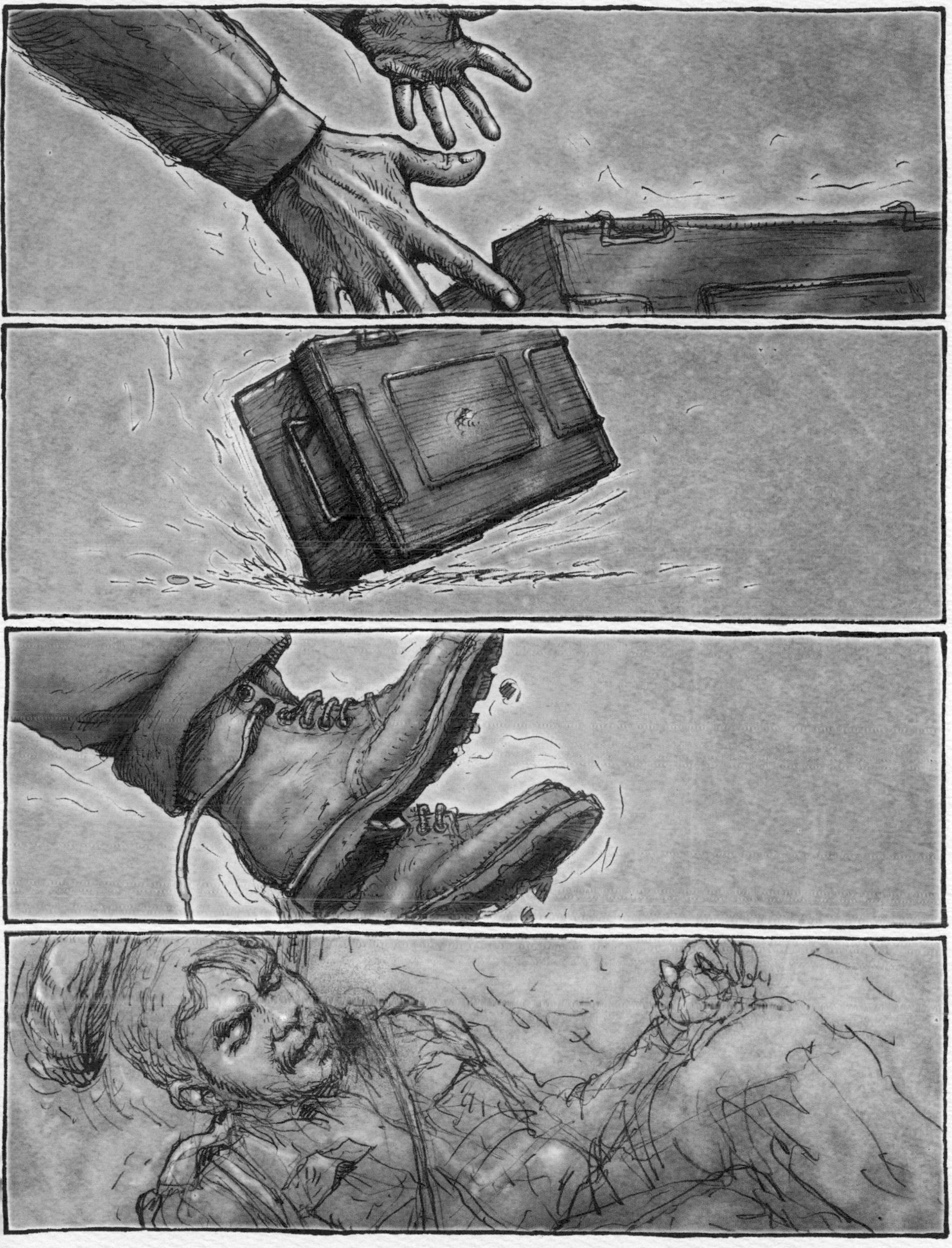

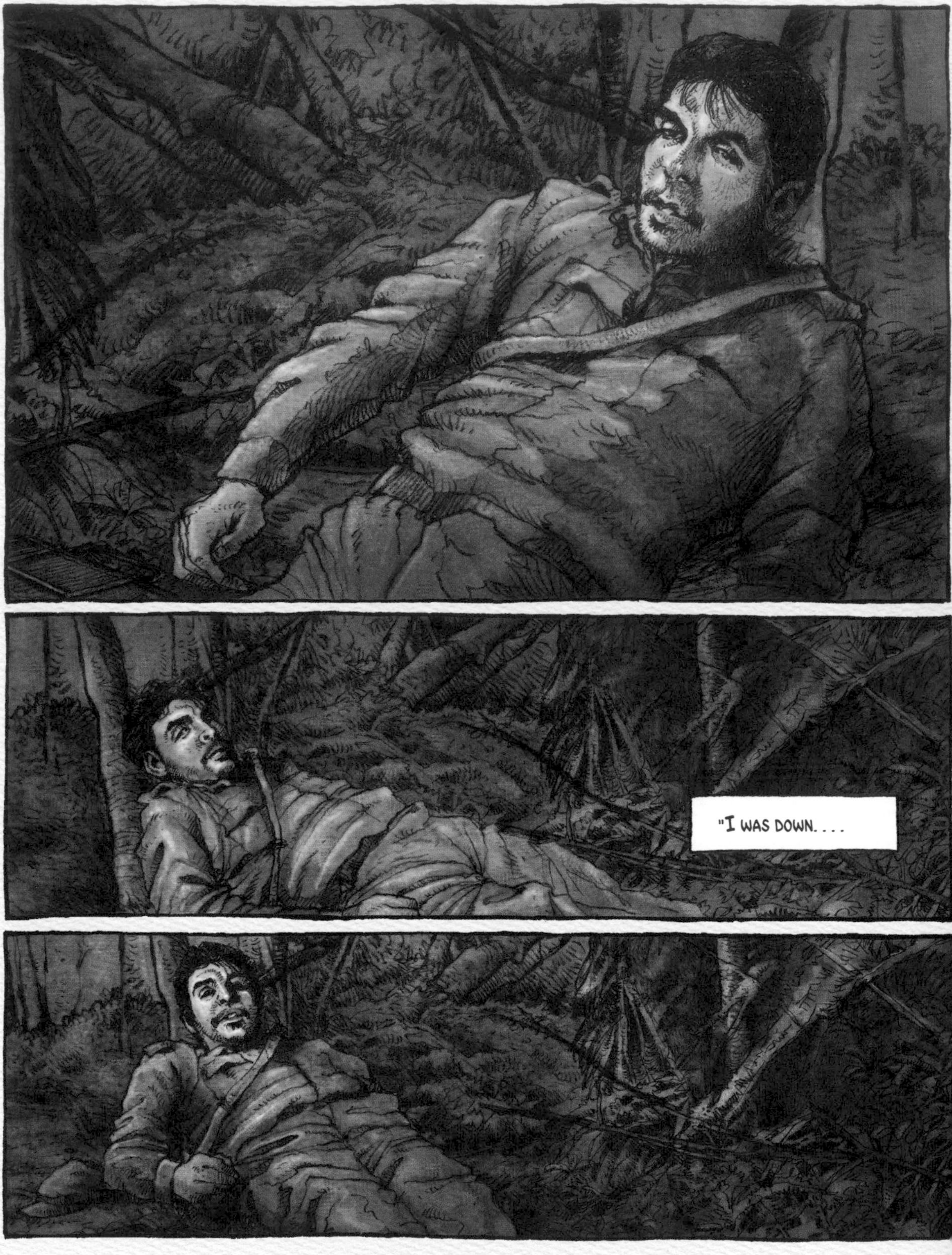
"I WAS DOWN. . . .

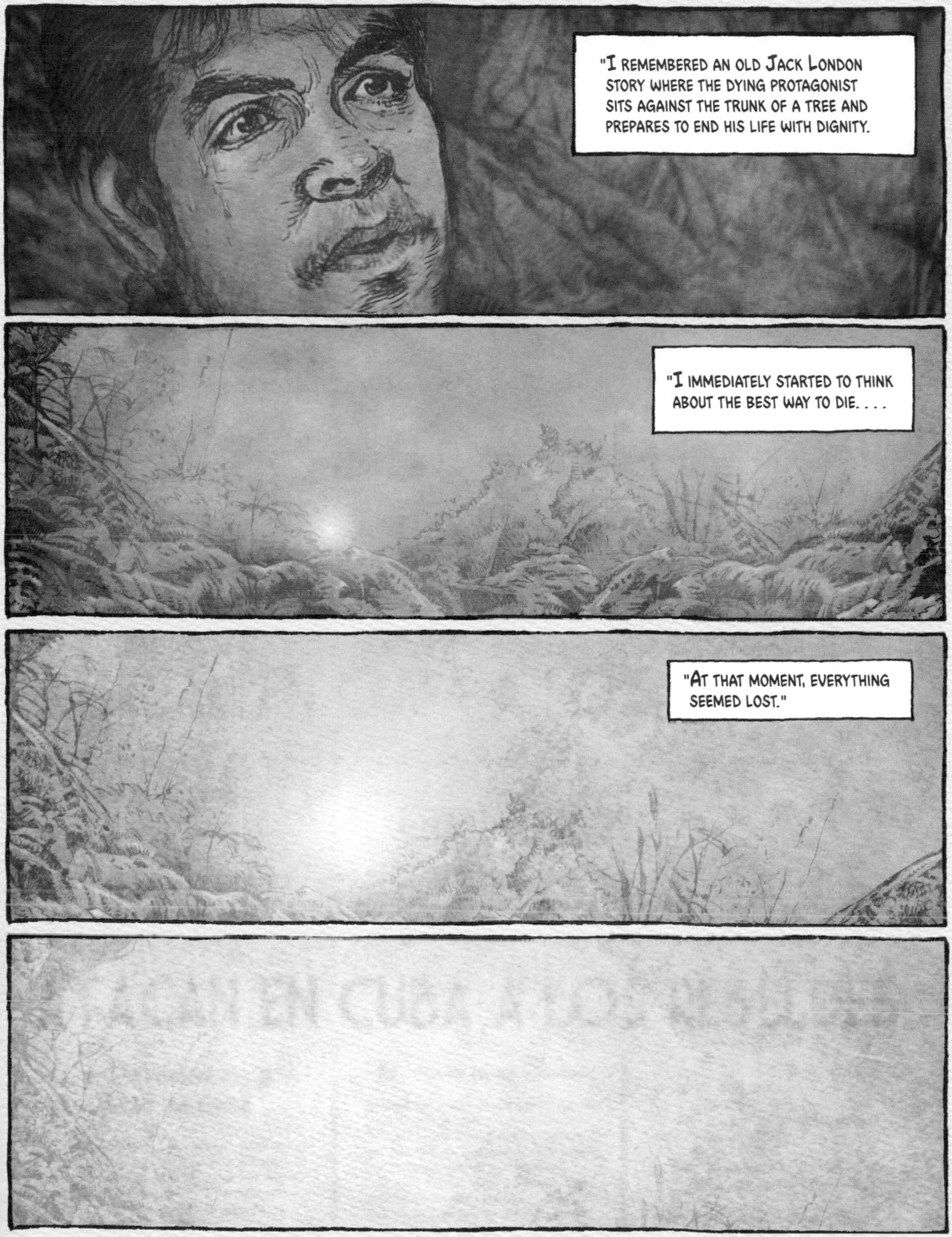
"I REMEMBERED AN OLD JACK LONDON STORY WHERE THE DYING PROTAGONIST SITS AGAINST THE TRUNK OF A TREE AND PREPARES TO END HIS LIFE WITH DIGNITY.
"I IMMEDIATELY STARTED TO THINK ABOUT THE BEST WAY TO DIE. . . .
"AT THAT MOMENT, EVERYTHING SEEMED LOST."

ATACAN EN CUBA A LOS REBELDES

La sublevación de Santiago de Cuba

Santiago de Cuba.– El presidente Batista ha suspendido las garantías constitucionales en cuatro de las seis provincias y ha enviado, en avión a Santiago, setecientos soldados entrenados en el combate para terminar con la revolución contra su Gobierno.

En días pasados, diez personas resultaron

La rebelión parece aplastada

Santiago de Cuba.– Han llegado refuerzos del Ejército para unirse a la guarnición de esta plaza, foco de la esporádica rebelión que ha originado la muerte de once personas durante el pasado fin de semana.

A pesar de la promesa rebelde de combatir hasta la muerte contra el presidente Batista, la resistencia parece virtualmente aplastada.

Se escucha todavía algún tiro, pero la

por ahora no se puede calcular el número de heridos ni de prisioneros.

Agregó que 13 de los 65 penados que huyeron de la prisión de Boniato habían sido capturados.– EFE.

Han muerto los principales jefes de la revolución

Santiago de Cuba.– Junto con el jefe de la revolución cubana, Fidel Castro, que según informes recibidos, resultó muerto

"THE MAIN LEADERS OF THE REVOLUTION ARE DEAD

ALONG WITH THE LEADER OF THE CUBAN REVOLUTION, FIDEL CASTRO . . . DEATHS INCLUDE HIS BROTHER RAÚL, JOSÉ MANUEL MERCO, AND THE ARGENTINE DOCTOR ERNESTO GUEVARA DE LA SERNA."

huyeron . . .
sido capturados.– EFE.

Han muerto los principales jefes de la revolución

Santiago de Cuba.– Junto con el jefe de la revolución cubana, Fidel Castro, que según informes recibidos, resultó muerto la pasada noche en el curso de un bombardeo con las fuerzas aéreas gubernamentales, han perecido su hermano Raúl, José Manuel Merco y el médico argentino Ernesto Guevara de la Serna.

El bombardeo ocurrió en un punto de la costa sur de Cuba, entre el Puerto de Niquero y Manzanillo.

Los revolucionarios fueron cogidos por sorpresa después de haber desembarcado de un barco mejicano.

Fidel Castro había declarado a la Prensa, antes de salir de Méjico, que él y sus seguidores serían, antes de que terminara el año, héroes o mártires. – AP.

deo con las fuerzas aéreas guberna[mentales], tales, han perecido su hermano Raúl, Manuel Merco y el médico argentino Ernesto Guevara de la Serna.

El bombardeo ocurrió en un punto costa sur de Cuba, entre el Puerto d[e Ni]quero y Manzanillo.

Los revolucionarios fueron cogid[os] [sor]presa después de haber desemba[rcado]

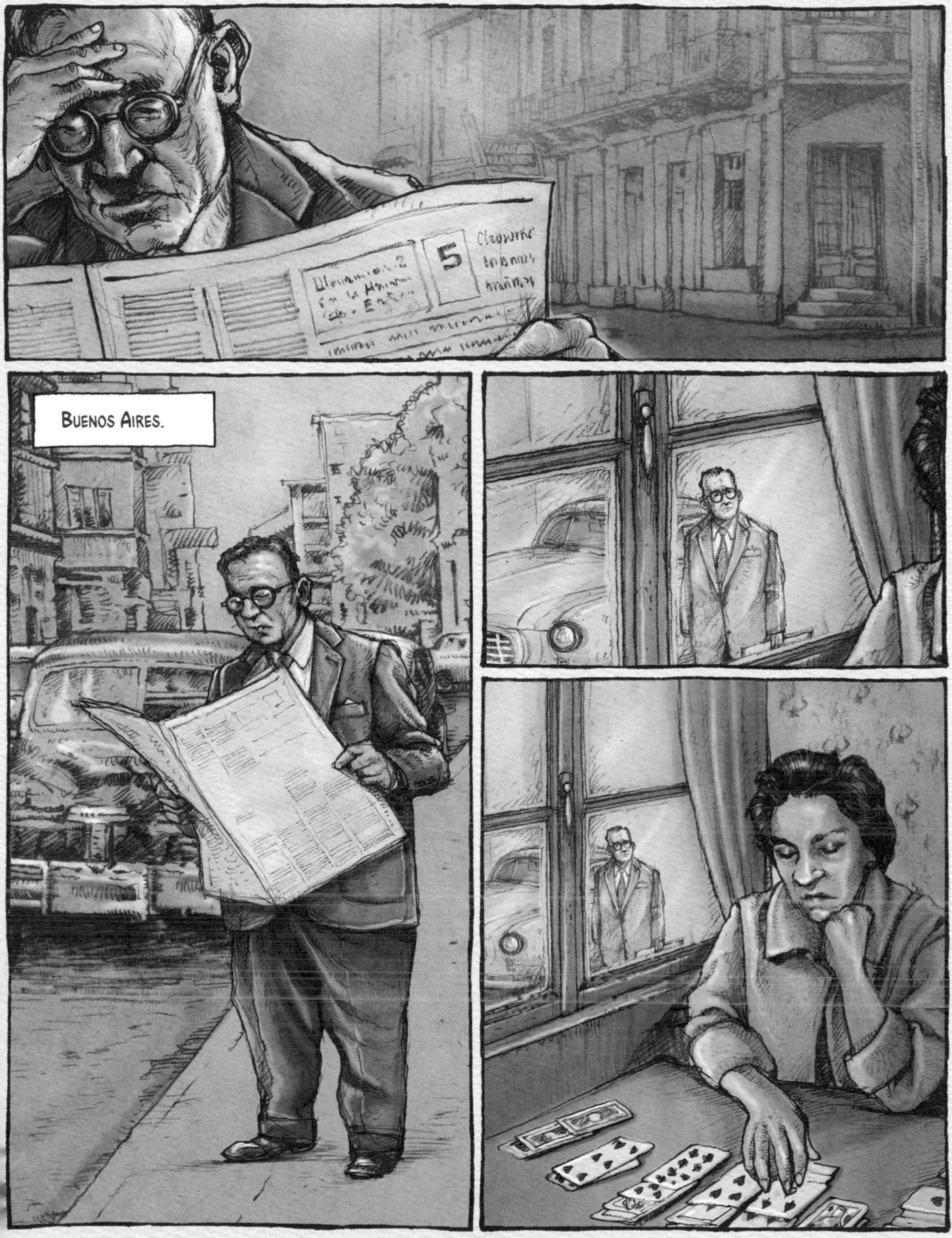
Buenos Aires.

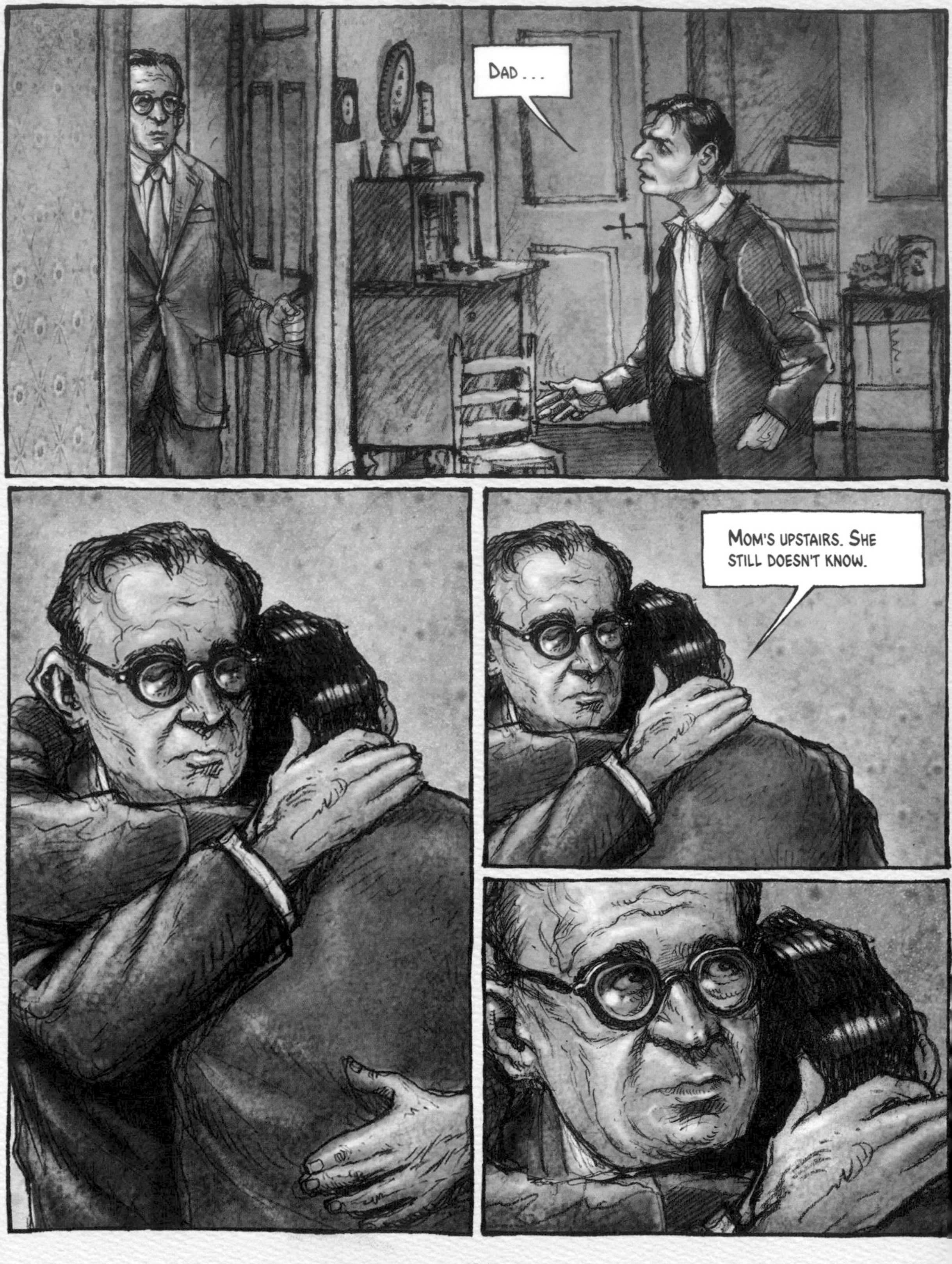
DAD . . .
MOM'S UPSTAIRS. SHE STILL DOESN'T KNOW.

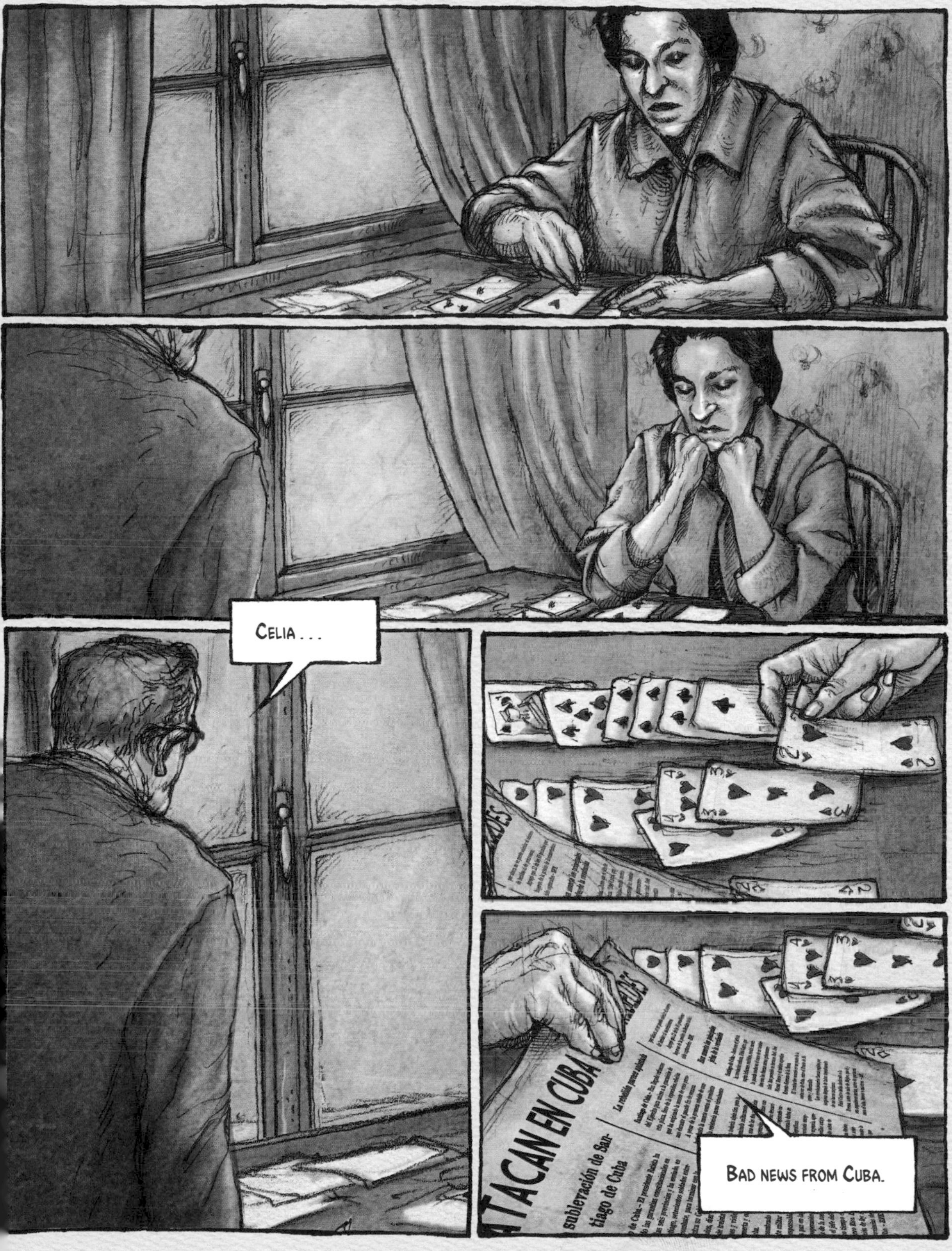

Celia . . .
Bad news from Cuba.

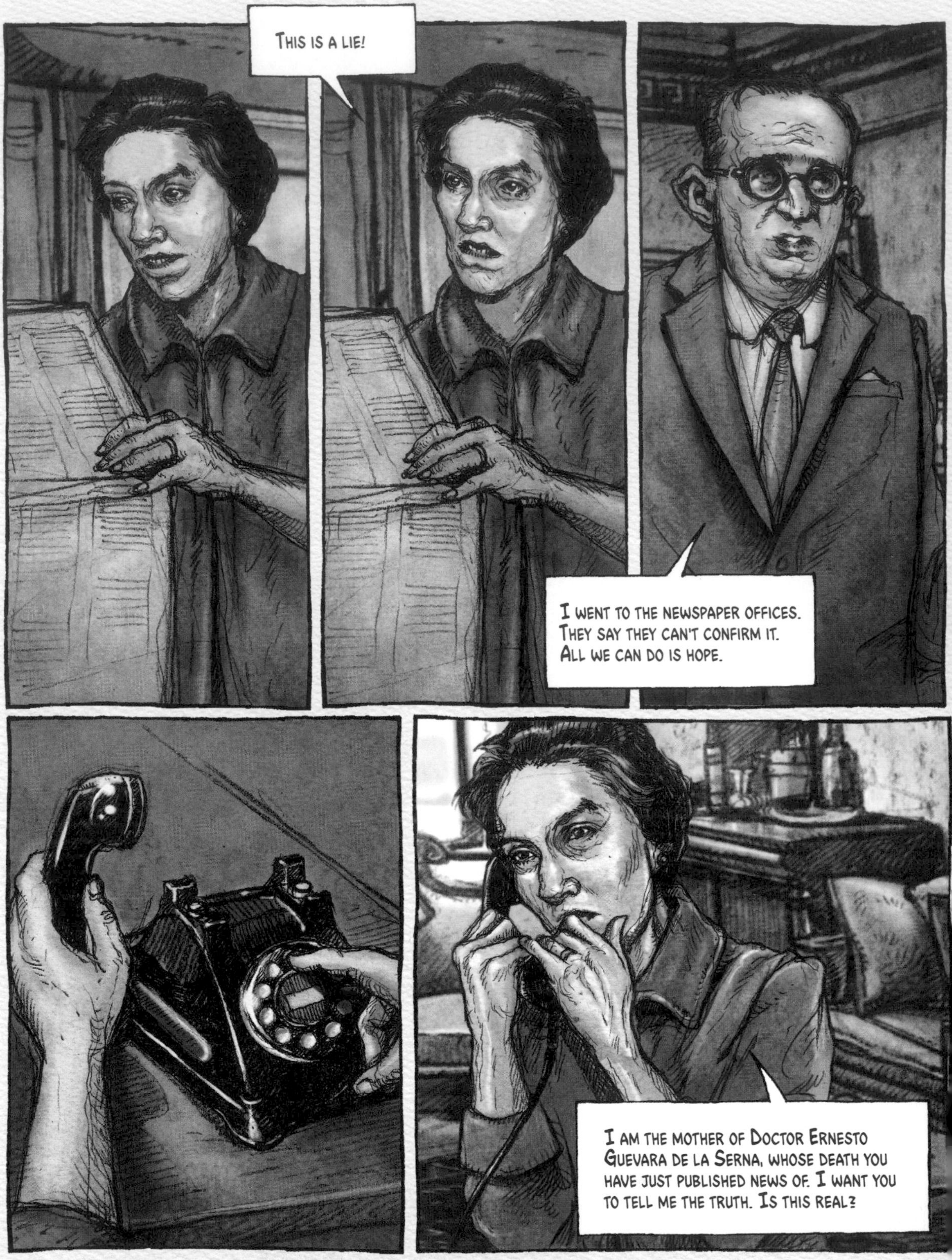
This is a lie!
I went to the newspaper offices. They say they can't confirm it. All we can do is hope.
I am the mother of Doctor Ernesto Guevara de la Serna, whose death you have just published news of. I want you to tell me the truth. Is this real?

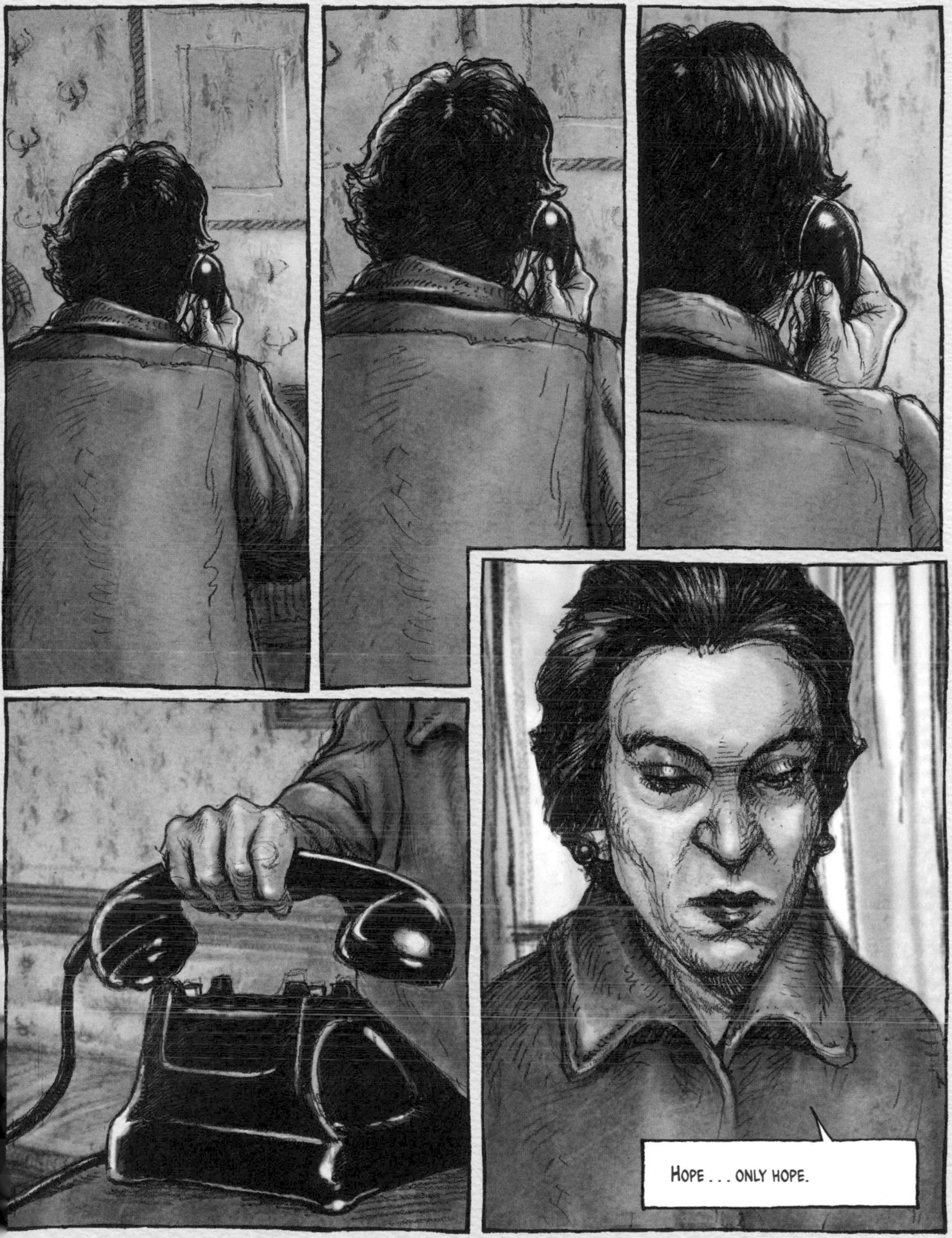
Hope . . . only hope.

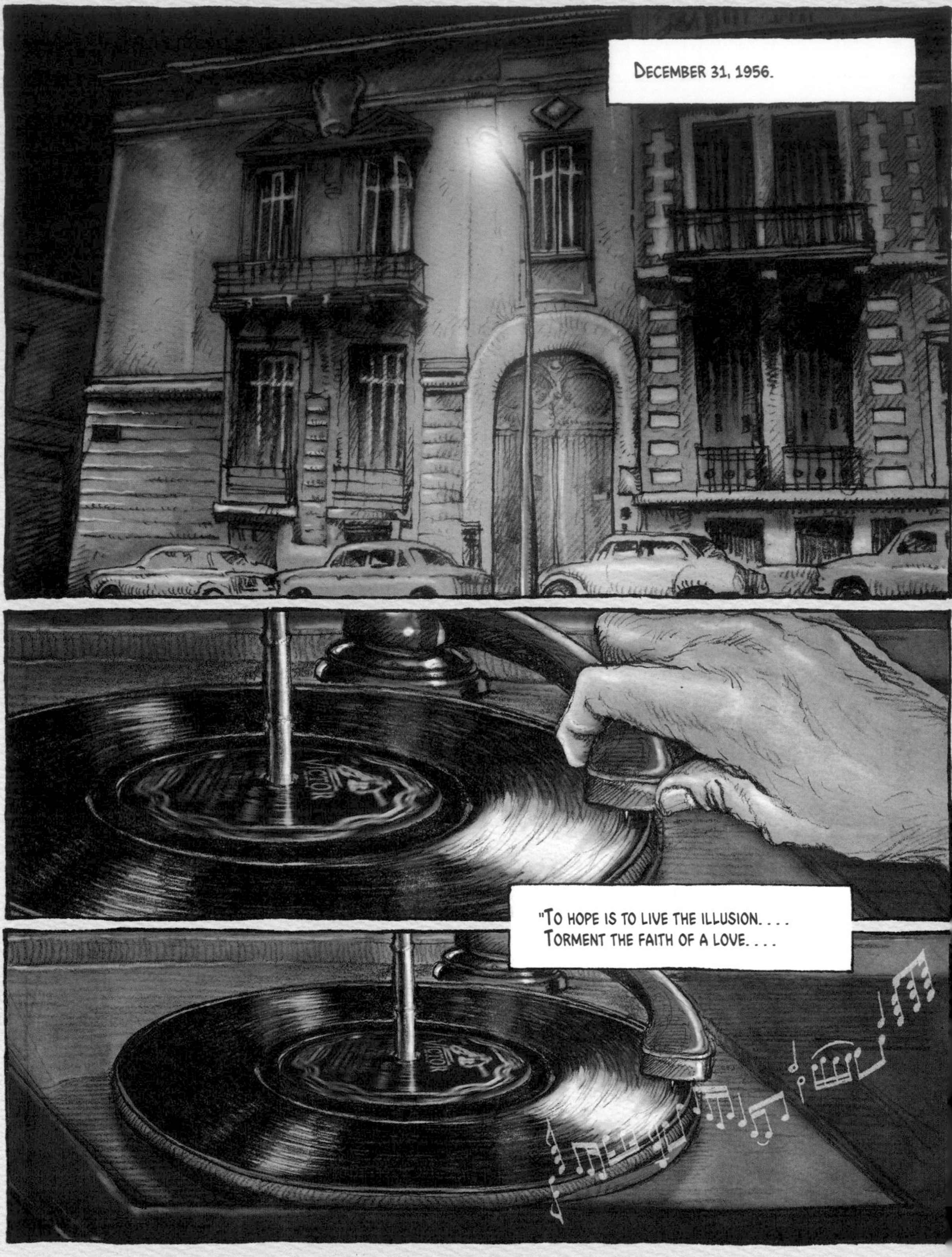
December 31, 1956.
"To hope is to live the illusion. . . .
Torment the faith of a love. . . .

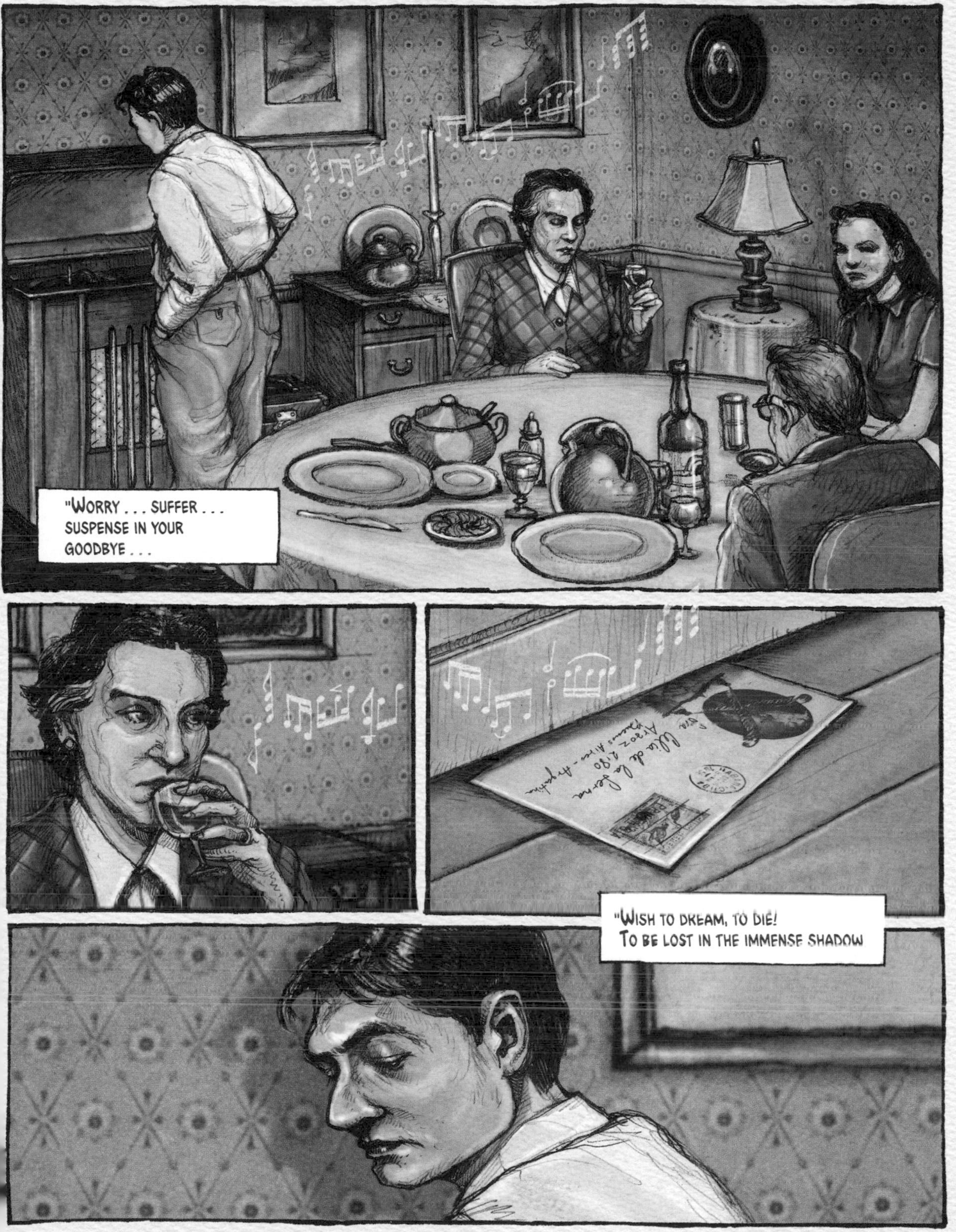
"WORRY . . . SUFFER . . . SUSPENSE IN YOUR GOODBYE . . .
"WISH TO DREAM, TO DIE! TO BE LOST IN THE IMMENSE SHADOW

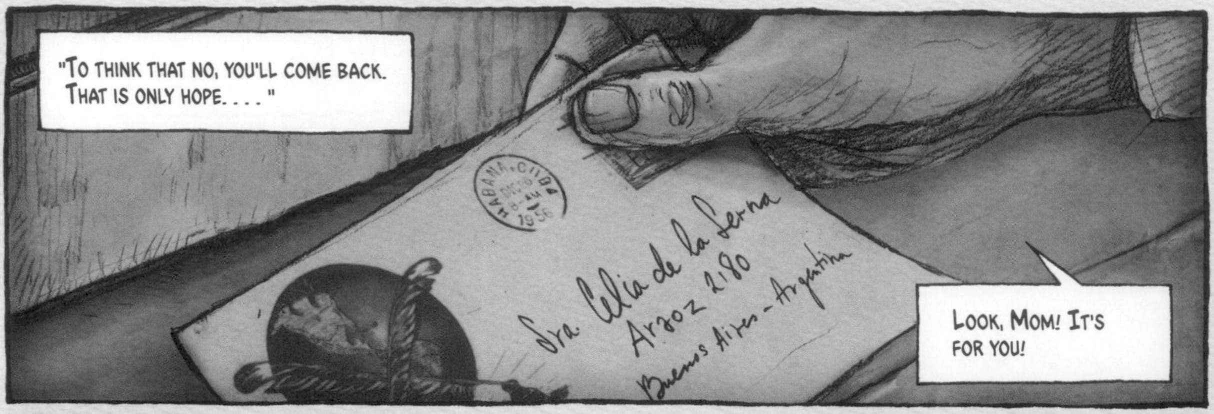
"TO THINK THAT NO, YOU'LL COME BACK. THAT IS ONLY HOPE. . . ."
Sra Celia de la Serna
Araoz 2180
Buenos Aires - Argentina
LOOK, MOM! IT'S FOR YOU!

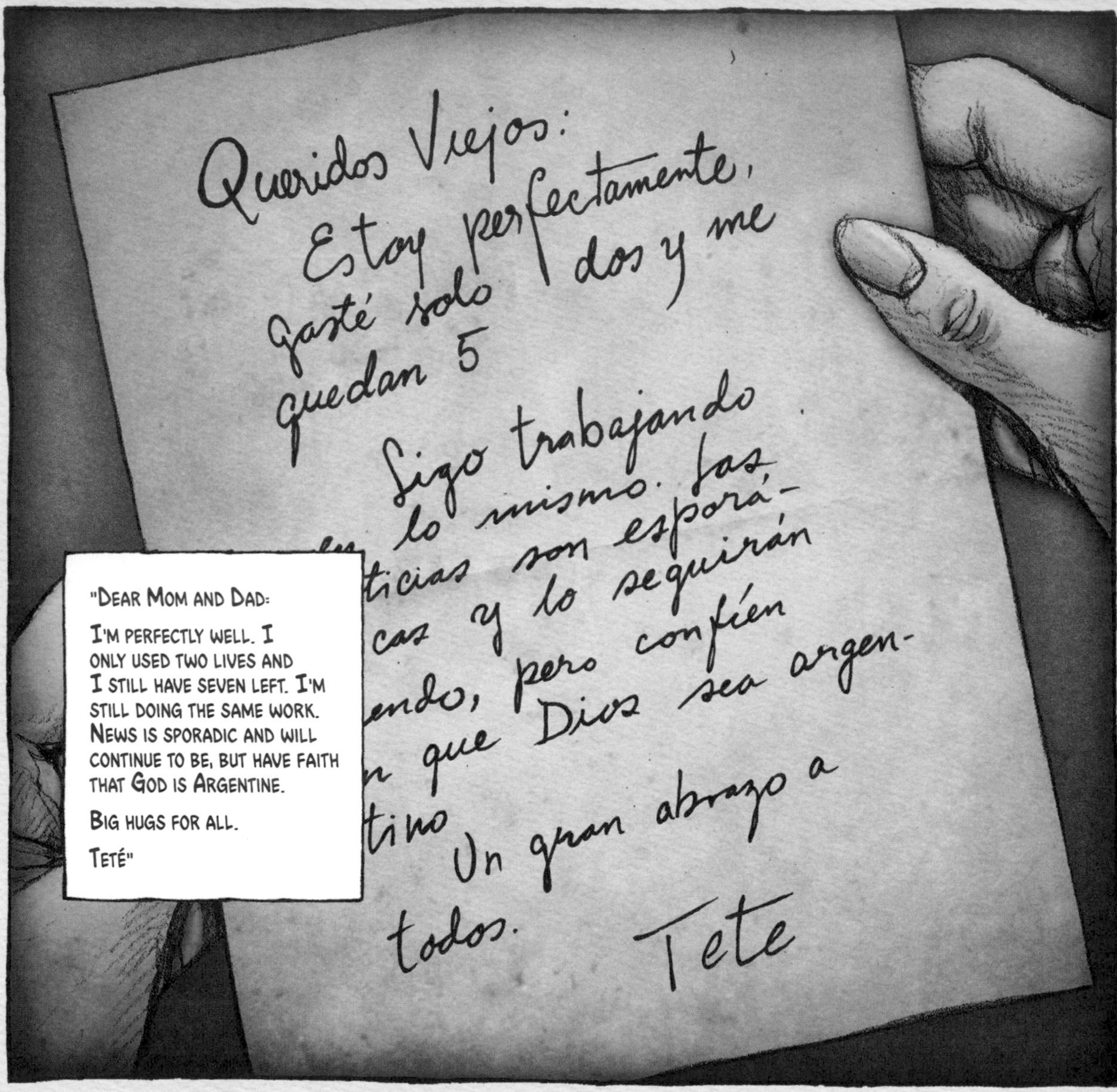
Queridos Viejos:
Estoy perfectamente,
gasté solo dos y me
quedan 5
Sigo trabajando
lo mismo. Las
ticias son esporá-
cas y lo seguirán
endo, pero confíen
que Dios sea argen-
tino
Un gran abrazo a
todos.
Tete
"DEAR MOM AND DAD:
I'M PERFECTLY WELL. I ONLY USED TWO LIVES AND I STILL HAVE SEVEN LEFT. I'M STILL DOING THE SAME WORK. NEWS IS SPORADIC AND WILL CONTINUE TO BE, BUT HAVE FAITH THAT GOD IS ARGENTINE.
BIG HUGS FOR ALL.
TETÉ"

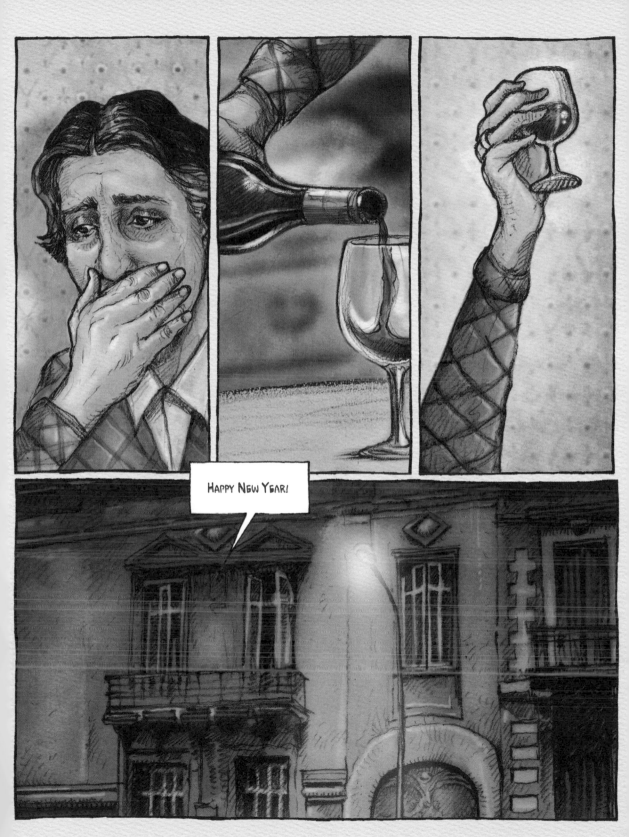

HAPPY NEW YEAR!

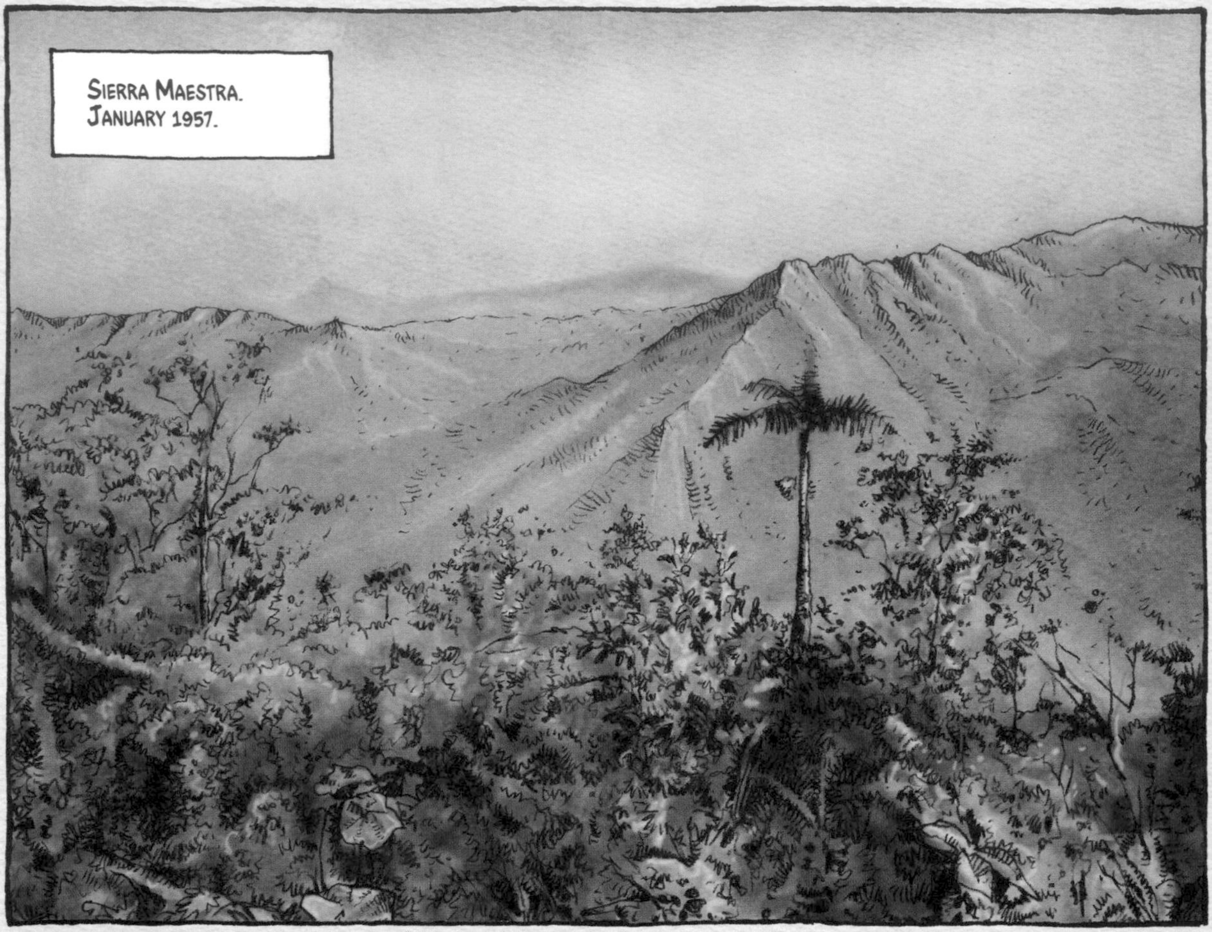
Sierra Maestra.
January 1957.

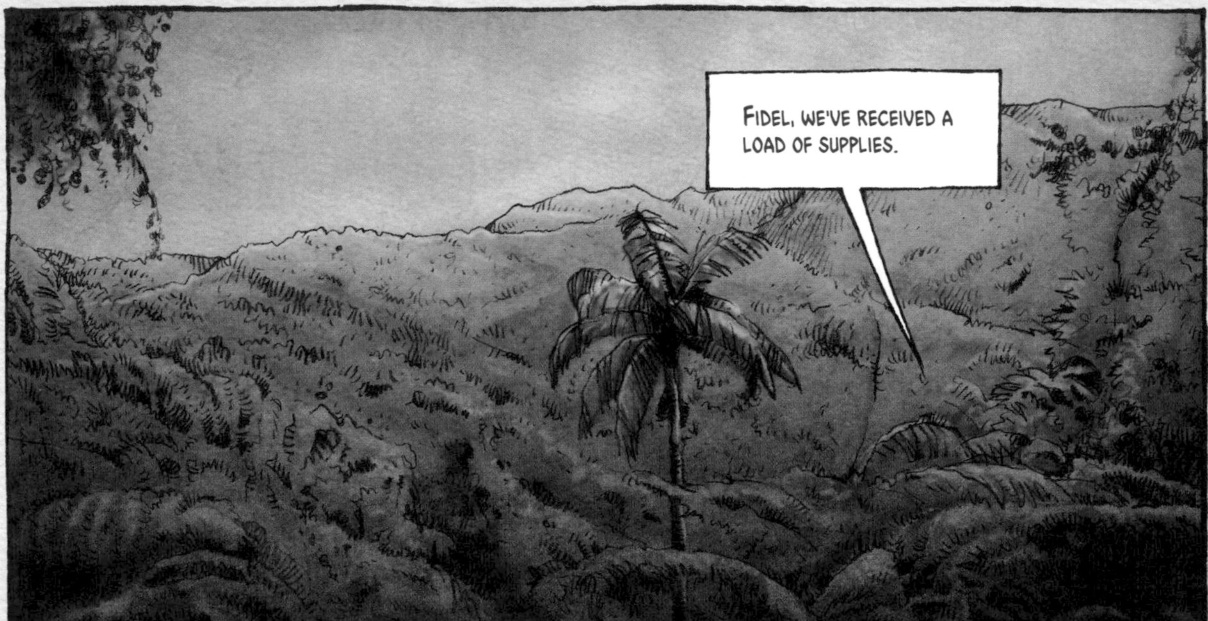
Fidel, we've received a load of supplies.

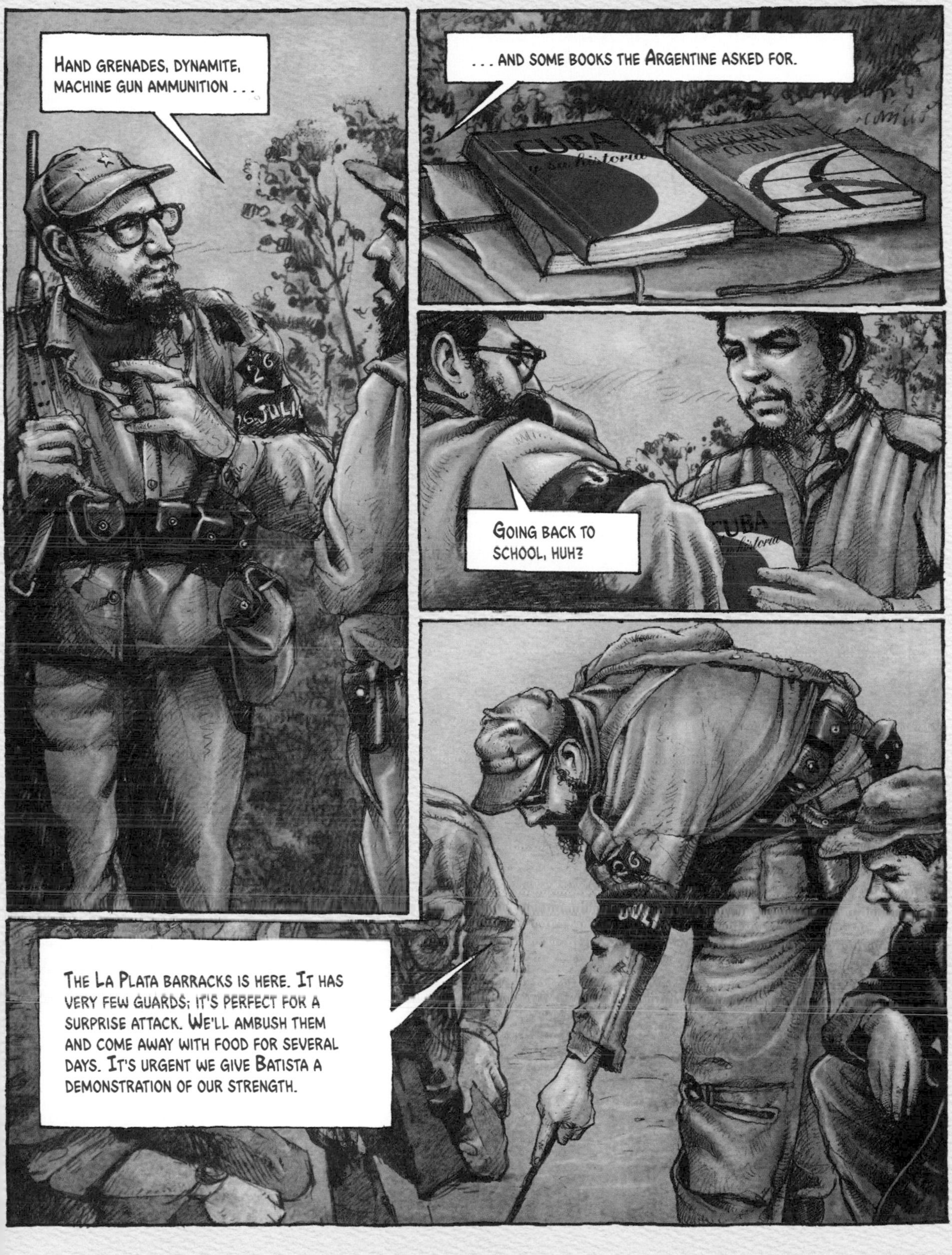
Hand grenades, dynamite, machine gun ammunition . . .
. . . and some books the Argentine asked for.
CUBA y su historia
Going back to school, huh?
The La Plata barracks is here. It has very few guards; it's perfect for a surprise attack. We'll ambush them and come away with food for several days. It's urgent we give Batista a demonstration of our strength.

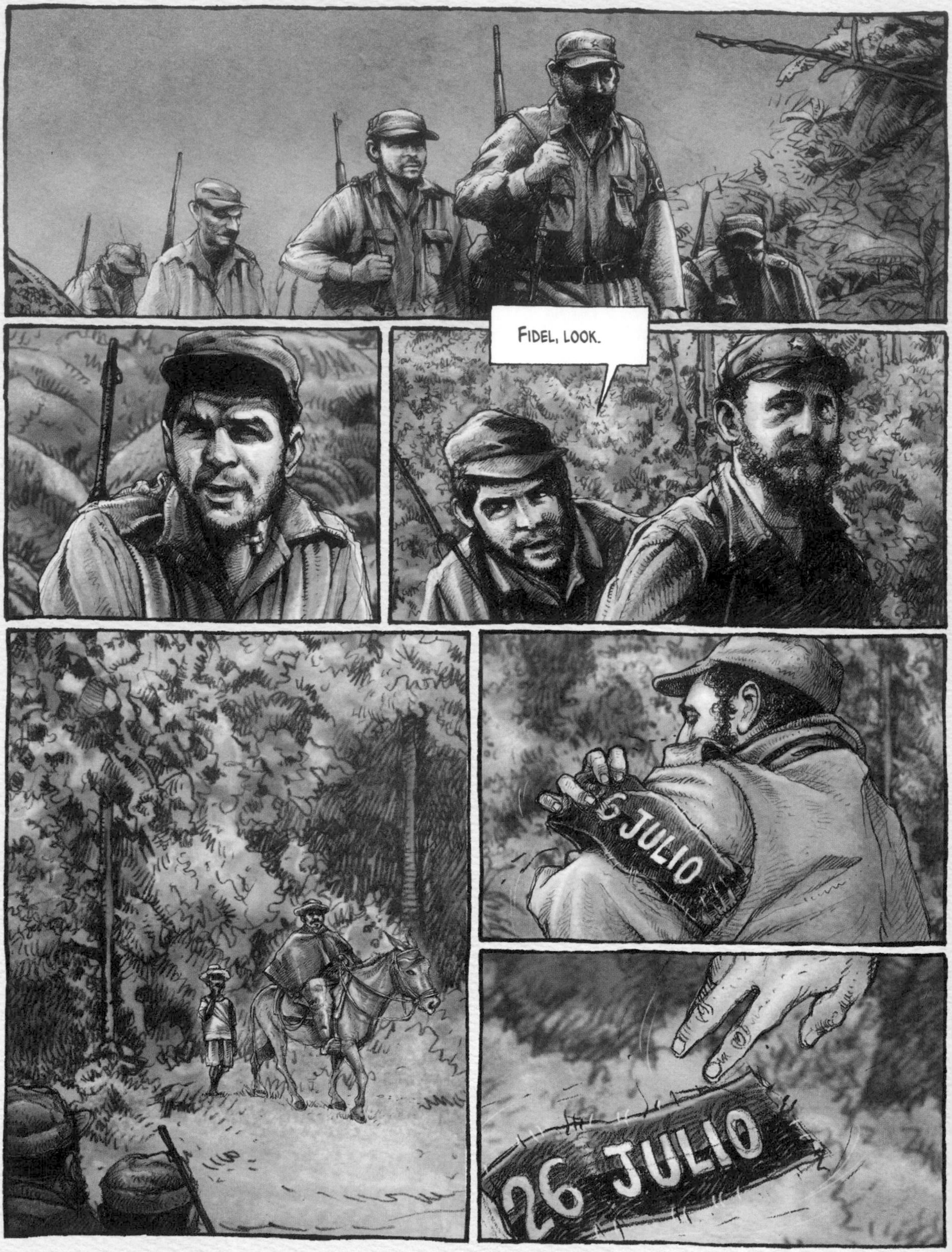
FIDEL, LOOK.
26 JULIO
26 JULIO

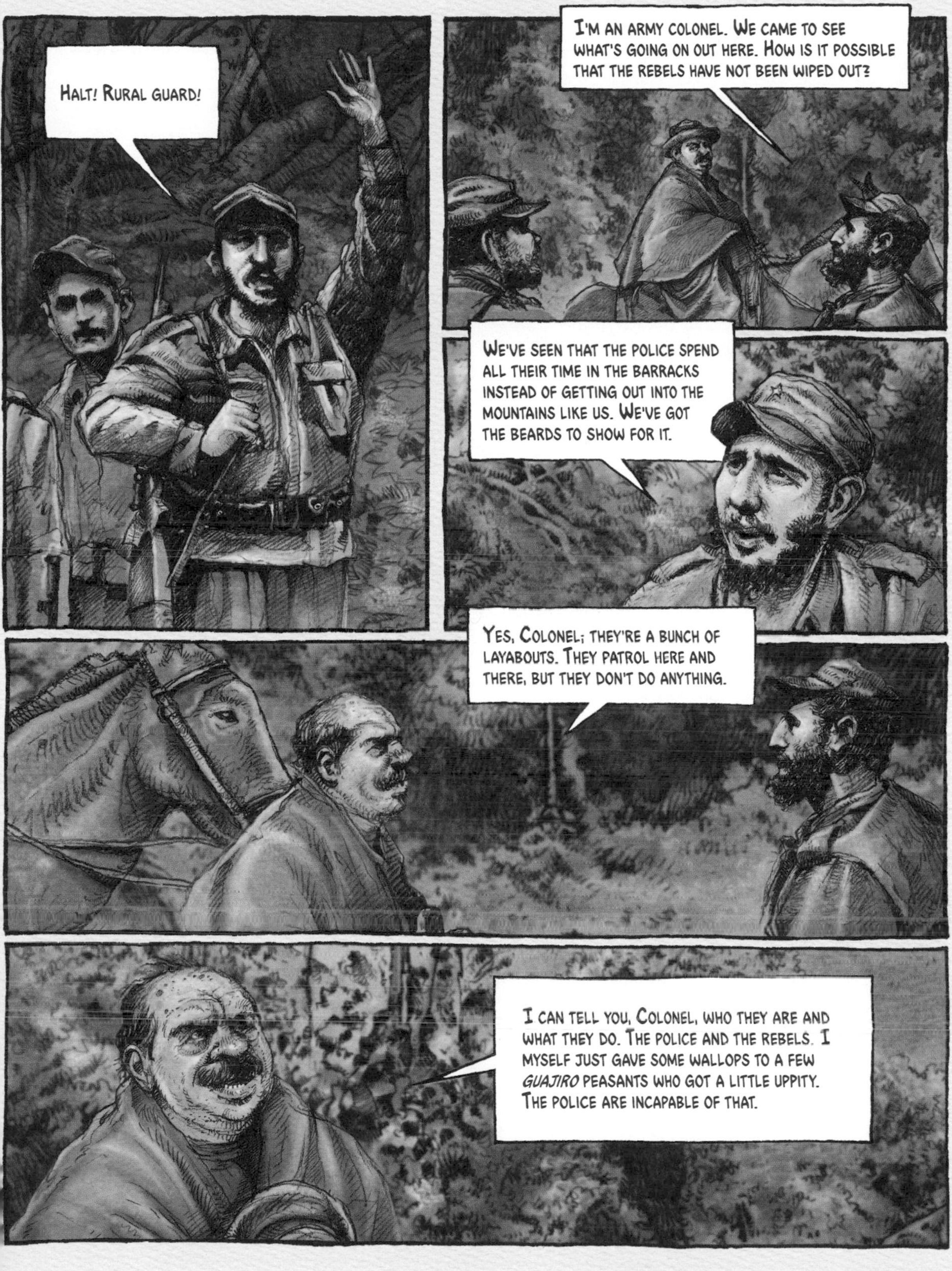
HALT! RURAL GUARD!
I'M AN ARMY COLONEL. WE CAME TO SEE WHAT'S GOING ON OUT HERE. HOW IS IT POSSIBLE THAT THE REBELS HAVE NOT BEEN WIPED OUT?
WE'VE SEEN THAT THE POLICE SPEND ALL THEIR TIME IN THE BARRACKS INSTEAD OF GETTING OUT INTO THE MOUNTAINS LIKE US. WE'VE GOT THE BEARDS TO SHOW FOR IT.
YES, COLONEL; THEY'RE A BUNCH OF LAYABOUTS. THEY PATROL HERE AND THERE, BUT THEY DON'T DO ANYTHING.
I CAN TELL YOU, COLONEL, WHO THEY ARE AND WHAT THEY DO. THE POLICE AND THE REBELS. I MYSELF JUST GAVE SOME WALLOPS TO A FEW *GUAJIRO* PEASANTS WHO GOT A LITTLE UPPITY. THE POLICE ARE INCAPABLE OF THAT.

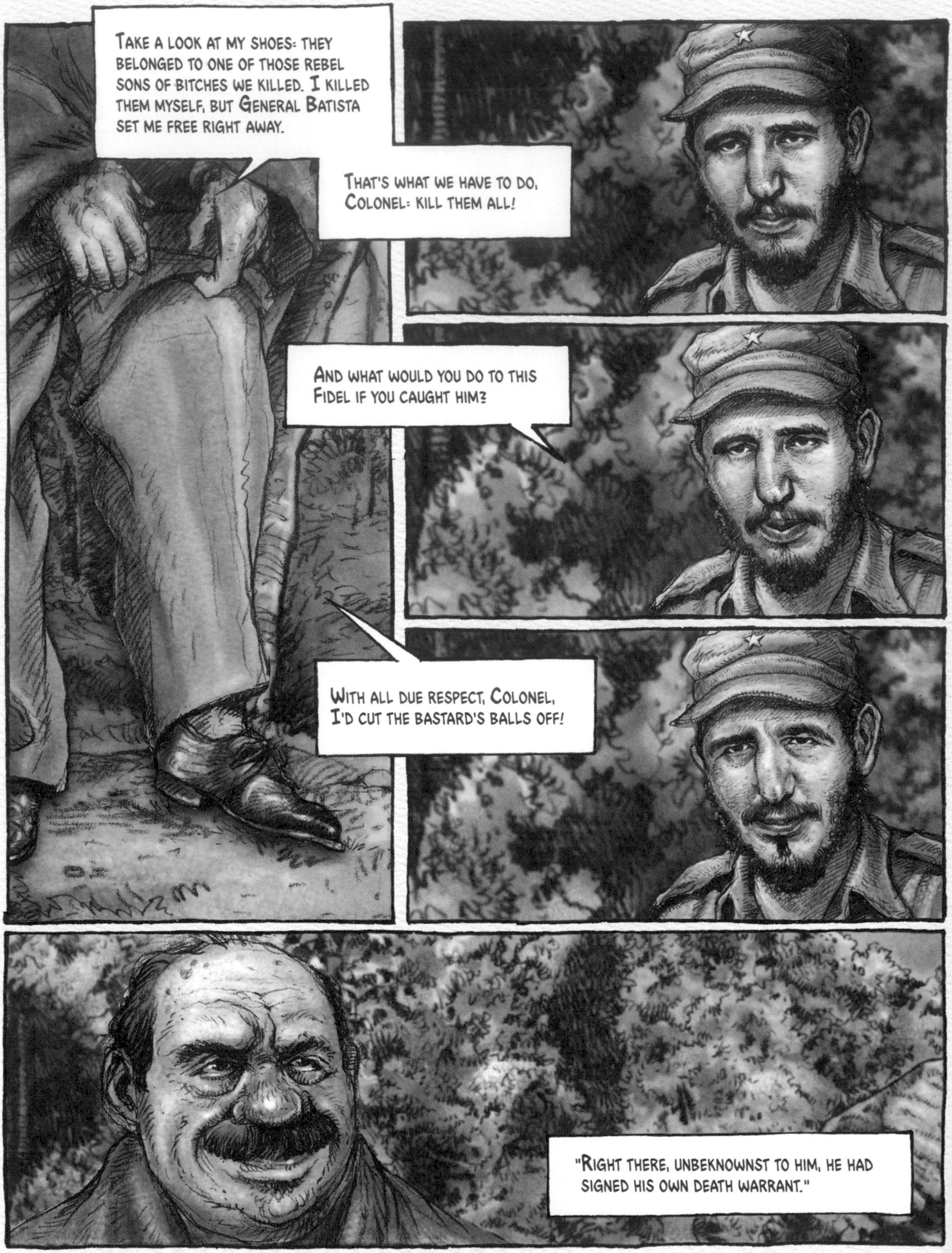
TAKE A LOOK AT MY SHOES: THEY BELONGED TO ONE OF THOSE REBEL SONS OF BITCHES WE KILLED. I KILLED THEM MYSELF, BUT GENERAL BATISTA SET ME FREE RIGHT AWAY.
THAT'S WHAT WE HAVE TO DO, COLONEL: KILL THEM ALL!
AND WHAT WOULD YOU DO TO THIS FIDEL IF YOU CAUGHT HIM?
WITH ALL DUE RESPECT, COLONEL, I'D CUT THE BASTARD'S BALLS OFF!
"RIGHT THERE, UNBEKNOWNST TO HIM, HE HAD SIGNED HIS OWN DEATH WARRANT."

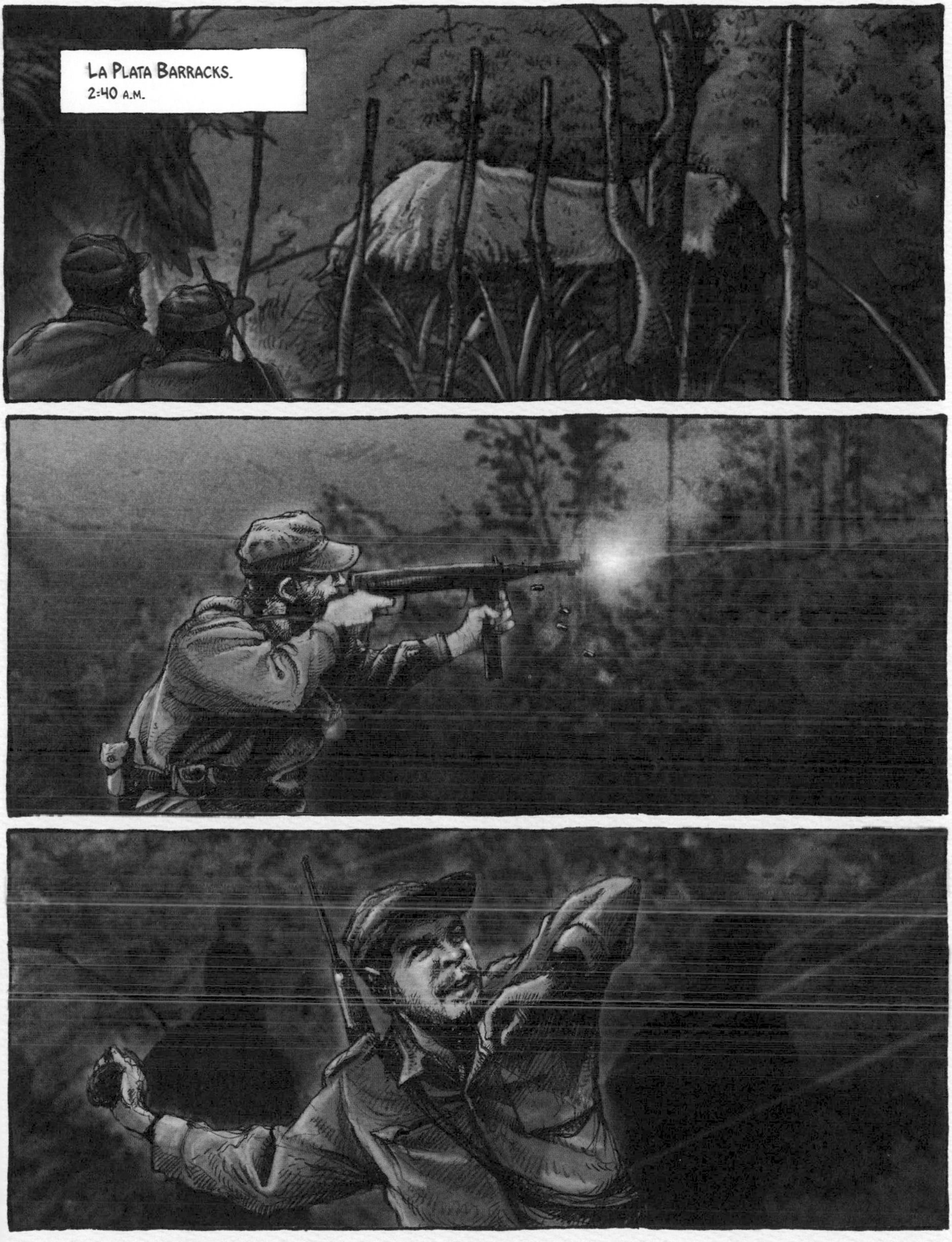
LA PLATA BARRACKS.
2:40 A.M.

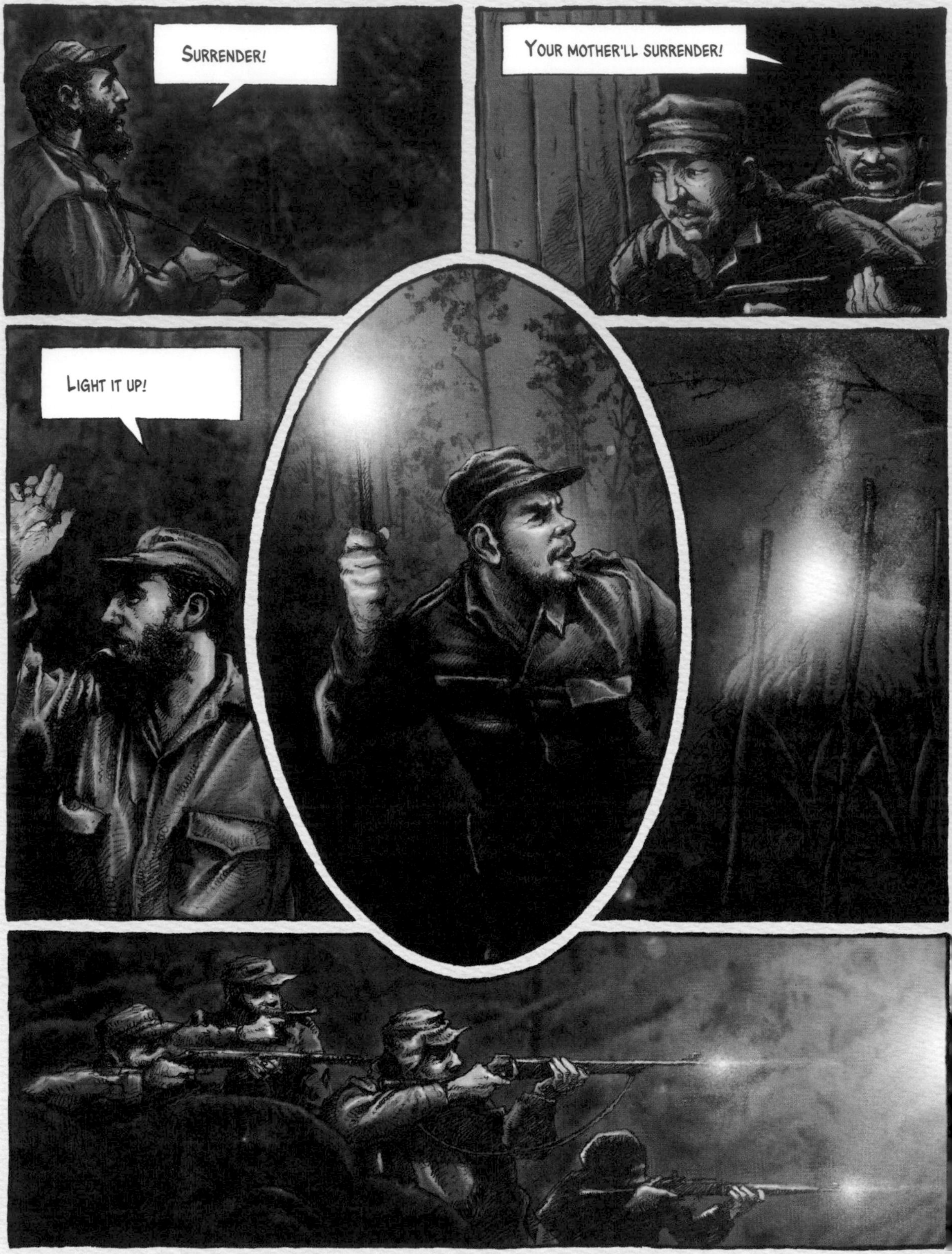
SURRENDER!
YOUR MOTHER'LL SURRENDER!
LIGHT IT UP!

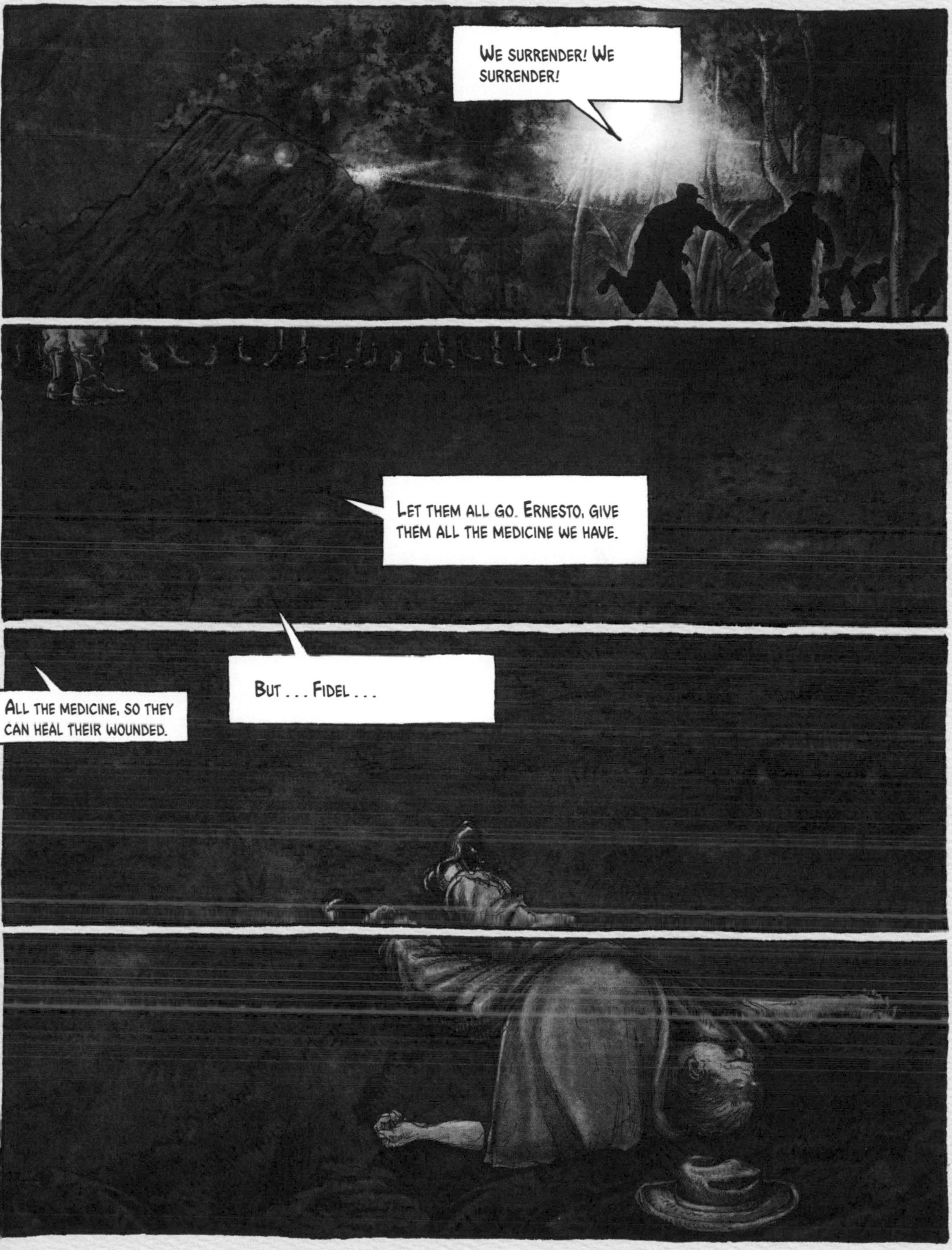
WE SURRENDER! WE SURRENDER!
LET THEM ALL GO. ERNESTO, GIVE THEM ALL THE MEDICINE WE HAVE.
BUT . . . FIDEL . . .
ALL THE MEDICINE, SO THEY CAN HEAL THEIR WOUNDED.

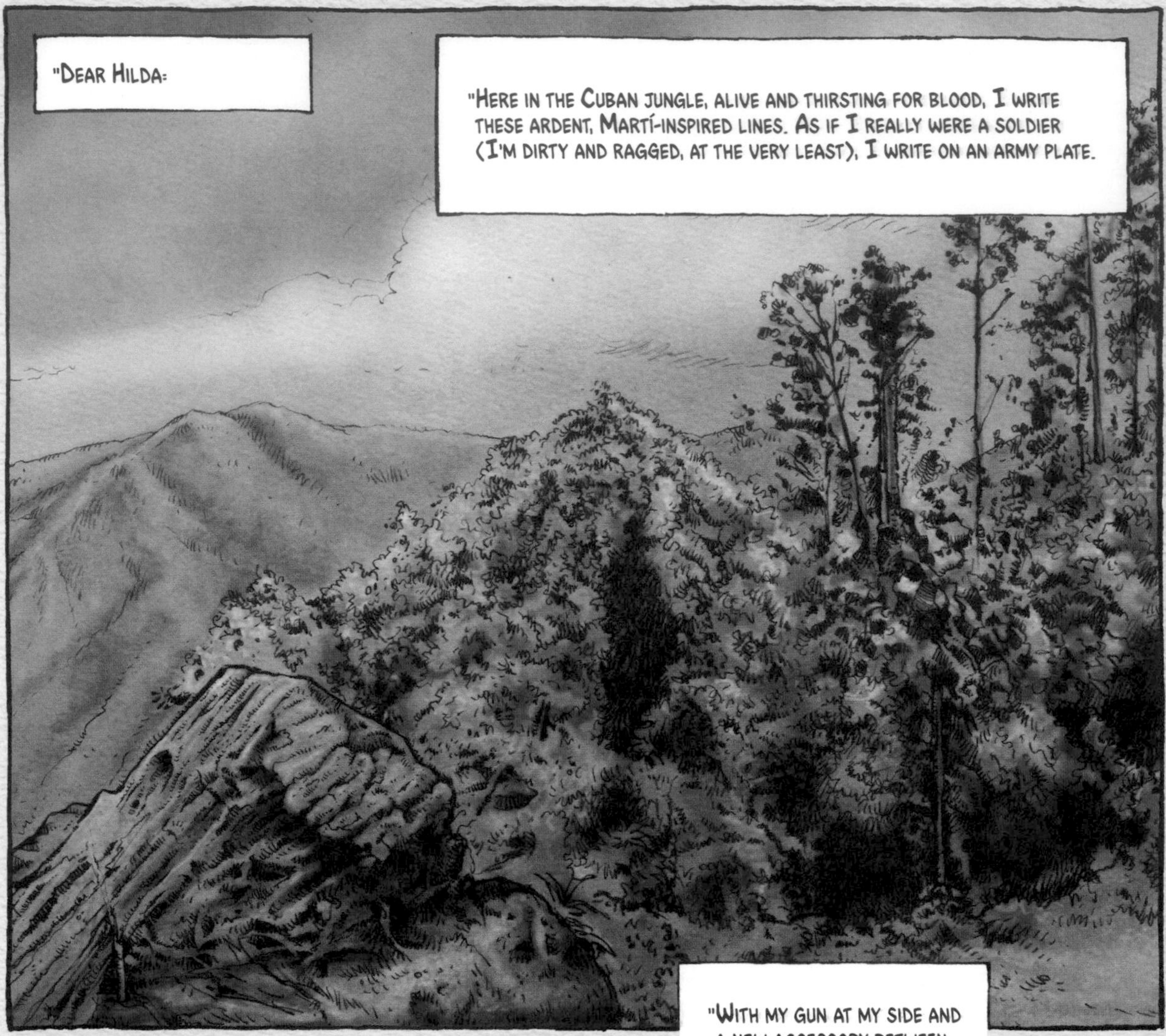
"Dear Hilda:
"Here in the Cuban jungle, alive and thirsting for blood, I write these ardent, Martí-inspired lines. As if I really were a soldier (I'm dirty and ragged, at the very least), I write on an army plate.

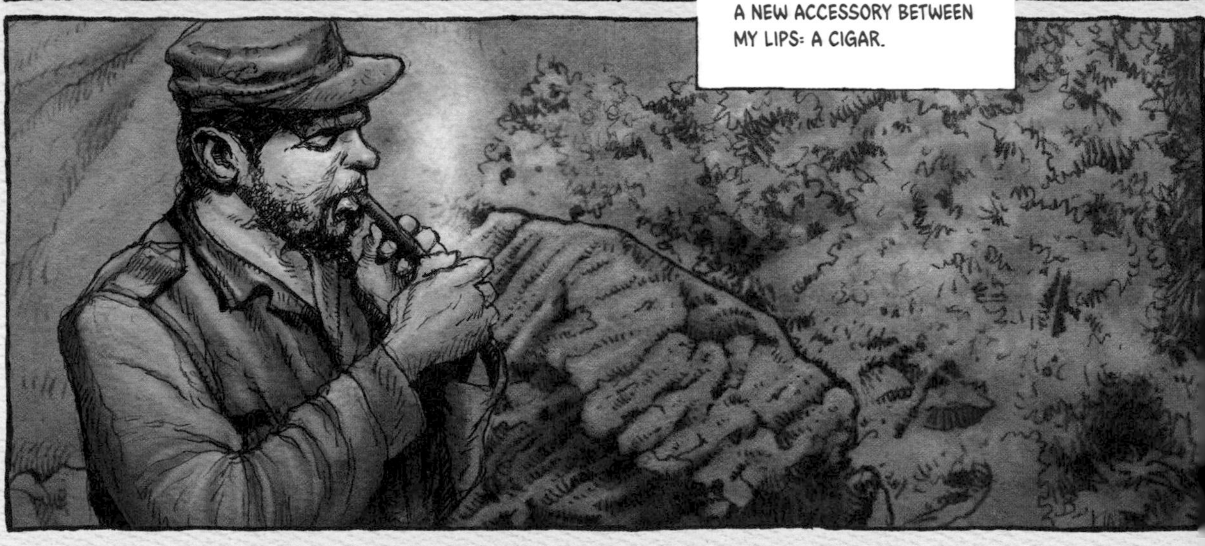
"With my gun at my side and a new accessory between my lips: a cigar.

"THEY WOUNDED ME IN THE NECK AND I SURVIVED THANKS ONLY TO MY CATLIKE LUCK.

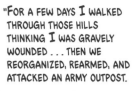

"FOR A FEW DAYS I WALKED THROUGH THOSE HILLS THINKING I WAS GRAVELY WOUNDED . . . THEN WE REORGANIZED, REARMED, AND ATTACKED AN ARMY OUTPOST.

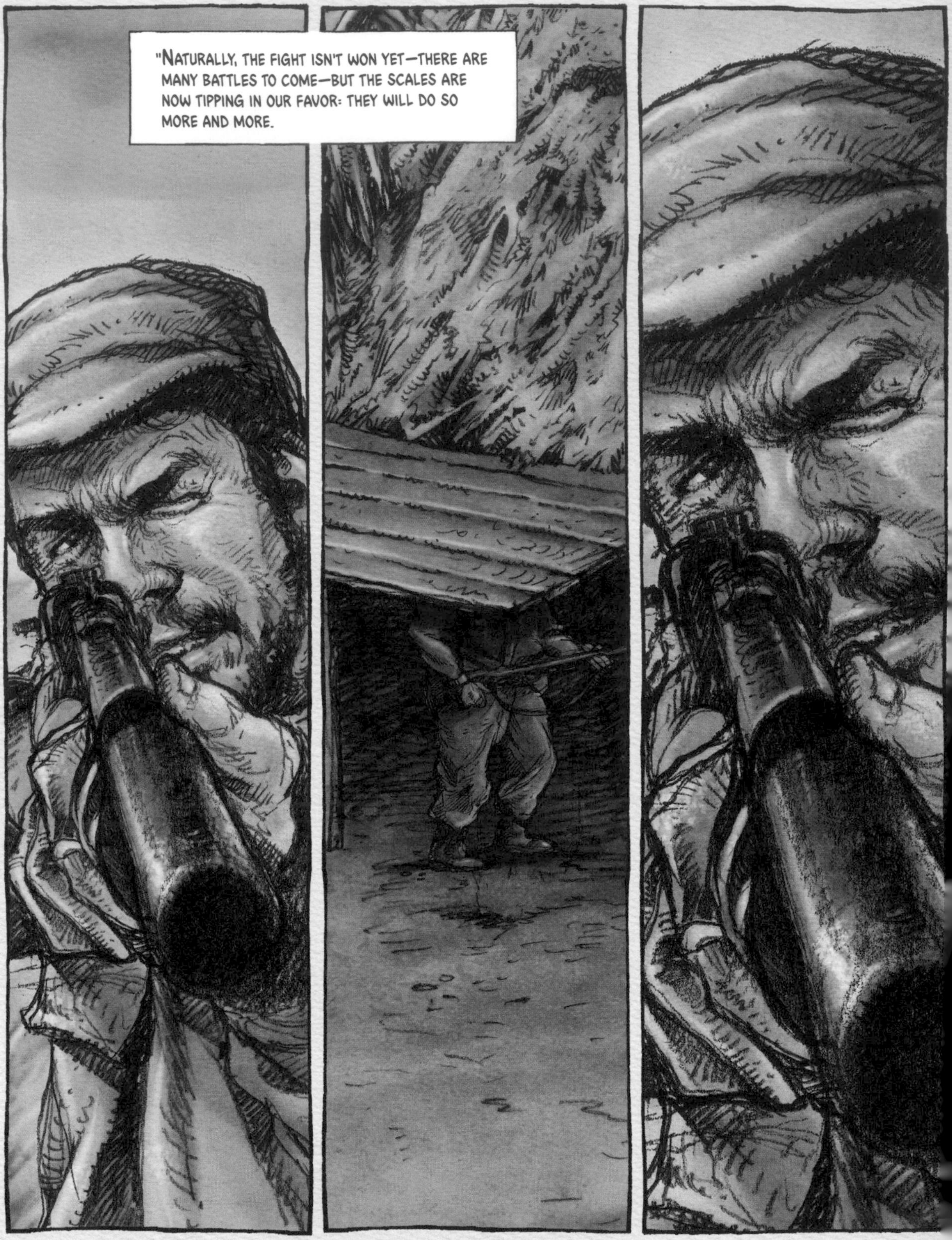
"NATURALLY, THE FIGHT ISN'T WON YET—THERE ARE MANY BATTLES TO COME—BUT THE SCALES ARE NOW TIPPING IN OUR FAVOR: THEY WILL DO SO MORE AND MORE.

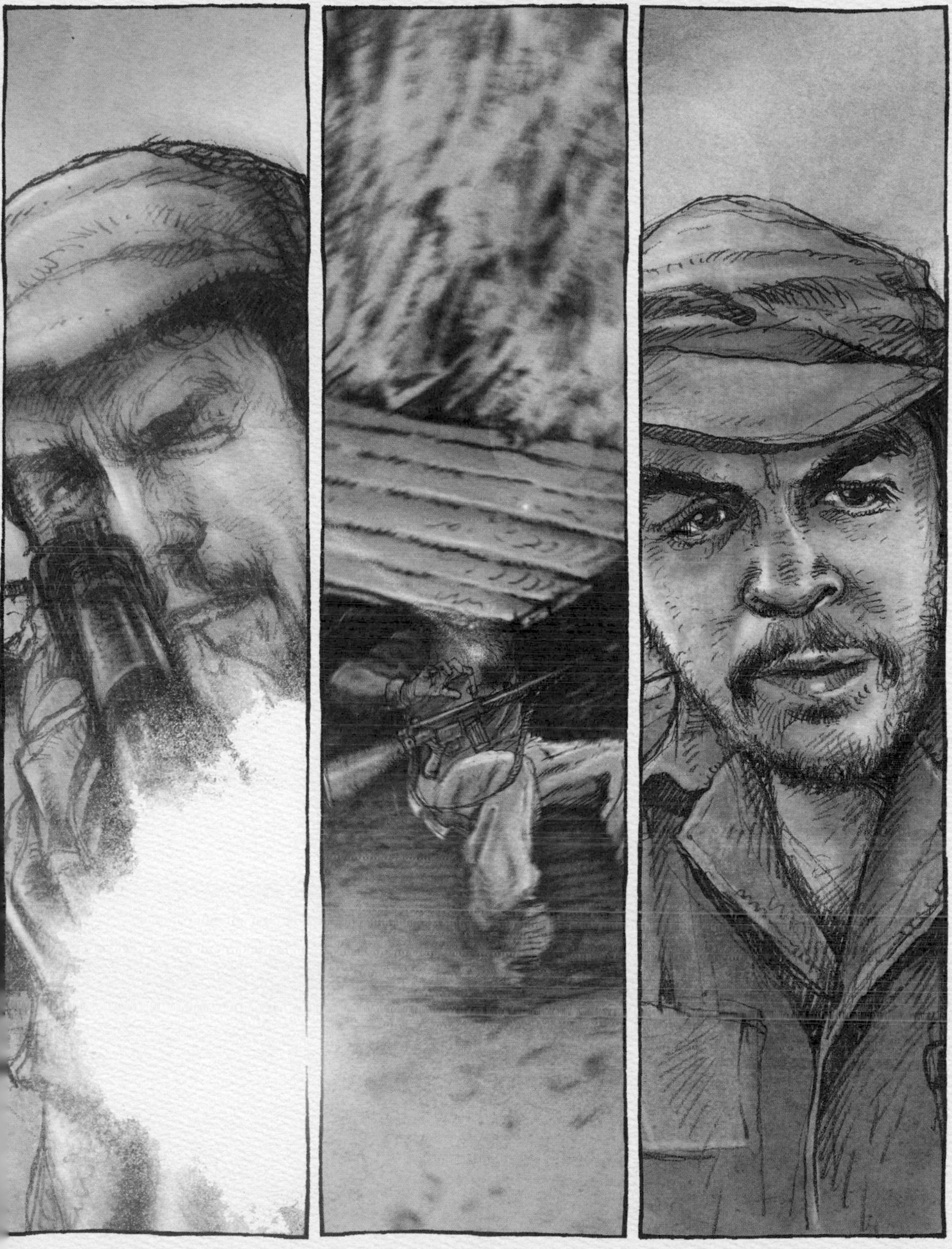

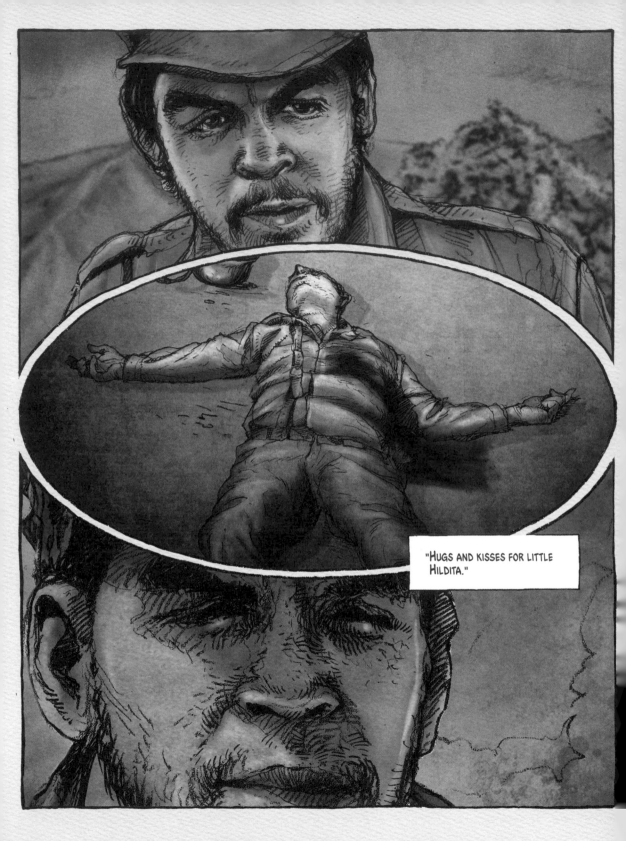

"HUGS AND KISSES FOR LITTLE HILDITA."

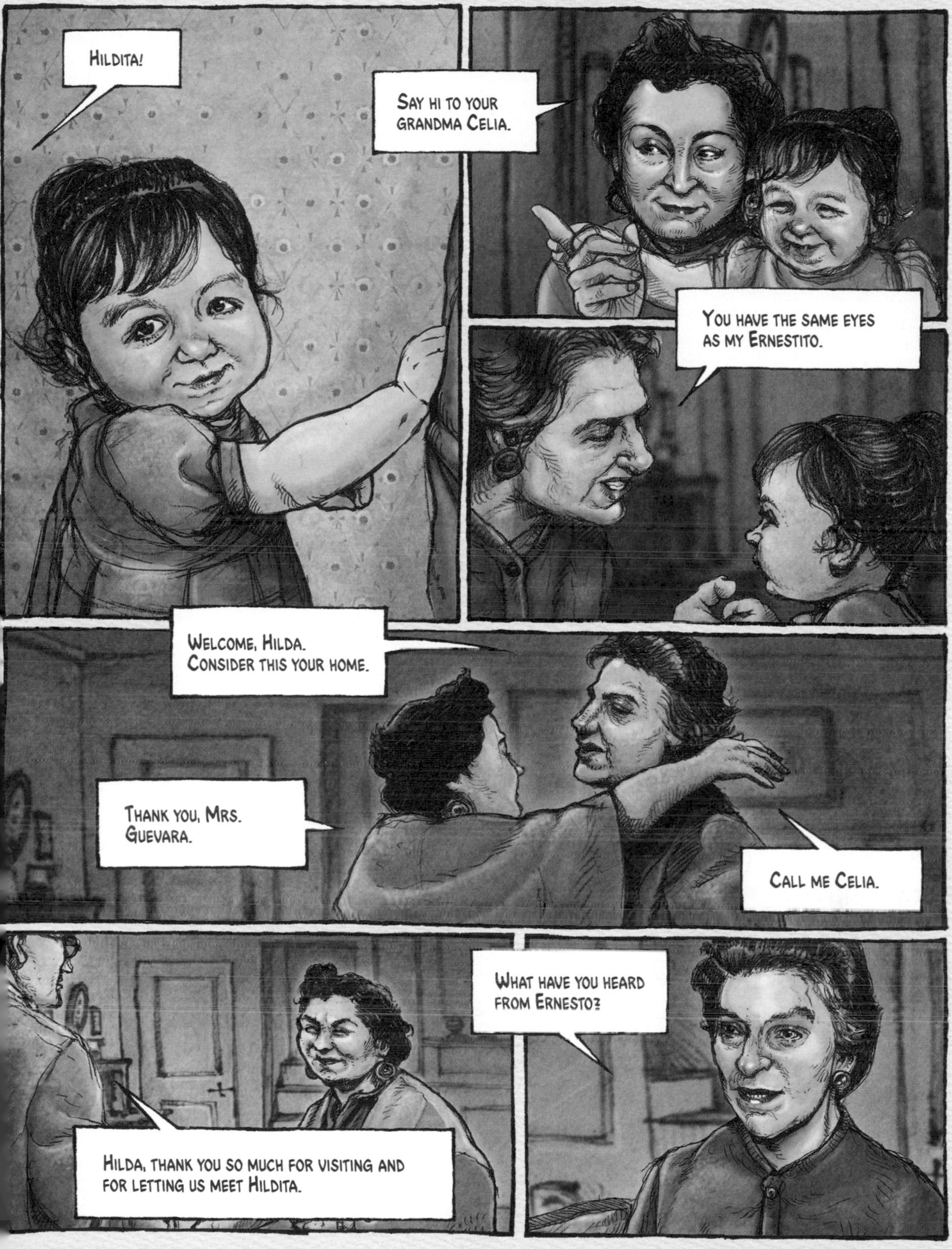

Hildita!
Say hi to your grandma Celia.
You have the same eyes as my Ernestito.
Welcome, Hilda. Consider this your home.
Thank you, Mrs. Guevara.
Call me Celia.
Hilda, thank you so much for visiting and for letting us meet Hildita.
What have you heard from Ernesto?

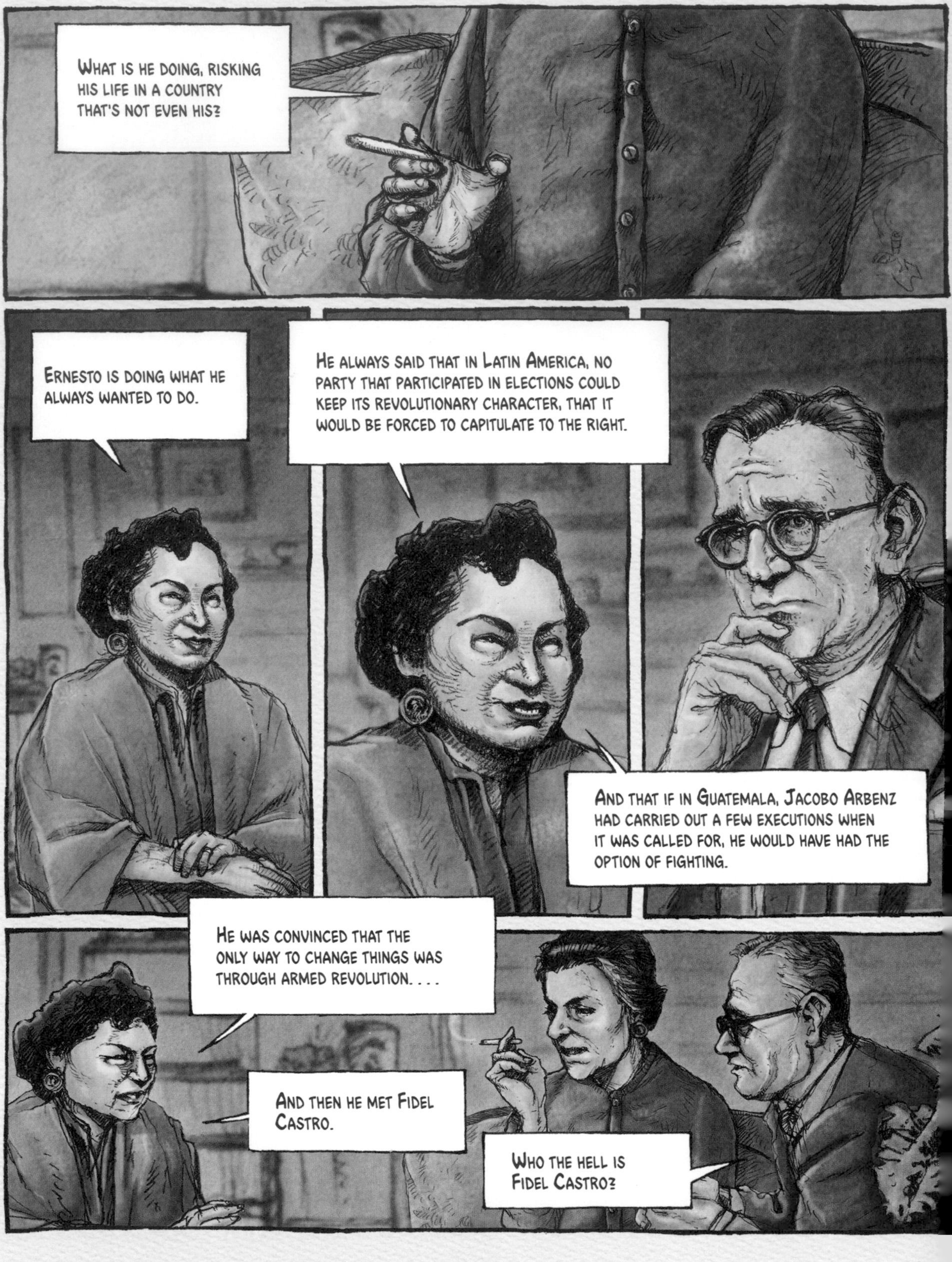
WHAT IS HE DOING, RISKING HIS LIFE IN A COUNTRY THAT'S NOT EVEN HIS?
ERNESTO IS DOING WHAT HE ALWAYS WANTED TO DO.
HE ALWAYS SAID THAT IN LATIN AMERICA, NO PARTY THAT PARTICIPATED IN ELECTIONS COULD KEEP ITS REVOLUTIONARY CHARACTER, THAT IT WOULD BE FORCED TO CAPITULATE TO THE RIGHT.
AND THAT IF IN GUATEMALA, JACOBO ARBENZ HAD CARRIED OUT A FEW EXECUTIONS WHEN IT WAS CALLED FOR, HE WOULD HAVE HAD THE OPTION OF FIGHTING.
HE WAS CONVINCED THAT THE ONLY WAY TO CHANGE THINGS WAS THROUGH ARMED REVOLUTION. . . .
AND THEN HE MET FIDEL CASTRO.
WHO THE HELL IS FIDEL CASTRO?

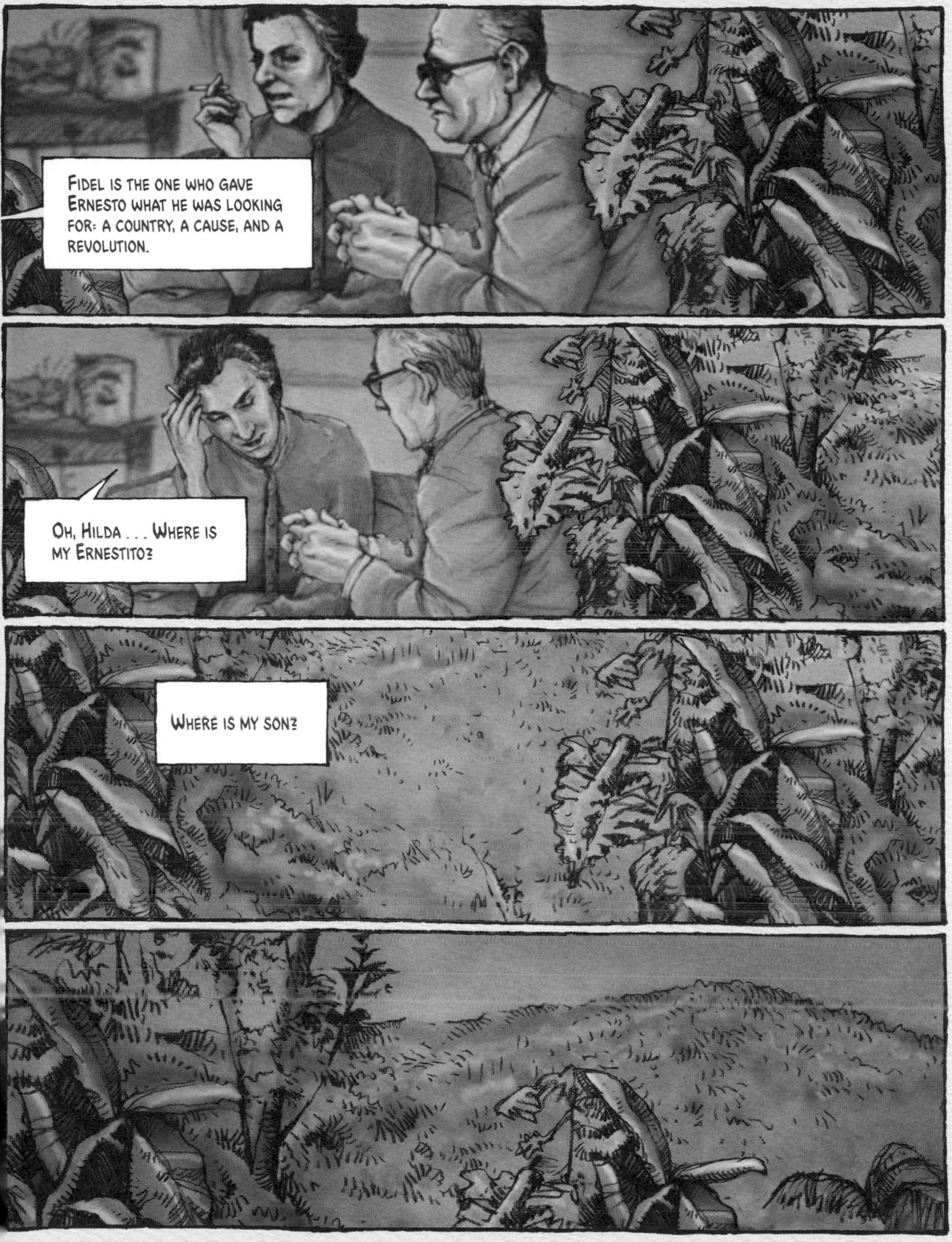
FIDEL IS THE ONE WHO GAVE ERNESTO WHAT HE WAS LOOKING FOR: A COUNTRY, A CAUSE, AND A REVOLUTION.
OH, HILDA . . . WHERE IS MY ERNESTITO?
WHERE IS MY SON?

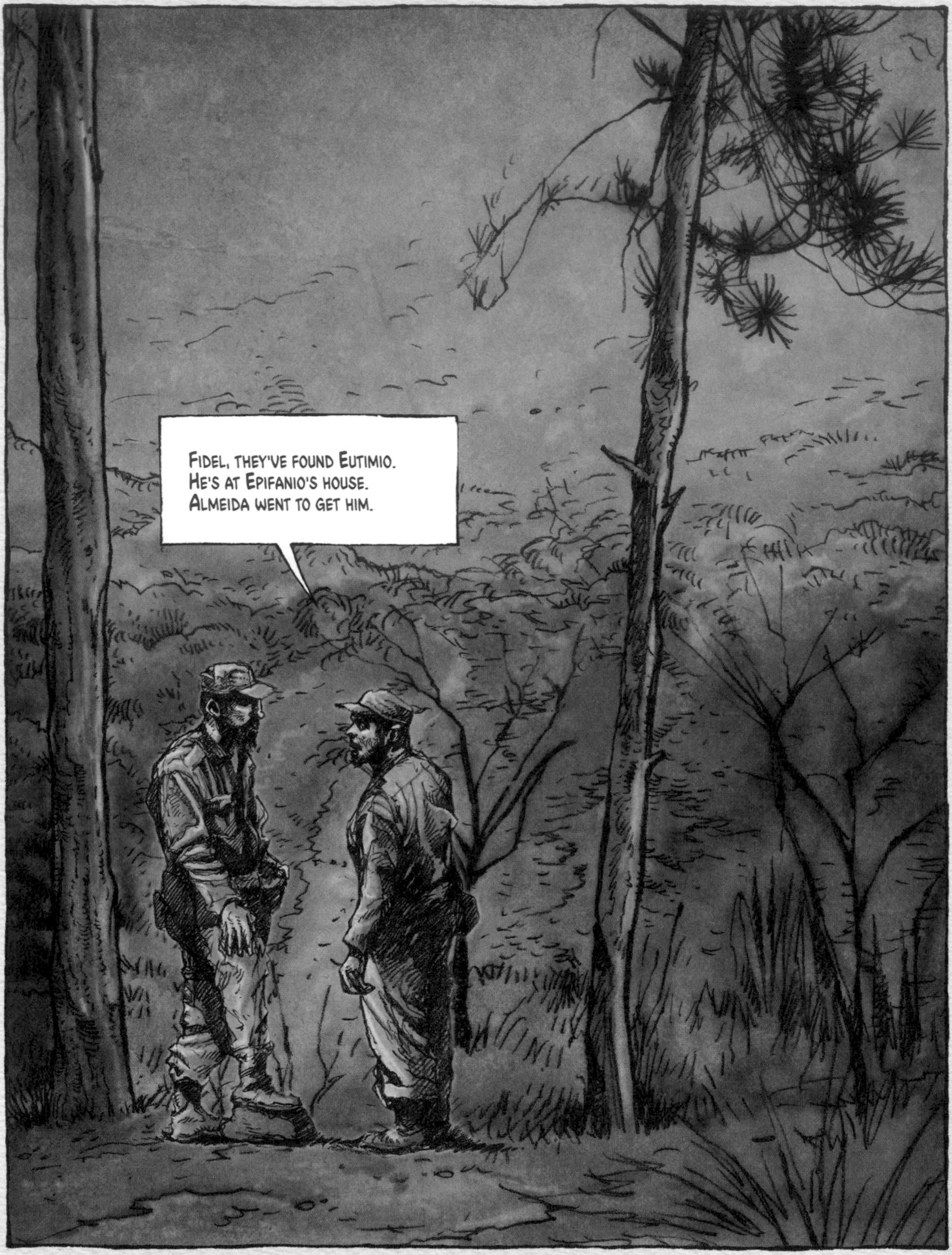
FIDEL, THEY'VE FOUND EUTIMIO.
HE'S AT EPIFANIO'S HOUSE.
ALMEIDA WENT TO GET HIM.

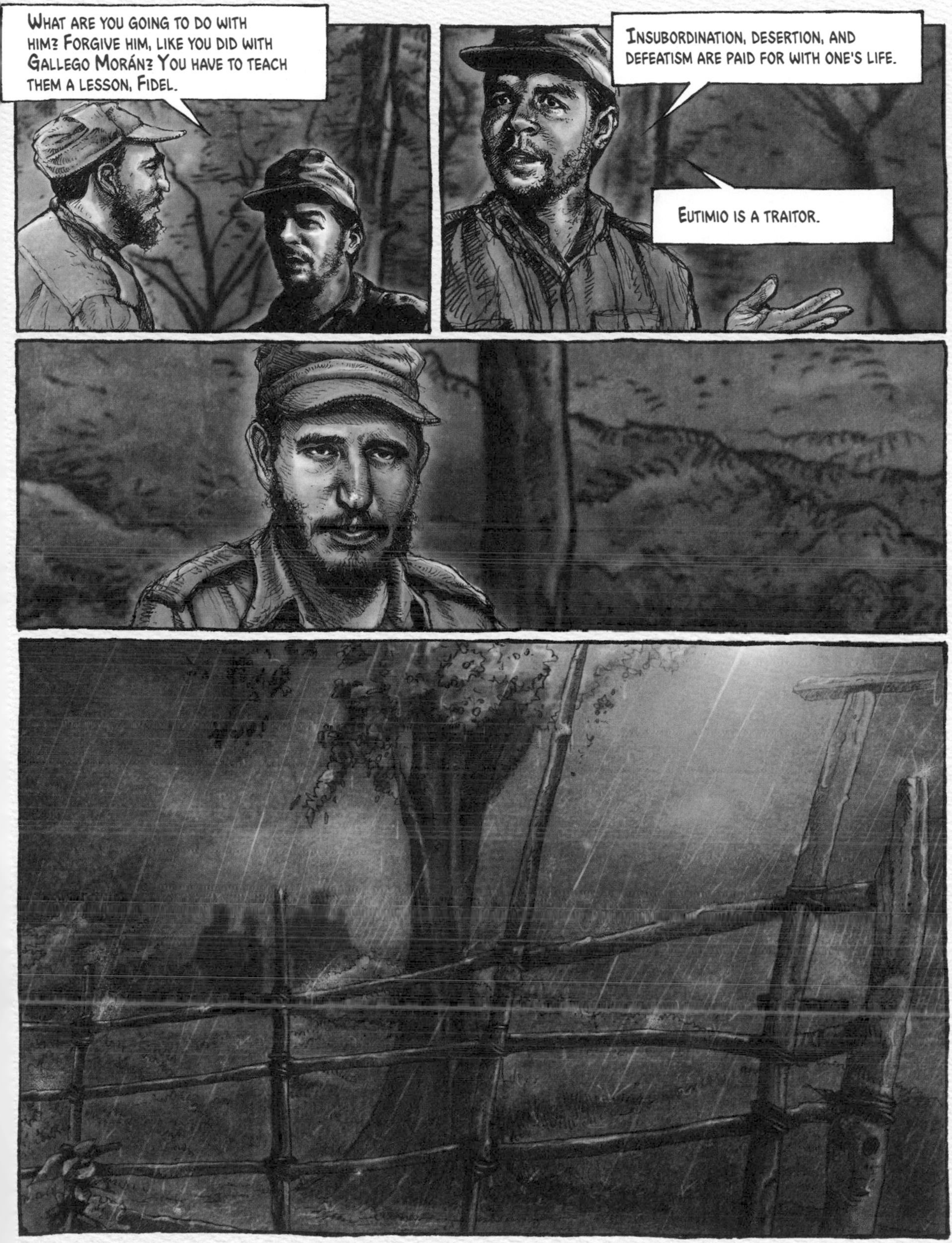
WHAT ARE YOU GOING TO DO WITH HIM? FORGIVE HIM, LIKE YOU DID WITH GALLEGO MORÁN? YOU HAVE TO TEACH THEM A LESSON, FIDEL.
INSUBORDINATION, DESERTION, AND DEFEATISM ARE PAID FOR WITH ONE'S LIFE.
EUTIMIO IS A TRAITOR.

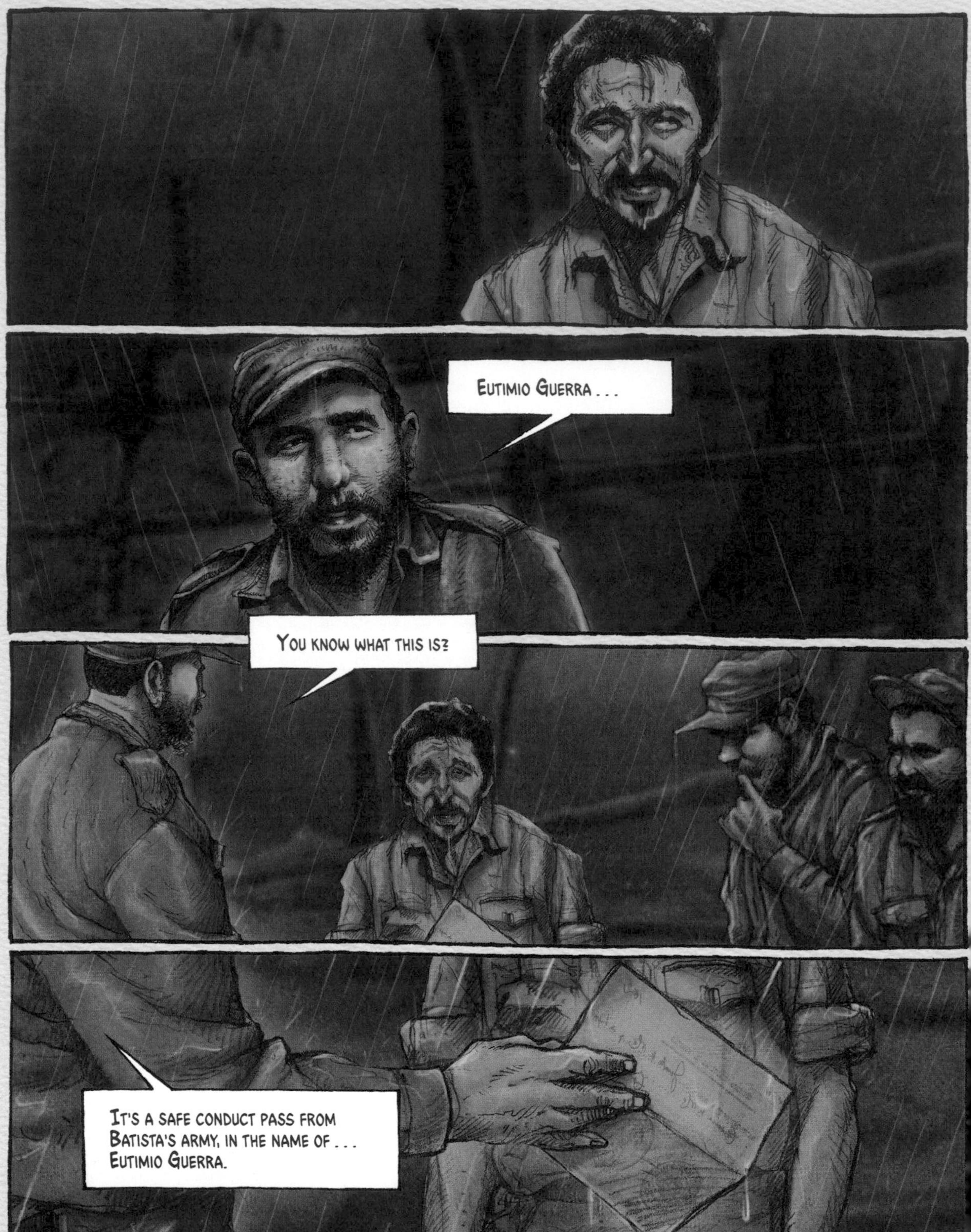
EUTIMIO GUERRA . . .
YOU KNOW WHAT THIS IS?
IT'S A SAFE CONDUCT PASS FROM BATISTA'S ARMY, IN THE NAME OF . . . EUTIMIO GUERRA.

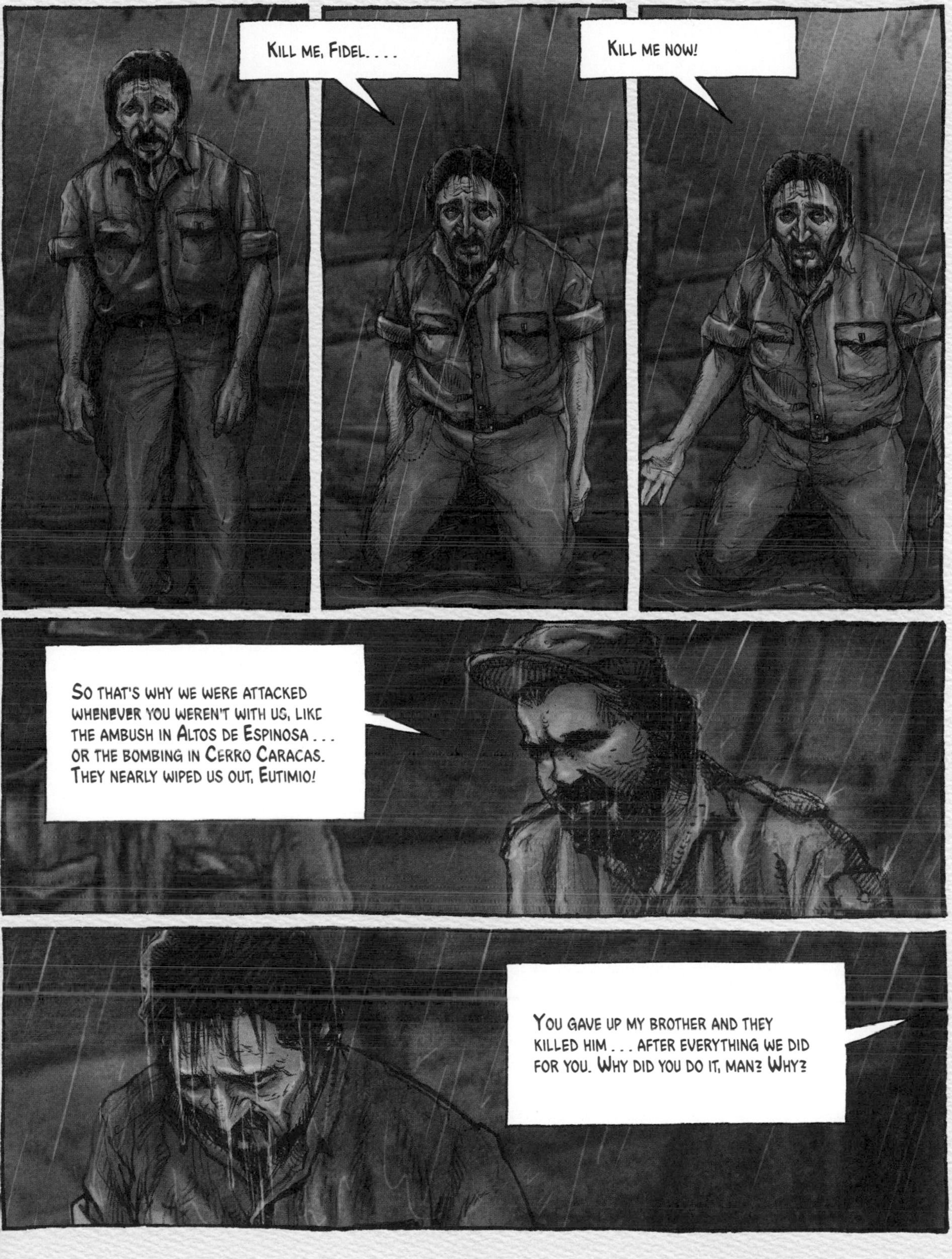
Kill me, Fidel. . . .
Kill me now!
So that's why we were attacked whenever you weren't with us, like the ambush in Altos de Espinosa . . . or the bombing in Cerro Caracas. They nearly wiped us out, Eutimio!
You gave up my brother and they killed him . . . after everything we did for you. Why did you do it, man? Why?

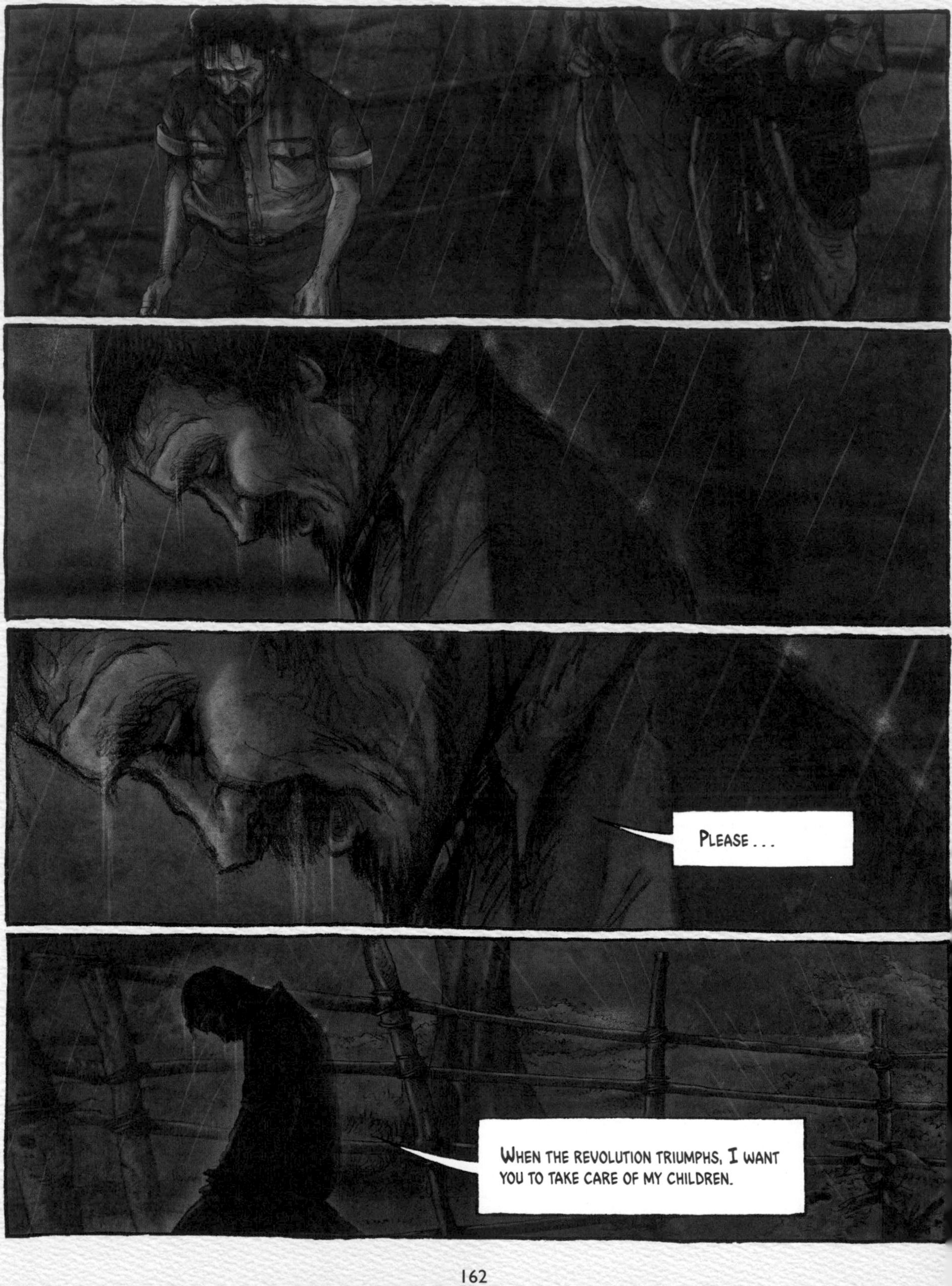
PLEASE . . .
WHEN THE REVOLUTION TRIUMPHS, I WANT YOU TO TAKE CARE OF MY CHILDREN.

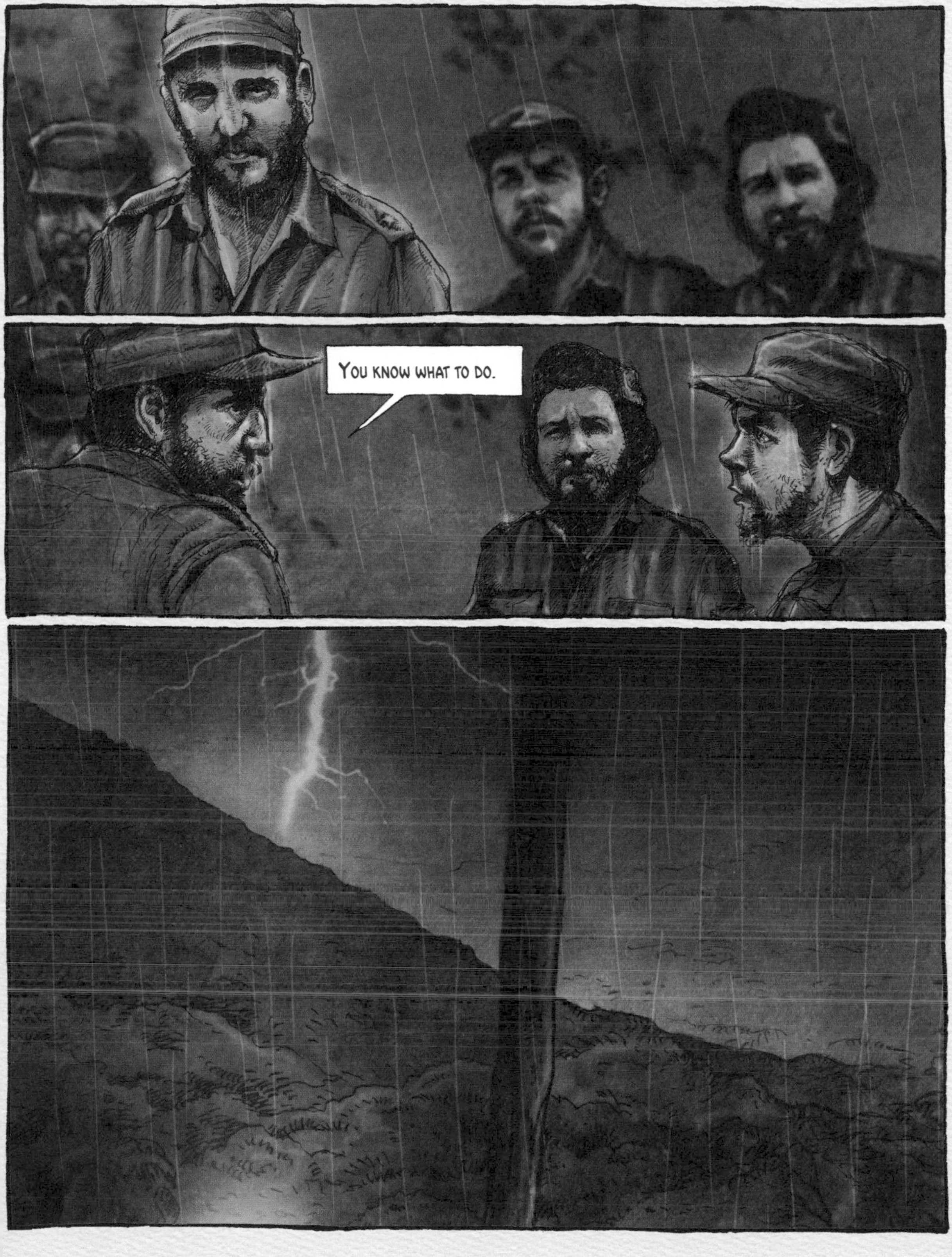
YOU KNOW WHAT TO DO.

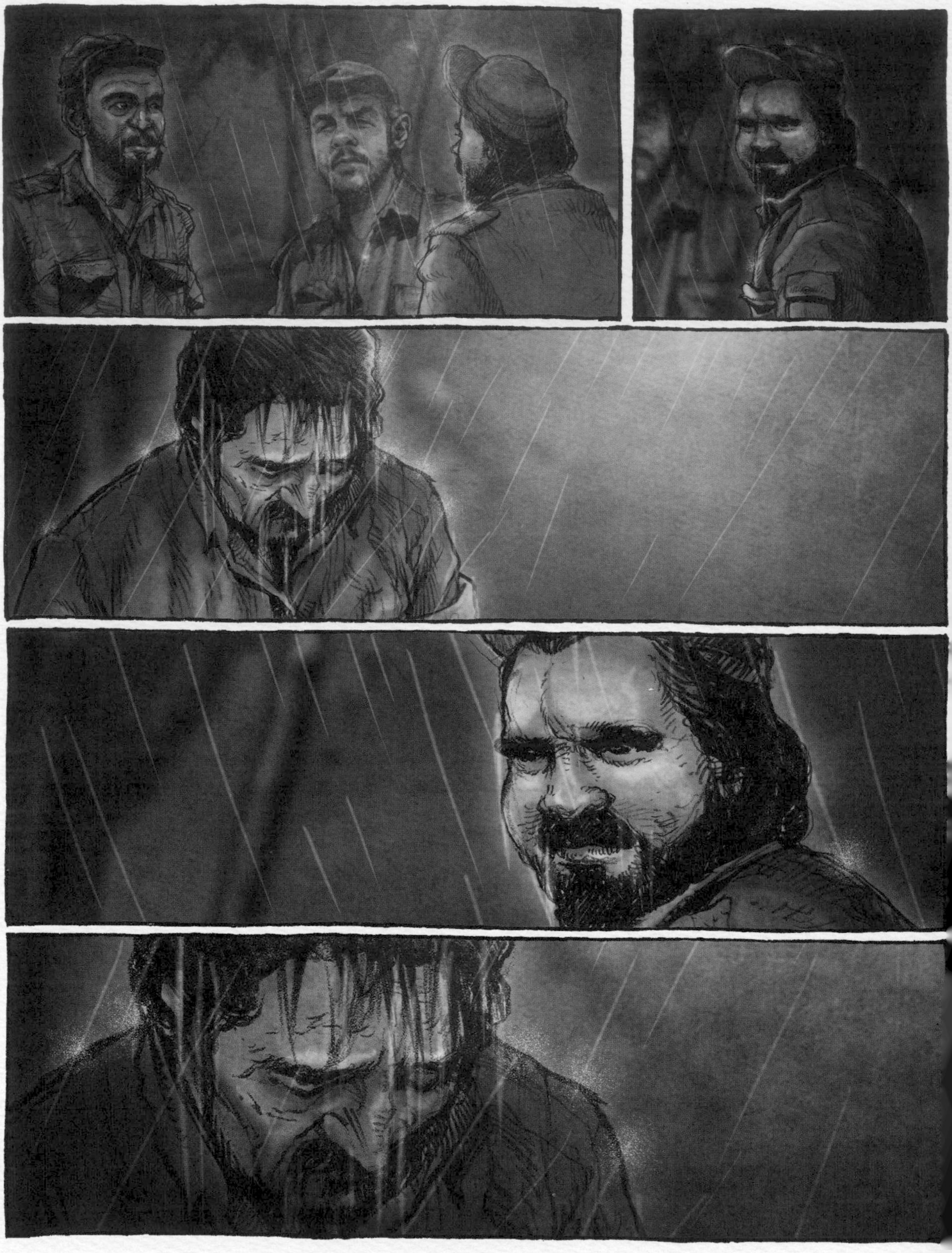

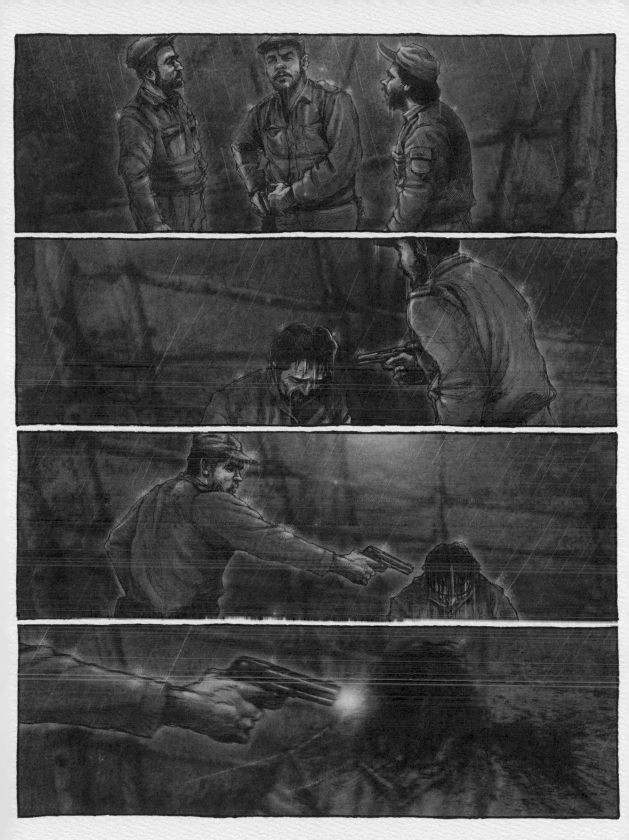

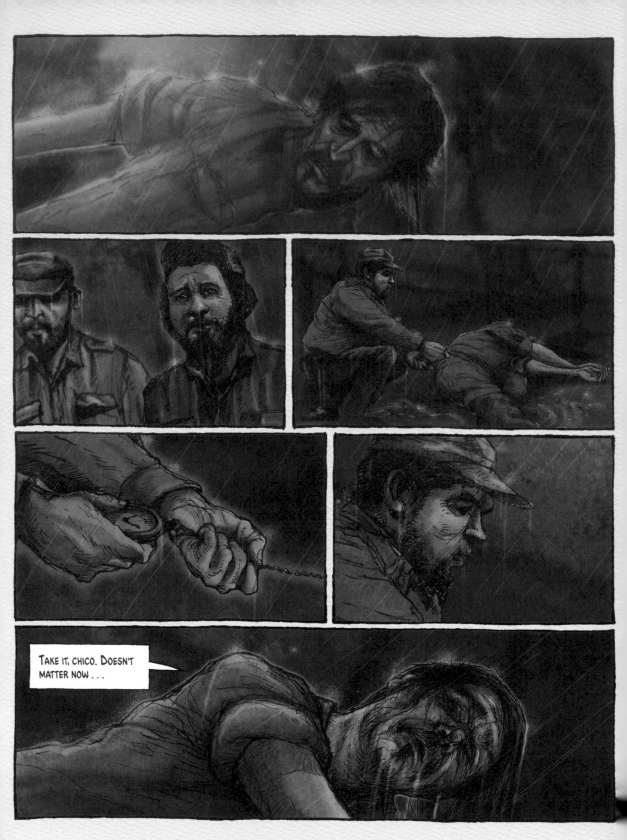

TAKE IT, CHICO. DOESN'T MATTER NOW . . .

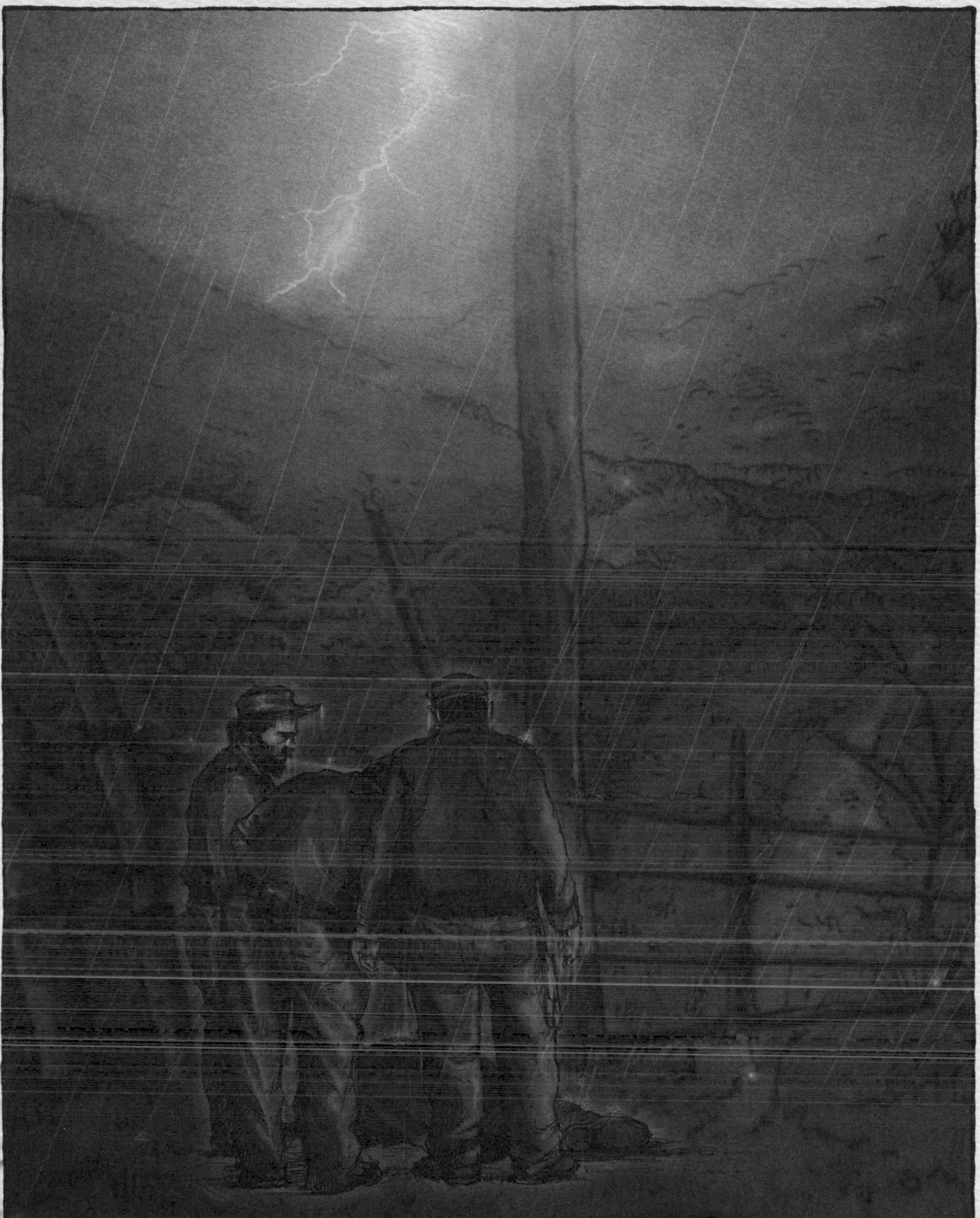

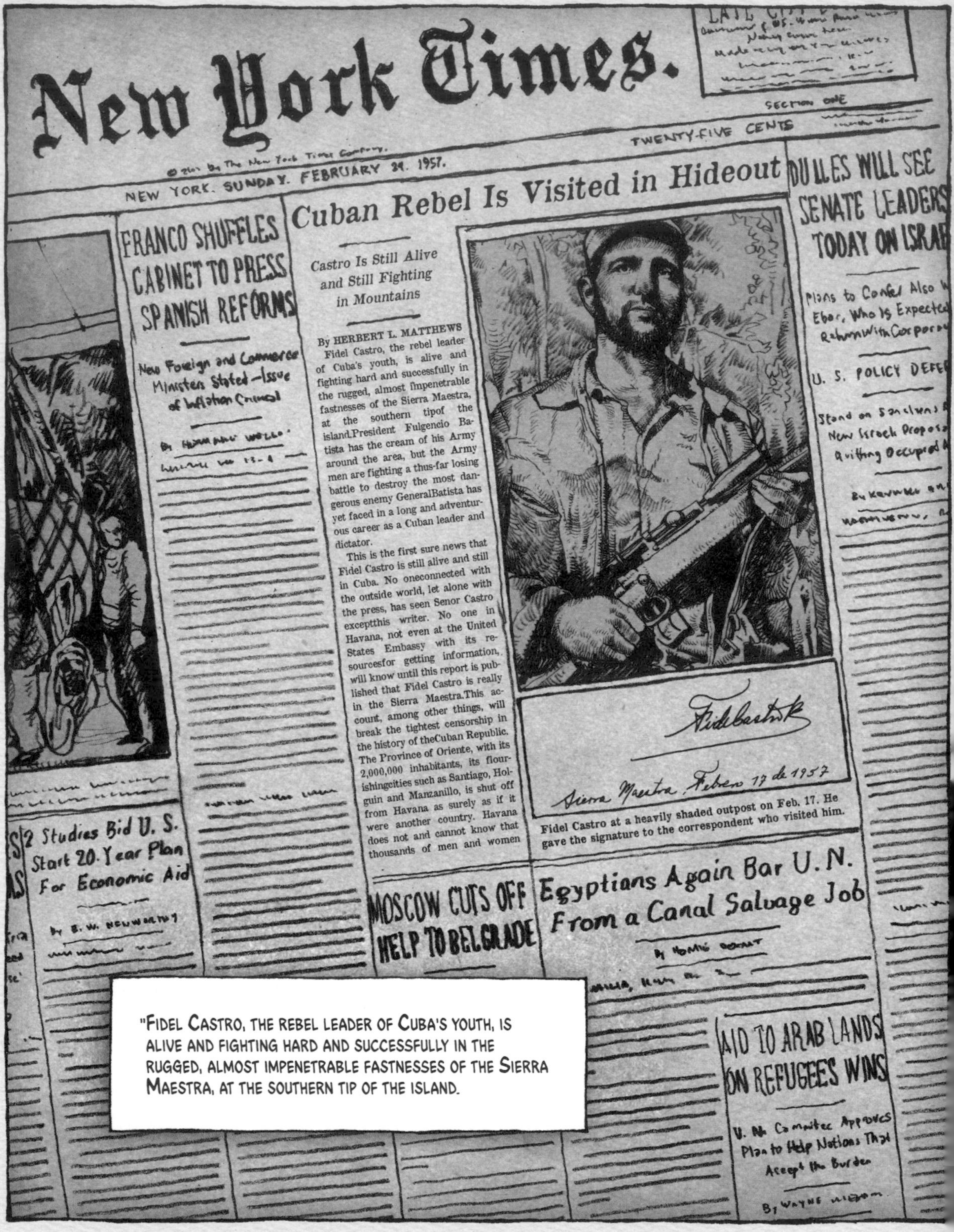
New York Times.
SECTION ONE
TWENTY-FIVE CENTS
NEW YORK, SUNDAY, FEBRUARY 24, 1957.
Cuban Rebel Is Visited in Hideout
Castro Is Still Alive and Still Fighting in Mountains
By HERBERT L. MATTHEWS
Fidel Castro, the rebel leader of Cuba's youth, is alive and fighting hard and successfully in the rugged, almost impenetrable fastnesses of the Sierra Maestra, at the southern tipof the island.President Fulgencio Batista has the cream of his Army around the area, but the Army men are fighting a thus-far losing battle to destroy the most dangerous enemy GeneralBatista has yet faced in a long and adventurous career as a Cuban leader and dictator.
This is the first sure news that Fidel Castro is still alive and still in Cuba. No oneconnected with the outside world, let alone with the press, has seen Senor Castro exceptthis writer. No one in Havana, not even at the United States Embassy with its resourcesfor getting information, will know until this report is published that Fidel Castro is really in the Sierra Maestra.This account, among other things, will break the tightest censorship in the history of theCuban Republic. The Province of Oriente, with its 2,000,000 inhabitants, its flourishingcities such as Santiago, Holguin and Manzanillo, is shut off from Havana as surely as if it were another country. Havana does not and cannot know that thousands of men and women
Fidel Castro
Sierra Maestra, Febrero 17 de 1957
Fidel Castro at a heavily shaded outpost on Feb. 17. He gave the signature to the correspondent who visited him.
FRANCO SHUFFLES CABINET TO PRESS SPANISH REFORMS
New Foreign and Commerce Ministers Stated—Issue of Inflation Critical
DULLES WILL SEE SENATE LEADERS TODAY ON ISRAE
U. S. POLICY DEFE
2 Studies Bid U. S. Start 20-Year Plan For Economic Aid
MOSCOW CUTS OFF HELP TO BELGRADE
Egyptians Again Bar U. N. From a Canal Salvage Job
AID TO ARAB LANDS ON REFUGEES WINS
U. N. Committee Approves Plan to Help Nations That Accept the Burden
"FIDEL CASTRO, THE REBEL LEADER OF CUBA'S YOUTH, IS ALIVE AND FIGHTING HARD AND SUCCESSFULLY IN THE RUGGED, ALMOST IMPENETRABLE FASTNESSES OF THE SIERRA MAESTRA, AT THE SOUTHERN TIP OF THE ISLAND.

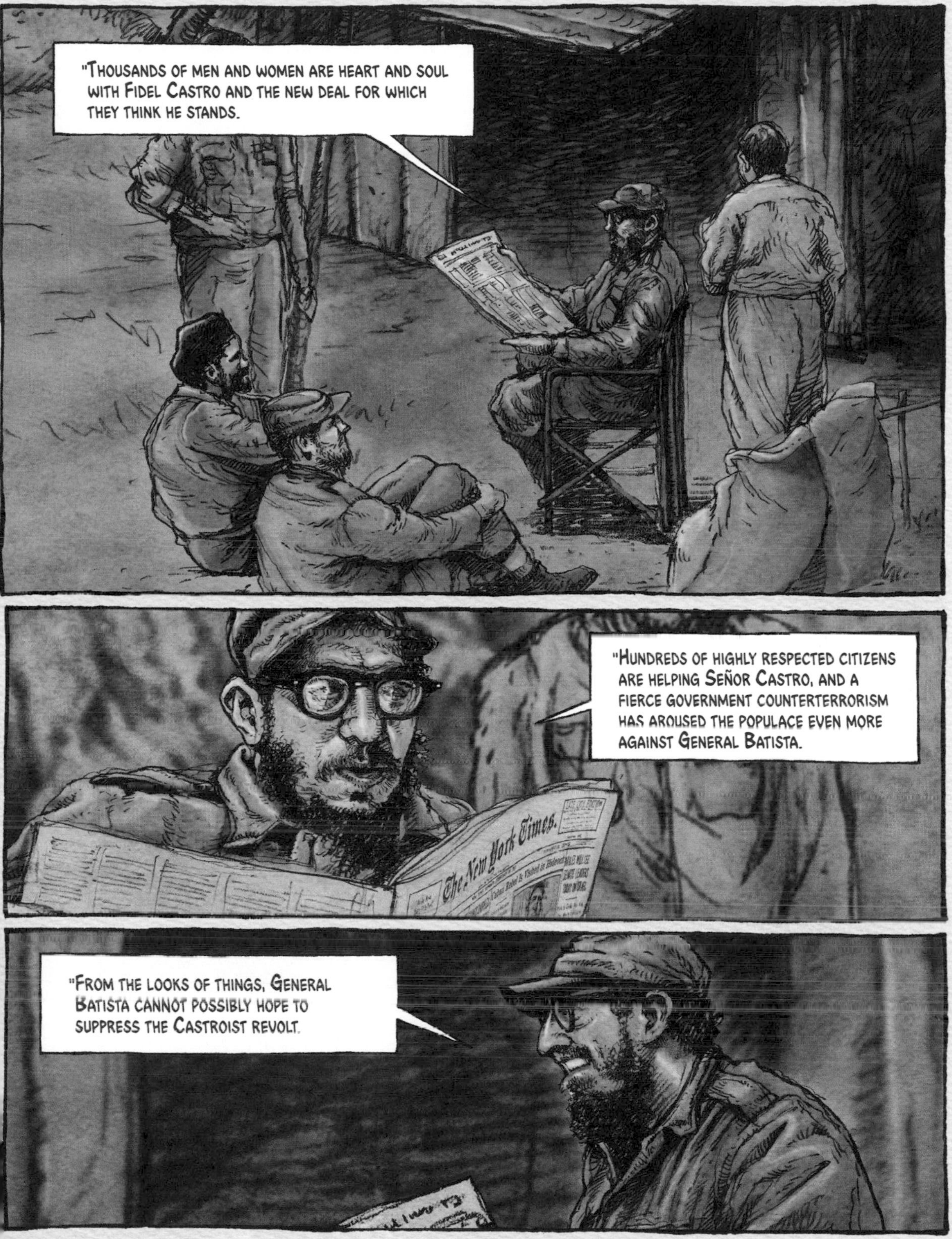
"THOUSANDS OF MEN AND WOMEN ARE HEART AND SOUL WITH FIDEL CASTRO AND THE NEW DEAL FOR WHICH THEY THINK HE STANDS.
"HUNDREDS OF HIGHLY RESPECTED CITIZENS ARE HELPING SEÑOR CASTRO, AND A FIERCE GOVERNMENT COUNTERTERRORISM HAS AROUSED THE POPULACE EVEN MORE AGAINST GENERAL BATISTA.
"FROM THE LOOKS OF THINGS, GENERAL BATISTA CANNOT POSSIBLY HOPE TO SUPPRESS THE CASTROIST REVOLT.

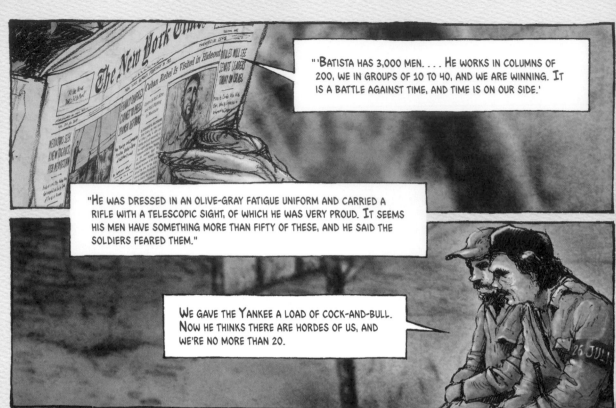

" 'BATISTA HAS 3,000 MEN. . . . HE WORKS IN COLUMNS OF 200, WE IN GROUPS OF 10 TO 40, AND WE ARE WINNING. IT IS A BATTLE AGAINST TIME, AND TIME IS ON OUR SIDE.' "

"HE WAS DRESSED IN AN OLIVE-GRAY FATIGUE UNIFORM AND CARRIED A RIFLE WITH A TELESCOPIC SIGHT, OF WHICH HE WAS VERY PROUD. IT SEEMS HIS MEN HAVE SOMETHING MORE THAN FIFTY OF THESE, AND HE SAID THE SOLDIERS FEARED THEM."

WE GAVE THE YANKEE A LOAD OF COCK-AND-BULL. NOW HE THINKS THERE ARE HORDES OF US, AND WE'RE NO MORE THAN 20.

I DIDN'T LIE TO THE YANKEE, I JUST GAVE HIM A LITTLE ADVANCE ON WHAT'S COMING. TODAY WE ARE FEW, BUT IT WON'T BE LIKE THAT FOREVER.

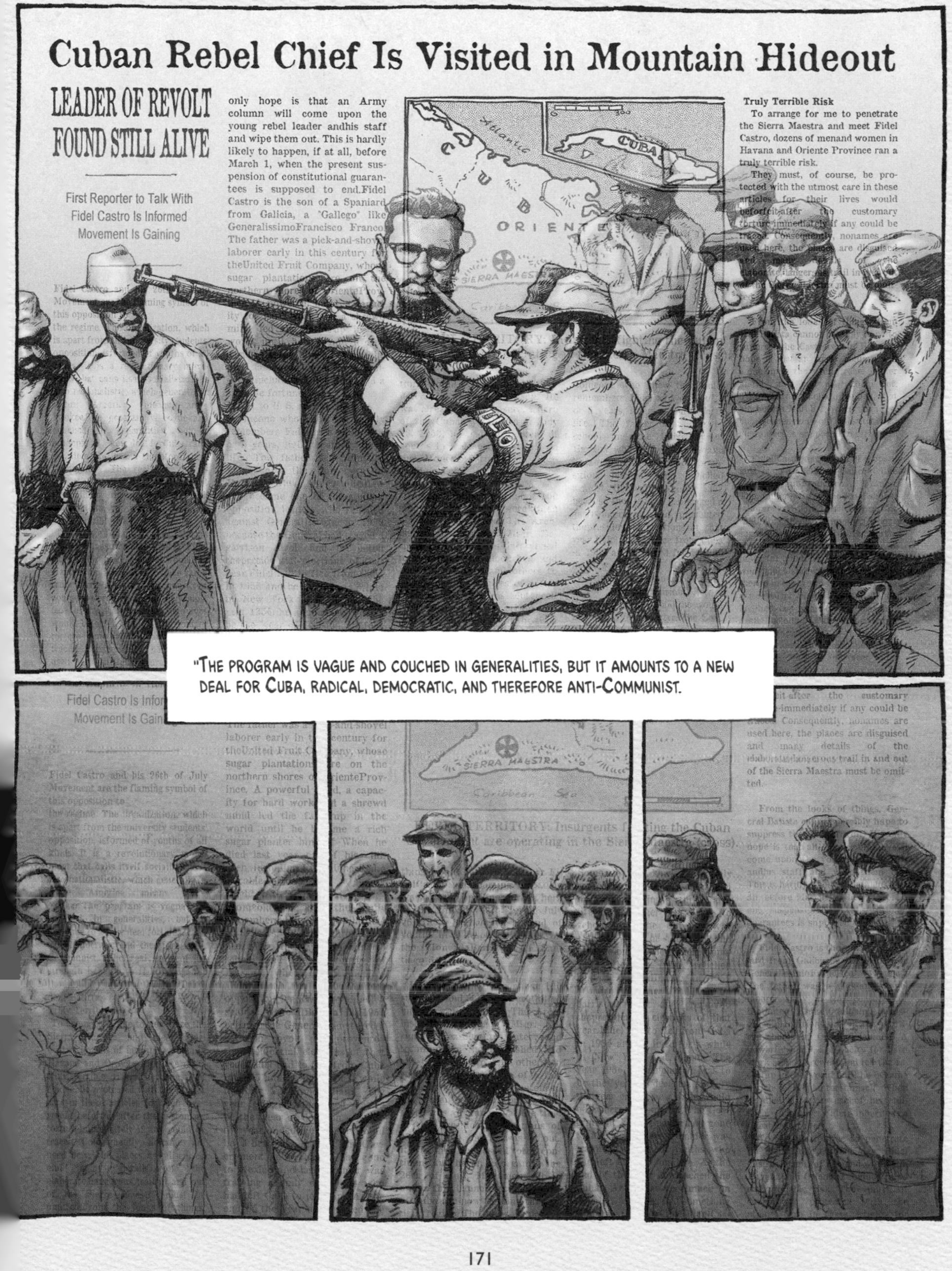
Cuban Rebel Chief Is Visited in Mountain Hideout
LEADER OF REVOLT FOUND STILL ALIVE
First Reporter to Talk With Fidel Castro Is Informed Movement Is Gaining
only hope is that an Army column will come upon the young rebel leader andhis staff and wipe them out. This is hardly likely to happen, if at all, before March 1, when the present suspension of constitutional guarantees is supposed to end.Fidel Castro is the son of a Spaniard from Galicia, a "Gallego" like GeneralissimoFrancisco Franco. The father was a pick-and-shov laborer early in this century f theUnited Fruit Company, who sugar plantati
CUBA
Atlantic
ORIENTE
SIERRA MAESTRA
Truly Terrible Risk
To arrange for me to penetrate the Sierra Maestra and meet Fidel Castro, dozens of menand women in Havana and Oriente Province ran a truly terrible risk.
They must, of course, be protected with the utmost care in these articles for their lives would
"The program is vague and couched in generalities, but it amounts to a new deal for Cuba, radical, democratic, and therefore anti-Communist.
laborer early in this century for theUnited Fruit Company, whose sugar plantations are on the northern shores of OrienteProvince. A powerful ... a capacity for hard work ... a shrewd
Fidel Castro and his 26th of July Movement are the flaming symbol of this opposition to
ORIENTE
SIERRA MAESTRA
Caribbean Sea
used here, the places are disguised and many details of the
of the Sierra Maestra must be omitted.

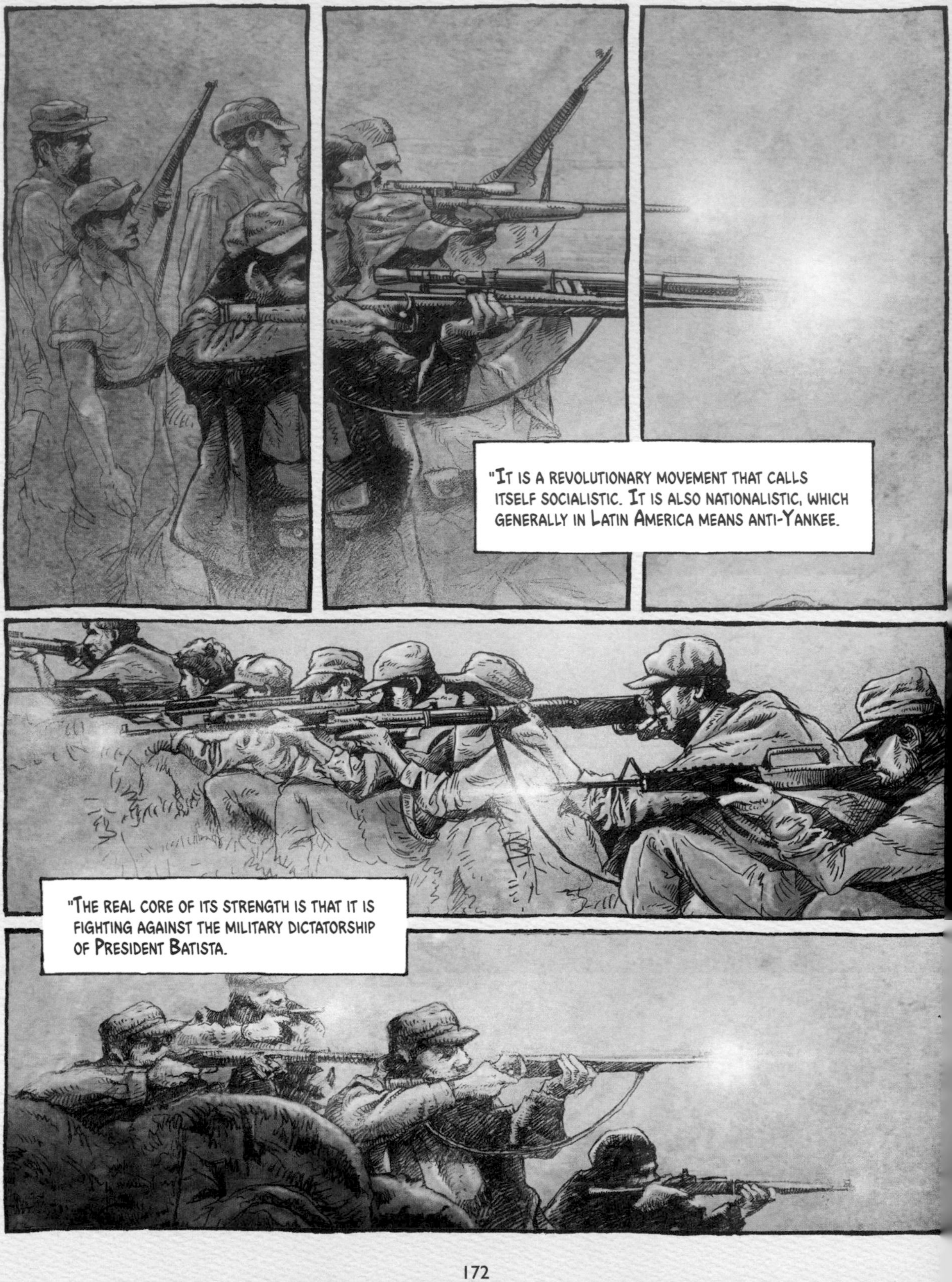
"It is a revolutionary movement that calls itself socialistic. It is also nationalistic, which generally in Latin America means anti-Yankee.
"The real core of its strength is that it is fighting against the military dictatorship of President Batista.

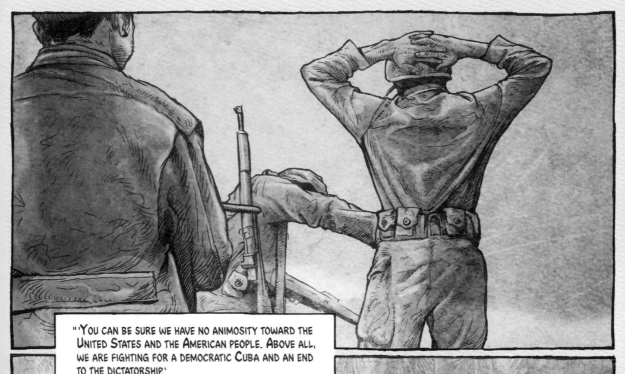

"'YOU CAN BE SURE WE HAVE NO ANIMOSITY TOWARD THE UNITED STATES AND THE AMERICAN PEOPLE. ABOVE ALL, WE ARE FIGHTING FOR A DEMOCRATIC CUBA AND AN END TO THE DICTATORSHIP.'

"FIDEL HAS FIRM IDEAS OF LIBERTY, DEMOCRACY, SOCIAL JUSTICE, THE NEED TO RESTORE THE CONSTITUTION, TO HOLD ELECTIONS."

... deal far too radi-... throne... cal and therefore still Communist. The real core of its strength isthat it is fighting against the military dictatorship of President Batista.

Truly Terrible Risk

To arrange for me to penetrate the Sierra Maestra and meet Fidel Castro, dozens of menand women in Havana and Oriente Province ran a truly terrible risk. They must, of course, be protected with the utmost care in these articles for their lives would beforfeit-after the customary torture-immediately if any could be traced. Consequently, nonames are used here, the places are disguised and many details of the elaborate,dangerous trail in and out of the Sierra Maestra must be ...

...a chief of ...he's years, living a sturdy farm life. The father sent him to school and the University of Havana, where he studiedlaw and became one of the student opposition leaders who rebelled against GeneralBatista in 1952 because the General had staged a garrison revolt and prevented thepresidential elections of that year.Fidel had to flee from Cuba in 1955 and he lived for a while in New York and Miami. The year 1956, he announced, was to be the "year of decision." Before the year ended, hesaid, he would be "a hero or a martyr."The Government knew that he had gone to Mexico and last summer was training a body of youths who had left Cuba to join him. As the

28, 1953, he had led a band of youths in a desperate attack on the MonedaBarracks in Santiago de Cuba.

In the fighting then about 100 students and soldiers were killed but the revolt failed. The Archbishop of Santiago, Msgr. Enrique Perez Serantes, intervened to minimize the bloodshed and got Senor Castro and others to surrender on pro... trial. FidelCastro ... to fifteen years ... there was an amn... of the Presidenti... Nov. 1, 1954, and ... It was then he cro... tinent and began ... 26th of July M... under this bannerthat the youth of Cuba are now fighting the Ba-

school and the University of Havana, where he studiedlaw and became one of the student opposition leaders who rebelled against GeneralBatista in 1952 because the General had staged a garrison revolt and prevented thepresidential elections of that year.Fidel had to flee from Cuba in 1955 and he lived for a while in New York and Miami. The ...

Cuban Army was very much on the alert, knowing that something

Fidel ... ...tart f... General... The father... laborer o... sugar plantation... ern shores of OrienteProvince. A powerful build, a capacity for hard work and a shrewd mind led the fa-...e became ...lf When ...his chil-...herited a ...penetrate ...eet Fidel ...women in ...nce ran a truly terrible risk. They must, of course.

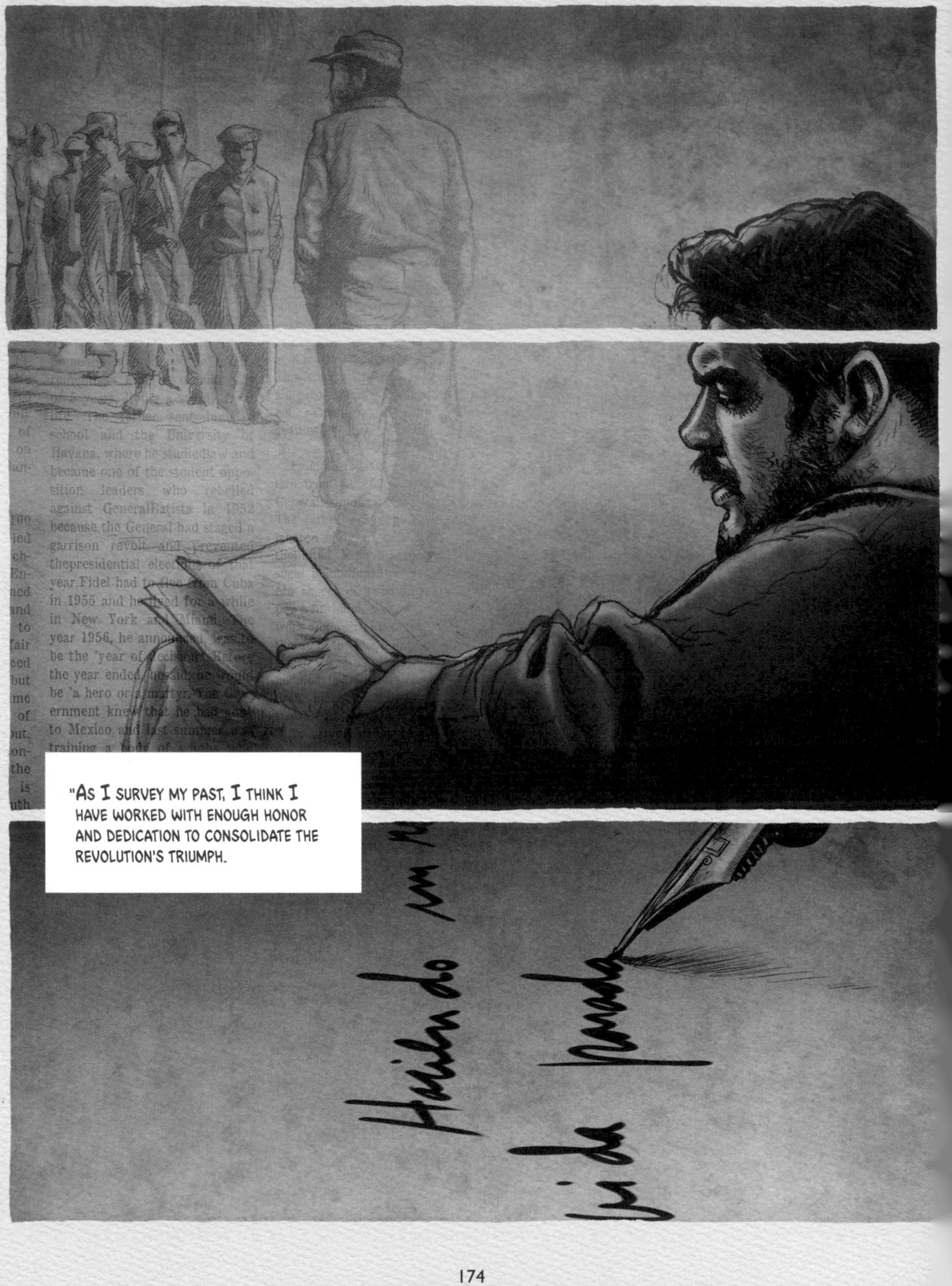
"AS I SURVEY MY PAST, I THINK I HAVE WORKED WITH ENOUGH HONOR AND DEDICATION TO CONSOLIDATE THE REVOLUTION'S TRIUMPH.

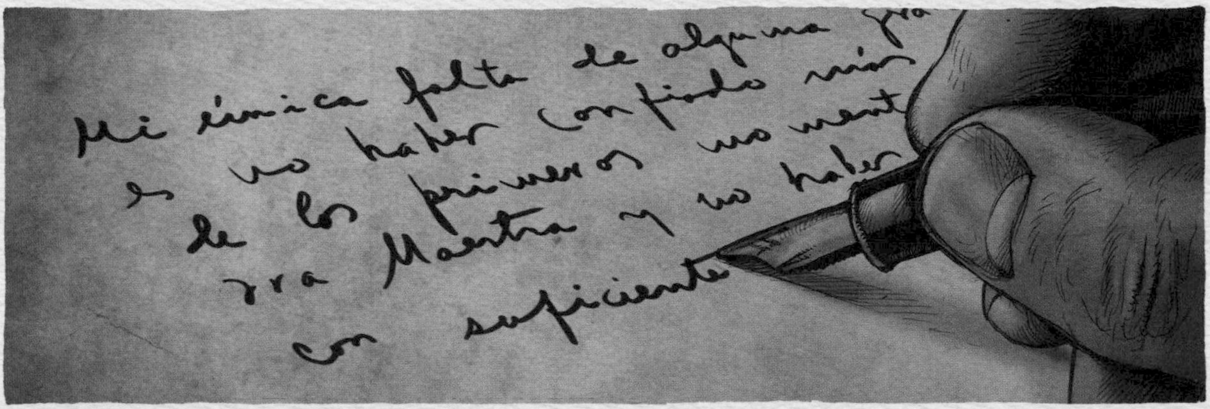
Mi única falta de alguna gra
es no haber confiado más
de los primeros moment
rra Maestra y no haber
con suficiente

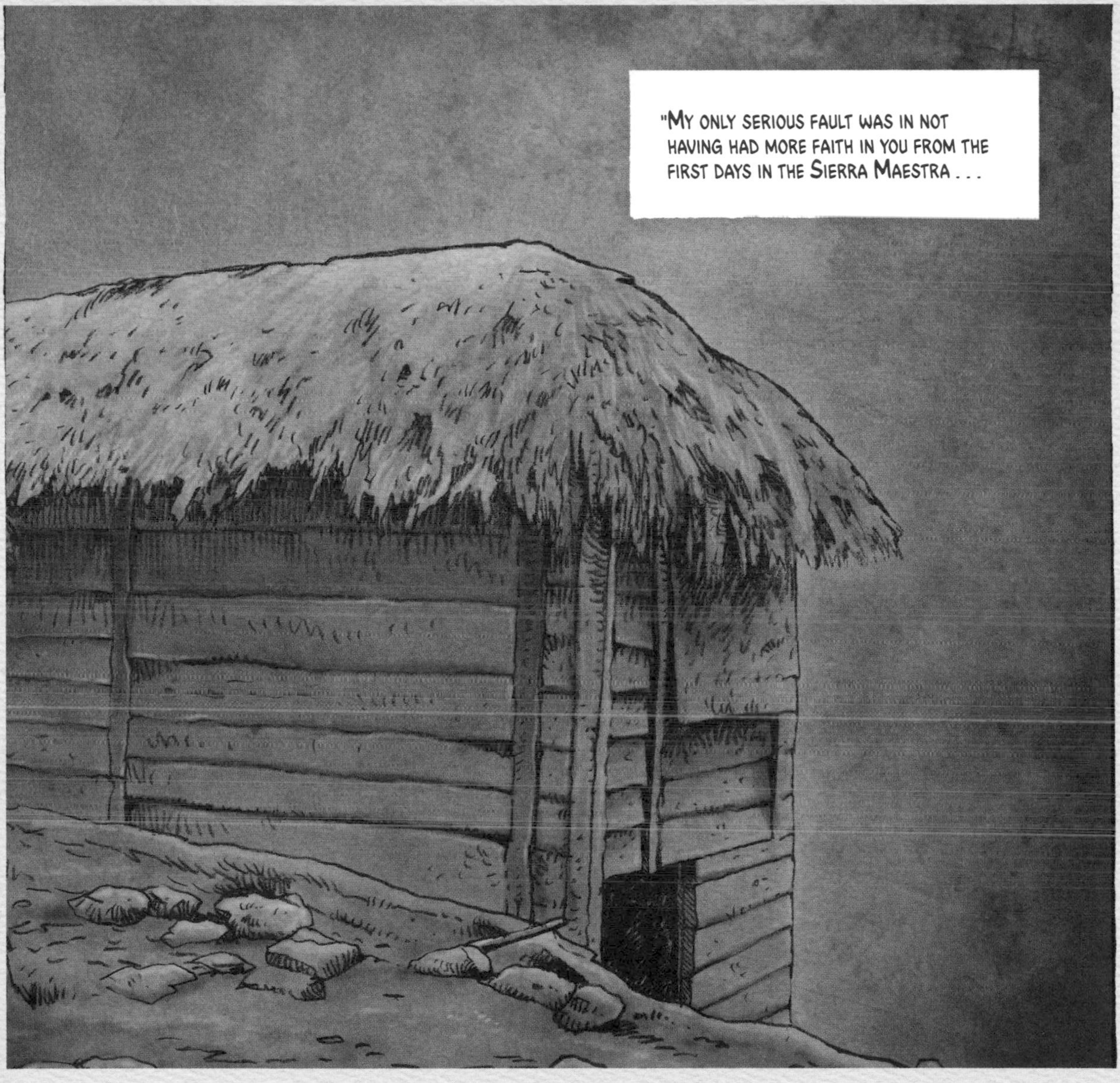
"My only serious fault was in not having had more faith in you from the first days in the Sierra Maestra . . .

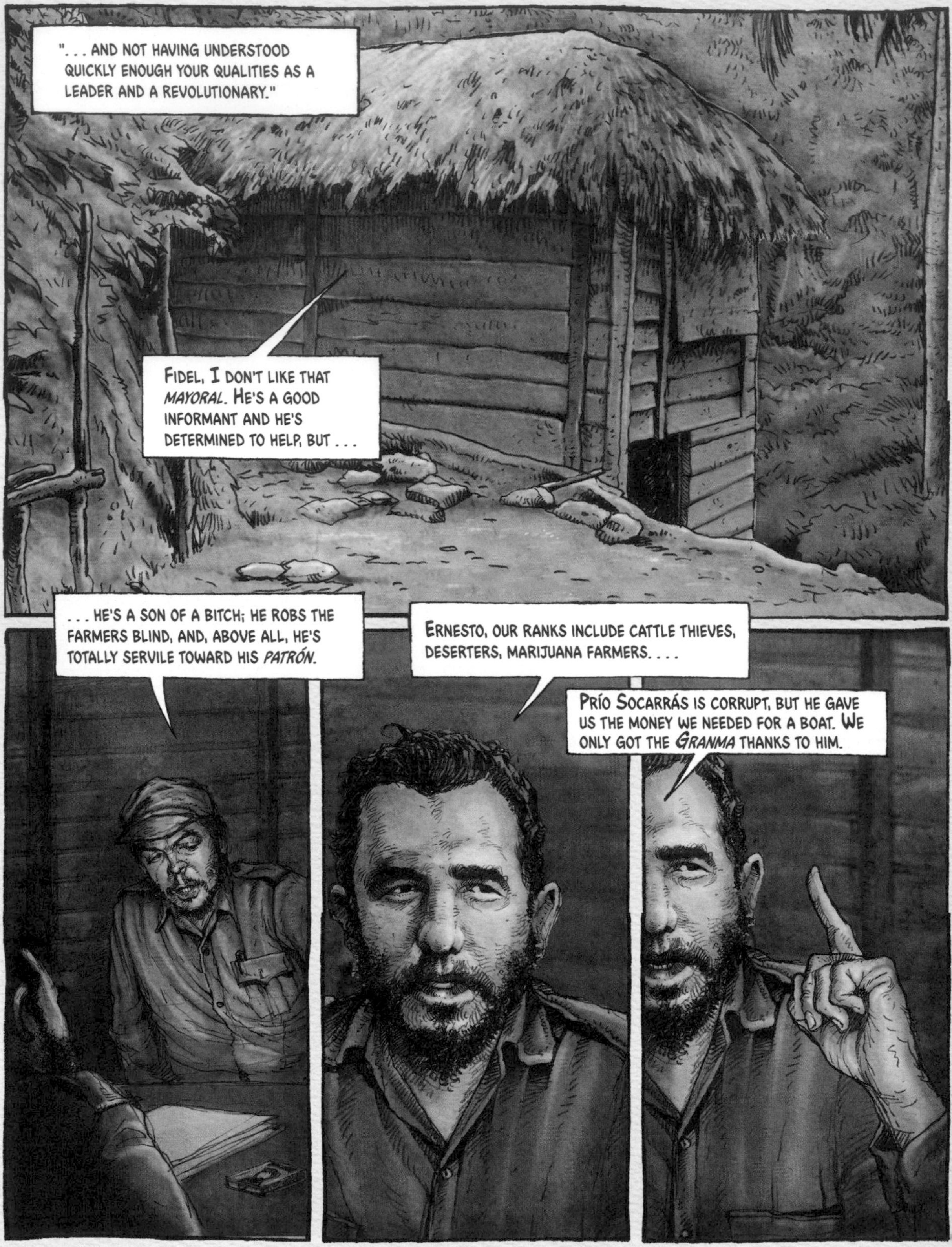
". . . AND NOT HAVING UNDERSTOOD QUICKLY ENOUGH YOUR QUALITIES AS A LEADER AND A REVOLUTIONARY."
FIDEL, I DON'T LIKE THAT *MAYORAL*. HE'S A GOOD INFORMANT AND HE'S DETERMINED TO HELP, BUT . . .
. . . HE'S A SON OF A BITCH; HE ROBS THE FARMERS BLIND, AND, ABOVE ALL, HE'S TOTALLY SERVILE TOWARD HIS *PATRÓN*.
ERNESTO, OUR RANKS INCLUDE CATTLE THIEVES, DESERTERS, MARIJUANA FARMERS. . . .
PRÍO SOCARRÁS IS CORRUPT, BUT HE GAVE US THE MONEY WE NEEDED FOR A BOAT. WE ONLY GOT THE *GRANMA* THANKS TO HIM.

THE REVOLUTION IS NOT CARRIED OUT WITH SAINTS, ERNESTO; IT'S MADE BY REAL PEOPLE.

FIDEL, HERE'S THE CONDOLENCE LETTER FOR FRANK PAÍS.

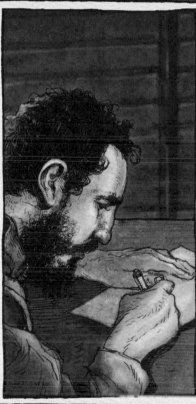

YOU SIGN IT TOO, ERNESTO.

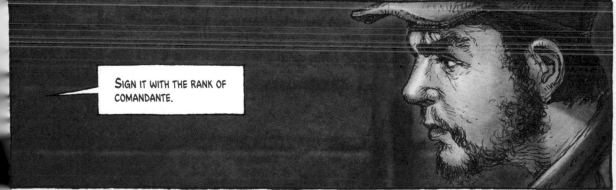

SIGN IT WITH THE RANK OF COMANDANTE.

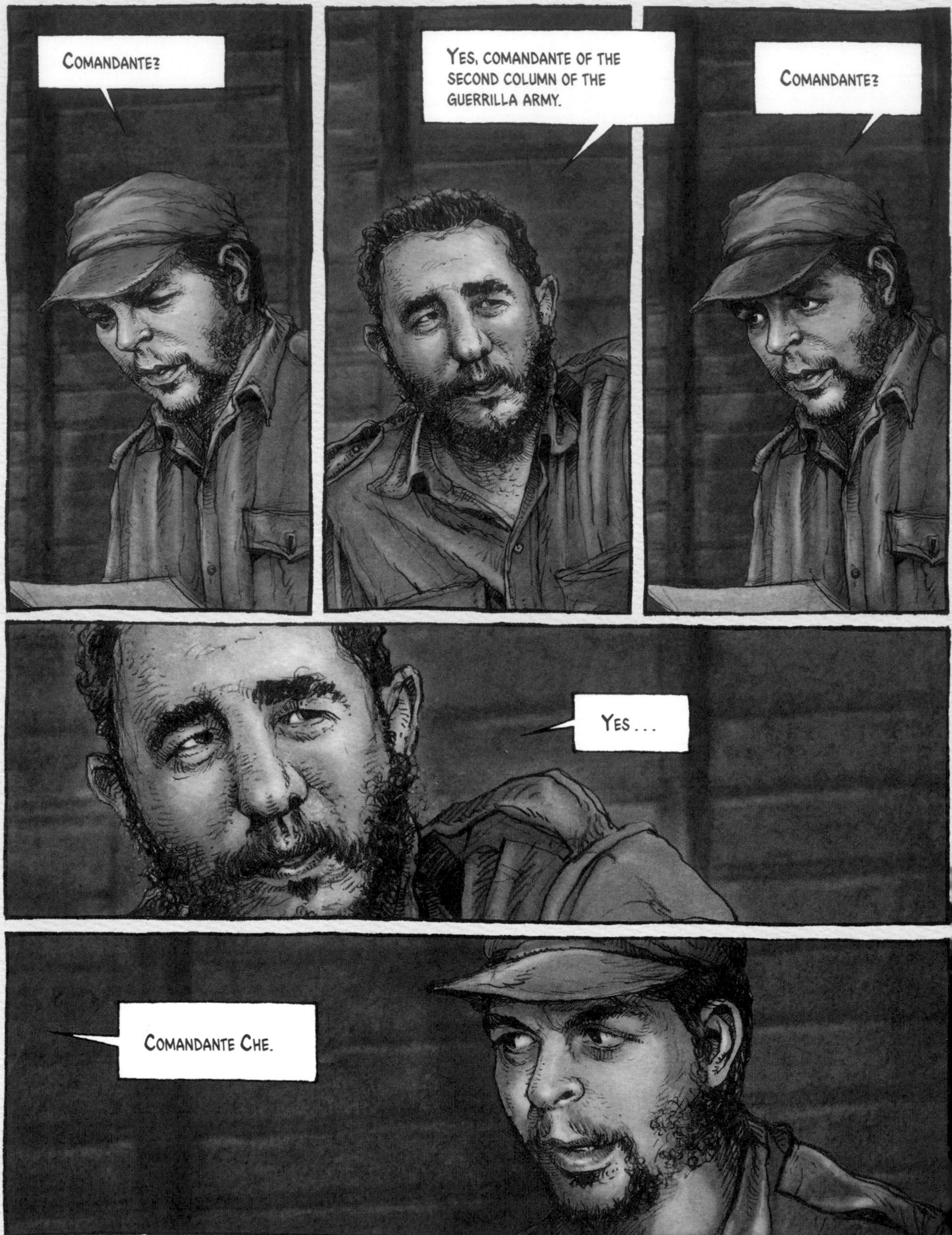
Comandante?
Yes, comandante of the second column of the guerrilla army.
Comandante?
Yes...
Comandante Che.

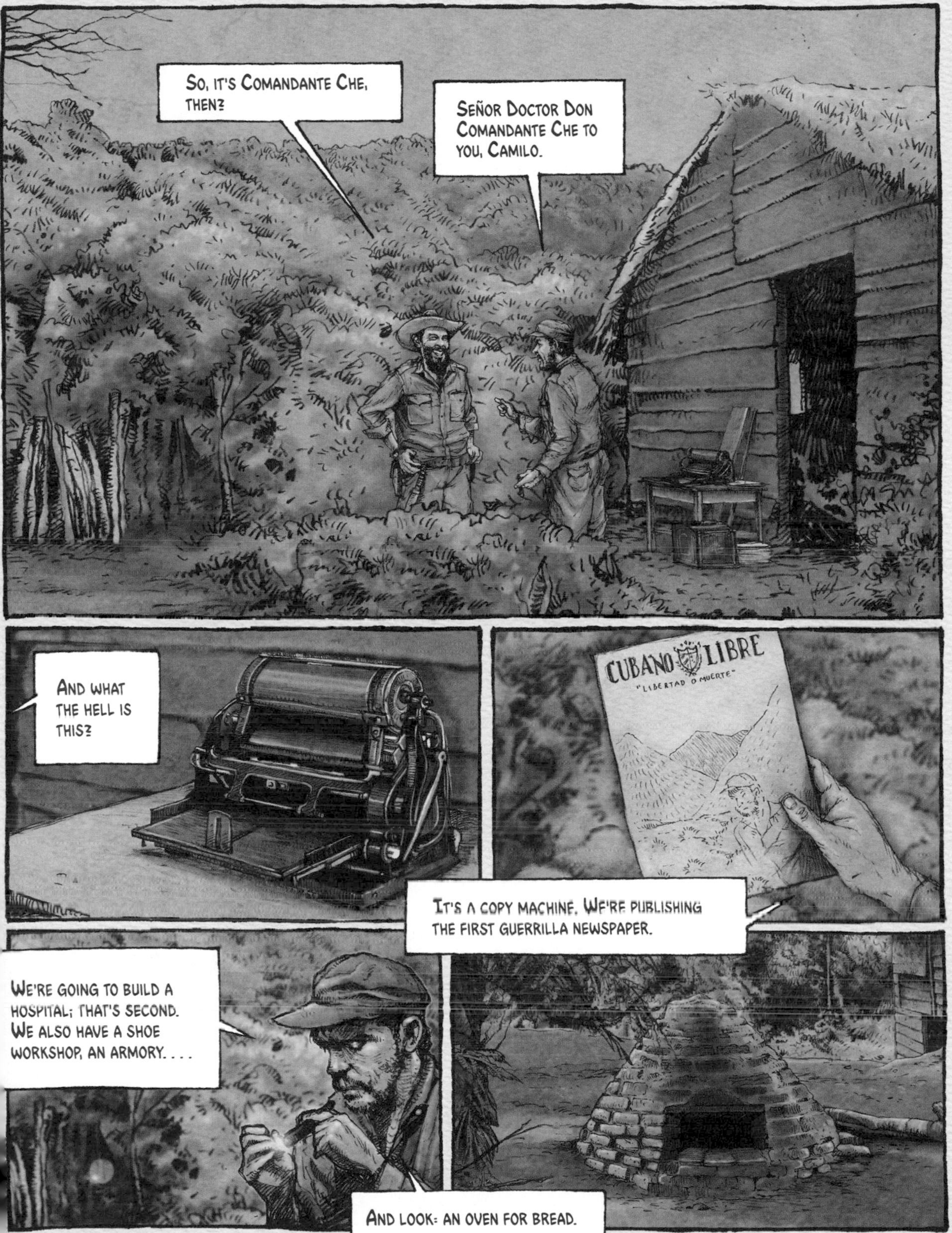
So, it's Comandante Che, then?
Señor Doctor Don Comandante Che to you, Camilo.
And what the hell is this?
CUBANO LIBRE
"LIBERTAD O MUERTE"
It's a copy machine. We're publishing the first guerrilla newspaper.
We're going to build a hospital; that's second. We also have a shoe workshop, an armory. . . .
And look: an oven for bread.

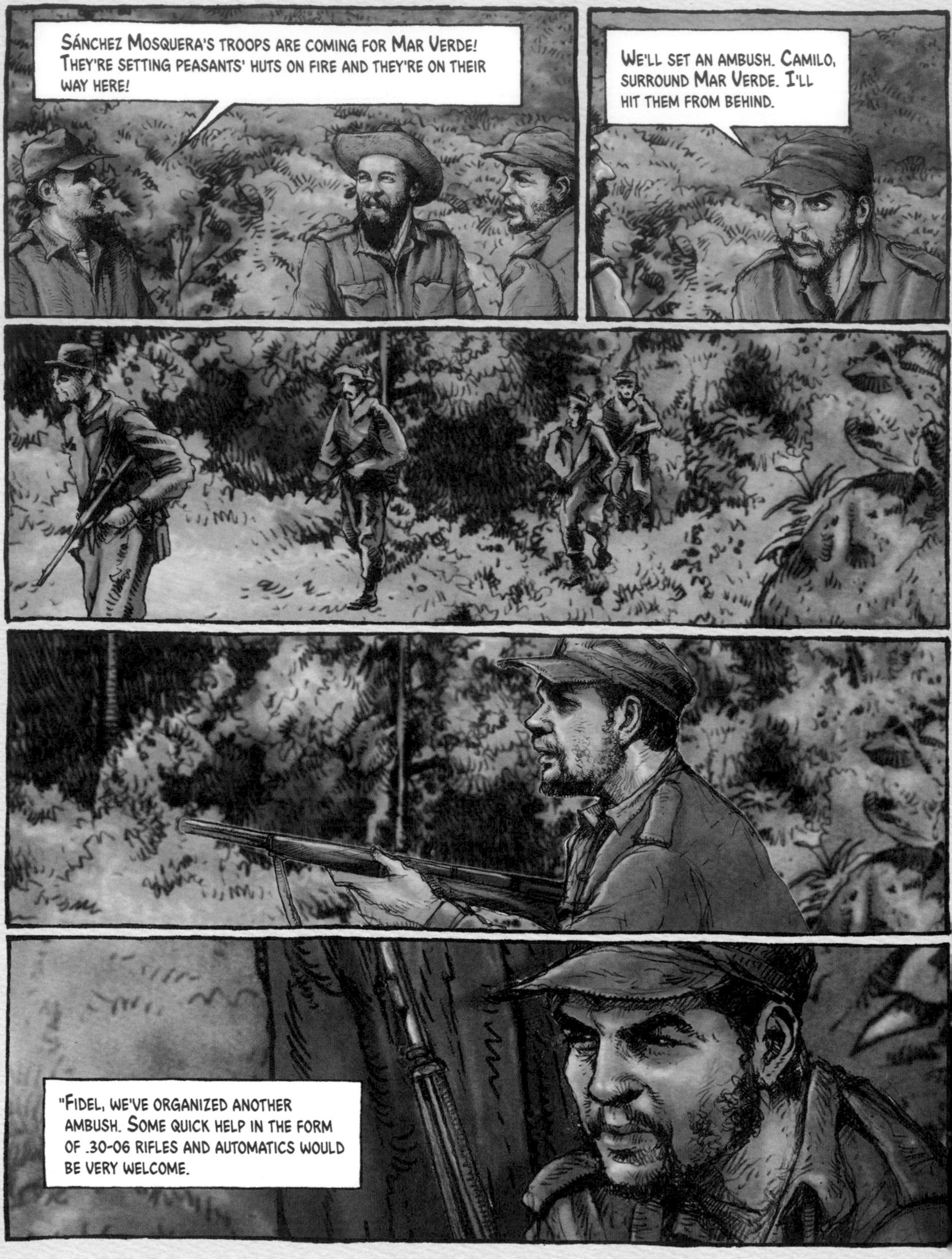
SÁNCHEZ MOSQUERA'S TROOPS ARE COMING FOR MAR VERDE! THEY'RE SETTING PEASANTS' HUTS ON FIRE AND THEY'RE ON THEIR WAY HERE!
WE'LL SET AN AMBUSH. CAMILO, SURROUND MAR VERDE. I'LL HIT THEM FROM BEHIND.
"FIDEL, WE'VE ORGANIZED ANOTHER AMBUSH. SOME QUICK HELP IN THE FORM OF .30-06 RIFLES AND AUTOMATICS WOULD BE VERY WELCOME.

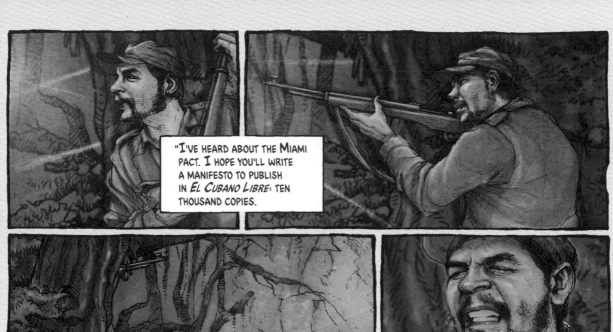

"I'VE HEARD ABOUT THE MIAMI PACT. I HOPE YOU'LL WRITE A MANIFESTO TO PUBLISH IN *EL CUBANO LIBRE*: TEN THOUSAND COPIES.

"IT'S SABOTAGE. I HOPE YOU'LL ALLOW ME TO TAKE STERN MEASURES. OTHERWISE, I'LL PRESENT MY RESIGNATION.

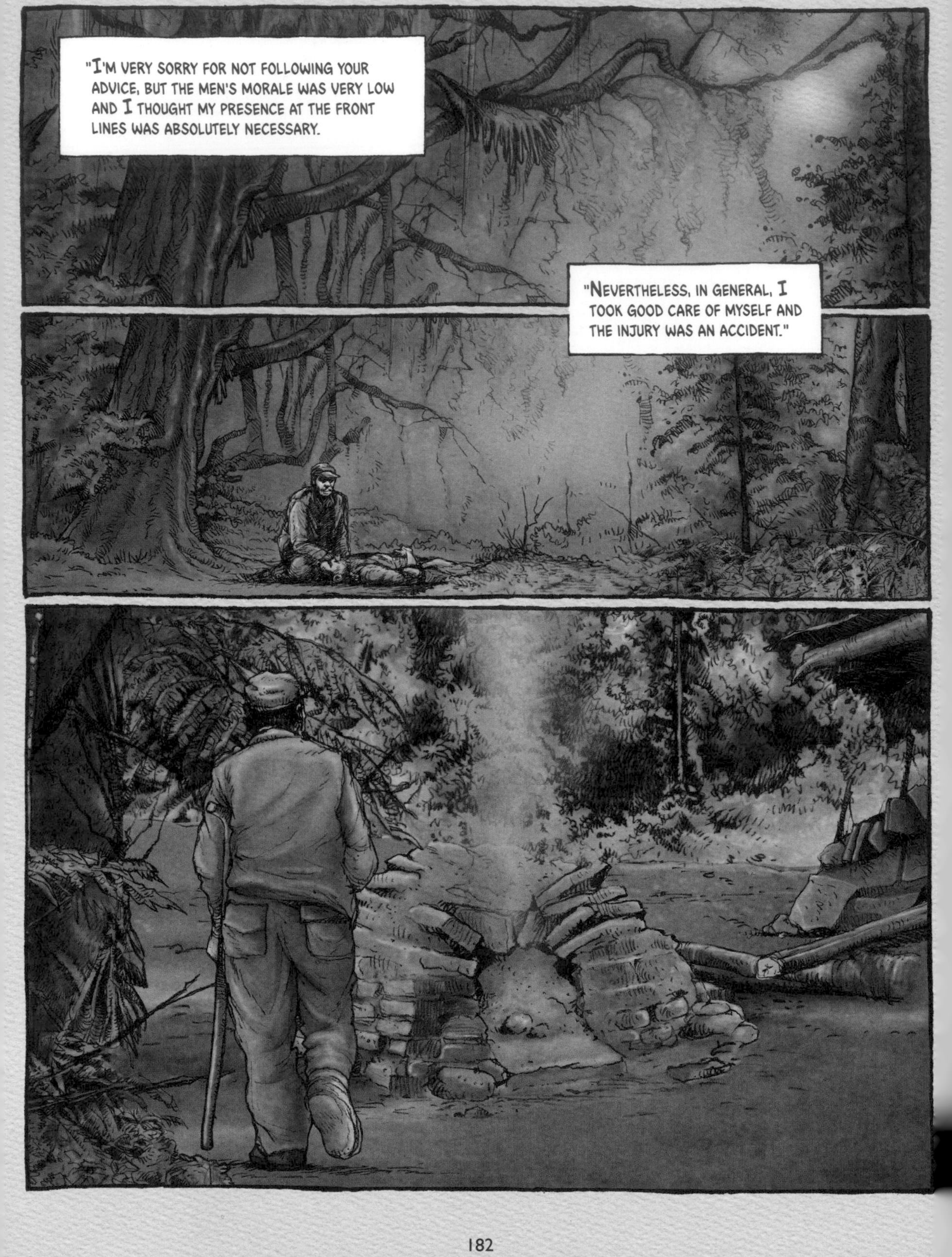
"I'M VERY SORRY FOR NOT FOLLOWING YOUR ADVICE, BUT THE MEN'S MORALE WAS VERY LOW AND I THOUGHT MY PRESENCE AT THE FRONT LINES WAS ABSOLUTELY NECESSARY.
"NEVERTHELESS, IN GENERAL, I TOOK GOOD CARE OF MYSELF AND THE INJURY WAS AN ACCIDENT."

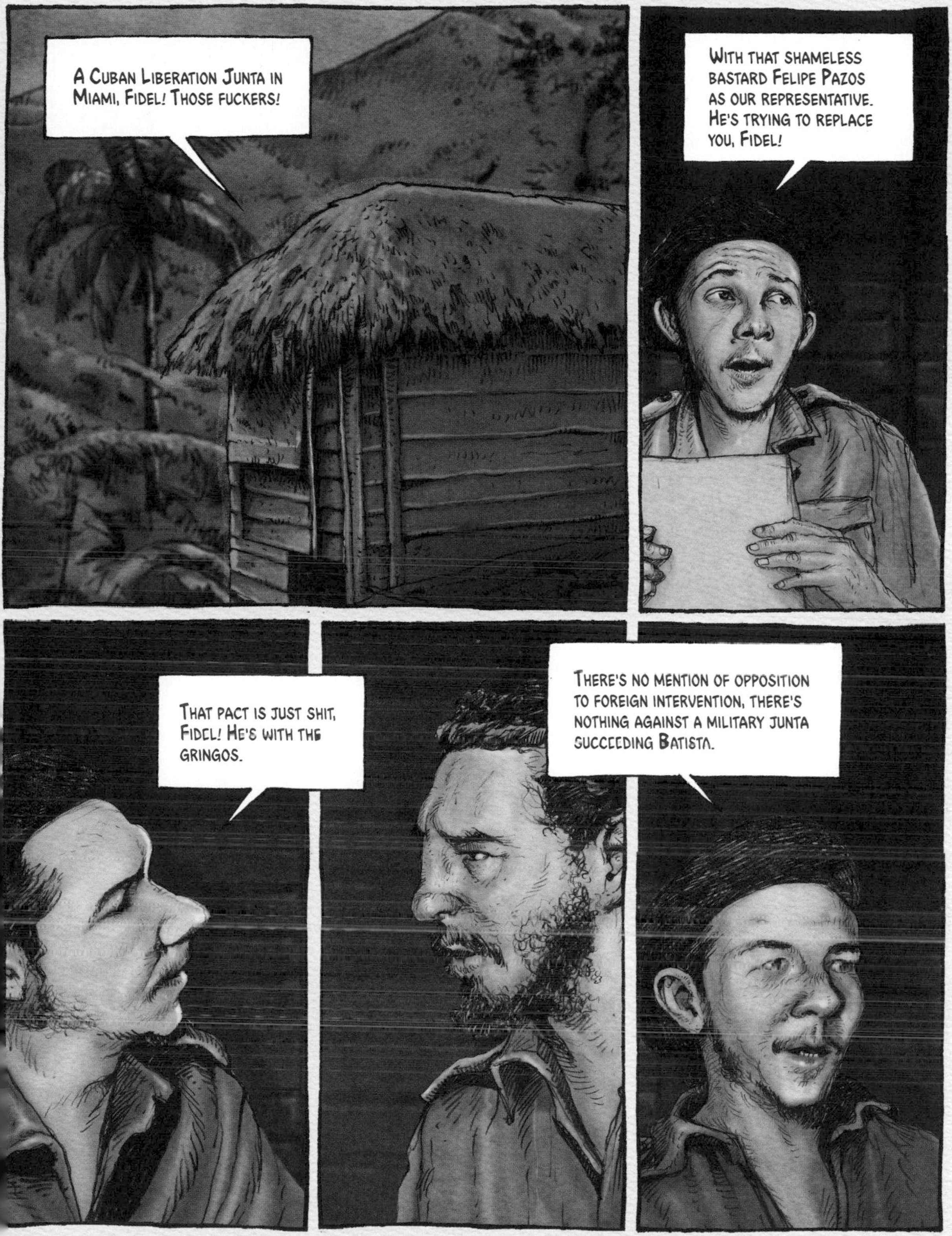
A Cuban Liberation Junta in Miami, Fidel! Those fuckers!
With that shameless bastard Felipe Pazos as our representative. He's trying to replace you, Fidel!
That pact is just shit, Fidel! He's with the gringos.
There's no mention of opposition to foreign intervention, there's nothing against a military junta succeeding Batista.

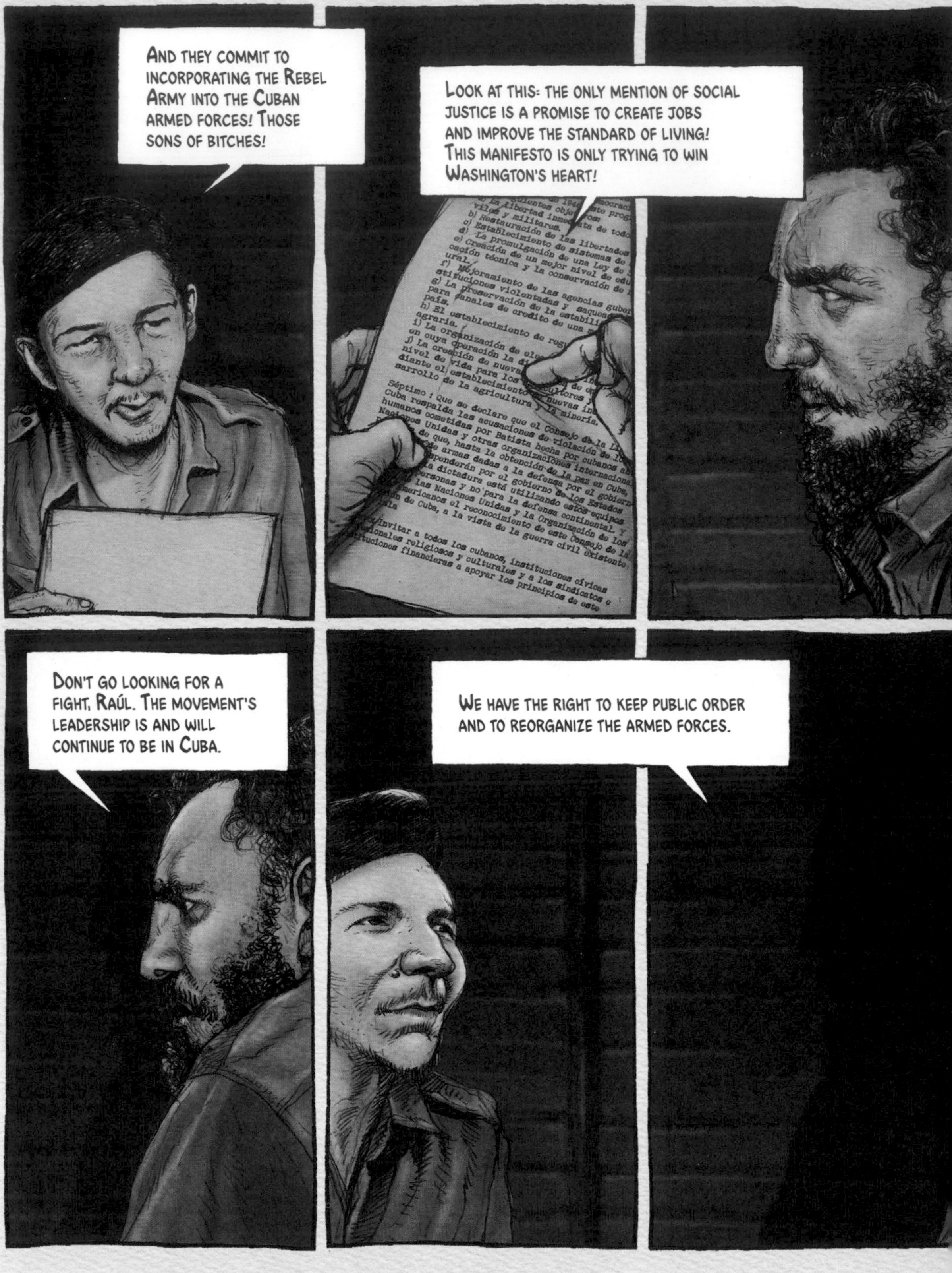
AND THEY COMMIT TO INCORPORATING THE REBEL ARMY INTO THE CUBAN ARMED FORCES! THOSE SONS OF BITCHES!
LOOK AT THIS: THE ONLY MENTION OF SOCIAL JUSTICE IS A PROMISE TO CREATE JOBS AND IMPROVE THE STANDARD OF LIVING! THIS MANIFESTO IS ONLY TRYING TO WIN WASHINGTON'S HEART!
DON'T GO LOOKING FOR A FIGHT, RAÚL. THE MOVEMENT'S LEADERSHIP IS AND WILL CONTINUE TO BE IN CUBA.
WE HAVE THE RIGHT TO KEEP PUBLIC ORDER AND TO REORGANIZE THE ARMED FORCES.

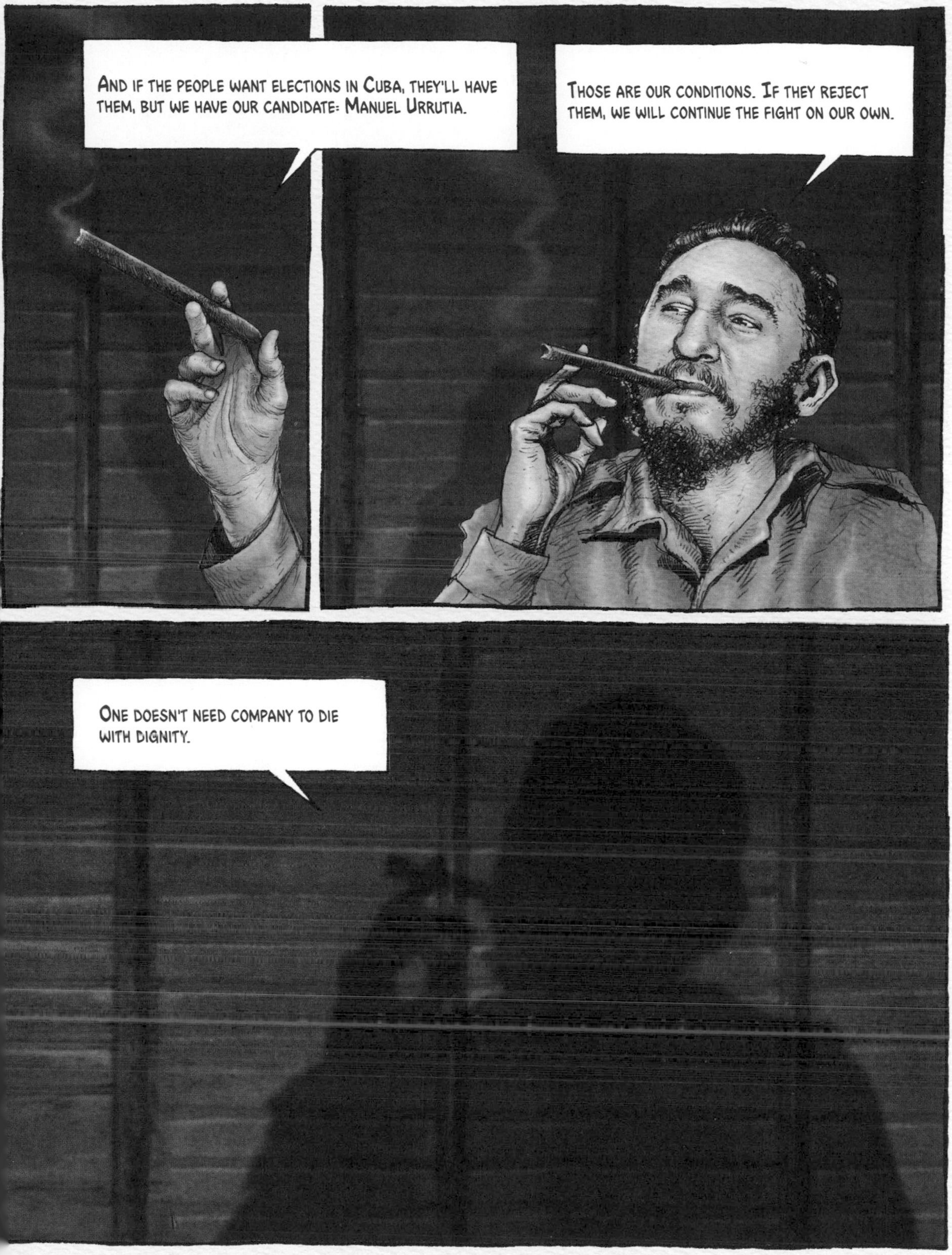
And if the people want elections in Cuba, they'll have them, but we have our candidate: Manuel Urrutia.
Those are our conditions. If they reject them, we will continue the fight on our own.
One doesn't need company to die with dignity.

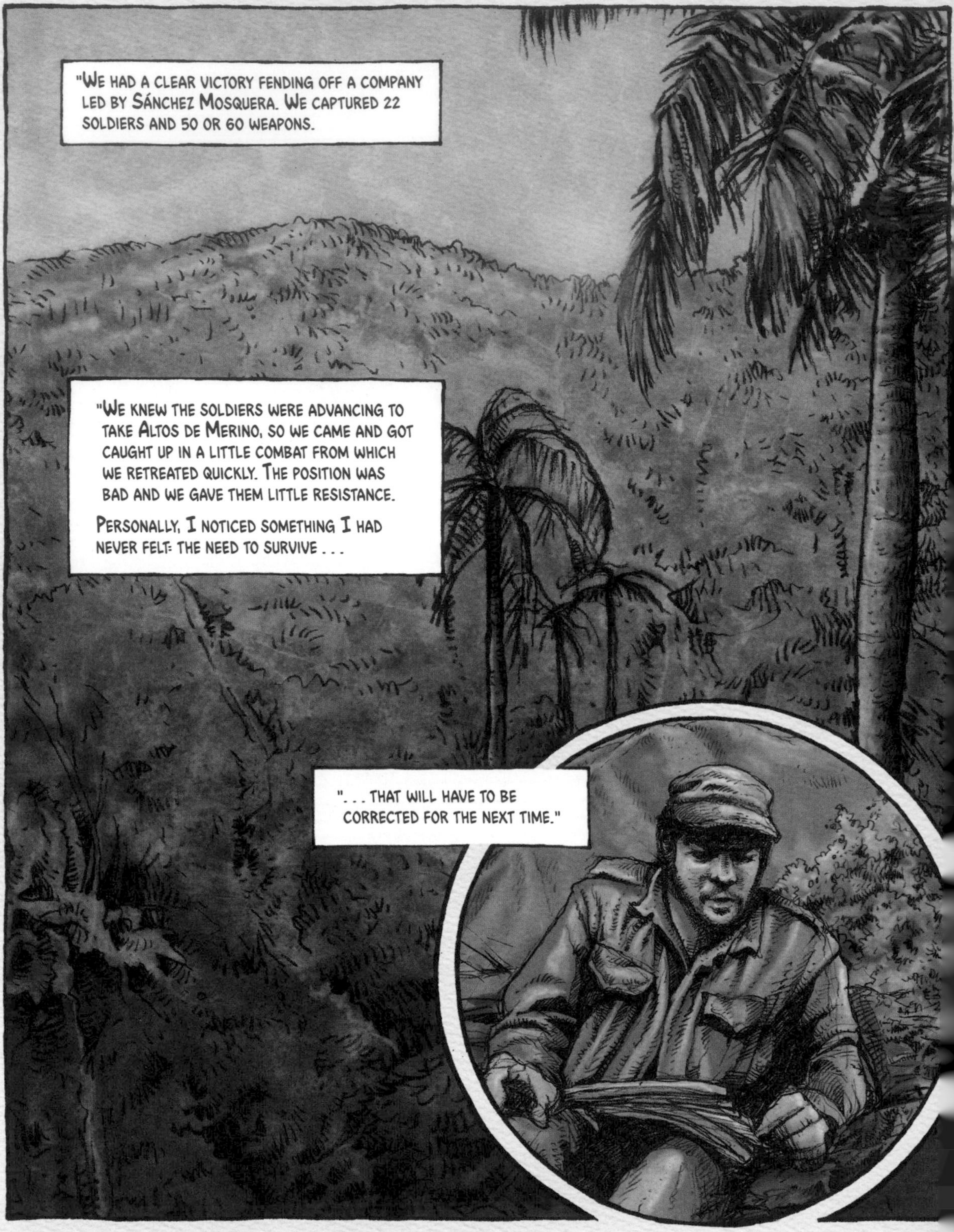
"We had a clear victory fending off a company led by Sánchez Mosquera. We captured 22 soldiers and 50 or 60 weapons.
"We knew the soldiers were advancing to take Altos de Merino, so we came and got caught up in a little combat from which we retreated quickly. The position was bad and we gave them little resistance.
Personally, I noticed something I had never felt: the need to survive . . .
". . . that will have to be corrected for the next time."

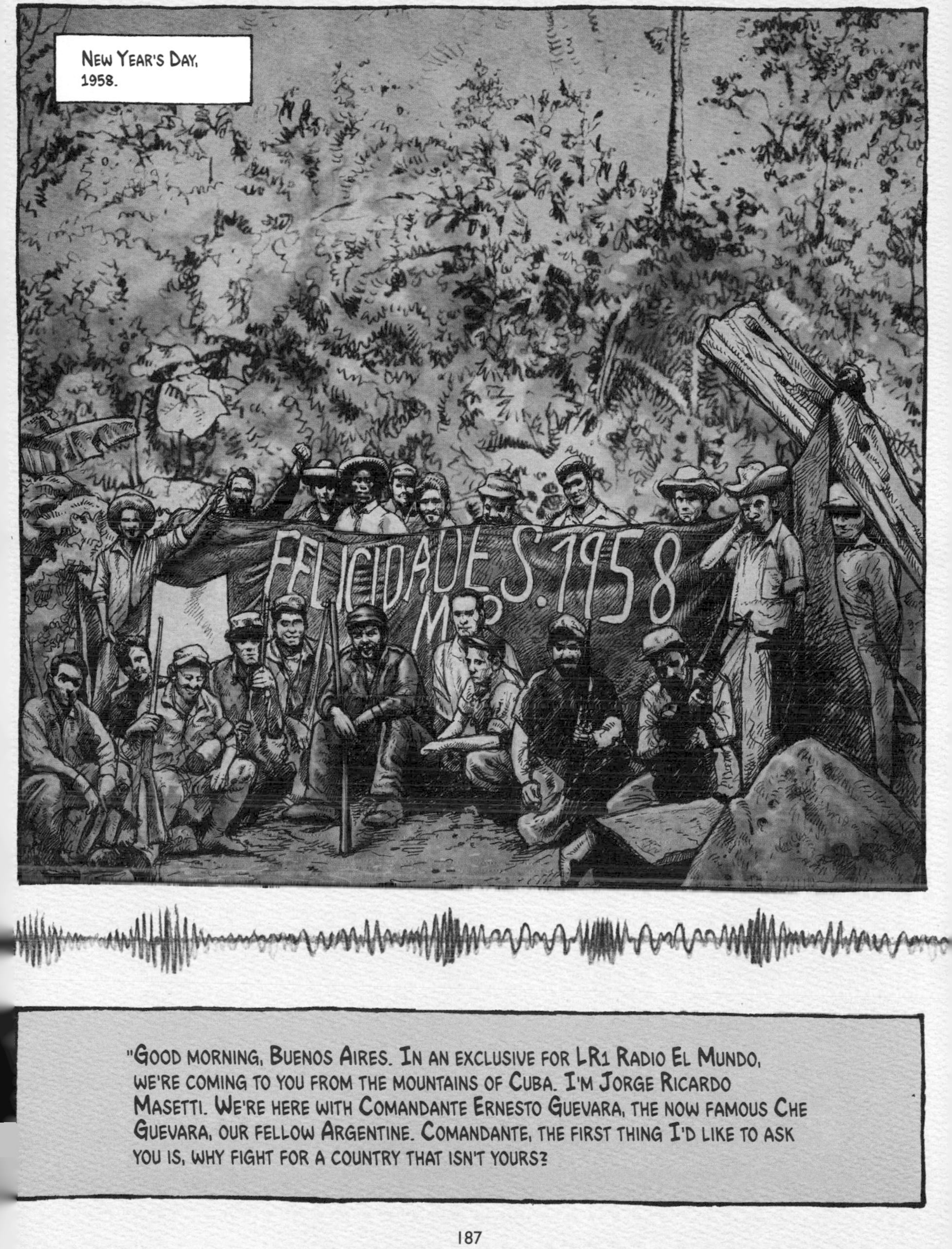
NEW YEAR'S DAY, 1958.

"GOOD MORNING, BUENOS AIRES. IN AN EXCLUSIVE FOR LR1 RADIO EL MUNDO, WE'RE COMING TO YOU FROM THE MOUNTAINS OF CUBA. I'M JORGE RICARDO MASETTI. WE'RE HERE WITH COMANDANTE ERNESTO GUEVARA, THE NOW FAMOUS CHE GUEVARA, OUR FELLOW ARGENTINE. COMANDANTE, THE FIRST THING I'D LIKE TO ASK YOU IS, WHY FIGHT FOR A COUNTRY THAT ISN'T YOURS?

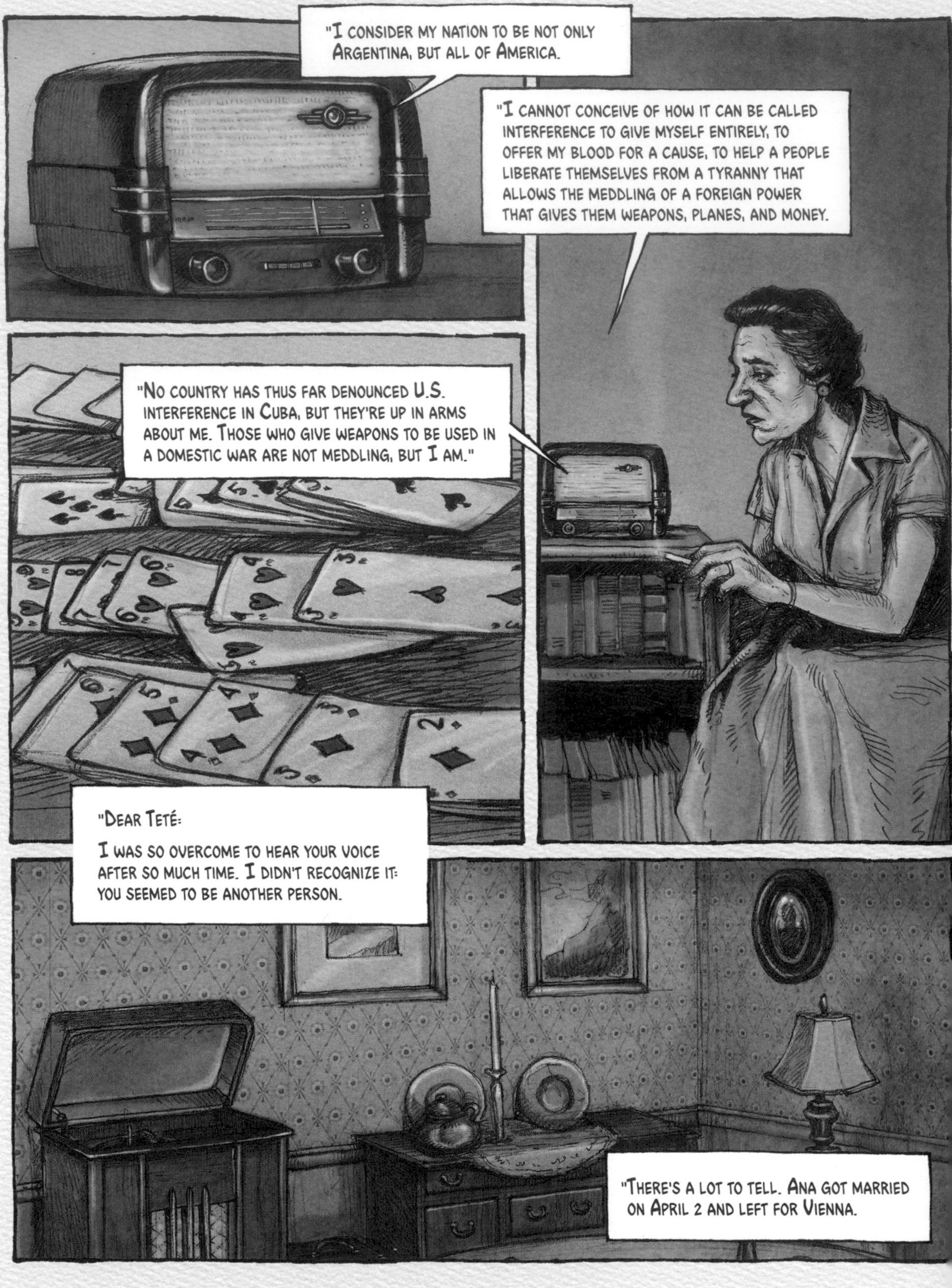
"I CONSIDER MY NATION TO BE NOT ONLY ARGENTINA, BUT ALL OF AMERICA.
"I CANNOT CONCEIVE OF HOW IT CAN BE CALLED INTERFERENCE TO GIVE MYSELF ENTIRELY, TO OFFER MY BLOOD FOR A CAUSE, TO HELP A PEOPLE LIBERATE THEMSELVES FROM A TYRANNY THAT ALLOWS THE MEDDLING OF A FOREIGN POWER THAT GIVES THEM WEAPONS, PLANES, AND MONEY.
"NO COUNTRY HAS THUS FAR DENOUNCED U.S. INTERFERENCE IN CUBA, BUT THEY'RE UP IN ARMS ABOUT ME. THOSE WHO GIVE WEAPONS TO BE USED IN A DOMESTIC WAR ARE NOT MEDDLING, BUT I AM."
"DEAR TETÉ:
I WAS SO OVERCOME TO HEAR YOUR VOICE AFTER SO MUCH TIME. I DIDN'T RECOGNIZE IT: YOU SEEMED TO BE ANOTHER PERSON.
"THERE'S A LOT TO TELL. ANA GOT MARRIED ON APRIL 2 AND LEFT FOR VIENNA.

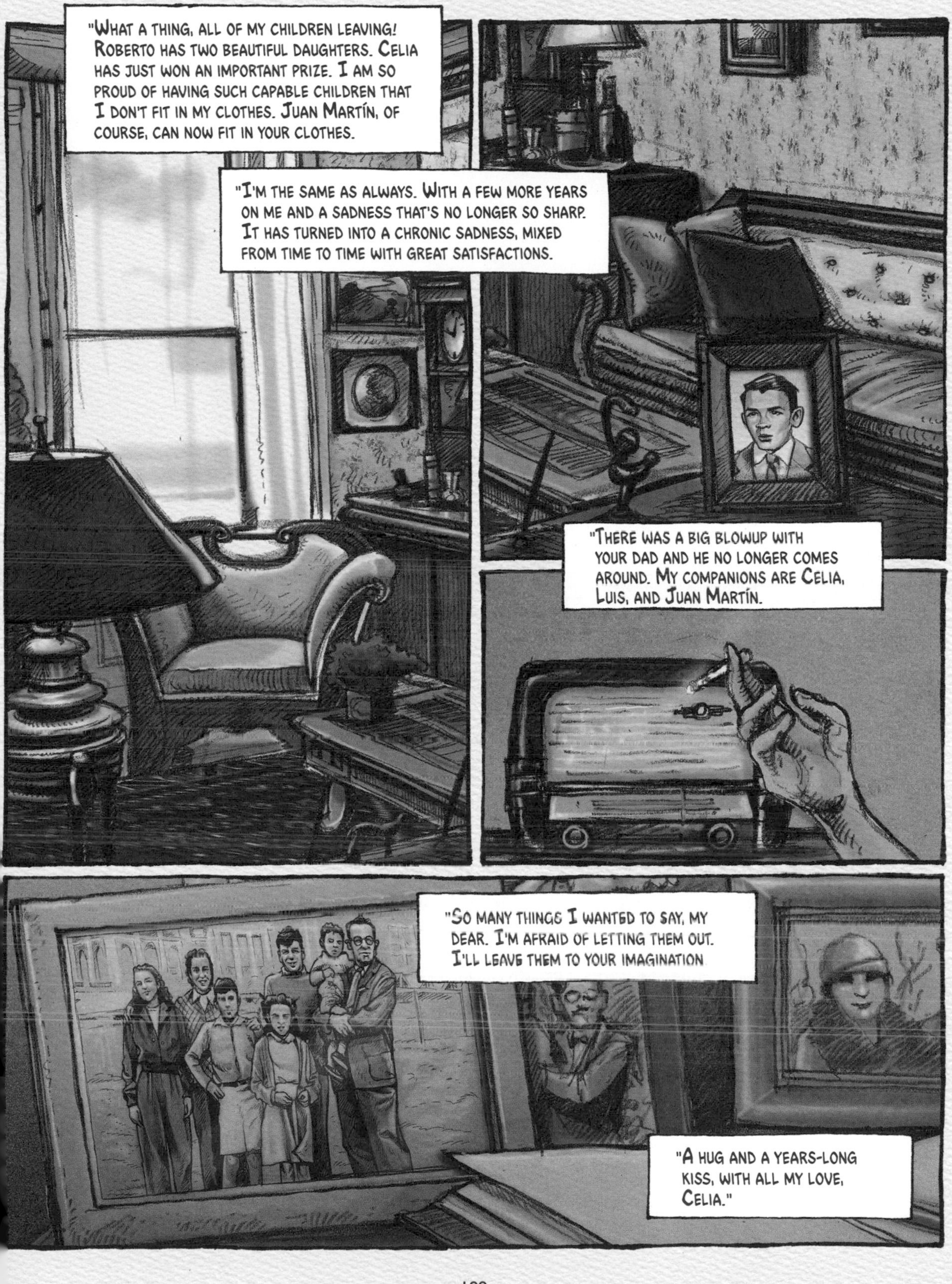
"What a thing, all of my children leaving! Roberto has two beautiful daughters. Celia has just won an important prize. I am so proud of having such capable children that I don't fit in my clothes. Juan Martín, of course, can now fit in your clothes.
"I'm the same as always. With a few more years on me and a sadness that's no longer so sharp. It has turned into a chronic sadness, mixed from time to time with great satisfactions.
"There was a big blowup with your dad and he no longer comes around. My companions are Celia, Luis, and Juan Martín.
"So many things I wanted to say, my dear. I'm afraid of letting them out. I'll leave them to your imagination
"A hug and a years-long kiss, with all my love, Celia."

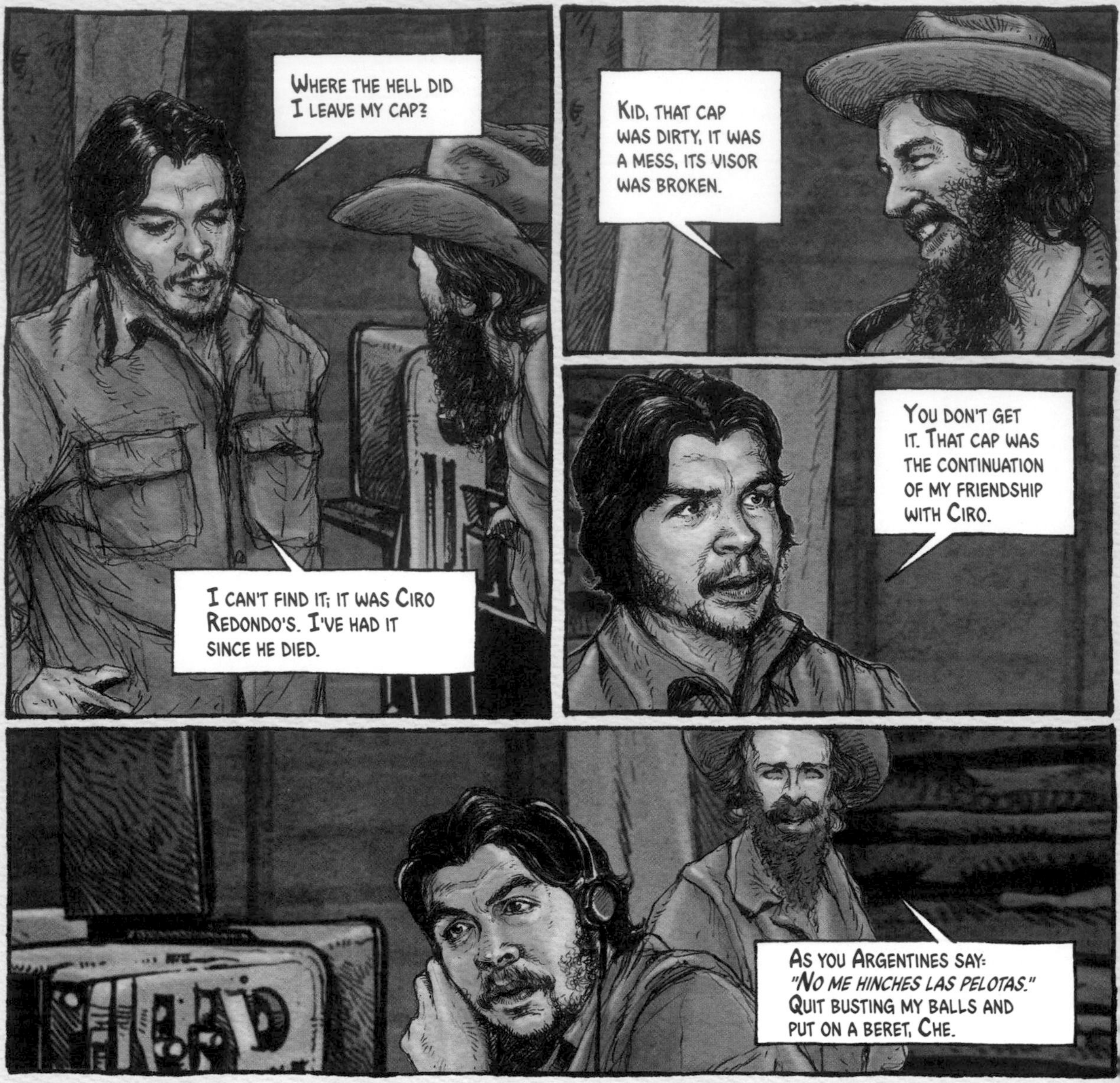
WHERE THE HELL DID I LEAVE MY CAP?
I CAN'T FIND IT; IT WAS CIRO REDONDO'S. I'VE HAD IT SINCE HE DIED.
KID, THAT CAP WAS DIRTY, IT WAS A MESS, ITS VISOR WAS BROKEN.
YOU DON'T GET IT. THAT CAP WAS THE CONTINUATION OF MY FRIENDSHIP WITH CIRO.
AS YOU ARGENTINES SAY: *"NO ME HINCHES LAS PELOTAS."* QUIT BUSTING MY BALLS AND PUT ON A BERET, CHE.

"RADIO REBELDE HERE, FROM THE EASTERN MOUNTAINS, FREE CUBAN TERRITORY! WE ARE CALLING FOR A GENERAL STRIKE, AND TOTAL WAR AGAINST THE REGIME. STARTING ON APRIL FIRST, NO TAXES ARE TO BE PAID. STARTING ON THE FIFTH, ANYONE STILL IN EXECUTIVE POWER WILL BE CONSIDERED A TRAITOR AND ANYONE WHO JOINS THE ARMED FORCES WILL BE CONSIDERED A CRIMINAL."

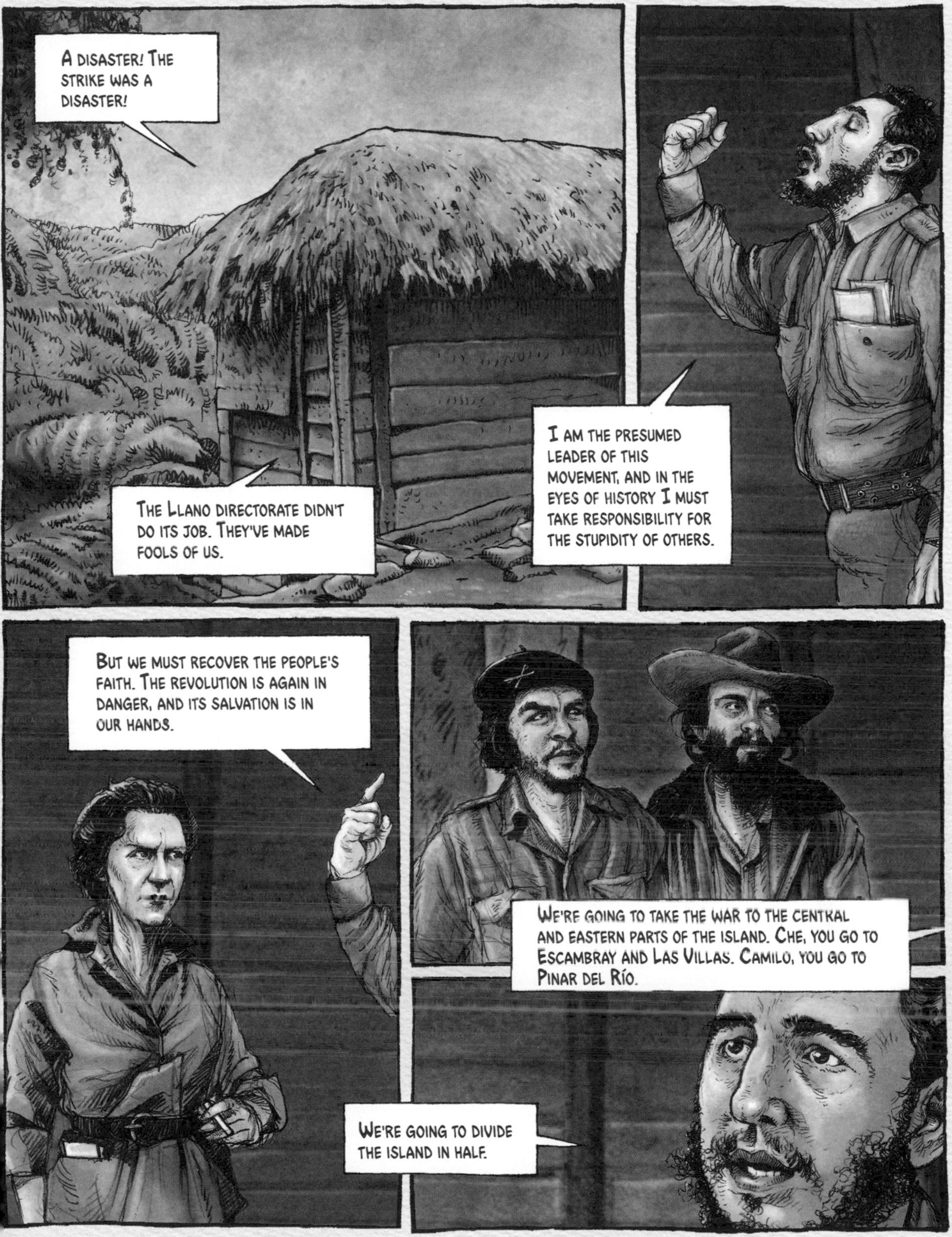
A DISASTER! THE STRIKE WAS A DISASTER!
THE LLANO DIRECTORATE DIDN'T DO ITS JOB. THEY'VE MADE FOOLS OF US.
I AM THE PRESUMED LEADER OF THIS MOVEMENT, AND IN THE EYES OF HISTORY I MUST TAKE RESPONSIBILITY FOR THE STUPIDITY OF OTHERS.
BUT WE MUST RECOVER THE PEOPLE'S FAITH. THE REVOLUTION IS AGAIN IN DANGER, AND ITS SALVATION IS IN OUR HANDS.
WE'RE GOING TO TAKE THE WAR TO THE CENTRAL AND EASTERN PARTS OF THE ISLAND. CHE, YOU GO TO ESCAMBRAY AND LAS VILLAS. CAMILO, YOU GO TO PINAR DEL RÍO.
WE'RE GOING TO DIVIDE THE ISLAND IN HALF.

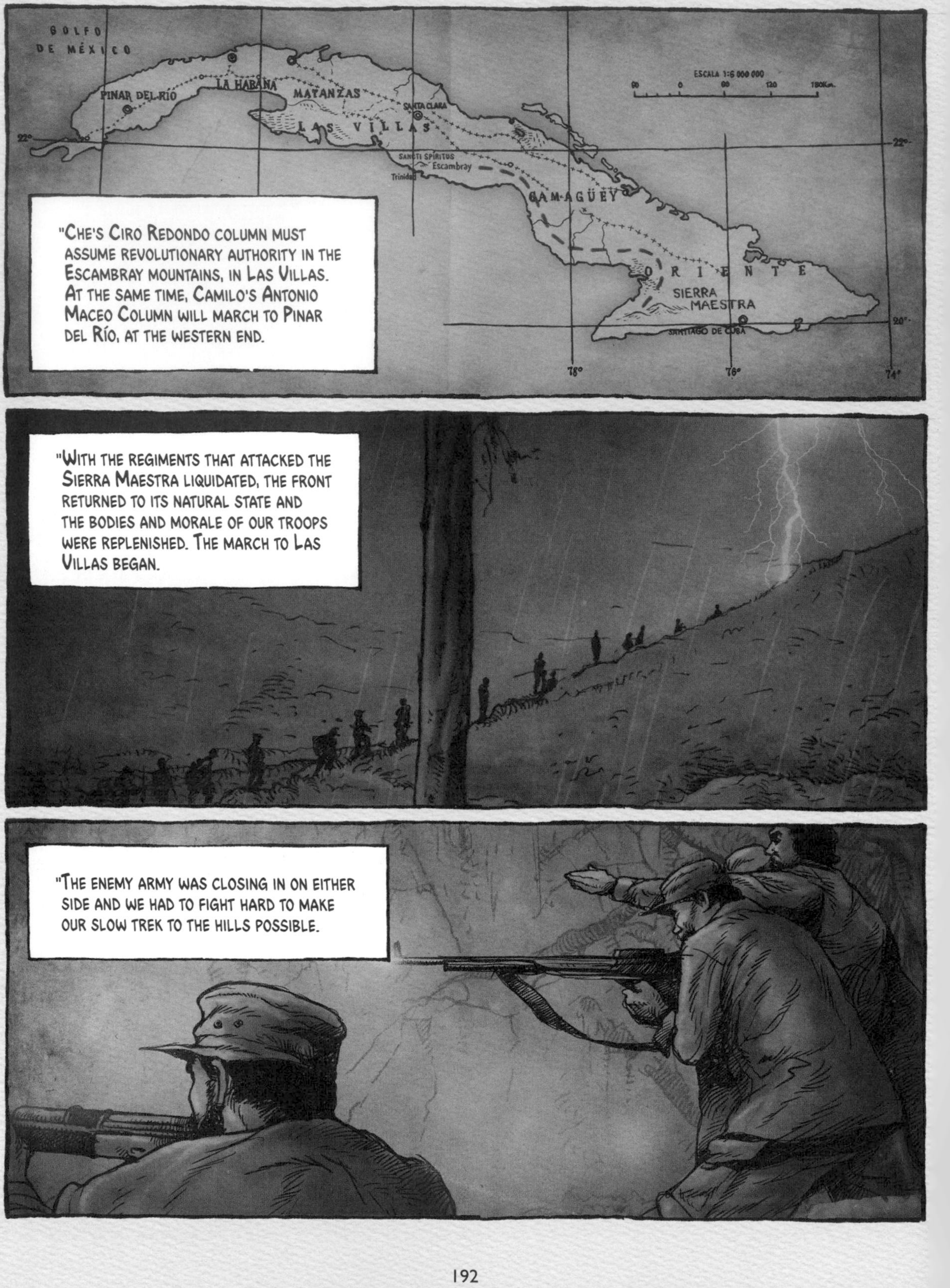
GOLFO DE MÉXICO
PINAR DEL RÍO
LA HABANA
MATANZAS
LAS VILLAS
SANTA CLARA
SANCTI SPIRITUS
Escambray
Trinidad
CAMAGÜEY
ORIENTE
SIERRA MAESTRA
SANTIAGO DE CUBA
ESCALA 1:6 000 000
"CHE'S CIRO REDONDO COLUMN MUST ASSUME REVOLUTIONARY AUTHORITY IN THE ESCAMBRAY MOUNTAINS, IN LAS VILLAS. AT THE SAME TIME, CAMILO'S ANTONIO MACEO COLUMN WILL MARCH TO PINAR DEL RÍO, AT THE WESTERN END.
"WITH THE REGIMENTS THAT ATTACKED THE SIERRA MAESTRA LIQUIDATED, THE FRONT RETURNED TO ITS NATURAL STATE AND THE BODIES AND MORALE OF OUR TROOPS WERE REPLENISHED. THE MARCH TO LAS VILLAS BEGAN.
"THE ENEMY ARMY WAS CLOSING IN ON EITHER SIDE AND WE HAD TO FIGHT HARD TO MAKE OUR SLOW TREK TO THE HILLS POSSIBLE.

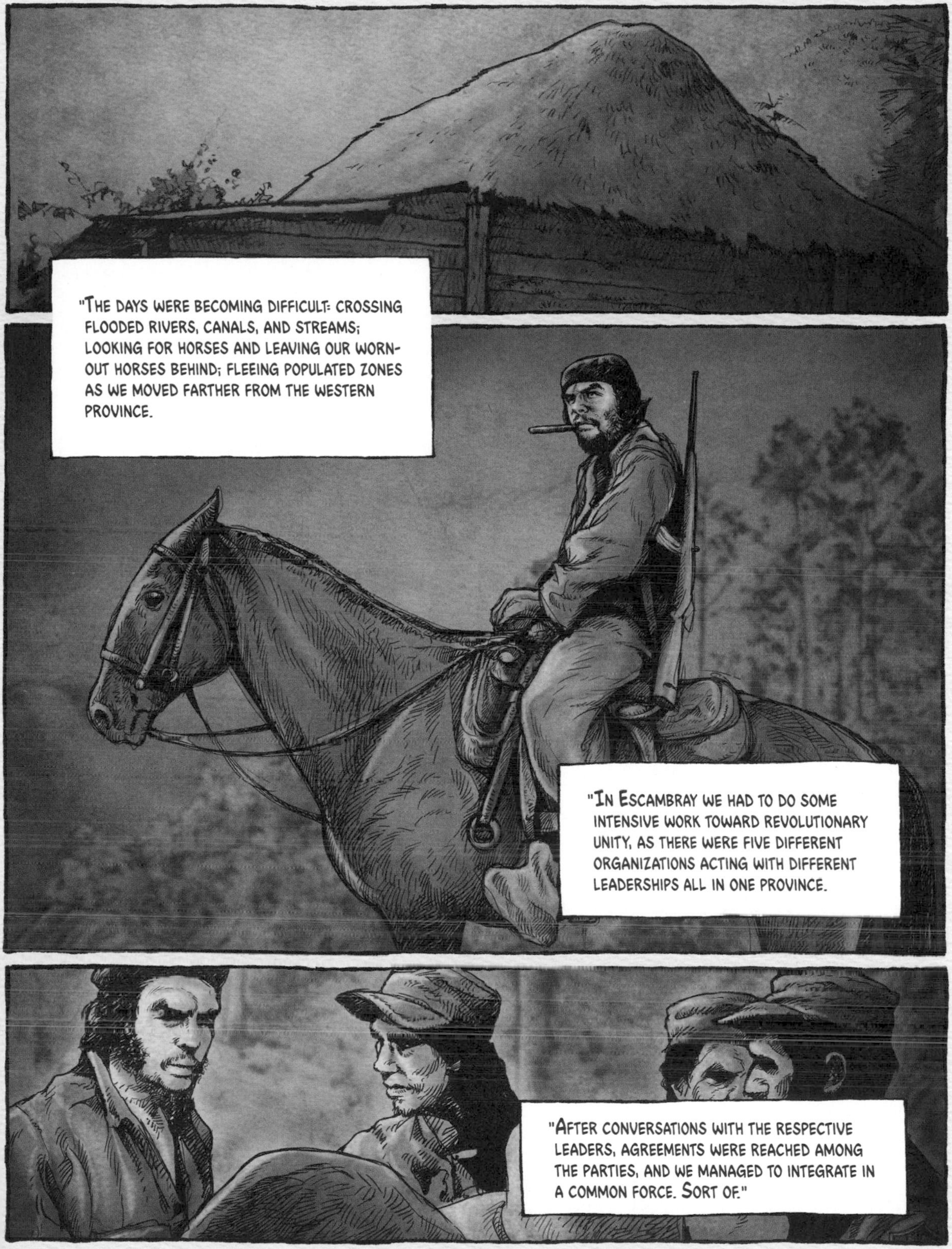
"THE DAYS WERE BECOMING DIFFICULT: CROSSING FLOODED RIVERS, CANALS, AND STREAMS; LOOKING FOR HORSES AND LEAVING OUR WORN-OUT HORSES BEHIND; FLEEING POPULATED ZONES AS WE MOVED FARTHER FROM THE WESTERN PROVINCE.
"IN ESCAMBRAY WE HAD TO DO SOME INTENSIVE WORK TOWARD REVOLUTIONARY UNITY, AS THERE WERE FIVE DIFFERENT ORGANIZATIONS ACTING WITH DIFFERENT LEADERSHIPS ALL IN ONE PROVINCE.
"AFTER CONVERSATIONS WITH THE RESPECTIVE LEADERS, AGREEMENTS WERE REACHED AMONG THE PARTIES, AND WE MANAGED TO INTEGRATE IN A COMMON FORCE. SORT OF."

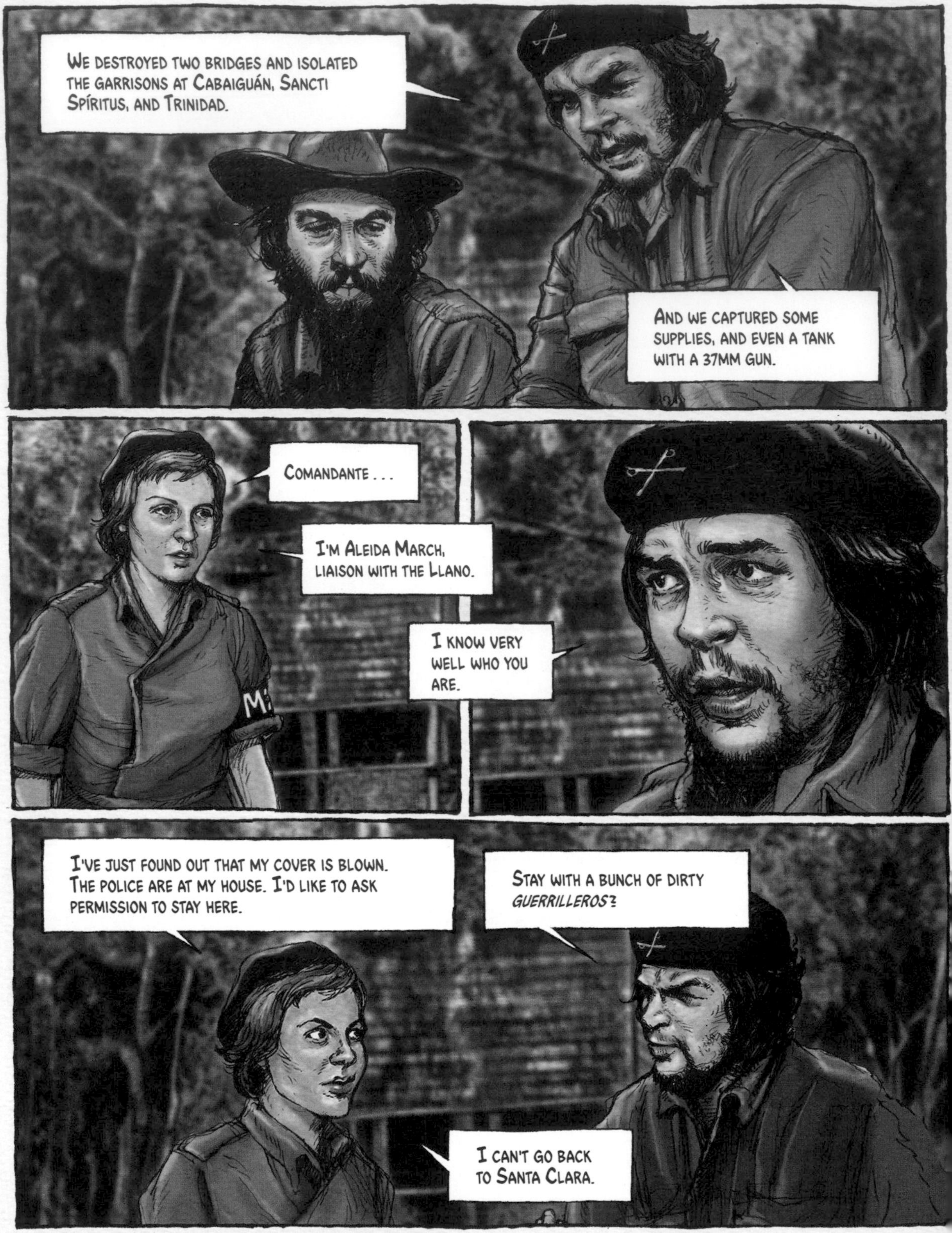
We destroyed two bridges and isolated the garrisons at Cabaiguán, Sancti Spíritus, and Trinidad.
And we captured some supplies, and even a tank with a 37mm gun.
Comandante . . .
I'm Aleida March, liaison with the Llano.
I know very well who you are.
I've just found out that my cover is blown. The police are at my house. I'd like to ask permission to stay here.
Stay with a bunch of dirty *guerrilleros*?
I can't go back to Santa Clara.

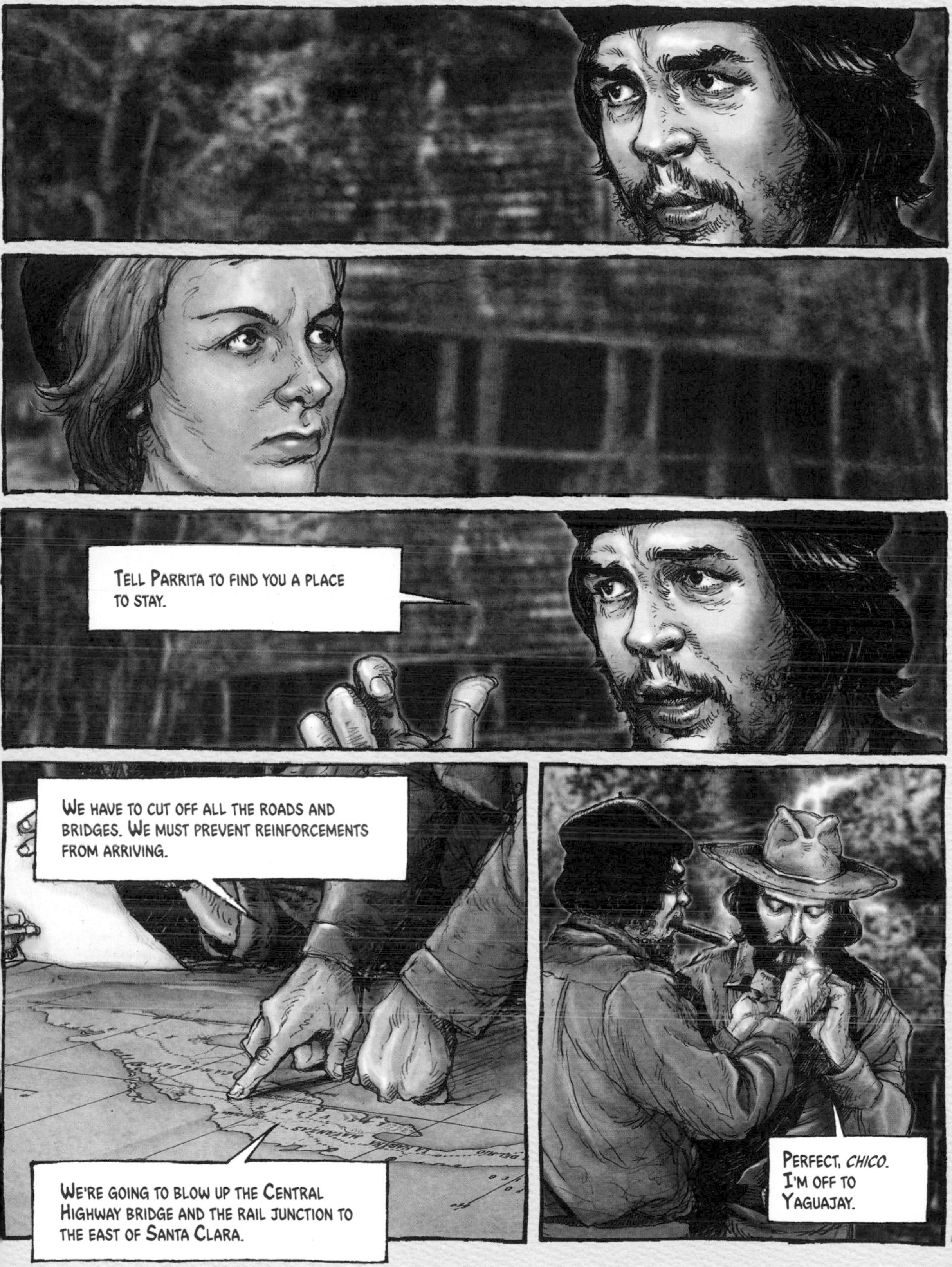
TELL PARRITA TO FIND YOU A PLACE TO STAY.
WE HAVE TO CUT OFF ALL THE ROADS AND BRIDGES. WE MUST PREVENT REINFORCEMENTS FROM ARRIVING.
WE'RE GOING TO BLOW UP THE CENTRAL HIGHWAY BRIDGE AND THE RAIL JUNCTION TO THE EAST OF SANTA CLARA.
PERFECT, *CHICO*. I'M OFF TO YAGUAJAY.

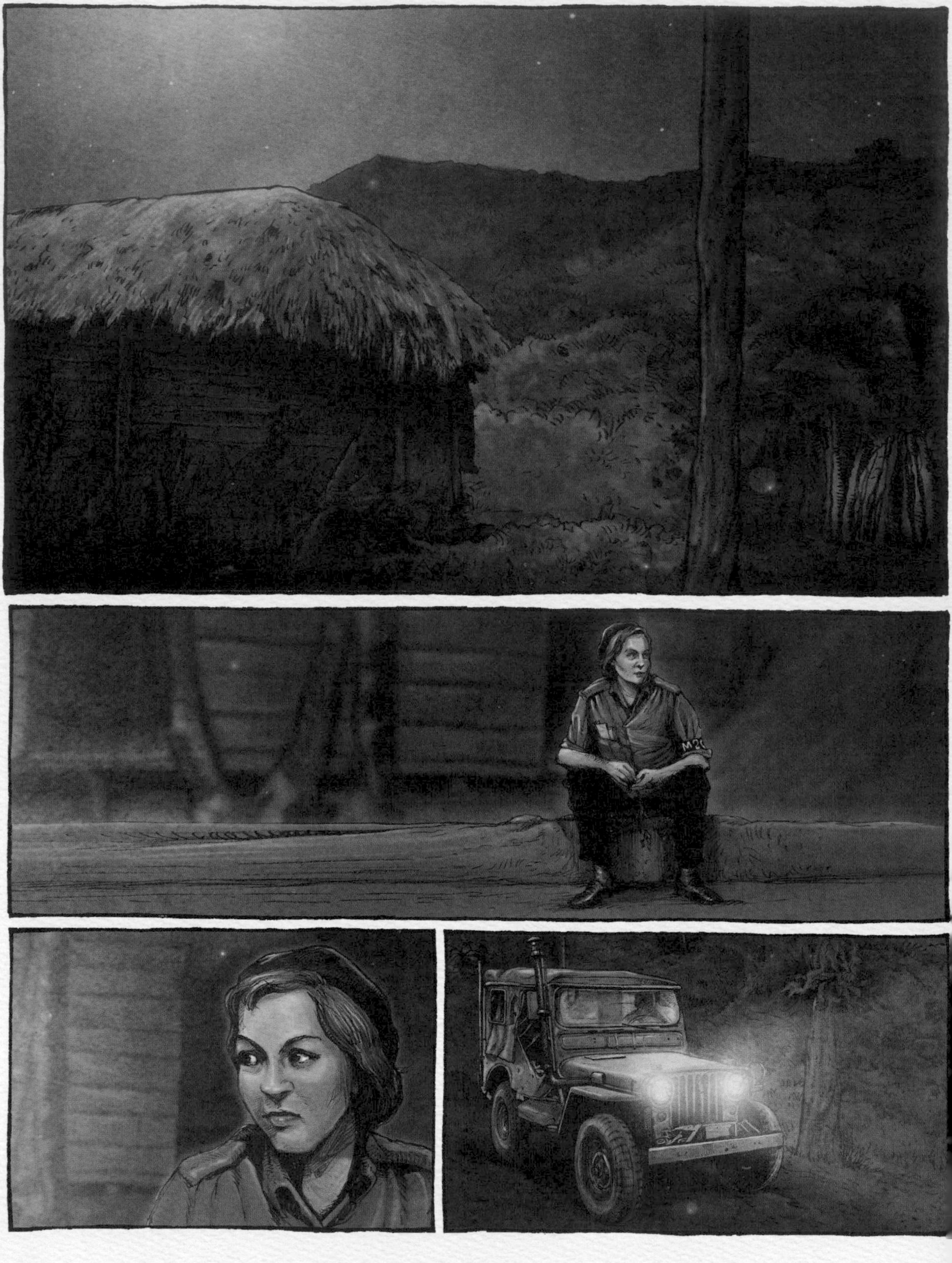

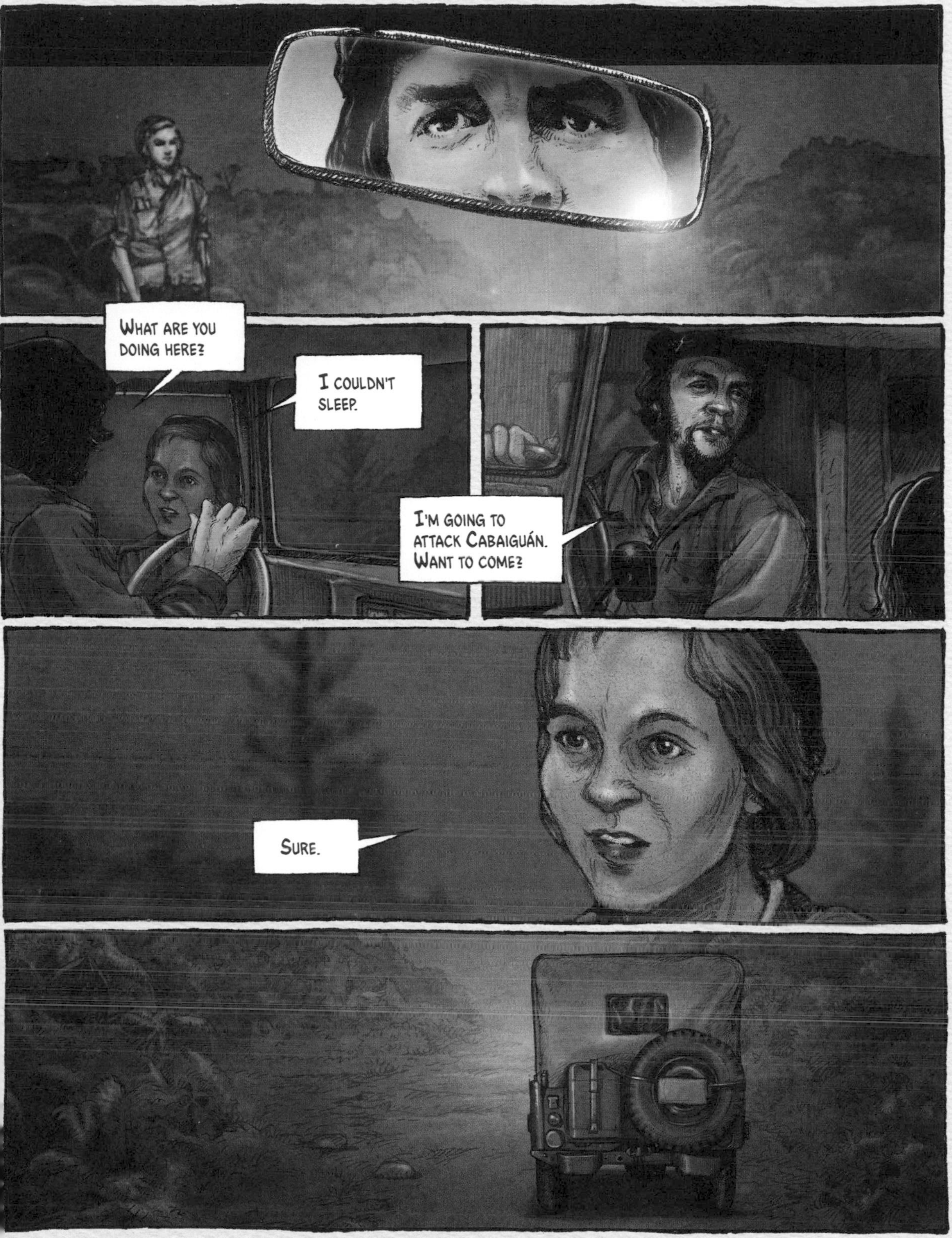
WHAT ARE YOU DOING HERE?
I COULDN'T SLEEP.
I'M GOING TO ATTACK CABAIGUÁN. WANT TO COME?
SURE.

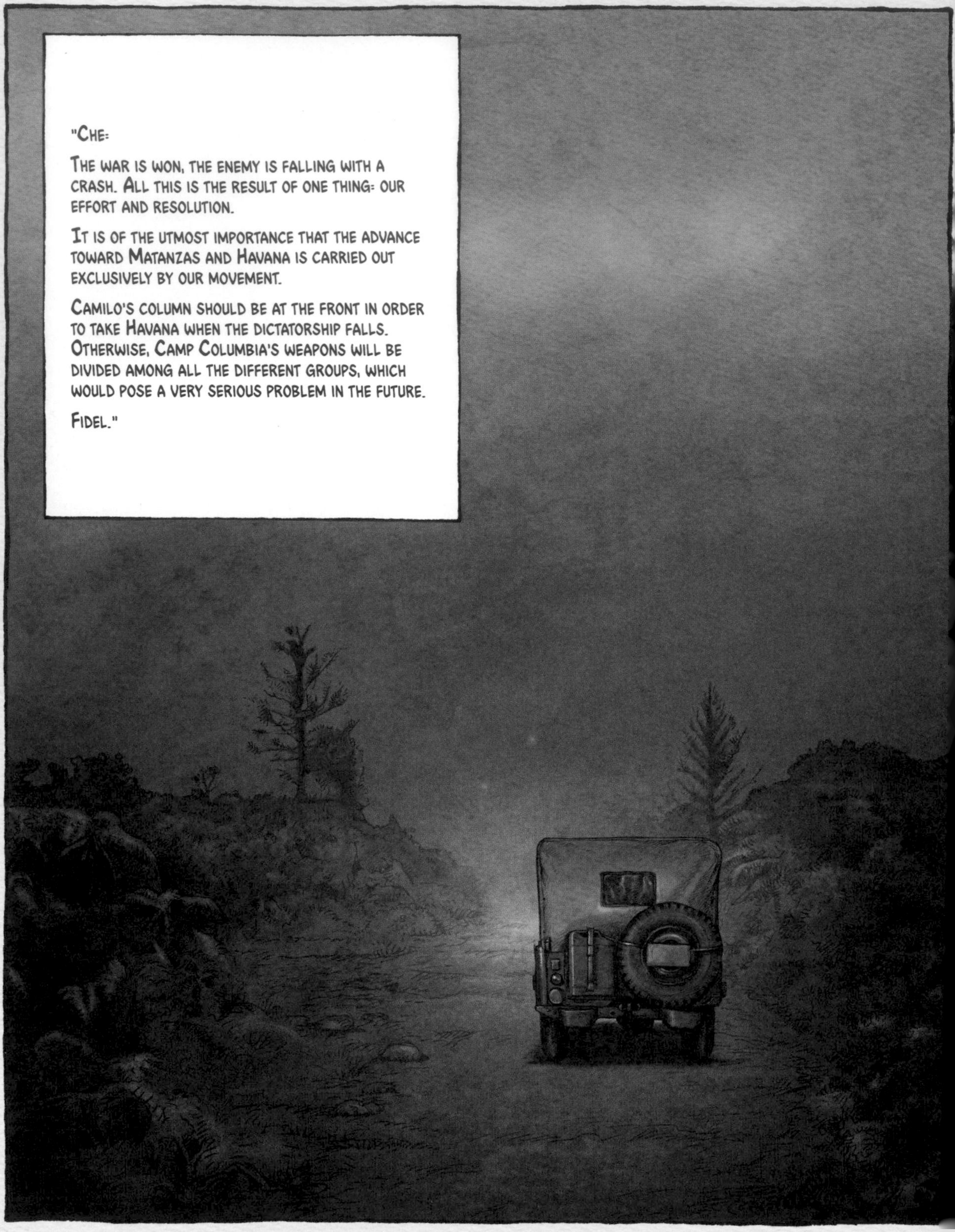
"CHE:
THE WAR IS WON, THE ENEMY IS FALLING WITH A CRASH. ALL THIS IS THE RESULT OF ONE THING: OUR EFFORT AND RESOLUTION.
IT IS OF THE UTMOST IMPORTANCE THAT THE ADVANCE TOWARD MATANZAS AND HAVANA IS CARRIED OUT EXCLUSIVELY BY OUR MOVEMENT.
CAMILO'S COLUMN SHOULD BE AT THE FRONT IN ORDER TO TAKE HAVANA WHEN THE DICTATORSHIP FALLS. OTHERWISE, CAMP COLUMBIA'S WEAPONS WILL BE DIVIDED AMONG ALL THE DIFFERENT GROUPS, WHICH WOULD POSE A VERY SERIOUS PROBLEM IN THE FUTURE.
FIDEL."

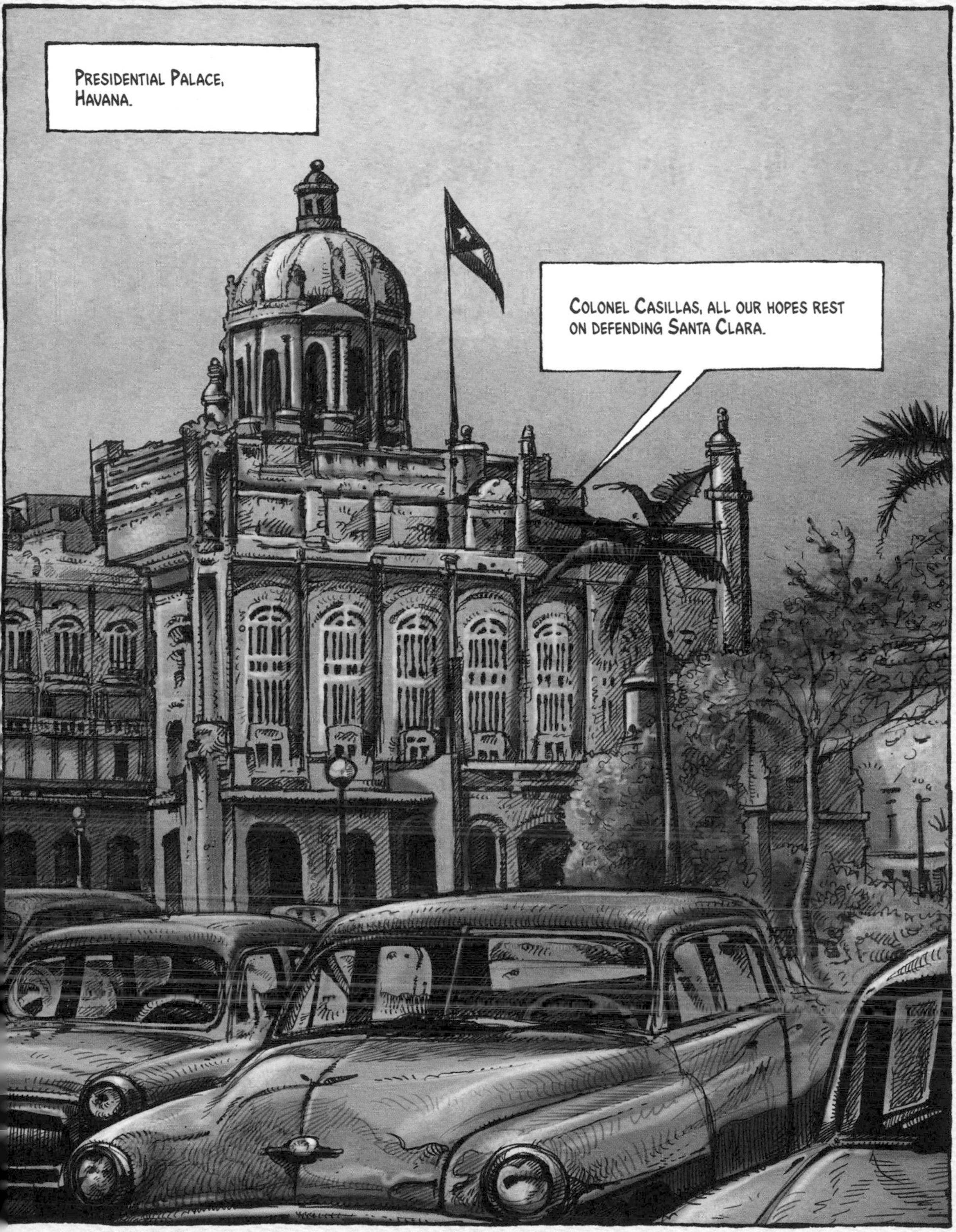
Presidential Palace,
Havana.
Colonel Casillas, all our hopes rest on defending Santa Clara.

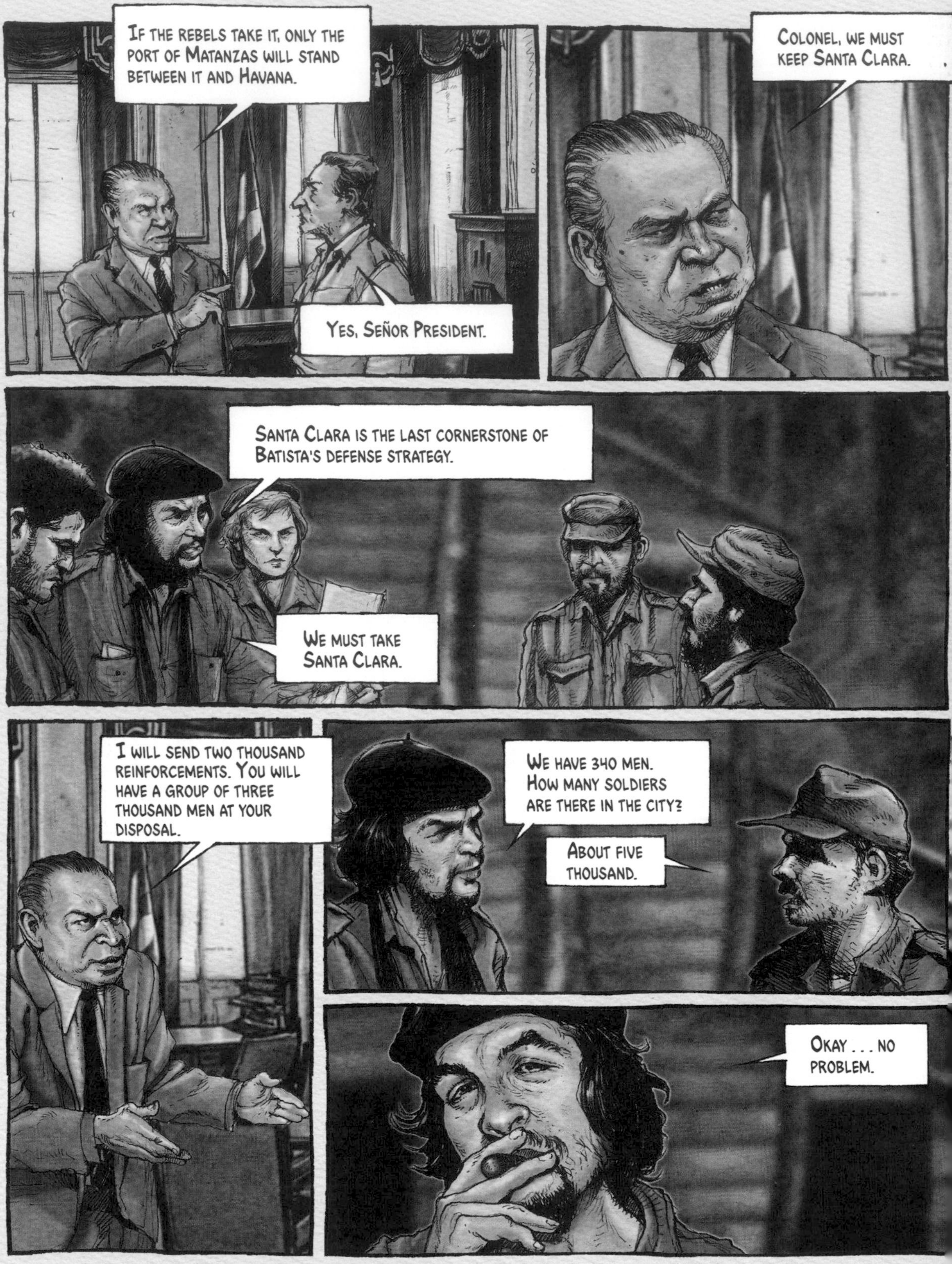
If the rebels take it, only the port of Matanzas will stand between it and Havana.
Yes, Señor President.
Colonel, we must keep Santa Clara.
Santa Clara is the last cornerstone of Batista's defense strategy.
We must take Santa Clara.
I will send two thousand reinforcements. You will have a group of three thousand men at your disposal.
We have 340 men. How many soldiers are there in the city?
About five thousand.
Okay . . . no problem.

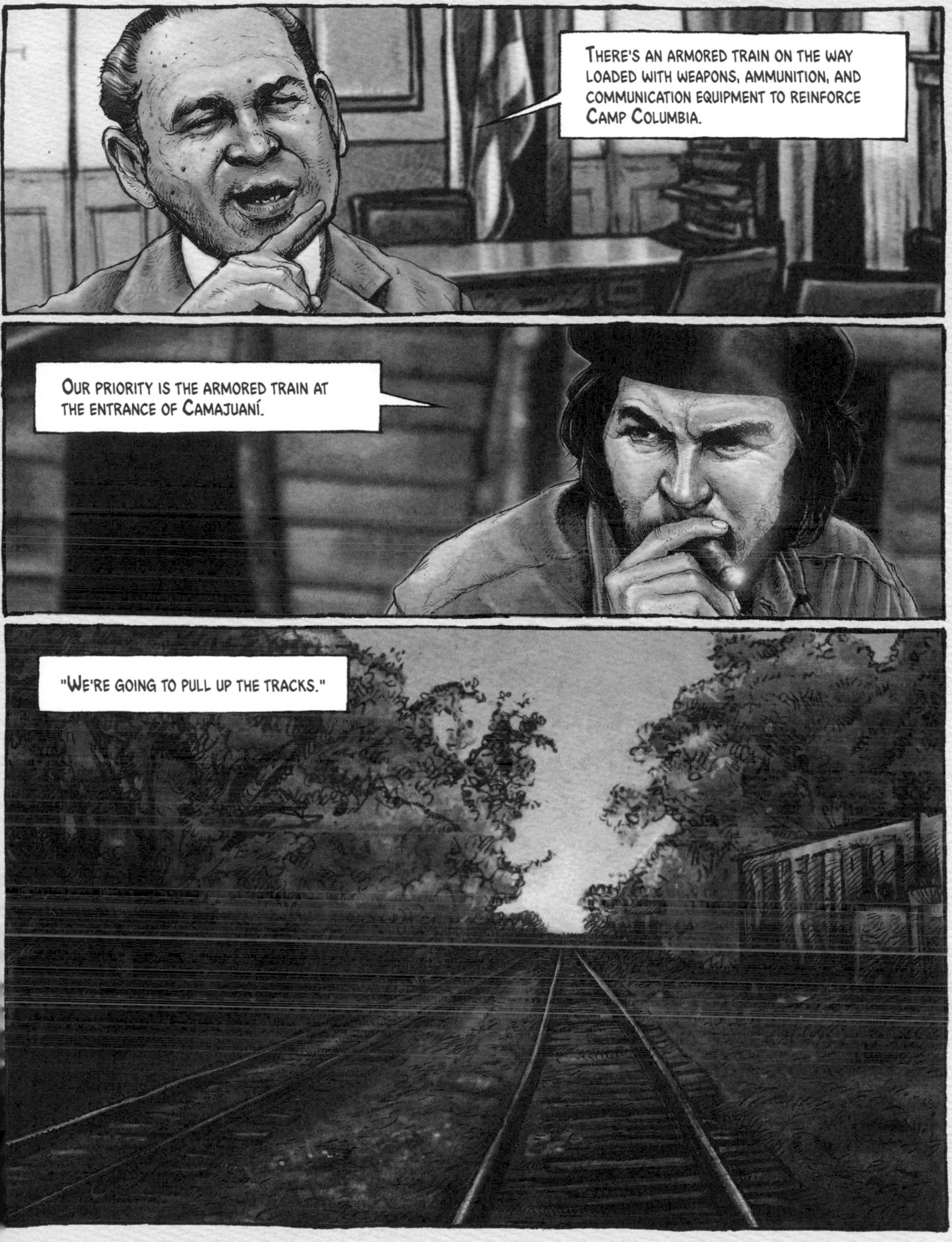
THERE'S AN ARMORED TRAIN ON THE WAY LOADED WITH WEAPONS, AMMUNITION, AND COMMUNICATION EQUIPMENT TO REINFORCE CAMP COLUMBIA.
OUR PRIORITY IS THE ARMORED TRAIN AT THE ENTRANCE OF CAMAJUANÍ.
"WE'RE GOING TO PULL UP THE TRACKS."

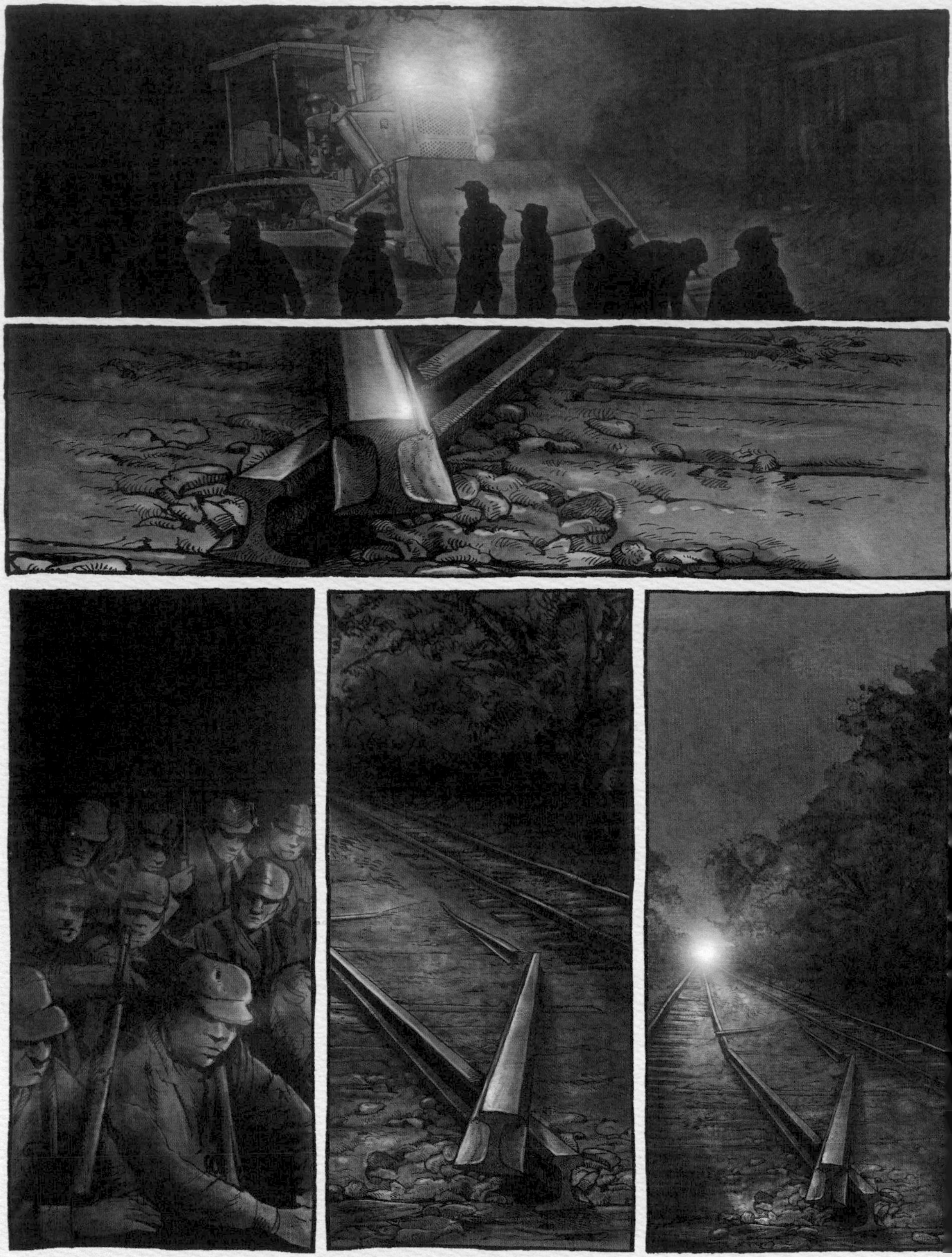

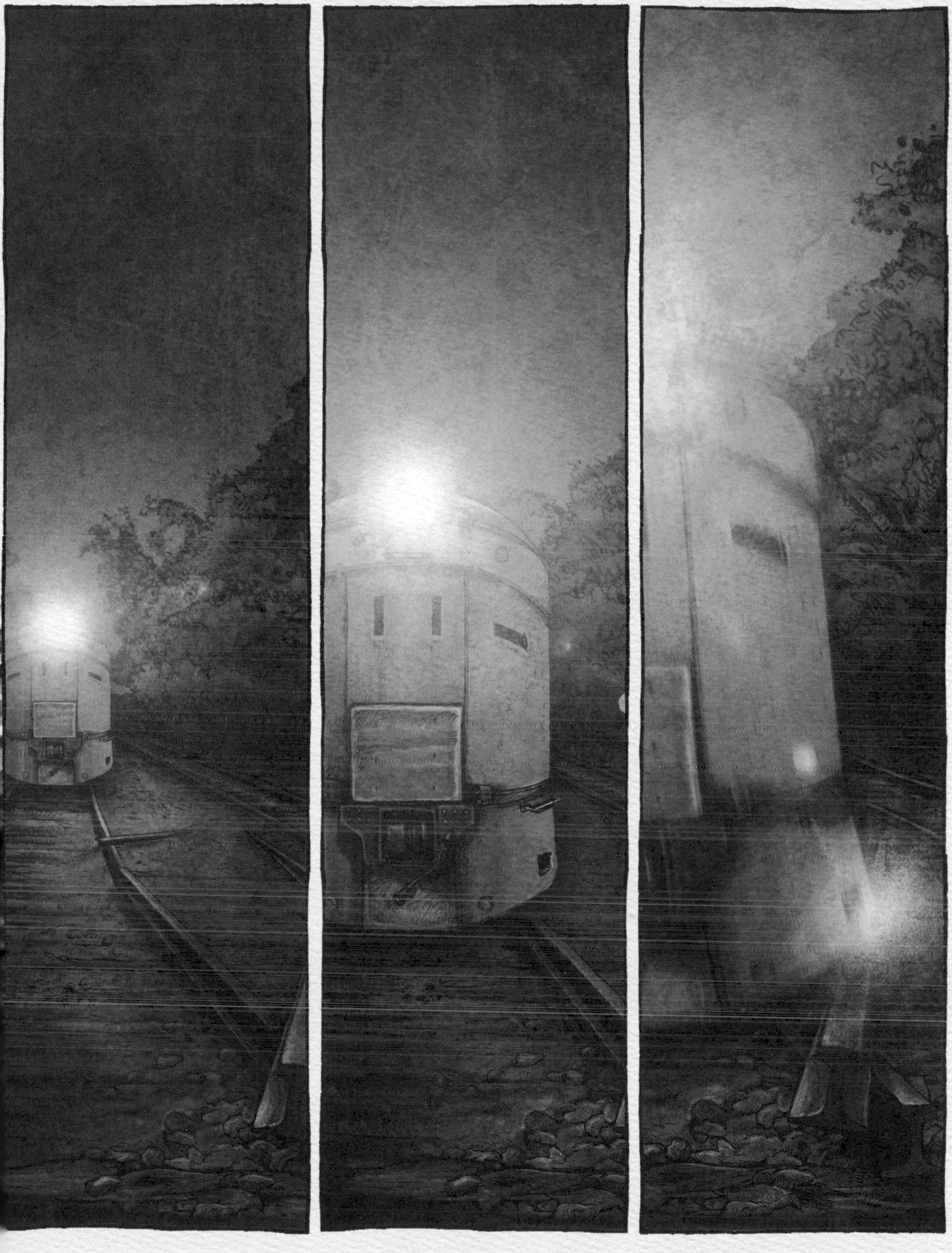

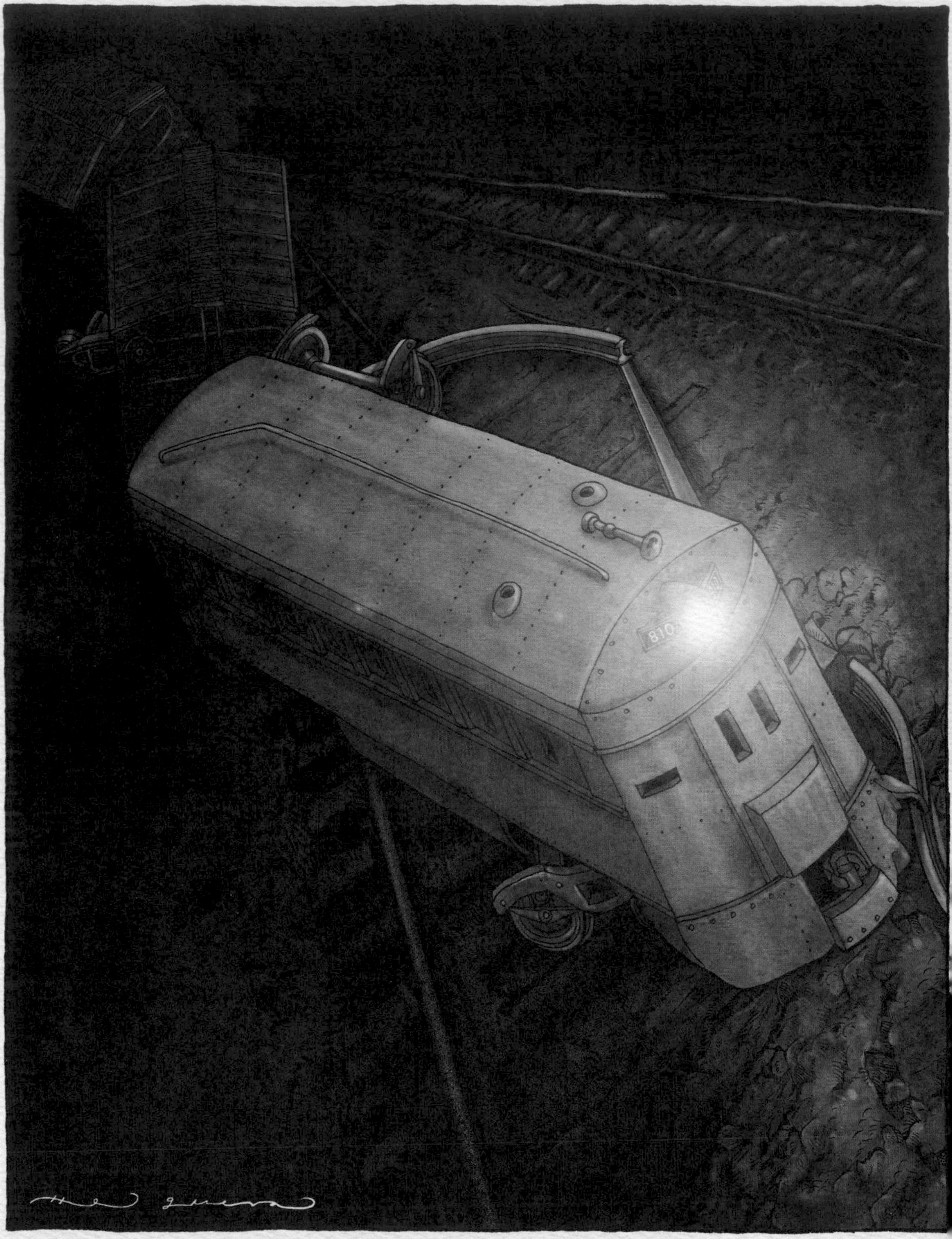
810

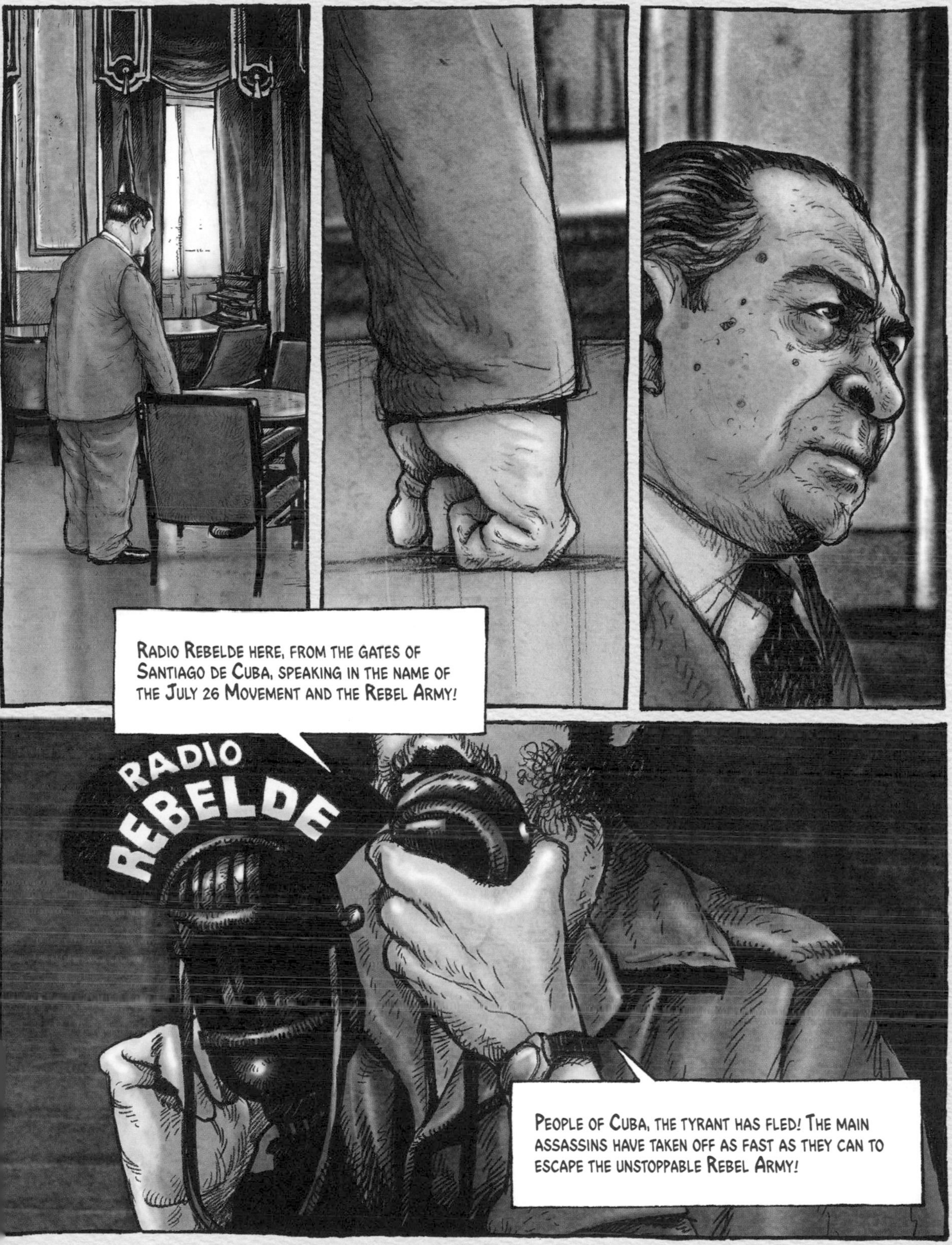
Radio Rebelde here, from the gates of Santiago de Cuba, speaking in the name of the July 26 Movement and the Rebel Army!
RADIO REBELDE
People of Cuba, the tyrant has fled! The main assassins have taken off as fast as they can to escape the unstoppable Rebel Army!

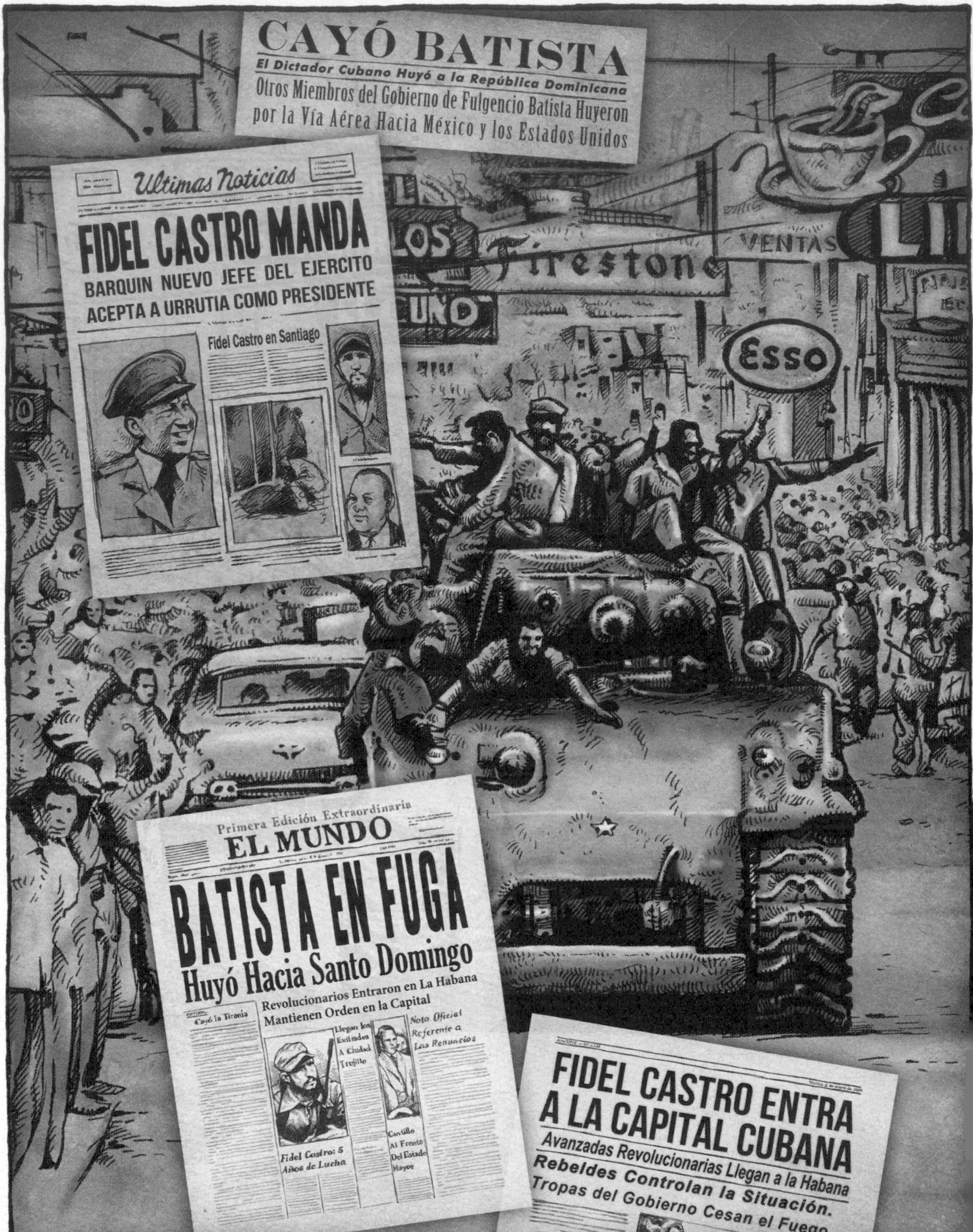

CAYÓ BATISTA
El Dictador Cubano Huyó a la República Dominicana
Otros Miembros del Gobierno de Fulgencio Batista Huyeron por la Vía Aérea Hacia México y los Estados Unidos
Ultimas Noticias
FIDEL CASTRO MANDA
BARQUIN NUEVO JEFE DEL EJERCITO
ACEPTA A URRUTIA COMO PRESIDENTE
Fidel Castro en Santiago
Firestone
VENTAS
Esso
Primera Edición Extraordinaria
EL MUNDO
BATISTA EN FUGA
Huyó Hacia Santo Domingo
Revolucionarios Entraron en La Habana
Mantienen Orden en la Capital
Cayó la Tiranía
Llegan los Exiliados A Ciudad Trujillo
Nota Oficial Referente a Las Renuncias
Fidel Castro: 5 Años de Lucha
Cantillo Al Frente Del Estado Mayor
FIDEL CASTRO ENTRA A LA CAPITAL CUBANA
Avanzadas Revolucionarias Llegan a la Habana
Rebeldes Controlan la Situación.
Tropas del Gobierno Cesan el Fuego.

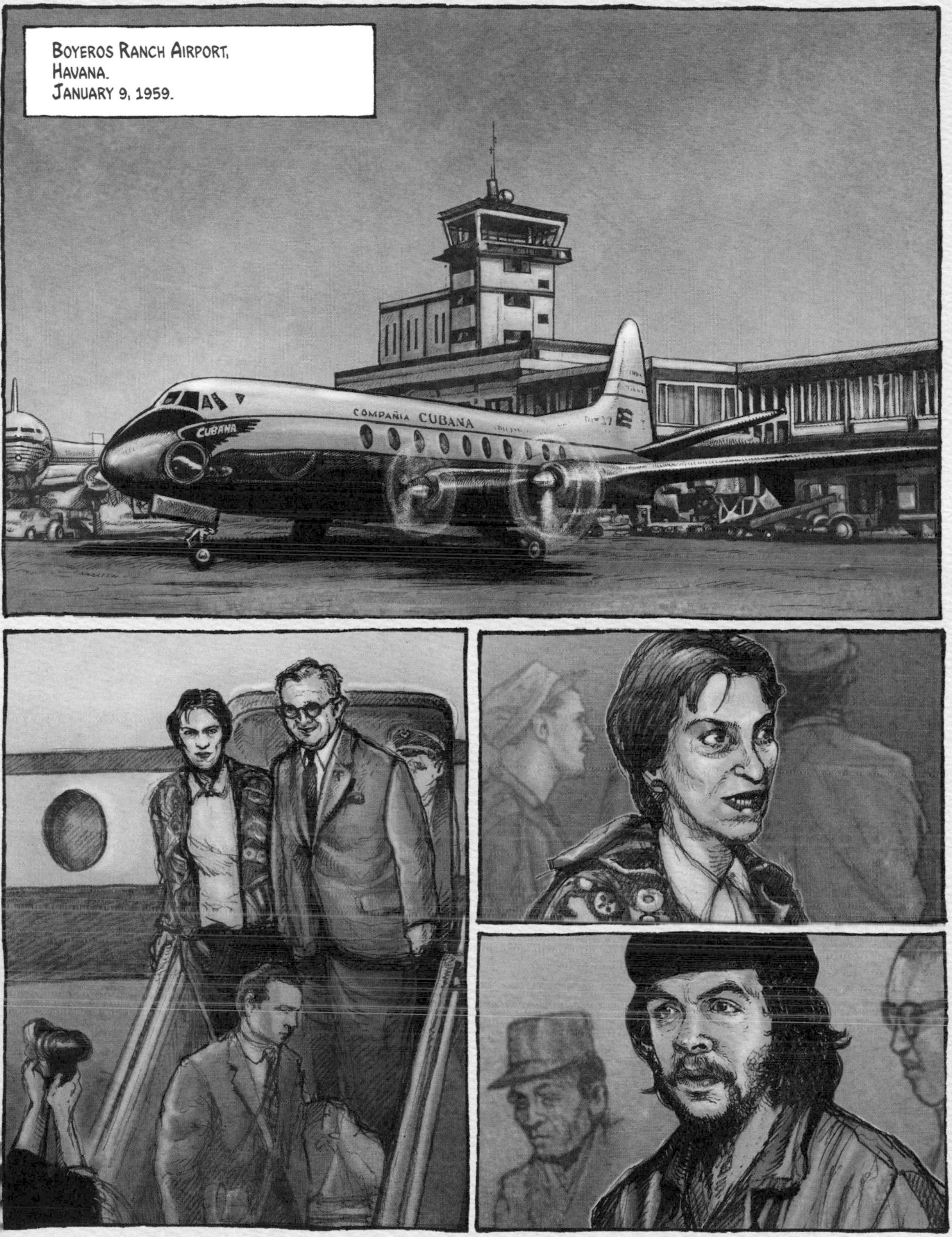
Boyeros Ranch Airport,
Havana.
January 9, 1959.
COMPAÑIA CUBANA
CUBANA

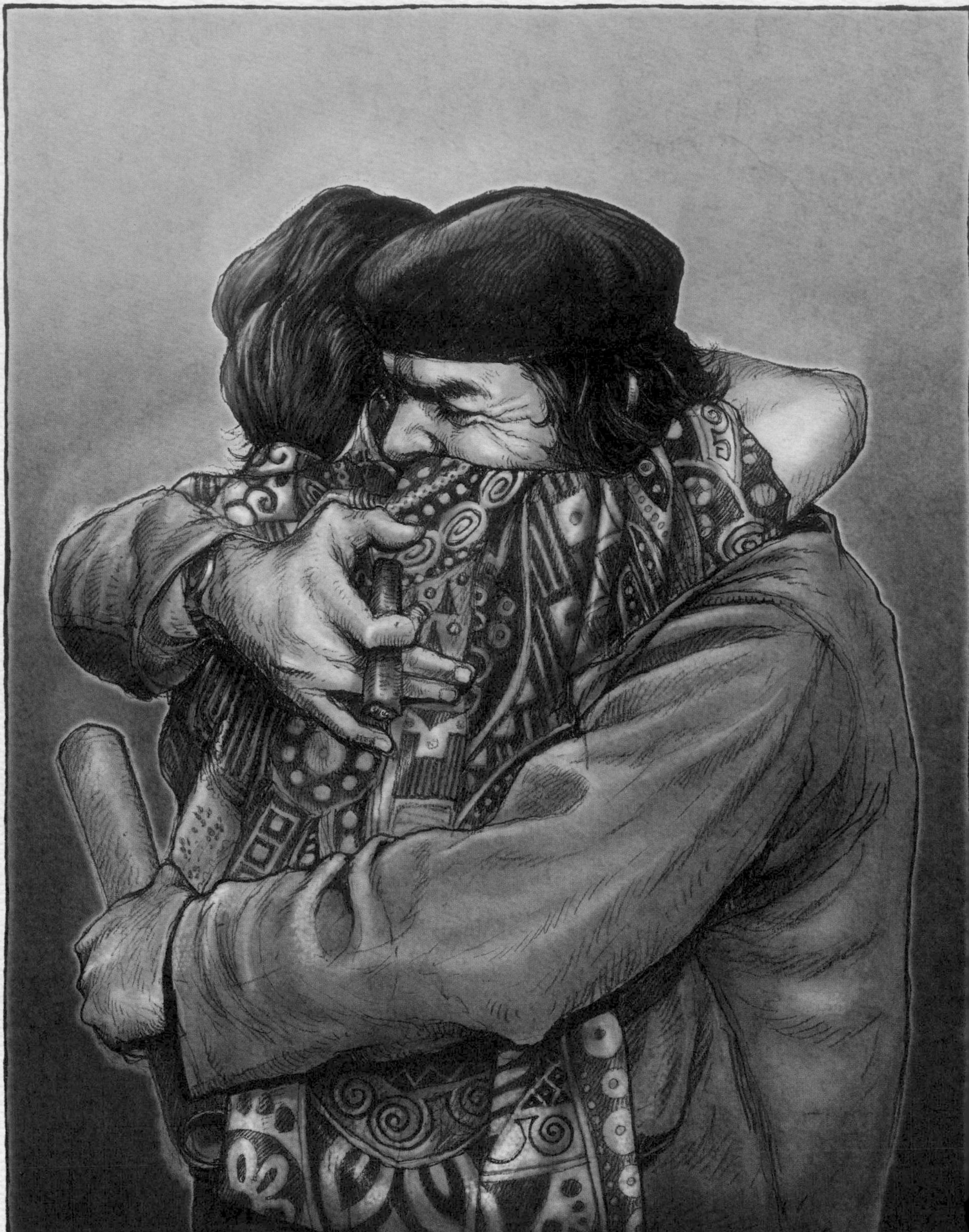

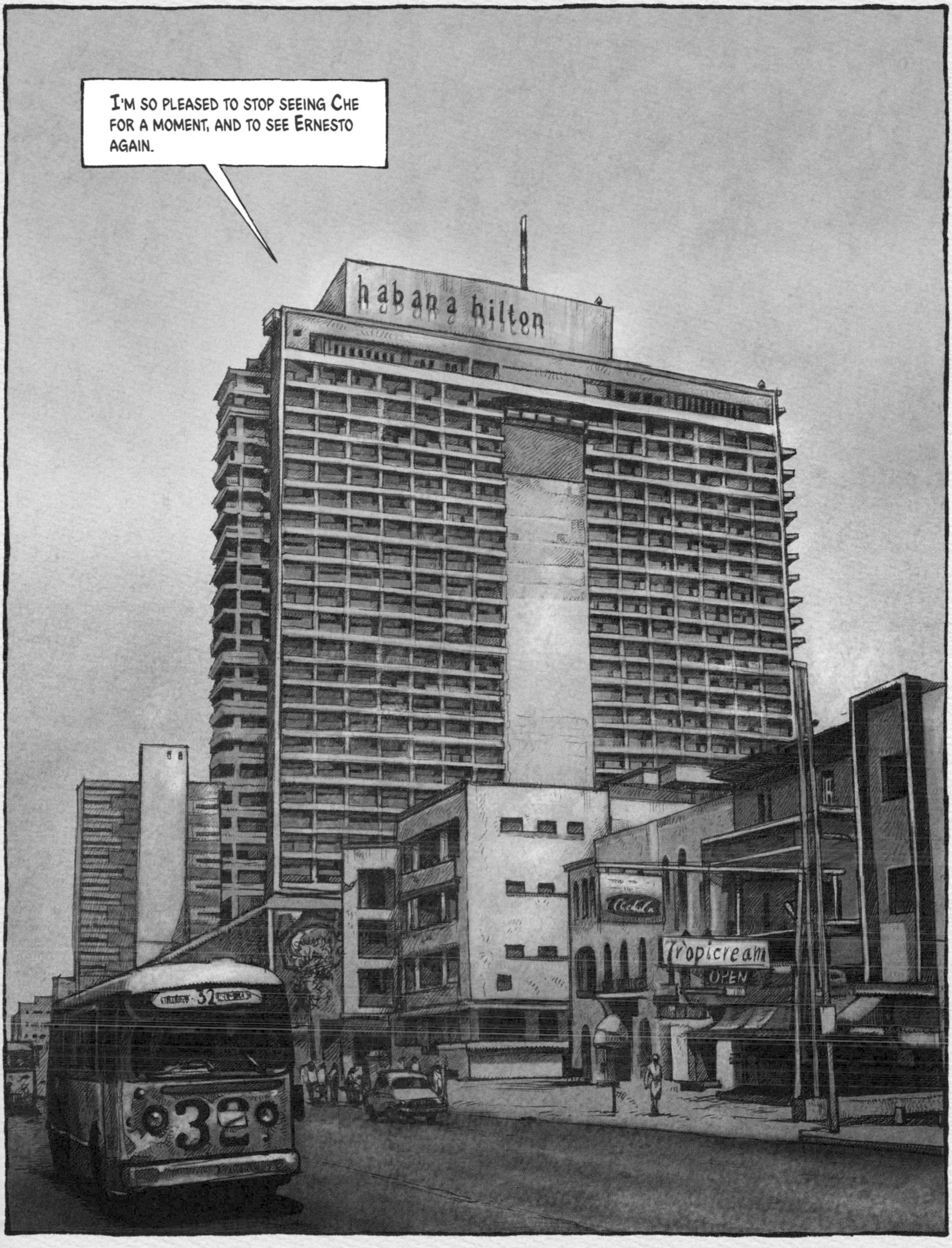
I'M SO PLEASED TO STOP SEEING CHE FOR A MOMENT, AND TO SEE ERNESTO AGAIN.
habana hilton
Tropicream
OPEN
32

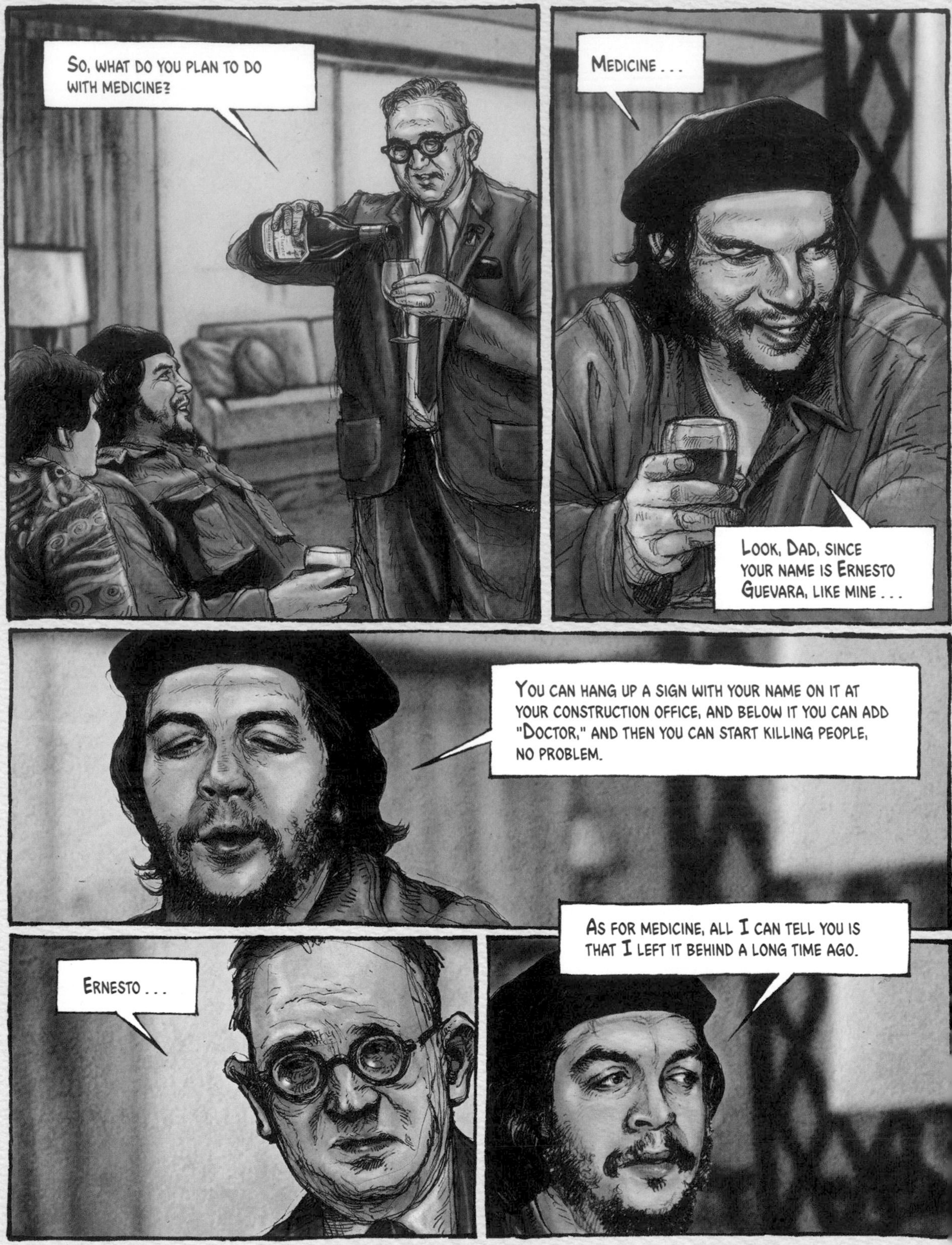
So, what do you plan to do with medicine?
Medicine . . .
Look, Dad, since your name is Ernesto Guevara, like mine . . .
You can hang up a sign with your name on it at your construction office, and below it you can add "Doctor," and then you can start killing people, no problem.
Ernesto . . .
As for medicine, all I can tell you is that I left it behind a long time ago.

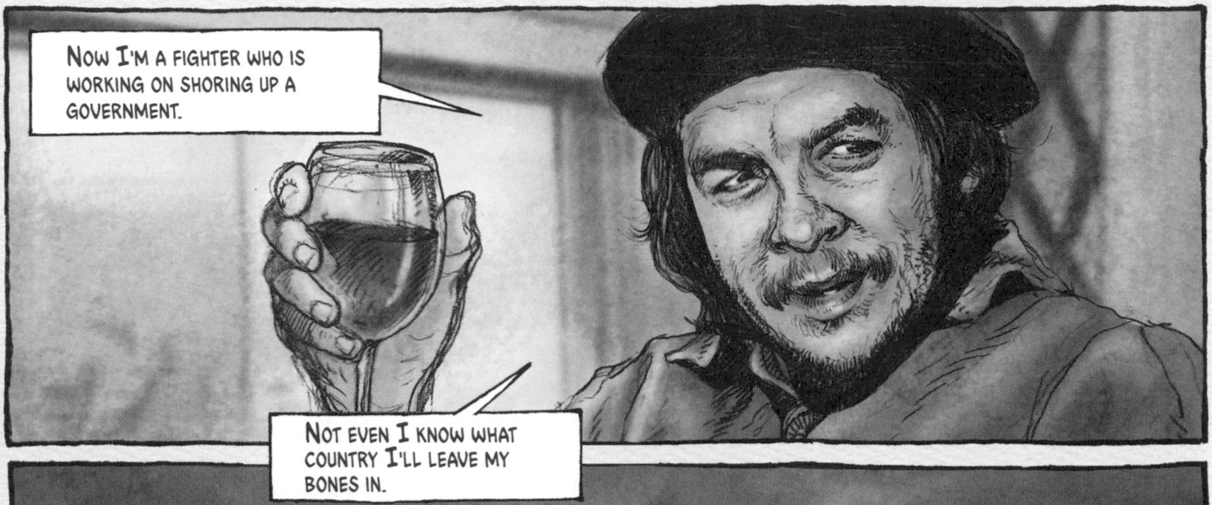
Now I'm a fighter who is working on shoring up a government.
Not even I know what country I'll leave my bones in.

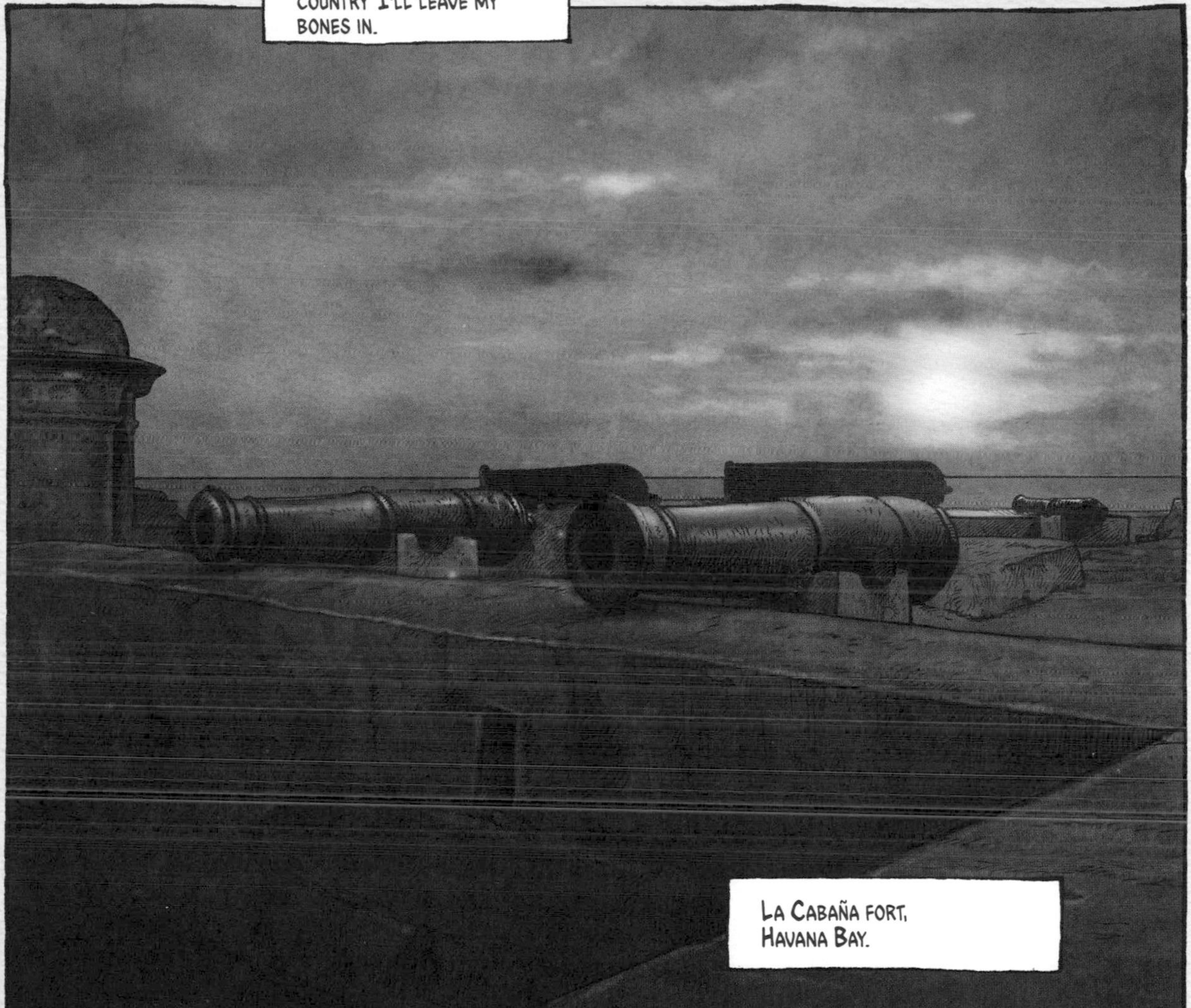
La Cabaña fort, Havana Bay.

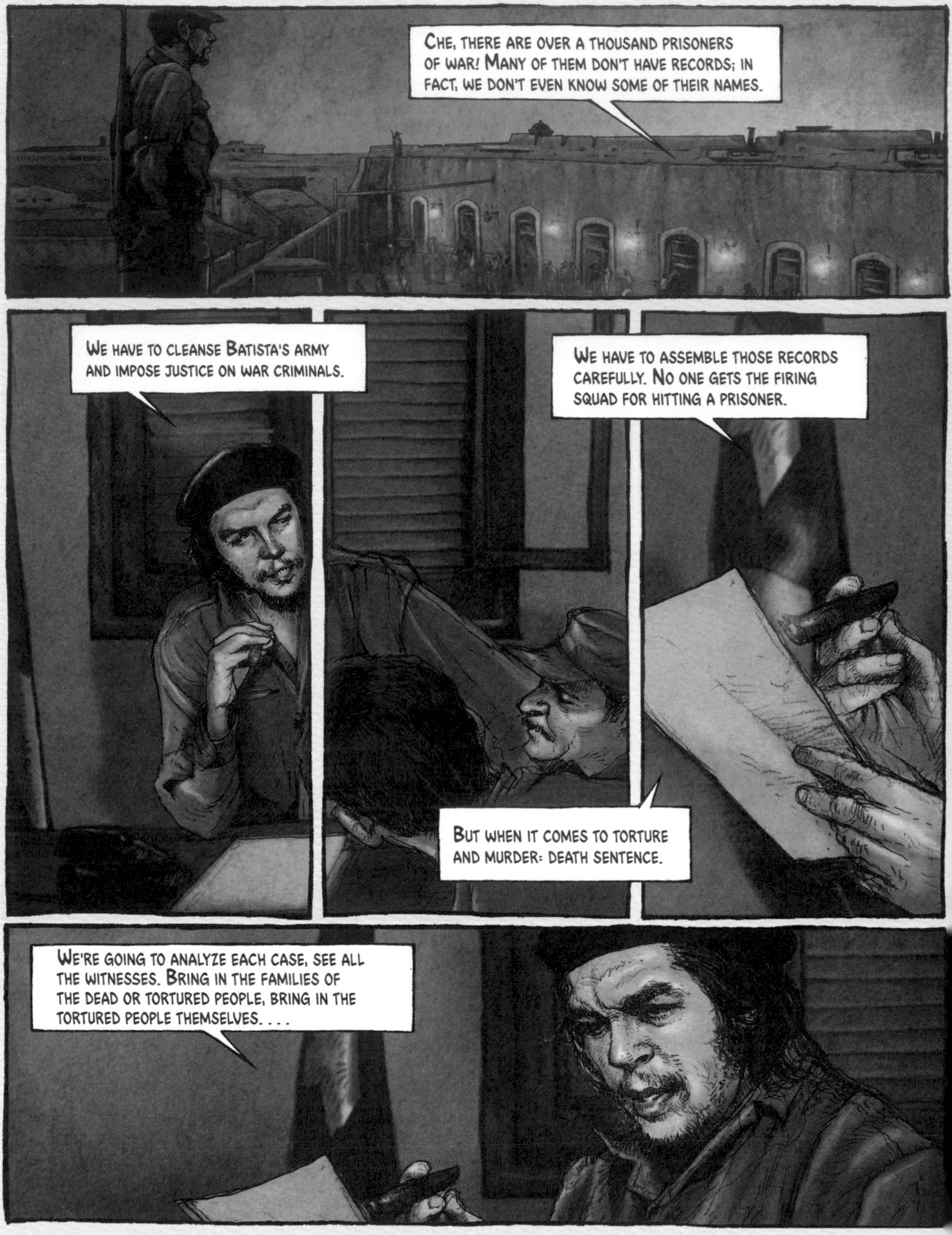
CHE, THERE ARE OVER A THOUSAND PRISONERS OF WAR! MANY OF THEM DON'T HAVE RECORDS; IN FACT, WE DON'T EVEN KNOW SOME OF THEIR NAMES.
WE HAVE TO CLEANSE BATISTA'S ARMY AND IMPOSE JUSTICE ON WAR CRIMINALS.
WE HAVE TO ASSEMBLE THOSE RECORDS CAREFULLY. NO ONE GETS THE FIRING SQUAD FOR HITTING A PRISONER.
BUT WHEN IT COMES TO TORTURE AND MURDER: DEATH SENTENCE.
WE'RE GOING TO ANALYZE EACH CASE, SEE ALL THE WITNESSES. BRING IN THE FAMILIES OF THE DEAD OR TORTURED PEOPLE, BRING IN THE TORTURED PEOPLE THEMSELVES. . . .

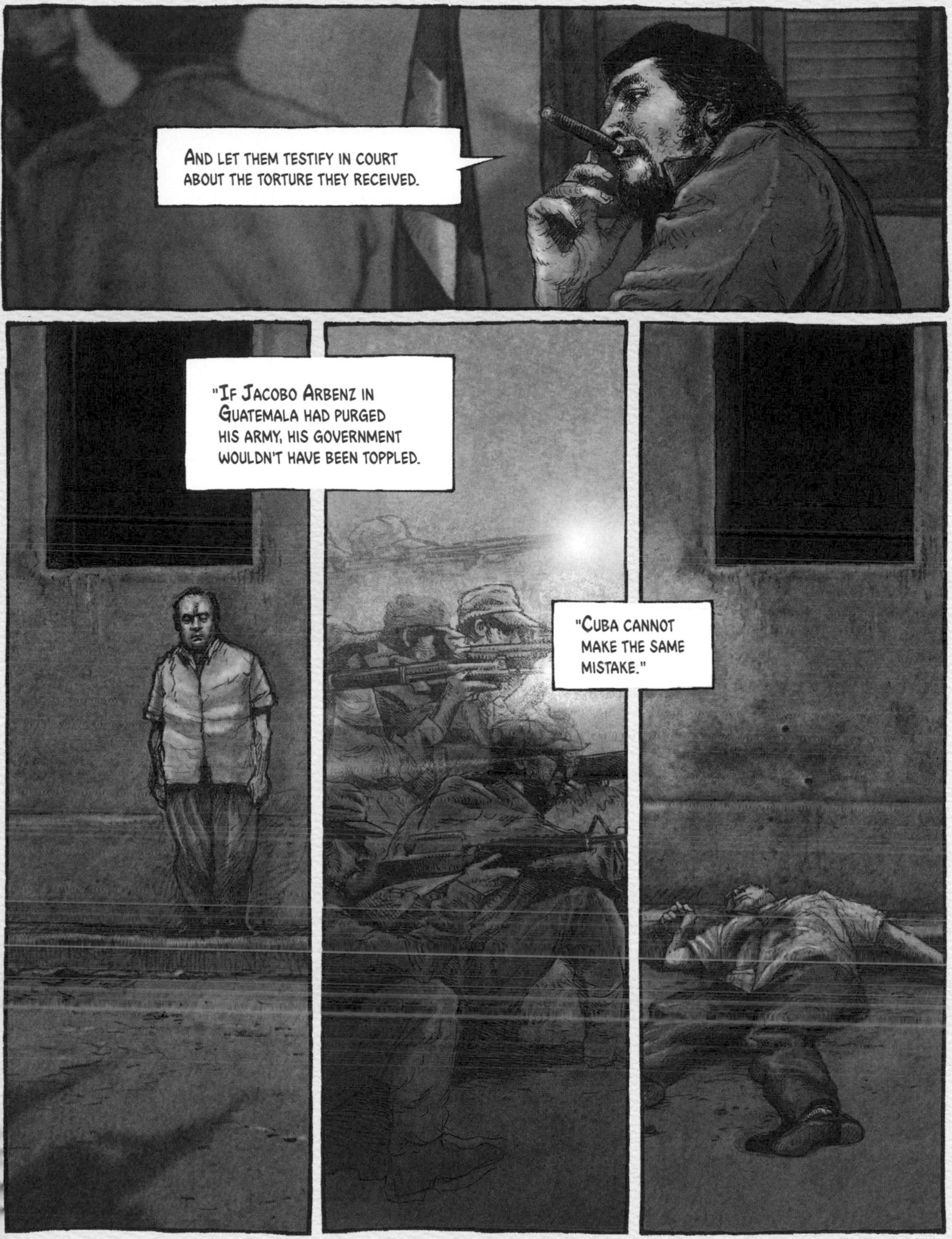
AND LET THEM TESTIFY IN COURT ABOUT THE TORTURE THEY RECEIVED.
"IF JACOBO ARBENZ IN GUATEMALA HAD PURGED HIS ARMY, HIS GOVERNMENT WOULDN'T HAVE BEEN TOPPLED.
"CUBA CANNOT MAKE THE SAME MISTAKE."

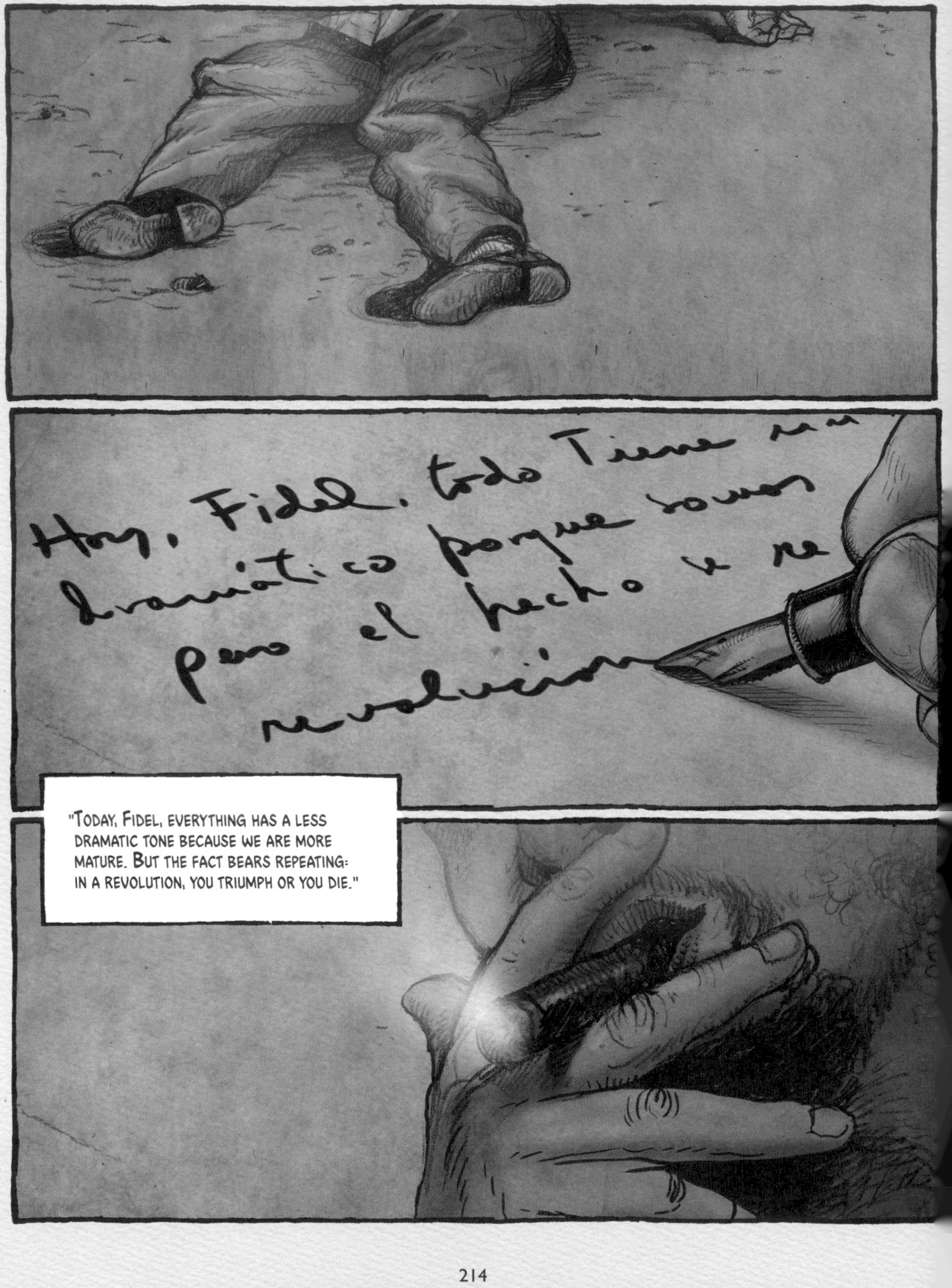
Hoy, Fidel, todo Tiene
dramático porque somos
pero el hecho.
"TODAY, FIDEL, EVERYTHING HAS A LESS DRAMATIC TONE BECAUSE WE ARE MORE MATURE. BUT THE FACT BEARS REPEATING: IN A REVOLUTION, YOU TRIUMPH OR YOU DIE."

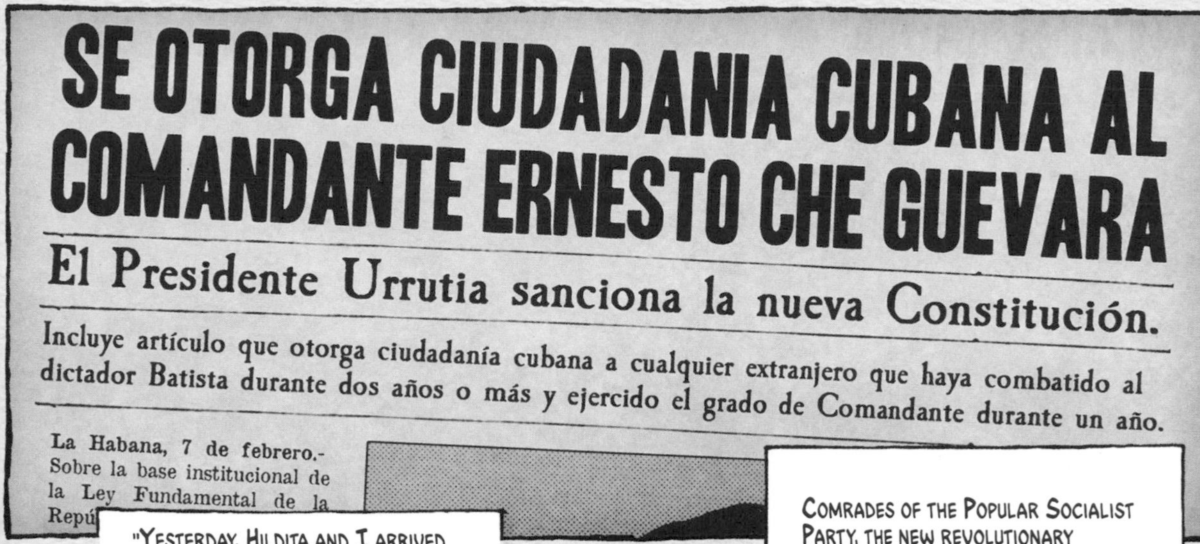

SE OTORGA CIUDADANIA CUBANA AL COMANDANTE ERNESTO CHE GUEVARA

El Presidente Urrutia sanciona la nueva Constitución.

Incluye artículo que otorga ciudadanía cubana a cualquier extranjero que haya combatido al dictador Batista durante dos años o más y ejercido el grado de Comandante durante un año.

La Habana, 7 de febrero.- Sobre la base institucional de la Ley Fundamental de la

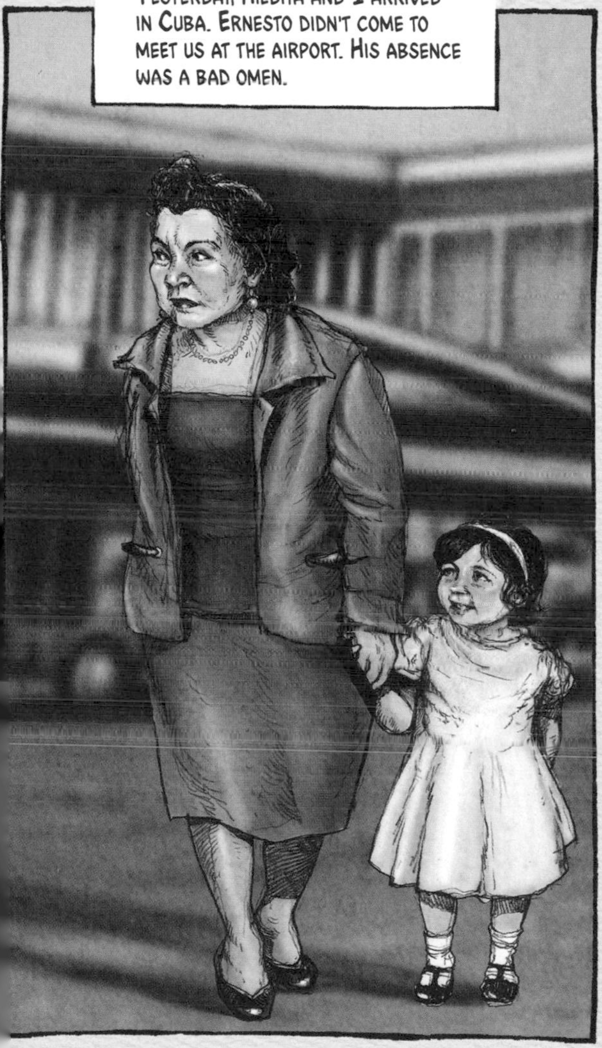
"YESTERDAY, HILDITA AND I ARRIVED IN CUBA. ERNESTO DIDN'T COME TO MEET US AT THE AIRPORT. HIS ABSENCE WAS A BAD OMEN.

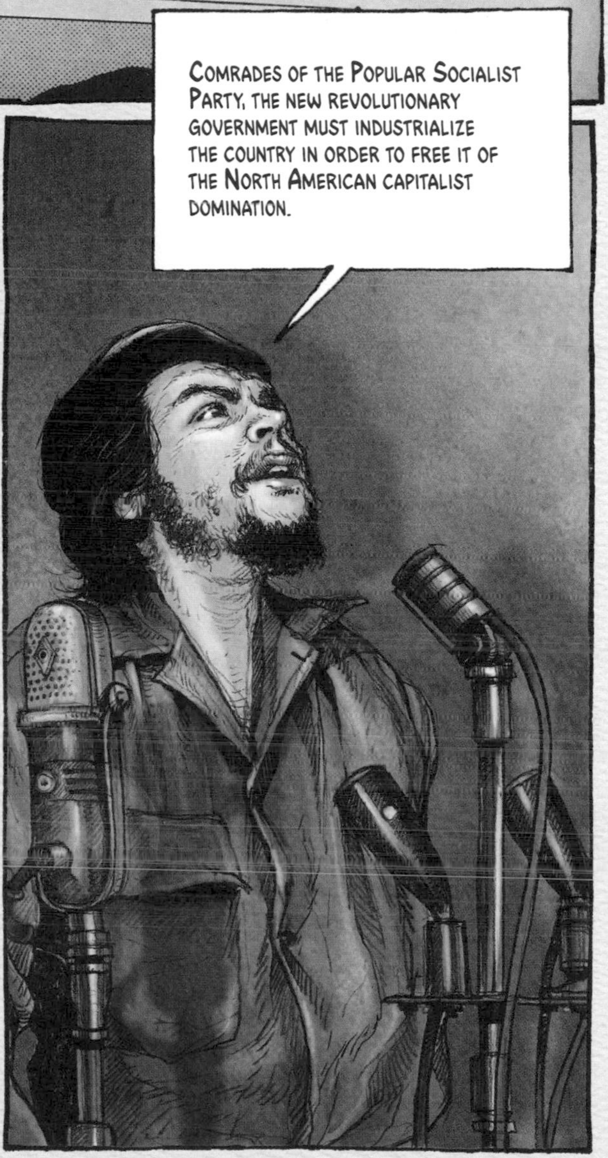
COMRADES OF THE POPULAR SOCIALIST PARTY, THE NEW REVOLUTIONARY GOVERNMENT MUST INDUSTRIALIZE THE COUNTRY IN ORDER TO FREE IT OF THE NORTH AMERICAN CAPITALIST DOMINATION.

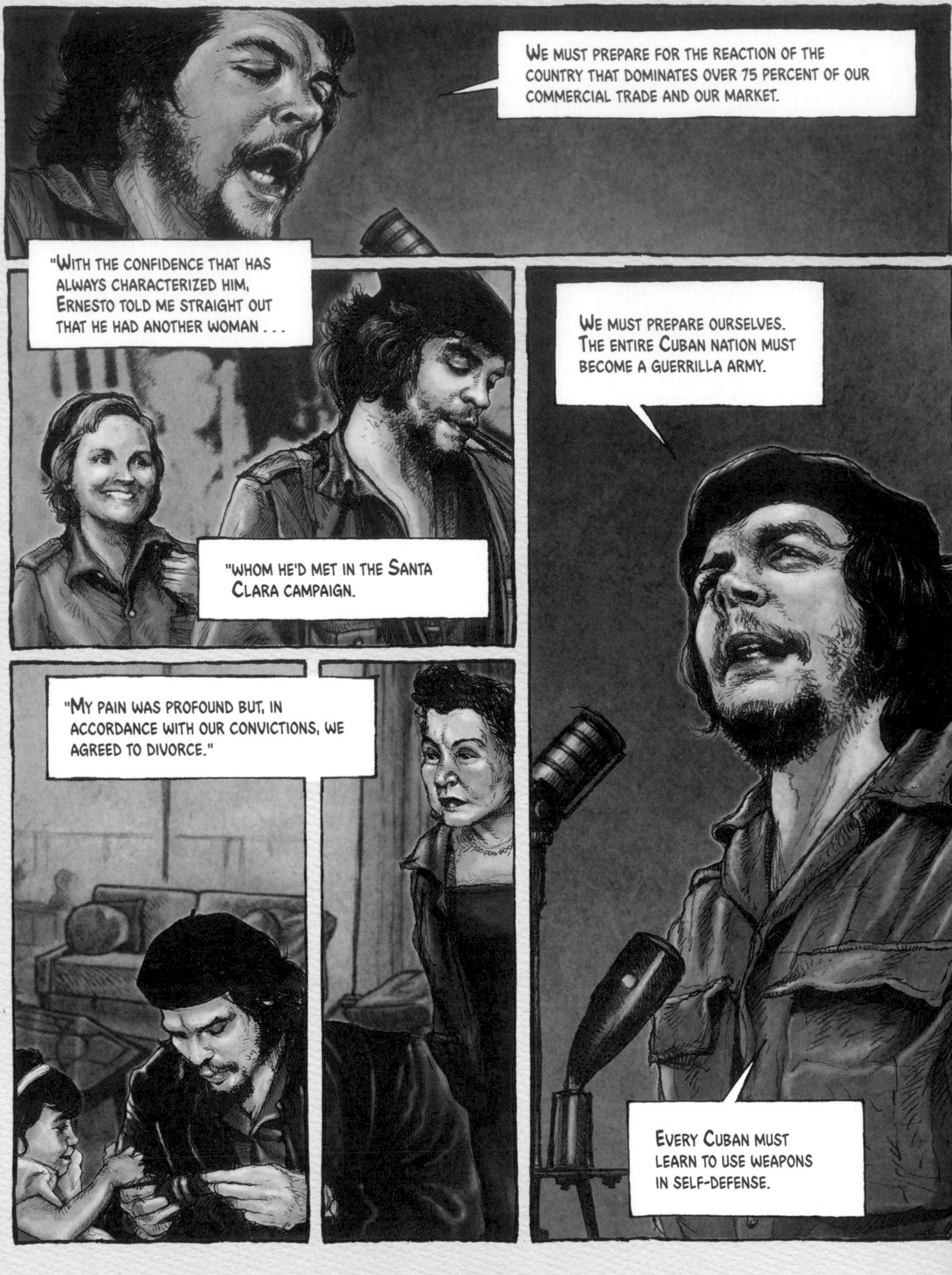
WE MUST PREPARE FOR THE REACTION OF THE COUNTRY THAT DOMINATES OVER 75 PERCENT OF OUR COMMERCIAL TRADE AND OUR MARKET.
"WITH THE CONFIDENCE THAT HAS ALWAYS CHARACTERIZED HIM, ERNESTO TOLD ME STRAIGHT OUT THAT HE HAD ANOTHER WOMAN . . .
"WHOM HE'D MET IN THE SANTA CLARA CAMPAIGN.
WE MUST PREPARE OURSELVES. THE ENTIRE CUBAN NATION MUST BECOME A GUERRILLA ARMY.
"MY PAIN WAS PROFOUND BUT, IN ACCORDANCE WITH OUR CONVICTIONS, WE AGREED TO DIVORCE."
EVERY CUBAN MUST LEARN TO USE WEAPONS IN SELF-DEFENSE.

TODAY, THE WHOLE CUBAN NATION IS ON A WAR FOOTING, AND IT MUST REMAIN SO! THIS IS THE FIRST STEP TOWARD A VICTORY FOR AMERICA!

WESTERN UNION
TELEGRAM
W. P. MARSHALL, PRESIDENT

FEB 2 1959

CLASSIFIED

A NUMBER OF LEADERS OF THE SUCCESSFUL REVOLUTIONARY MOVEMENT IN CUBA CONSIDER THAT EFFORTS SHOULD NOW BE UNDERTAKEN TO 'FREE' THE ... OF SOME OTHER LATIN AMERICAN NATIONS FROM THE ... ERNESTO 'CHE' GUEVARA SER... THE PRINCIPAL FORCE BEHIN...

IT CAN BE EXPECTED THAT ... REVOLUTIONARY SCHEMINGA... WITH CONSEQUENT CONCERN AND ... GOVERNMENTS INCLUDING OU...

"A NUMBER OF LEADERS OF THE SUCCESSFUL REVOLUTIONARY MOVEMENT IN CUBA CONSIDER THAT EFFORTS SHOULD NOW BE UNDERTAKEN TO 'FREE' THE PEOPLE OF SOME OTHER LATIN AMERICAN NATIONS FROM THEIR DICTATORIAL GOVERNMENTS. ERNESTO 'CHE' GUEVARA SERNA IS THE PRINCIPAL FORCE BEHIND SUCH THINKING.

IT CAN BE EXPECTED THAT CUBA WILL BE A CENTER OF REVOLUTIONARY SCHEMING, WITH SERIOUS CONSEQUENCES FOR OUR GOVERNMENT.

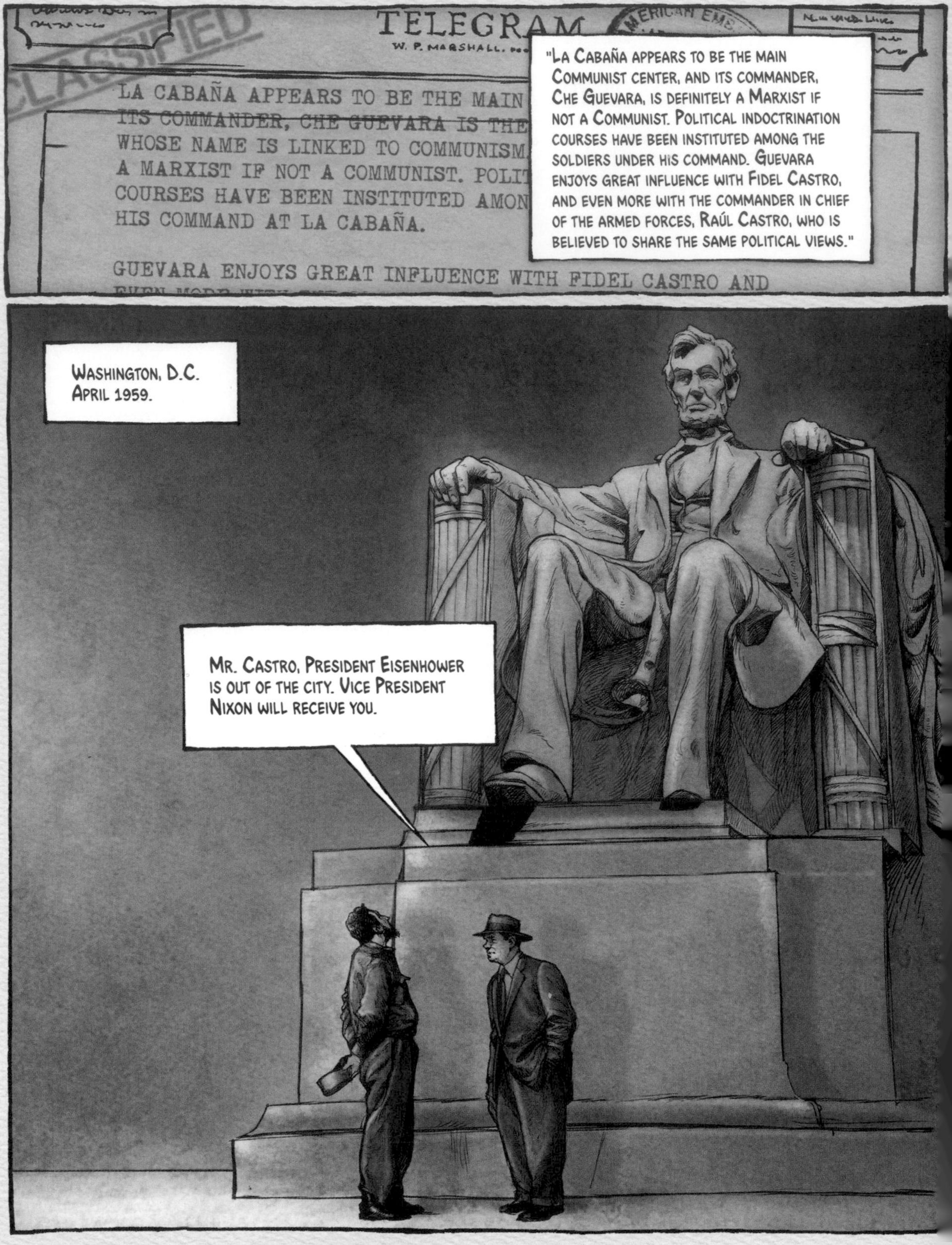
TELEGRAM
W. P. MARSHALL
CLASSIFIED
LA CABAÑA APPEARS TO BE THE MAIN
ITS COMMANDER, CHE GUEVARA IS THE
WHOSE NAME IS LINKED TO COMMUNISM
A MARXIST IF NOT A COMMUNIST. POLIT
COURSES HAVE BEEN INSTITUTED AMON
HIS COMMAND AT LA CABAÑA.
GUEVARA ENJOYS GREAT INFLUENCE WITH FIDEL CASTRO AND
"La Cabaña appears to be the main Communist center, and its commander, Che Guevara, is definitely a Marxist if not a Communist. Political indoctrination courses have been instituted among the soldiers under his command. Guevara enjoys great influence with Fidel Castro, and even more with the commander in chief of the armed forces, Raúl Castro, who is believed to share the same political views."
Washington, D.C. April 1959.
Mr. Castro, President Eisenhower is out of the city. Vice President Nixon will receive you.

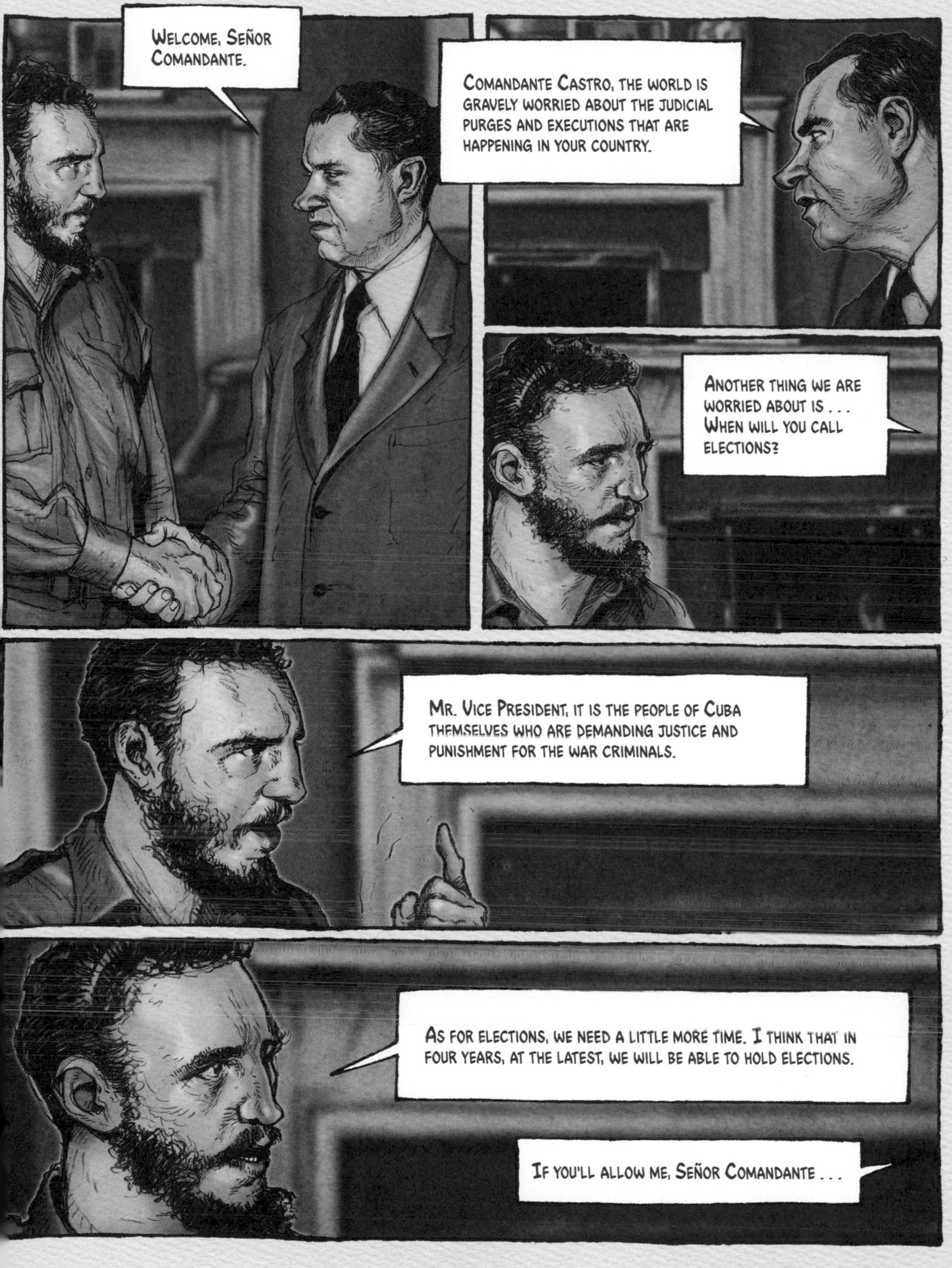

Welcome, Señor Comandante.
Comandante Castro, the world is gravely worried about the judicial purges and executions that are happening in your country.
Another thing we are worried about is . . . When will you call elections?
Mr. Vice President, it is the people of Cuba themselves who are demanding justice and punishment for the war criminals.
As for elections, we need a little more time. I think that in four years, at the latest, we will be able to hold elections.
If you'll allow me, Señor Comandante . . .

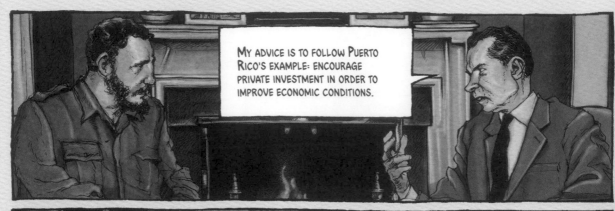

MY ADVICE IS TO FOLLOW PUERTO RICO'S EXAMPLE: ENCOURAGE PRIVATE INVESTMENT IN ORDER TO IMPROVE ECONOMIC CONDITIONS.

MR. VICE PRESIDENT, THE DAYS OF THE PLATT AMENDMENT ARE OVER, AND THE UNITED STATES NO LONGER HAS THE RIGHT TO INTERVENE IN CUBA.

"MR. PRESIDENT, THE MEETING WITH MR. CASTRO DIDN'T GO PARTICULARLY WELL. EITHER CASTRO IS COMMUNIST HIMSELF, OR HE'S A PUPPET WHO SHOWS INCREDIBLE NAÏVETÉ TOWARD THE COMMUNIST INFLUENCE IN HIS GOVERNMENT."

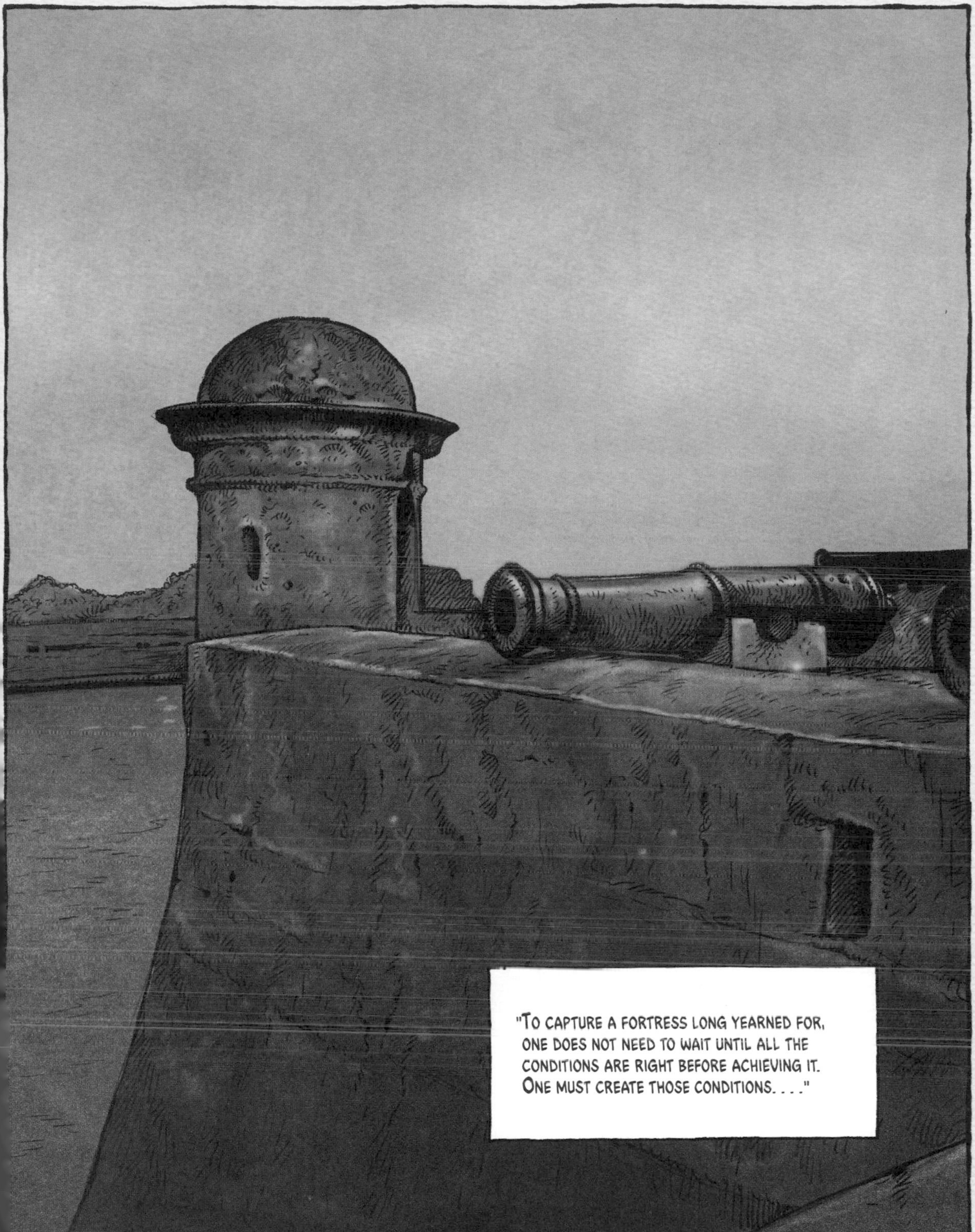
"To capture a fortress long yearned for, one does not need to wait until all the conditions are right before achieving it. One must create those conditions. . . ."

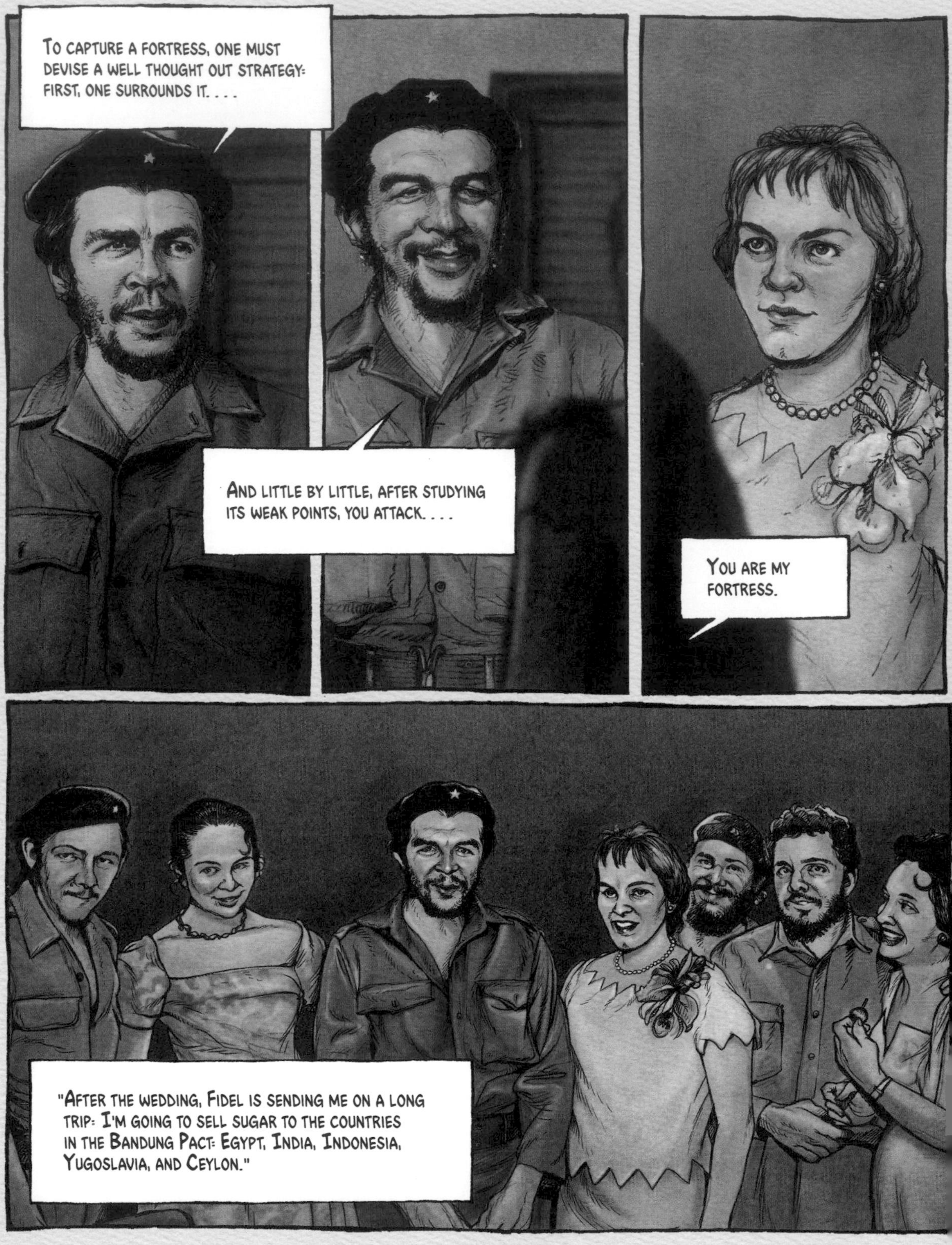
To capture a fortress, one must devise a well thought out strategy: first, one surrounds it. . . .
And little by little, after studying its weak points, you attack. . . .
You are my fortress.
"After the wedding, Fidel is sending me on a long trip: I'm going to sell sugar to the countries in the Bandung Pact: Egypt, India, Indonesia, Yugoslavia, and Ceylon."

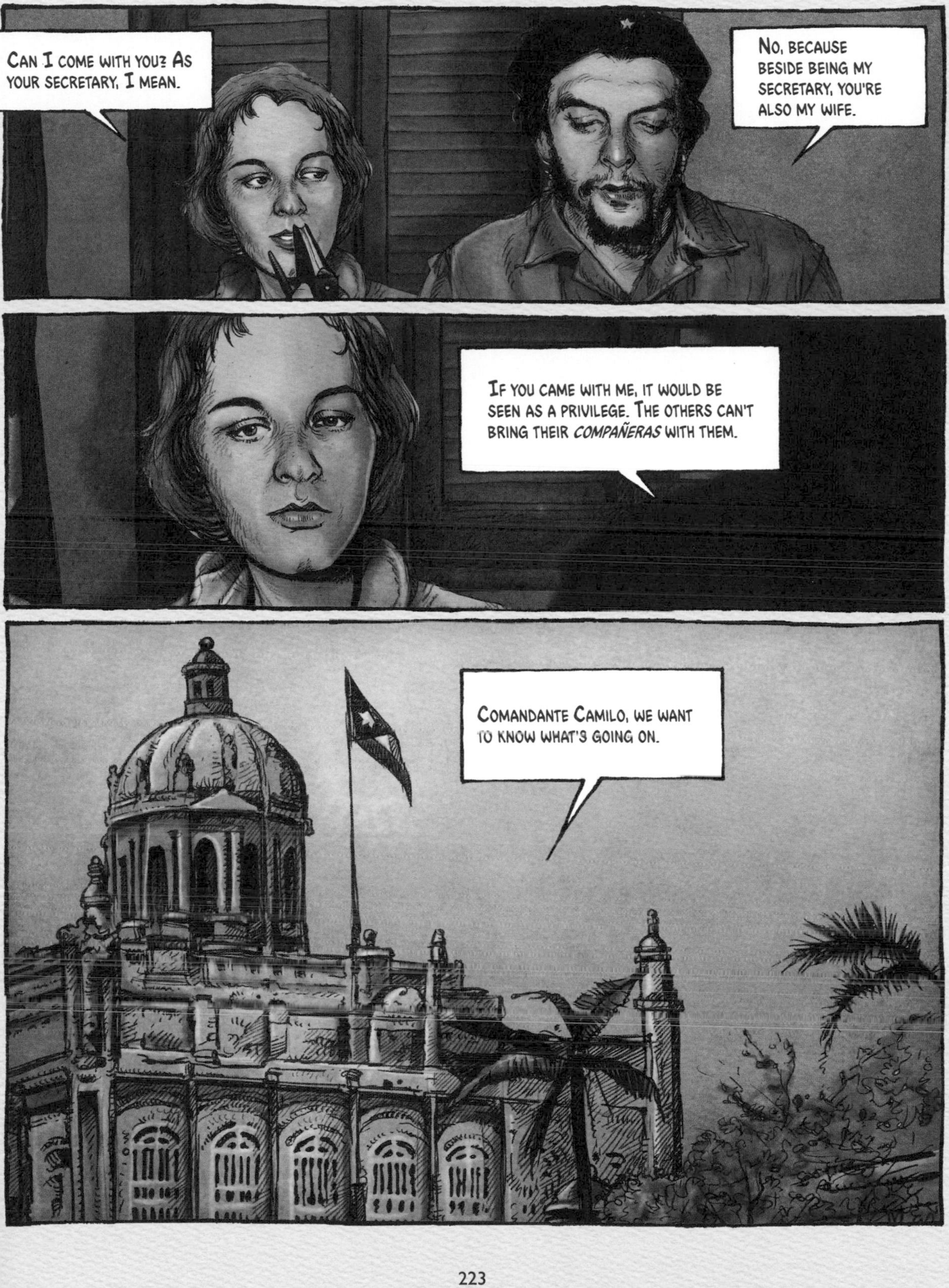

Can I come with you? As your secretary, I mean.
No, because beside being my secretary, you're also my wife.
If you came with me, it would be seen as a privilege. The others can't bring their *compañeras* with them.
Comandante Camilo, we want to know what's going on.

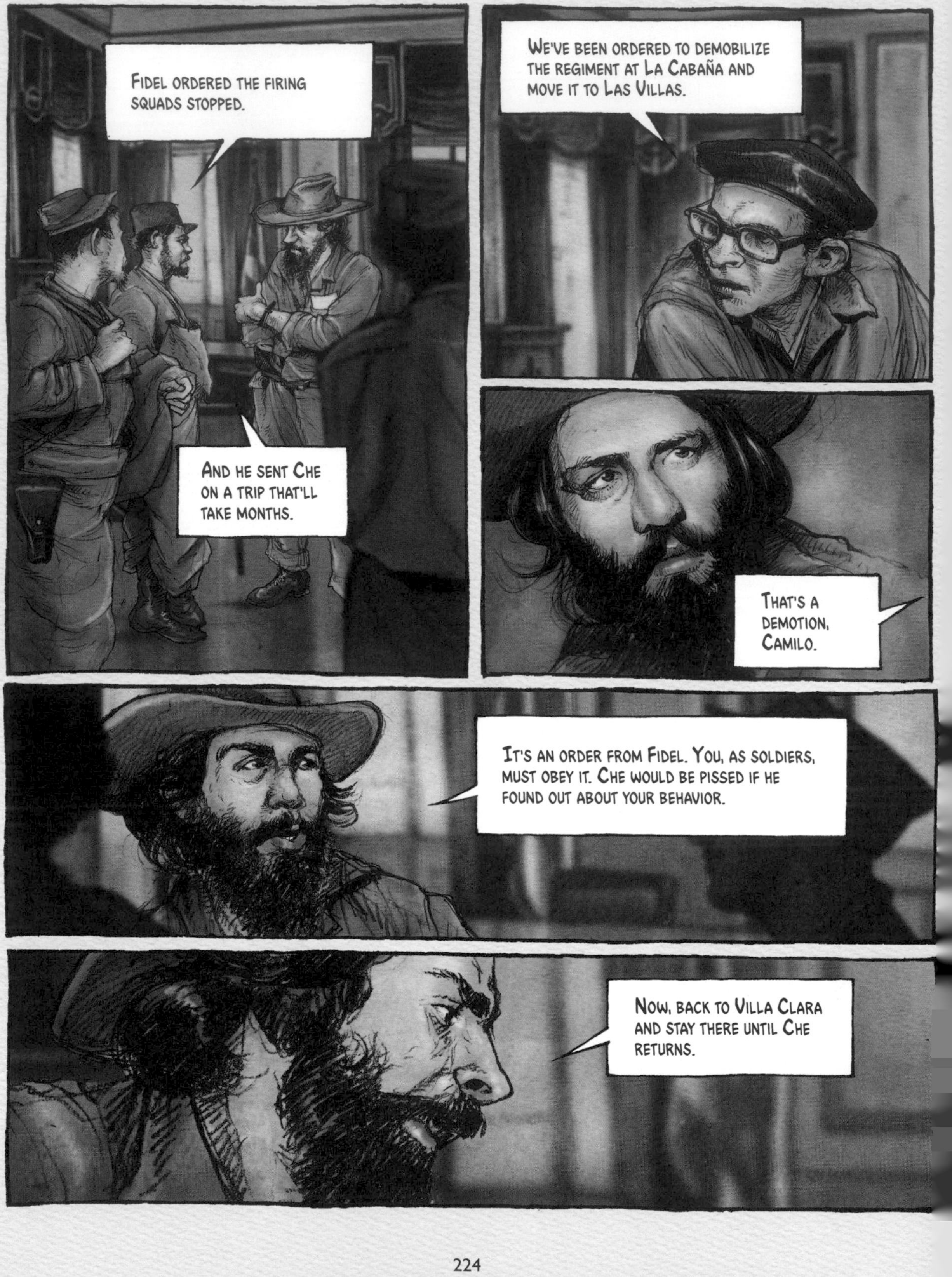
Fidel ordered the firing squads stopped.
And he sent Che on a trip that'll take months.
We've been ordered to demobilize the regiment at La Cabaña and move it to Las Villas.
That's a demotion, Camilo.
It's an order from Fidel. You, as soldiers, must obey it. Che would be pissed if he found out about your behavior.
Now, back to Villa Clara and stay there until Che returns.

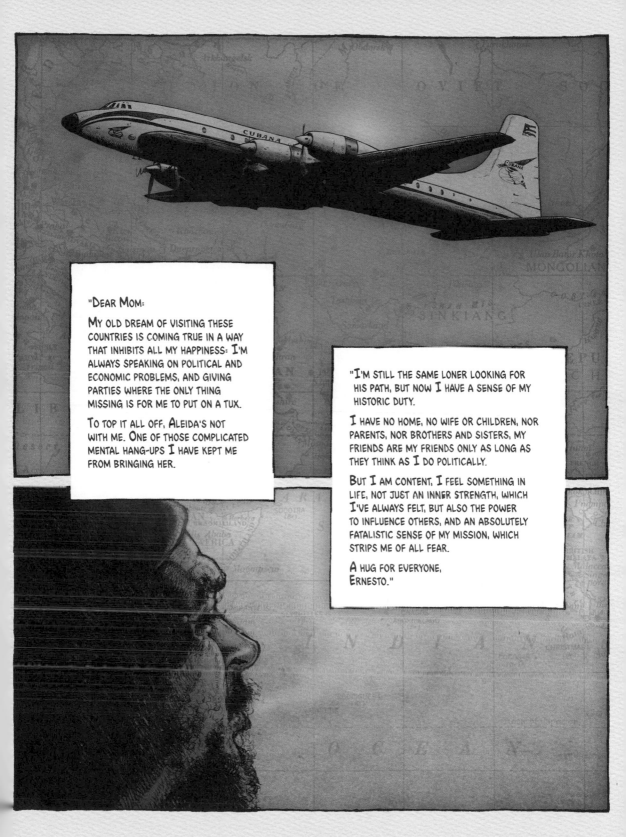

"Dear Mom:

My old dream of visiting these countries is coming true in a way that inhibits all my happiness: I'm always speaking on political and economic problems, and giving parties where the only thing missing is for me to put on a tux.

To top it all off, Aleida's not with me. One of those complicated mental hang-ups I have kept me from bringing her.

"I'm still the same loner looking for his path, but now I have a sense of my historic duty.

I have no home, no wife or children, nor parents, nor brothers and sisters, my friends are my friends only as long as they think as I do politically.

But I am content, I feel something in life, not just an inner strength, which I've always felt, but also the power to influence others, and an absolutely fatalistic sense of my mission, which strips me of all fear.

A hug for everyone,
Ernesto."

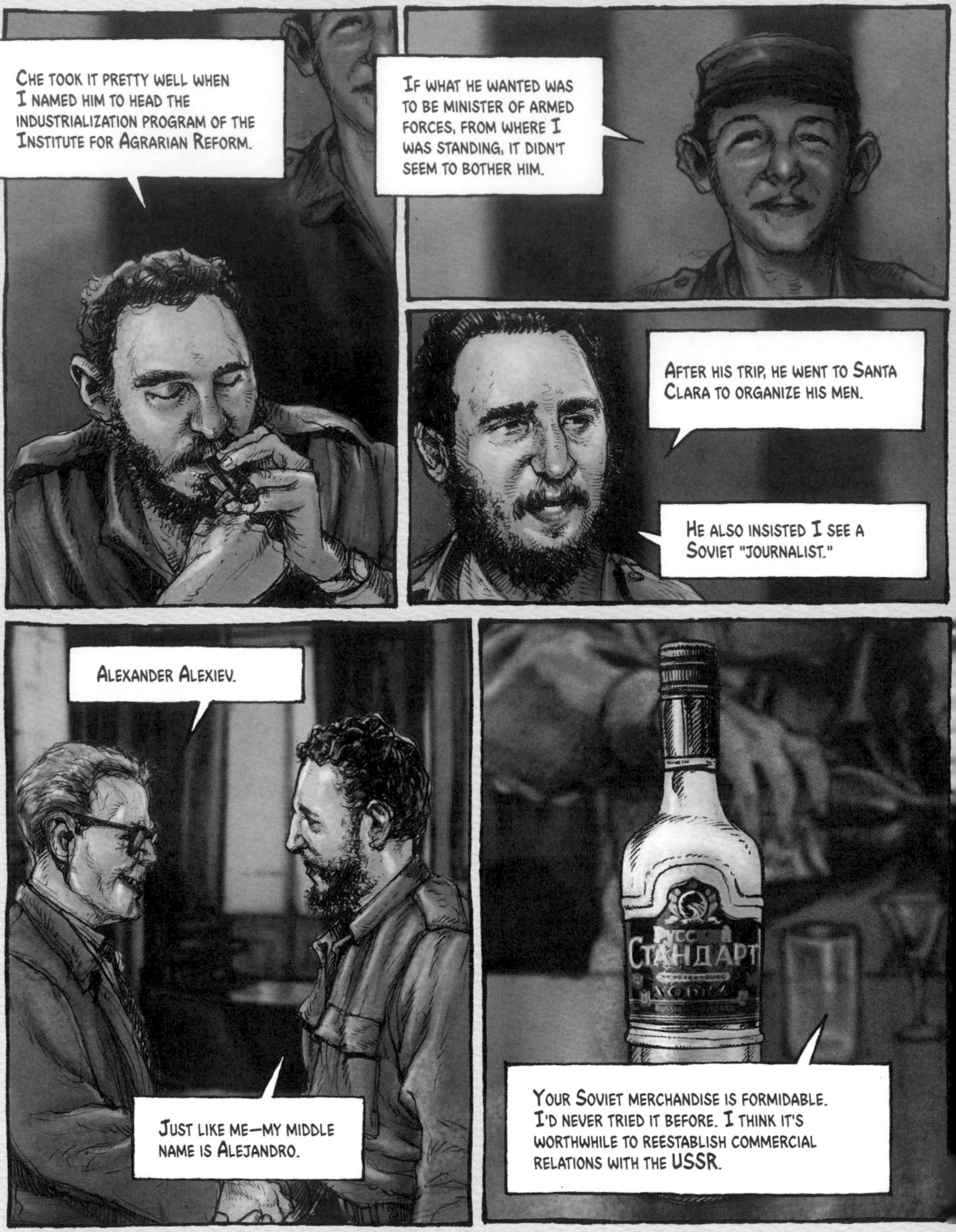
CHE TOOK IT PRETTY WELL WHEN I NAMED HIM TO HEAD THE INDUSTRIALIZATION PROGRAM OF THE INSTITUTE FOR AGRARIAN REFORM.
IF WHAT HE WANTED WAS TO BE MINISTER OF ARMED FORCES, FROM WHERE I WAS STANDING, IT DIDN'T SEEM TO BOTHER HIM.
AFTER HIS TRIP, HE WENT TO SANTA CLARA TO ORGANIZE HIS MEN.
HE ALSO INSISTED I SEE A SOVIET "JOURNALIST."
ALEXANDER ALEXIEV.
JUST LIKE ME—MY MIDDLE NAME IS ALEJANDRO.
СТАНДАРТ
YOUR SOVIET MERCHANDISE IS FORMIDABLE. I'D NEVER TRIED IT BEFORE. I THINK IT'S WORTHWHILE TO REESTABLISH COMMERCIAL RELATIONS WITH THE USSR.

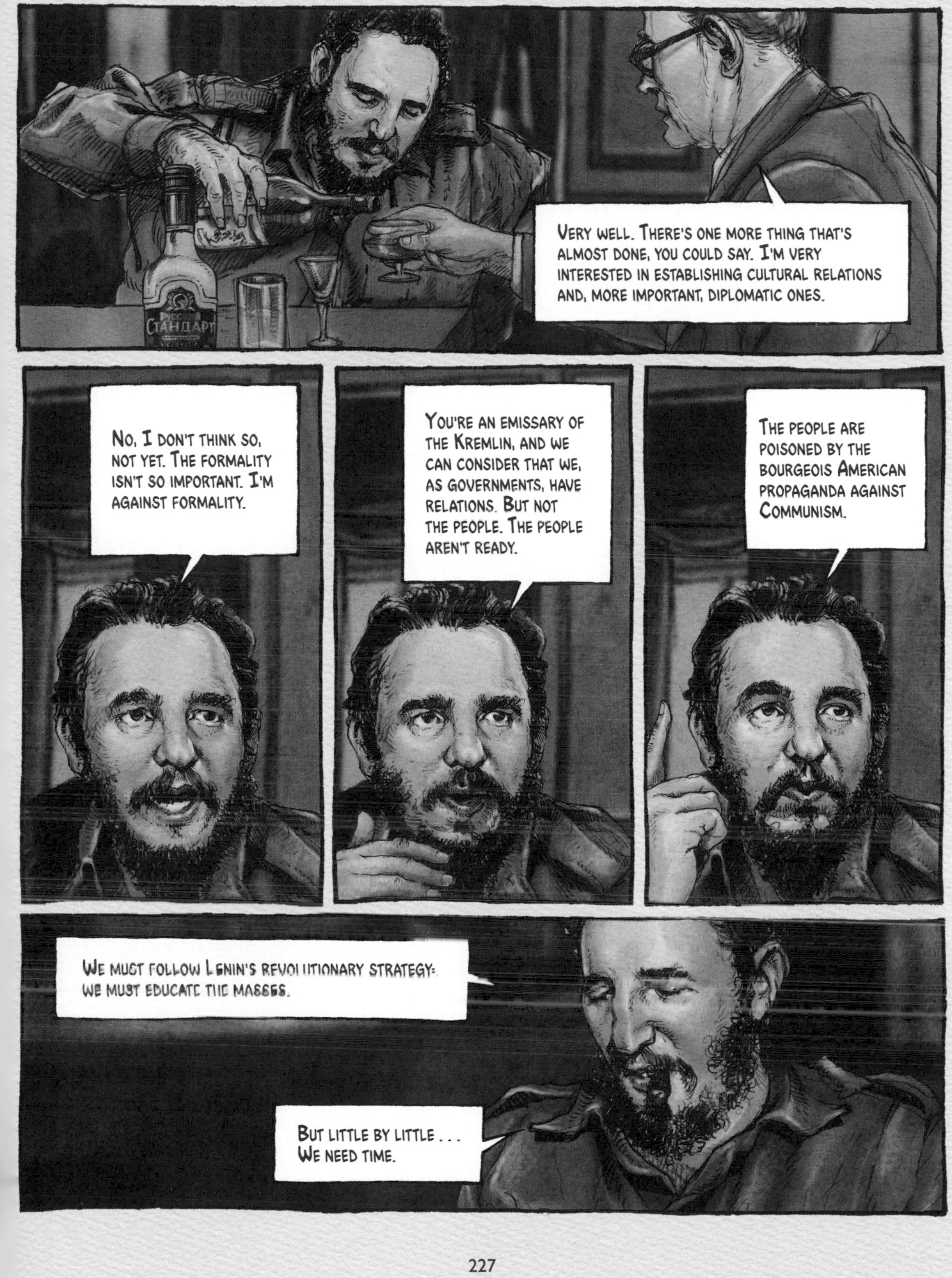
СТАНДАРТ
VERY WELL. THERE'S ONE MORE THING THAT'S ALMOST DONE, YOU COULD SAY. I'M VERY INTERESTED IN ESTABLISHING CULTURAL RELATIONS AND, MORE IMPORTANT, DIPLOMATIC ONES.
NO, I DON'T THINK SO, NOT YET. THE FORMALITY ISN'T SO IMPORTANT. I'M AGAINST FORMALITY.
YOU'RE AN EMISSARY OF THE KREMLIN, AND WE CAN CONSIDER THAT WE, AS GOVERNMENTS, HAVE RELATIONS. BUT NOT THE PEOPLE. THE PEOPLE AREN'T READY.
THE PEOPLE ARE POISONED BY THE BOURGEOIS AMERICAN PROPAGANDA AGAINST COMMUNISM.
WE MUST FOLLOW LENIN'S REVOLUTIONARY STRATEGY: WE MUST EDUCATE THE MASSES.
BUT LITTLE BY LITTLE . . . WE NEED TIME.

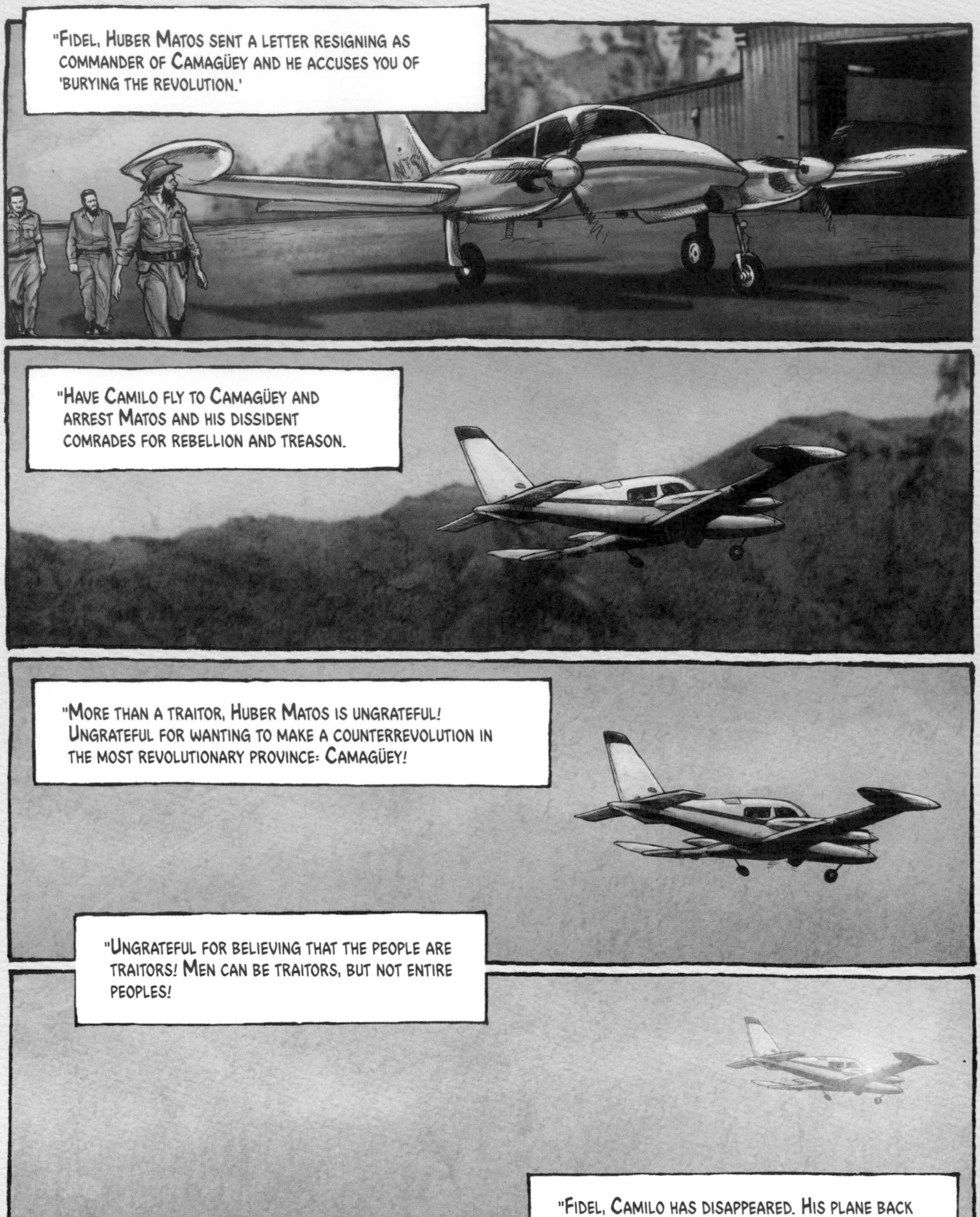
"FIDEL, HUBER MATOS SENT A LETTER RESIGNING AS COMMANDER OF CAMAGÜEY AND HE ACCUSES YOU OF 'BURYING THE REVOLUTION.'
"HAVE CAMILO FLY TO CAMAGÜEY AND ARREST MATOS AND HIS DISSIDENT COMRADES FOR REBELLION AND TREASON.
"MORE THAN A TRAITOR, HUBER MATOS IS UNGRATEFUL! UNGRATEFUL FOR WANTING TO MAKE A COUNTERREVOLUTION IN THE MOST REVOLUTIONARY PROVINCE: CAMAGÜEY!
"UNGRATEFUL FOR BELIEVING THAT THE PEOPLE ARE TRAITORS! MEN CAN BE TRAITORS, BUT NOT ENTIRE PEOPLES!
"FIDEL, CAMILO HAS DISAPPEARED. HIS PLANE BACK FROM CAMAGÜEY NEVER ARRIVED."

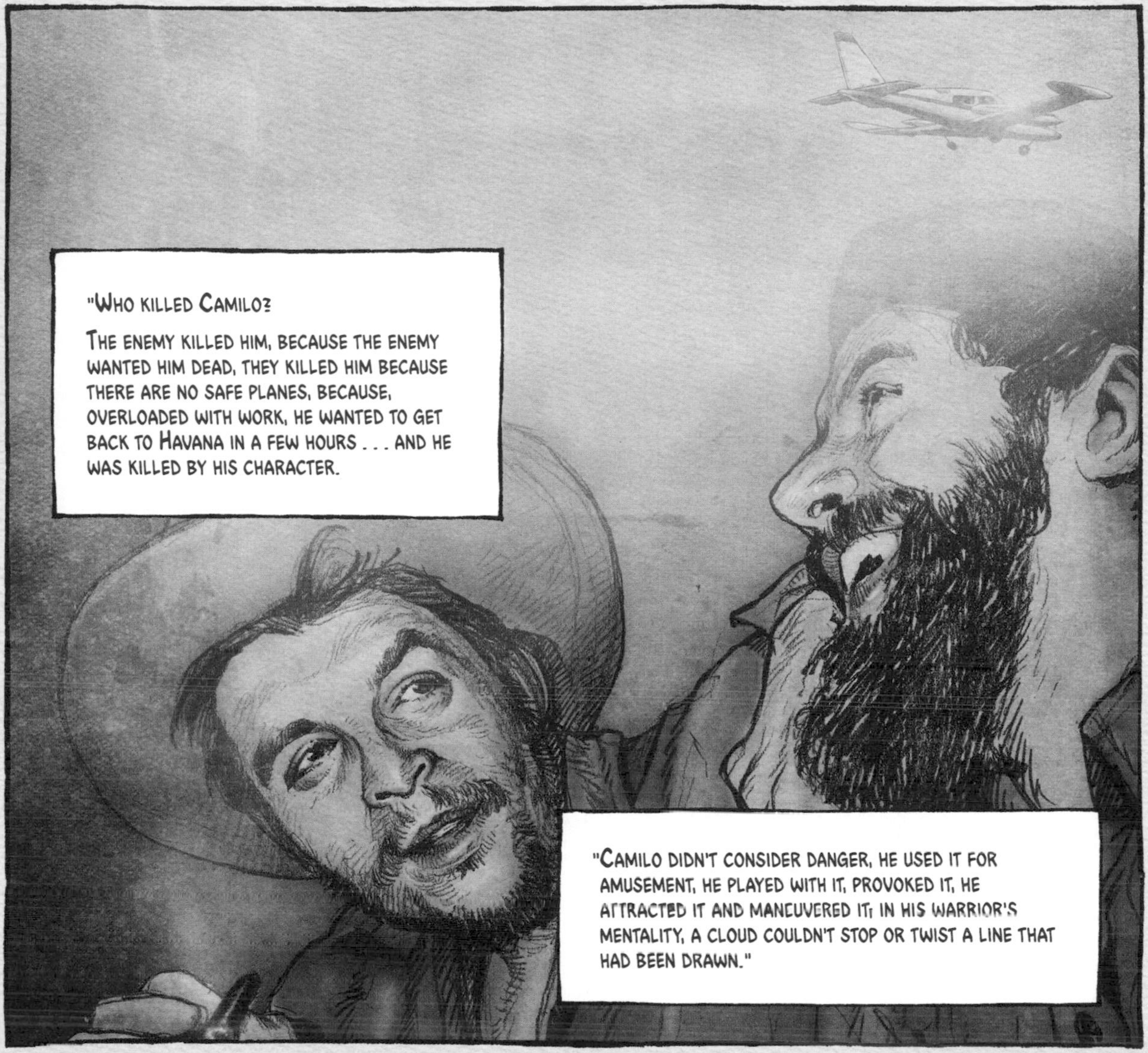
"Who killed Camilo?
The enemy killed him, because the enemy wanted him dead, they killed him because there are no safe planes, because, overloaded with work, he wanted to get back to Havana in a few hours . . . and he was killed by his character.
"Camilo didn't consider danger, he used it for amusement, he played with it, provoked it, he attracted it and maneuvered it; in his warrior's mentality, a cloud couldn't stop or twist a line that had been drawn."

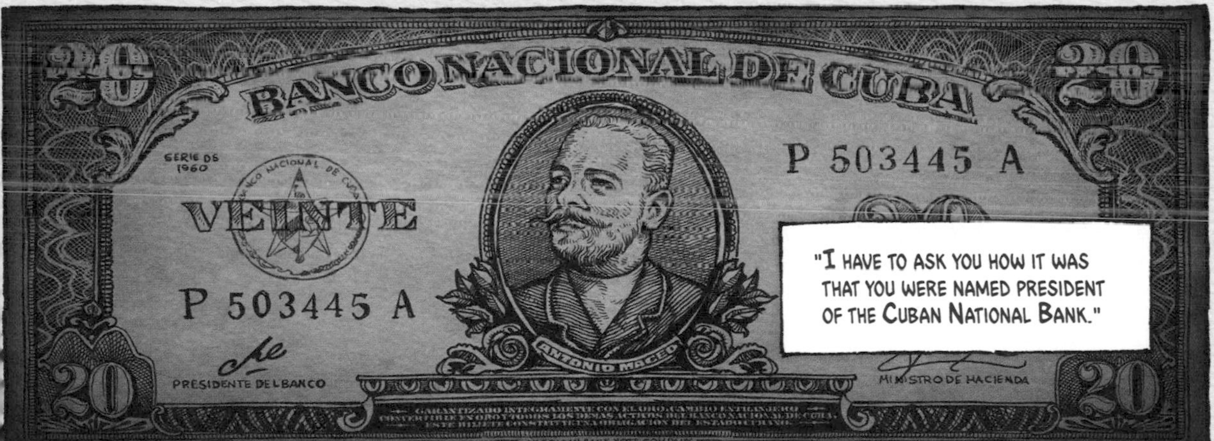
20
BANCO NACIONAL DE CUBA
20
SERIE DE 1960
BANCO NACIONAL DE CUBA
VEINTE
P 503445 A
P 503445 A
ANTONIO MACEO
PRESIDENTE DEL BANCO
MINISTRO DE HACIENDA
20
20
AMERICAN BANK NOTE COMPANY
"I have to ask you how it was that you were named president of the Cuban National Bank."

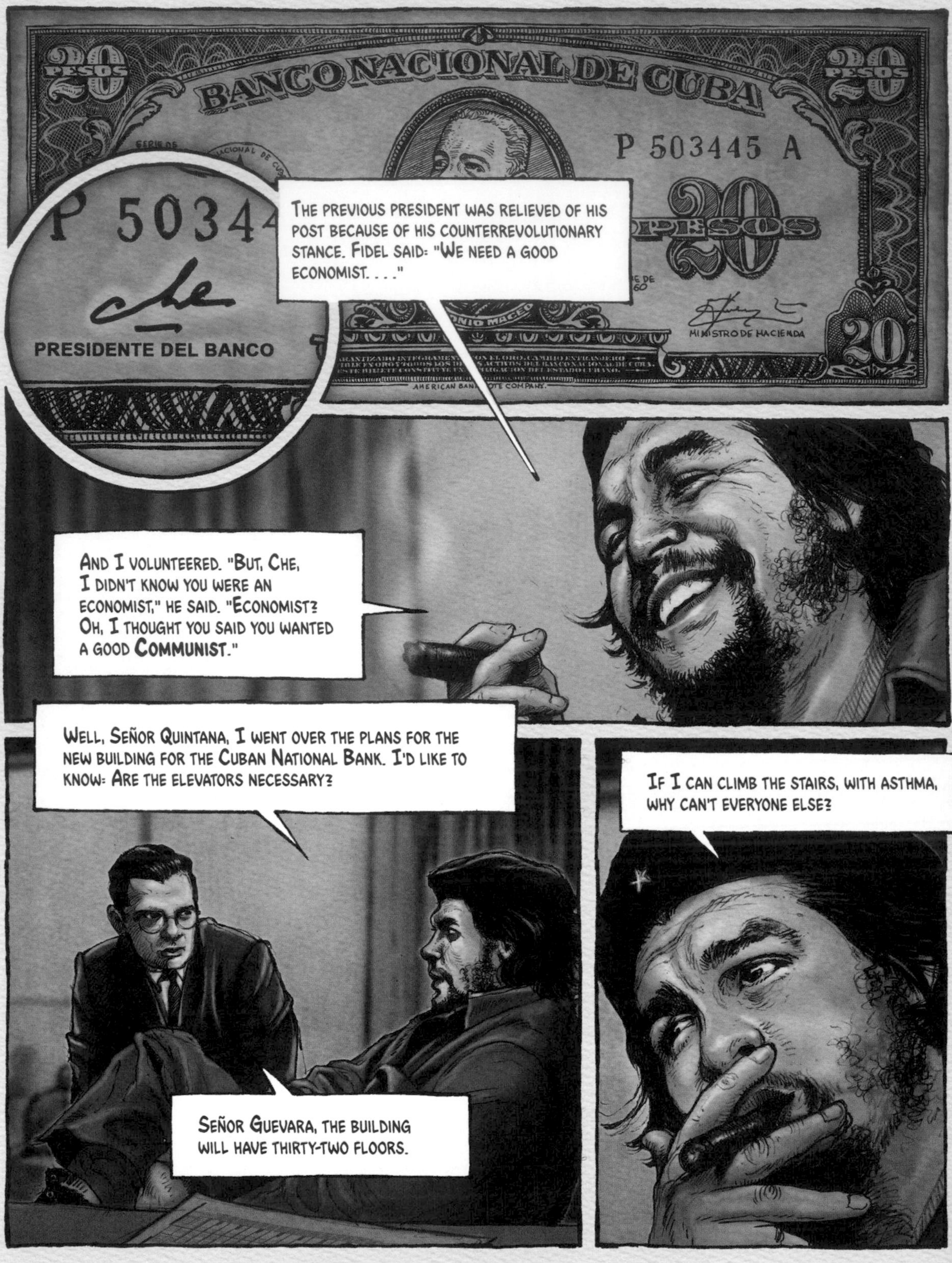
20 PESOS
BANCO NACIONAL DE CUBA
20 PESOS
P 503445 A
20 PESOS
PRESIDENTE DEL BANCO
MINISTRO DE HACIENDA
20
AMERICAN BANK NOTE COMPANY
THE PREVIOUS PRESIDENT WAS RELIEVED OF HIS POST BECAUSE OF HIS COUNTERREVOLUTIONARY STANCE. FIDEL SAID: "WE NEED A GOOD ECONOMIST. . . ."
AND I VOLUNTEERED. "BUT, CHE, I DIDN'T KNOW YOU WERE AN ECONOMIST," HE SAID. "ECONOMIST? OH, I THOUGHT YOU SAID YOU WANTED A GOOD COMMUNIST."
WELL, SEÑOR QUINTANA, I WENT OVER THE PLANS FOR THE NEW BUILDING FOR THE CUBAN NATIONAL BANK. I'D LIKE TO KNOW: ARE THE ELEVATORS NECESSARY?
SEÑOR GUEVARA, THE BUILDING WILL HAVE THIRTY-TWO FLOORS.
IF I CAN CLIMB THE STAIRS, WITH ASTHMA, WHY CAN'T EVERYONE ELSE?

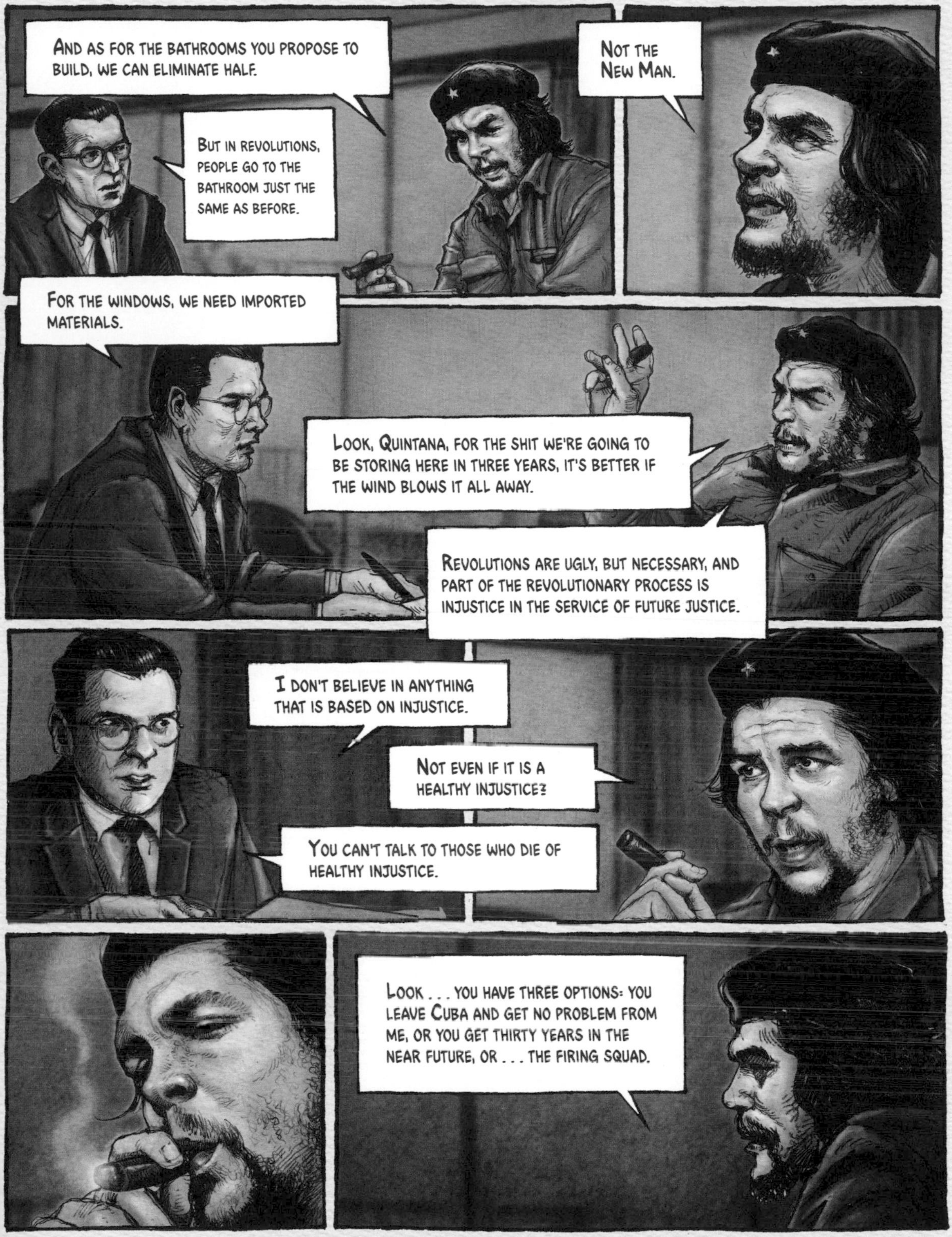
And as for the bathrooms you propose to build, we can eliminate half.
But in revolutions, people go to the bathroom just the same as before.
Not the New Man.
For the windows, we need imported materials.
Look, Quintana, for the shit we're going to be storing here in three years, it's better if the wind blows it all away.
Revolutions are ugly, but necessary, and part of the revolutionary process is injustice in the service of future justice.
I don't believe in anything that is based on injustice.
Not even if it is a healthy injustice?
You can't talk to those who die of healthy injustice.
Look . . . you have three options: you leave Cuba and get no problem from me, or you get thirty years in the near future, or . . . the firing squad.

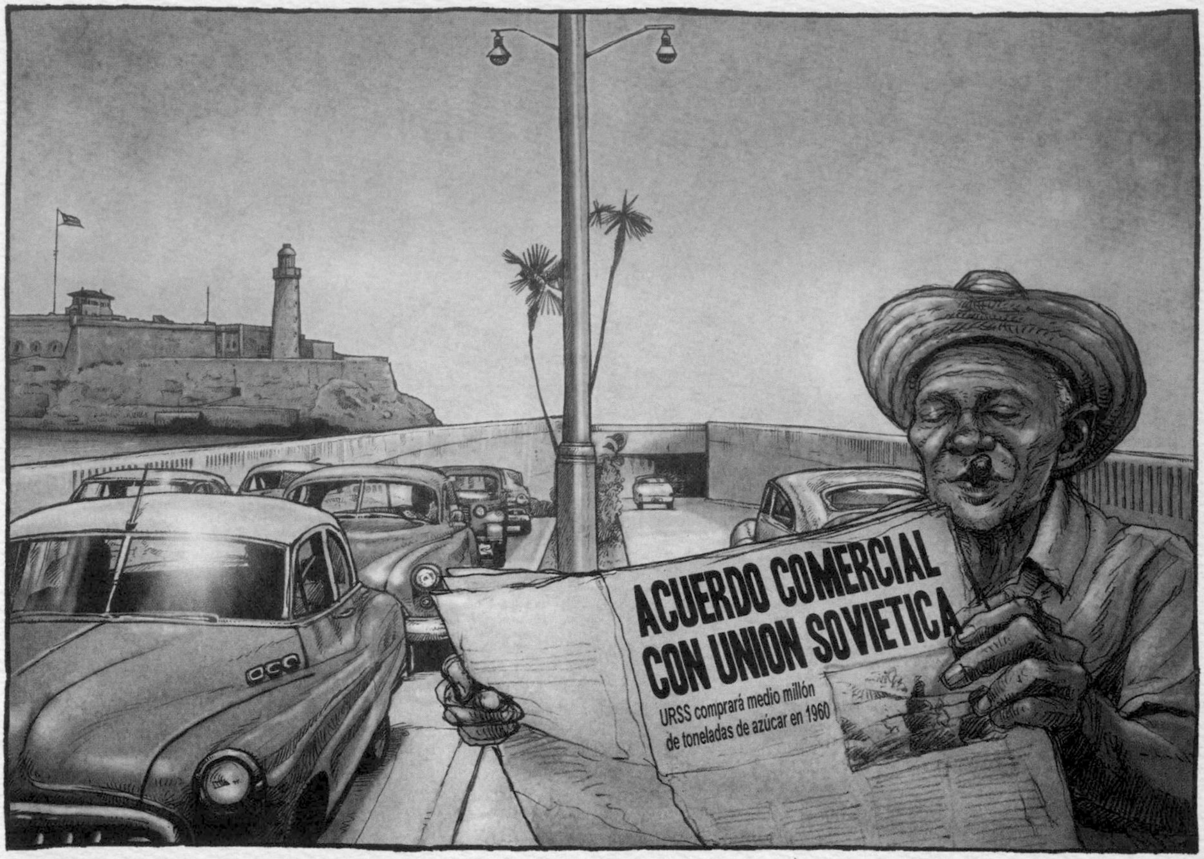
ACUERDO COMERCIAL CON UNION SOVIETICA
URSS comprará medio millón de toneladas de azúcar en 1960

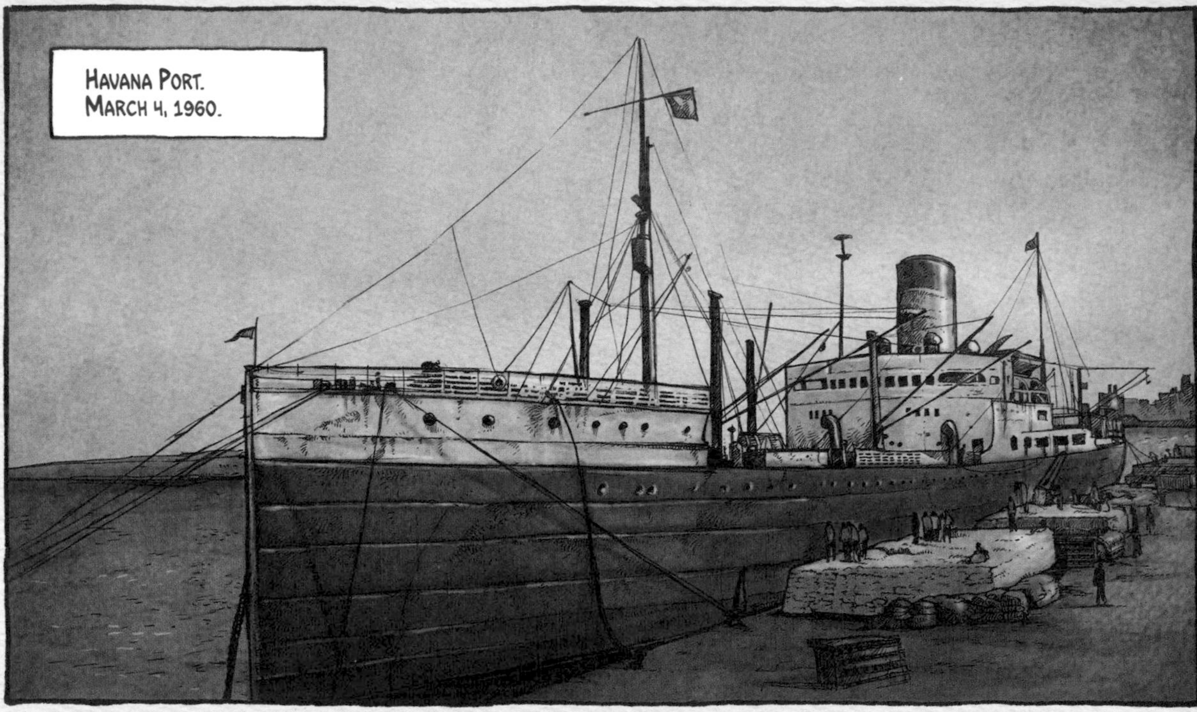
HAVANA PORT.
MARCH 4, 1960.

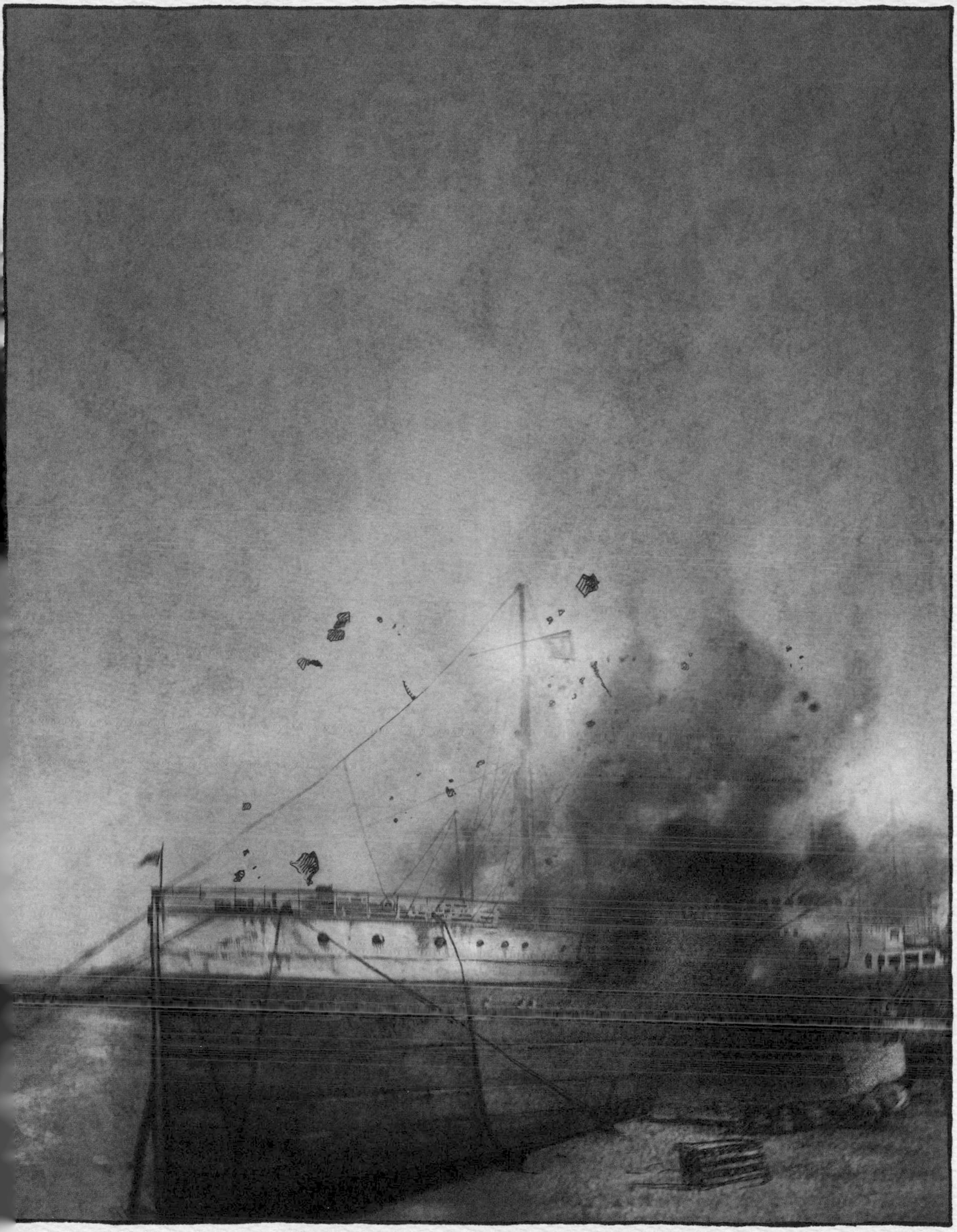

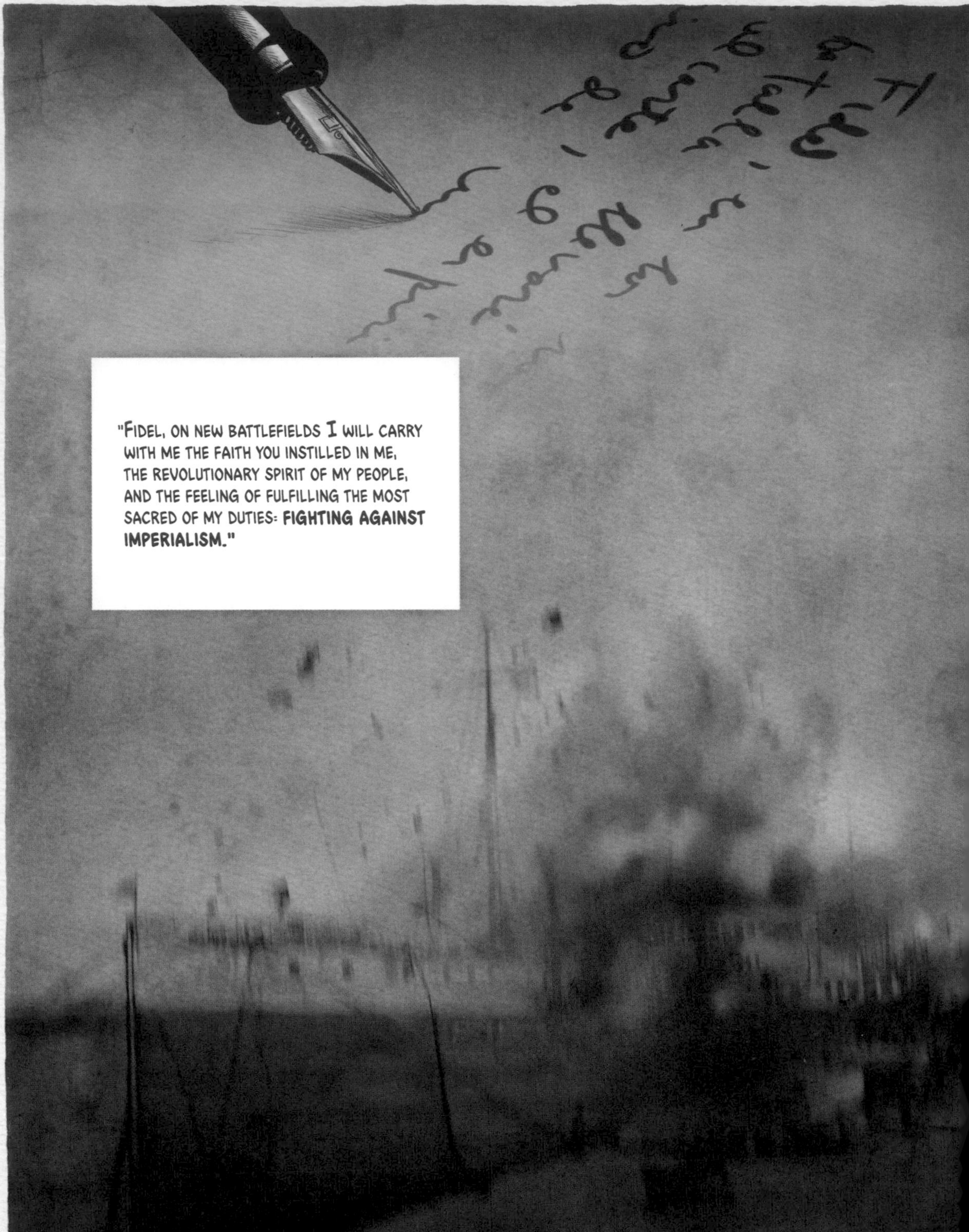
"FIDEL, ON NEW BATTLEFIELDS I WILL CARRY WITH ME THE FAITH YOU INSTILLED IN ME, THE REVOLUTIONARY SPIRIT OF MY PEOPLE, AND THE FEELING OF FULFILLING THE MOST SACRED OF MY DUTIES: **FIGHTING AGAINST IMPERIALISM.**"

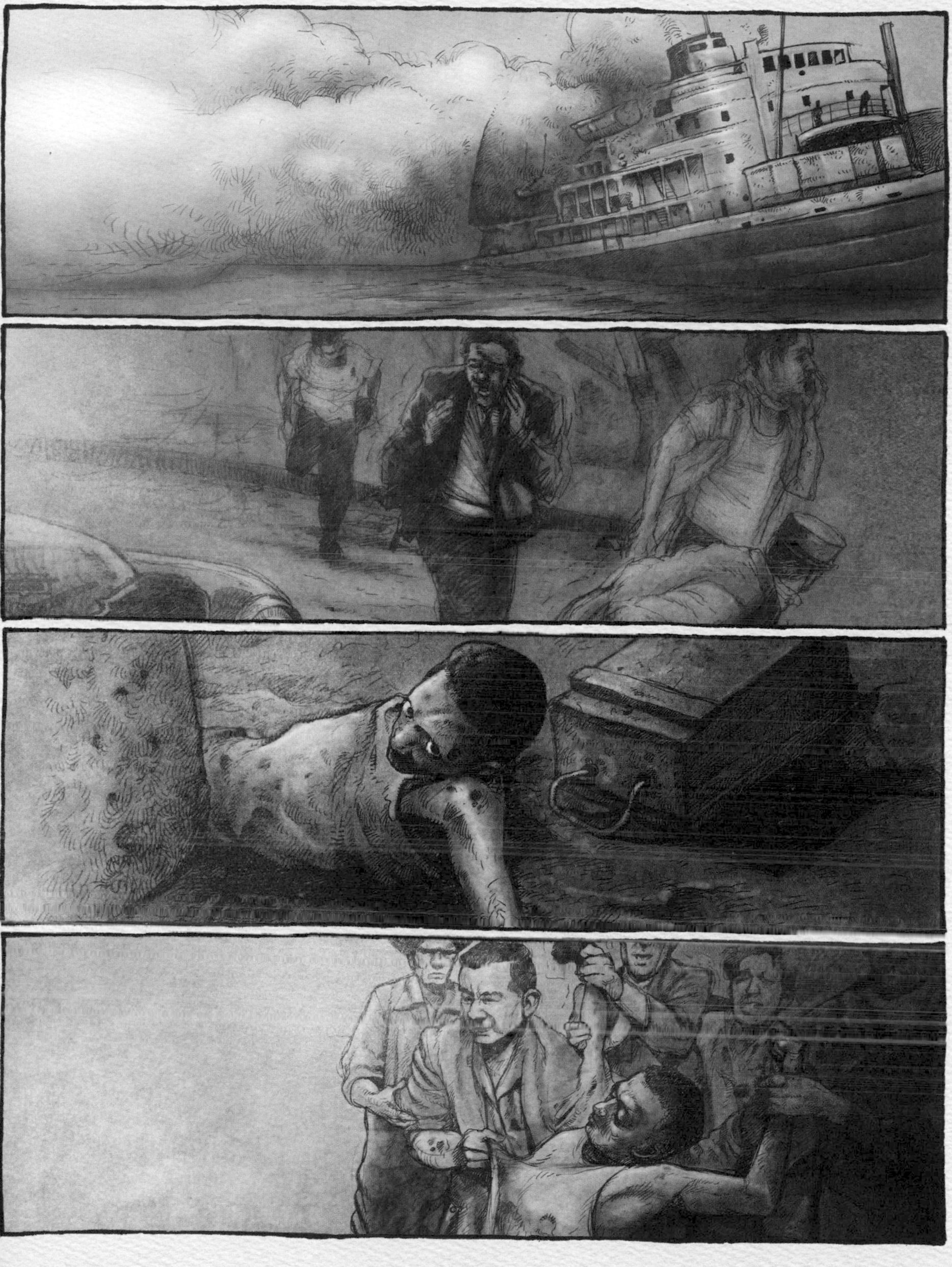

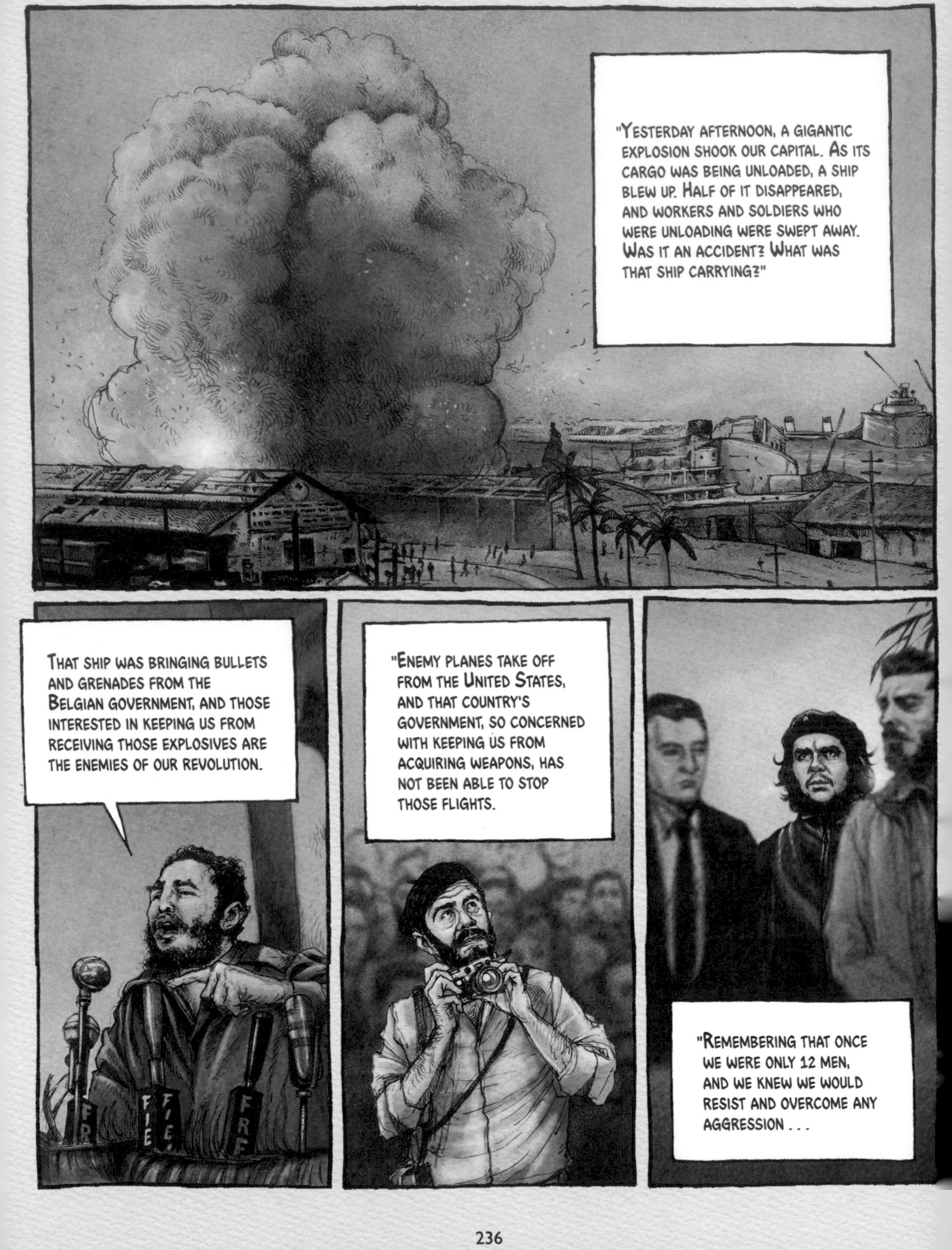
"YESTERDAY AFTERNOON, A GIGANTIC EXPLOSION SHOOK OUR CAPITAL. AS ITS CARGO WAS BEING UNLOADED, A SHIP BLEW UP. HALF OF IT DISAPPEARED, AND WORKERS AND SOLDIERS WHO WERE UNLOADING WERE SWEPT AWAY. WAS IT AN ACCIDENT? WHAT WAS THAT SHIP CARRYING?"
THAT SHIP WAS BRINGING BULLETS AND GRENADES FROM THE BELGIAN GOVERNMENT, AND THOSE INTERESTED IN KEEPING US FROM RECEIVING THOSE EXPLOSIVES ARE THE ENEMIES OF OUR REVOLUTION.
"ENEMY PLANES TAKE OFF FROM THE UNITED STATES, AND THAT COUNTRY'S GOVERNMENT, SO CONCERNED WITH KEEPING US FROM ACQUIRING WEAPONS, HAS NOT BEEN ABLE TO STOP THOSE FLIGHTS.
"REMEMBERING THAT ONCE WE WERE ONLY 12 MEN, AND WE KNEW WE WOULD RESIST AND OVERCOME ANY AGGRESSION . . .

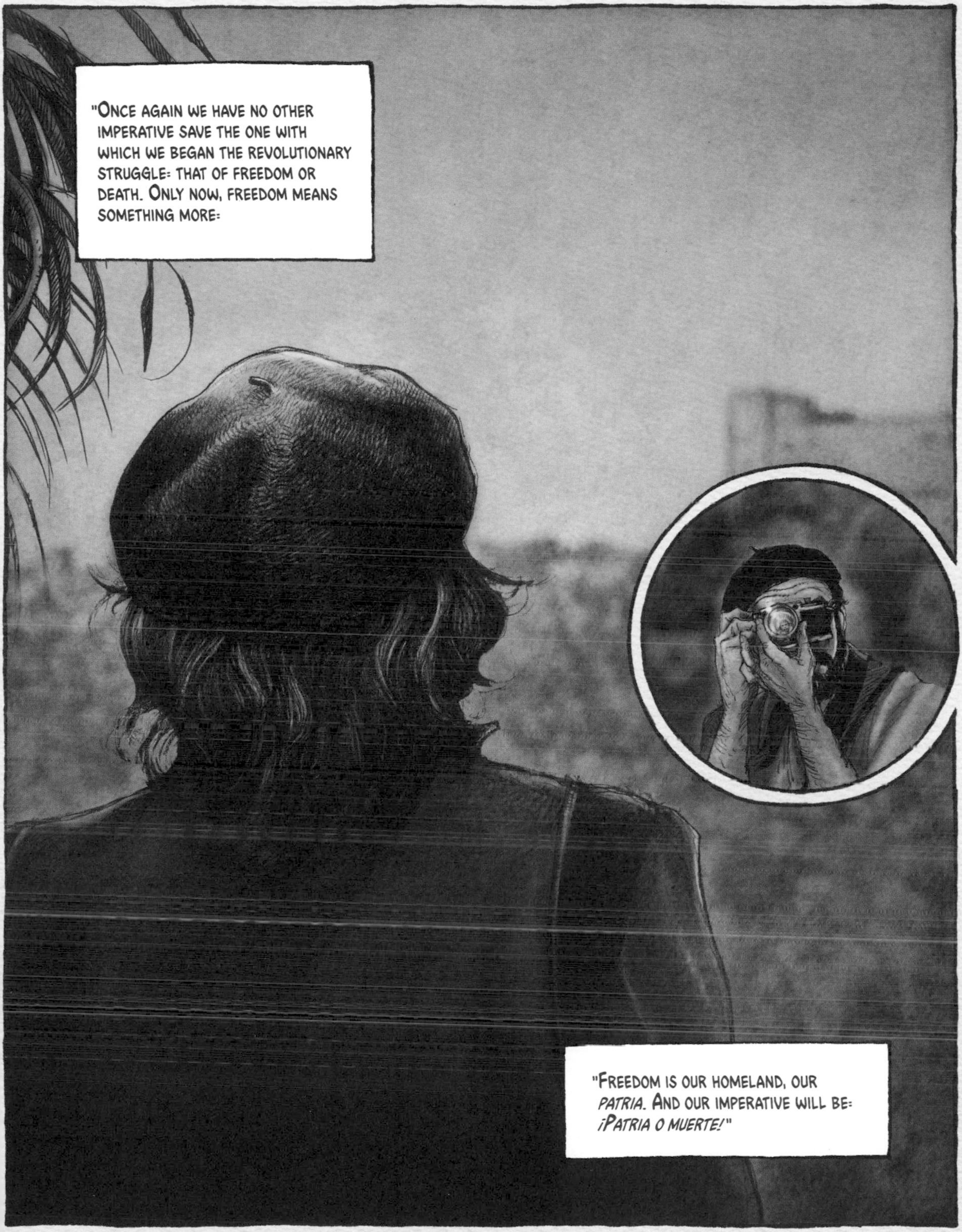
"Once again we have no other imperative save the one with which we began the revolutionary struggle: that of freedom or death. Only now, freedom means something more:
"Freedom is our homeland, our *patria*. And our imperative will be: *¡Patria o muerte!*"

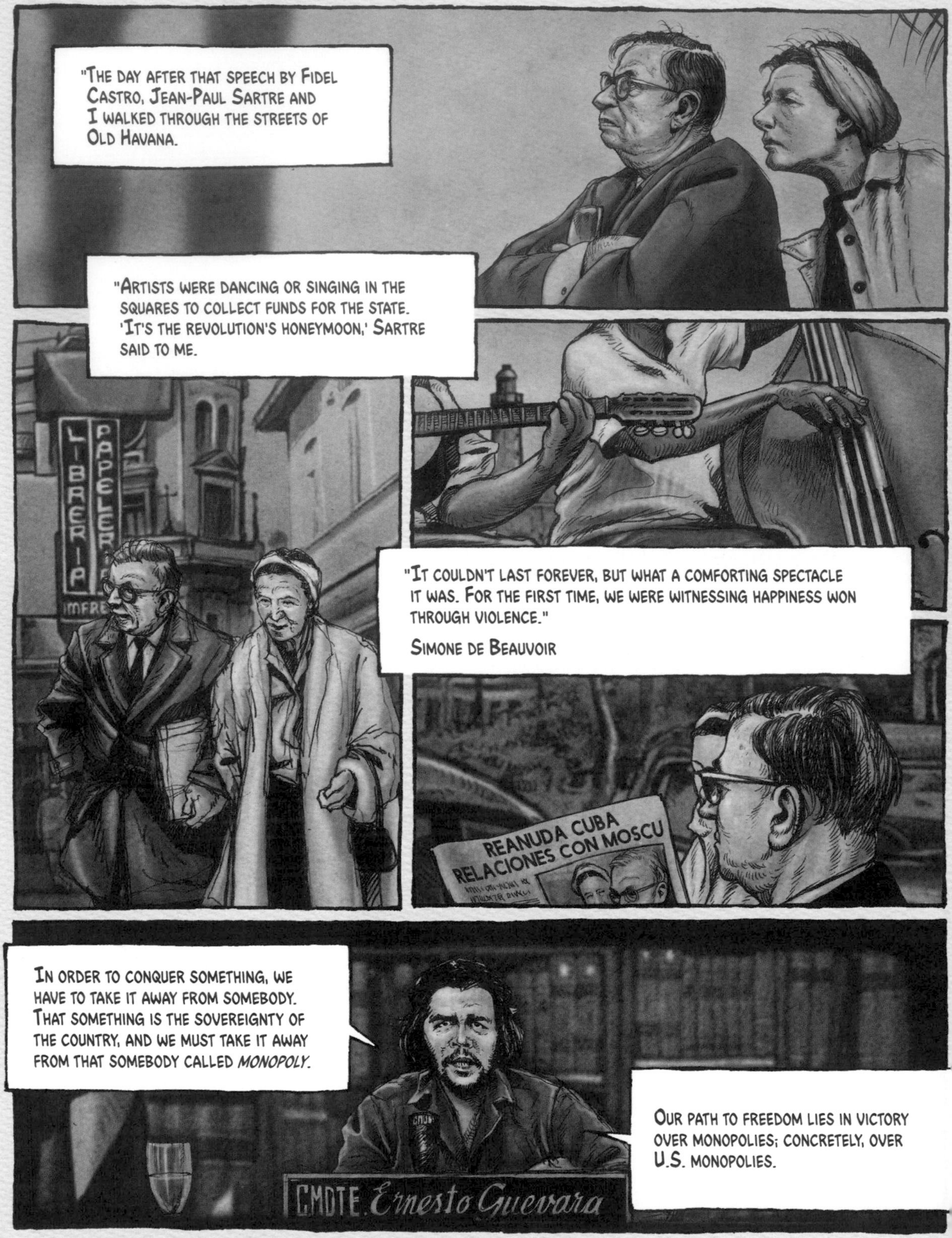
"THE DAY AFTER THAT SPEECH BY FIDEL CASTRO, JEAN-PAUL SARTRE AND I WALKED THROUGH THE STREETS OF OLD HAVANA.
"ARTISTS WERE DANCING OR SINGING IN THE SQUARES TO COLLECT FUNDS FOR THE STATE. 'IT'S THE REVOLUTION'S HONEYMOON,' SARTRE SAID TO ME.
LIBRERIA
PAPELERIA
"IT COULDN'T LAST FOREVER, BUT WHAT A COMFORTING SPECTACLE IT WAS. FOR THE FIRST TIME, WE WERE WITNESSING HAPPINESS WON THROUGH VIOLENCE."
SIMONE DE BEAUVOIR
REANUDA CUBA RELACIONES CON MOSCU
IN ORDER TO CONQUER SOMETHING, WE HAVE TO TAKE IT AWAY FROM SOMEBODY. THAT SOMETHING IS THE SOVEREIGNTY OF THE COUNTRY, AND WE MUST TAKE IT AWAY FROM THAT SOMEBODY CALLED *MONOPOLY*.
CMDTE. Ernesto Guevara
OUR PATH TO FREEDOM LIES IN VICTORY OVER MONOPOLIES; CONCRETELY, OVER U.S. MONOPOLIES.

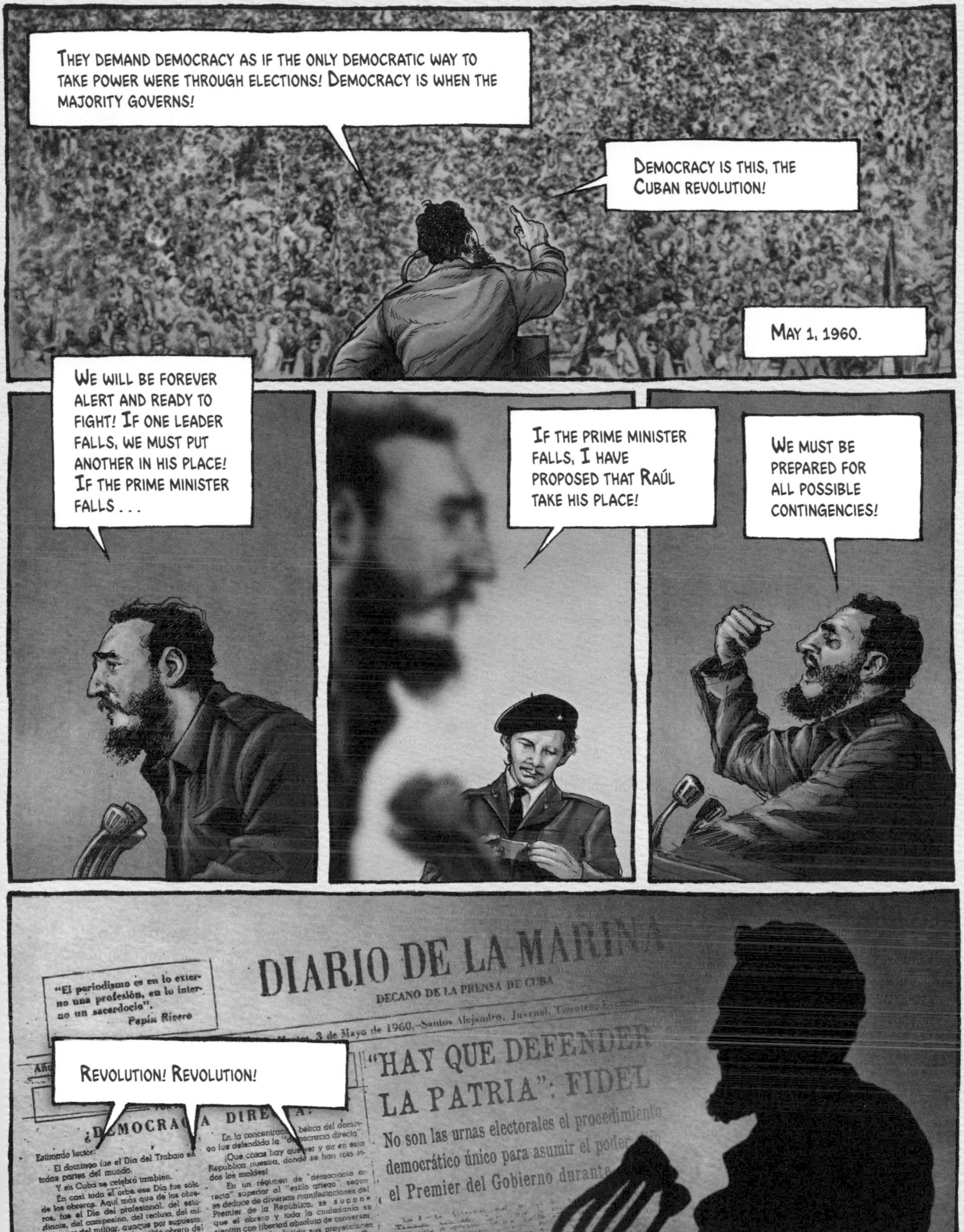
THEY DEMAND DEMOCRACY AS IF THE ONLY DEMOCRATIC WAY TO TAKE POWER WERE THROUGH ELECTIONS! DEMOCRACY IS WHEN THE MAJORITY GOVERNS!
DEMOCRACY IS THIS, THE CUBAN REVOLUTION!
MAY 1, 1960.
WE WILL BE FOREVER ALERT AND READY TO FIGHT! IF ONE LEADER FALLS, WE MUST PUT ANOTHER IN HIS PLACE! IF THE PRIME MINISTER FALLS . . .
IF THE PRIME MINISTER FALLS, I HAVE PROPOSED THAT RAÚL TAKE HIS PLACE!
WE MUST BE PREPARED FOR ALL POSSIBLE CONTINGENCIES!
DIARIO DE LA MARINA
DECANO DE LA PRENSA DE CUBA
"El periodismo es en lo externo una profesión, en lo interno un sacerdocio". Pepín Rivero
"HAY QUE DEFENDER LA PATRIA": FIDEL
No son las urnas electorales el procedimiento democrático único para asumir el poder
el Premier del Gobierno durante
REVOLUTION! REVOLUTION!

Slogans and more slogans, but none has the flavor of peace, tranquility, calm, of freedom or democracy. One of the many slogans was that of "No elections." The cry of "Elections, what for?" was repeated many times. Do you know of any Communist who does not fear elections? The Marxists detest the ballot box because they are aware that their ranks are an insignificant minority, and that the immense majority of our Christian and democratic republic repudiates them.

Either we do not understand well, dear readers, what a "direct democracy" is, or, convinced as we are that there is no democracy besides a truly representative one that honors universal suffrage, the kind of democracy here, "direct" or "superior to the Greeks, " looks very similar to that of Perón, Hitler, Mussolini, Khrushchev, or Mao Zedong.

NOTE.—The previous text is published at the will of this journalistic company in exercise of the freedom of the press, but the Local Committee of Freedom of the Press of Journalists and Artists of this labor center expresses that its contents, including a profusion of historical and bellicose phrases mixed in with the names of Hitler, Mussolini, Perón, etc., has only one common denominator: a savage attack on the Cuban Revolution.

PATRIA O MUERTE.

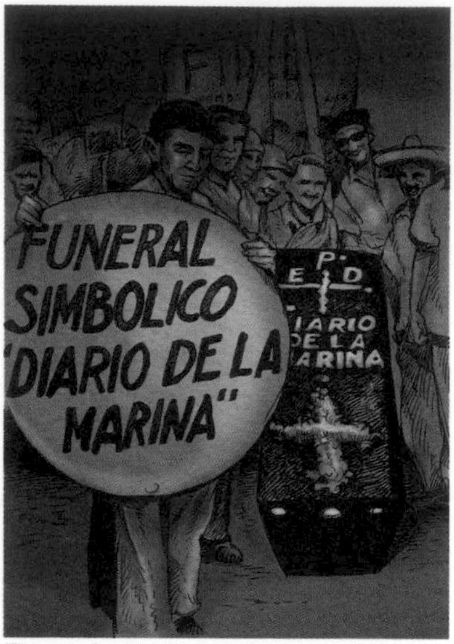

FIDEL
FUNERAL SIMBOLICO "DIARIO DE LA MARINA"
E.P.D.
DIARIO DE LA MARINA

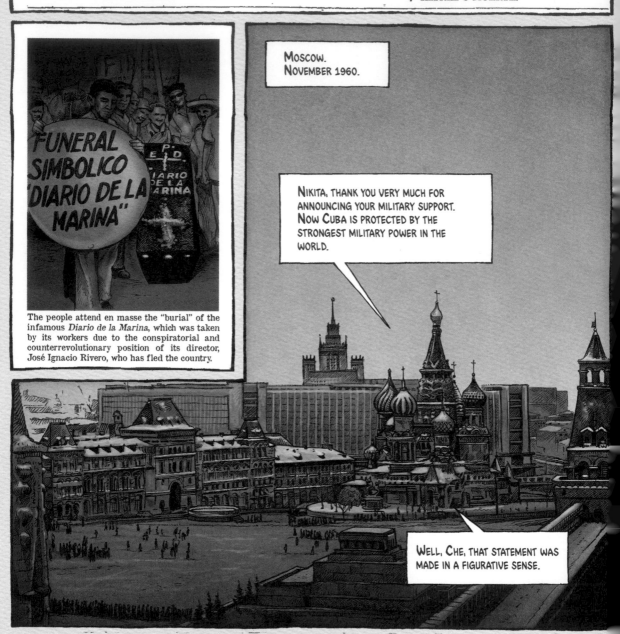

The people attend en masse the "burial" of the infamous *Diario de la Marina*, which was taken by its workers due to the conspiratorial and counterrevolutionary position of its director, José Ignacio Rivero, who has fled the country.

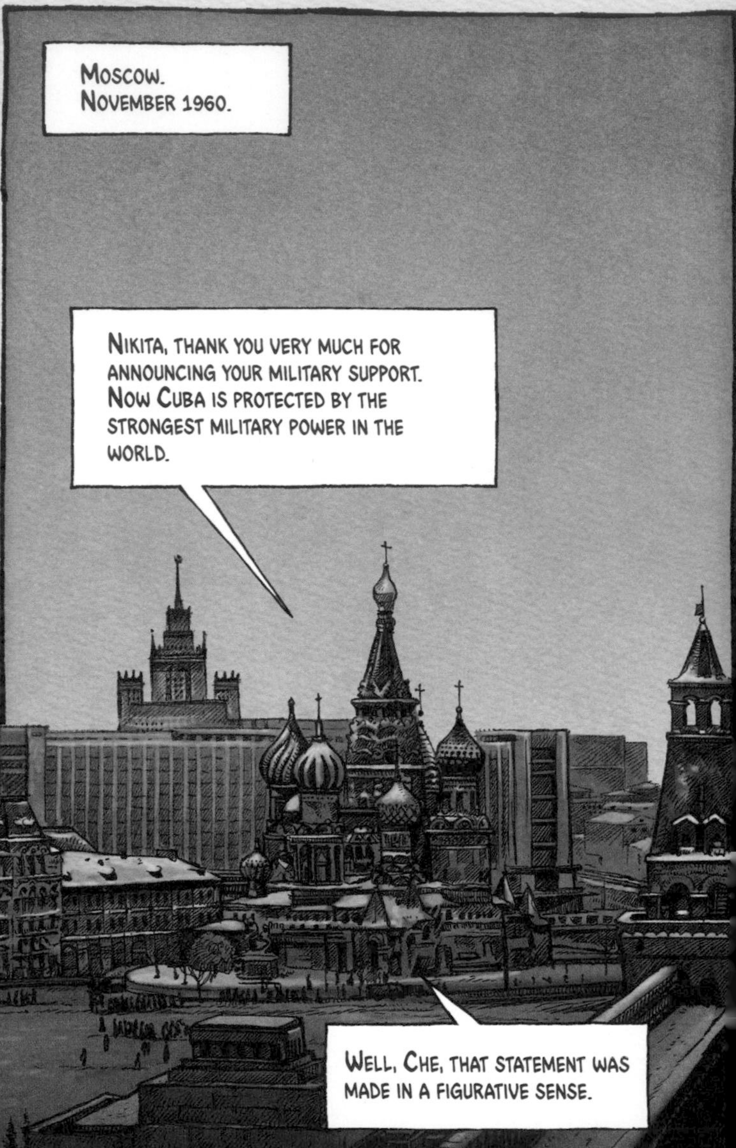

MOSCOW. NOVEMBER 1960.
NIKITA, THANK YOU VERY MUCH FOR ANNOUNCING YOUR MILITARY SUPPORT. NOW CUBA IS PROTECTED BY THE STRONGEST MILITARY POWER IN THE WORLD.
WELL, CHE, THAT STATEMENT WAS MADE IN A FIGURATIVE SENSE.

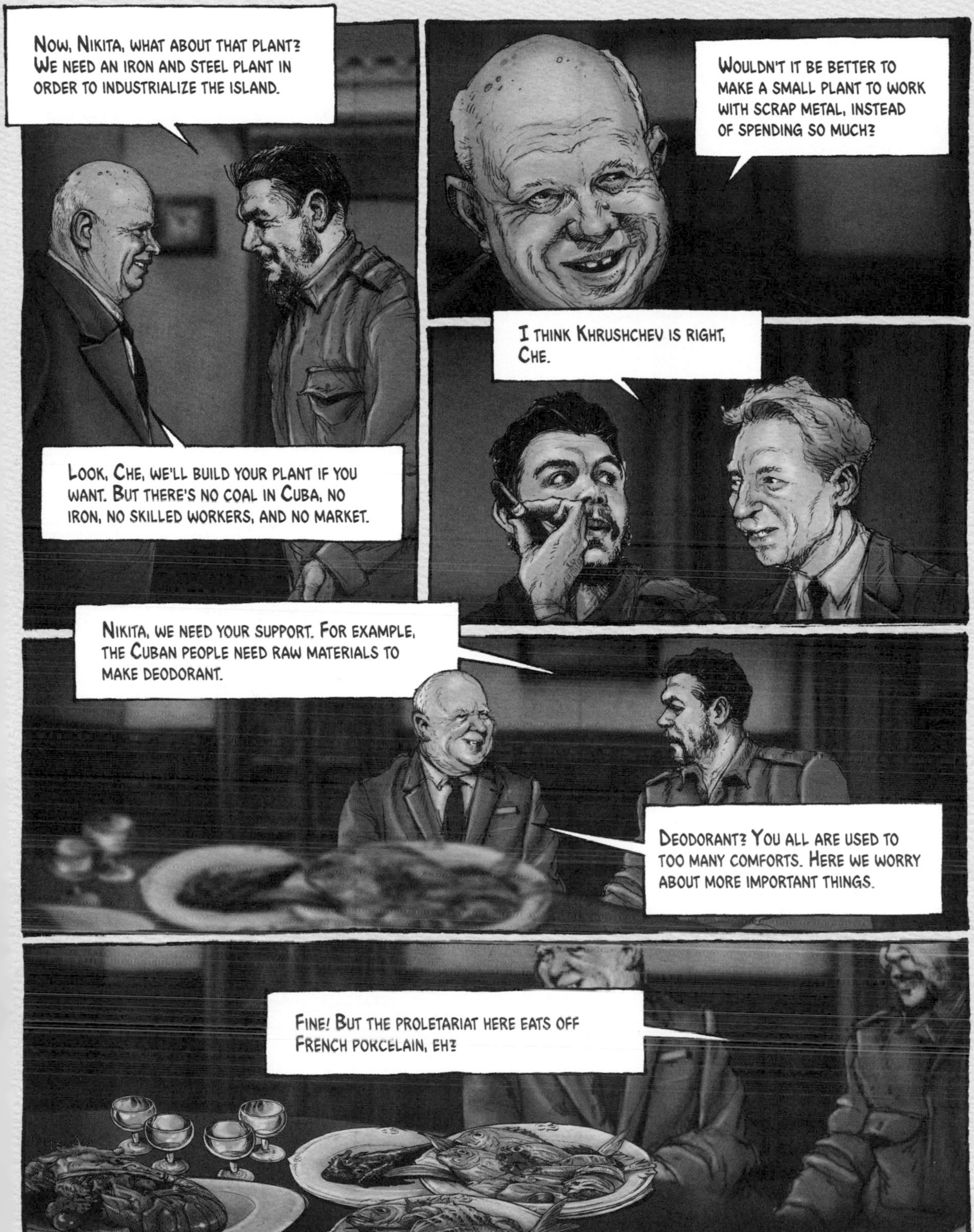

Now, Nikita, what about that plant? We need an iron and steel plant in order to industrialize the island.
Look, Che, we'll build your plant if you want. But there's no coal in Cuba, no iron, no skilled workers, and no market.
Wouldn't it be better to make a small plant to work with scrap metal, instead of spending so much?
I think Khrushchev is right, Che.
Nikita, we need your support. For example, the Cuban people need raw materials to make deodorant.
Deodorant? You all are used to too many comforts. Here we worry about more important things.
Fine! But the proletariat here eats off French porcelain, eh?

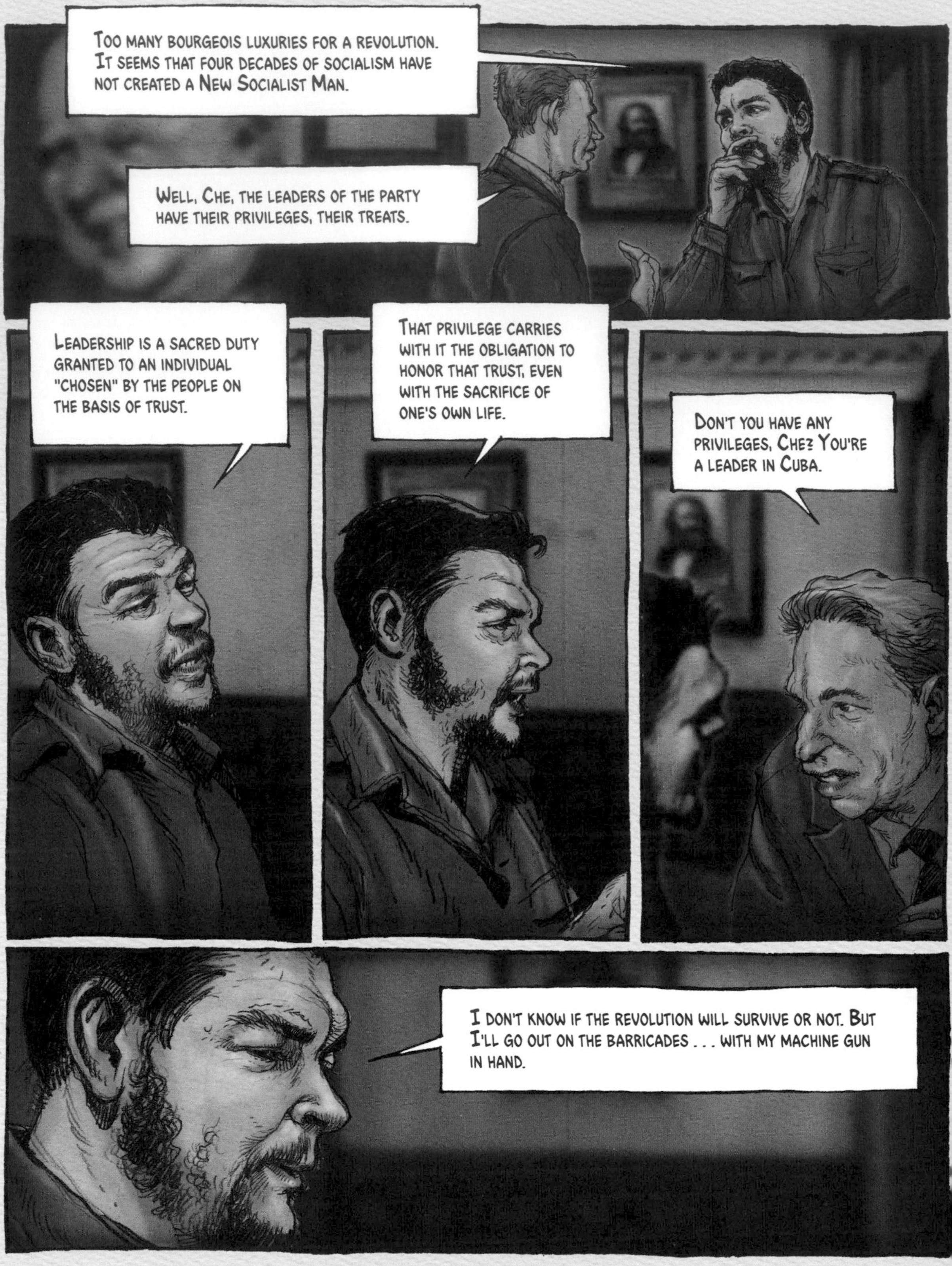

Too many bourgeois luxuries for a revolution. It seems that four decades of socialism have not created a New Socialist Man.
Well, Che, the leaders of the party have their privileges, their treats.
Leadership is a sacred duty granted to an individual "chosen" by the people on the basis of trust.
That privilege carries with it the obligation to honor that trust, even with the sacrifice of one's own life.
Don't you have any privileges, Che? You're a leader in Cuba.
I don't know if the revolution will survive or not. But I'll go out on the barricades . . . with my machine gun in hand.

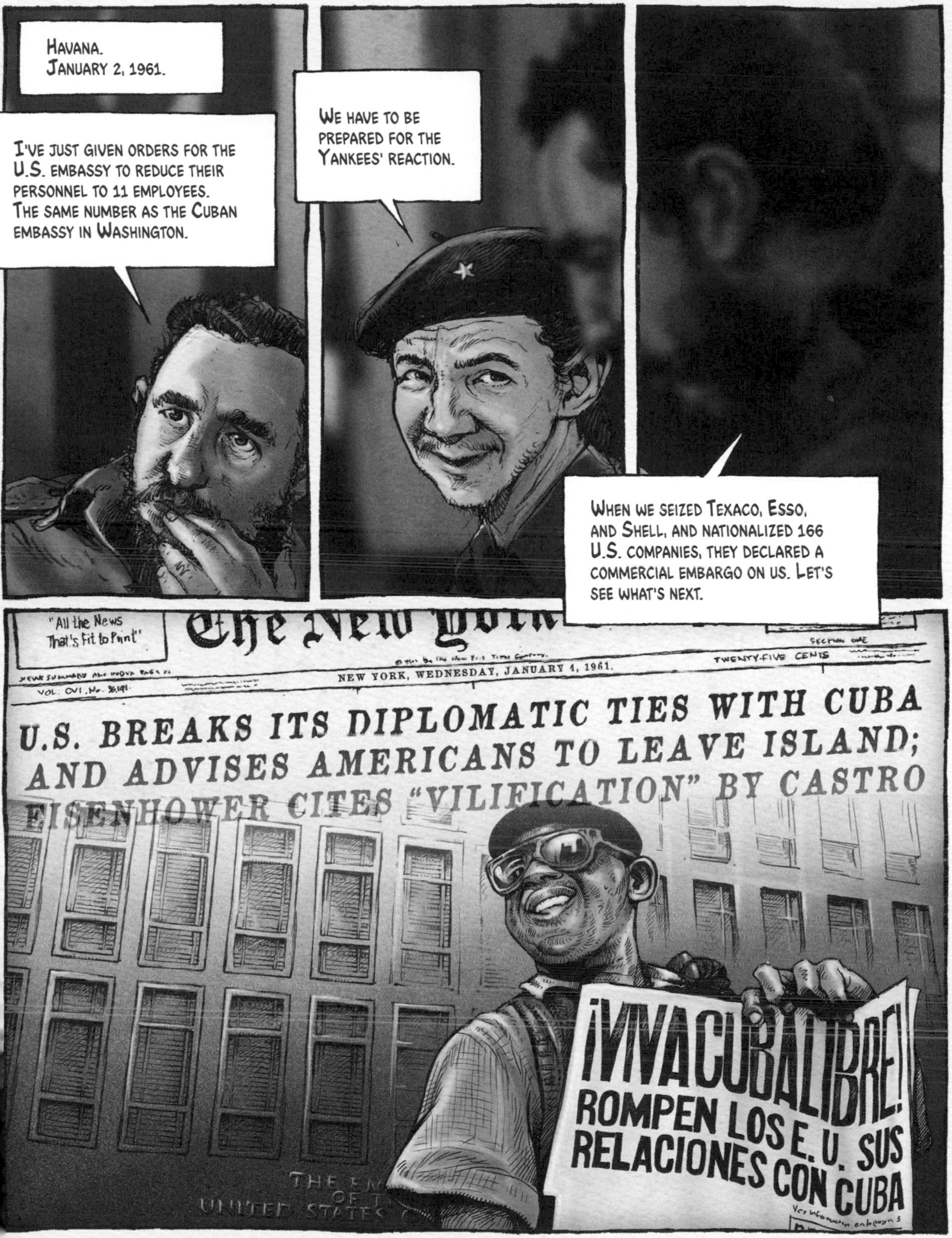
HAVANA.
JANUARY 2, 1961.
I'VE JUST GIVEN ORDERS FOR THE U.S. EMBASSY TO REDUCE THEIR PERSONNEL TO 11 EMPLOYEES. THE SAME NUMBER AS THE CUBAN EMBASSY IN WASHINGTON.
WE HAVE TO BE PREPARED FOR THE YANKEES' REACTION.
WHEN WE SEIZED TEXACO, ESSO, AND SHELL, AND NATIONALIZED 166 U.S. COMPANIES, THEY DECLARED A COMMERCIAL EMBARGO ON US. LET'S SEE WHAT'S NEXT.
"All the News That's Fit to Print"
The New York
SECTION ONE
TWENTY-FIVE CENTS
NEW YORK, WEDNESDAY, JANUARY 4, 1961.
U.S. BREAKS ITS DIPLOMATIC TIES WITH CUBA
AND ADVISES AMERICANS TO LEAVE ISLAND;
EISENHOWER CITES "VILIFICATION" BY CASTRO
¡VIVA CUBA LIBRE!
ROMPEN LOS E. U. SUS RELACIONES CON CUBA

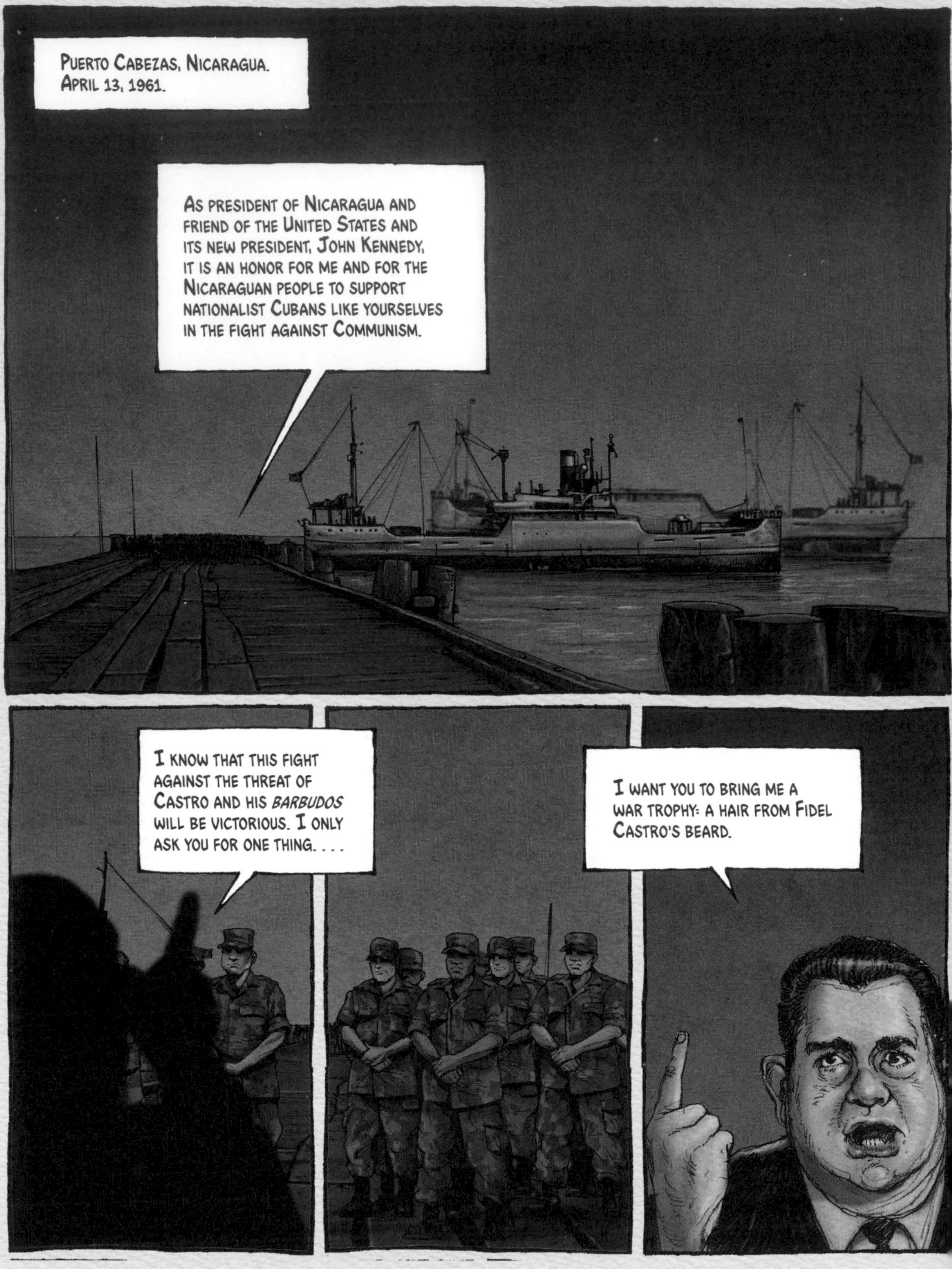
PUERTO CABEZAS, NICARAGUA.
APRIL 13, 1961.
AS PRESIDENT OF NICARAGUA AND FRIEND OF THE UNITED STATES AND ITS NEW PRESIDENT, JOHN KENNEDY, IT IS AN HONOR FOR ME AND FOR THE NICARAGUAN PEOPLE TO SUPPORT NATIONALIST CUBANS LIKE YOURSELVES IN THE FIGHT AGAINST COMMUNISM.
I KNOW THAT THIS FIGHT AGAINST THE THREAT OF CASTRO AND HIS *BARBUDOS* WILL BE VICTORIOUS. I ONLY ASK YOU FOR ONE THING. . . .
I WANT YOU TO BRING ME A WAR TROPHY: A HAIR FROM FIDEL CASTRO'S BEARD.

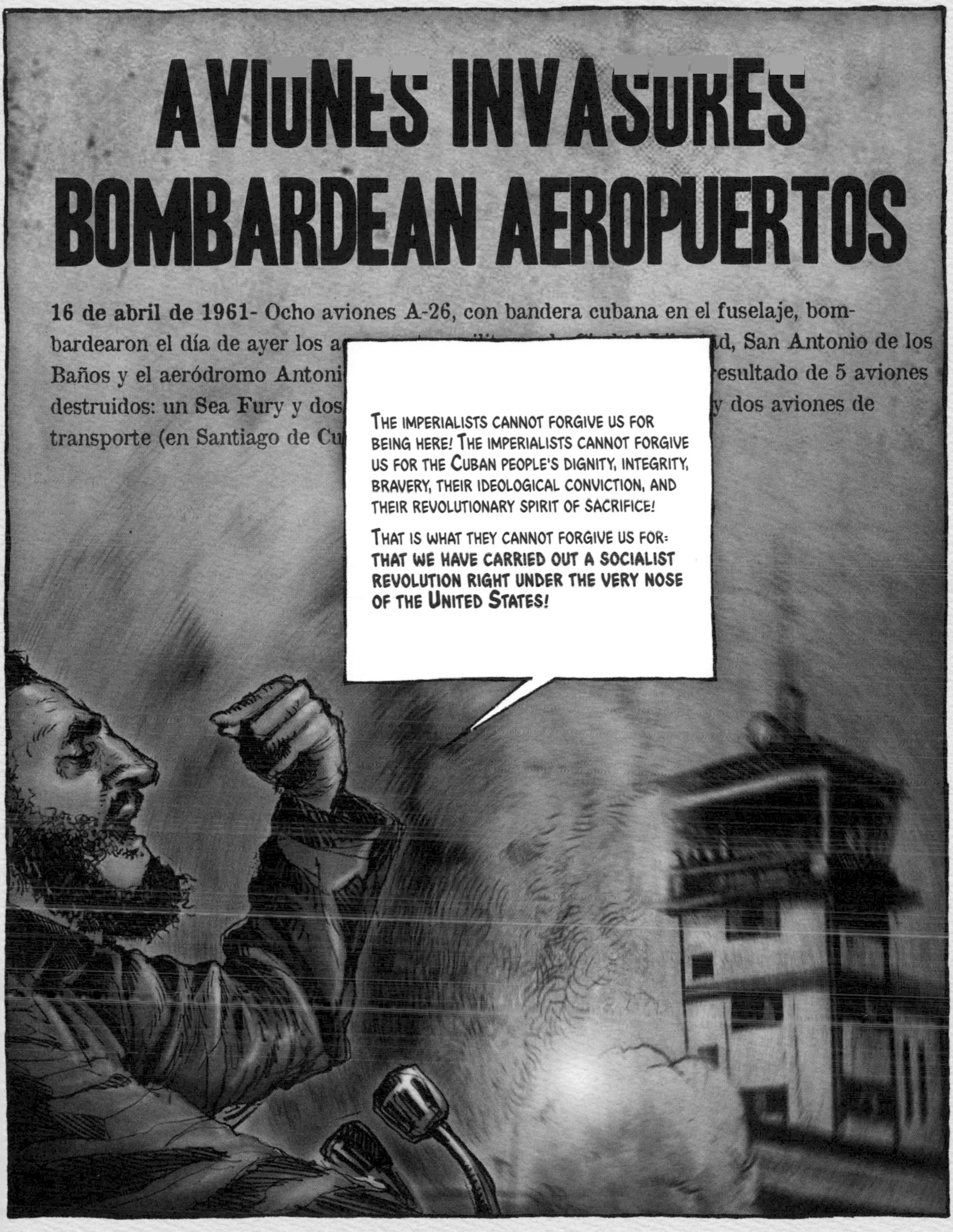
AVIONES INVASORES
BOMBARDEAN AEROPUERTOS
16 de abril de 1961- Ocho aviones A-26, con bandera cubana en el fuselaje, bom-
bardearon el día de ayer los a
Baños y el aeródromo Antoni
destruidos: un Sea Fury y dos
transporte (en Santiago de Cu
d, San Antonio de los
resultado de 5 aviones
y dos aviones de
THE IMPERIALISTS CANNOT FORGIVE US FOR BEING HERE! THE IMPERIALISTS CANNOT FORGIVE US FOR THE CUBAN PEOPLE'S DIGNITY, INTEGRITY, BRAVERY, THEIR IDEOLOGICAL CONVICTION, AND THEIR REVOLUTIONARY SPIRIT OF SACRIFICE!
THAT IS WHAT THEY CANNOT FORGIVE US FOR: THAT WE HAVE CARRIED OUT A SOCIALIST REVOLUTION RIGHT UNDER THE VERY NOSE OF THE UNITED STATES!

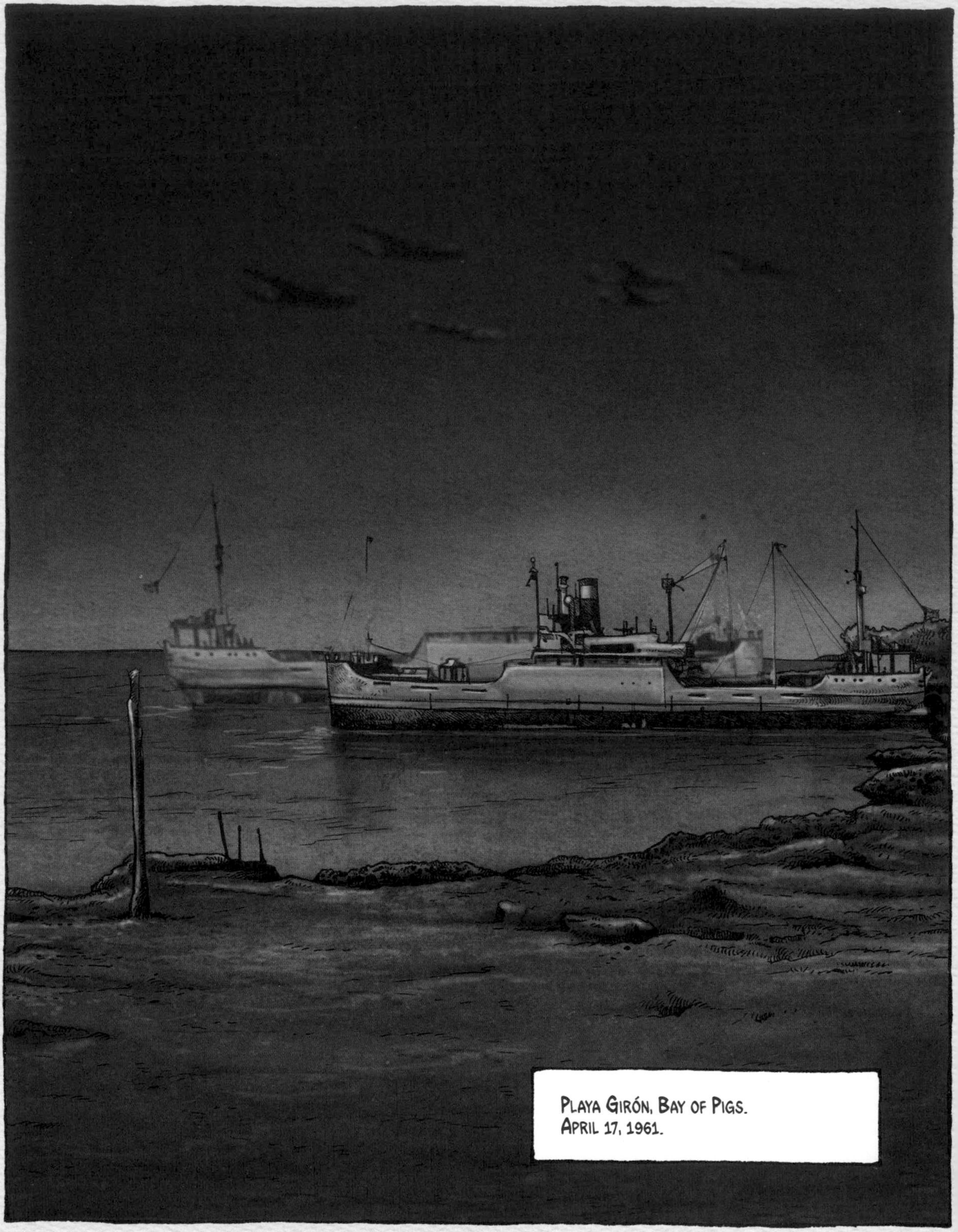
PLAYA GIRÓN, BAY OF PIGS.
APRIL 17, 1961.

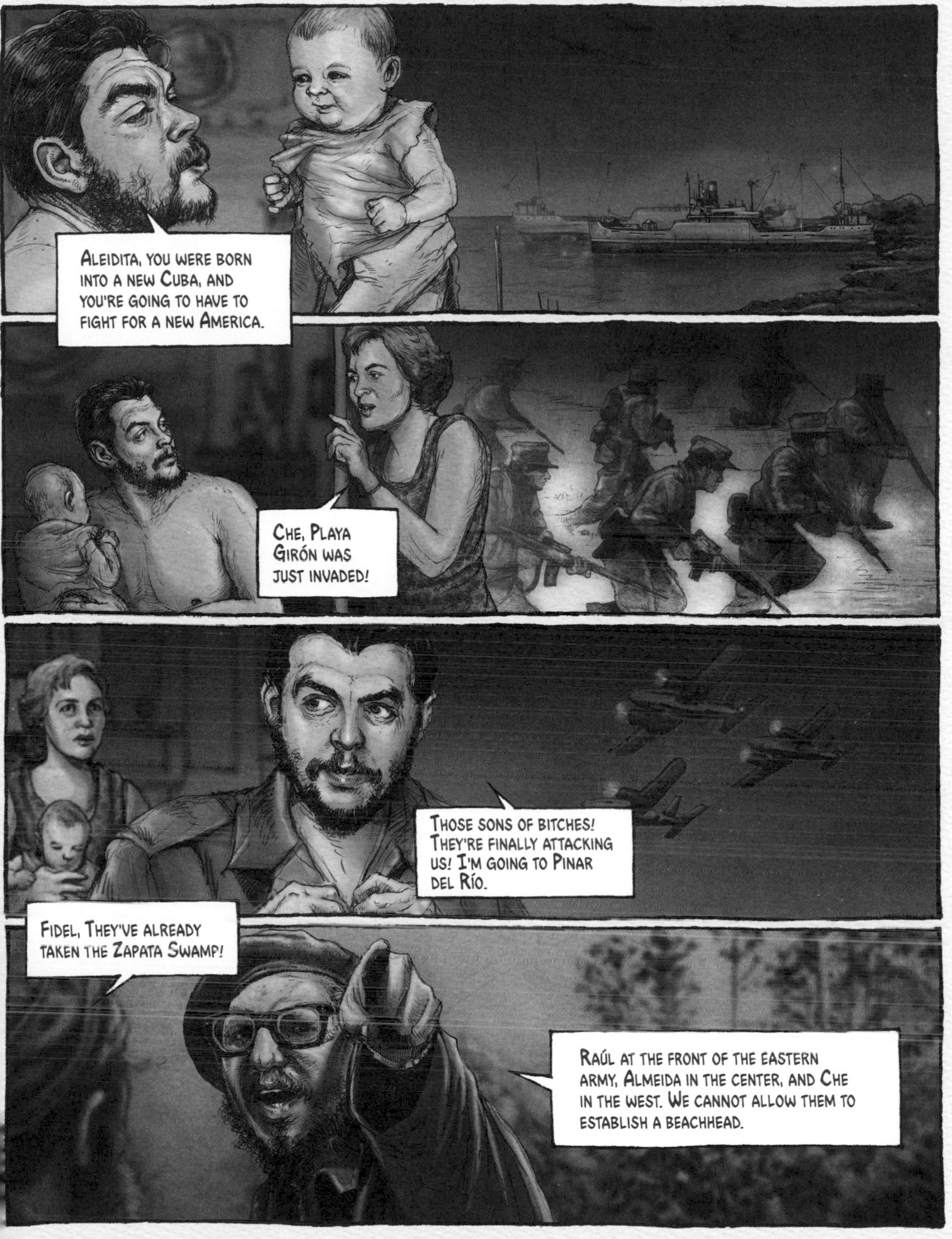
ALEIDITA, YOU WERE BORN INTO A NEW CUBA, AND YOU'RE GOING TO HAVE TO FIGHT FOR A NEW AMERICA.
CHE, PLAYA GIRÓN WAS JUST INVADED!
THOSE SONS OF BITCHES! THEY'RE FINALLY ATTACKING US! I'M GOING TO PINAR DEL RÍO.
FIDEL, THEY'VE ALREADY TAKEN THE ZAPATA SWAMP!
RAÚL AT THE FRONT OF THE EASTERN ARMY, ALMEIDA IN THE CENTER, AND CHE IN THE WEST. WE CANNOT ALLOW THEM TO ESTABLISH A BEACHHEAD.

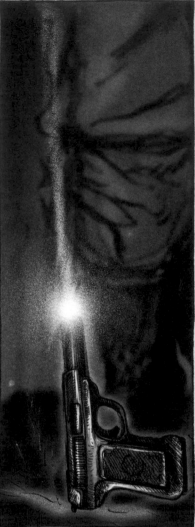

ALEIDA, CHE HAD AN ACCIDENT; HIS GUN WENT OFF. IT'S OKAY; IT WAS ONLY A SUPERFICIAL WOUND, BUT HE'S IN THE HOSPITAL. A CAR WILL TAKE YOU TO SEE HIM. I'LL TAKE ALEIDITA TO MY HOUSE.

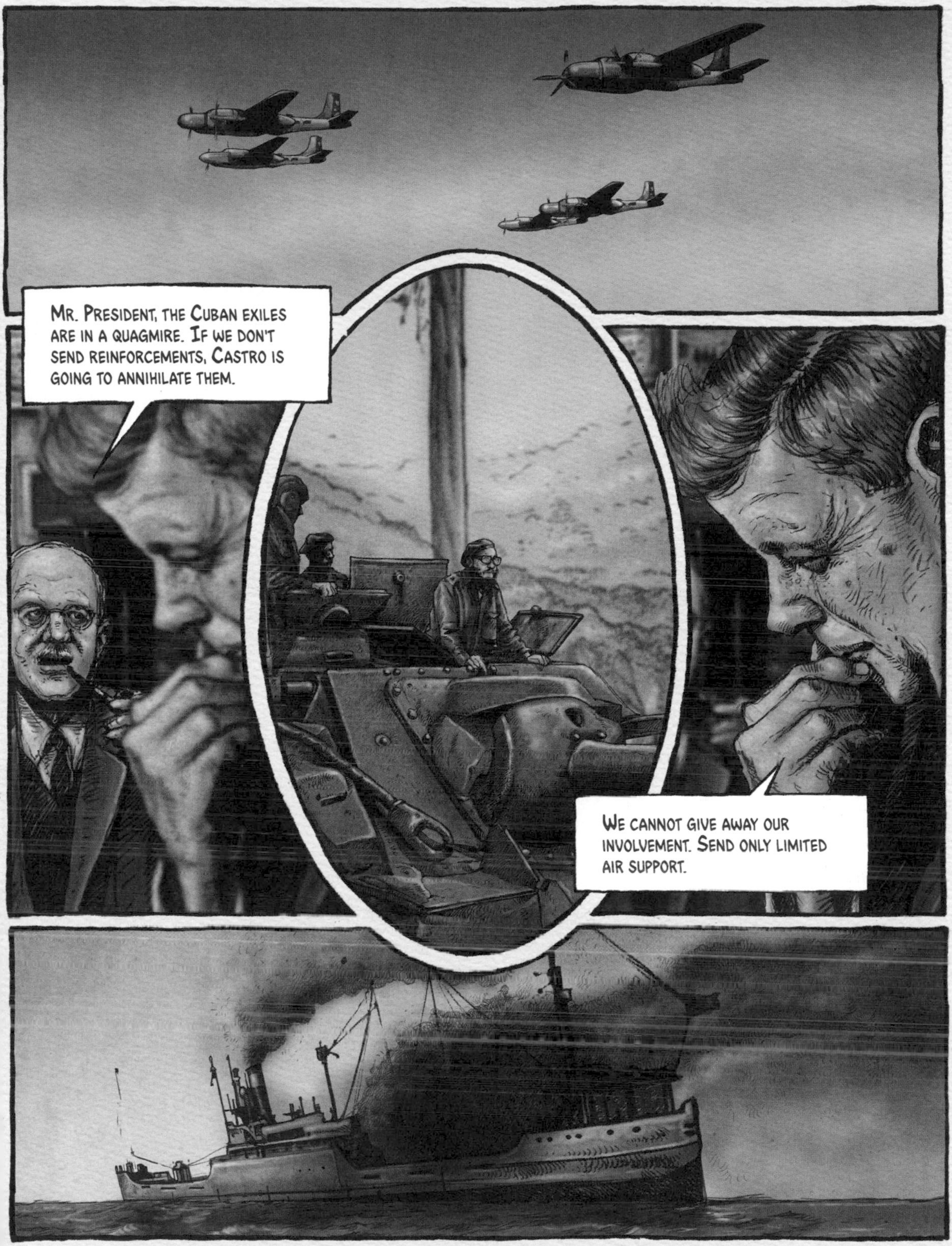
MR. PRESIDENT, THE CUBAN EXILES ARE IN A QUAGMIRE. IF WE DON'T SEND REINFORCEMENTS, CASTRO IS GOING TO ANNIHILATE THEM.
WE CANNOT GIVE AWAY OUR INVOLVEMENT. SEND ONLY LIMITED AIR SUPPORT.

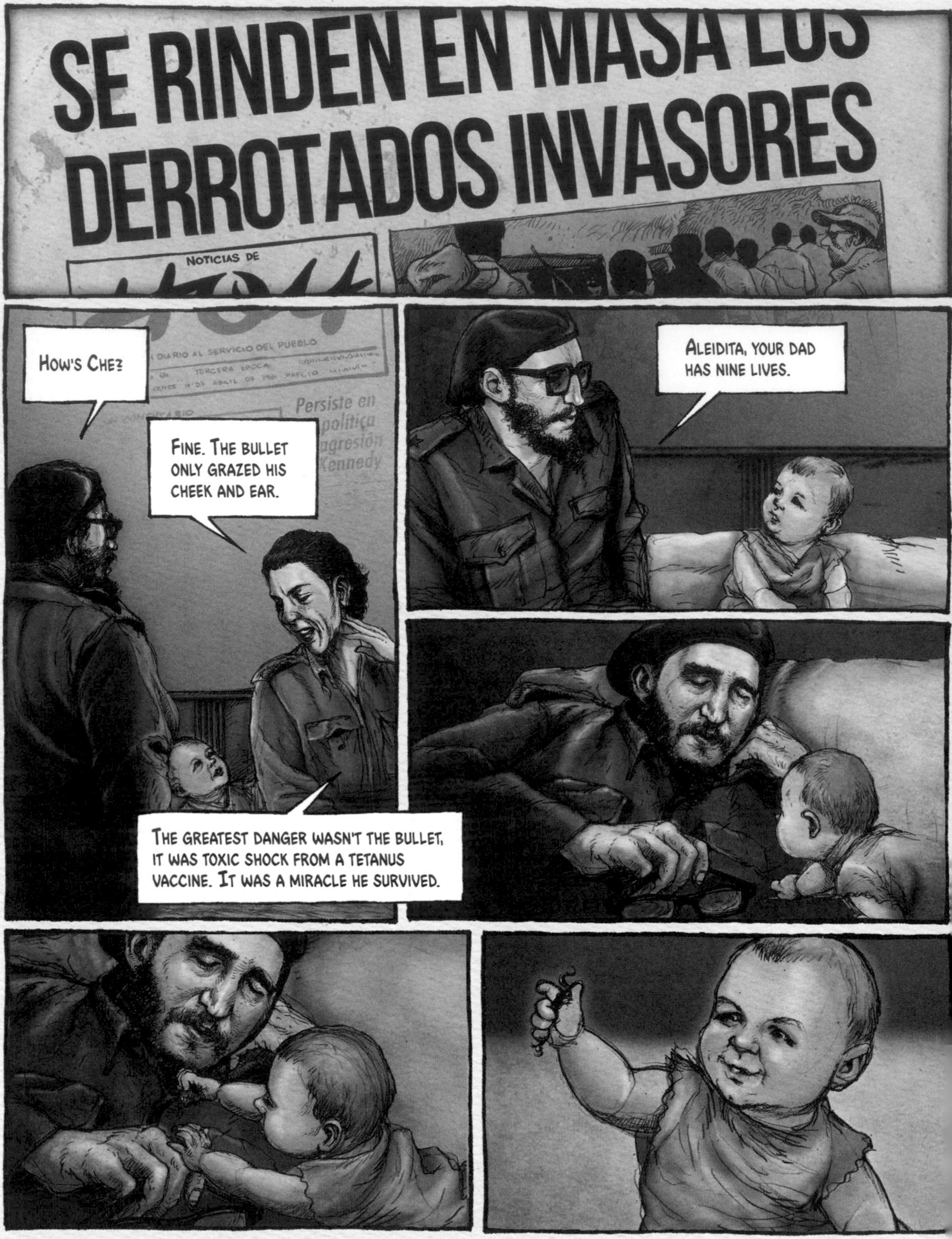
SE RINDEN EN MASA LOS
DERROTADOS INVASORES
NOTICIAS DE
HOW'S CHE?
FINE. THE BULLET ONLY GRAZED HIS CHEEK AND EAR.
THE GREATEST DANGER WASN'T THE BULLET, IT WAS TOXIC SHOCK FROM A TETANUS VACCINE. IT WAS A MIRACLE HE SURVIVED.
ALEIDITA, YOUR DAD HAS NINE LIVES.

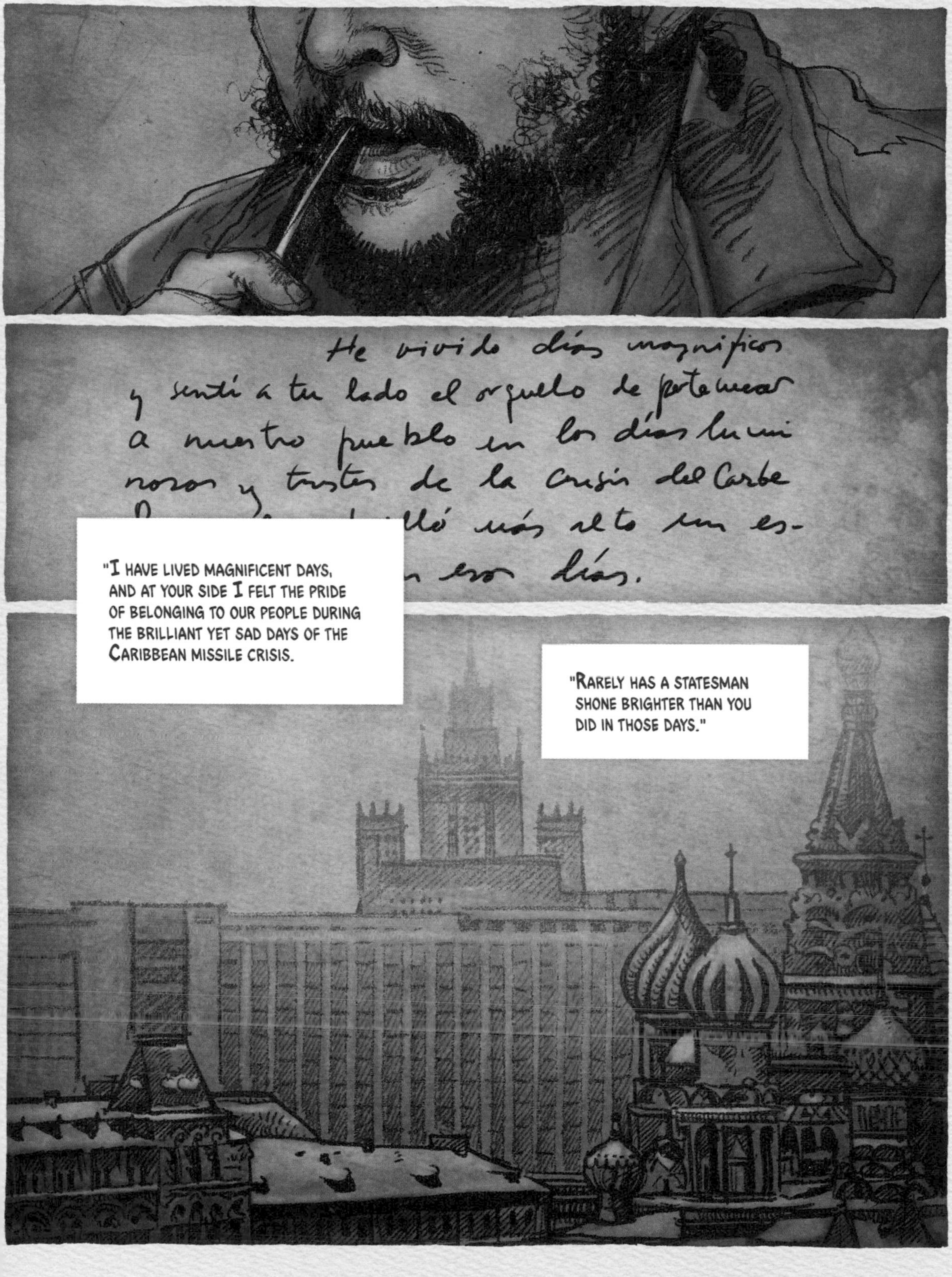
He vivido días magníficos
y sentí a tu lado el orgullo de pertenecer
a nuestro pueblo en los días lumi
nosos y tristes de la crisis del Caribe
brilló más alto un es-
esos días.
"I HAVE LIVED MAGNIFICENT DAYS, AND AT YOUR SIDE I FELT THE PRIDE OF BELONGING TO OUR PEOPLE DURING THE BRILLIANT YET SAD DAYS OF THE CARIBBEAN MISSILE CRISIS.
"RARELY HAS A STATESMAN SHONE BRIGHTER THAN YOU DID IN THOSE DAYS."

COMRADE ALEXIEV, TO HELP CUBA AND TO SAVE THE CUBAN REVOLUTION, WE HAVE DECIDED THAT WE WILL PLACE MISSILES ON THE ISLAND. DO YOU THINK FIDEL WILL AGREE?

IN MY OPINION, NO, I DON'T THINK SO. HE HAS ALWAYS PUBLICLY DEFENDED THE GOAL THAT HIS REVOLUTION WILL ACHIEVE CUBAN INDEPENDENCE.

SOVIET NUCLEAR MISSILES IN CUBA.

I SEE NO OTHER WAY TO IMPEDE A U.S. INVASION.

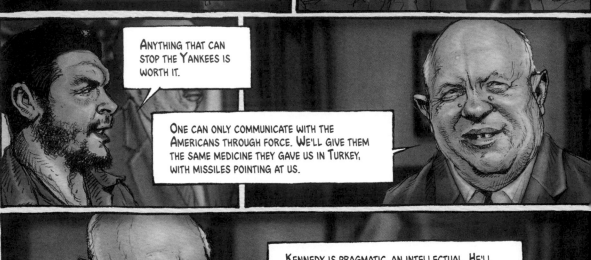

ANYTHING THAT CAN STOP THE YANKEES IS WORTH IT.

ONE CAN ONLY COMMUNICATE WITH THE AMERICANS THROUGH FORCE. WE'LL GIVE THEM THE SAME MEDICINE THEY GAVE US IN TURKEY, WITH MISSILES POINTING AT US.

KENNEDY IS PRAGMATIC, AN INTELLECTUAL. HE'LL UNDERSTAND AND HE WON'T DARE START A WAR, BECAUSE WAR IS WAR.

ANY IDIOT CAN START A WAR, BUT IT'S NOT ABOUT THAT. IT'S ABOUT GIVING THEM A SCARE, NOTHING MORE.

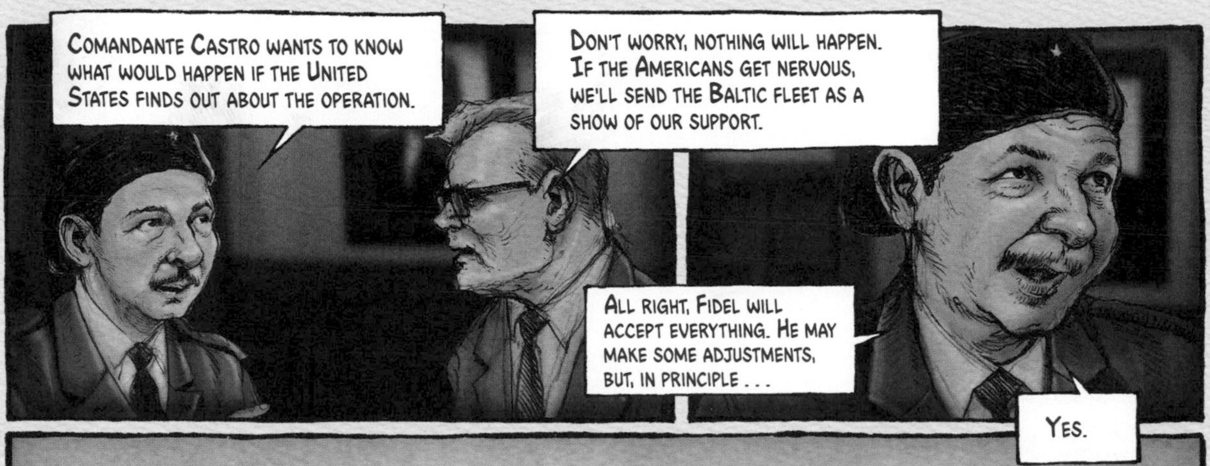

Comandante Castro wants to know what would happen if the United States finds out about the operation.
Don't worry, nothing will happen. If the Americans get nervous, we'll send the Baltic fleet as a show of our support.
All right, Fidel will accept everything. He may make some adjustments, but, in principle . . .
Yes.

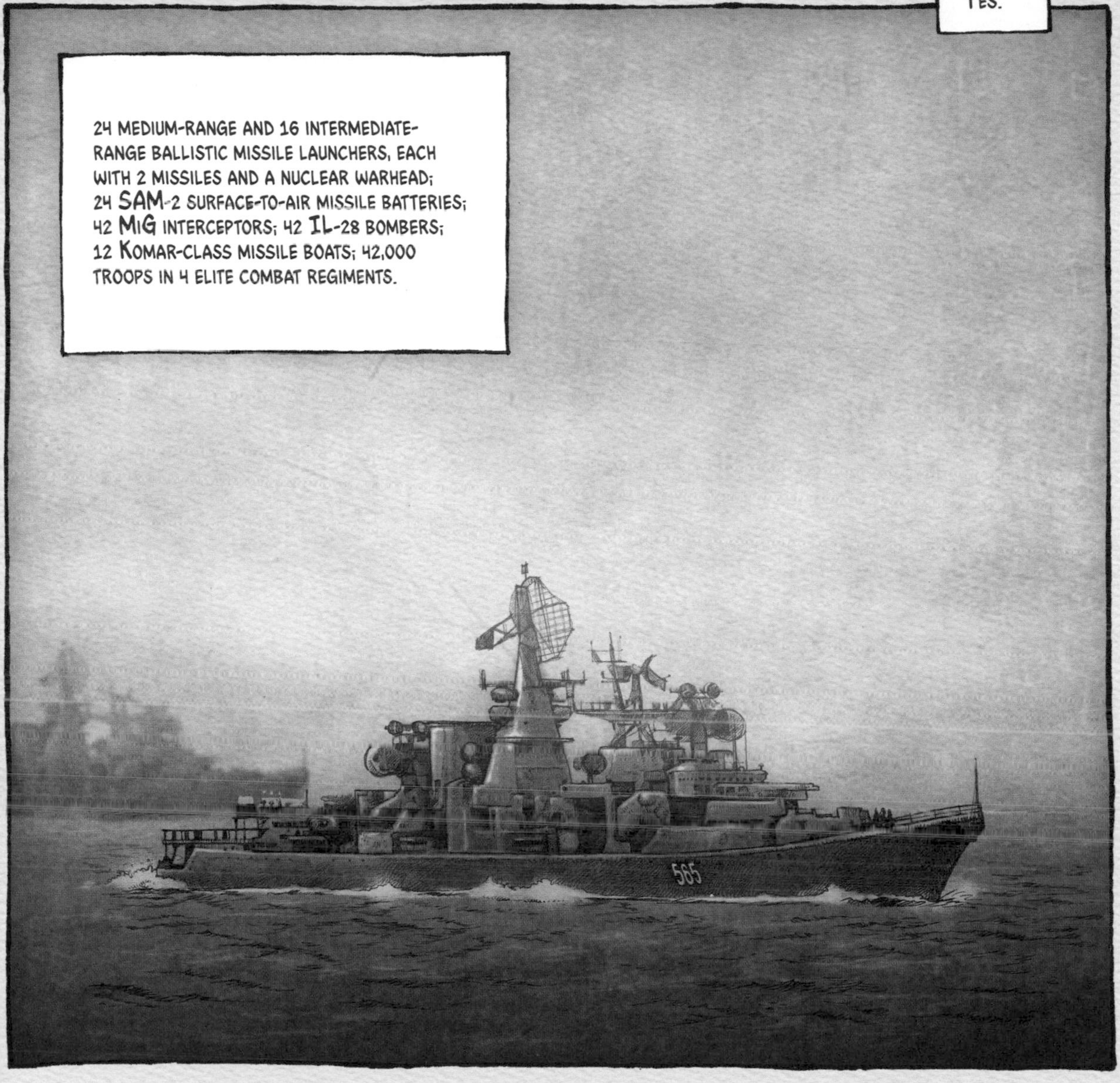

24 medium-range and 16 intermediate-range ballistic missile launchers, each with 2 missiles and a nuclear warhead; 24 SAM-2 surface-to-air missile batteries; 42 MiG interceptors; 42 IL-28 bombers; 12 Komar-class missile boats; 42,000 troops in 4 elite combat regiments.
565

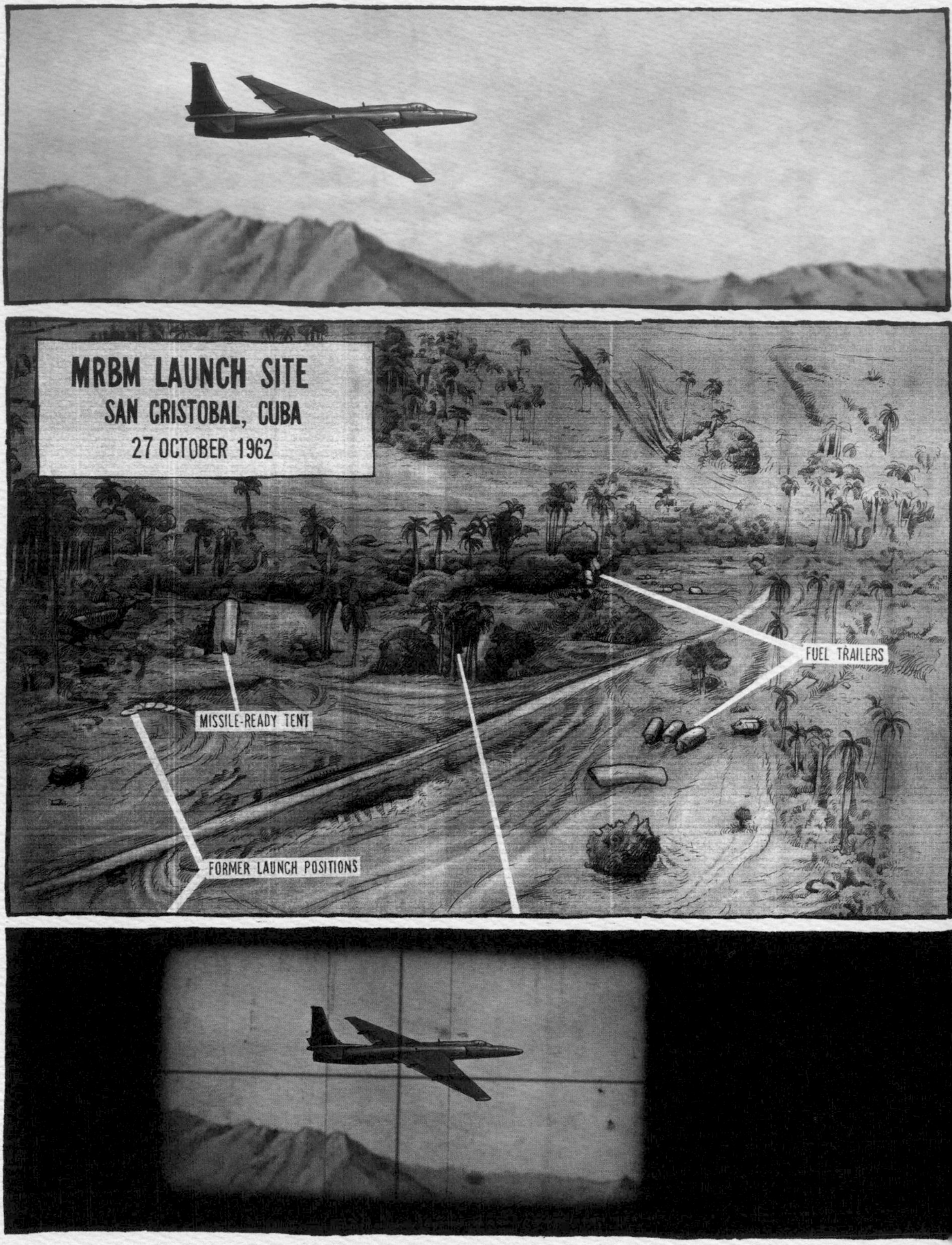
MRBM LAUNCH SITE
SAN CRISTOBAL, CUBA
27 OCTOBER 1962
MISSILE-READY TENT
FUEL TRAILERS
FORMER LAUNCH POSITIONS

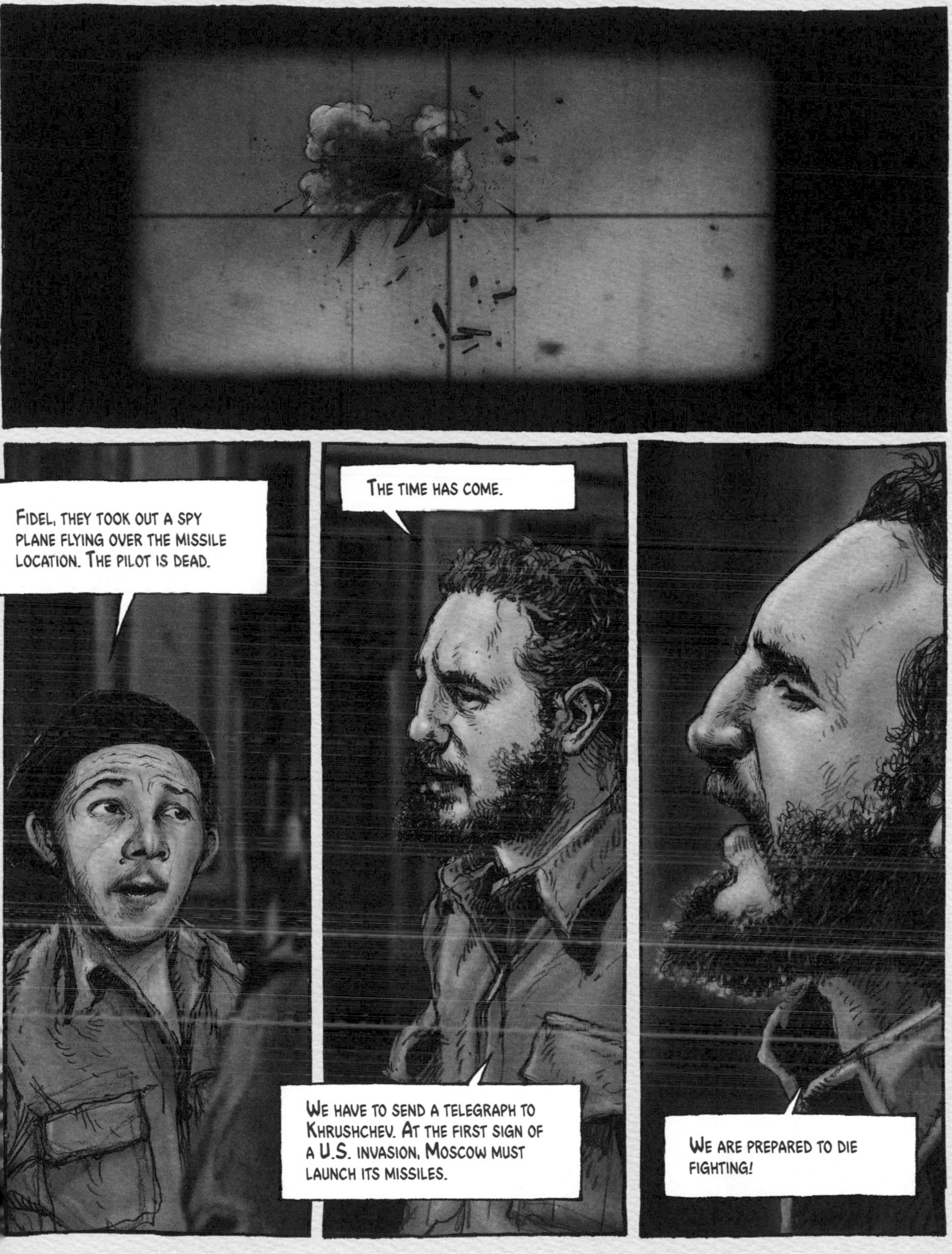
FIDEL, THEY TOOK OUT A SPY PLANE FLYING OVER THE MISSILE LOCATION. THE PILOT IS DEAD.
THE TIME HAS COME.
WE HAVE TO SEND A TELEGRAPH TO KHRUSHCHEV. AT THE FIRST SIGN OF A U.S. INVASION, MOSCOW MUST LAUNCH ITS MISSILES.
WE ARE PREPARED TO DIE FIGHTING!

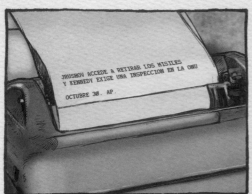

JRUSHOV ACCEDE A RETIRAR LOS MISILES
Y KENNEDY EXIGE UNA INSPECCION EN LA ONU

OCTUBRE 30. AP.

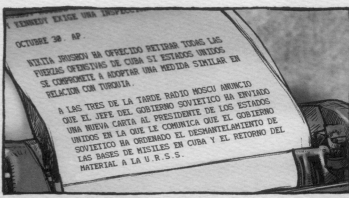

Y KENNEDY EXIGE UNA INSPECCIO

OCTUBRE 30. AP.

NIKITA JRUSHOV HA OFRECIDO RETIRAR TODAS LAS
FUERZAS OFENSIVAS DE CUBA SI ESTADOS UNIDOS
SE COMPROMETE A ADOPTAR UNA MEDIDA SIMILAR EN
RELACION CON TURQUIA.

A LAS TRES DE LA TARDE RADIO MOSCU ANUNCIO
QUE EL JEFE DEL GOBIERNO SOVIETICO HA ENVIADO
UNA NUEVA CARTA AL PRESIDENTE DE LOS ESTADOS
UNIDOS EN LA QUE LE COMUNICA QUE EL GOBIERNO DE
SOVIETICO HA ORDENADO EL DESMANTELAMIENTO DE
LAS BASES DE MISILES EN CUBA Y EL RETORNO DEL
MATERIAL A LA U.R.S.S.

BASTARD! FUCKER! HE ONLY USED US TO NEGOTIATE WITH KENNEDY!

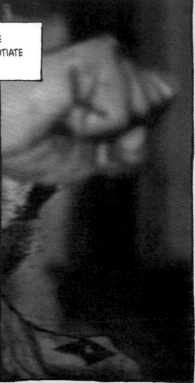

WHAT A SON OF A BITCH!

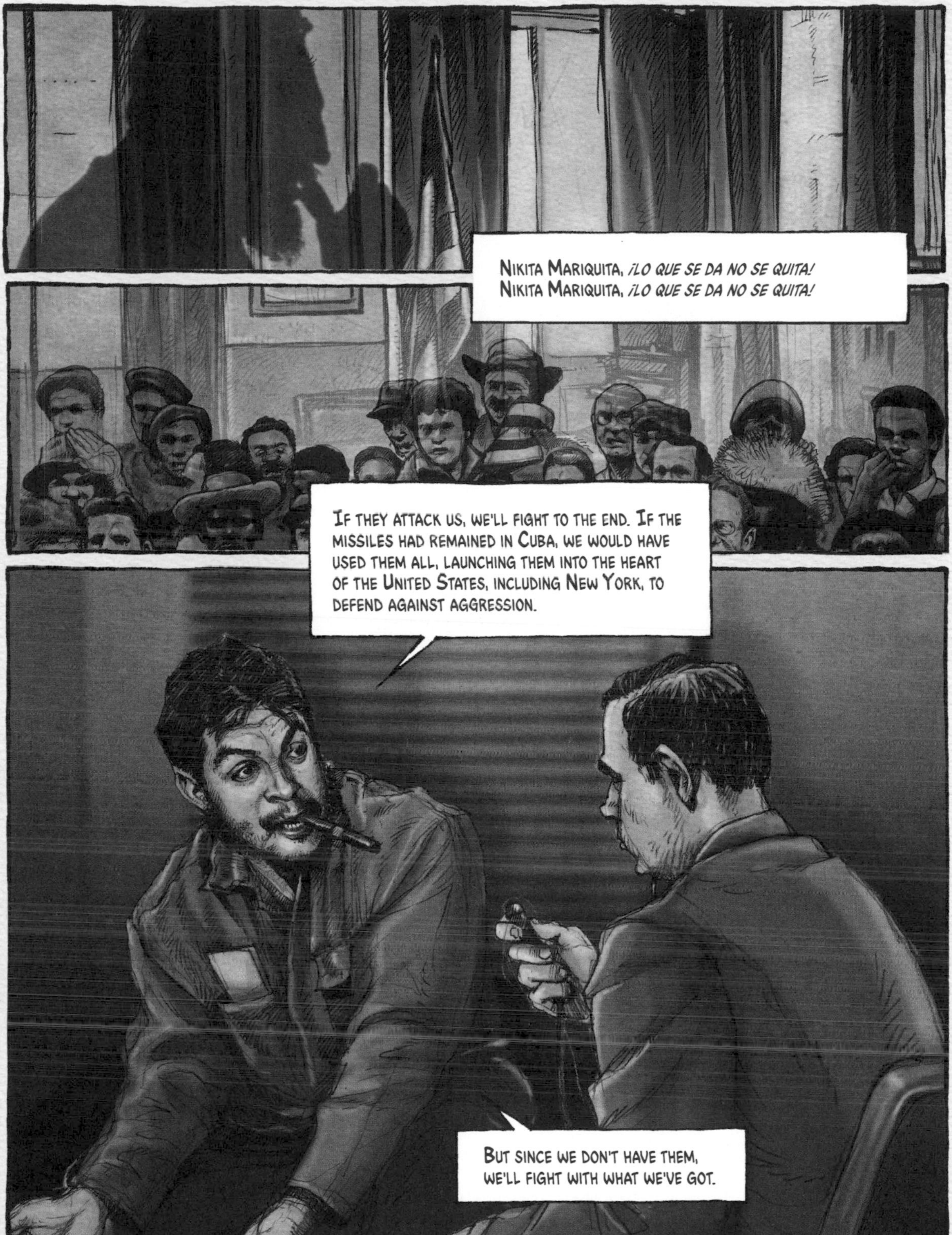
NIKITA MARIQUITA, ¡LO QUE SE DA NO SE QUITA!
NIKITA MARIQUITA, ¡LO QUE SE DA NO SE QUITA!
IF THEY ATTACK US, WE'LL FIGHT TO THE END. IF THE MISSILES HAD REMAINED IN CUBA, WE WOULD HAVE USED THEM ALL, LAUNCHING THEM INTO THE HEART OF THE UNITED STATES, INCLUDING NEW YORK, TO DEFEND AGAINST AGGRESSION.
BUT SINCE WE DON'T HAVE THEM, WE'LL FIGHT WITH WHAT WE'VE GOT.

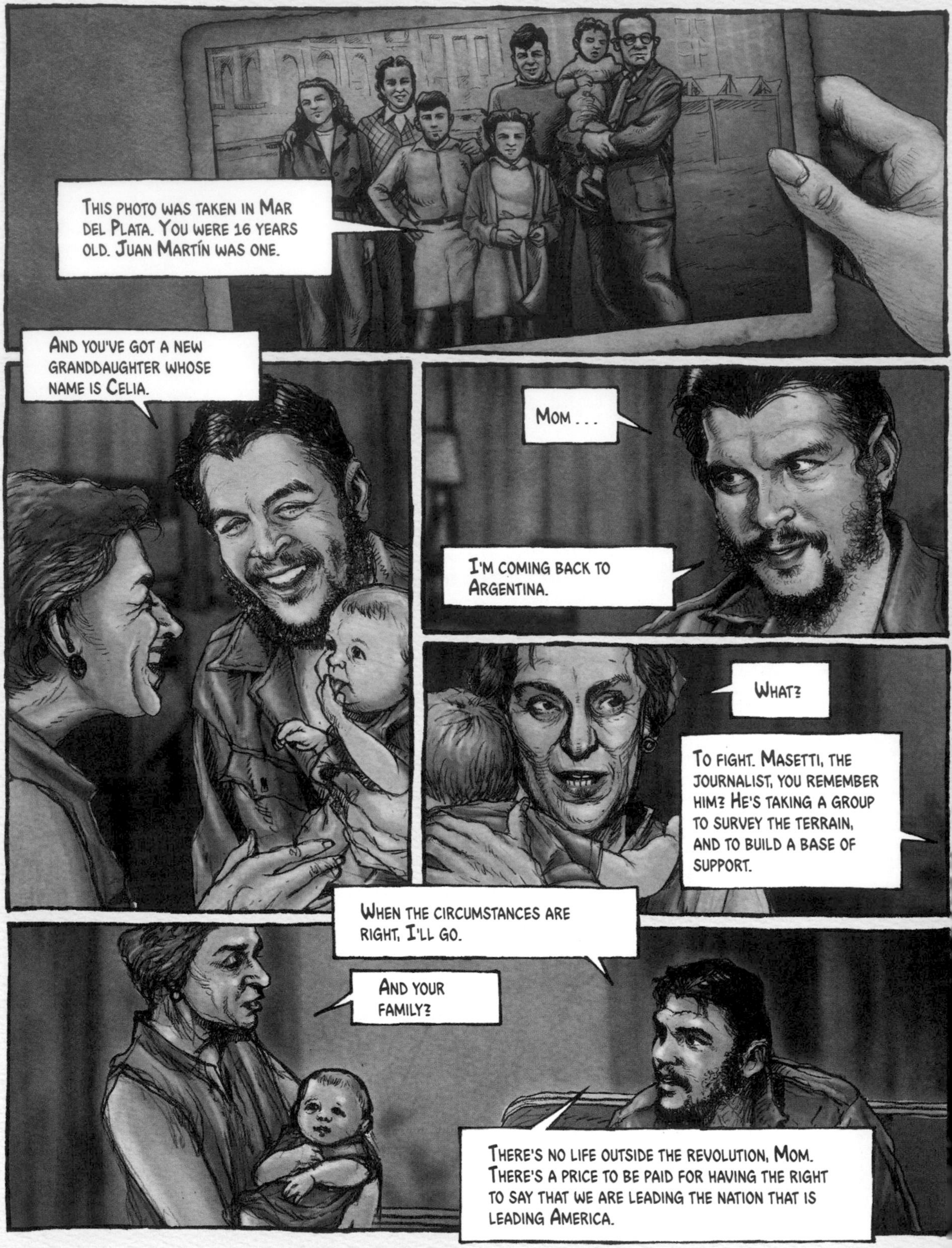
THIS PHOTO WAS TAKEN IN MAR DEL PLATA. YOU WERE 16 YEARS OLD. JUAN MARTÍN WAS ONE.
AND YOU'VE GOT A NEW GRANDDAUGHTER WHOSE NAME IS CELIA.
MOM . . .
I'M COMING BACK TO ARGENTINA.
WHAT?
TO FIGHT. MASETTI, THE JOURNALIST, YOU REMEMBER HIM? HE'S TAKING A GROUP TO SURVEY THE TERRAIN, AND TO BUILD A BASE OF SUPPORT.
WHEN THE CIRCUMSTANCES ARE RIGHT, I'LL GO.
AND YOUR FAMILY?
THERE'S NO LIFE OUTSIDE THE REVOLUTION, MOM. THERE'S A PRICE TO BE PAID FOR HAVING THE RIGHT TO SAY THAT WE ARE LEADING THE NATION THAT IS LEADING AMERICA.

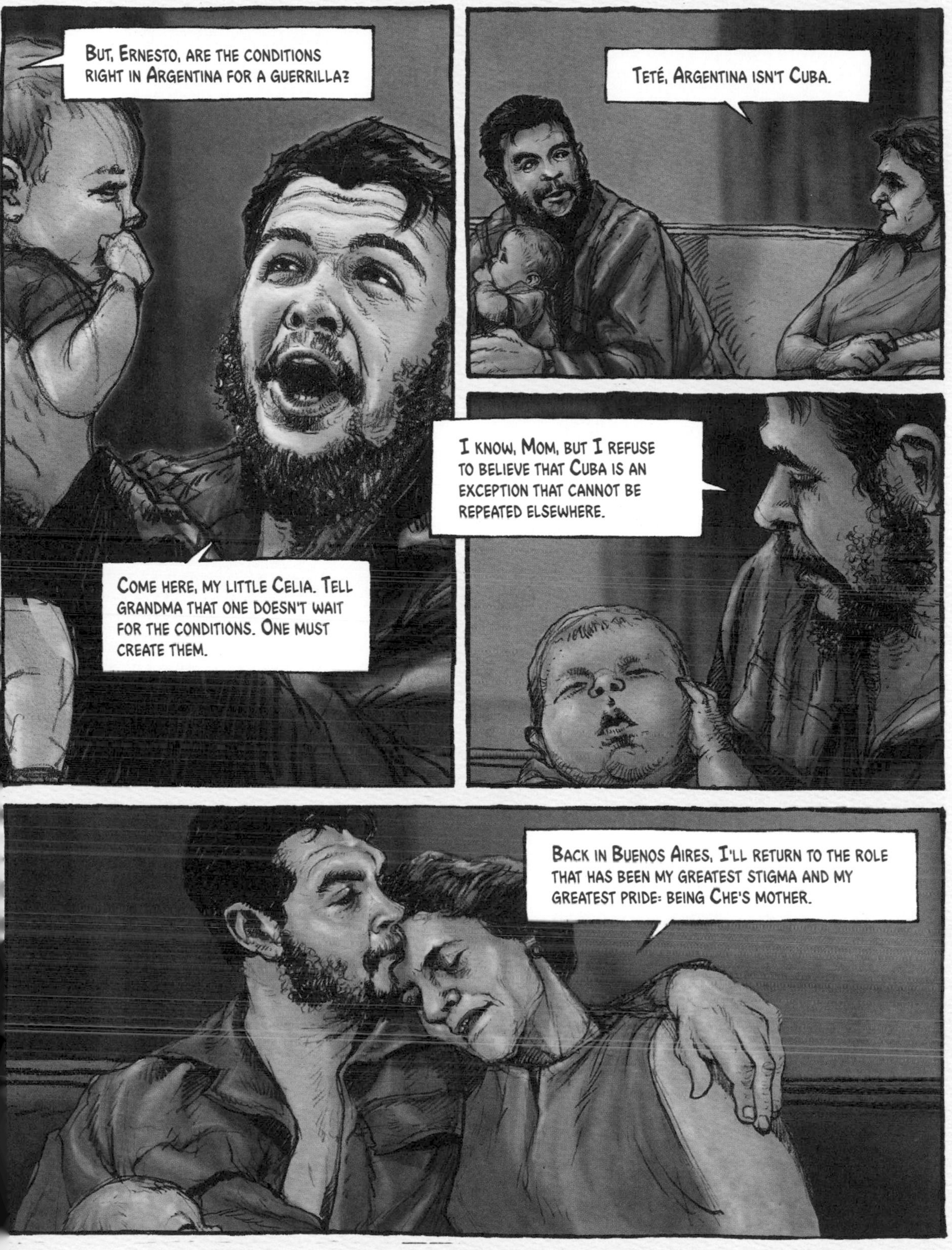

But, Ernesto, are the conditions right in Argentina for a guerrilla?
Come here, my little Celia. Tell grandma that one doesn't wait for the conditions. One must create them.
Teté, Argentina isn't Cuba.
I know, Mom, but I refuse to believe that Cuba is an exception that cannot be repeated elsewhere.
Back in Buenos Aires, I'll return to the role that has been my greatest stigma and my greatest pride: being Che's mother.

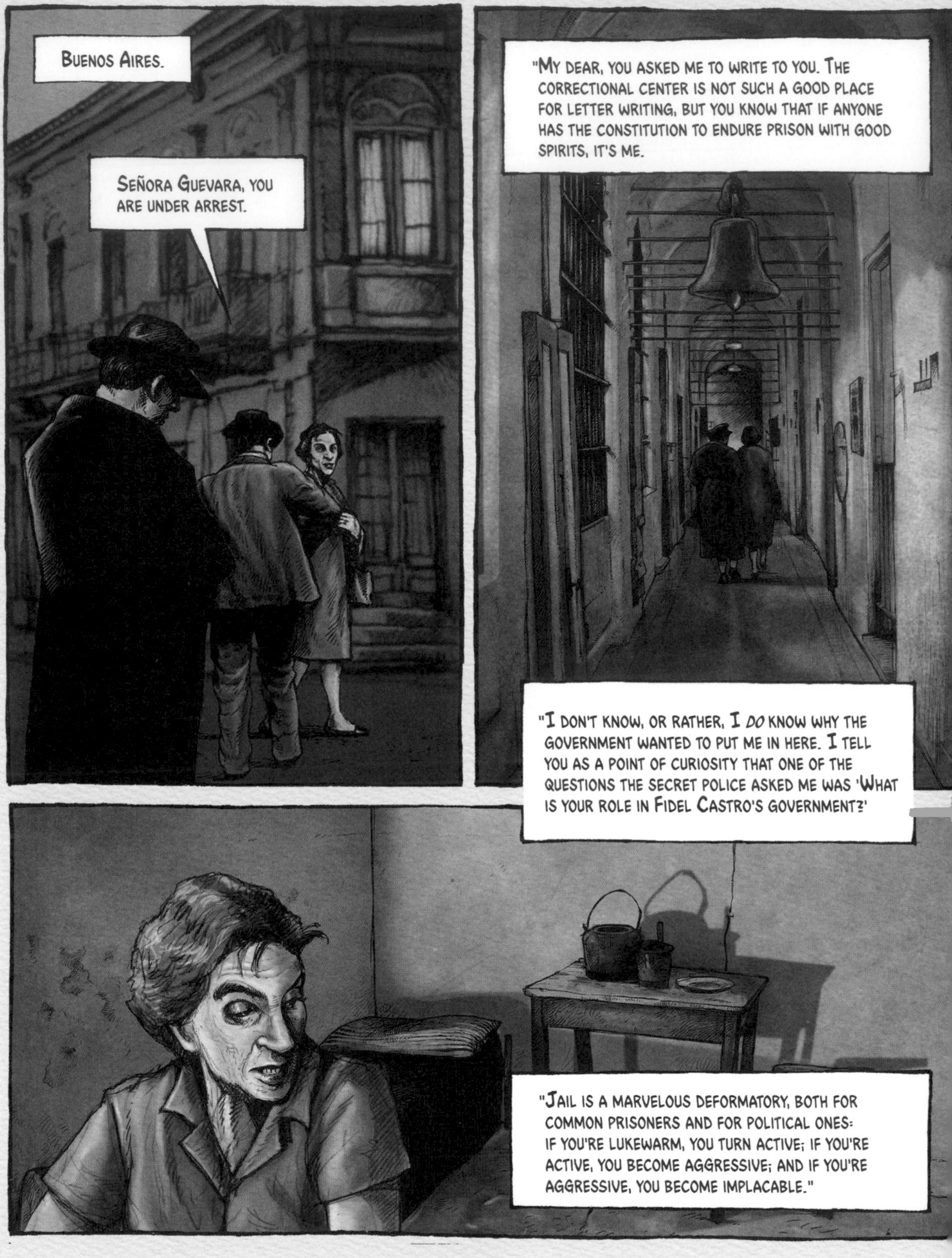
BUENOS AIRES.
SEÑORA GUEVARA, YOU ARE UNDER ARREST.
"MY DEAR, YOU ASKED ME TO WRITE TO YOU. THE CORRECTIONAL CENTER IS NOT SUCH A GOOD PLACE FOR LETTER WRITING, BUT YOU KNOW THAT IF ANYONE HAS THE CONSTITUTION TO ENDURE PRISON WITH GOOD SPIRITS, IT'S ME.
"I DON'T KNOW, OR RATHER, I *DO* KNOW WHY THE GOVERNMENT WANTED TO PUT ME IN HERE. I TELL YOU AS A POINT OF CURIOSITY THAT ONE OF THE QUESTIONS THE SECRET POLICE ASKED ME WAS 'WHAT IS YOUR ROLE IN FIDEL CASTRO'S GOVERNMENT?'
"JAIL IS A MARVELOUS DEFORMATORY, BOTH FOR COMMON PRISONERS AND FOR POLITICAL ONES: IF YOU'RE LUKEWARM, YOU TURN ACTIVE; IF YOU'RE ACTIVE, YOU BECOME AGGRESSIVE; AND IF YOU'RE AGGRESSIVE, YOU BECOME IMPLACABLE."

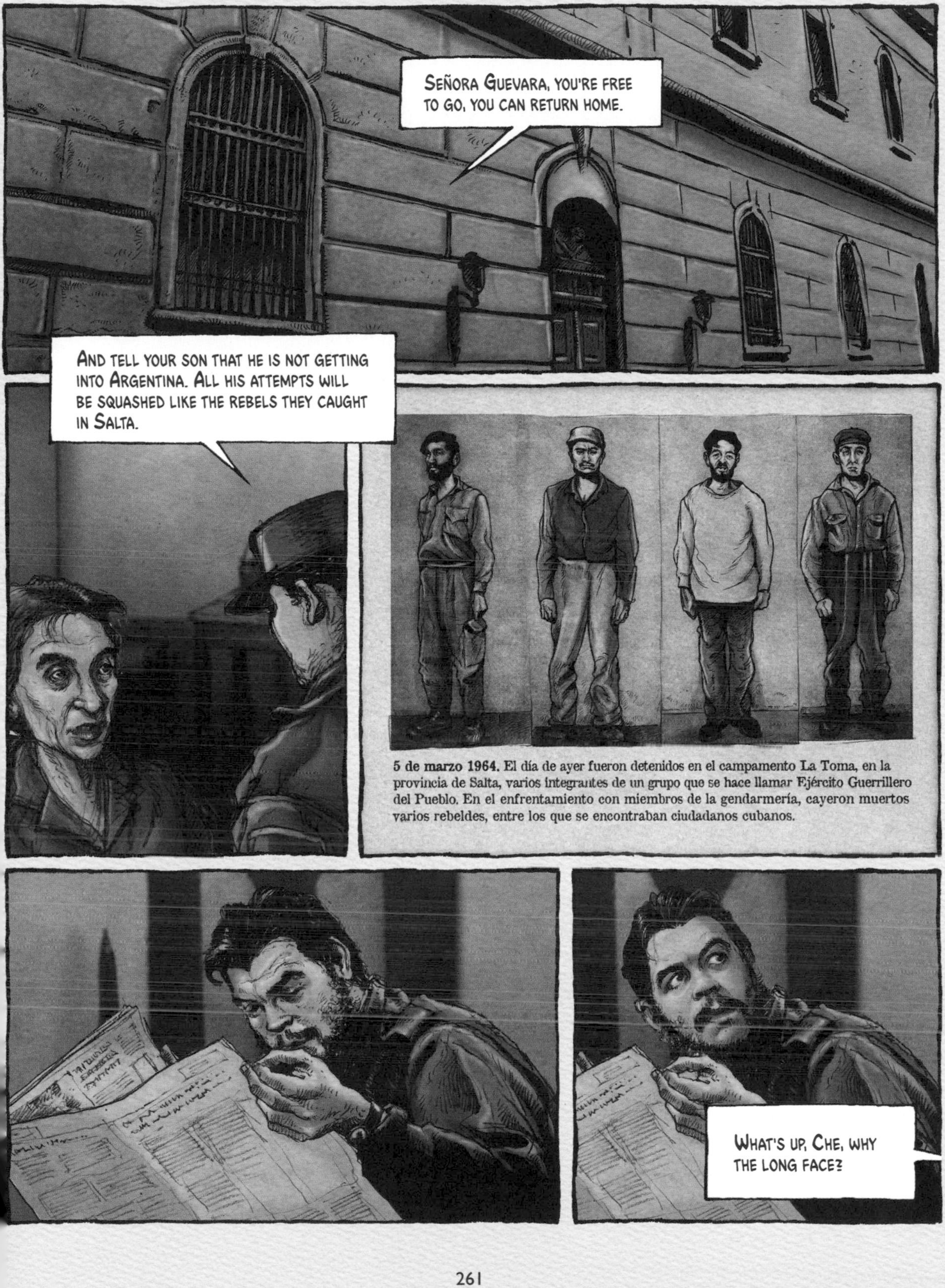
SEÑORA GUEVARA, YOU'RE FREE TO GO, YOU CAN RETURN HOME.
AND TELL YOUR SON THAT HE IS NOT GETTING INTO ARGENTINA. ALL HIS ATTEMPTS WILL BE SQUASHED LIKE THE REBELS THEY CAUGHT IN SALTA.
5 de marzo 1964. El día de ayer fueron detenidos en el campamento La Toma, en la provincia de Salta, varios integrantes de un grupo que se hace llamar Ejército Guerrillero del Pueblo. En el enfrentamiento con miembros de la gendarmería, cayeron muertos varios rebeldes, entre los que se encontraban ciudadanos cubanos.
WHAT'S UP, CHE, WHY THE LONG FACE?

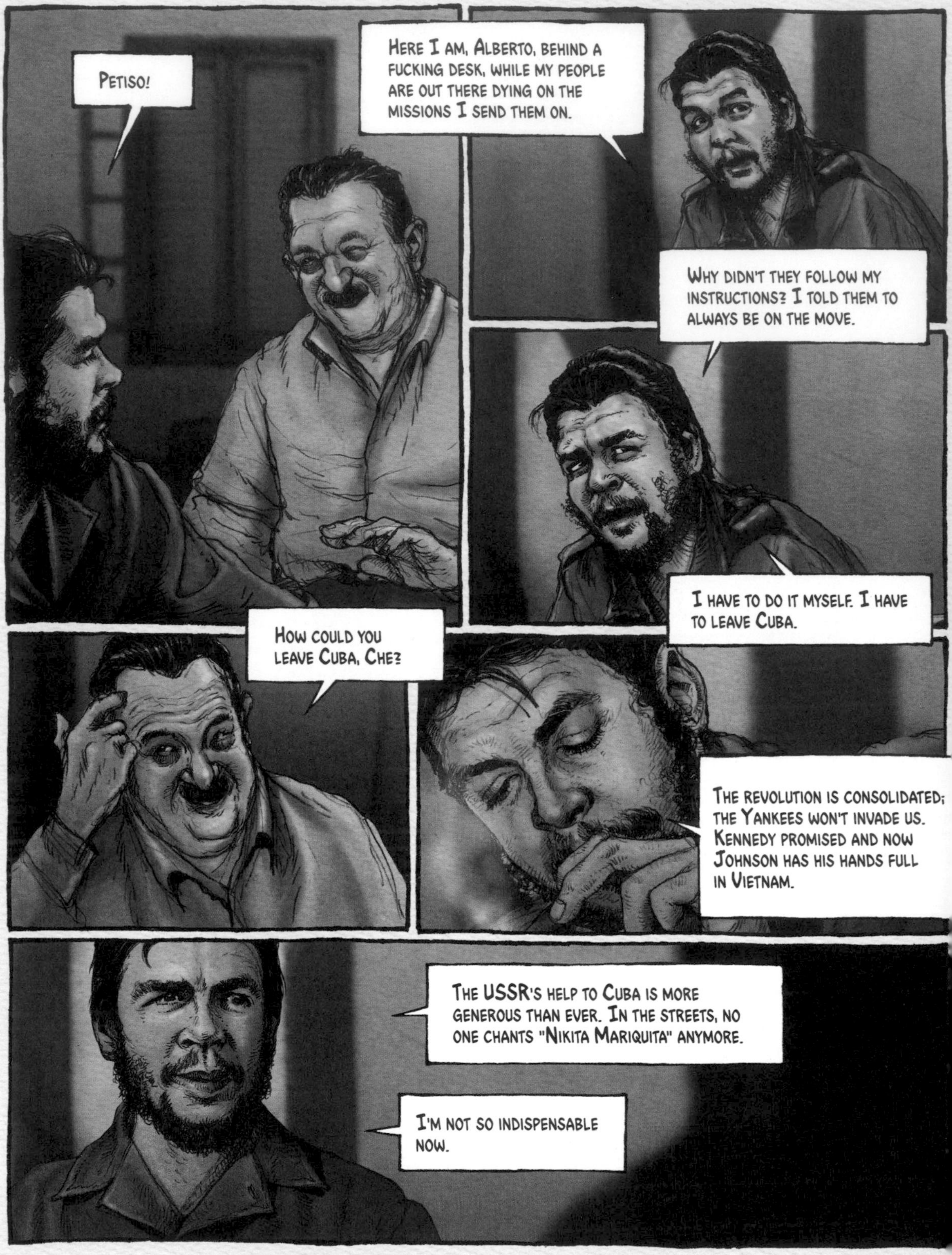
PETISO!
HERE I AM, ALBERTO, BEHIND A FUCKING DESK, WHILE MY PEOPLE ARE OUT THERE DYING ON THE MISSIONS I SEND THEM ON.
WHY DIDN'T THEY FOLLOW MY INSTRUCTIONS? I TOLD THEM TO ALWAYS BE ON THE MOVE.
I HAVE TO DO IT MYSELF. I HAVE TO LEAVE CUBA.
HOW COULD YOU LEAVE CUBA, CHE?
THE REVOLUTION IS CONSOLIDATED; THE YANKEES WON'T INVADE US. KENNEDY PROMISED AND NOW JOHNSON HAS HIS HANDS FULL IN VIETNAM.
THE USSR'S HELP TO CUBA IS MORE GENEROUS THAN EVER. IN THE STREETS, NO ONE CHANTS "NIKITA MARIQUITA" ANYMORE.
I'M NOT SO INDISPENSABLE NOW.

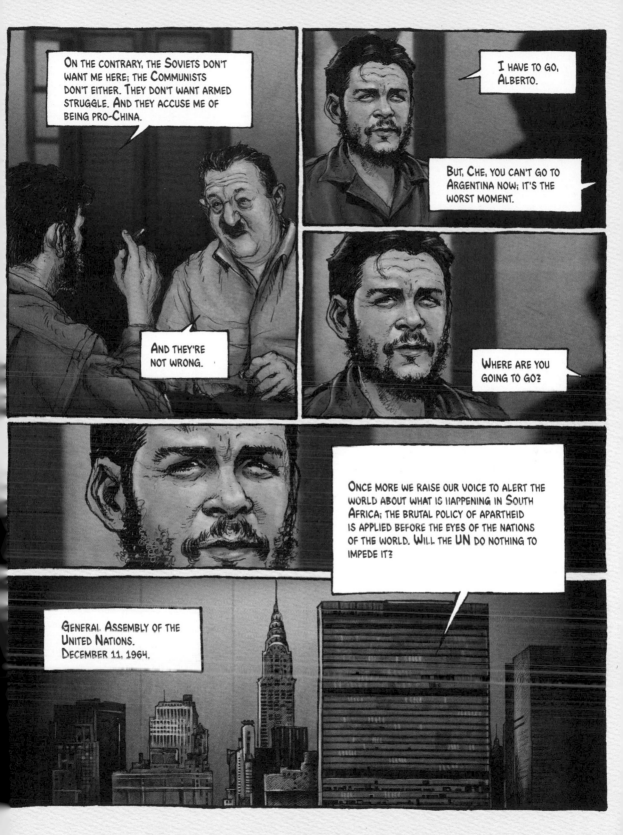

ON THE CONTRARY, THE SOVIETS DON'T WANT ME HERE; THE COMMUNISTS DON'T EITHER. THEY DON'T WANT ARMED STRUGGLE. AND THEY ACCUSE ME OF BEING PRO-CHINA.

AND THEY'RE NOT WRONG.

I HAVE TO GO, ALBERTO.

BUT, CHE, YOU CAN'T GO TO ARGENTINA NOW; IT'S THE WORST MOMENT.

WHERE ARE YOU GOING TO GO?

ONCE MORE WE RAISE OUR VOICE TO ALERT THE WORLD ABOUT WHAT IS HAPPENING IN SOUTH AFRICA; THE BRUTAL POLICY OF APARTHEID IS APPLIED BEFORE THE EYES OF THE NATIONS OF THE WORLD. WILL THE UN DO NOTHING TO IMPEDE IT?

GENERAL ASSEMBLY OF THE UNITED NATIONS. DECEMBER 11, 1964.

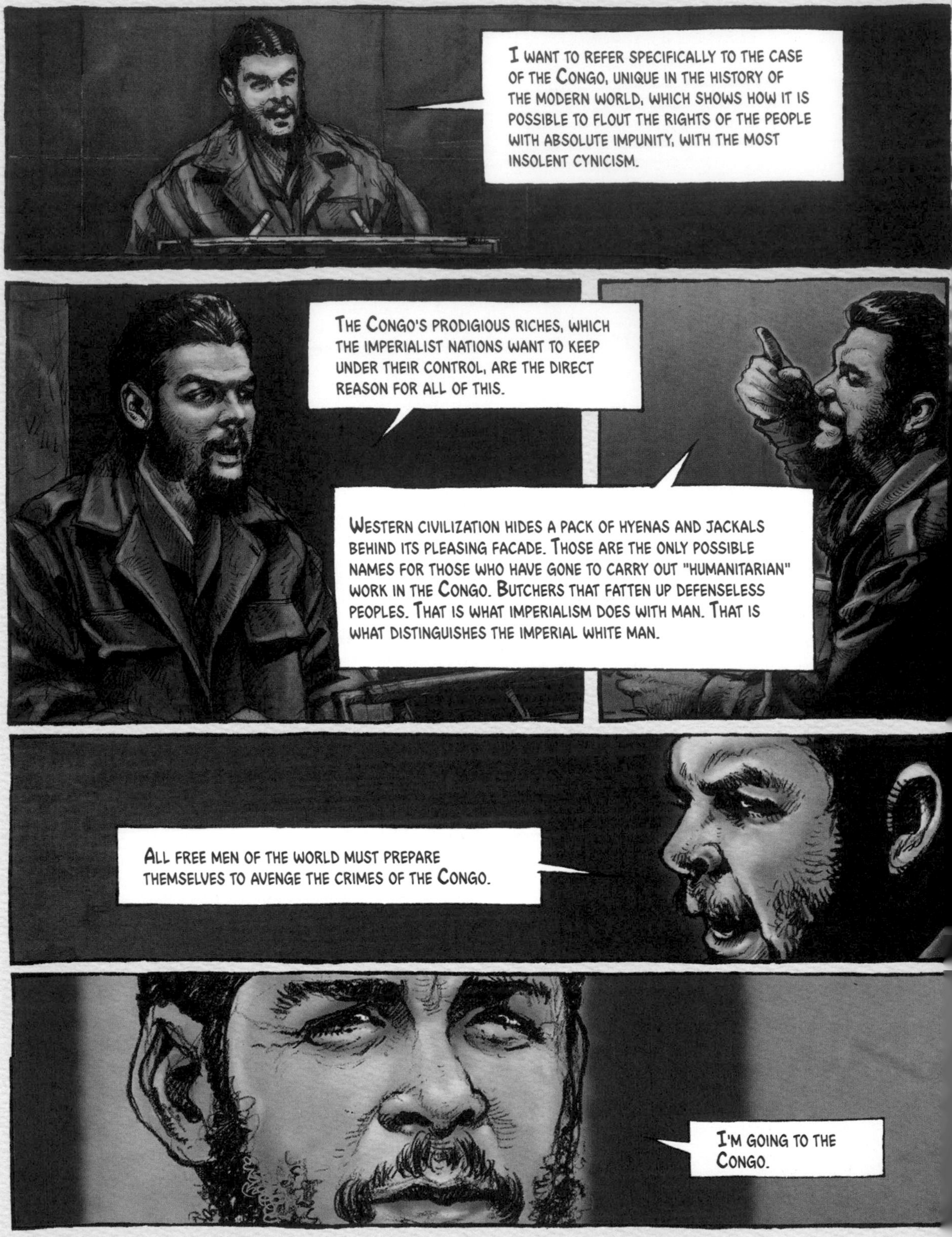
I WANT TO REFER SPECIFICALLY TO THE CASE OF THE CONGO, UNIQUE IN THE HISTORY OF THE MODERN WORLD, WHICH SHOWS HOW IT IS POSSIBLE TO FLOUT THE RIGHTS OF THE PEOPLE WITH ABSOLUTE IMPUNITY, WITH THE MOST INSOLENT CYNICISM.
THE CONGO'S PRODIGIOUS RICHES, WHICH THE IMPERIALIST NATIONS WANT TO KEEP UNDER THEIR CONTROL, ARE THE DIRECT REASON FOR ALL OF THIS.
WESTERN CIVILIZATION HIDES A PACK OF HYENAS AND JACKALS BEHIND ITS PLEASING FACADE. THOSE ARE THE ONLY POSSIBLE NAMES FOR THOSE WHO HAVE GONE TO CARRY OUT "HUMANITARIAN" WORK IN THE CONGO. BUTCHERS THAT FATTEN UP DEFENSELESS PEOPLES. THAT IS WHAT IMPERIALISM DOES WITH MAN. THAT IS WHAT DISTINGUISHES THE IMPERIAL WHITE MAN.
ALL FREE MEN OF THE WORLD MUST PREPARE THEMSELVES TO AVENGE THE CRIMES OF THE CONGO.
I'M GOING TO THE CONGO.

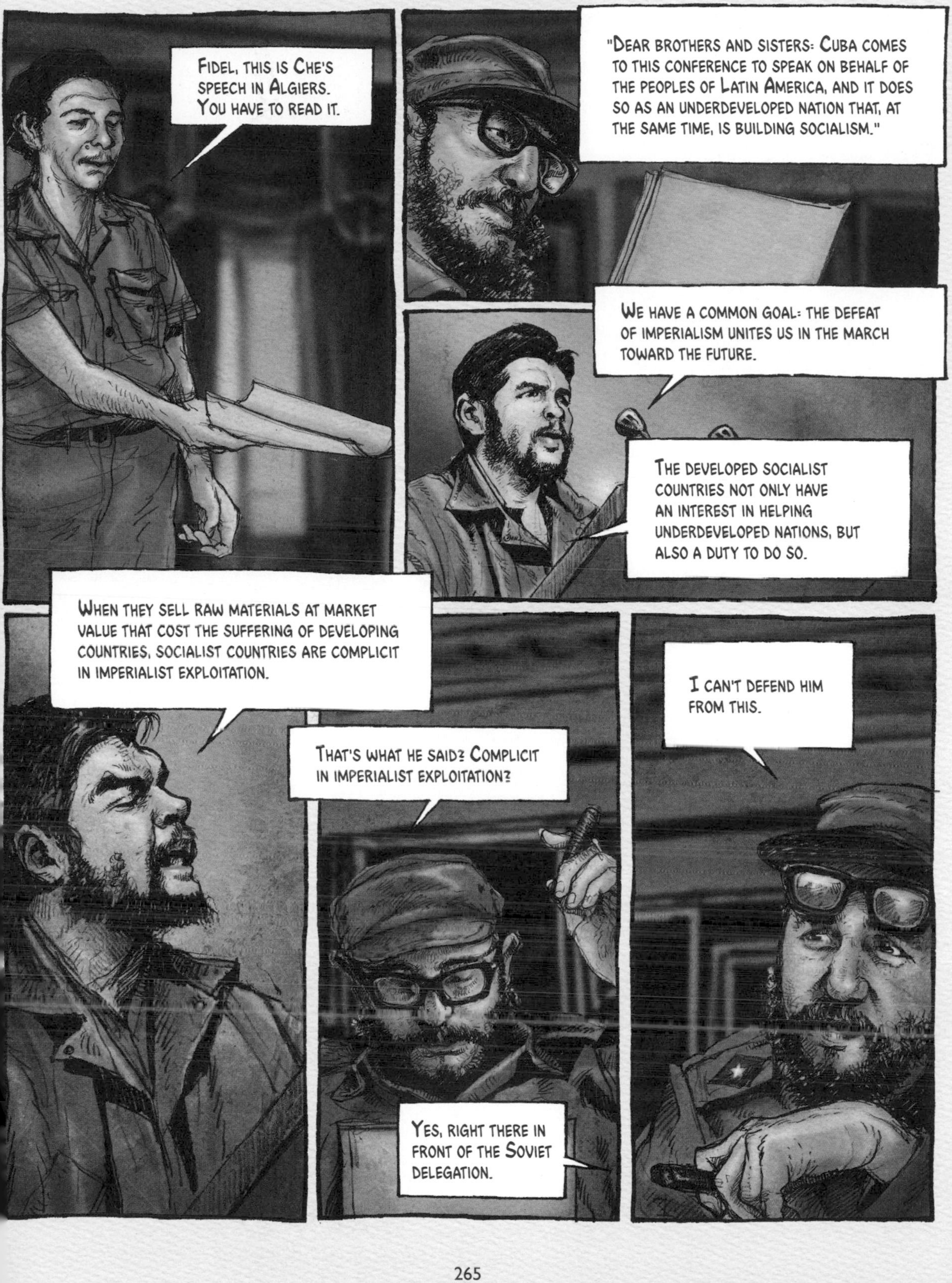
Fidel, this is Che's speech in Algiers. You have to read it.
"Dear brothers and sisters: Cuba comes to this conference to speak on behalf of the peoples of Latin America, and it does so as an underdeveloped nation that, at the same time, is building socialism."
We have a common goal: the defeat of imperialism unites us in the march toward the future.
The developed socialist countries not only have an interest in helping underdeveloped nations, but also a duty to do so.
When they sell raw materials at market value that cost the suffering of developing countries, socialist countries are complicit in imperialist exploitation.
That's what he said? Complicit in imperialist exploitation?
Yes, right there in front of the Soviet delegation.
I can't defend him from this.

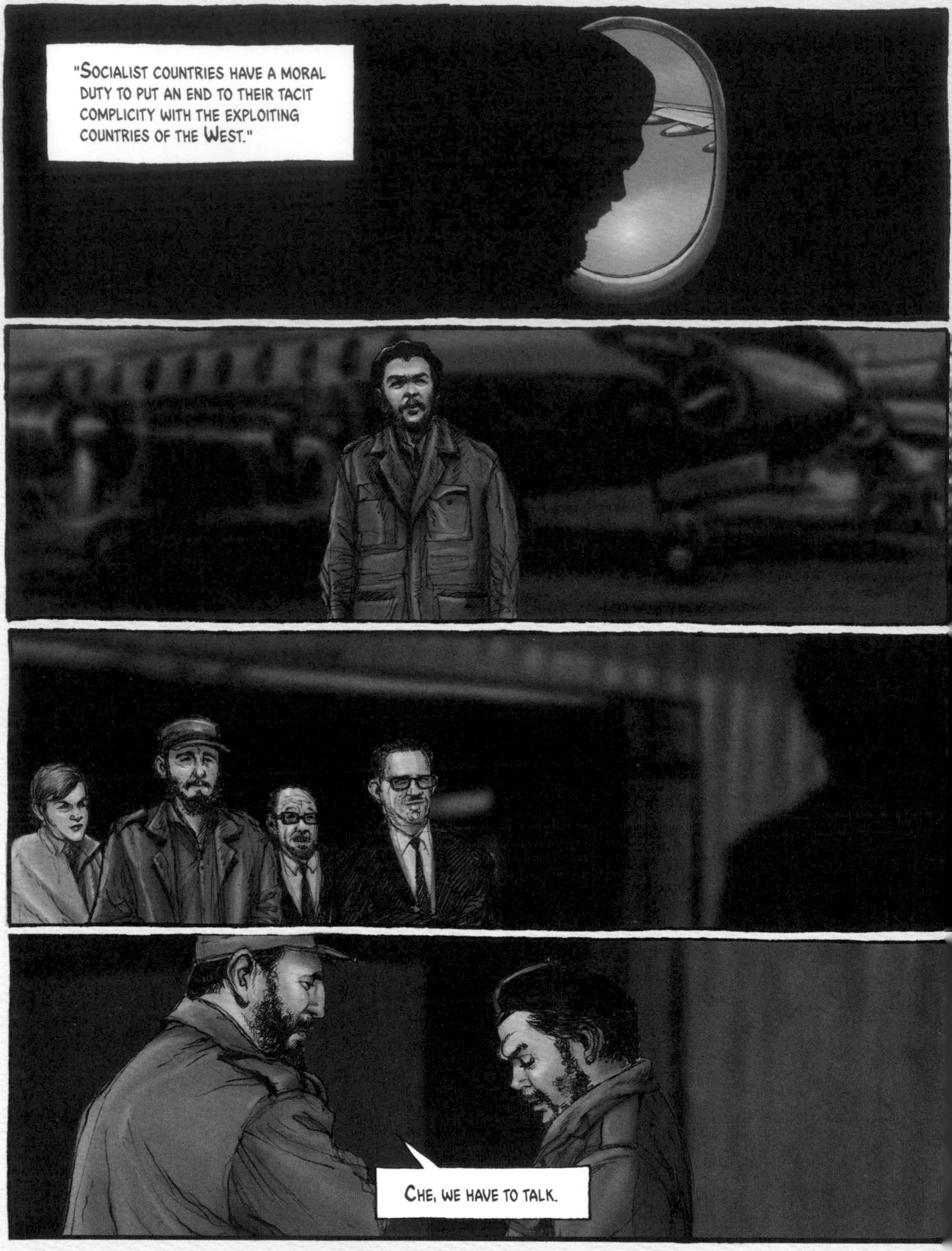
"Socialist countries have a moral duty to put an end to their tacit complicity with the exploiting countries of the West."
Che, we have to talk.

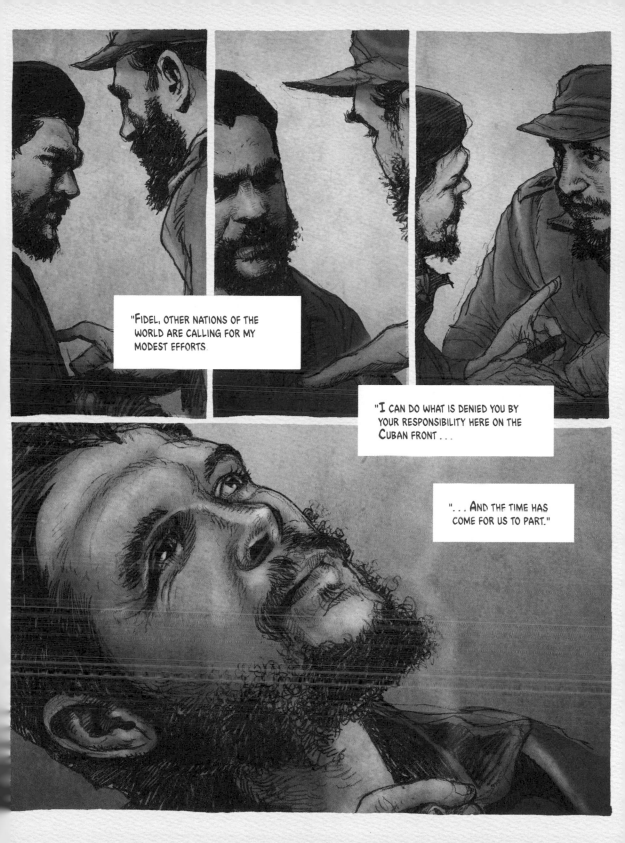

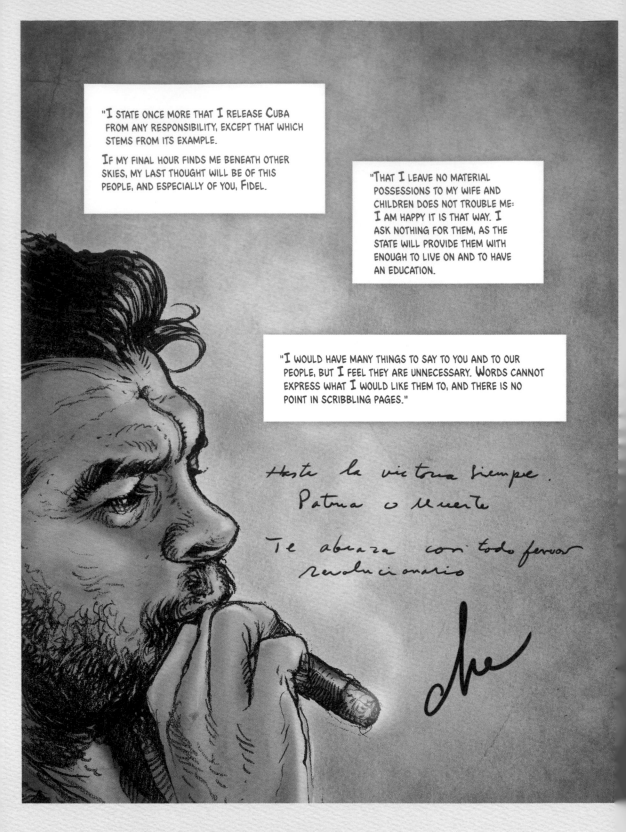

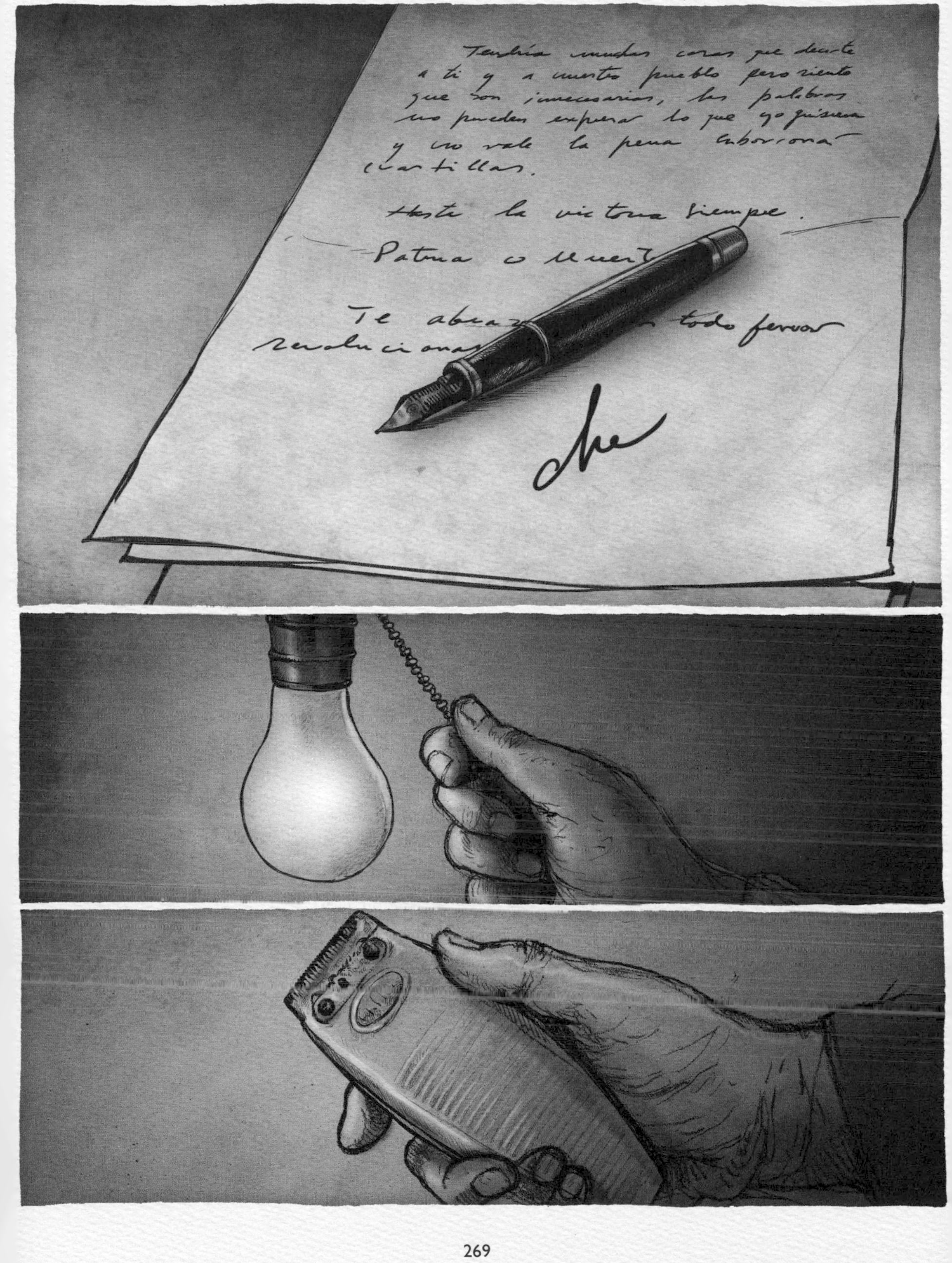
Tendría muchas cosas que decirte a ti y a nuestro pueblo pero siento que son innecesarias, las palabras no pueden expresar lo que yo quisiera y no vale la pena emborronar cuartillas.
Hasta la victoria siempre.
Patria o muert
Te abraz todo fervor
revolucionar
Che

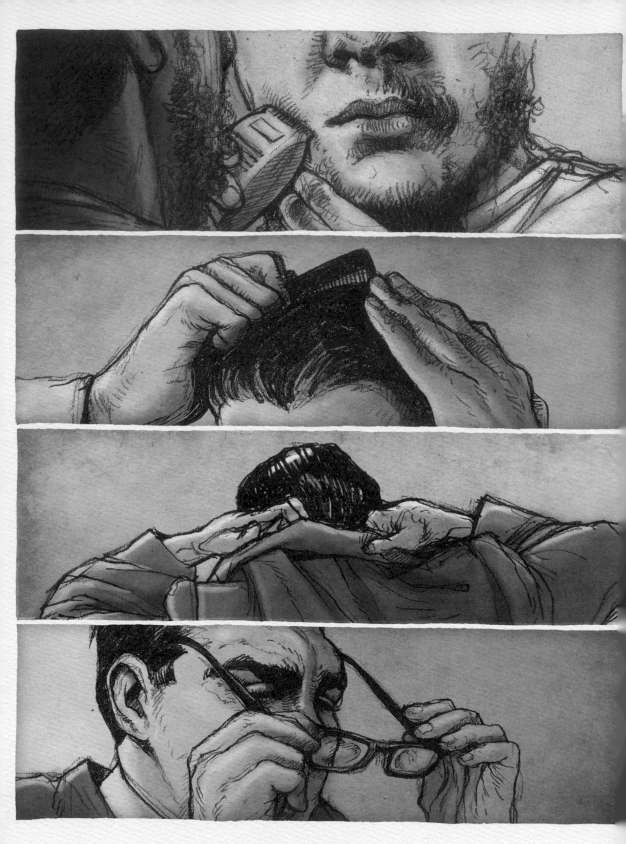

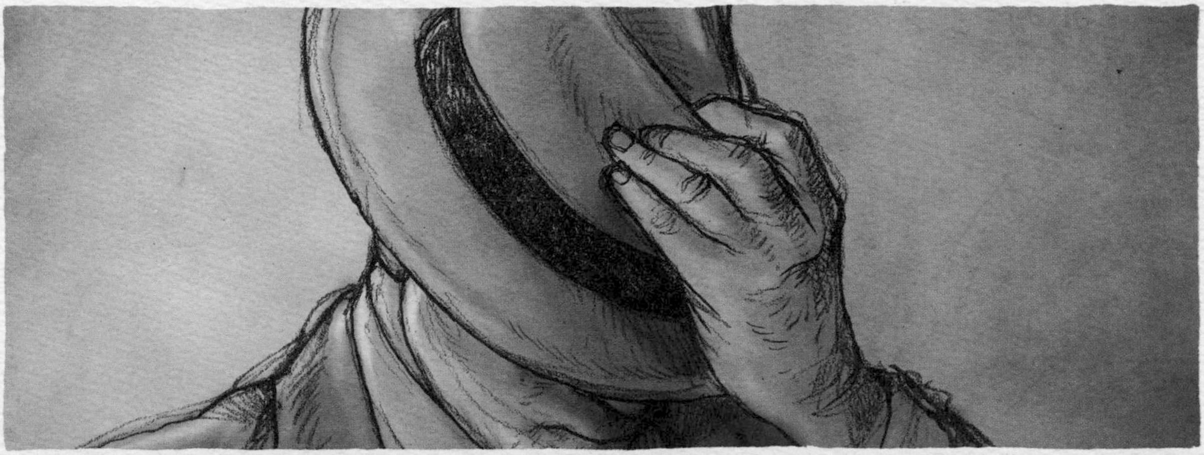

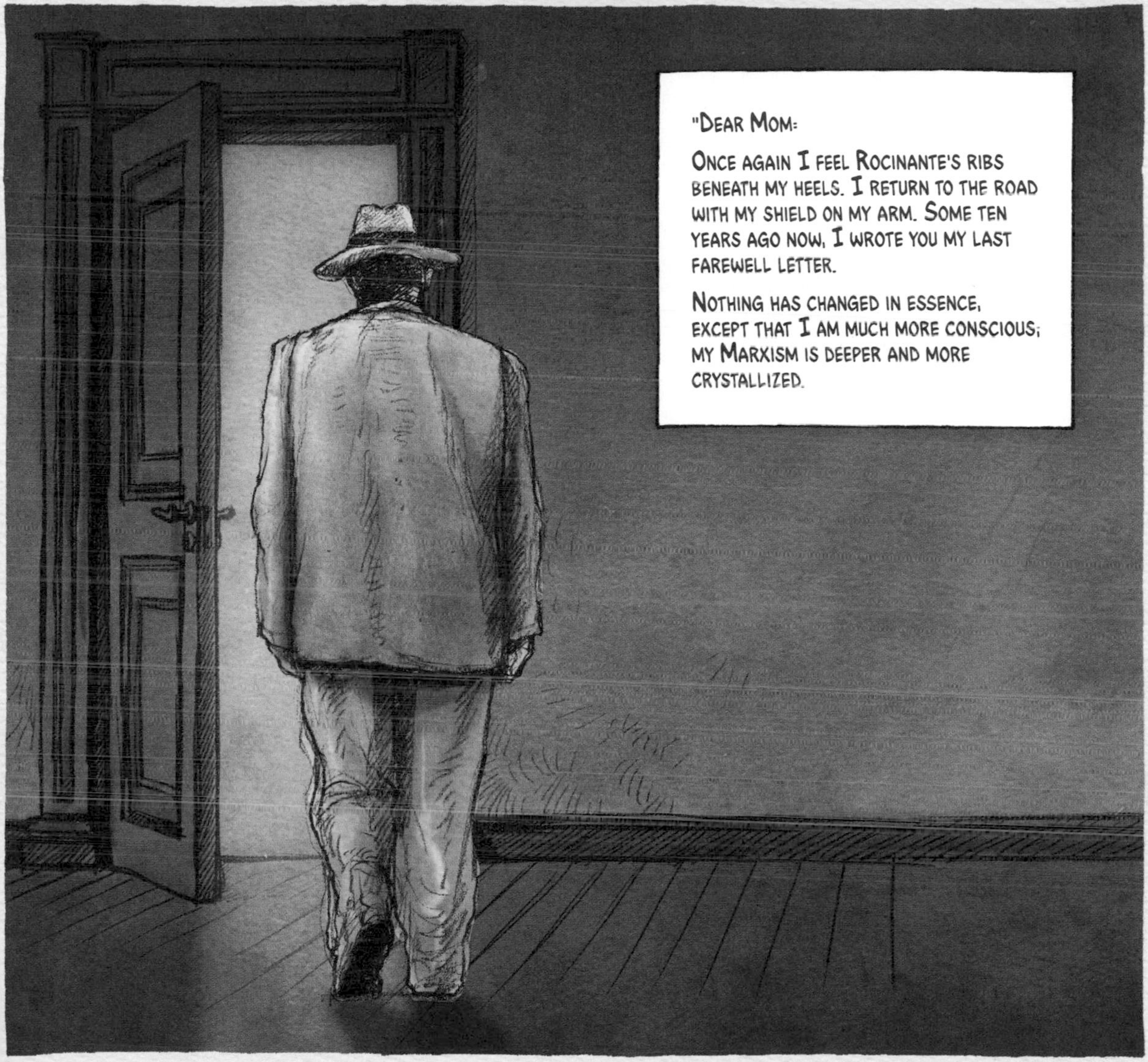
"Dear Mom:
Once again I feel Rocinante's ribs beneath my heels. I return to the road with my shield on my arm. Some ten years ago now, I wrote you my last farewell letter.
Nothing has changed in essence, except that I am much more conscious; my Marxism is deeper and more crystallized.

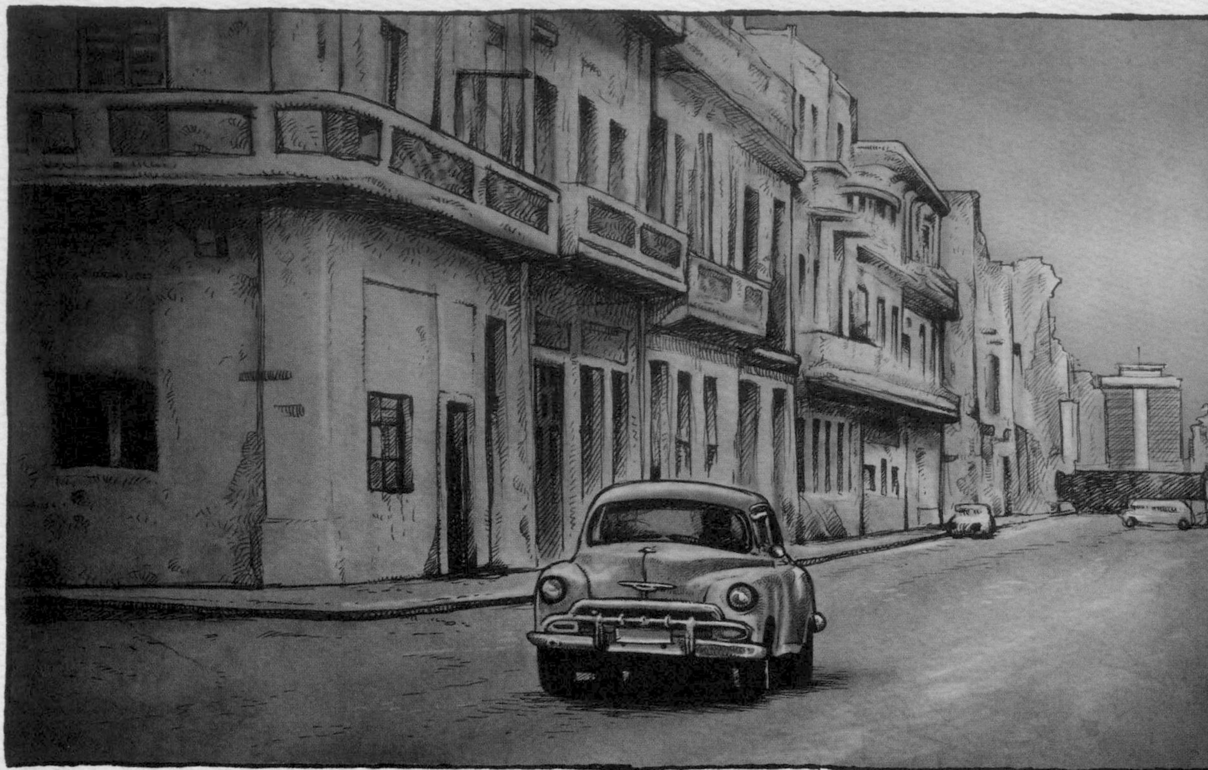

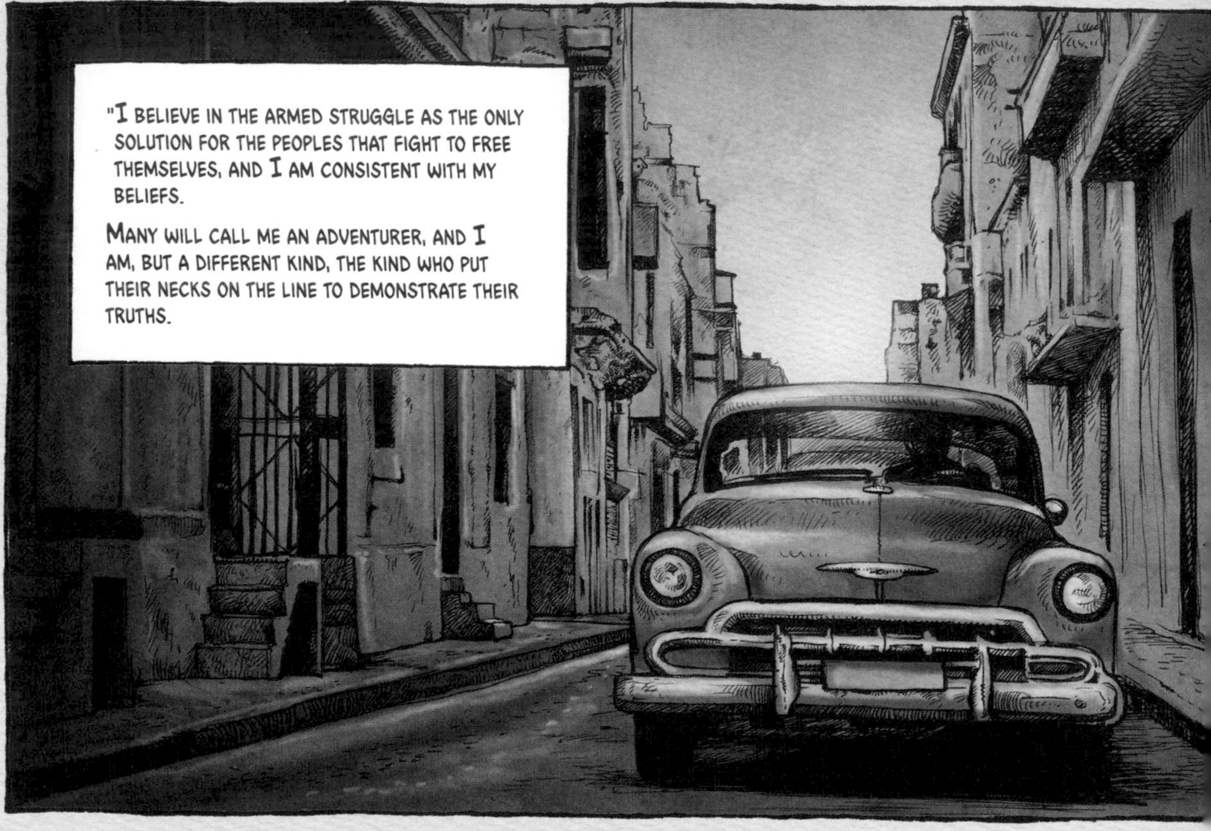
"I BELIEVE IN THE ARMED STRUGGLE AS THE ONLY SOLUTION FOR THE PEOPLES THAT FIGHT TO FREE THEMSELVES, AND I AM CONSISTENT WITH MY BELIEFS.
MANY WILL CALL ME AN ADVENTURER, AND I AM, BUT A DIFFERENT KIND, THE KIND WHO PUT THEIR NECKS ON THE LINE TO DEMONSTRATE THEIR TRUTHS.

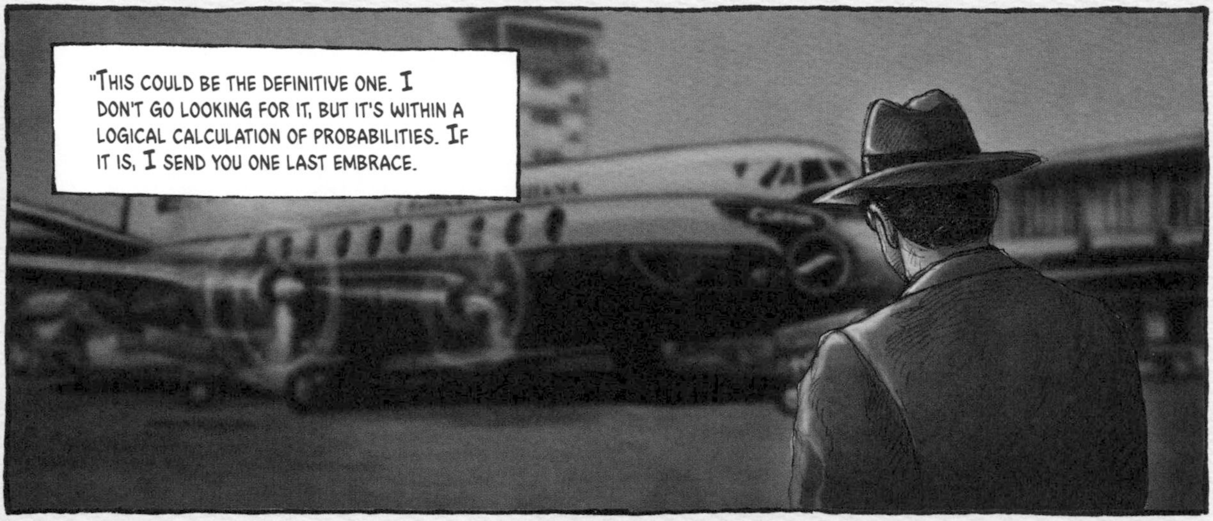
"THIS COULD BE THE DEFINITIVE ONE. I DON'T GO LOOKING FOR IT, BUT IT'S WITHIN A LOGICAL CALCULATION OF PROBABILITIES. IF IT IS, I SEND YOU ONE LAST EMBRACE.

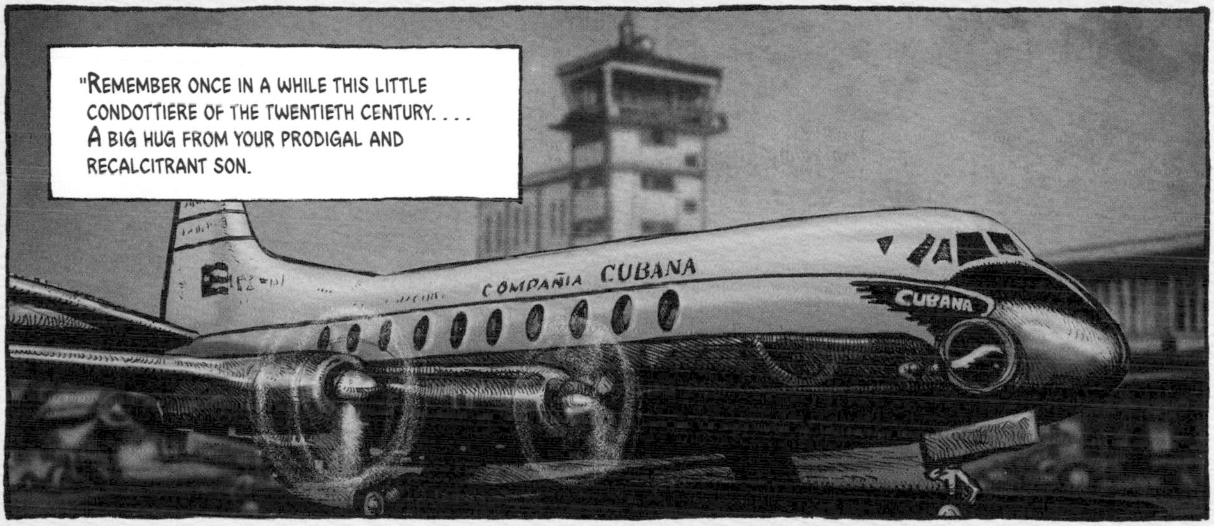
"REMEMBER ONCE IN A WHILE THIS LITTLE CONDOTTIERE OF THE TWENTIETH CENTURY. . . . A BIG HUG FROM YOUR PRODIGAL AND RECALCITRANT SON.
COMPAÑIA CUBANA
CUBANA

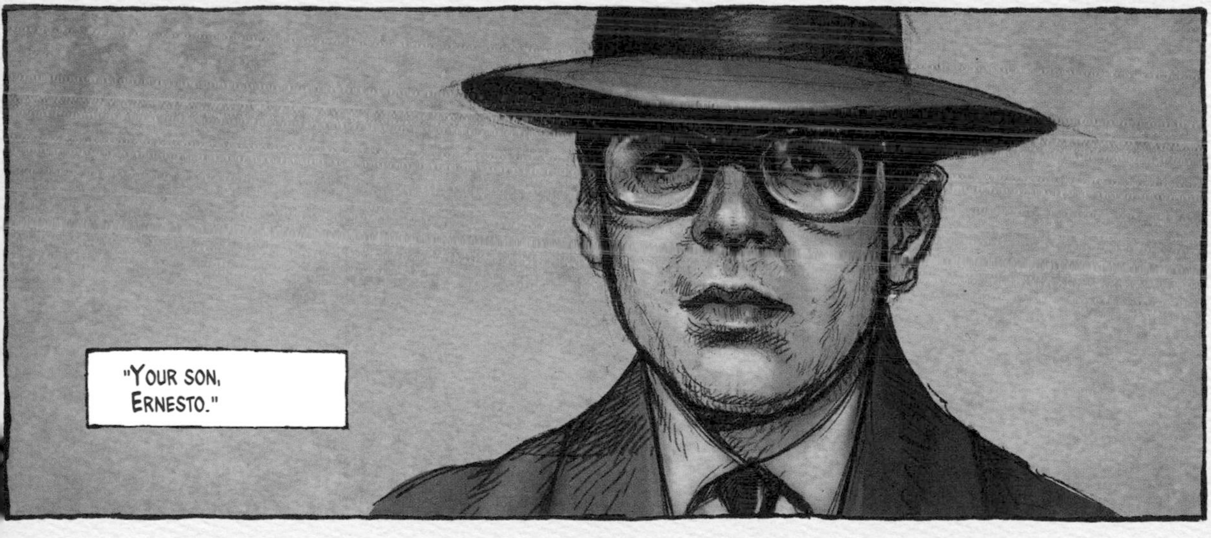
"YOUR SON, ERNESTO."

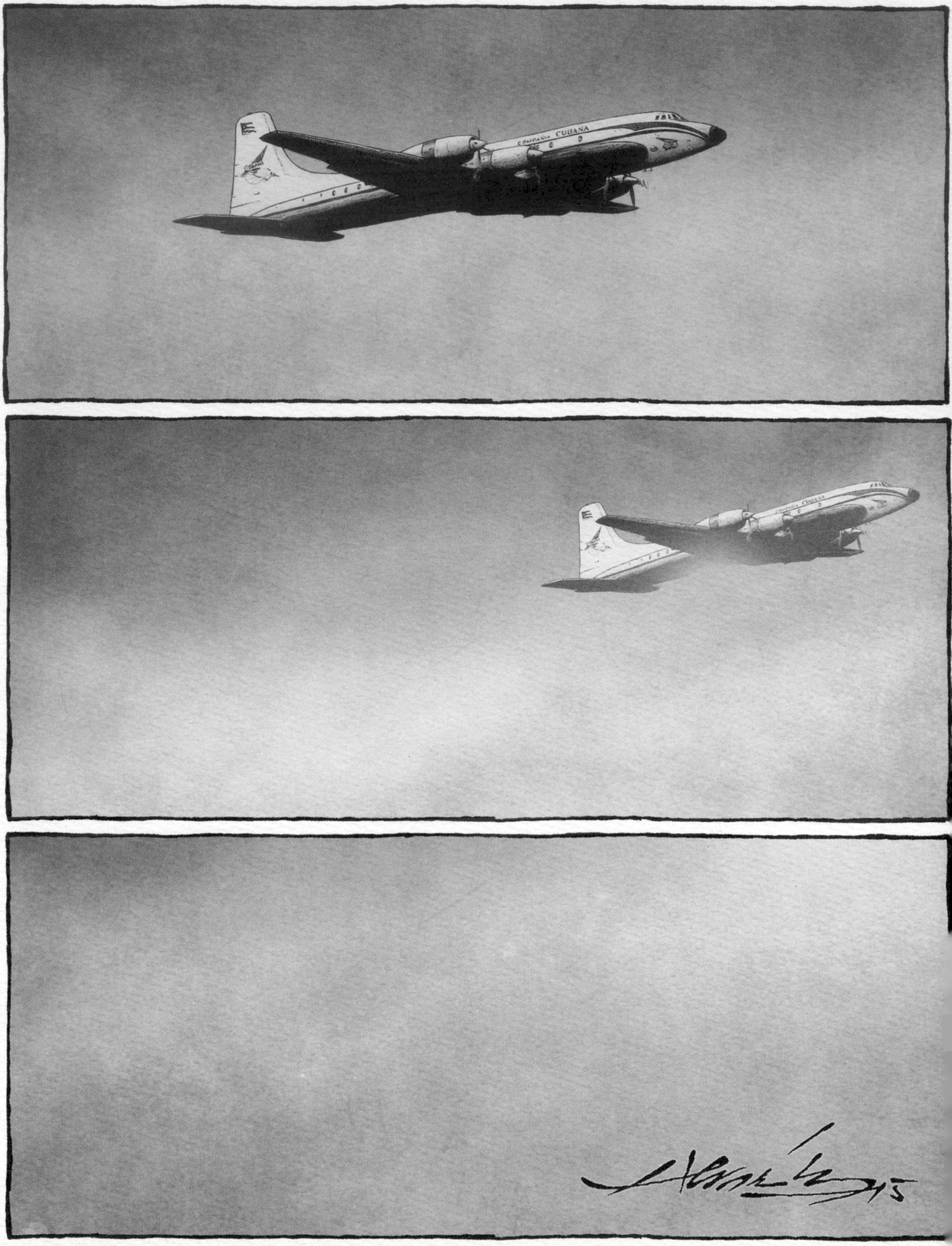
COMPAÑIA CUBANA

"MY ROVING HOME WILL HAVE TWO
FEET ONCE AGAIN, AND MY DREAMS
NO FRONTIERS, AT LEAST UNTIL THE
BULLETS HAVE THEIR SAY."

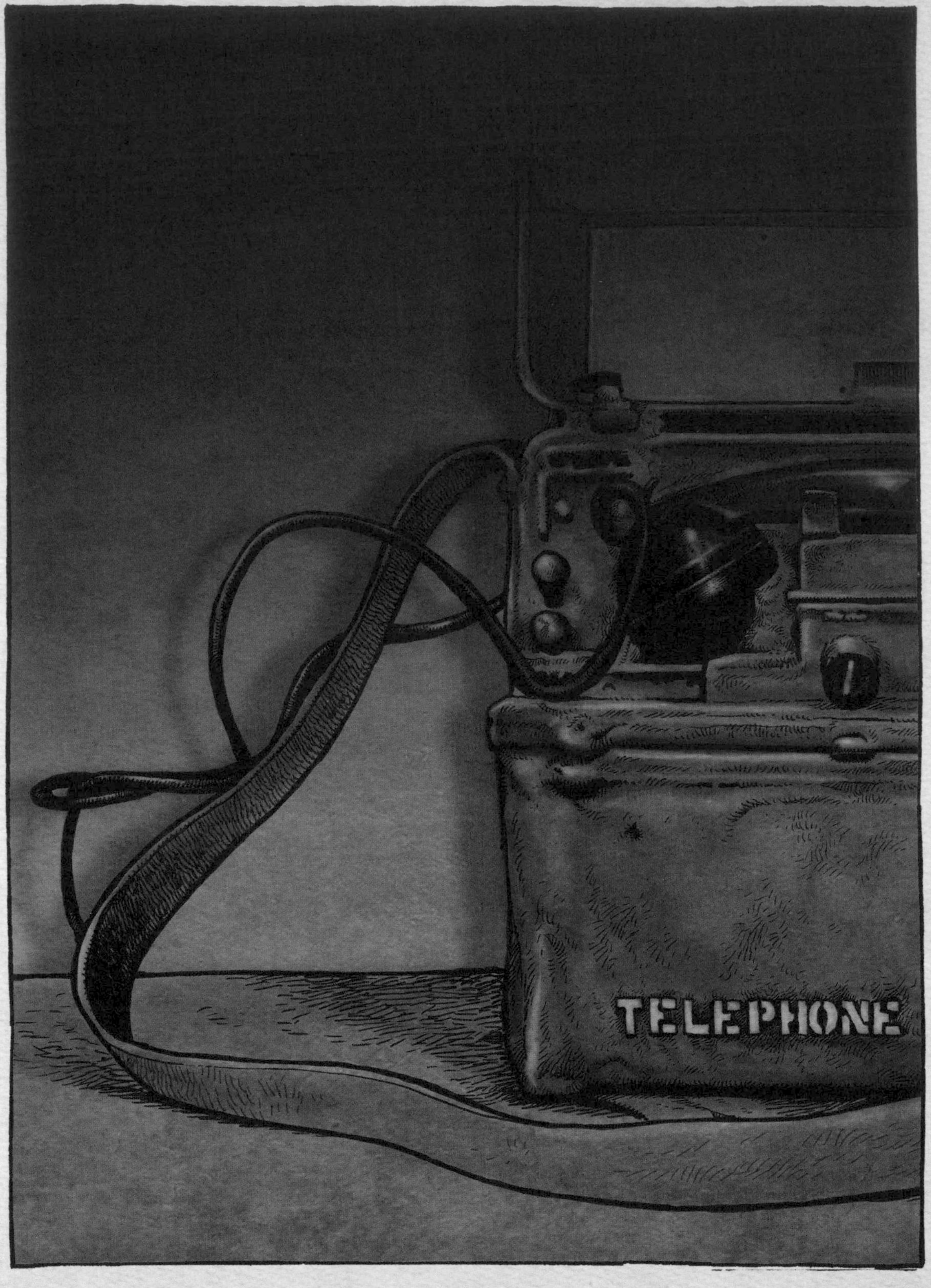
TELEPHONE

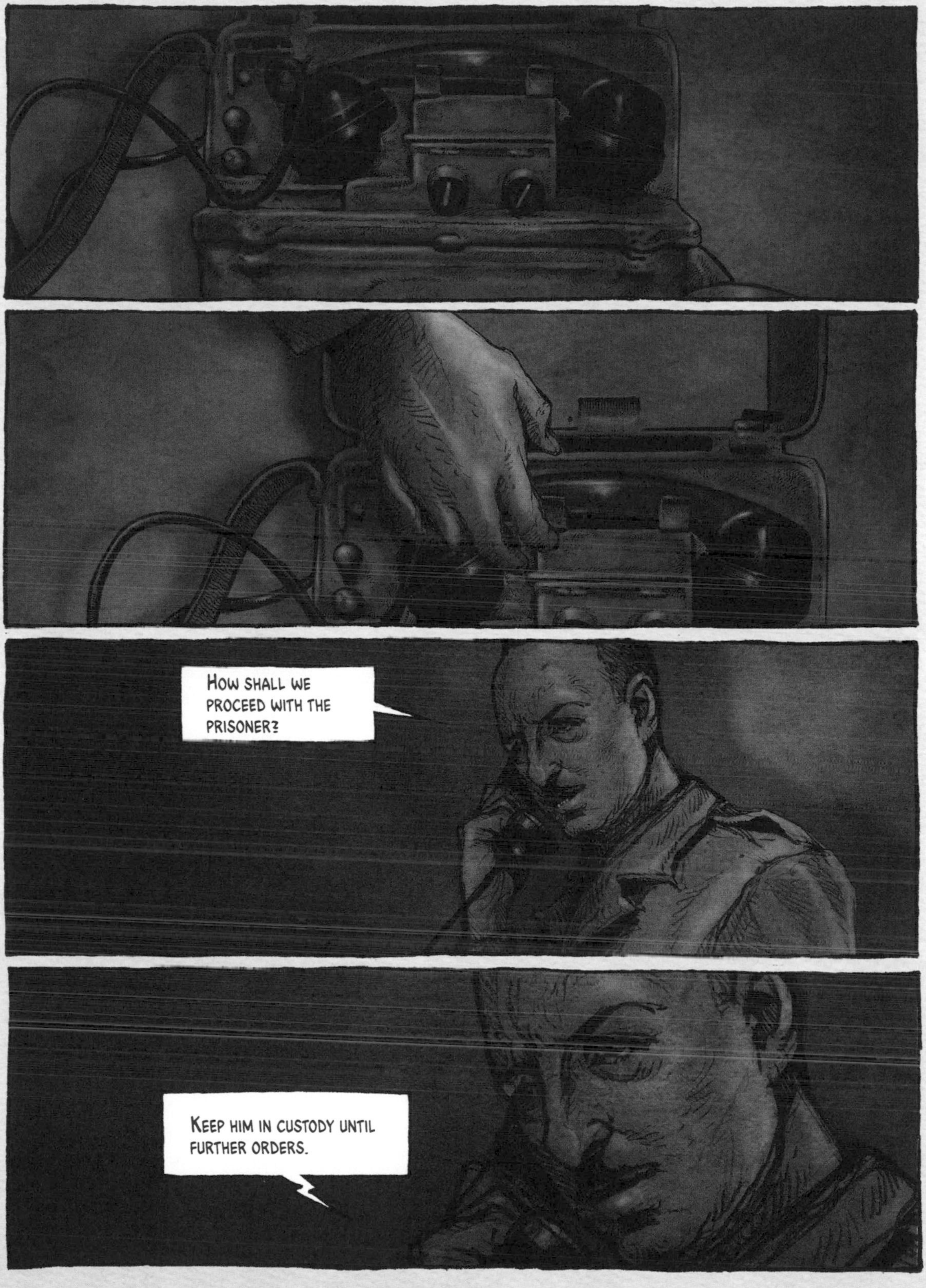
HOW SHALL WE PROCEED WITH THE PRISONER?
KEEP HIM IN CUSTODY UNTIL FURTHER ORDERS.

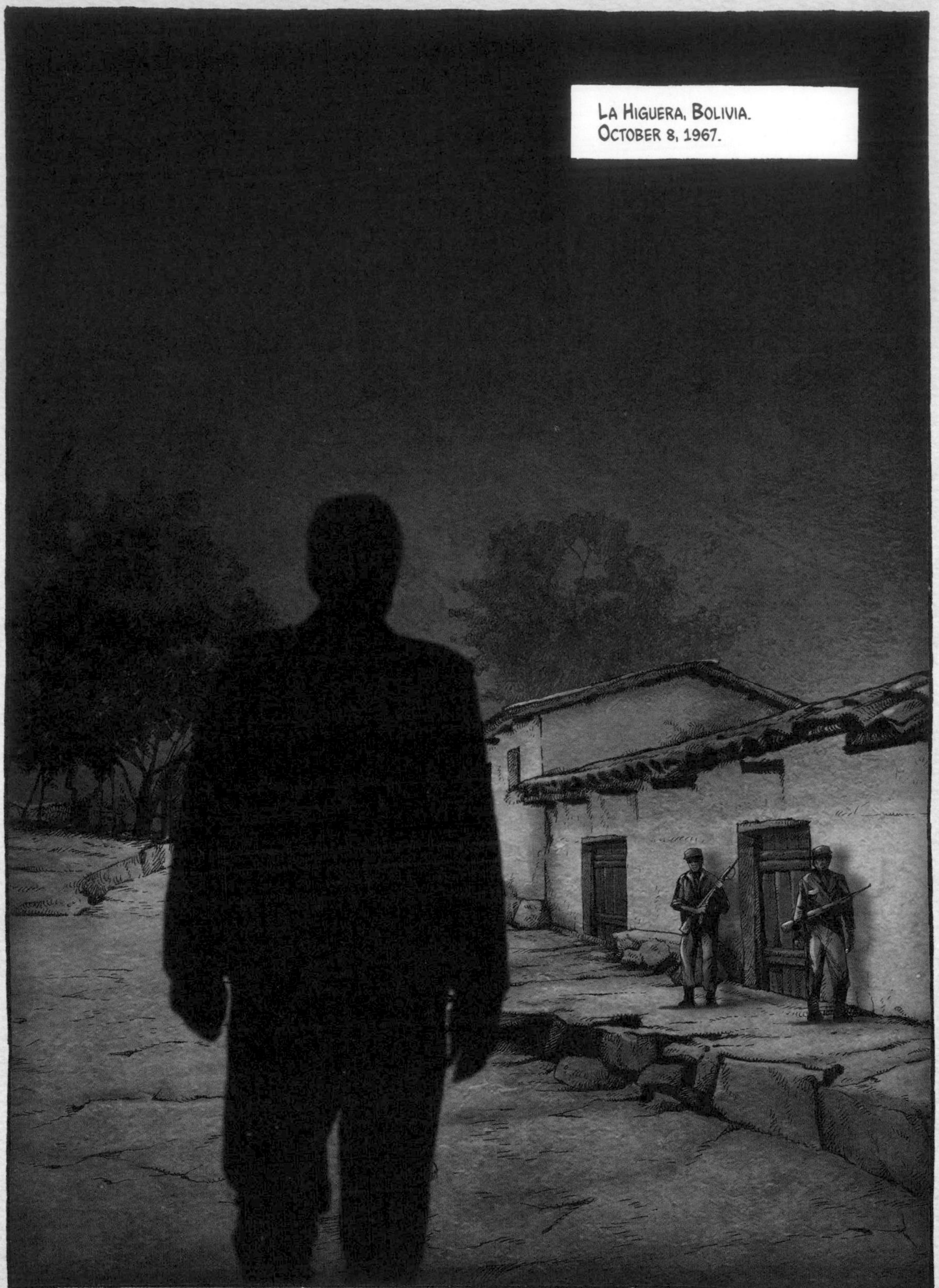
La Higuera, Bolivia.
October 8, 1967.

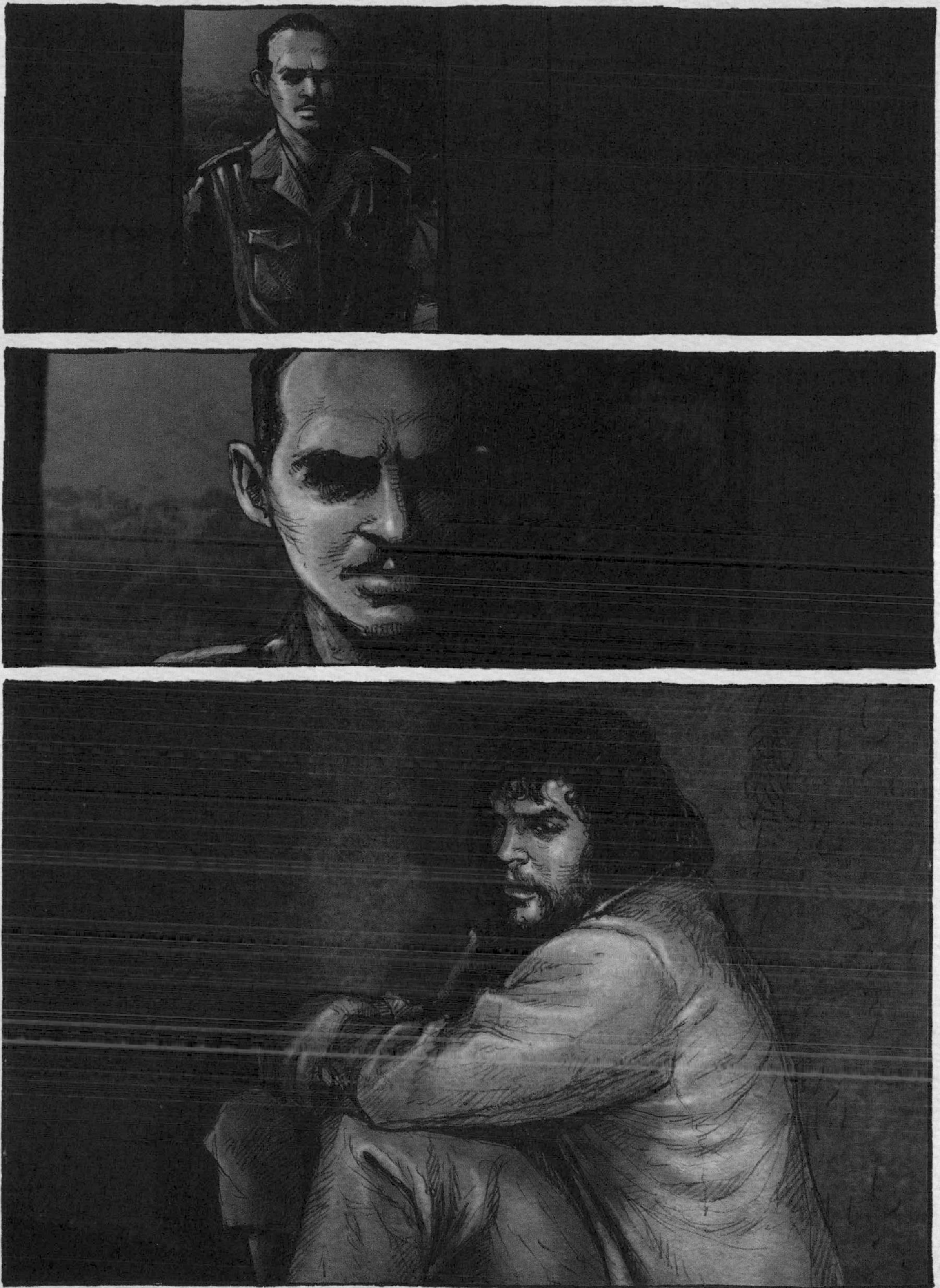

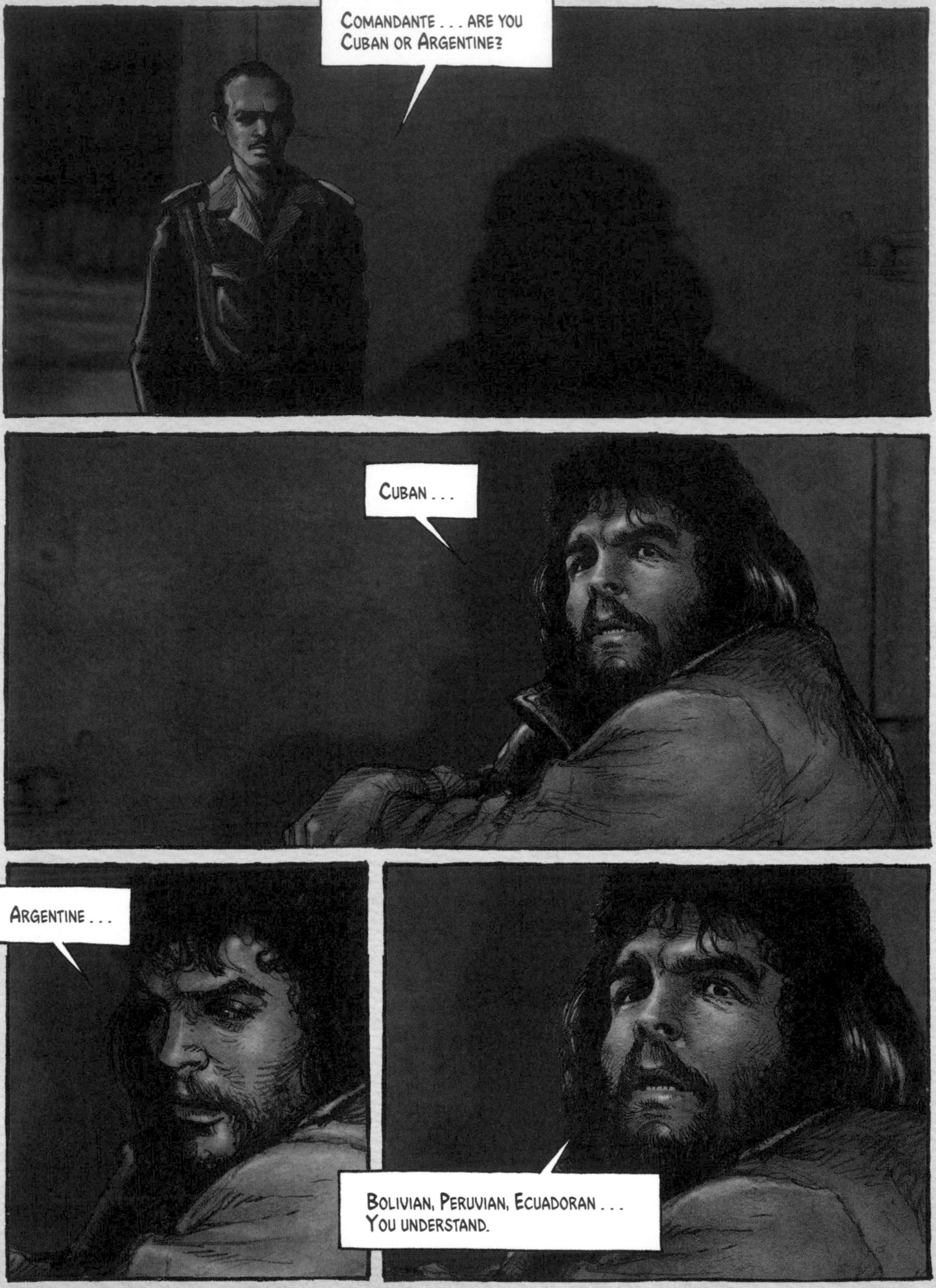
COMANDANTE . . . ARE YOU CUBAN OR ARGENTINE?
CUBAN . . .
ARGENTINE . . .
BOLIVIAN, PERUVIAN, ECUADORAN . . . YOU UNDERSTAND.

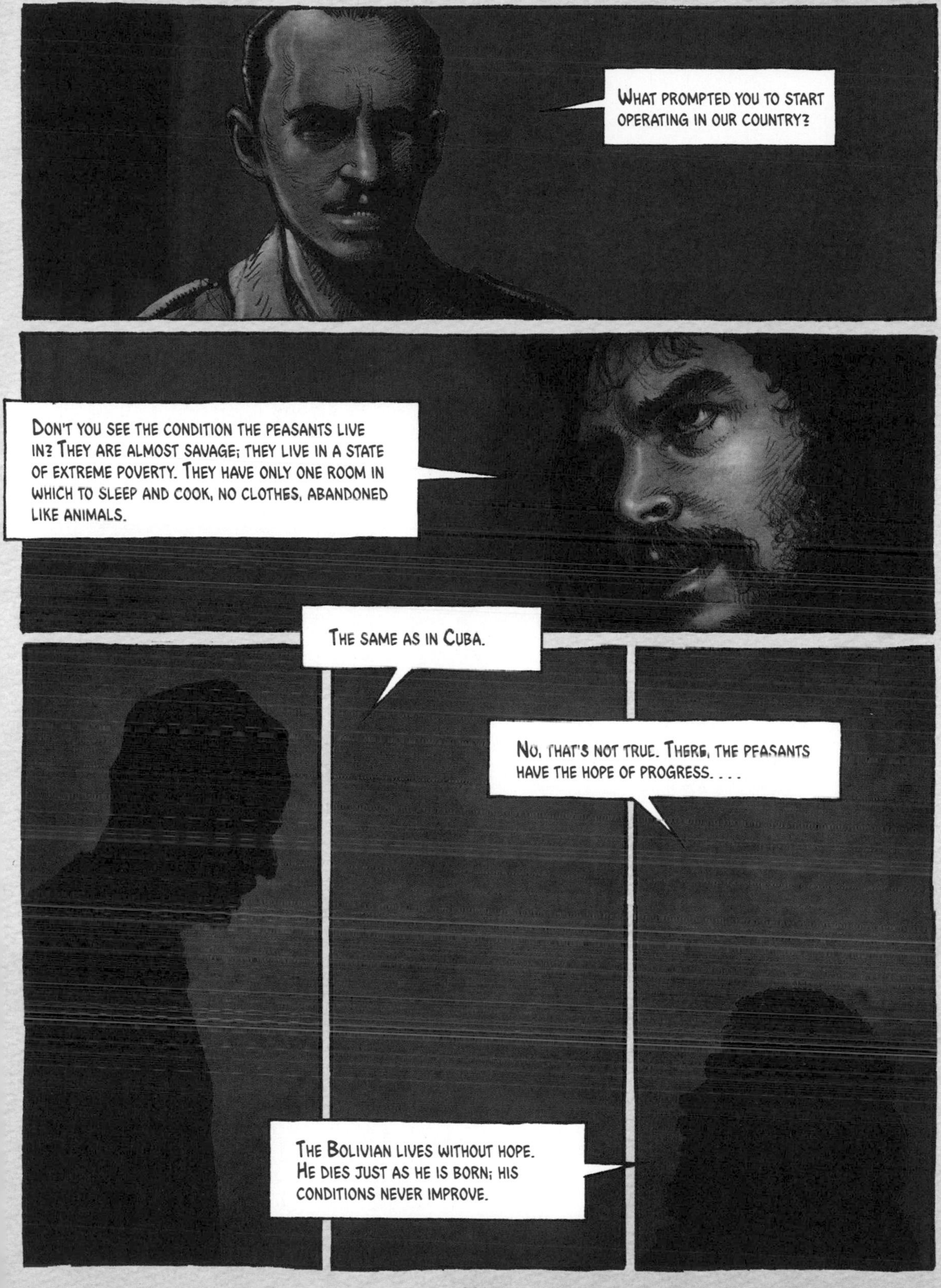
What prompted you to start operating in our country?
Don't you see the condition the peasants live in? They are almost savage; they live in a state of extreme poverty. They have only one room in which to sleep and cook, no clothes, abandoned like animals.
The same as in Cuba.
No, that's not true. There, the peasants have the hope of progress. . . .
The Bolivian lives without hope. He dies just as he is born; his conditions never improve.

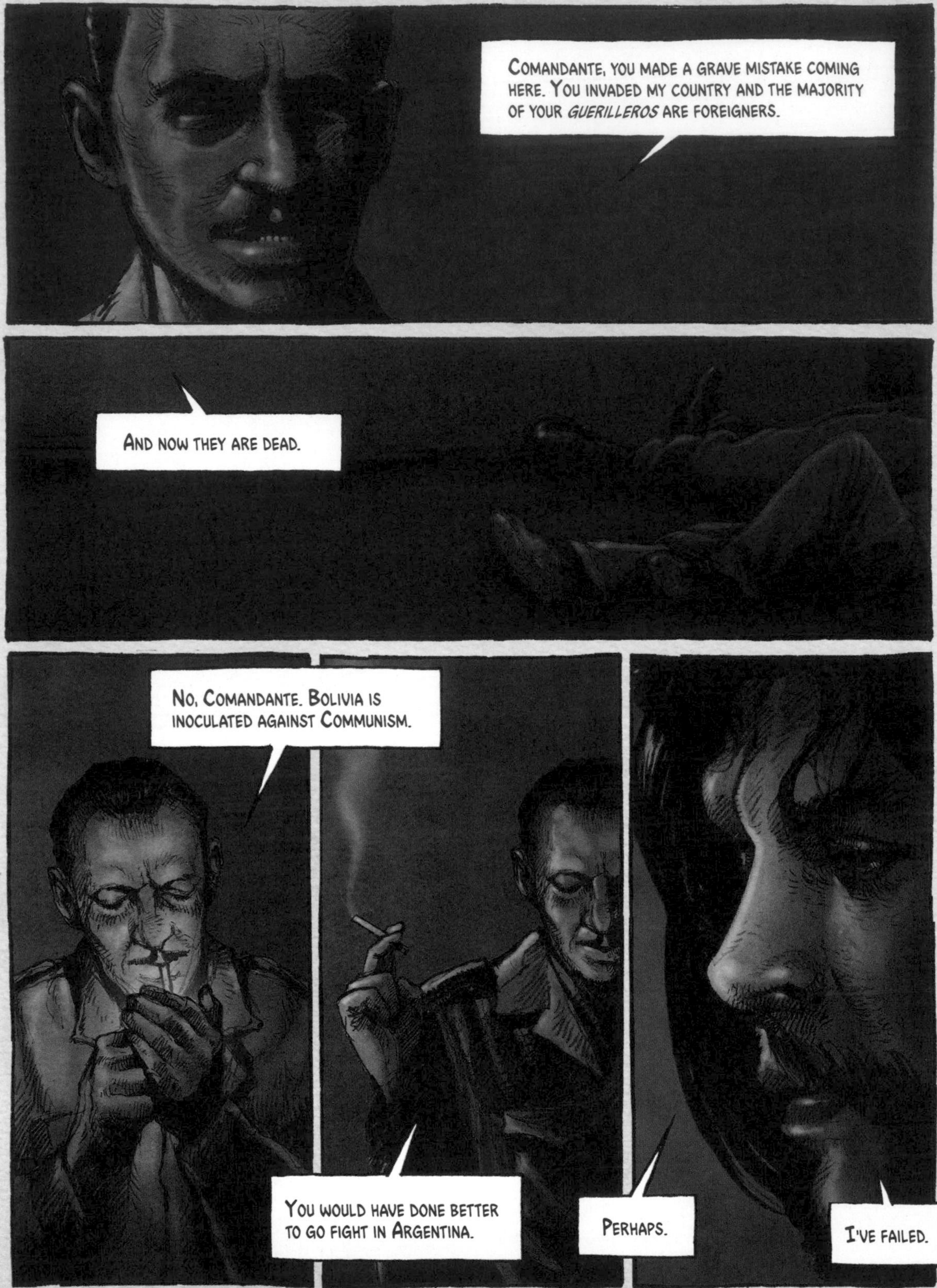
COMANDANTE, YOU MADE A GRAVE MISTAKE COMING HERE. YOU INVADED MY COUNTRY AND THE MAJORITY OF YOUR *GUERILLEROS* ARE FOREIGNERS.
AND NOW THEY ARE DEAD.
NO, COMANDANTE. BOLIVIA IS INOCULATED AGAINST COMMUNISM.
YOU WOULD HAVE DONE BETTER TO GO FIGHT IN ARGENTINA.
PERHAPS.
I'VE FAILED.

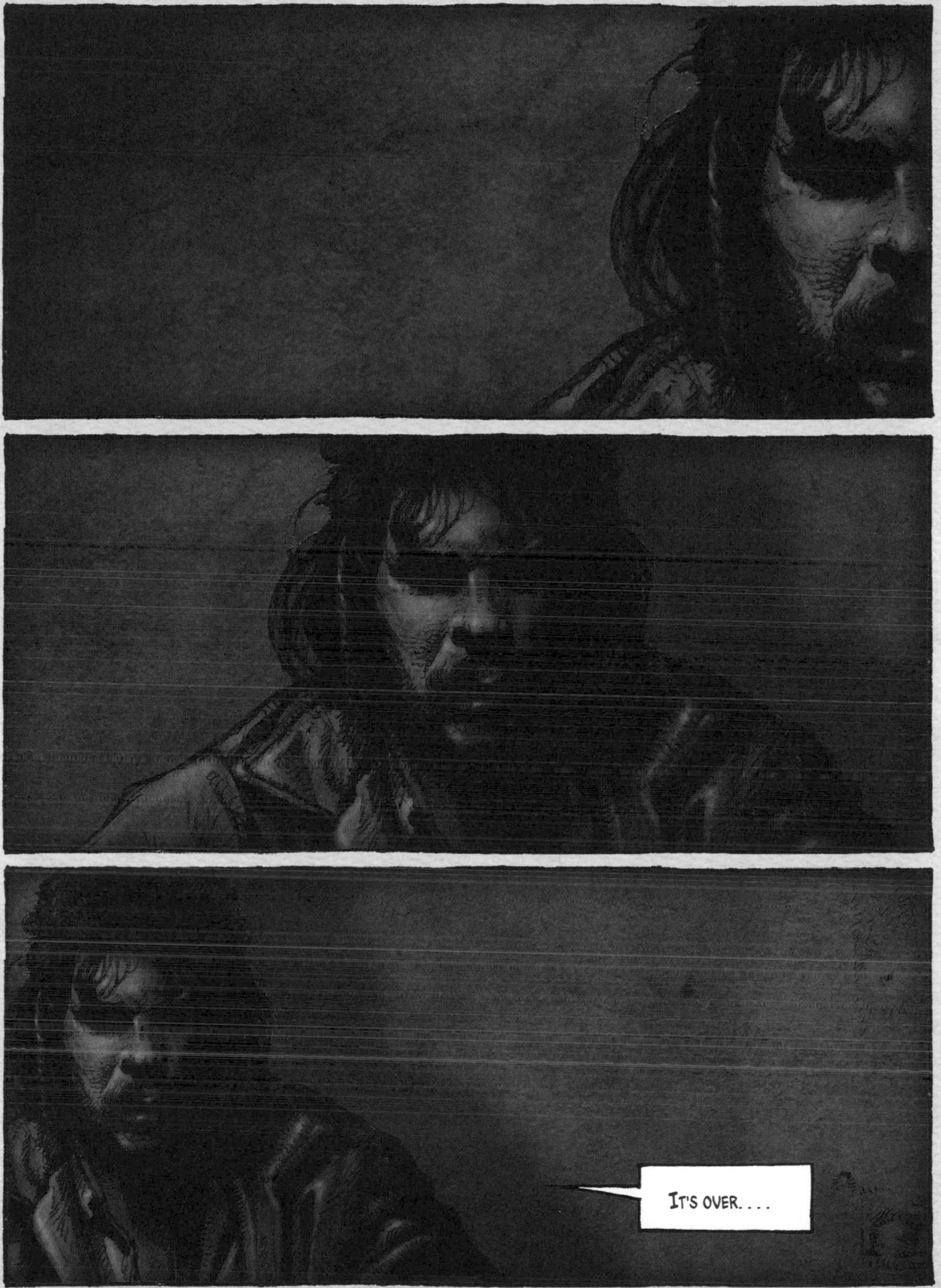
IT'S OVER. . . .

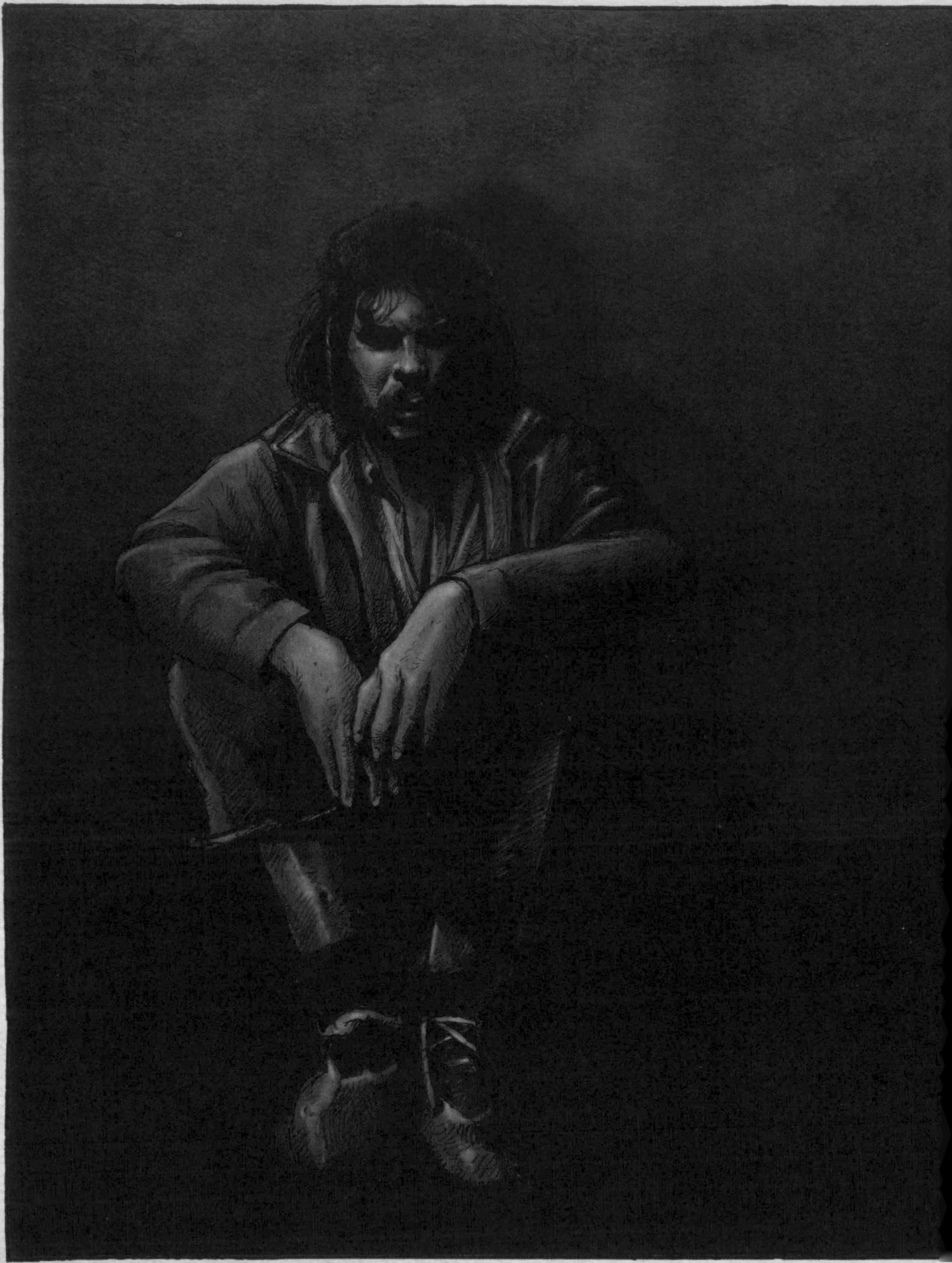

CHE

UNA VIDA REVOLUCIONARIA

LIBRO 3

EL SACRIFICIO NECESARIO

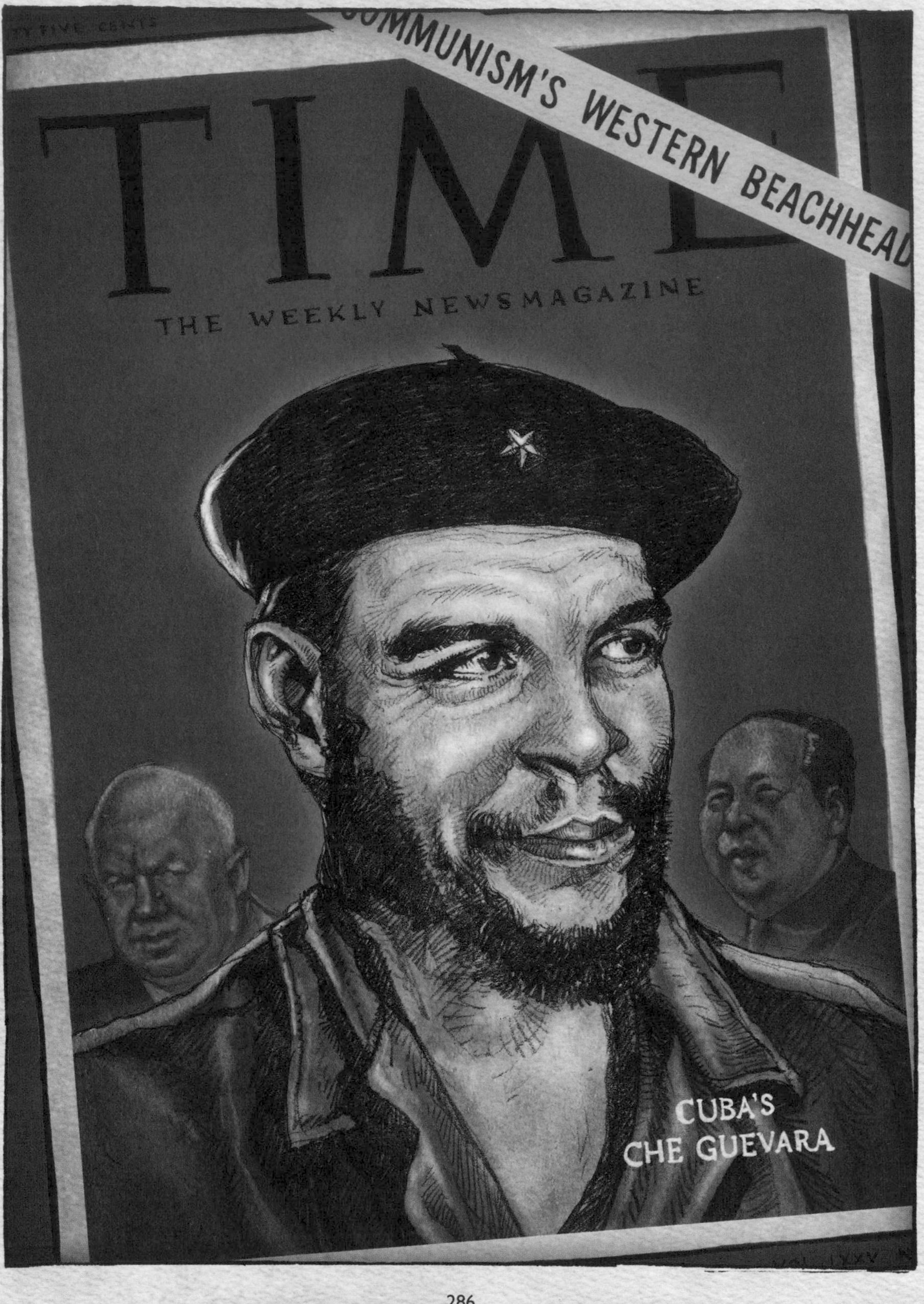
COMMUNISM'S WESTERN BEACHHEAD
TIME
THE WEEKLY NEWSMAGAZINE
CUBA'S
CHE GUEVARA

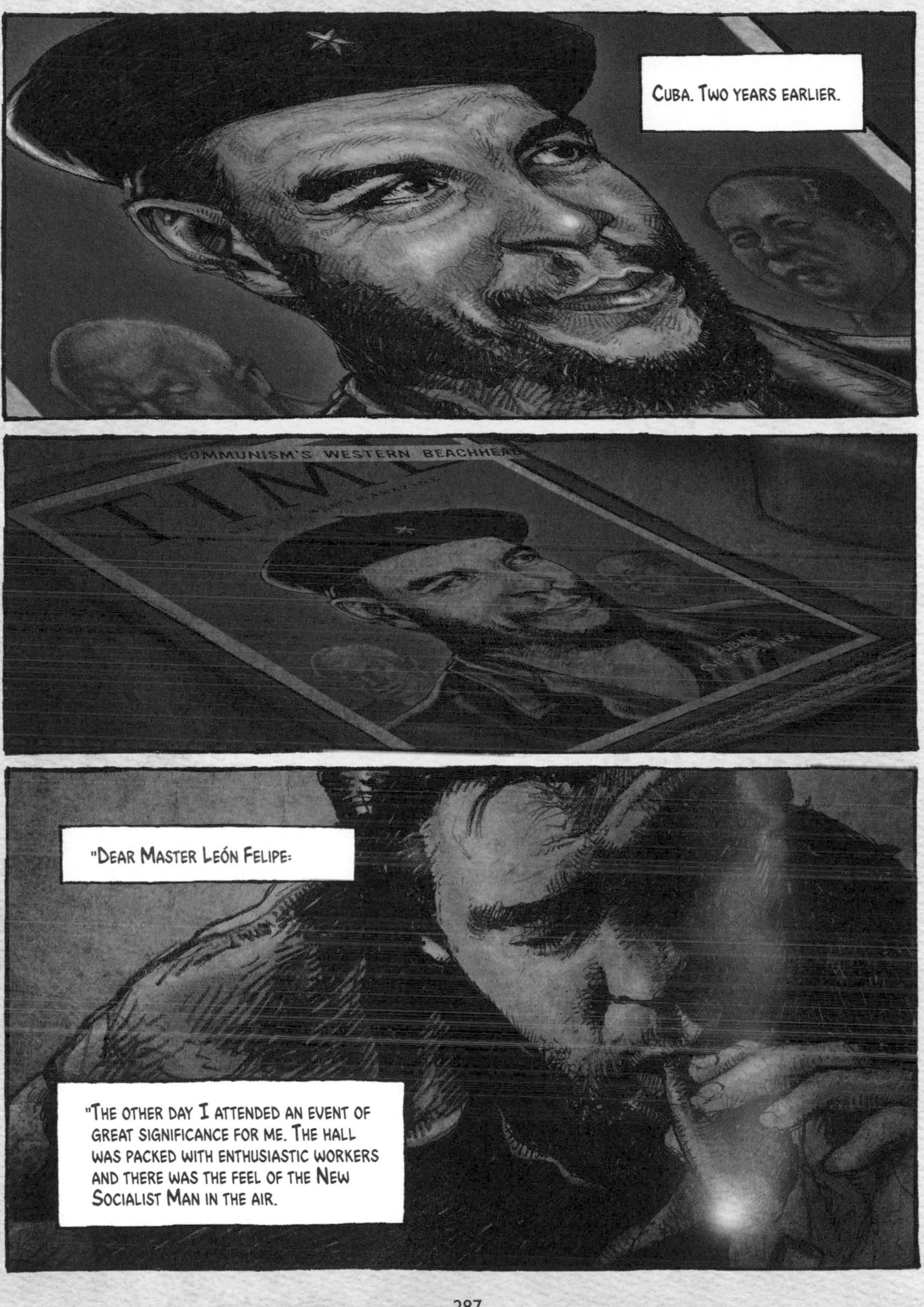
Cuba. Two years earlier.
COMMUNISM'S WESTERN BEACHHEA
"Dear Master León Felipe:
"The other day I attended an event of great significance for me. The hall was packed with enthusiastic workers and there was the feel of the New Socialist Man in the air.

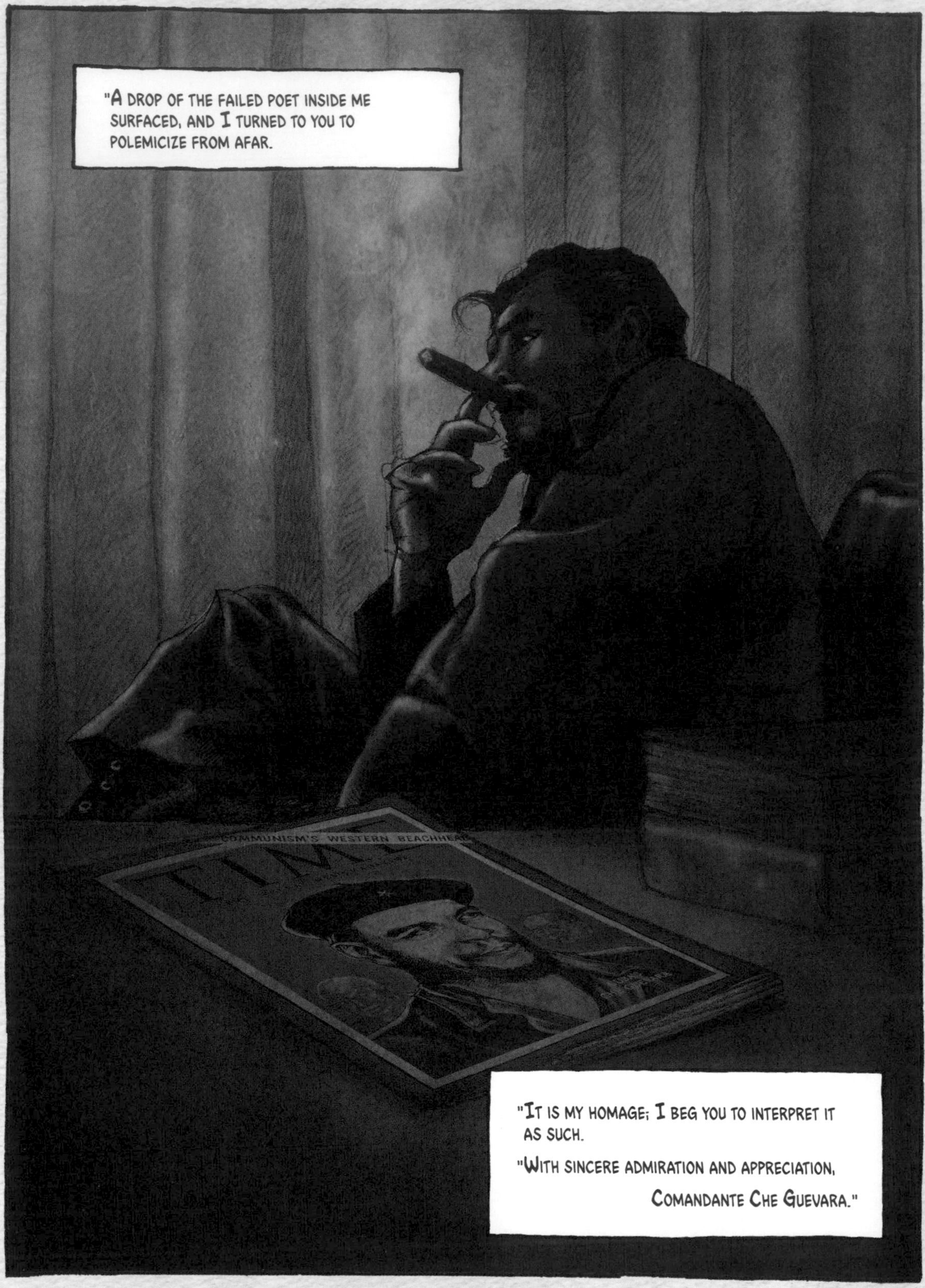
"A DROP OF THE FAILED POET INSIDE ME SURFACED, AND I TURNED TO YOU TO POLEMICIZE FROM AFAR.
COMMUNISM'S WESTERN BEACHHEAD
TIME
"IT IS MY HOMAGE; I BEG YOU TO INTERPRET IT AS SUCH.
"WITH SINCERE ADMIRATION AND APPRECIATION,
COMANDANTE CHE GUEVARA."

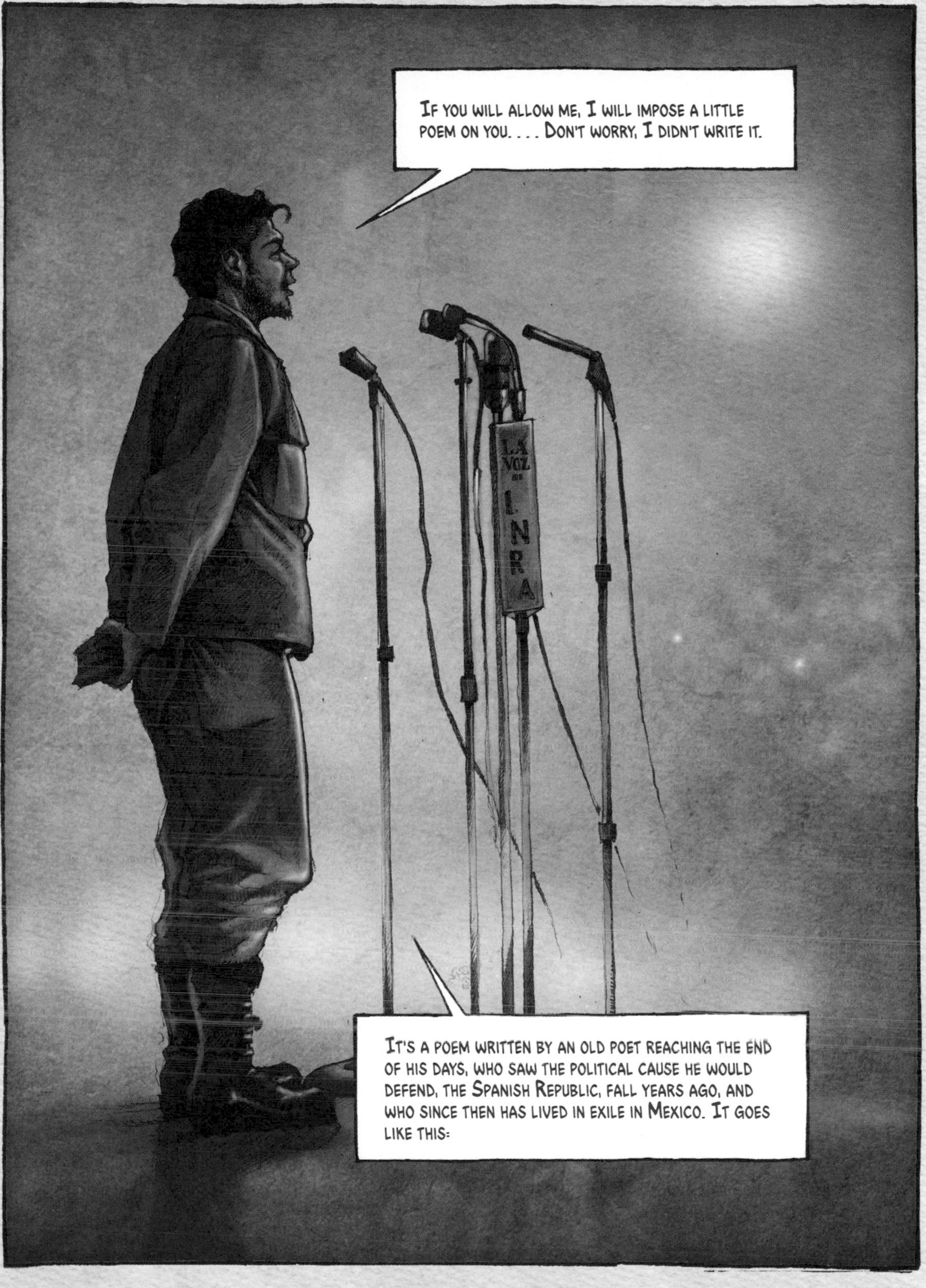
If you will allow me, I will impose a little poem on you. . . . Don't worry, I didn't write it.
LA VOZ
INRA
It's a poem written by an old poet reaching the end of his days, who saw the political cause he would defend, the Spanish Republic, fall years ago, and who since then has lived in exile in Mexico. It goes like this:

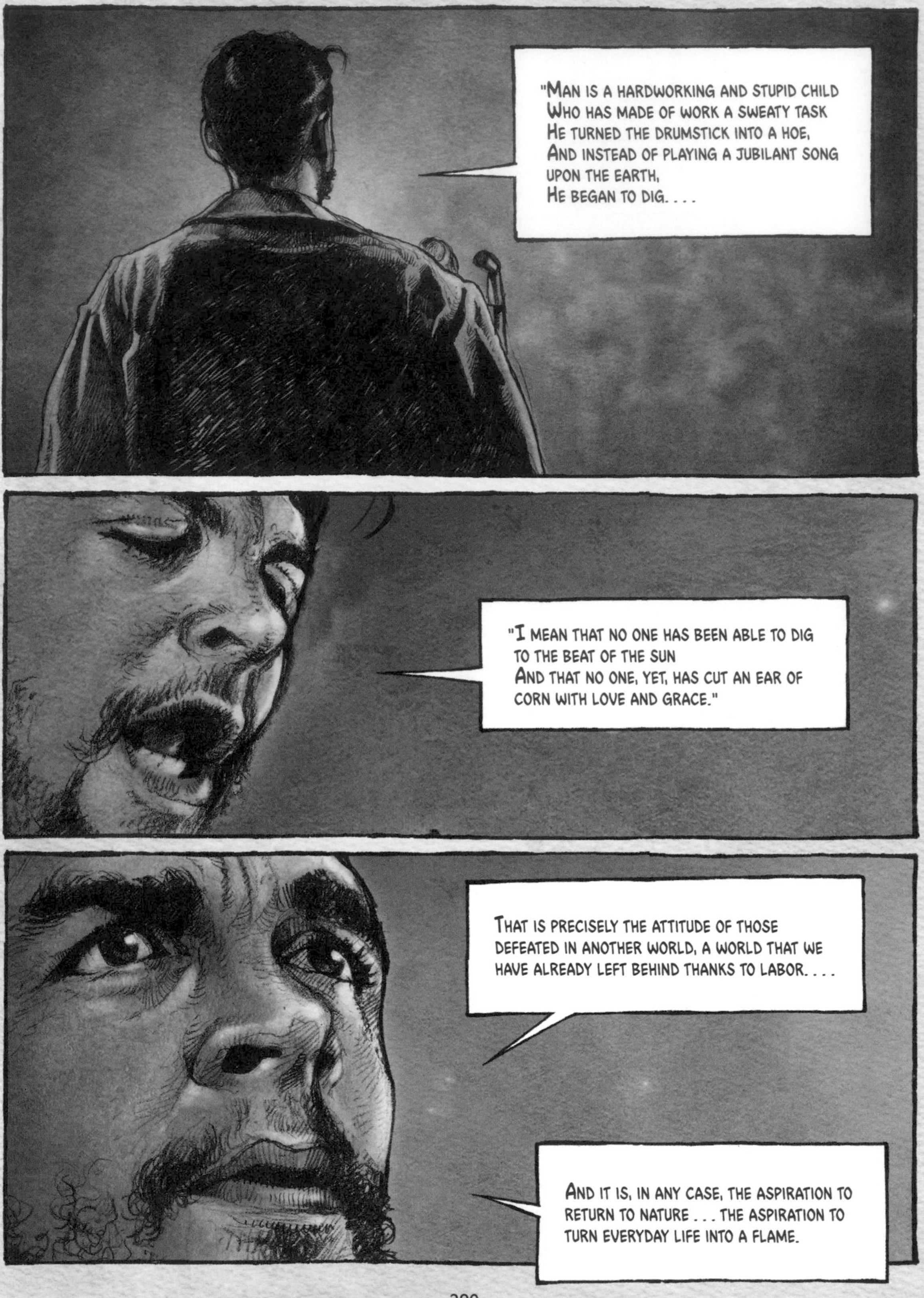
"MAN IS A HARDWORKING AND STUPID CHILD
WHO HAS MADE OF WORK A SWEATY TASK
HE TURNED THE DRUMSTICK INTO A HOE,
AND INSTEAD OF PLAYING A JUBILANT SONG
UPON THE EARTH,
HE BEGAN TO DIG. . . .
"I MEAN THAT NO ONE HAS BEEN ABLE TO DIG TO THE BEAT OF THE SUN AND THAT NO ONE, YET, HAS CUT AN EAR OF CORN WITH LOVE AND GRACE."
THAT IS PRECISELY THE ATTITUDE OF THOSE DEFEATED IN ANOTHER WORLD, A WORLD THAT WE HAVE ALREADY LEFT BEHIND THANKS TO LABOR. . . .
AND IT IS, IN ANY CASE, THE ASPIRATION TO RETURN TO NATURE . . . THE ASPIRATION TO TURN EVERYDAY LIFE INTO A FLAME.

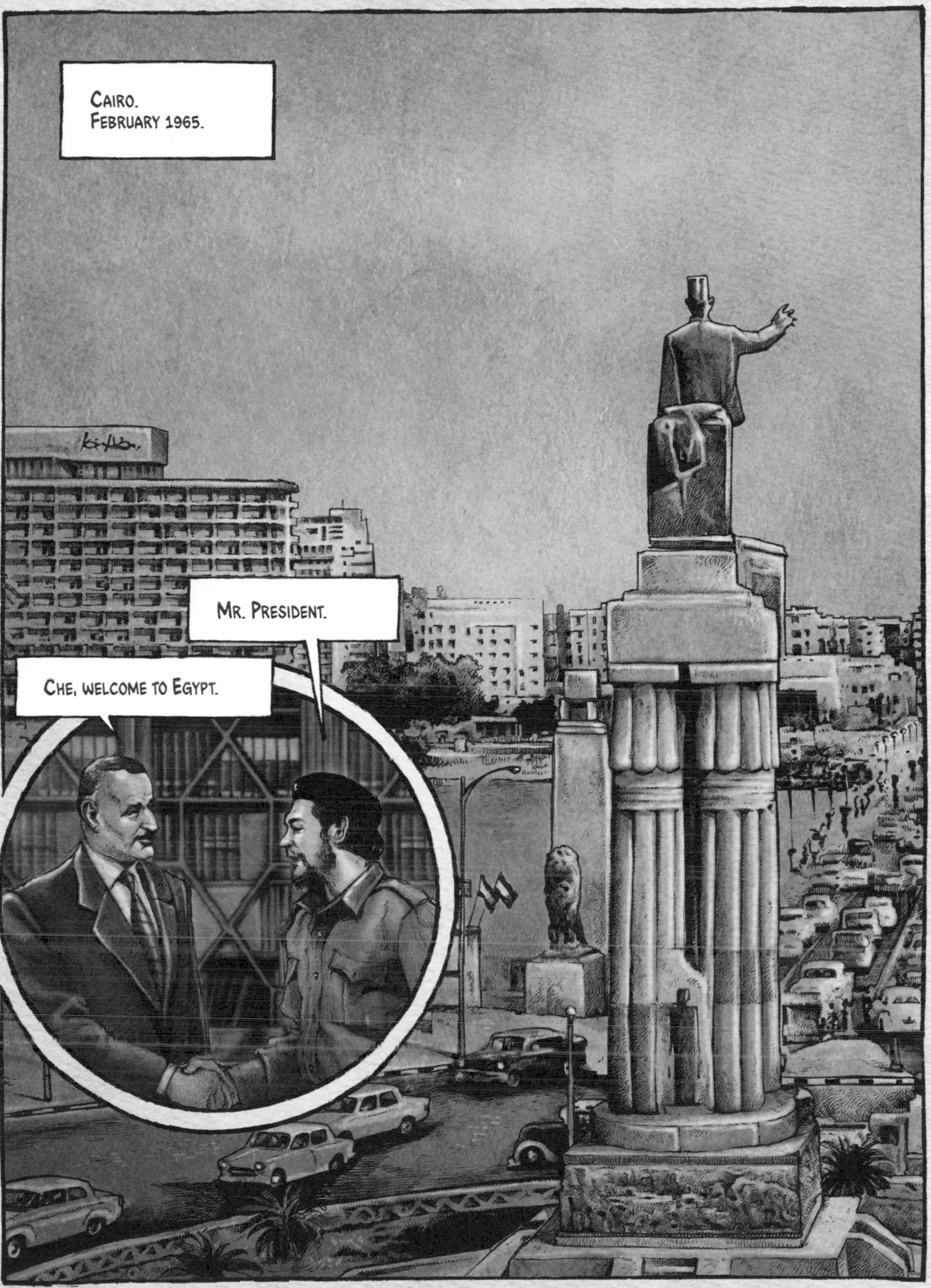
Cairo.
February 1965.
Che, welcome to Egypt.
Mr. President.

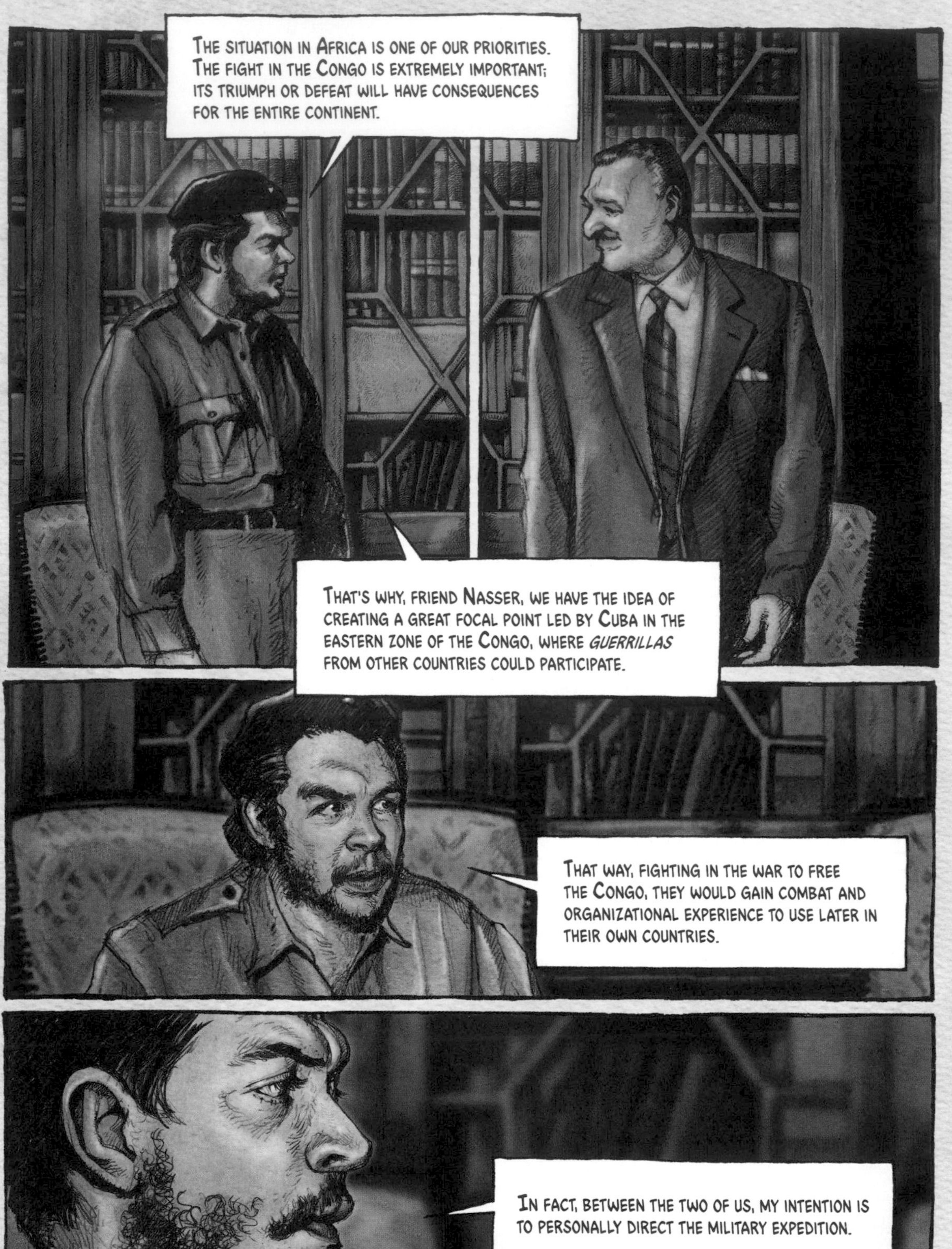
THE SITUATION IN AFRICA IS ONE OF OUR PRIORITIES. THE FIGHT IN THE CONGO IS EXTREMELY IMPORTANT; ITS TRIUMPH OR DEFEAT WILL HAVE CONSEQUENCES FOR THE ENTIRE CONTINENT.
THAT'S WHY, FRIEND NASSER, WE HAVE THE IDEA OF CREATING A GREAT FOCAL POINT LED BY CUBA IN THE EASTERN ZONE OF THE CONGO, WHERE *GUERRILLAS* FROM OTHER COUNTRIES COULD PARTICIPATE.
THAT WAY, FIGHTING IN THE WAR TO FREE THE CONGO, THEY WOULD GAIN COMBAT AND ORGANIZATIONAL EXPERIENCE TO USE LATER IN THEIR OWN COUNTRIES.
IN FACT, BETWEEN THE TWO OF US, MY INTENTION IS TO PERSONALLY DIRECT THE MILITARY EXPEDITION.

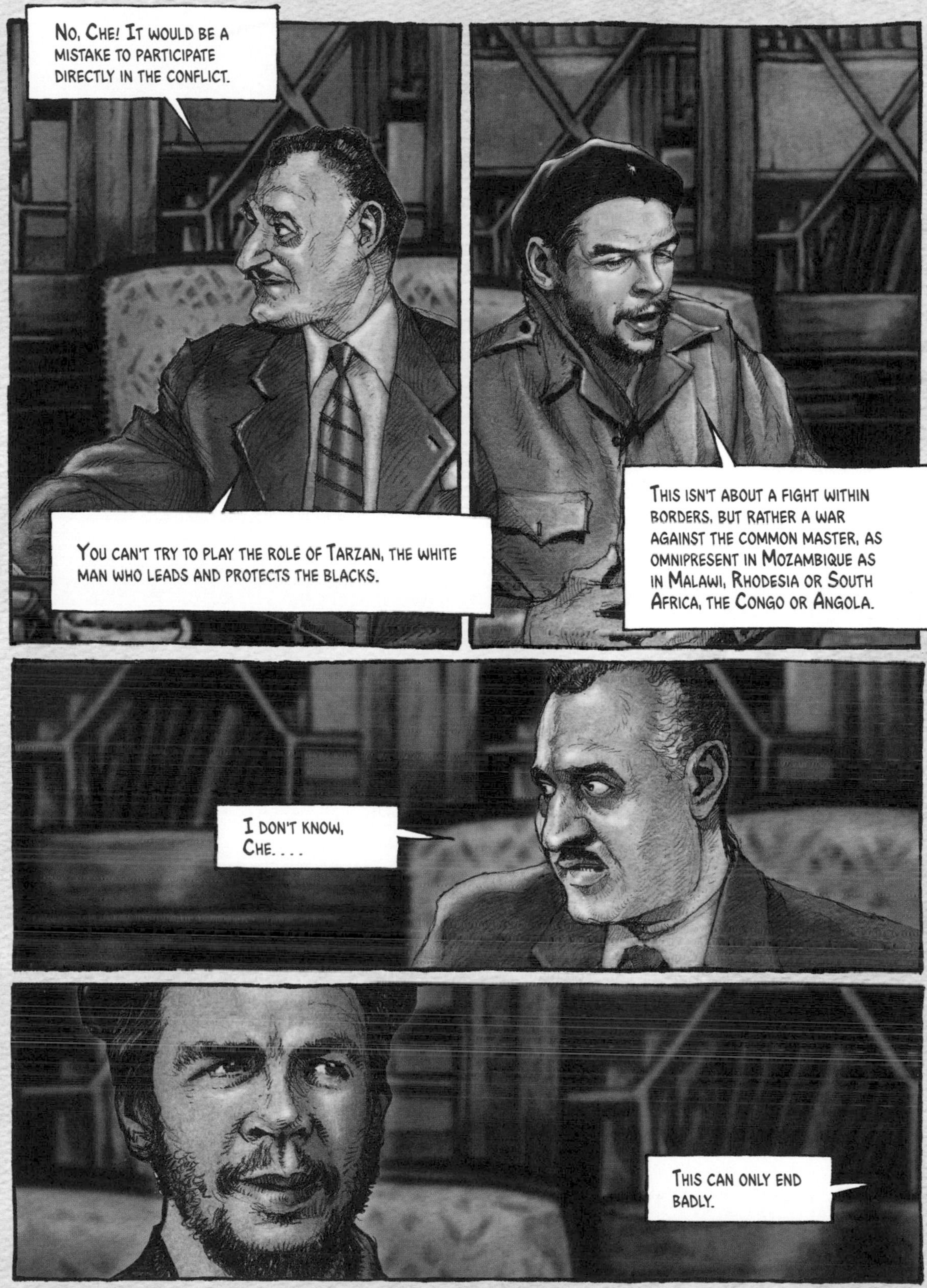
No, Che! It would be a mistake to participate directly in the conflict.
You can't try to play the role of Tarzan, the white man who leads and protects the blacks.
This isn't about a fight within borders, but rather a war against the common master, as omnipresent in Mozambique as in Malawi, Rhodesia or South Africa, the Congo or Angola.
I don't know, Che. . . .
This can only end badly.

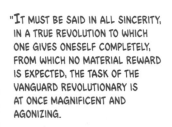

"IT MUST BE SAID IN ALL SINCERITY, IN A TRUE REVOLUTION TO WHICH ONE GIVES ONESELF COMPLETELY, FROM WHICH NO MATERIAL REWARD IS EXPECTED, THE TASK OF THE VANGUARD REVOLUTIONARY IS AT ONCE MAGNIFICENT AND AGONIZING.

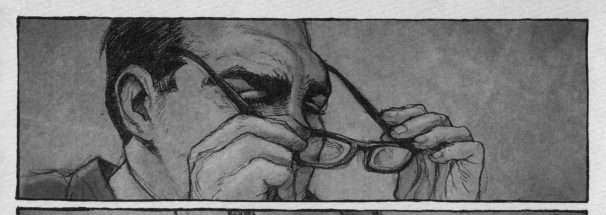

"THE TRUE REVOLUTIONARY IS GUIDED BY GREAT FEELINGS OF LOVE. IT IS IMPOSSIBLE TO IMAGINE AN AUTHENTIC REVOLUTIONARY WITHOUT THIS QUALITY.

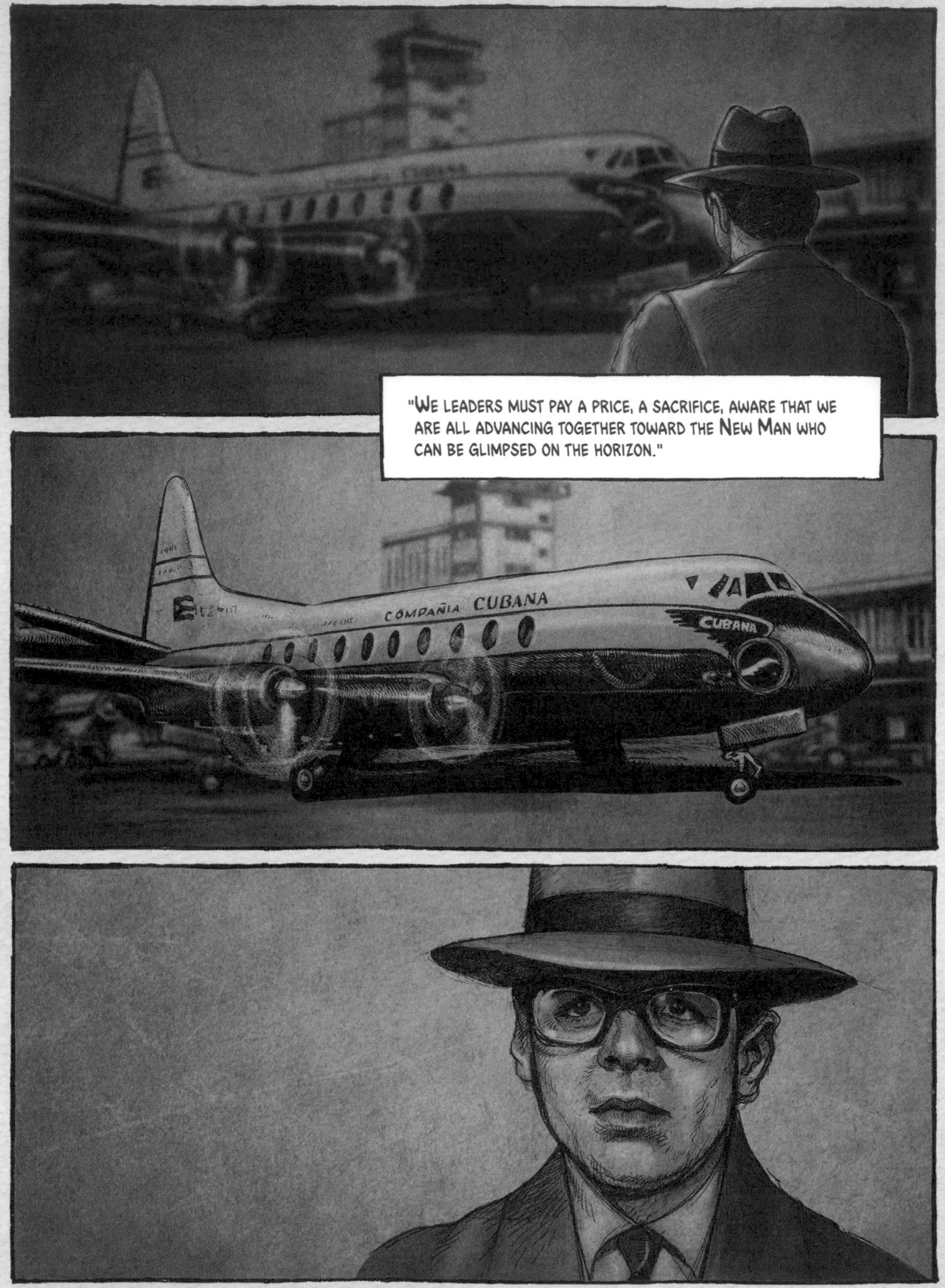
"We leaders must pay a price, a sacrifice, aware that we are all advancing together toward the New Man who can be glimpsed on the horizon."
COMPAÑIA CUBANA
CUBANA

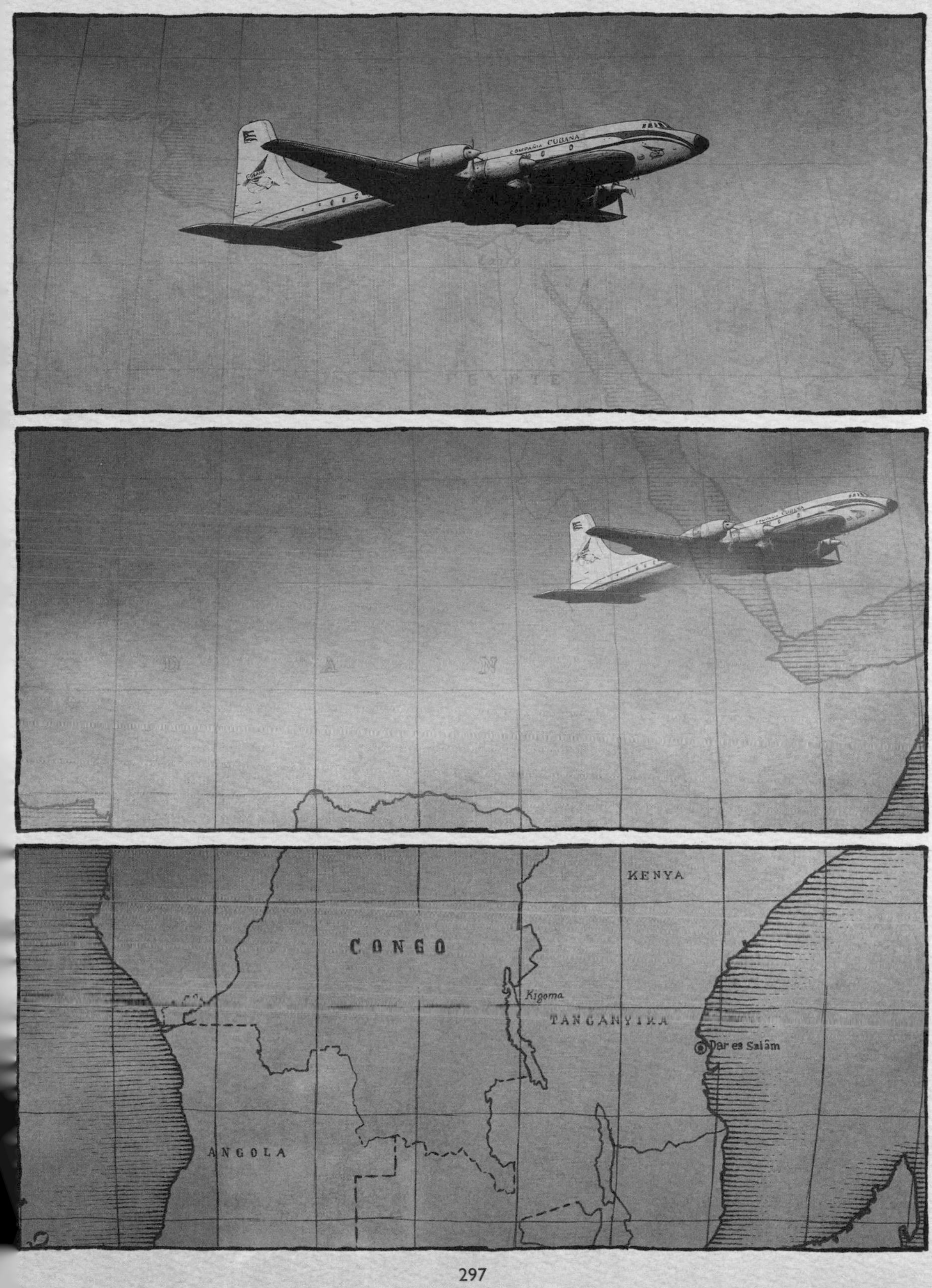
COMPAÑIA CUBANA
EGYPTE
KENYA
CONGO
Kigoma
TANGANYIKA
Dar es Salâm
ANGOLA

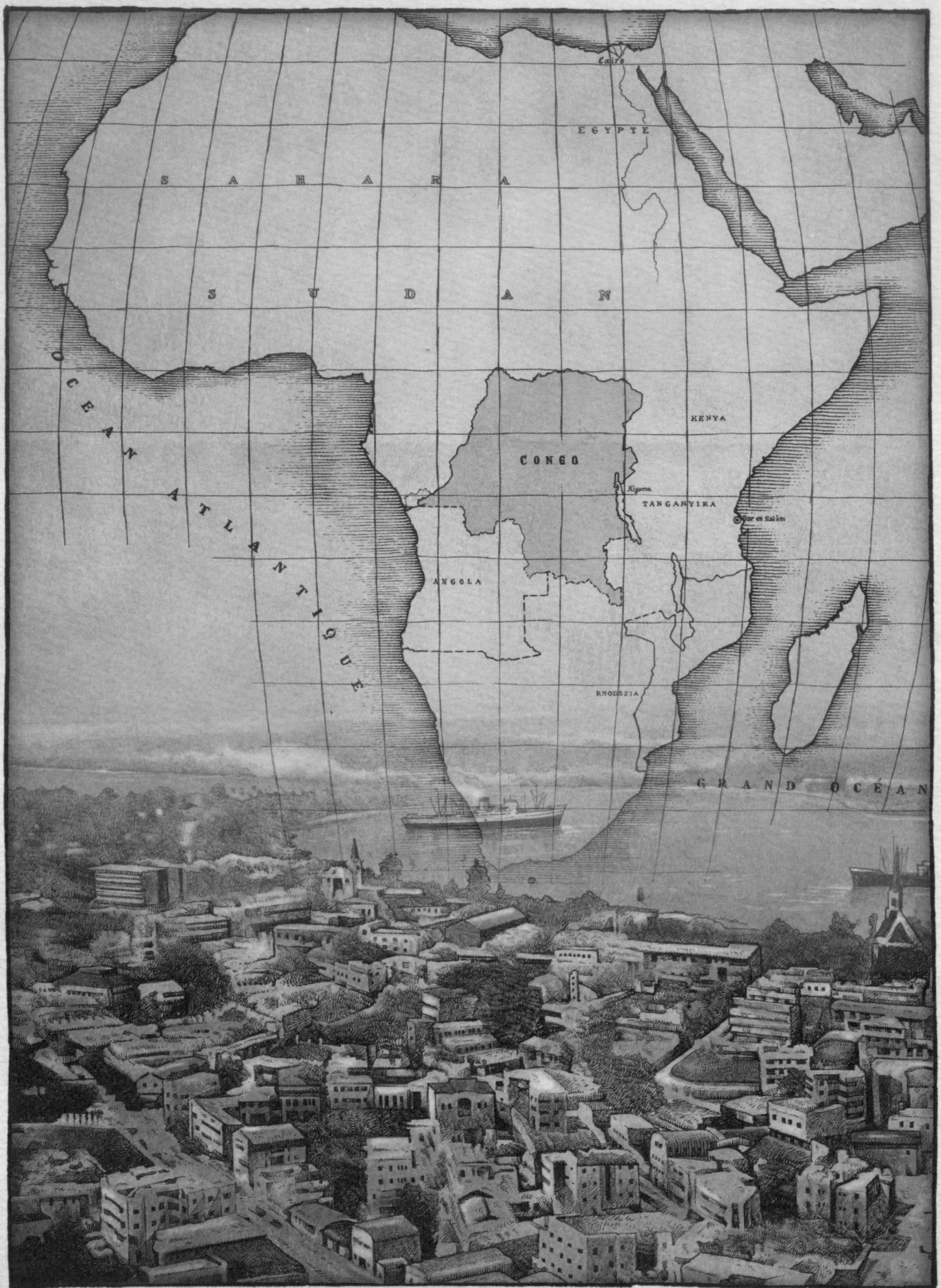
Caïro
EGYPTE
S A H A R A
S U D A N
OCEAN ATLANTIQUE
CONGO
KENYA
Kigoma
TANGANYIKA
Dar es Salâm
ANGOLA
RHODESIA
GRAND OCÉAN

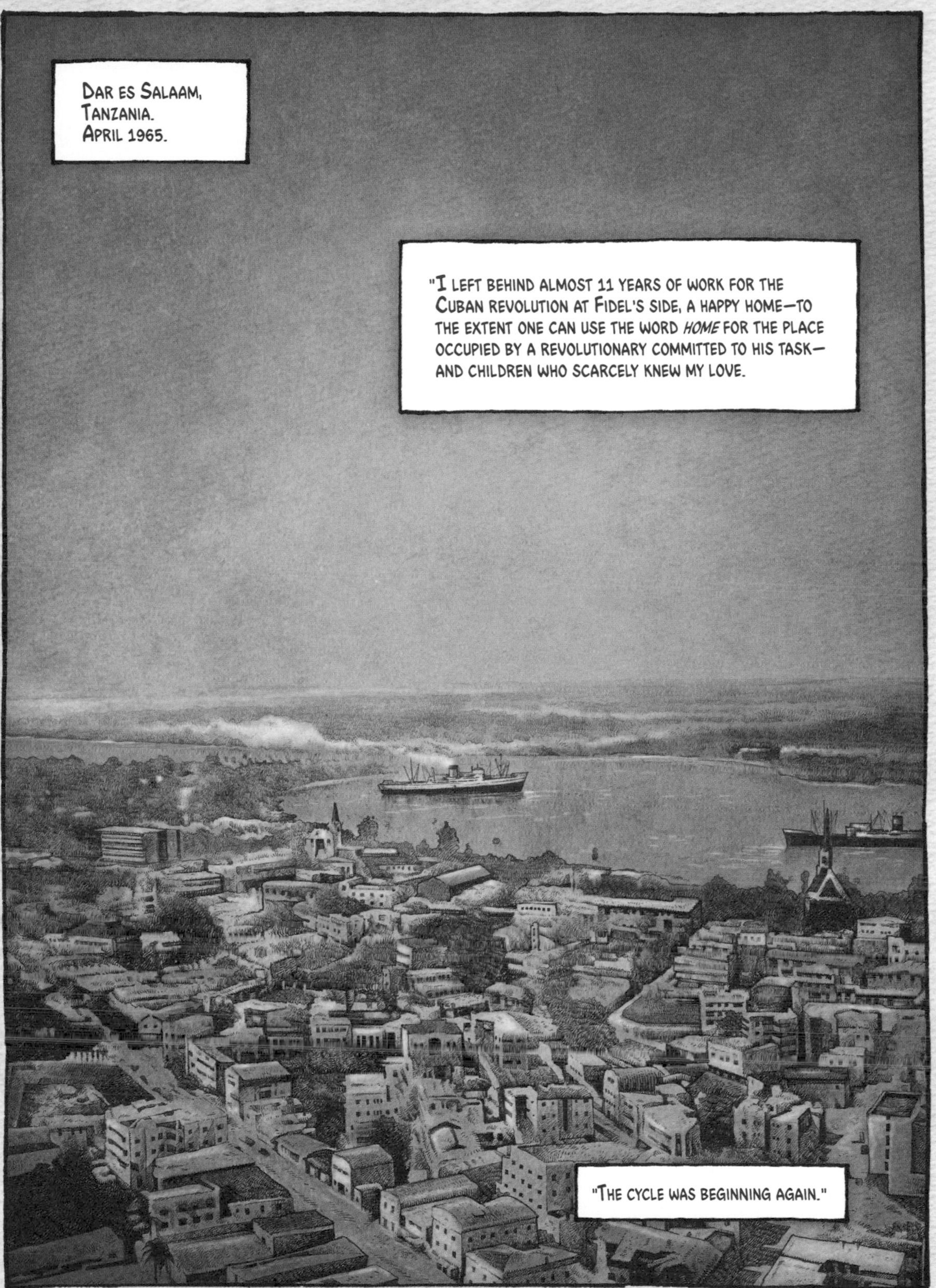
Dar es Salaam,
Tanzania.
April 1965.
"I left behind almost 11 years of work for the Cuban revolution at Fidel's side, a happy home—to the extent one can use the word *home* for the place occupied by a revolutionary committed to his task—and children who scarcely knew my love.
"The cycle was beginning again."

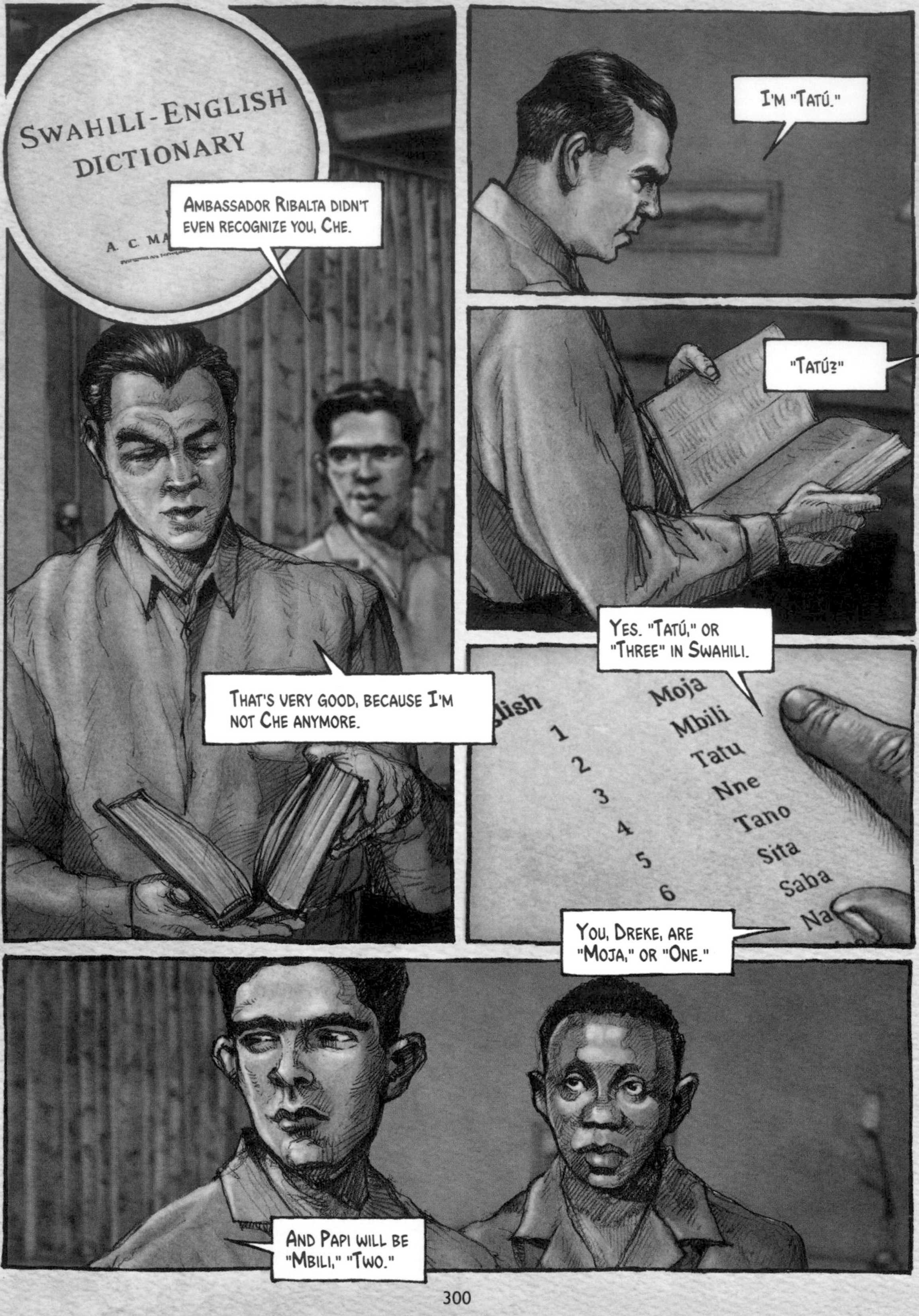

SWAHILI-ENGLISH DICTIONARY
A. C. MA
AMBASSADOR RIBALTA DIDN'T EVEN RECOGNIZE YOU, CHE.
I'M "TATÚ."
"TATÚ?"
THAT'S VERY GOOD, BECAUSE I'M NOT CHE ANYMORE.
YES. "TATÚ," OR "THREE" IN SWAHILI.
Moja
Mbili
Tatu
Nne
Tano
Sita
Saba
1
2
3
4
5
6
YOU, DREKE, ARE "MOJA," OR "ONE."
AND PAPI WILL BE "MBILI," "TWO."

HOW LONG ARE WE GOING TO WAIT HERE, CHE?

NOT CHE, TATÚ.

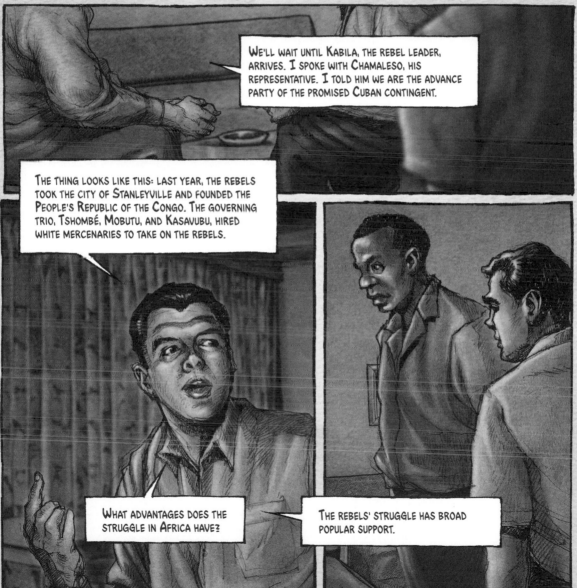

WE'LL WAIT UNTIL KABILA, THE REBEL LEADER, ARRIVES. I SPOKE WITH CHAMALESO, HIS REPRESENTATIVE. I TOLD HIM WE ARE THE ADVANCE PARTY OF THE PROMISED CUBAN CONTINGENT.

THE THING LOOKS LIKE THIS: LAST YEAR, THE REBELS TOOK THE CITY OF STANLEYVILLE AND FOUNDED THE PEOPLE'S REPUBLIC OF THE CONGO. THE GOVERNING TRIO, TSHOMBÉ, MOBUTU, AND KASAVUBU, HIRED WHITE MERCENARIES TO TAKE ON THE REBELS.

WHAT ADVANTAGES DOES THE STRUGGLE IN AFRICA HAVE?

THE REBELS' STRUGGLE HAS BROAD POPULAR SUPPORT.

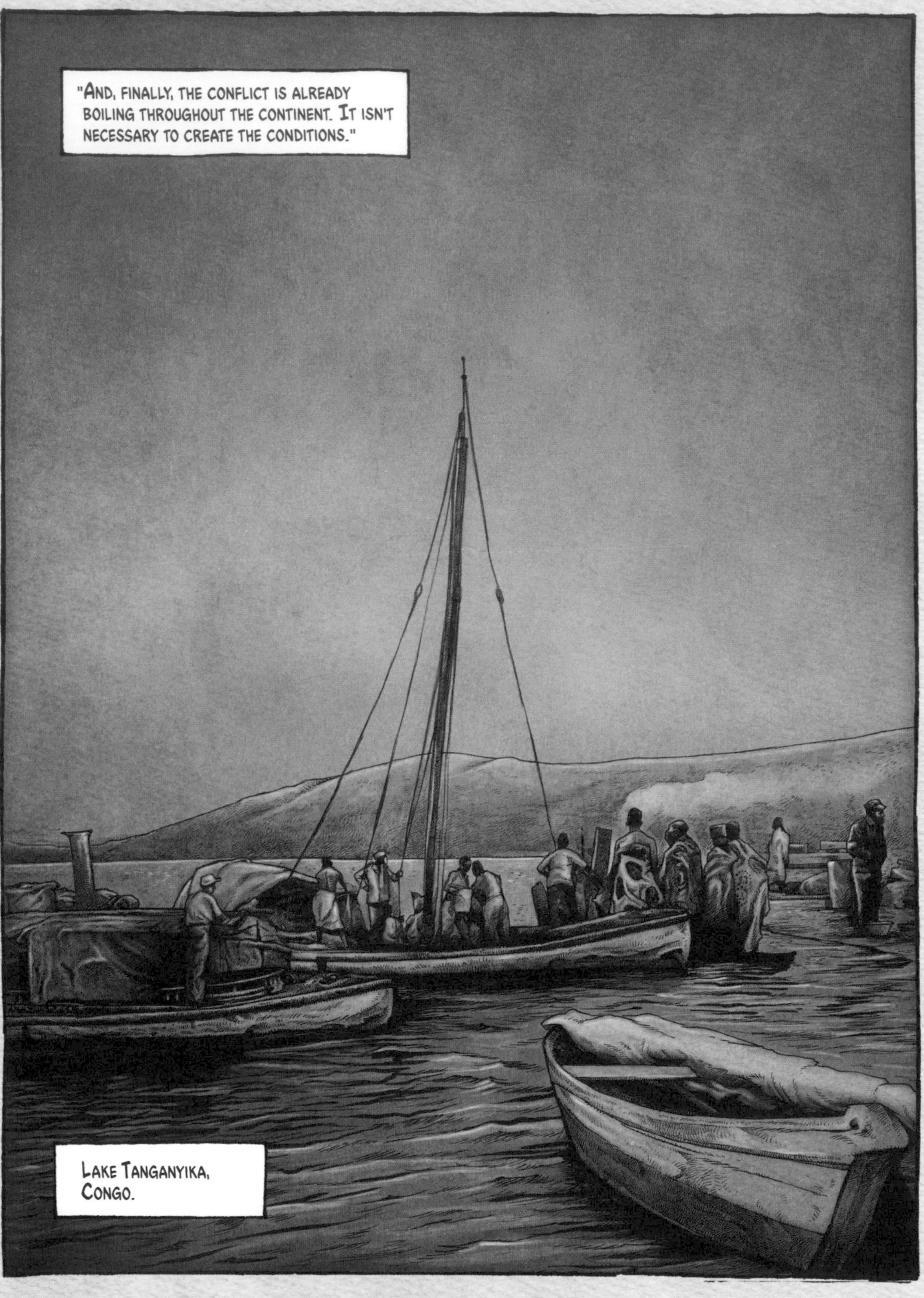
"AND, FINALLY, THE CONFLICT IS ALREADY BOILING THROUGHOUT THE CONTINENT. IT ISN'T NECESSARY TO CREATE THE CONDITIONS."
LAKE TANGANYIKA, CONGO.

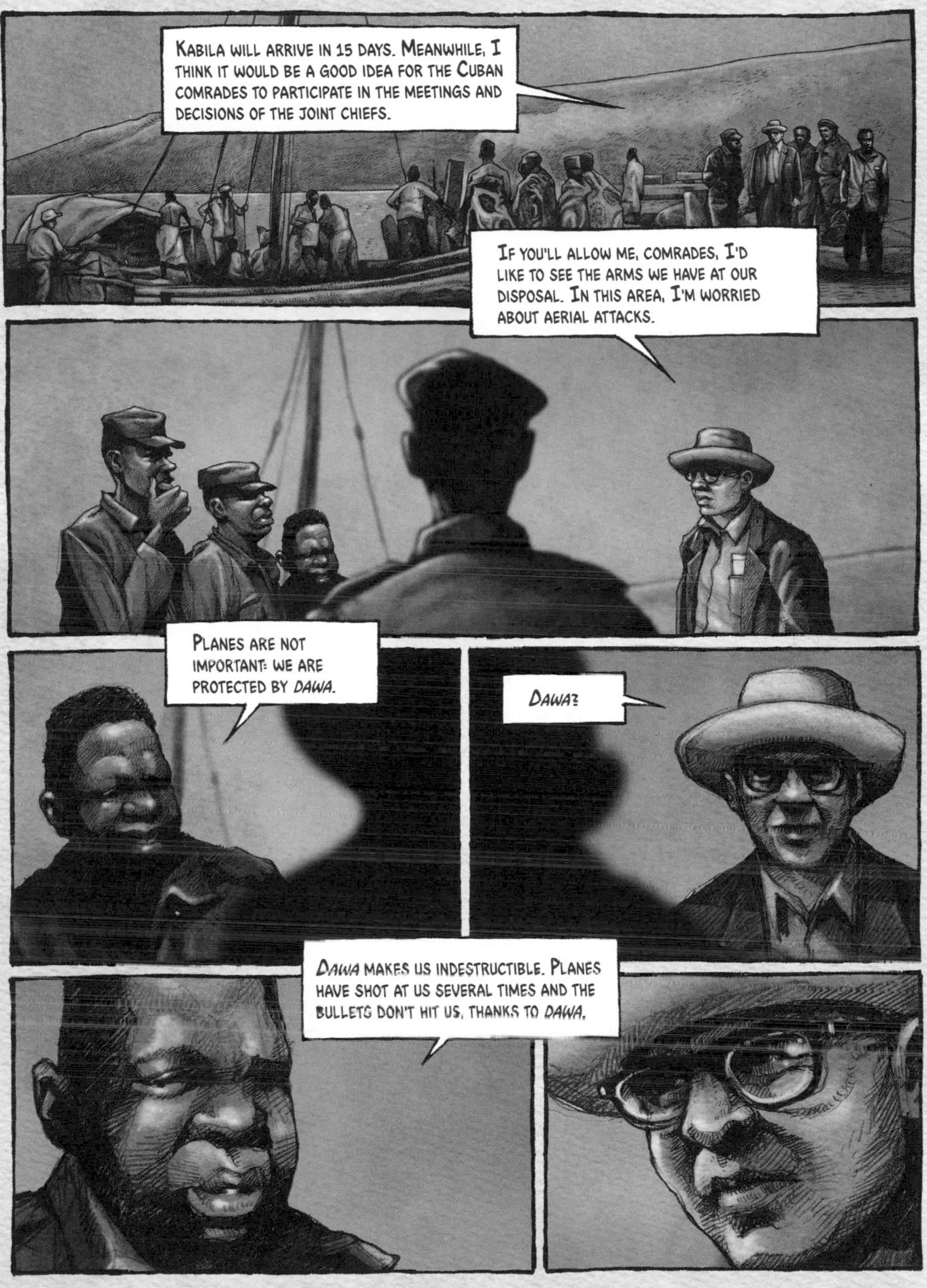
KABILA WILL ARRIVE IN 15 DAYS. MEANWHILE, I THINK IT WOULD BE A GOOD IDEA FOR THE CUBAN COMRADES TO PARTICIPATE IN THE MEETINGS AND DECISIONS OF THE JOINT CHIEFS.
IF YOU'LL ALLOW ME, COMRADES, I'D LIKE TO SEE THE ARMS WE HAVE AT OUR DISPOSAL. IN THIS AREA, I'M WORRIED ABOUT AERIAL ATTACKS.
PLANES ARE NOT IMPORTANT: WE ARE PROTECTED BY *DAWA*.
DAWA?
DAWA MAKES US INDESTRUCTIBLE. PLANES HAVE SHOT AT US SEVERAL TIMES AND THE BULLETS DON'T HIT US, THANKS TO *DAWA*.

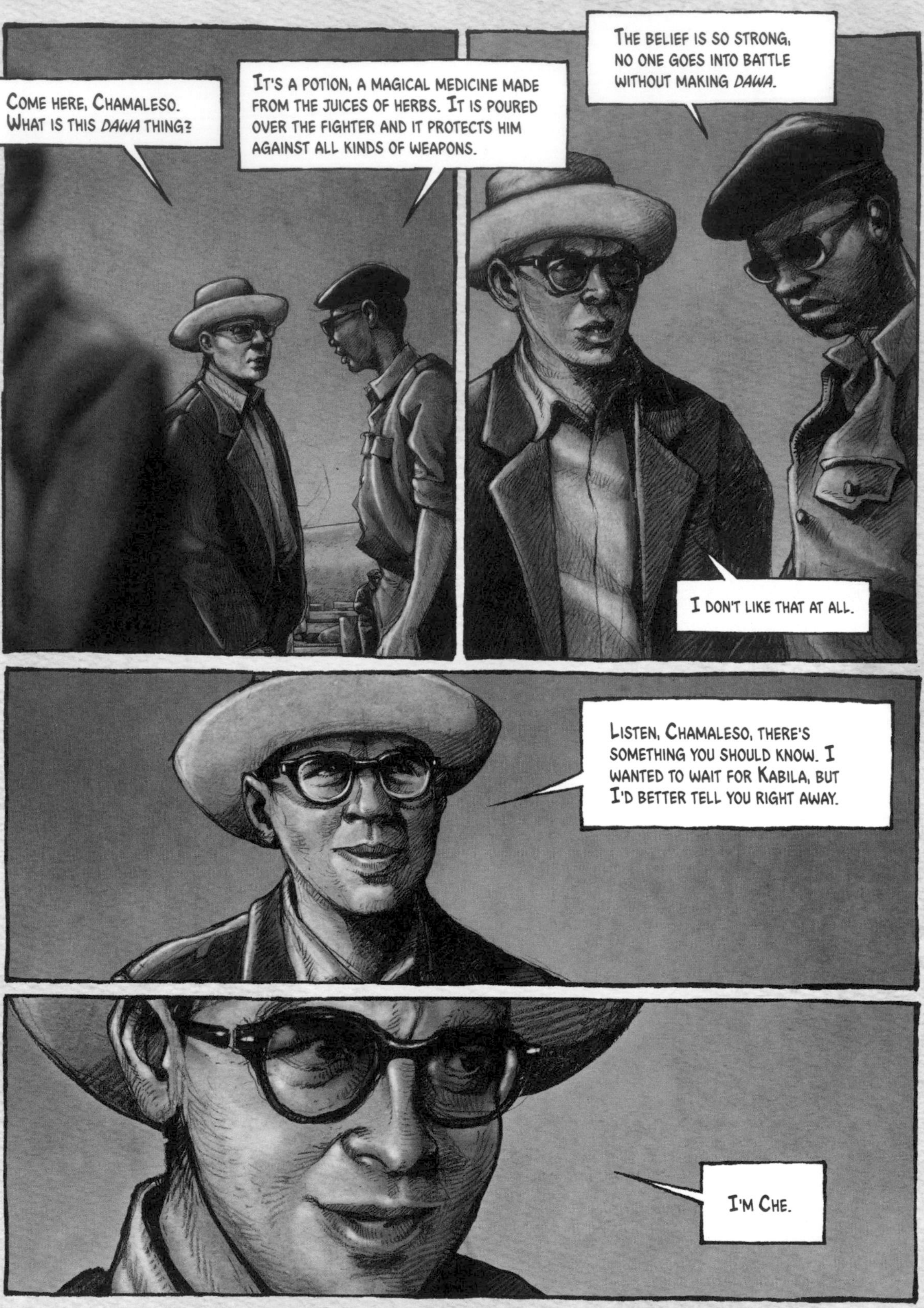
Come here, Chamaleso. What is this *dawa* thing?
It's a potion, a magical medicine made from the juices of herbs. It is poured over the fighter and it protects him against all kinds of weapons.
The belief is so strong, no one goes into battle without making *dawa*.
I don't like that at all.
Listen, Chamaleso, there's something you should know. I wanted to wait for Kabila, but I'd better tell you right away.
I'm Che.

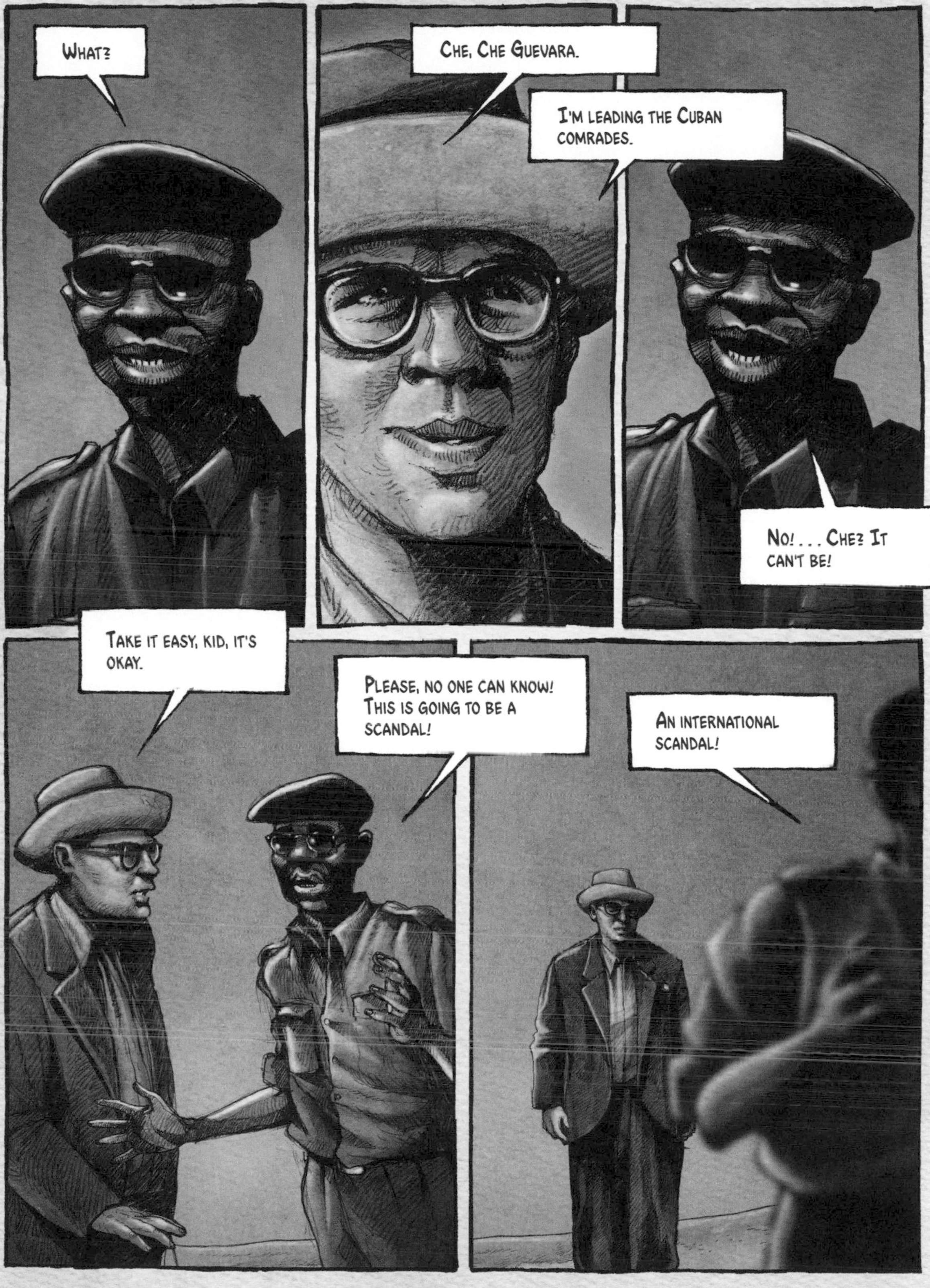
WHAT?
CHE, CHE GUEVARA.
I'M LEADING THE CUBAN COMRADES.
NO! . . . CHE? IT CAN'T BE!
TAKE IT EASY, KID, IT'S OKAY.
PLEASE, NO ONE CAN KNOW! THIS IS GOING TO BE A SCANDAL!
AN INTERNATIONAL SCANDAL!

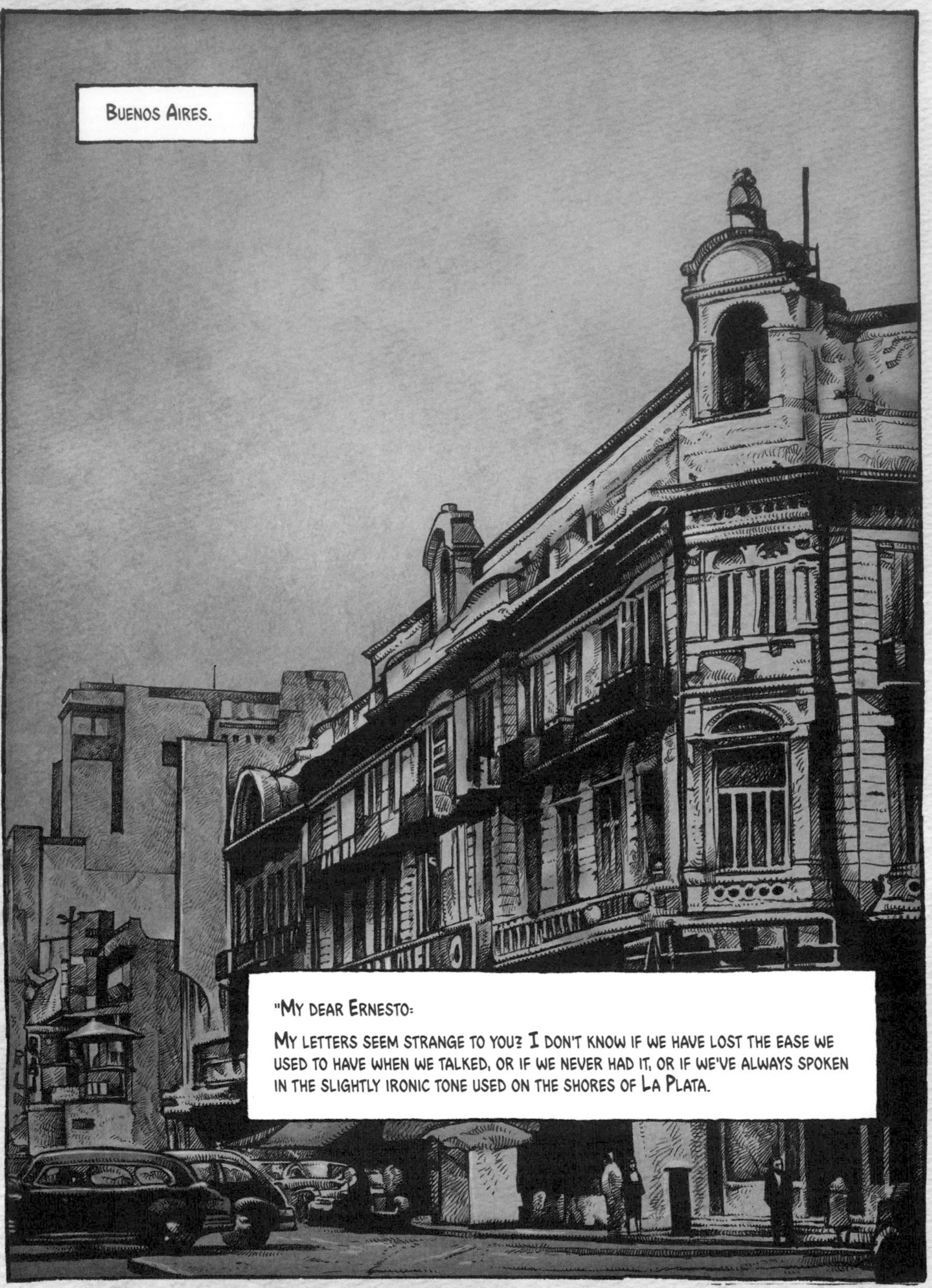
Buenos Aires.
"My dear Ernesto:
My letters seem strange to you? I don't know if we have lost the ease we used to have when we talked, or if we never had it, or if we've always spoken in the slightly ironic tone used on the shores of La Plata.

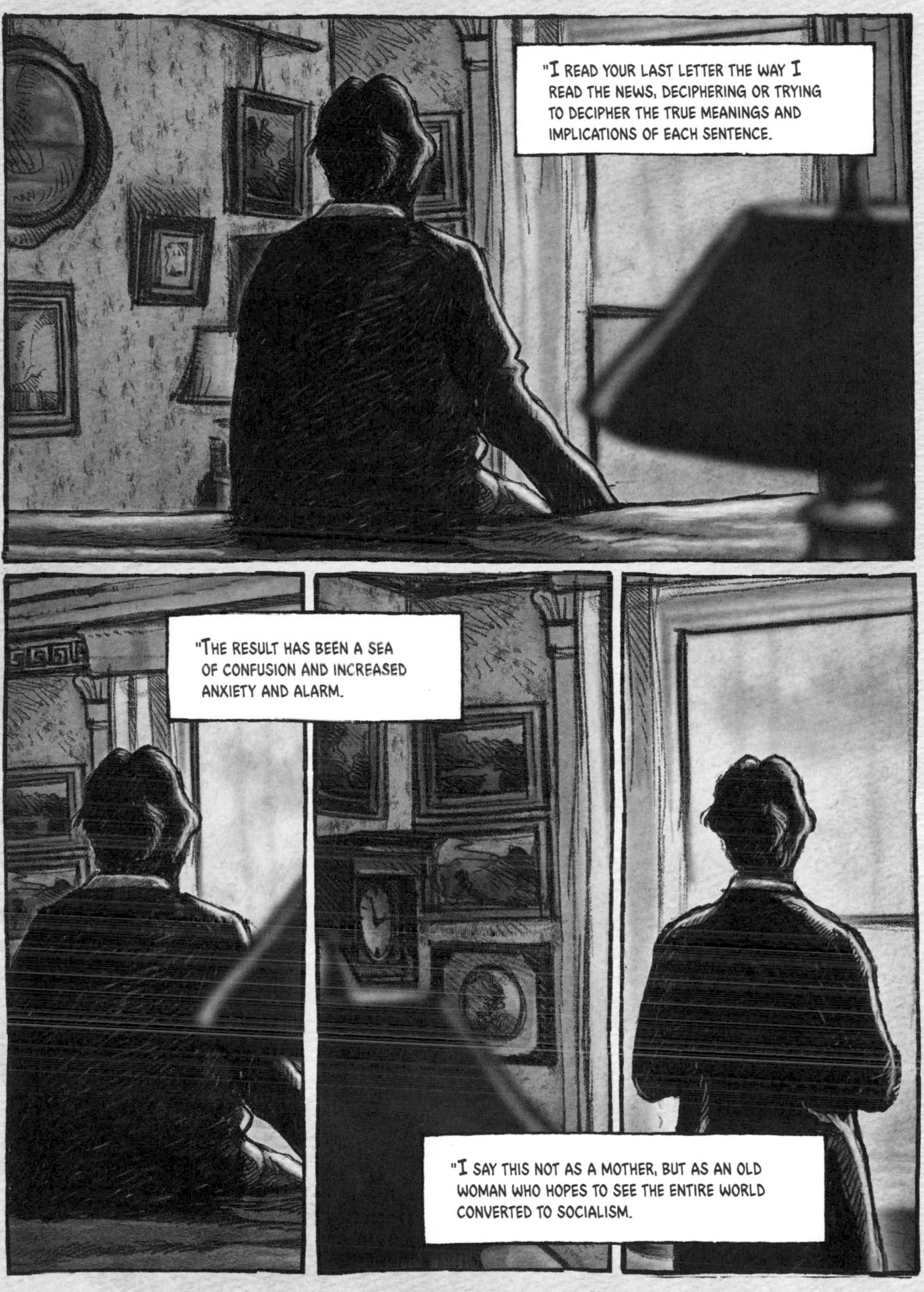
"I READ YOUR LAST LETTER THE WAY I READ THE NEWS, DECIPHERING OR TRYING TO DECIPHER THE TRUE MEANINGS AND IMPLICATIONS OF EACH SENTENCE.
"THE RESULT HAS BEEN A SEA OF CONFUSION AND INCREASED ANXIETY AND ALARM.
"I SAY THIS NOT AS A MOTHER, BUT AS AN OLD WOMAN WHO HOPES TO SEE THE ENTIRE WORLD CONVERTED TO SOCIALISM.

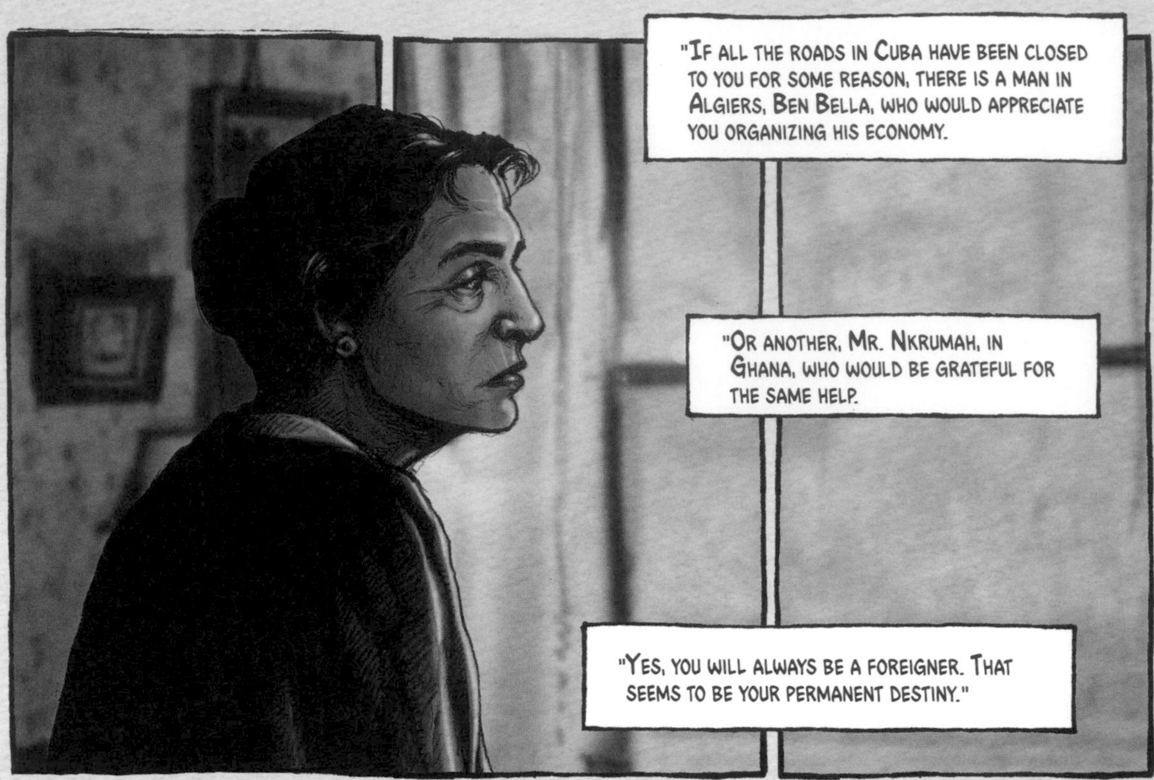
"IF ALL THE ROADS IN CUBA HAVE BEEN CLOSED TO YOU FOR SOME REASON, THERE IS A MAN IN ALGIERS, BEN BELLA, WHO WOULD APPRECIATE YOU ORGANIZING HIS ECONOMY.
"OR ANOTHER, MR. NKRUMAH, IN GHANA, WHO WOULD BE GRATEFUL FOR THE SAME HELP.
"YES, YOU WILL ALWAYS BE A FOREIGNER. THAT SEEMS TO BE YOUR PERMANENT DESTINY."

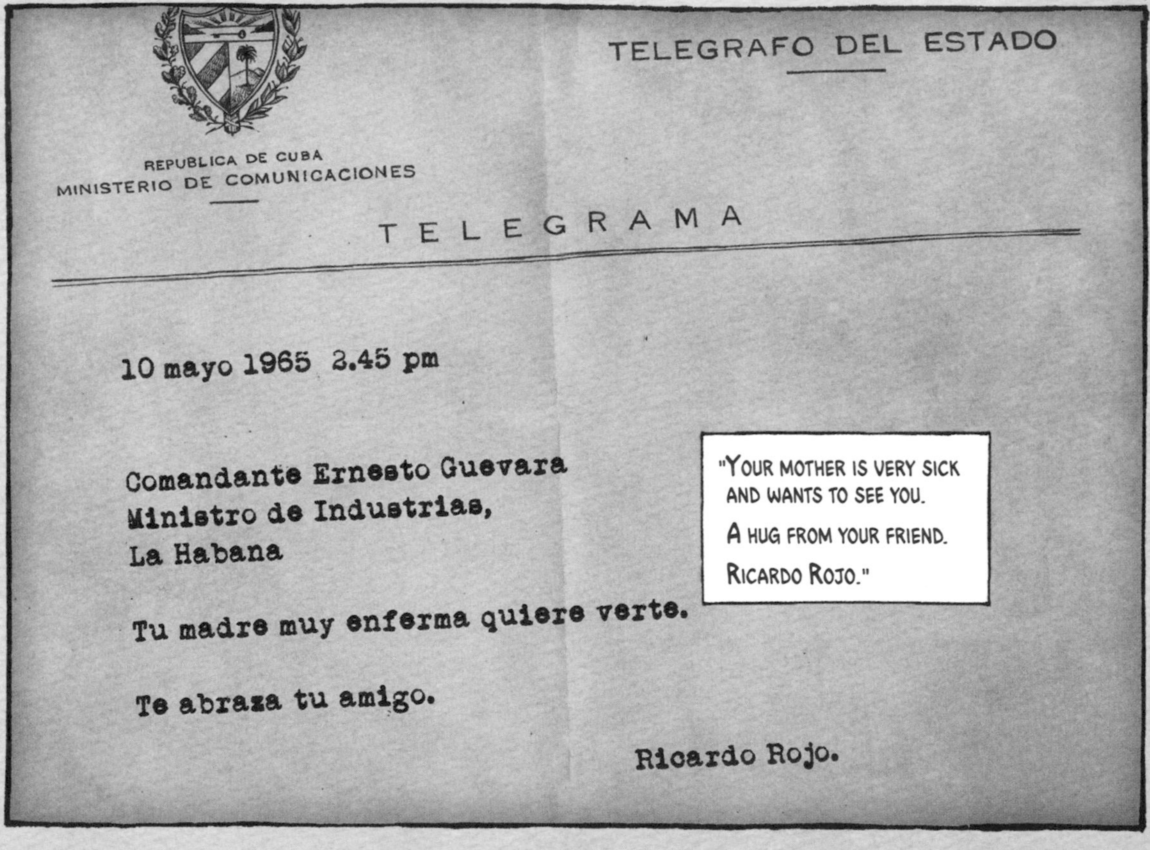

TELEGRAFO DEL ESTADO

REPUBLICA DE CUBA
MINISTERIO DE COMUNICACIONES

TELEGRAMA

10 mayo 1965 2.45 pm

Comandante Ernesto Guevara
Ministro de Industrias,
La Habana

Tu madre muy enferma quiere verte.

Te abraza tu amigo.

Ricardo Rojo.

"YOUR MOTHER IS VERY SICK AND WANTS TO SEE YOU.
A HUG FROM YOUR FRIEND.
RICARDO ROJO."

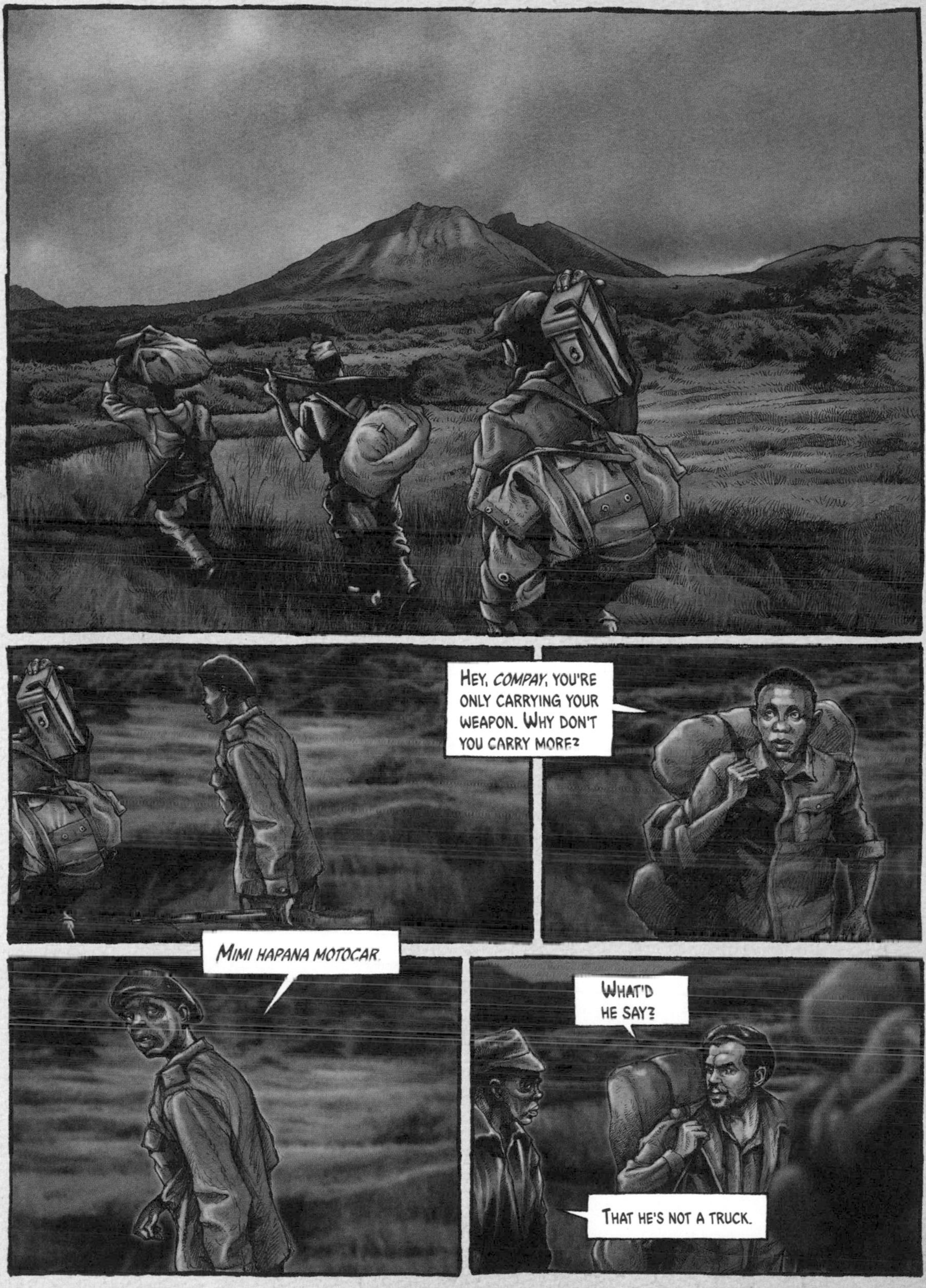
HEY, *COMPAY*, YOU'RE ONLY CARRYING YOUR WEAPON. WHY DON'T YOU CARRY MORE?
MIMI HAPANA MOTOCAR.
WHAT'D HE SAY?
THAT HE'S NOT A TRUCK.

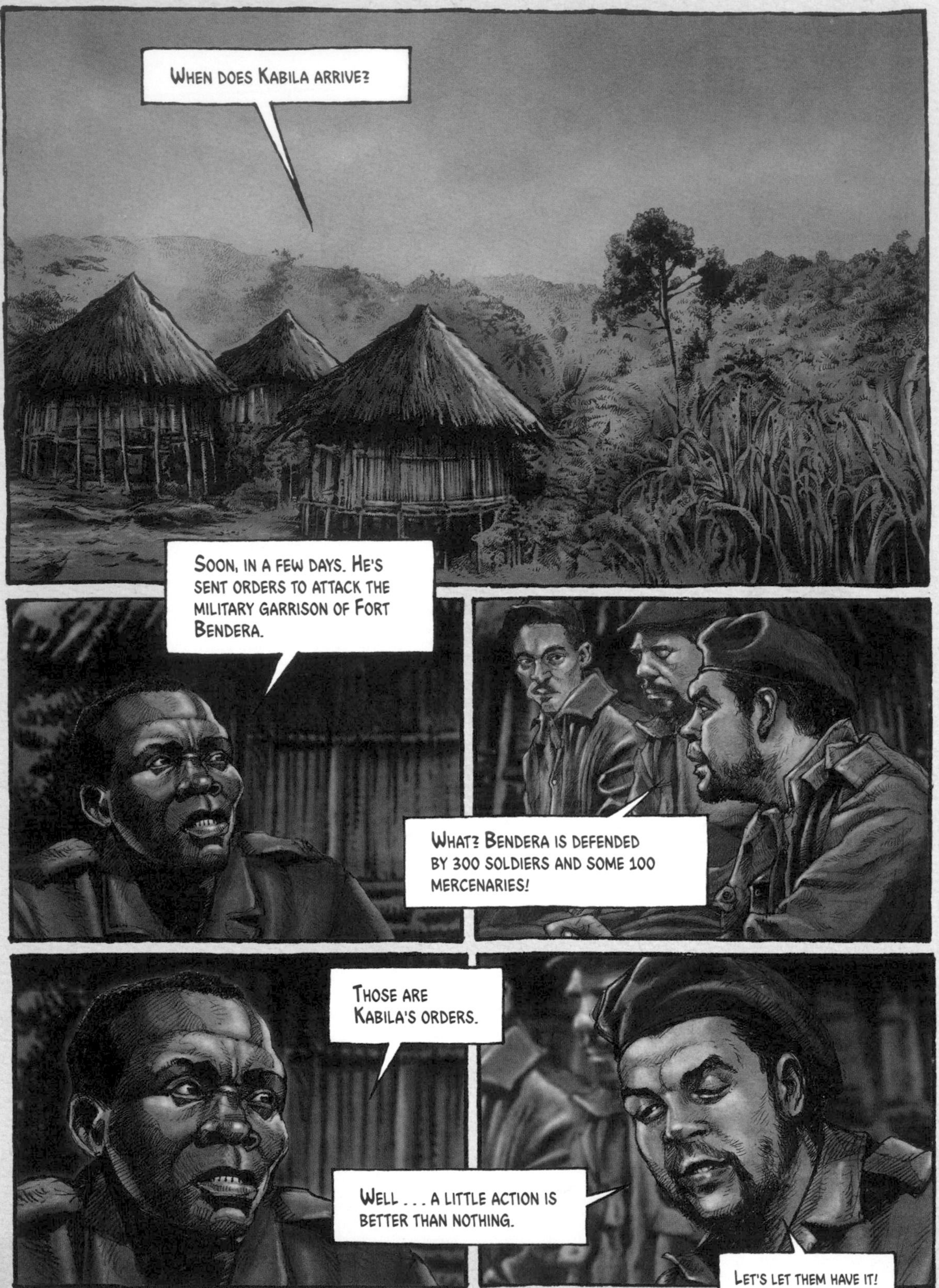
When does Kabila arrive?
Soon, in a few days. He's sent orders to attack the military garrison of Fort Bendera.
What? Bendera is defended by 300 soldiers and some 100 mercenaries!
Those are Kabila's orders.
Well . . . a little action is better than nothing.
Let's let them have it!

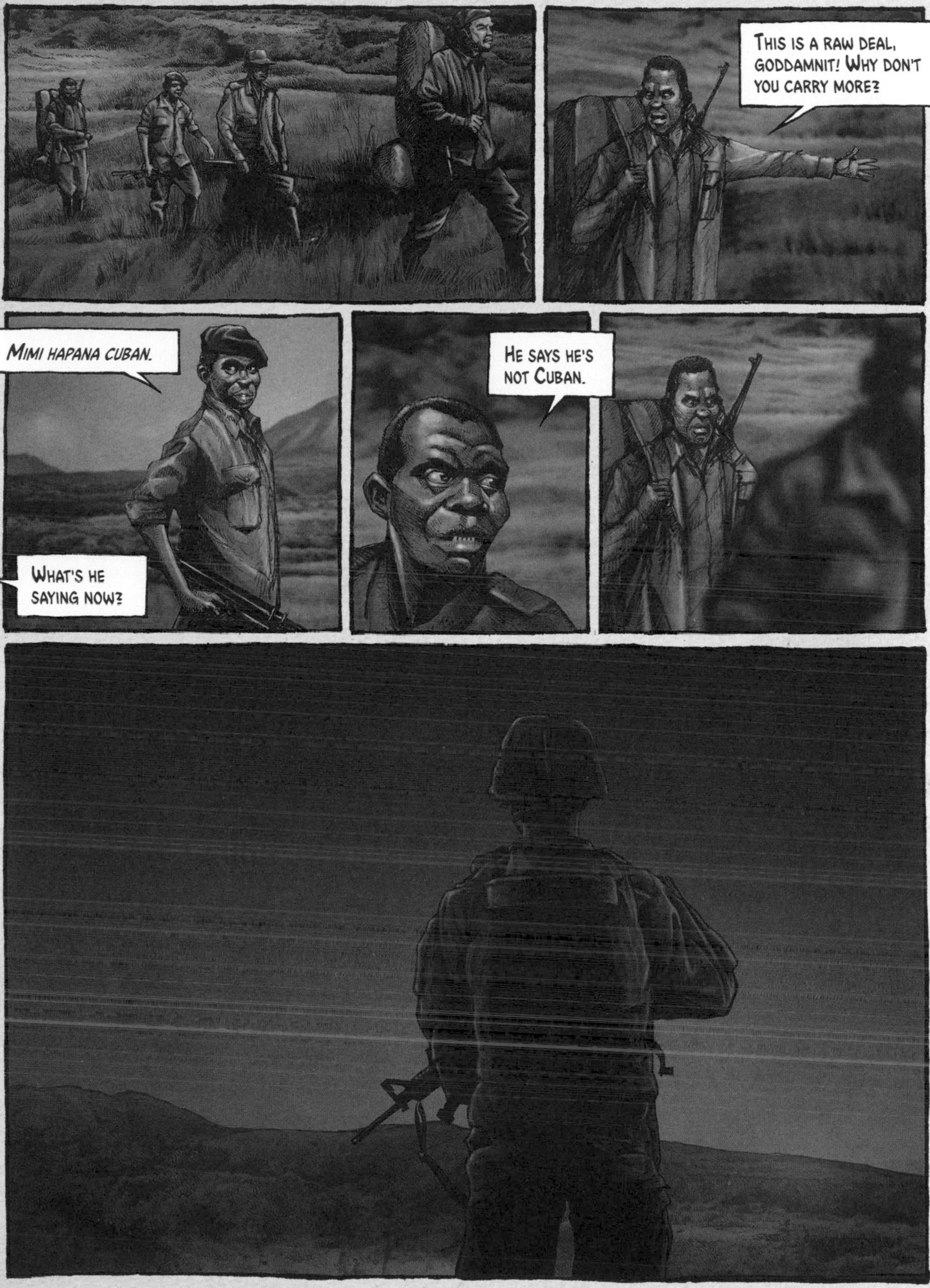
THIS IS A RAW DEAL, GODDAMNIT! WHY DON'T YOU CARRY MORE?
MIMI HAPANA CUBAN.
WHAT'S HE SAYING NOW?
HE SAYS HE'S NOT CUBAN.

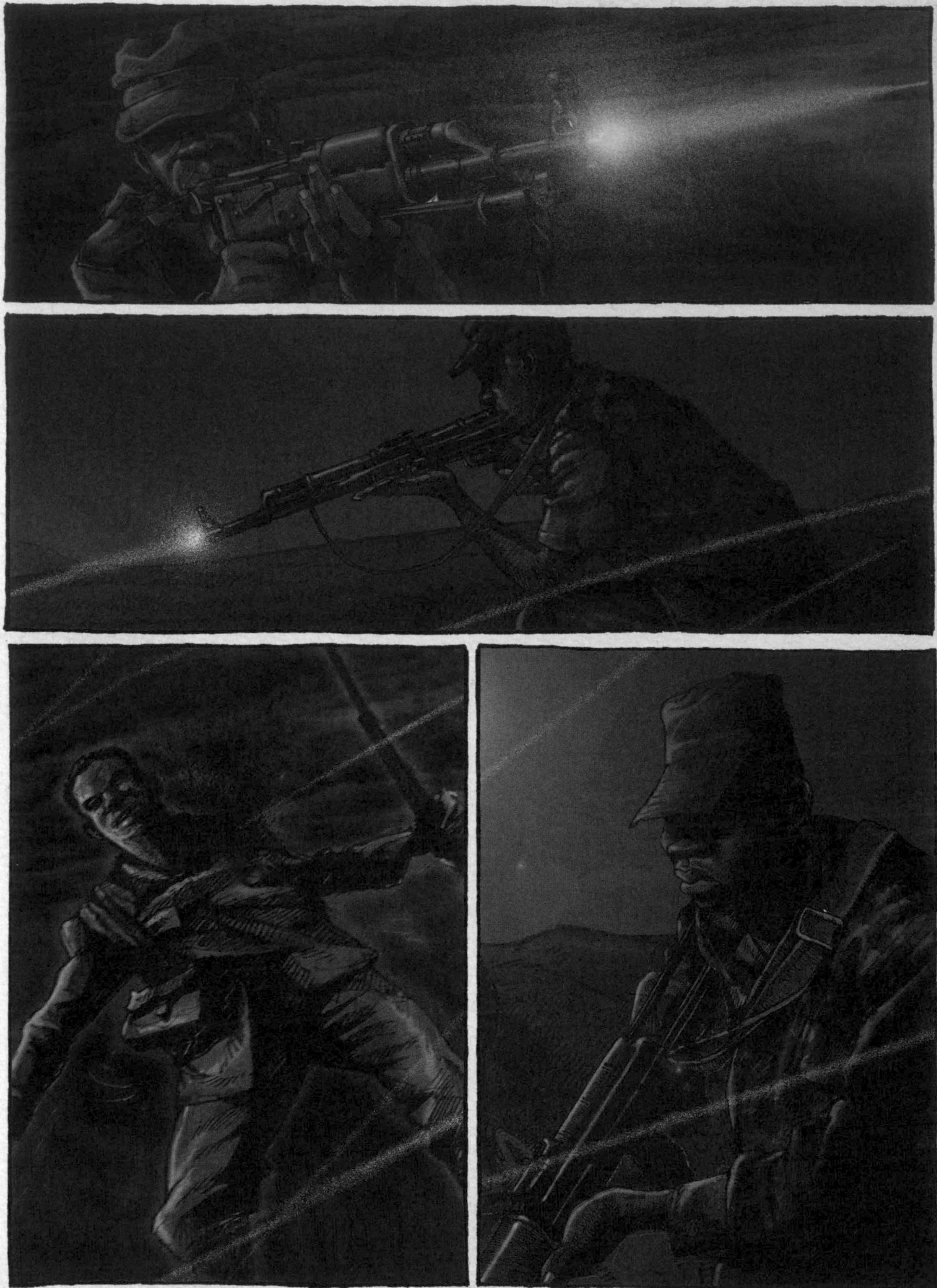

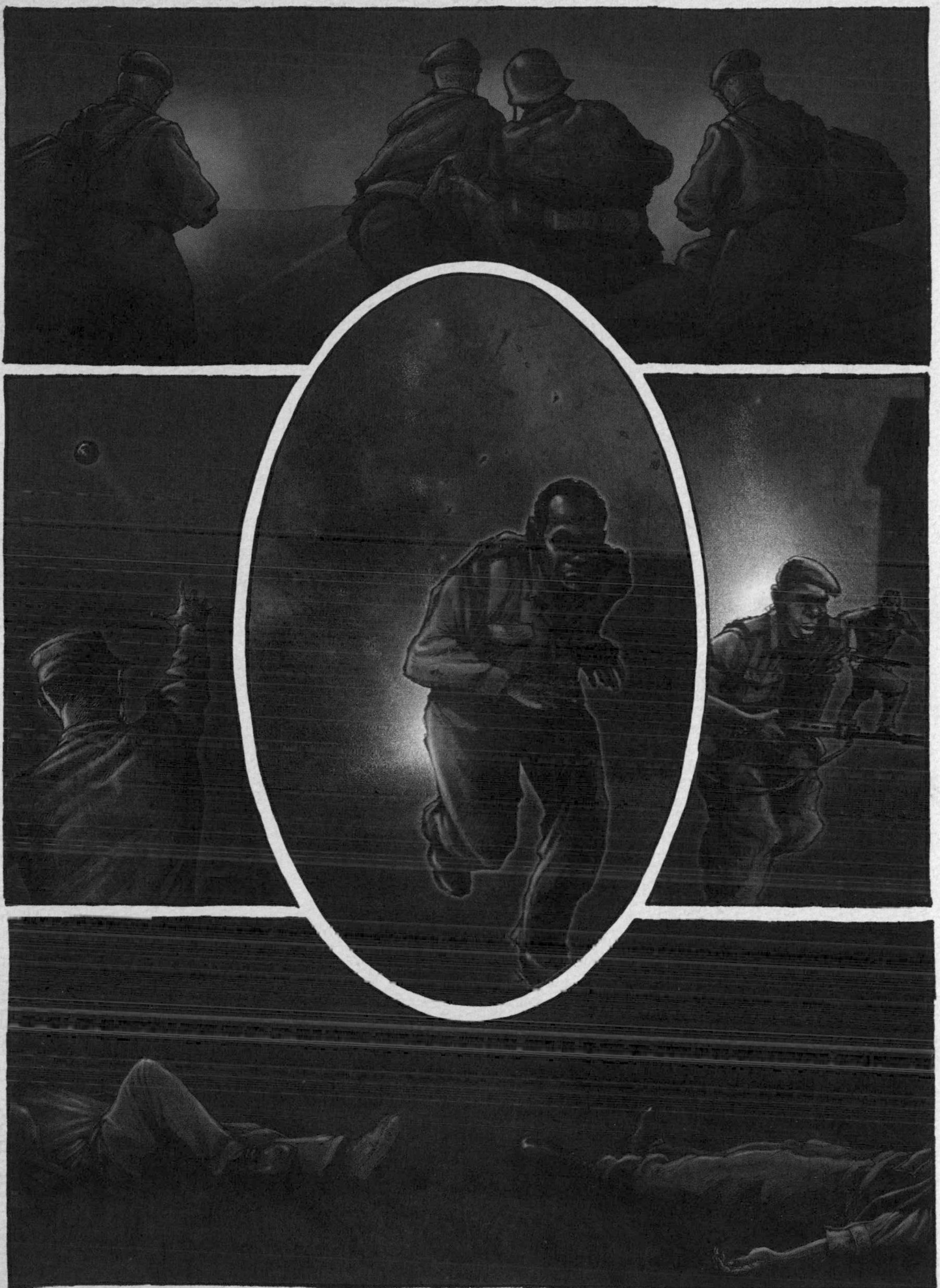

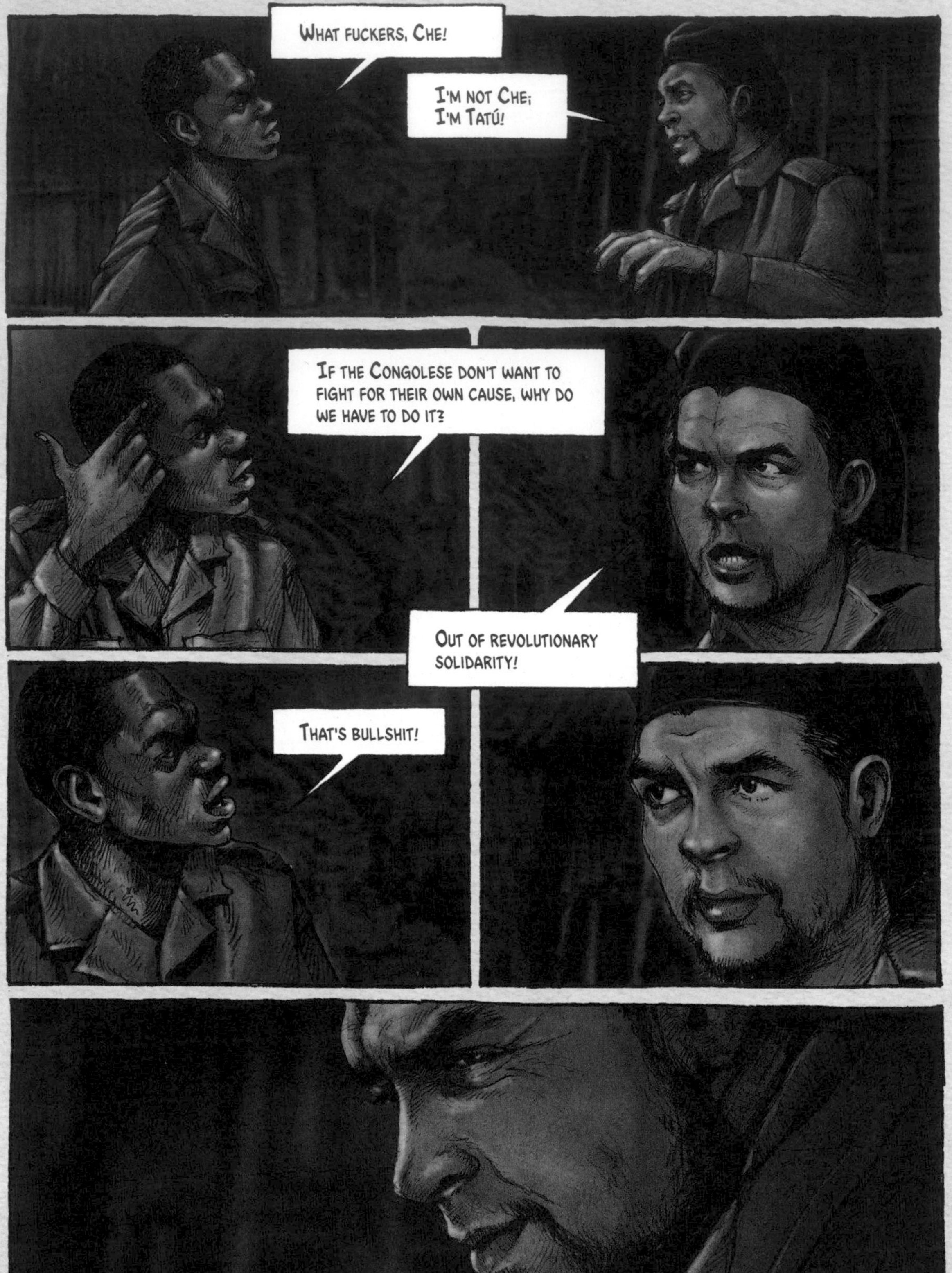
WHAT FUCKERS, CHE!
I'M NOT CHE; I'M TATÚ!
IF THE CONGOLESE DON'T WANT TO FIGHT FOR THEIR OWN CAUSE, WHY DO WE HAVE TO DO IT?
OUT OF REVOLUTIONARY SOLIDARITY!
THAT'S BULLSHIT!

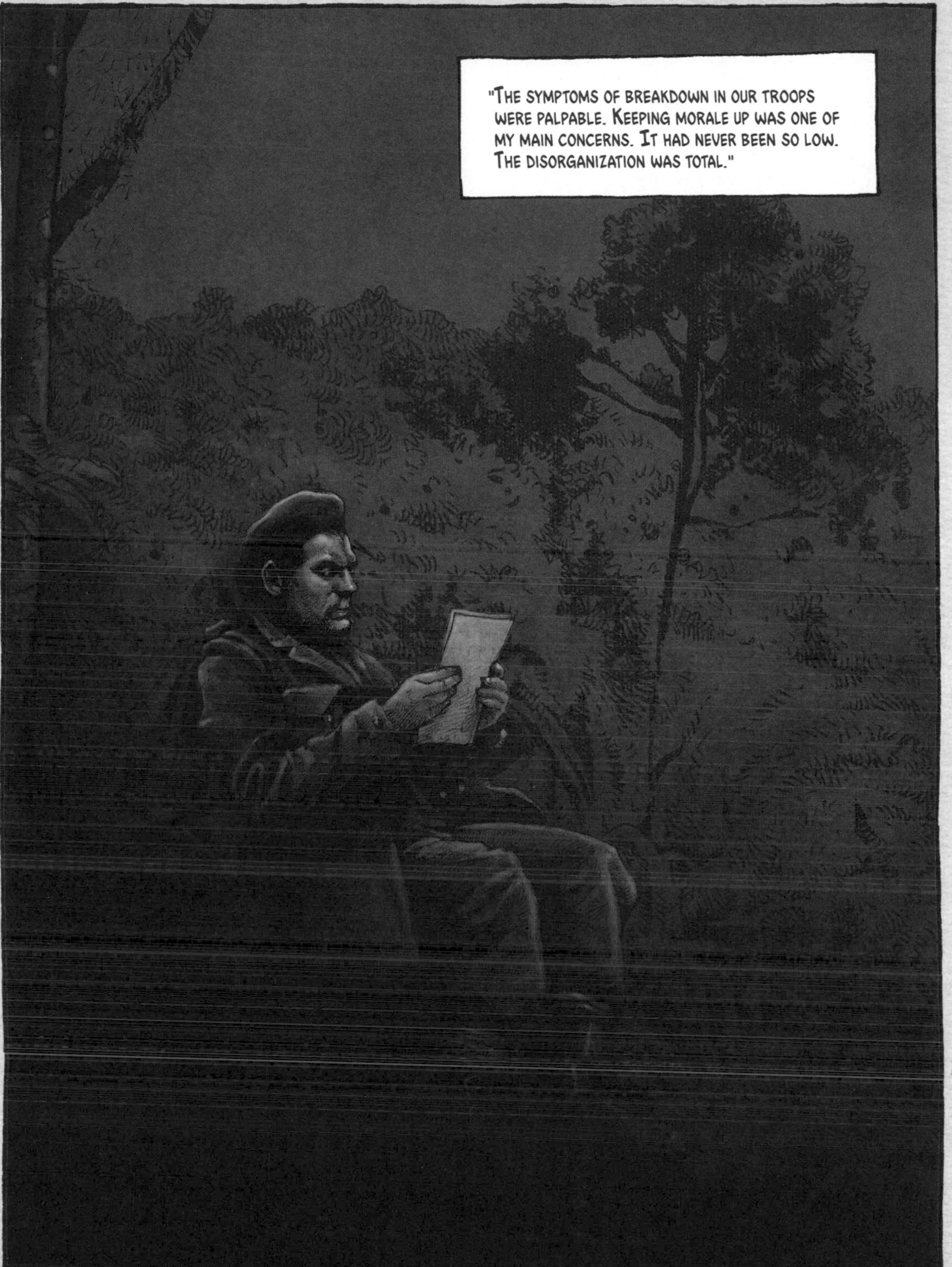
"THE SYMPTOMS OF BREAKDOWN IN OUR TROOPS WERE PALPABLE. KEEPING MORALE UP WAS ONE OF MY MAIN CONCERNS. IT HAD NEVER BEEN SO LOW. THE DISORGANIZATION WAS TOTAL."

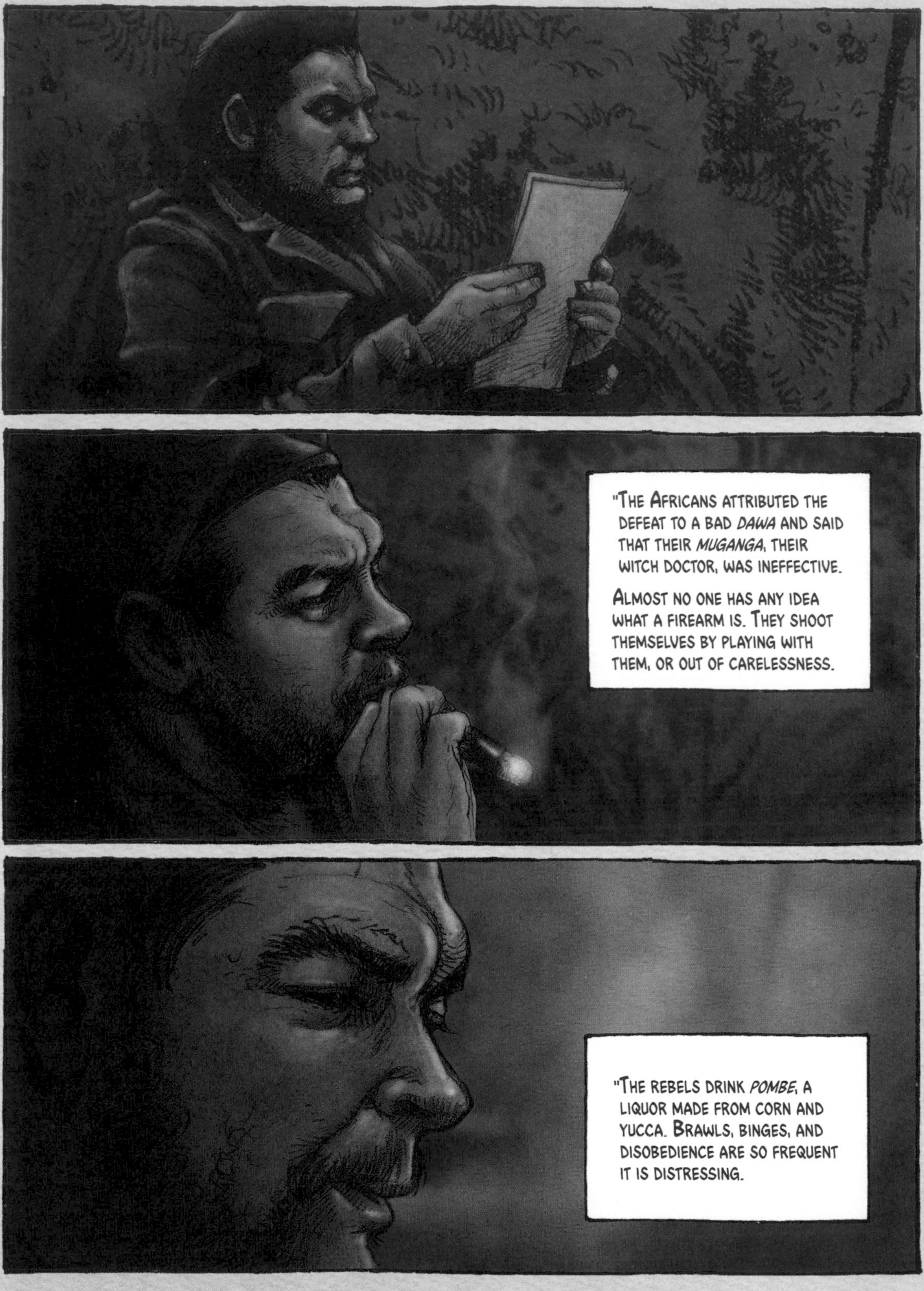
"The Africans attributed the defeat to a bad *dawa* and said that their *muganga*, their witch doctor, was ineffective.
Almost no one has any idea what a firearm is. They shoot themselves by playing with them, or out of carelessness.
"The rebels drink *pombe*, a liquor made from corn and yucca. Brawls, binges, and disobedience are so frequent it is distressing.

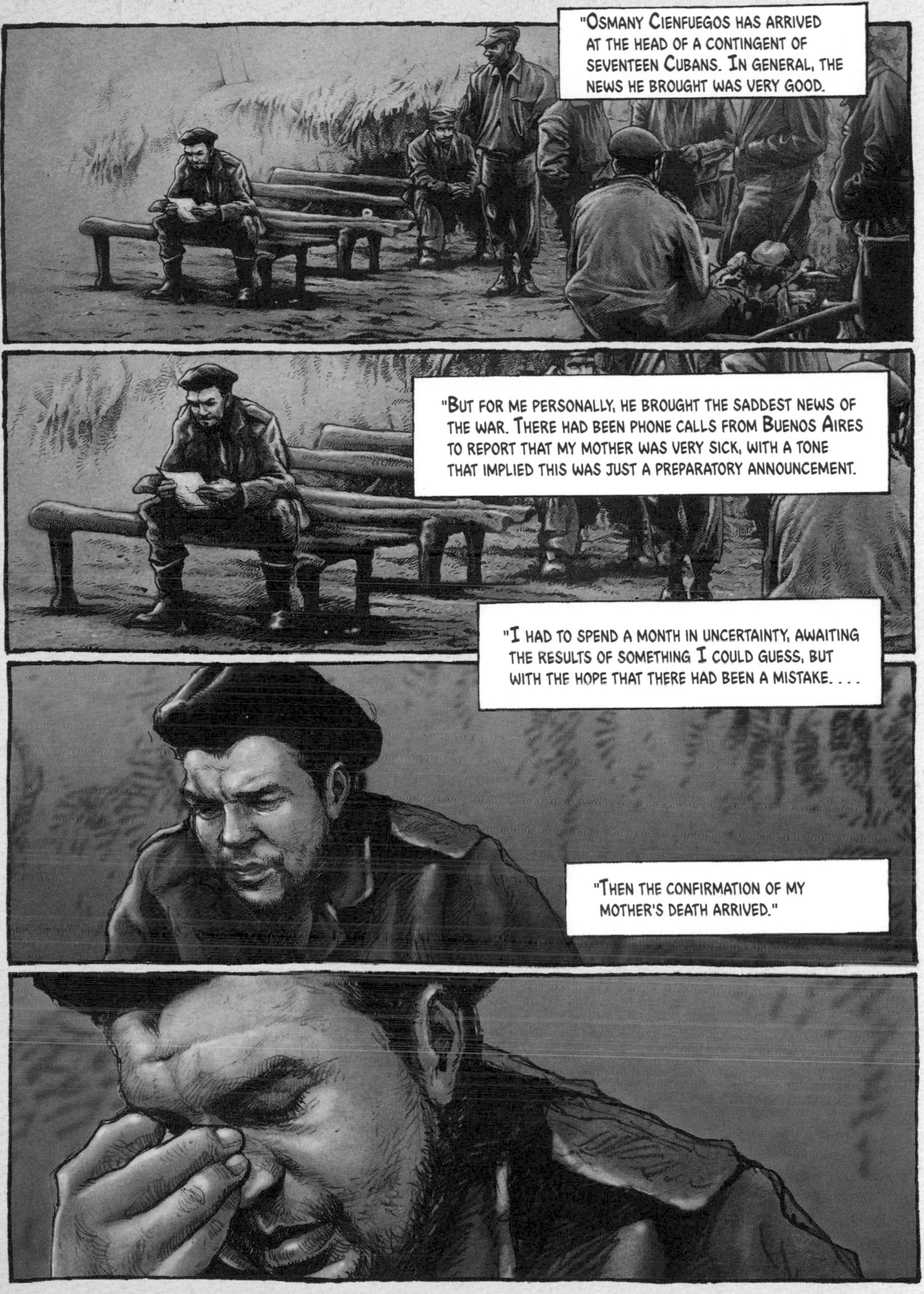
"OSMANY CIENFUEGOS HAS ARRIVED AT THE HEAD OF A CONTINGENT OF SEVENTEEN CUBANS. IN GENERAL, THE NEWS HE BROUGHT WAS VERY GOOD.
"BUT FOR ME PERSONALLY, HE BROUGHT THE SADDEST NEWS OF THE WAR. THERE HAD BEEN PHONE CALLS FROM BUENOS AIRES TO REPORT THAT MY MOTHER WAS VERY SICK, WITH A TONE THAT IMPLIED THIS WAS JUST A PREPARATORY ANNOUNCEMENT.
"I HAD TO SPEND A MONTH IN UNCERTAINTY, AWAITING THE RESULTS OF SOMETHING I COULD GUESS, BUT WITH THE HOPE THAT THERE HAD BEEN A MISTAKE. . . .
"THEN THE CONFIRMATION OF MY MOTHER'S DEATH ARRIVED."

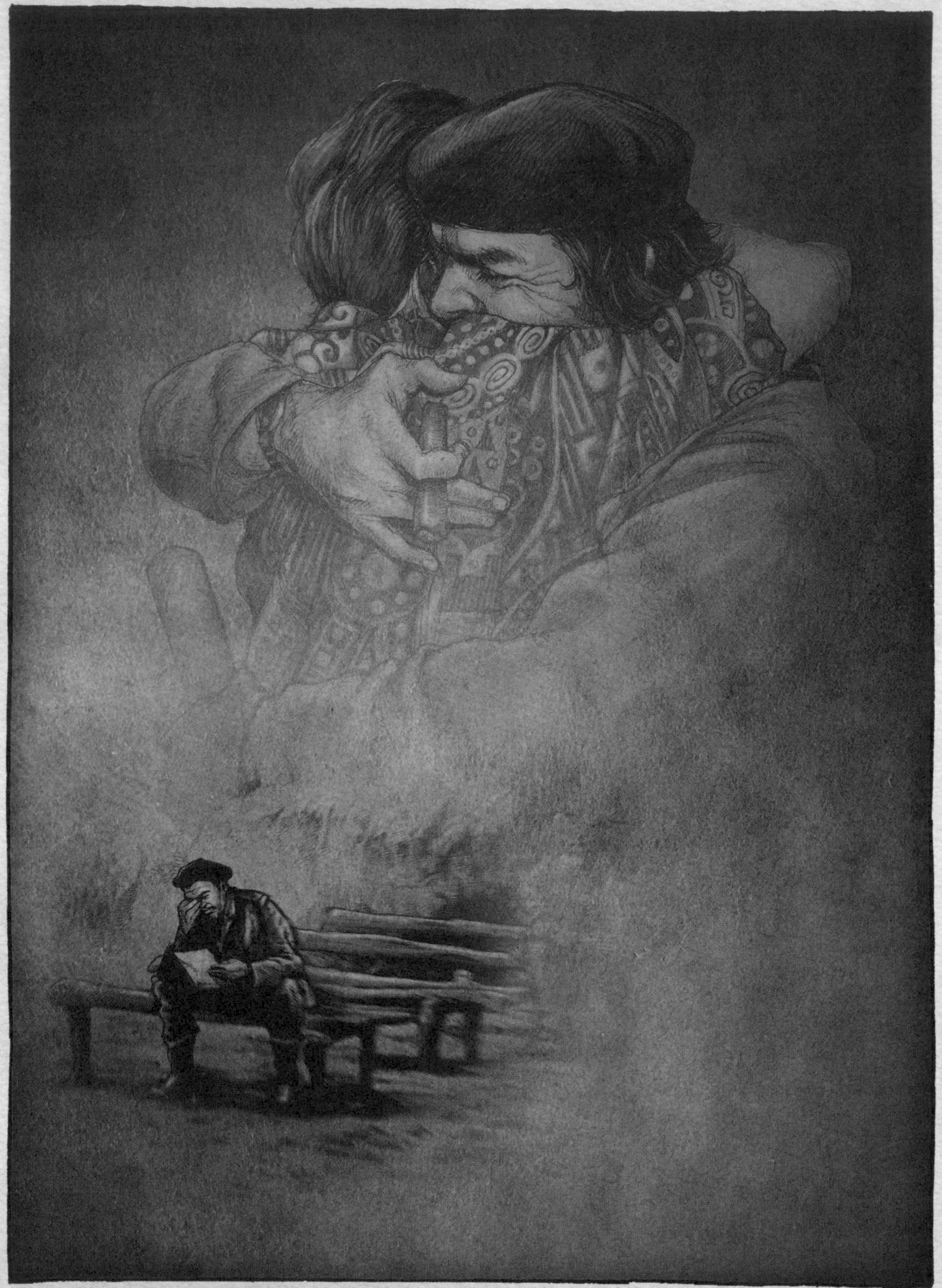

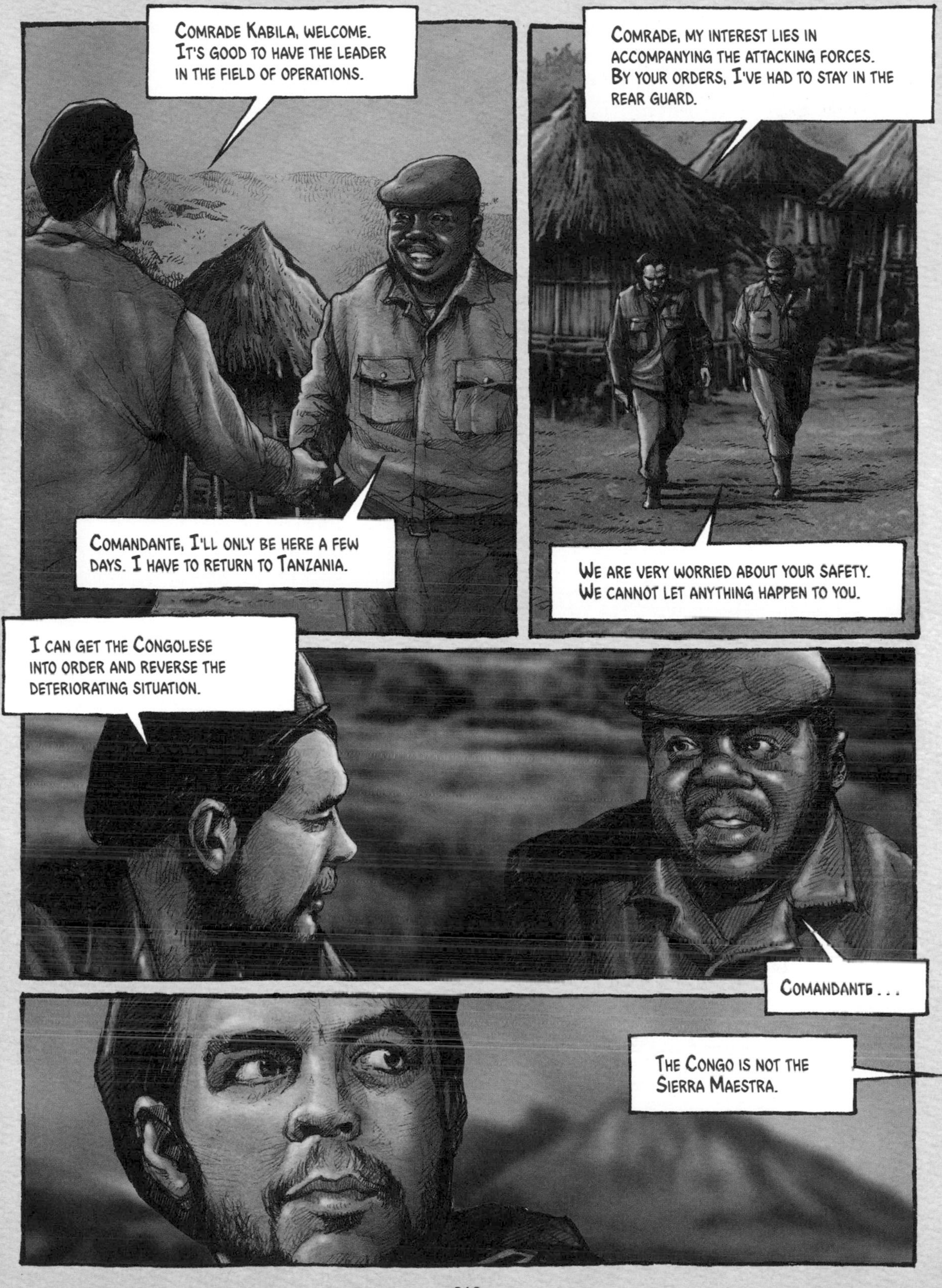

Comrade Kabila, welcome. It's good to have the leader in the field of operations.
Comandante, I'll only be here a few days. I have to return to Tanzania.
Comrade, my interest lies in accompanying the attacking forces. By your orders, I've had to stay in the rear guard.
We are very worried about your safety. We cannot let anything happen to you.
I can get the Congolese into order and reverse the deteriorating situation.
Comandante . . .
The Congo is not the Sierra Maestra.

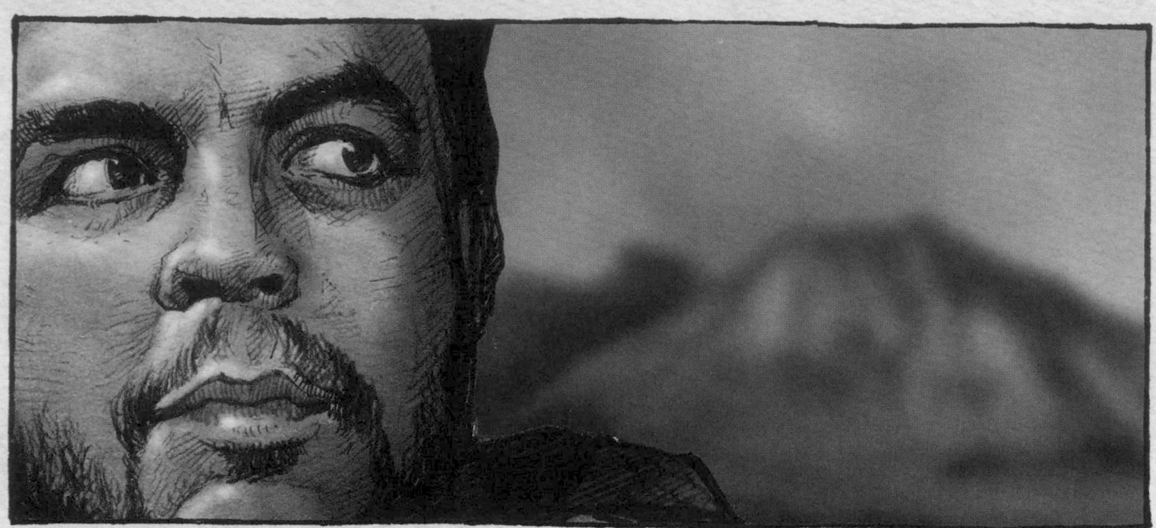

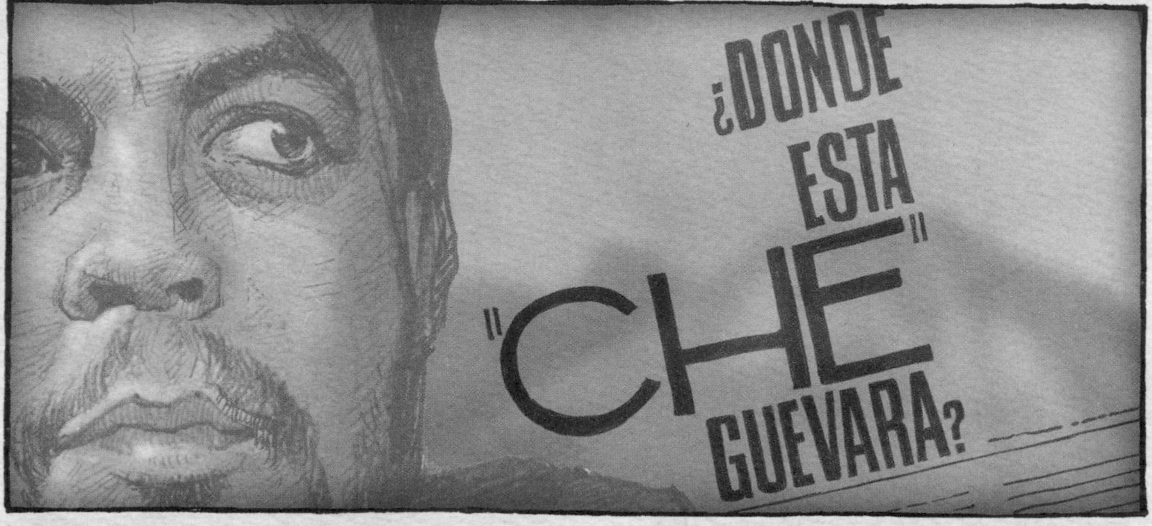
¿DONDE ESTA "CHE" GUEVARA?

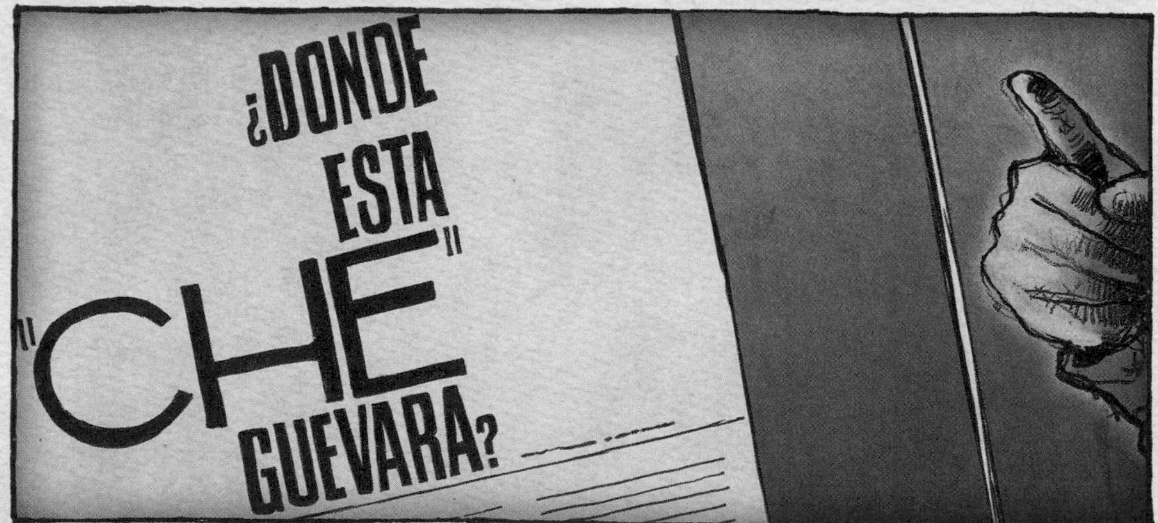
¿DONDE ESTA "CHE" GUEVARA?

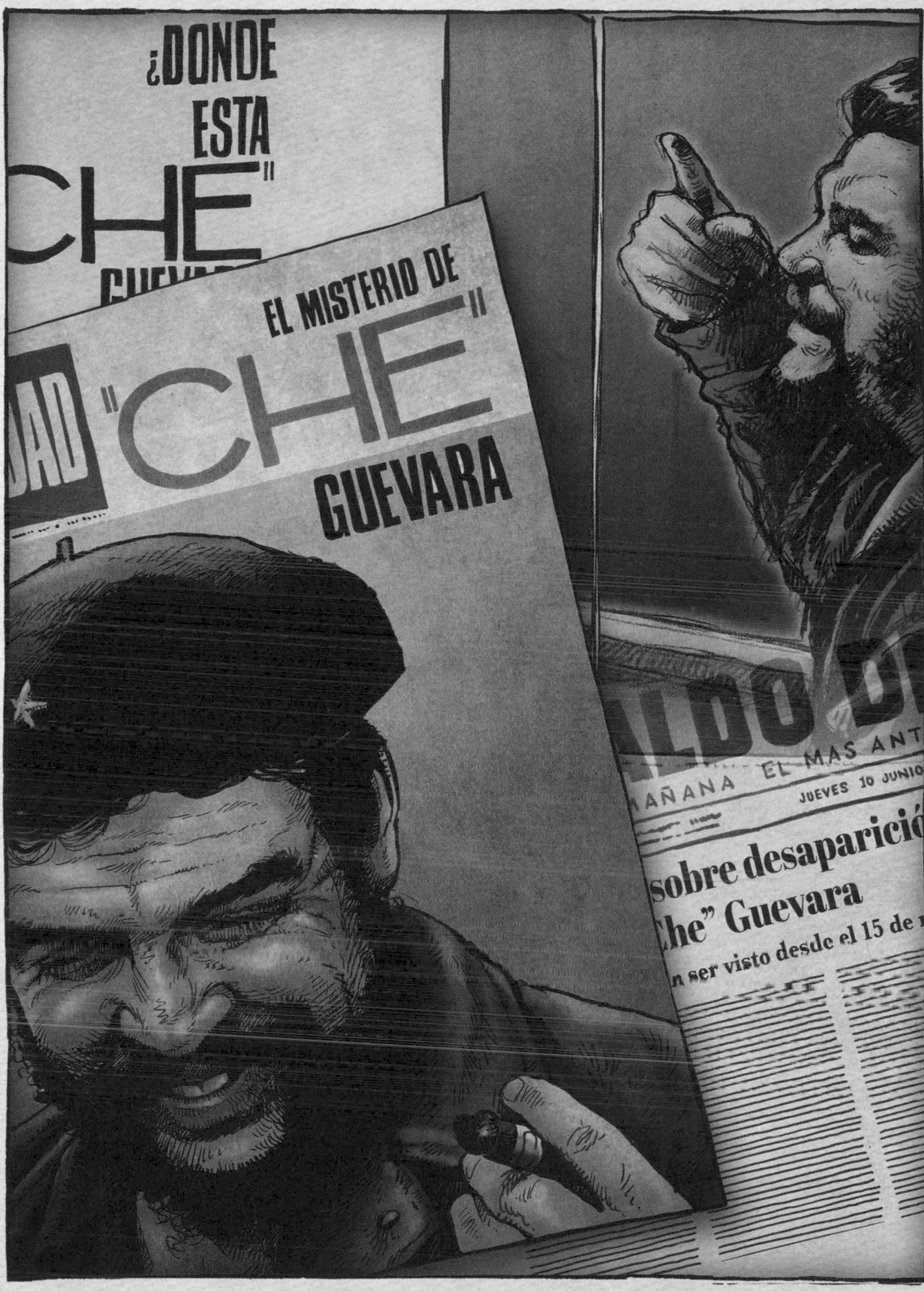

¿DONDE
ESTA
CHE"
EL MISTERIO DE
"CHE"
GUEVARA
ALDO D
MAÑANA EL MAS ANT
JUEVES 10 JUNIO
sobre desaparició
Che" Guevara
n ser visto desde el 15 de

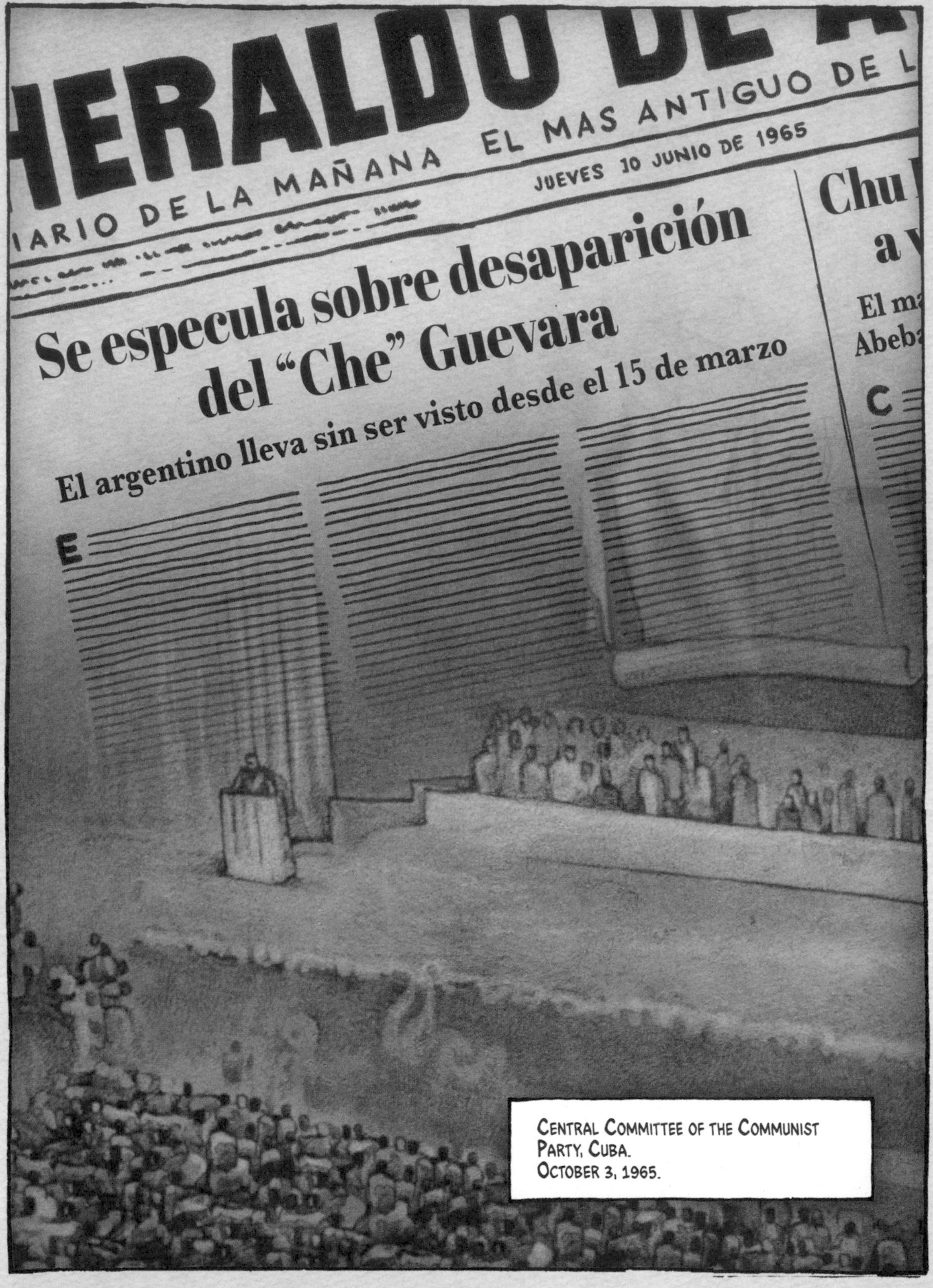
HERALDO DE A
DIARIO DE LA MAÑANA EL MAS ANTIGUO DE L
JUEVES 10 JUNIO DE 1965
Se especula sobre desaparición del "Che" Guevara
El argentino lleva sin ser visto desde el 15 de marzo
Chu
a
El m
Abeb
CENTRAL COMMITTEE OF THE COMMUNIST PARTY, CUBA.
OCTOBER 3, 1965.

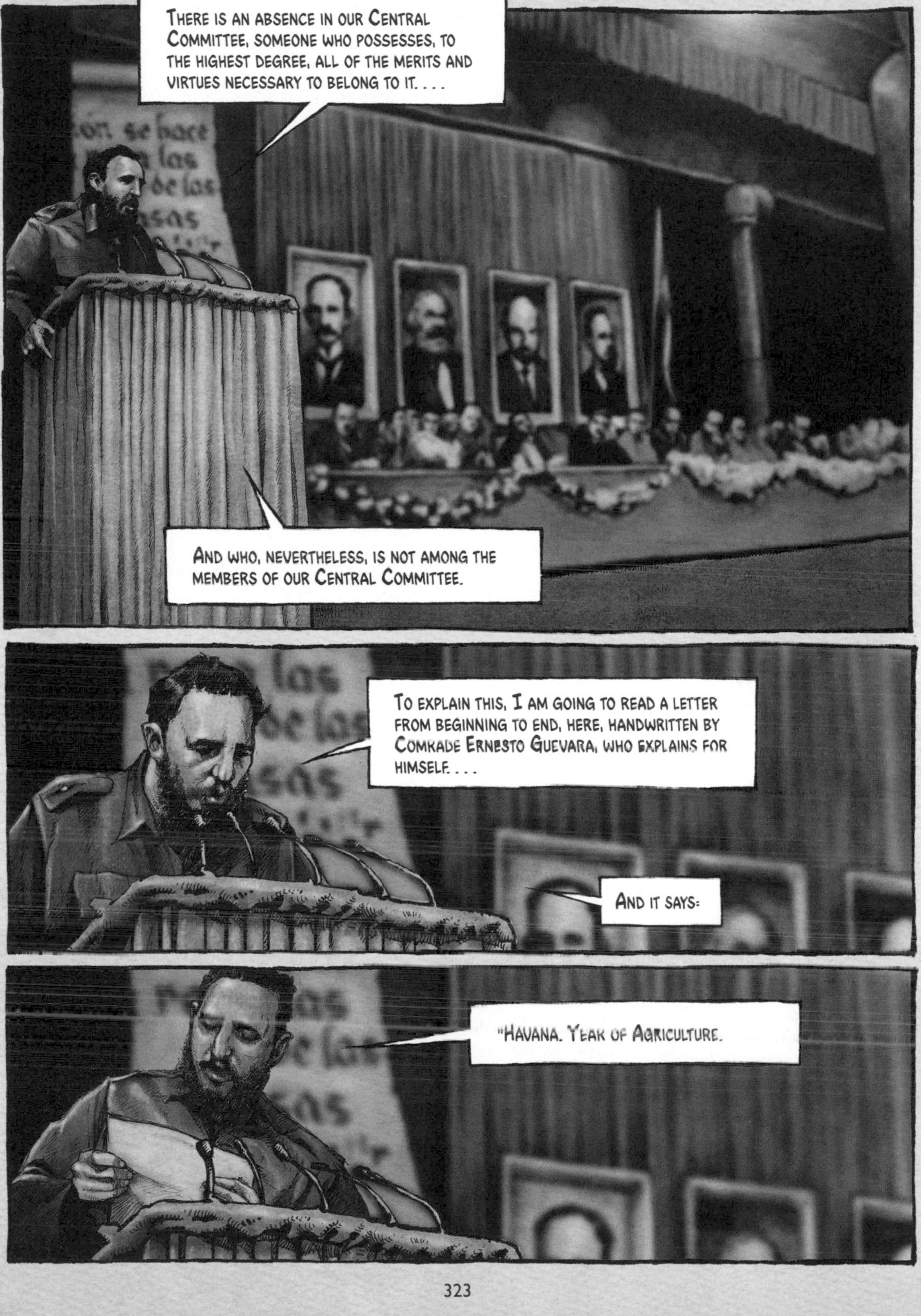
There is an absence in our Central Committee, someone who possesses, to the highest degree, all of the merits and virtues necessary to belong to it. . . .
And who, nevertheless, is not among the members of our Central Committee.
To explain this, I am going to read a letter from beginning to end, here, handwritten by Comrade Ernesto Guevara, who explains for himself. . . .
And it says:
"Havana. Year of Agriculture.

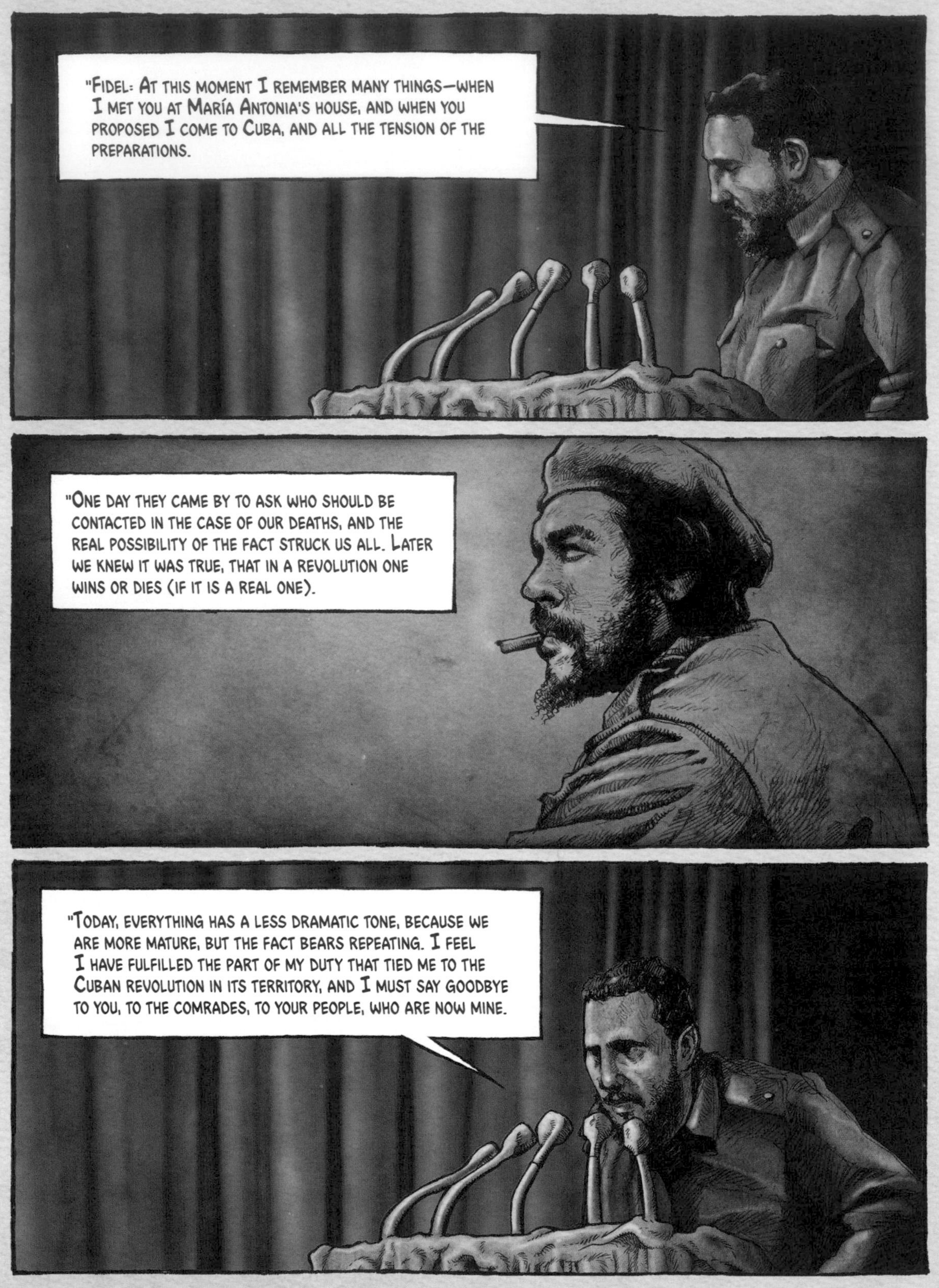
"Fidel: At this moment I remember many things—when I met you at María Antonia's house, and when you proposed I come to Cuba, and all the tension of the preparations.
"One day they came by to ask who should be contacted in the case of our deaths, and the real possibility of the fact struck us all. Later we knew it was true, that in a revolution one wins or dies (if it is a real one).
"Today, everything has a less dramatic tone, because we are more mature, but the fact bears repeating. I feel I have fulfilled the part of my duty that tied me to the Cuban revolution in its territory, and I must say goodbye to you, to the comrades, to your people, who are now mine.

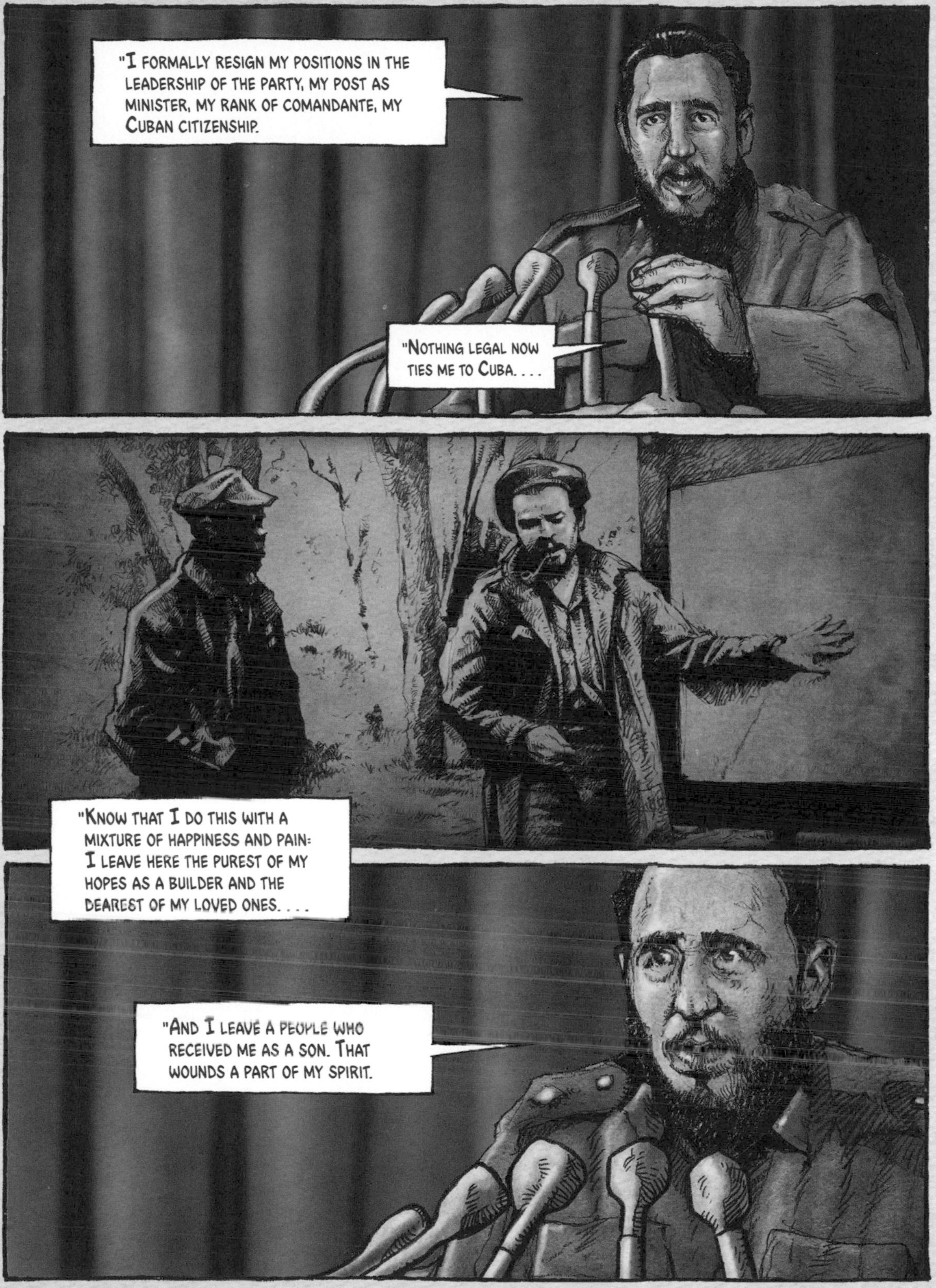
"I FORMALLY RESIGN MY POSITIONS IN THE LEADERSHIP OF THE PARTY, MY POST AS MINISTER, MY RANK OF COMANDANTE, MY CUBAN CITIZENSHIP.
"NOTHING LEGAL NOW TIES ME TO CUBA. . . .
"KNOW THAT I DO THIS WITH A MIXTURE OF HAPPINESS AND PAIN: I LEAVE HERE THE PUREST OF MY HOPES AS A BUILDER AND THE DEAREST OF MY LOVED ONES. . . .
"AND I LEAVE A PEOPLE WHO RECEIVED ME AS A SON. THAT WOUNDS A PART OF MY SPIRIT.

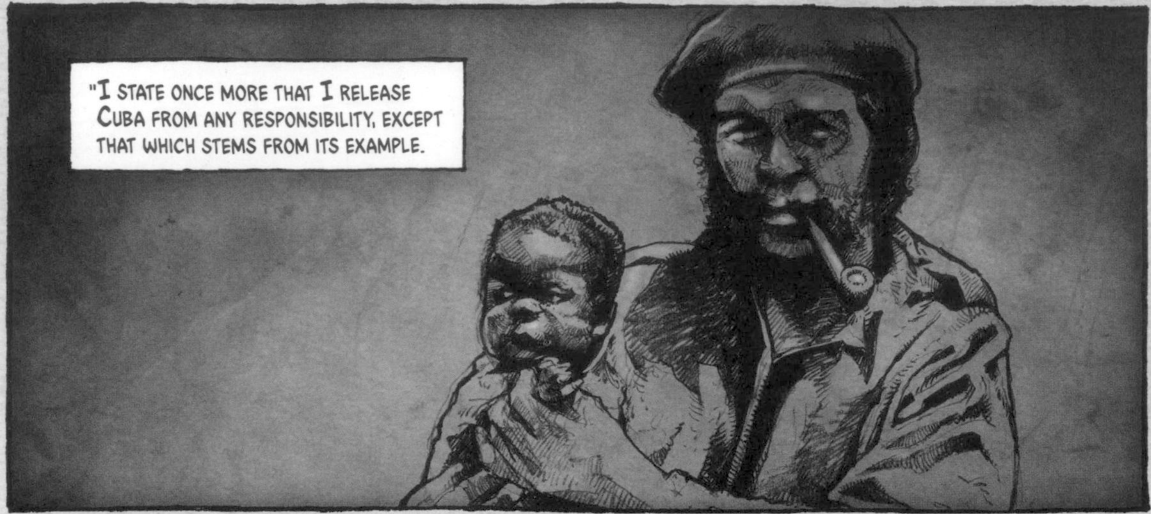
"I STATE ONCE MORE THAT I RELEASE CUBA FROM ANY RESPONSIBILITY, EXCEPT THAT WHICH STEMS FROM ITS EXAMPLE.

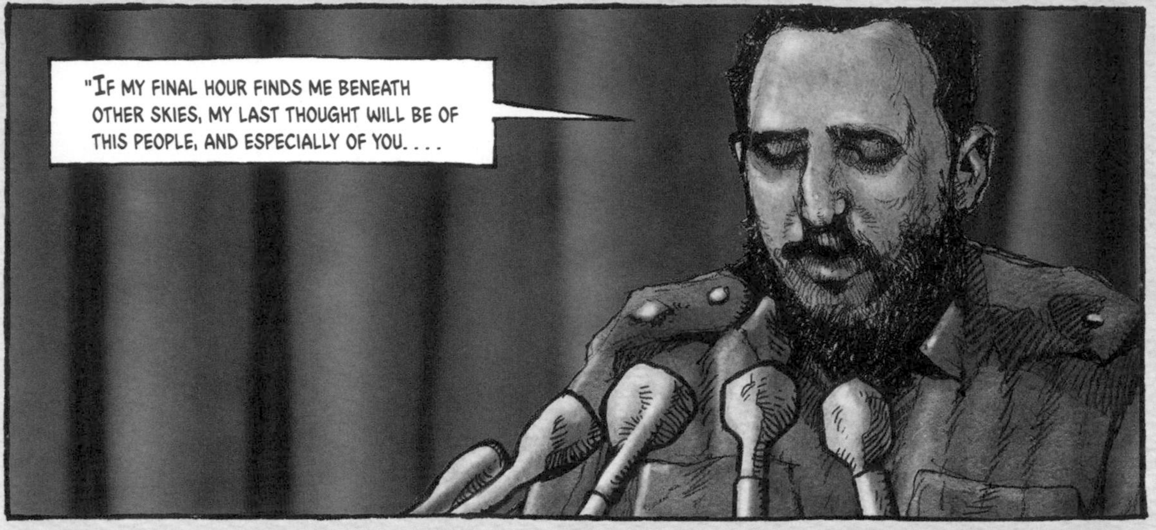
"IF MY FINAL HOUR FINDS ME BENEATH OTHER SKIES, MY LAST THOUGHT WILL BE OF THIS PEOPLE, AND ESPECIALLY OF YOU. . . .

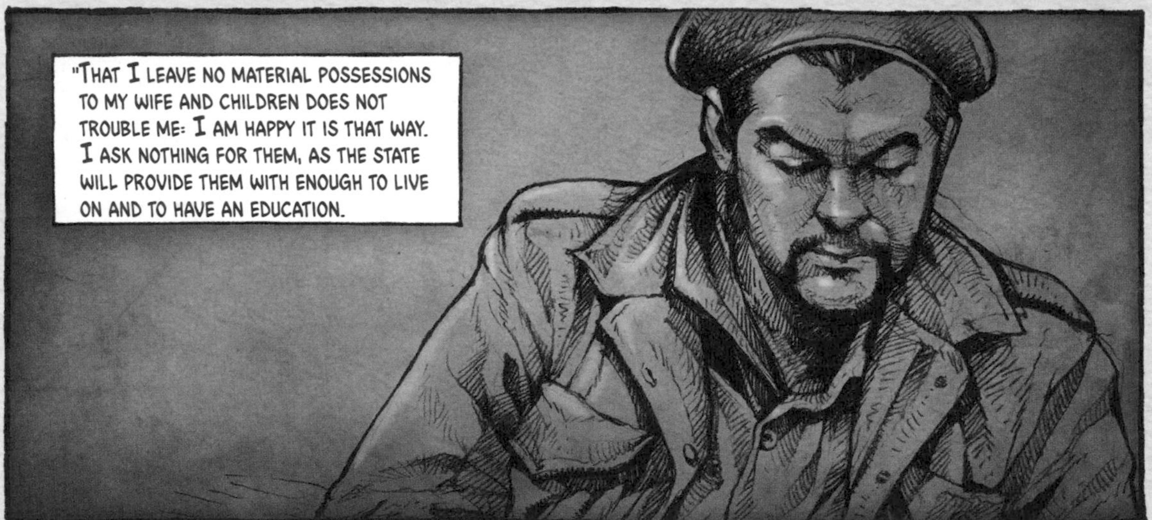
"THAT I LEAVE NO MATERIAL POSSESSIONS TO MY WIFE AND CHILDREN DOES NOT TROUBLE ME: I AM HAPPY IT IS THAT WAY. I ASK NOTHING FOR THEM, AS THE STATE WILL PROVIDE THEM WITH ENOUGH TO LIVE ON AND TO HAVE AN EDUCATION.

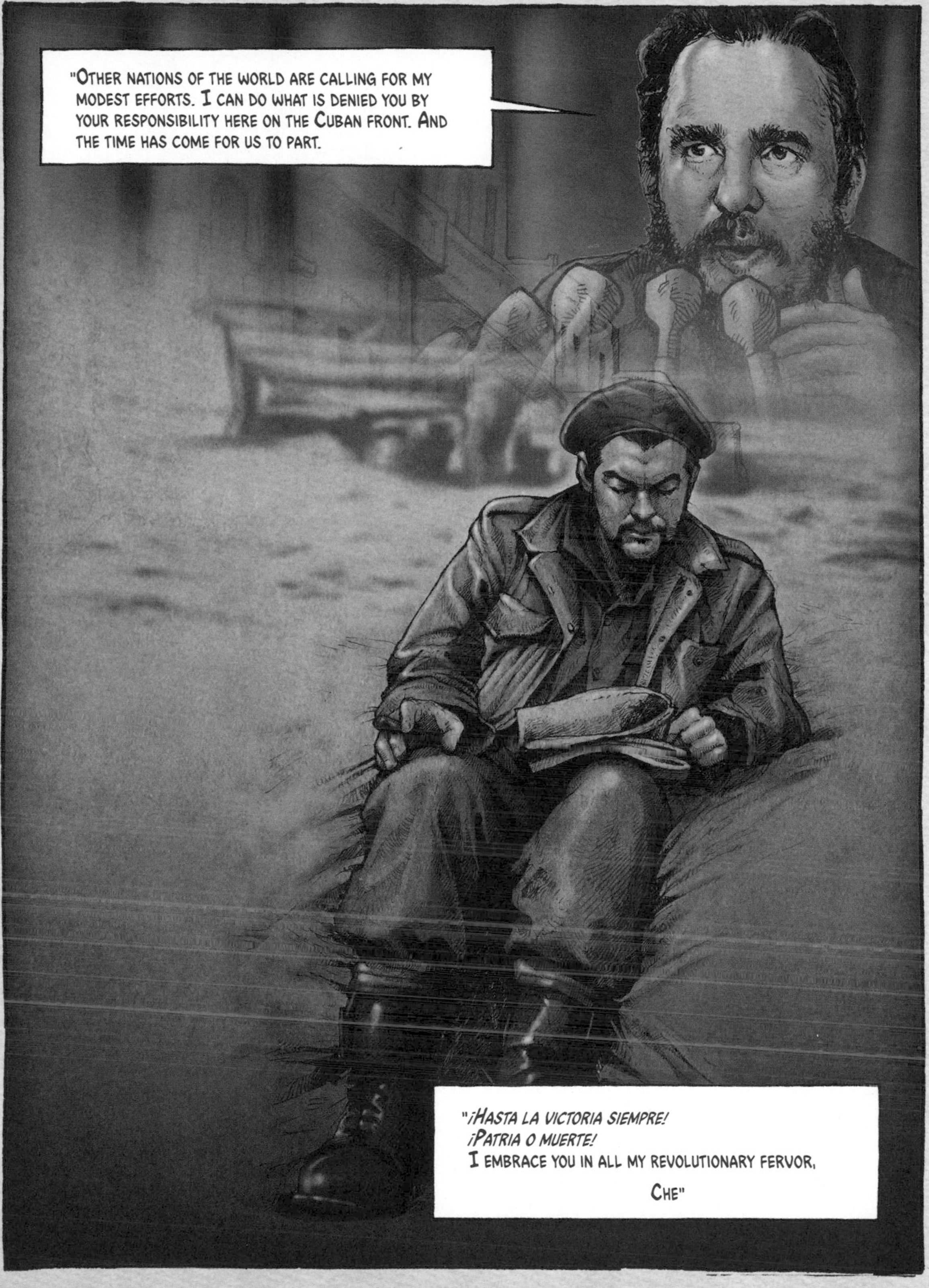
"Other nations of the world are calling for my modest efforts. I can do what is denied you by your responsibility here on the Cuban front. And the time has come for us to part.
"¡Hasta la victoria siempre! ¡Patria o muerte! I embrace you in all my revolutionary fervor, Che"

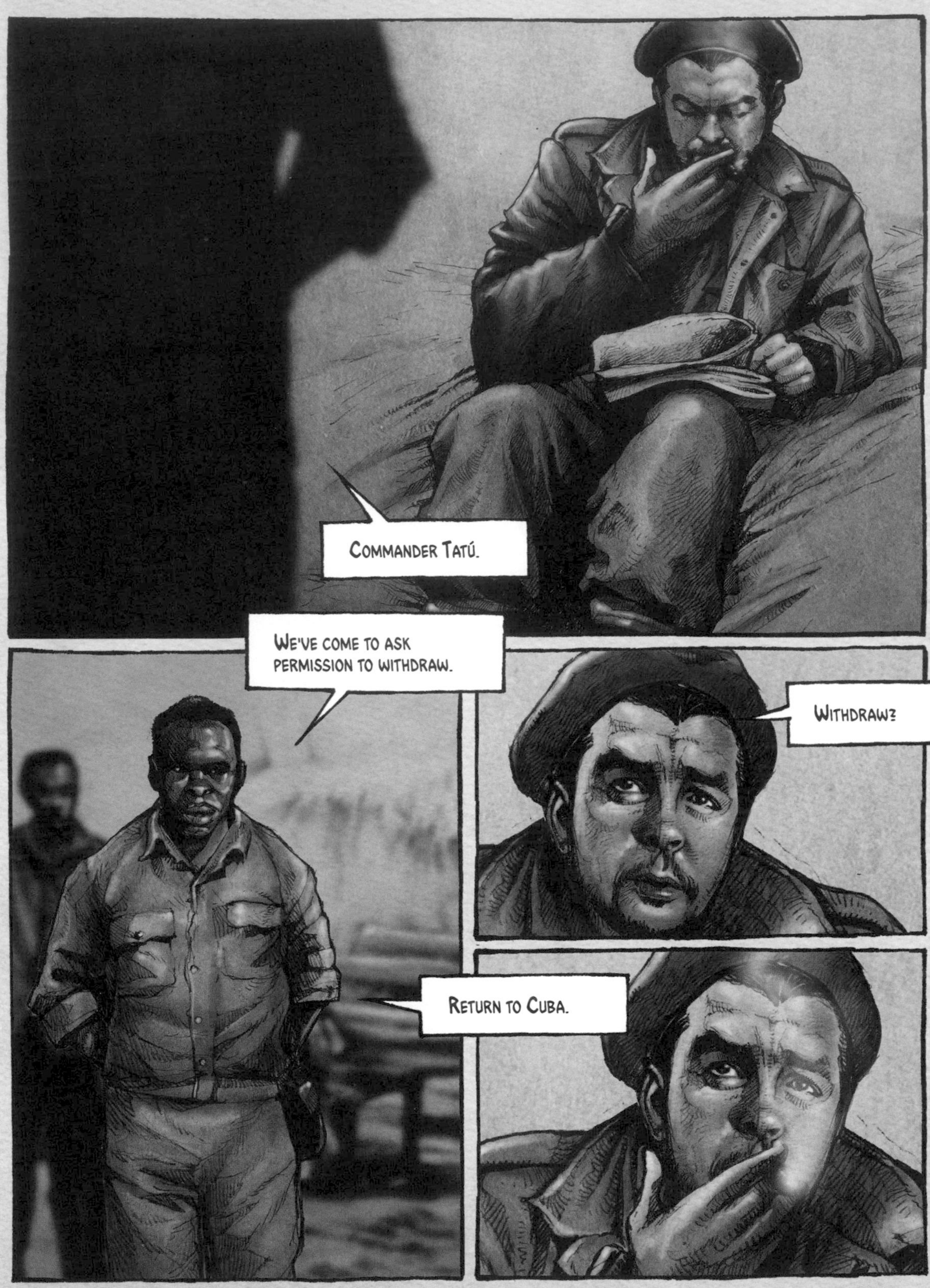
Commander Tatú.
We've come to ask permission to withdraw.
Withdraw?
Return to Cuba.

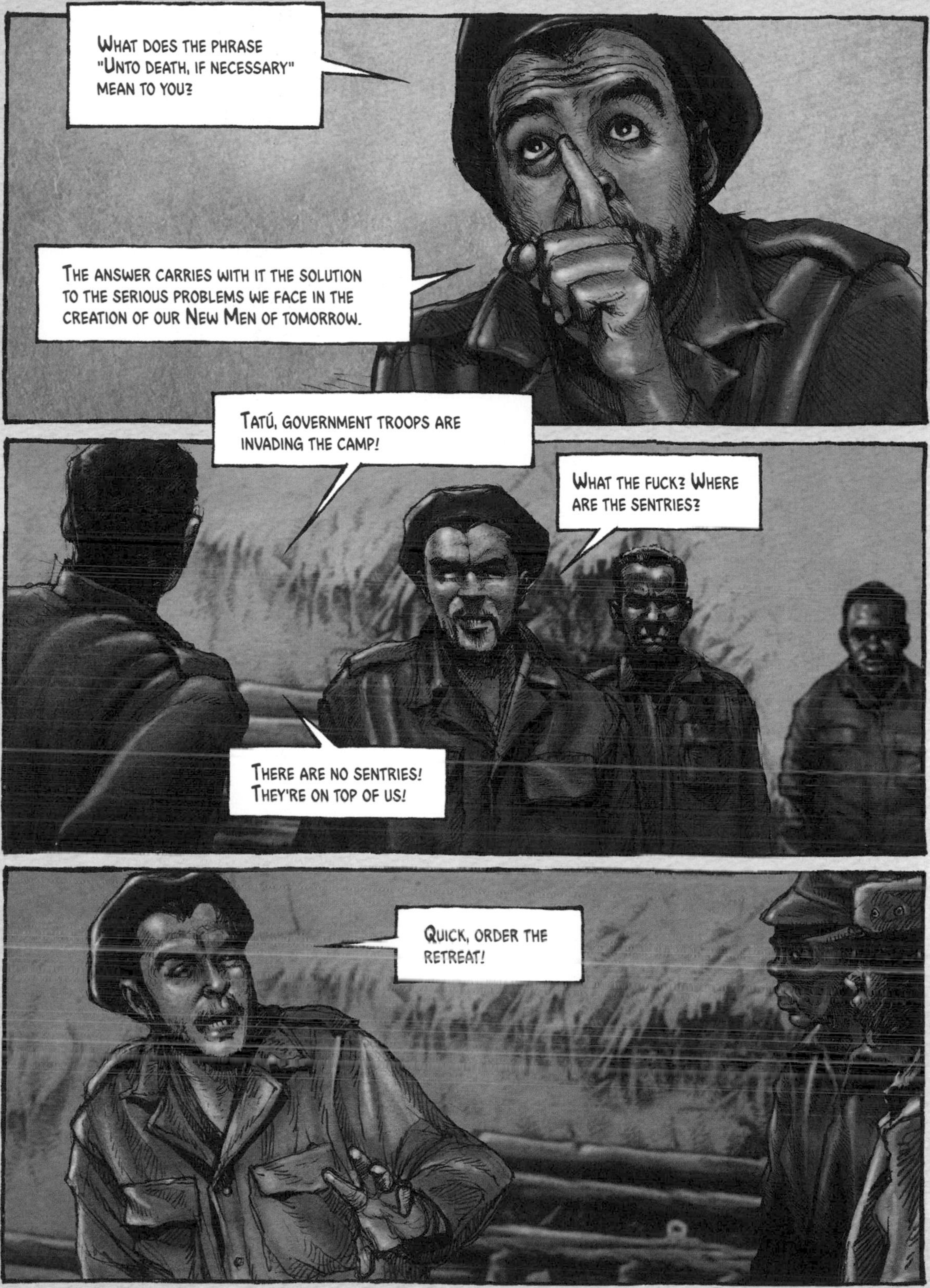
WHAT DOES THE PHRASE "UNTO DEATH, IF NECESSARY" MEAN TO YOU?
THE ANSWER CARRIES WITH IT THE SOLUTION TO THE SERIOUS PROBLEMS WE FACE IN THE CREATION OF OUR NEW MEN OF TOMORROW.
TATÚ, GOVERNMENT TROOPS ARE INVADING THE CAMP!
WHAT THE FUCK? WHERE ARE THE SENTRIES?
THERE ARE NO SENTRIES! THEY'RE ON TOP OF US!
QUICK, ORDER THE RETREAT!

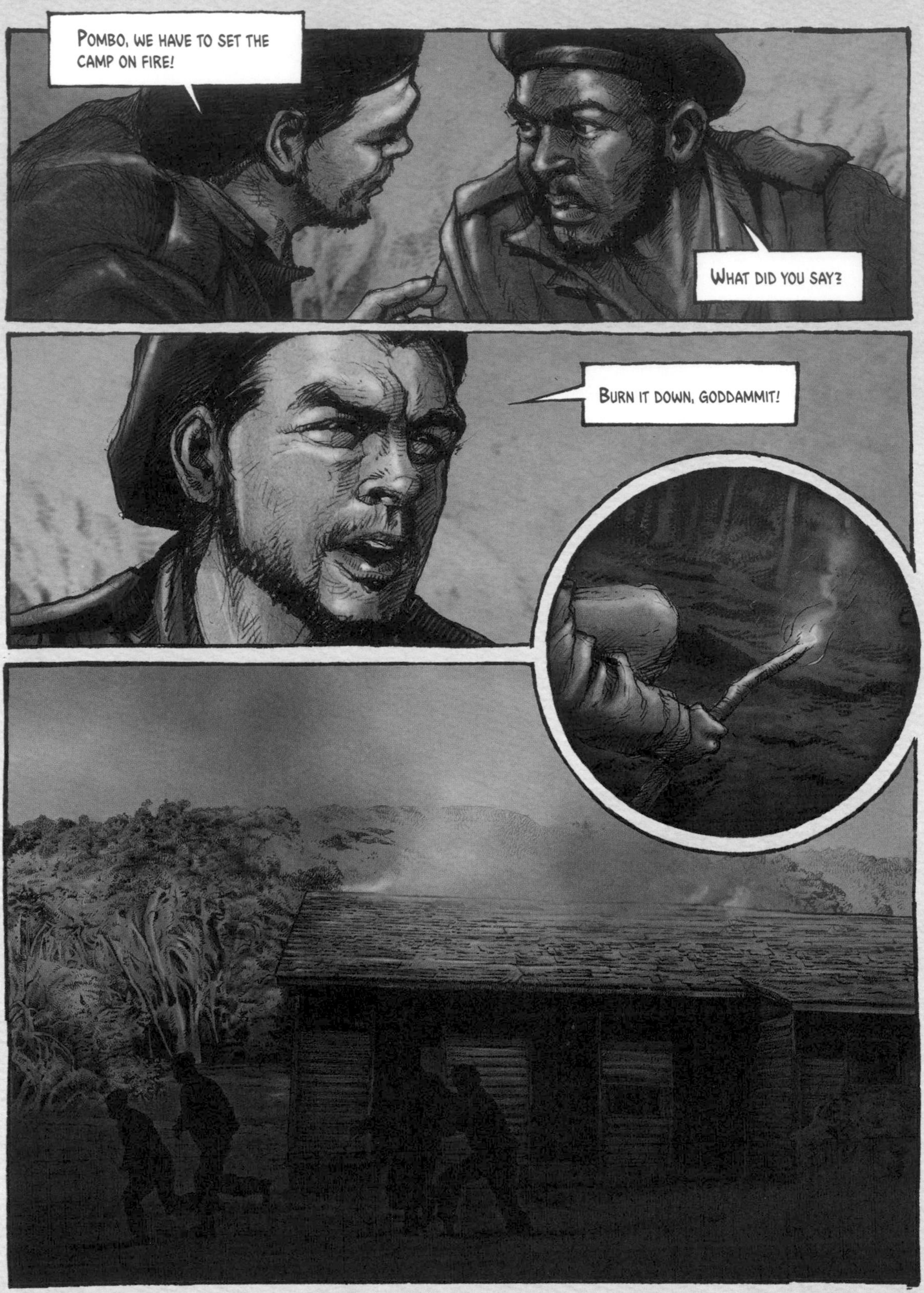

POMBO, WE HAVE TO SET THE CAMP ON FIRE!
WHAT DID YOU SAY?
BURN IT DOWN, GODDAMMIT!

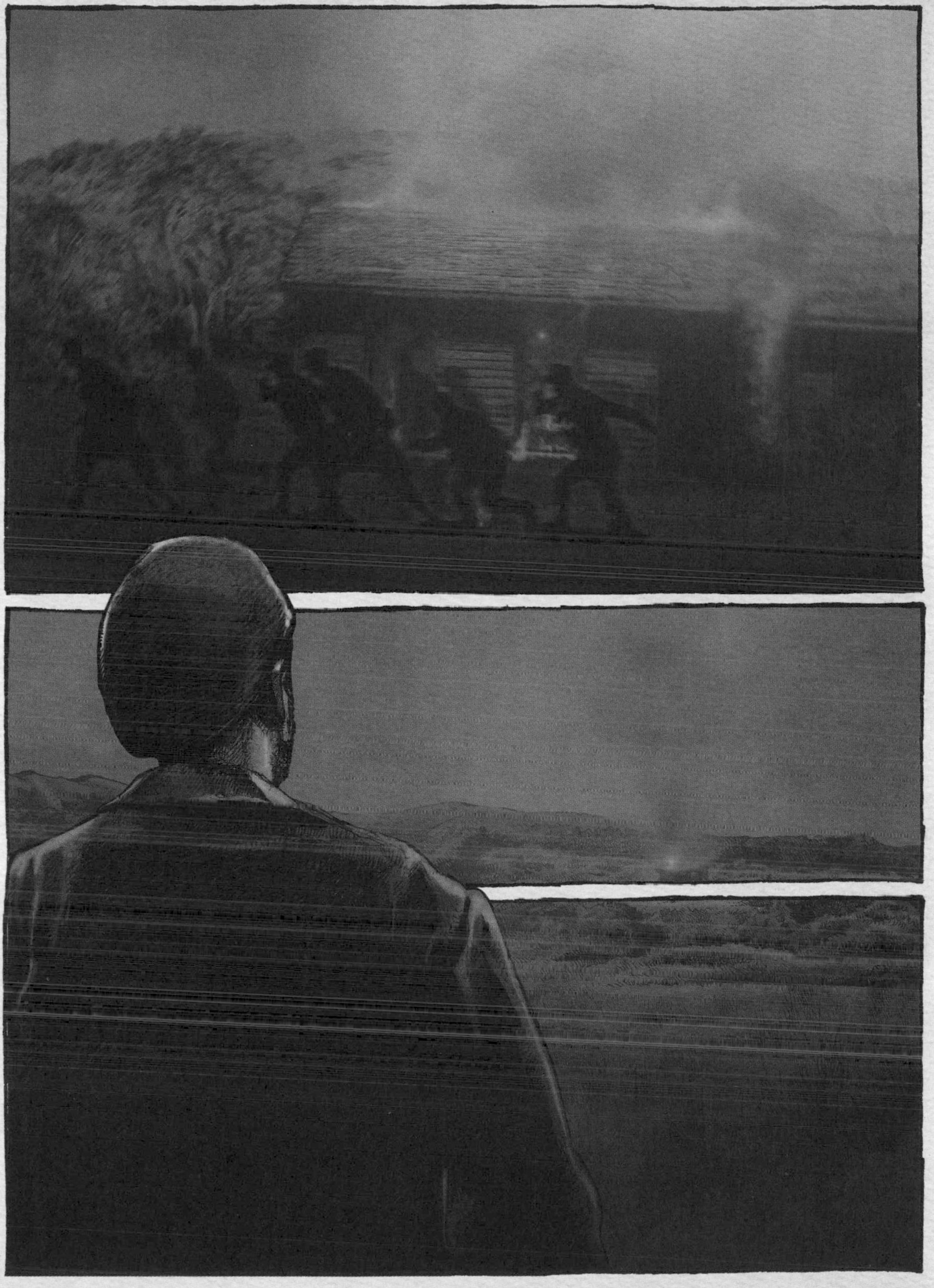

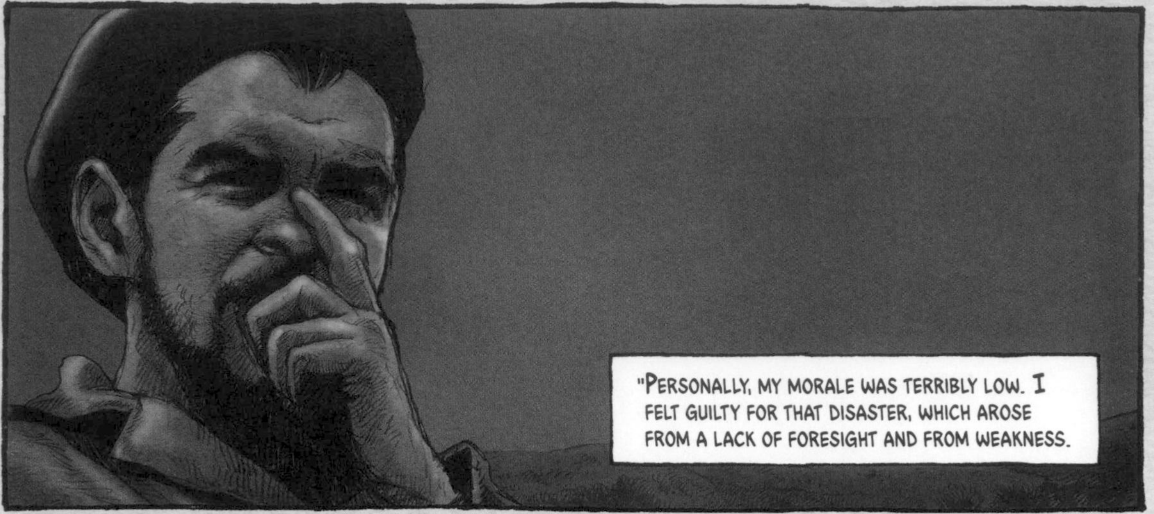
"PERSONALLY, MY MORALE WAS TERRIBLY LOW. I FELT GUILTY FOR THAT DISASTER, WHICH AROSE FROM A LACK OF FORESIGHT AND FROM WEAKNESS.

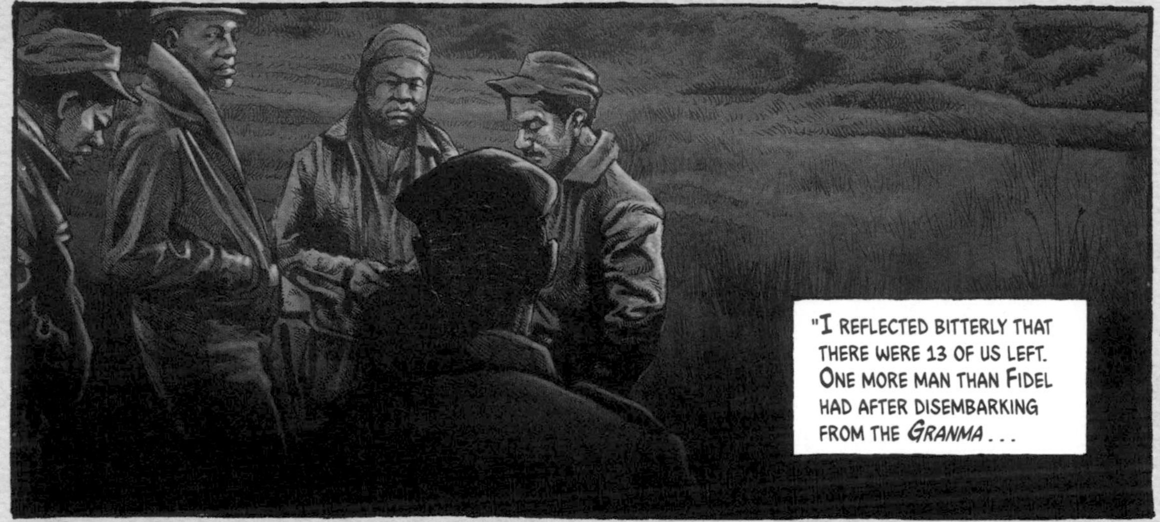
"I REFLECTED BITTERLY THAT THERE WERE 13 OF US LEFT. ONE MORE MAN THAN FIDEL HAD AFTER DISEMBARKING FROM THE *GRANMA* . . .

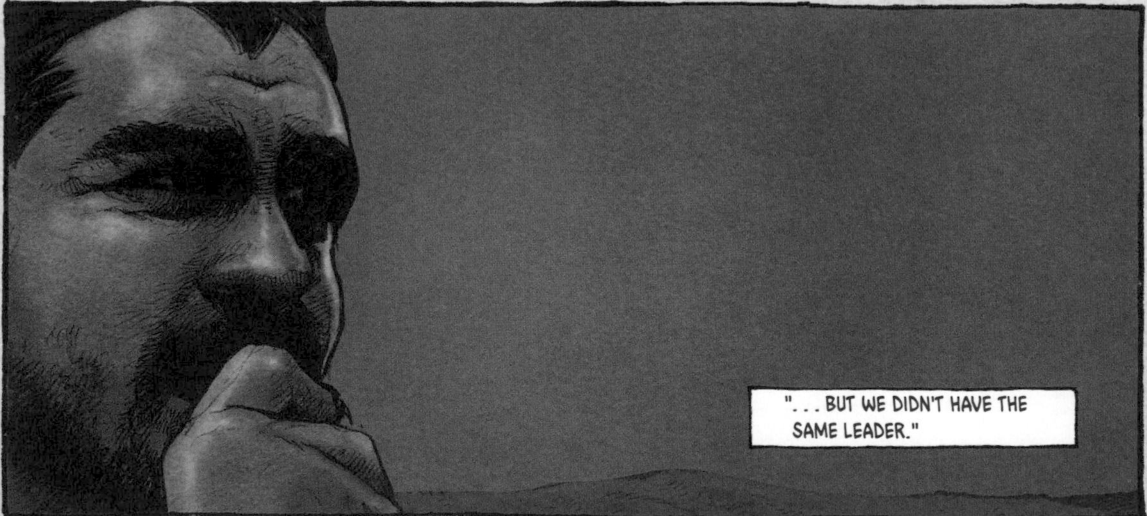
". . . BUT WE DIDN'T HAVE THE SAME LEADER."

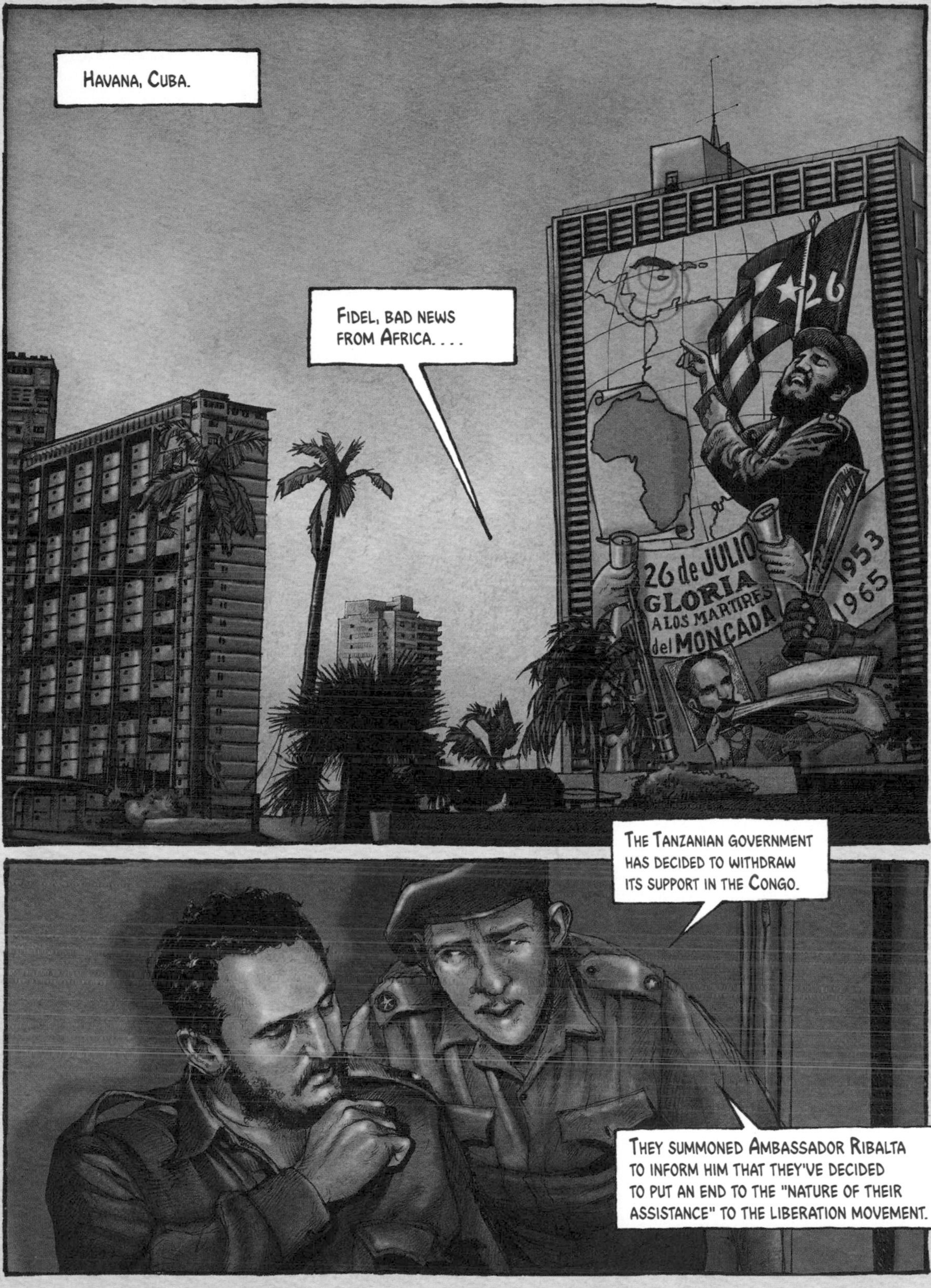

Havana, Cuba.
Fidel, bad news from Africa. . . .
26
26 de JULIO
GLORIA
A LOS MARTIRES
del MONCADA
1953
1965
The Tanzanian government has decided to withdraw its support in the Congo.
They summoned Ambassador Ribalta to inform him that they've decided to put an end to the "nature of their assistance" to the liberation movement.

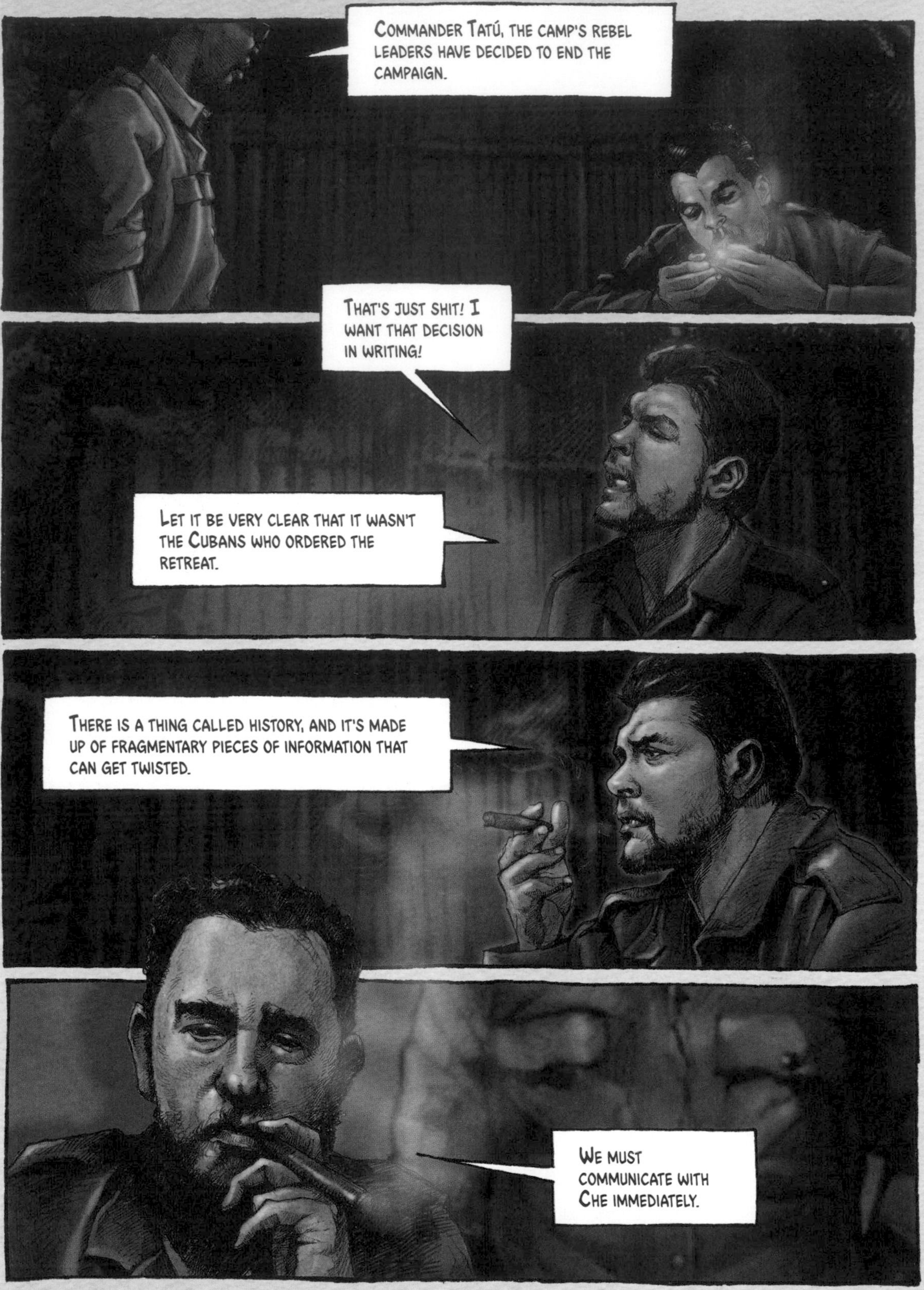
COMMANDER TATÚ, THE CAMP'S REBEL LEADERS HAVE DECIDED TO END THE CAMPAIGN.
THAT'S JUST SHIT! I WANT THAT DECISION IN WRITING!
LET IT BE VERY CLEAR THAT IT WASN'T THE CUBANS WHO ORDERED THE RETREAT.
THERE IS A THING CALLED HISTORY, AND IT'S MADE UP OF FRAGMENTARY PIECES OF INFORMATION THAT CAN GET TWISTED.
WE MUST COMMUNICATE WITH CHE IMMEDIATELY.

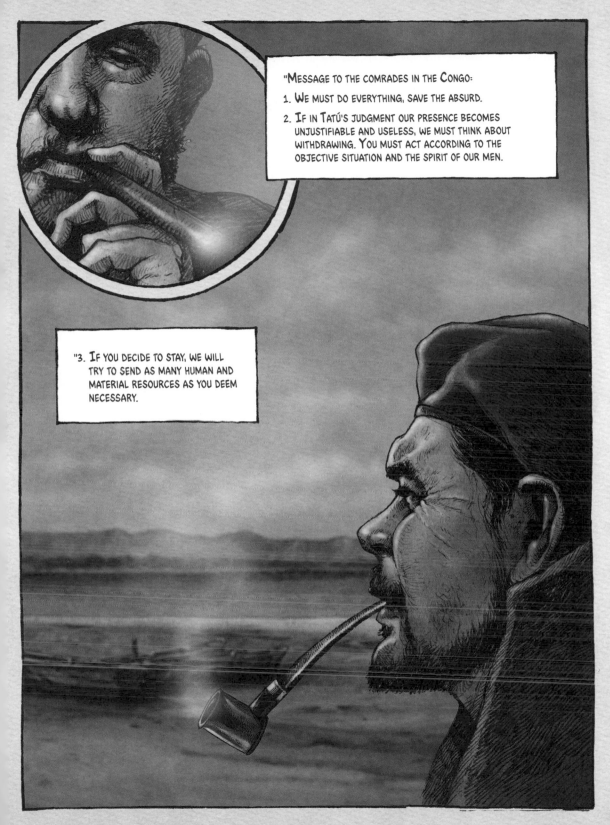

"MESSAGE TO THE COMRADES IN THE CONGO:

1. WE MUST DO EVERYTHING, SAVE THE ABSURD.

2. IF IN TATÚ'S JUDGMENT OUR PRESENCE BECOMES UNJUSTIFIABLE AND USELESS, WE MUST THINK ABOUT WITHDRAWING. YOU MUST ACT ACCORDING TO THE OBJECTIVE SITUATION AND THE SPIRIT OF OUR MEN.

"3. IF YOU DECIDE TO STAY, WE WILL TRY TO SEND AS MANY HUMAN AND MATERIAL RESOURCES AS YOU DEEM NECESSARY.

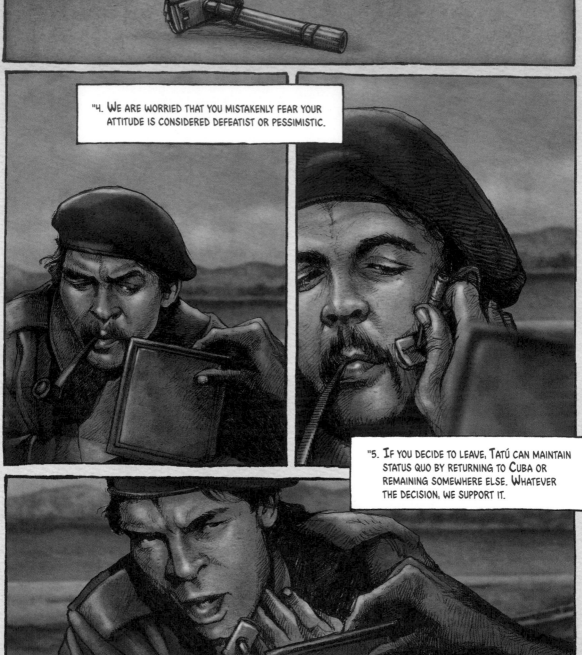

"4. We are worried that you mistakenly fear your attitude is considered defeatist or pessimistic.

"5. If you decide to leave, Tatú can maintain status quo by returning to Cuba or remaining somewhere else. Whatever the decision, we support it.

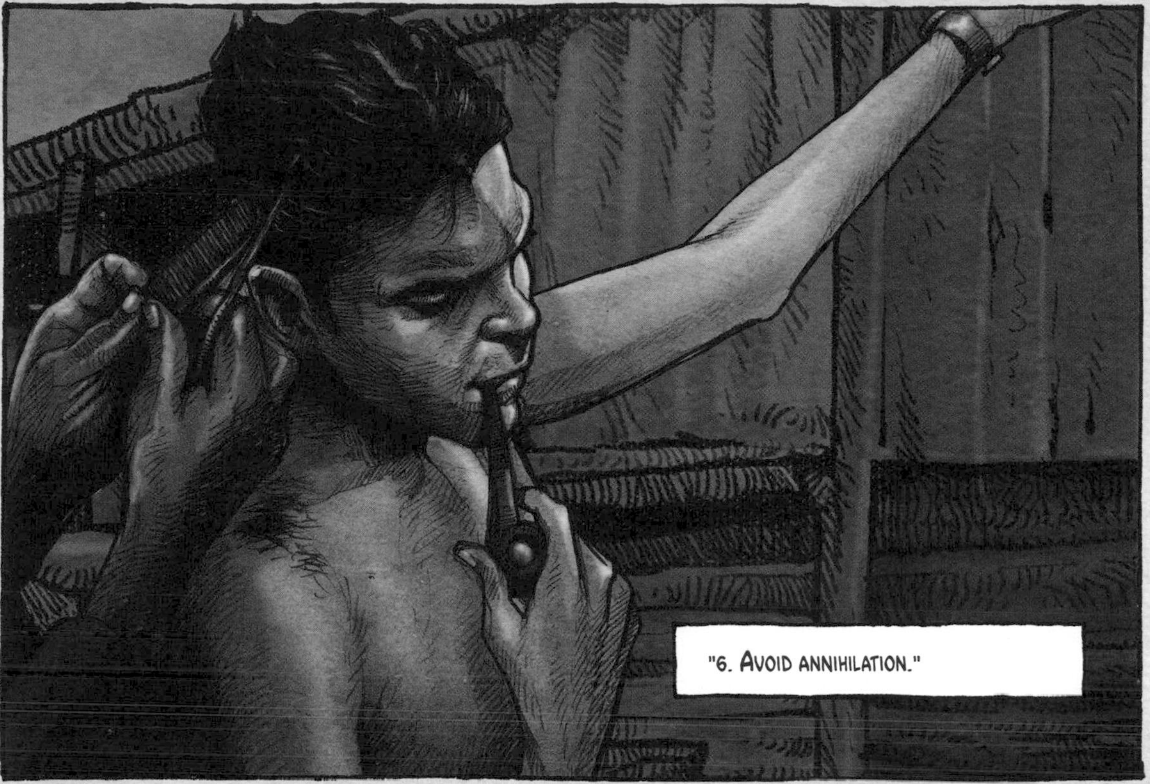
"6. Avoid annihilation."

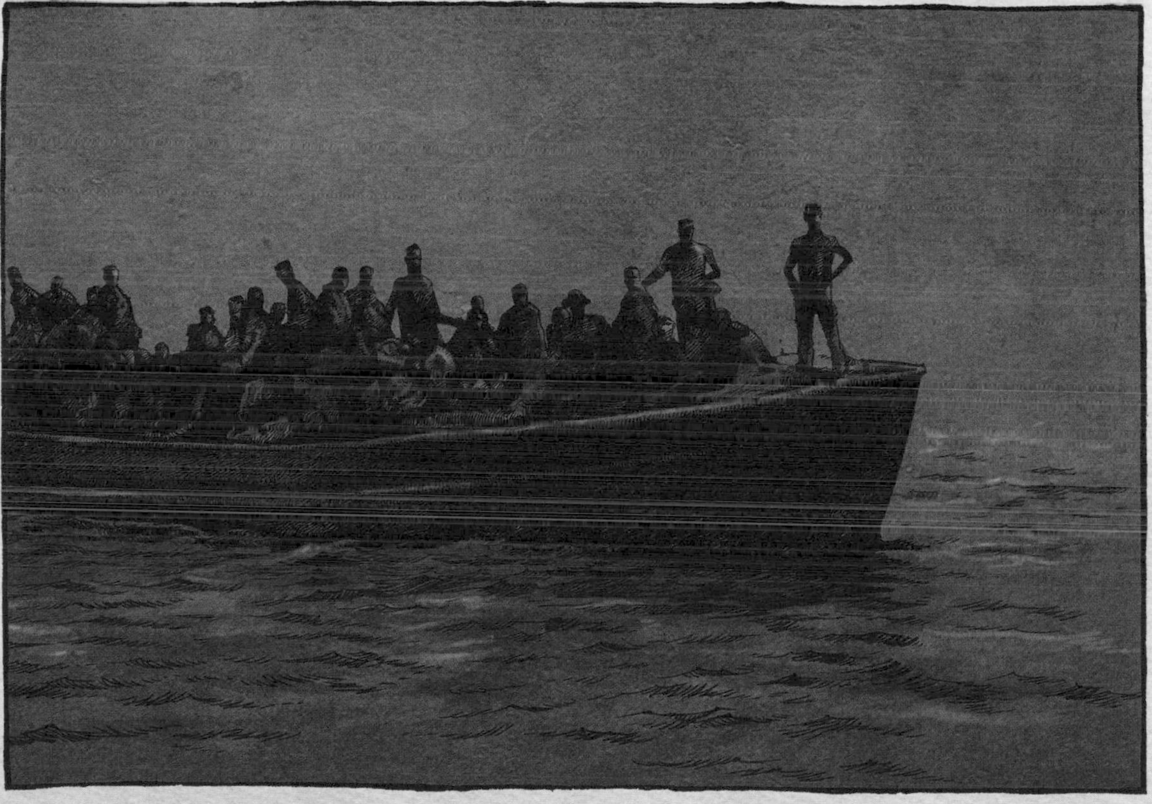

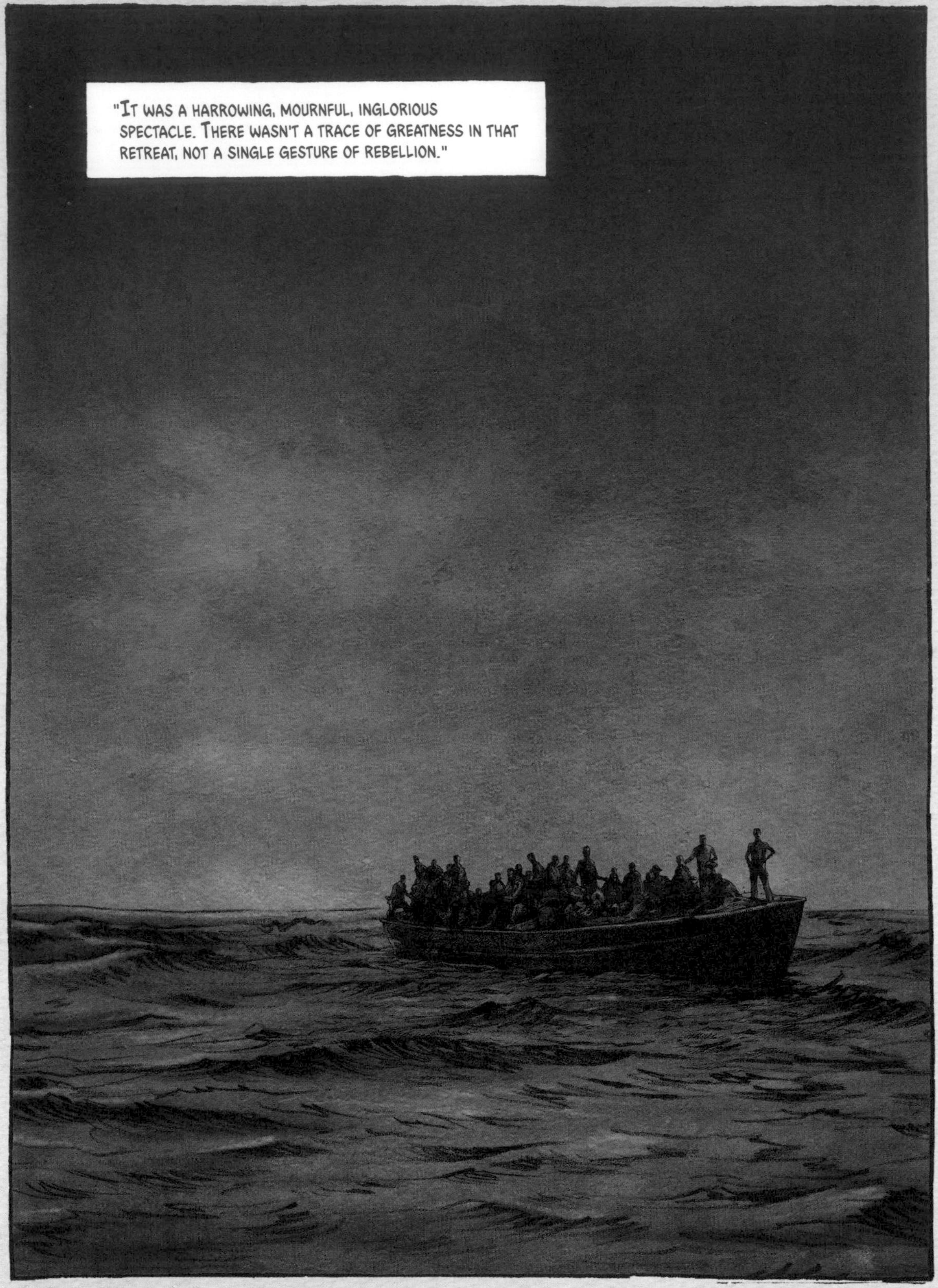
"It was a harrowing, mournful, inglorious spectacle. There wasn't a trace of greatness in that retreat, not a single gesture of rebellion."

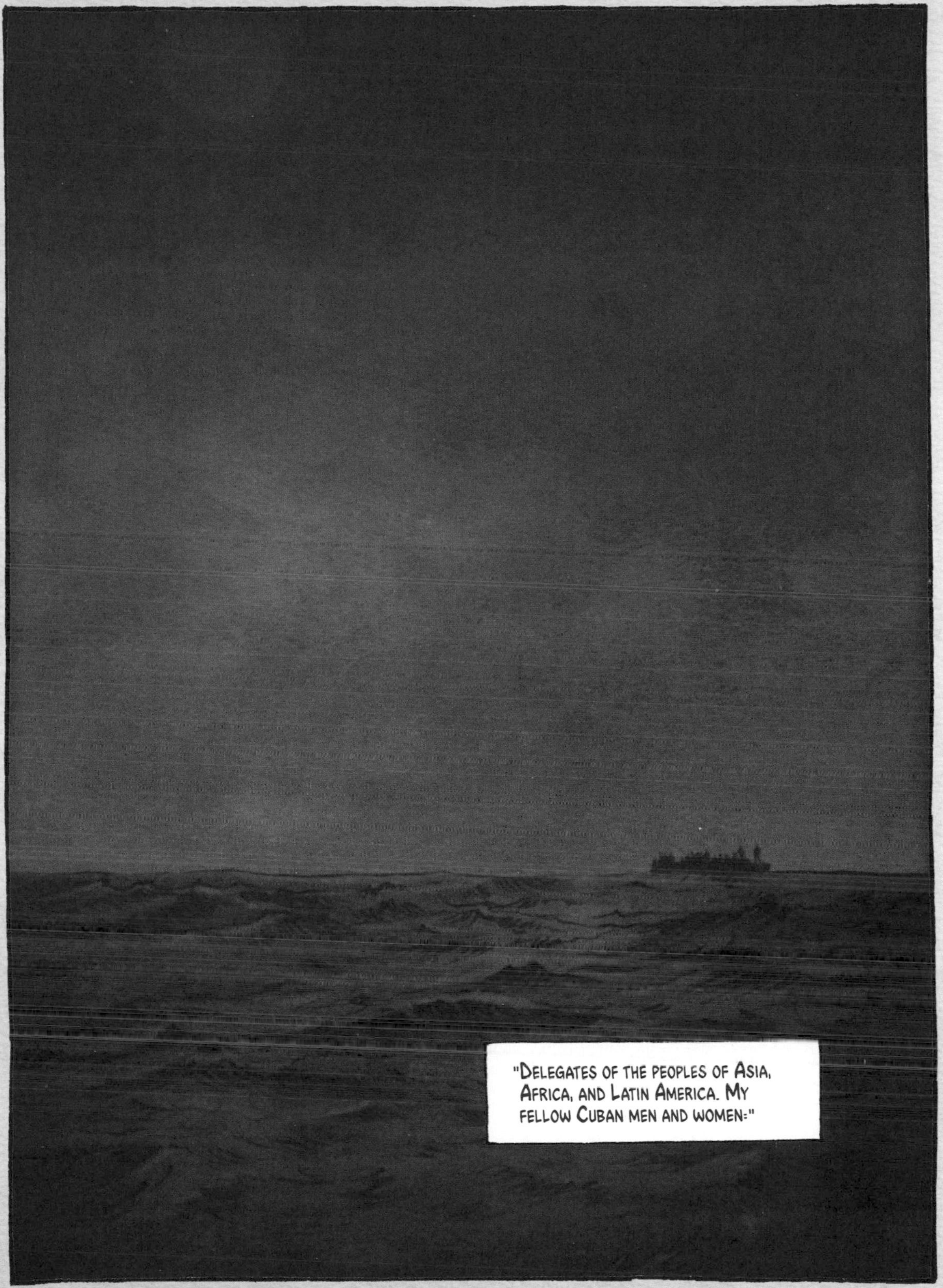
"Delegates of the peoples of Asia, Africa, and Latin America. My fellow Cuban men and women:"

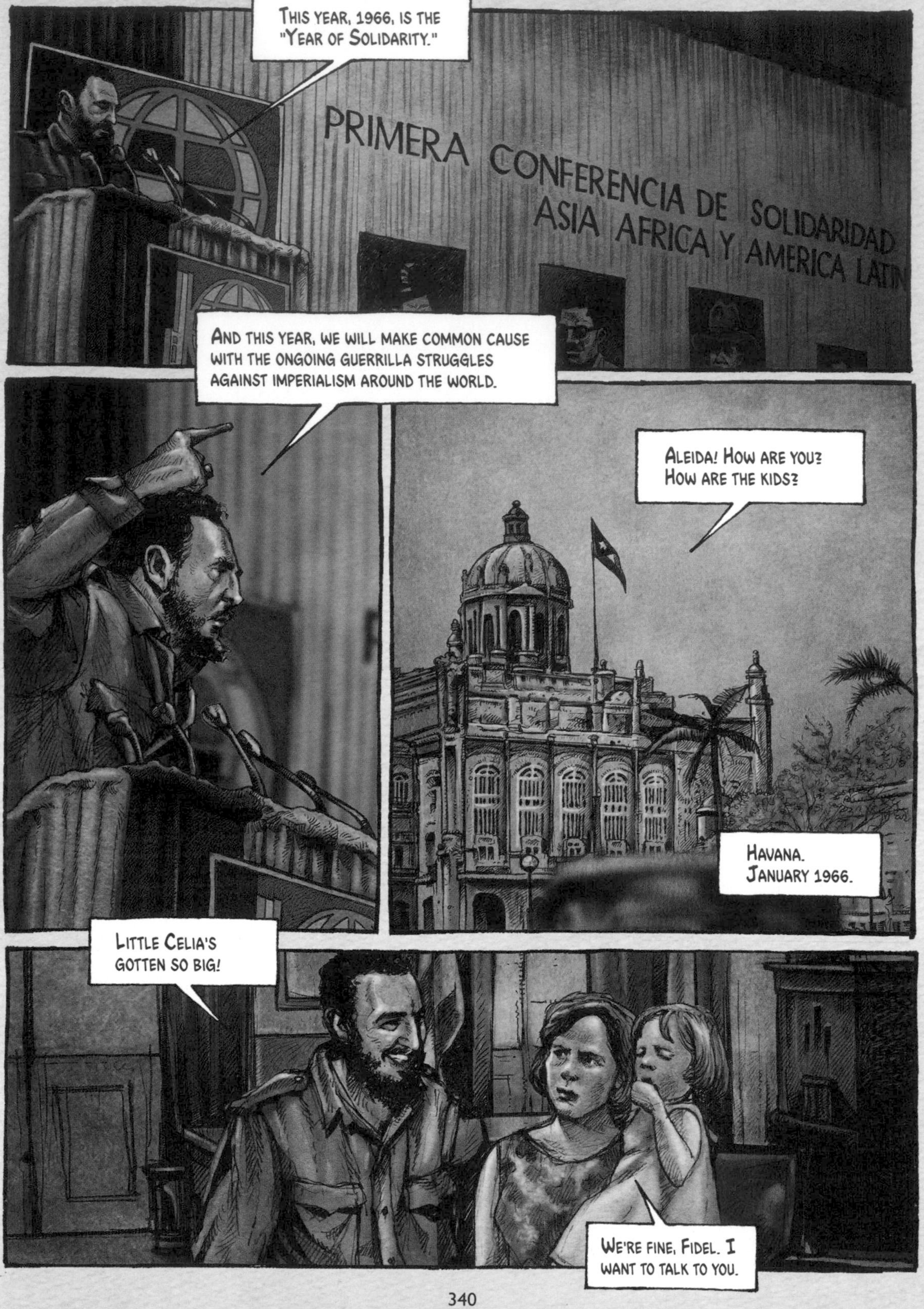
This year, 1966, is the "Year of Solidarity."
PRIMERA CONFERENCIA DE SOLIDARIDAD ASIA AFRICA Y AMERICA LATIN
And this year, we will make common cause with the ongoing guerrilla struggles against imperialism around the world.
Aleida! How are you? How are the kids?
Havana. January 1966.
Little Celia's gotten so big!
We're fine, Fidel. I want to talk to you.

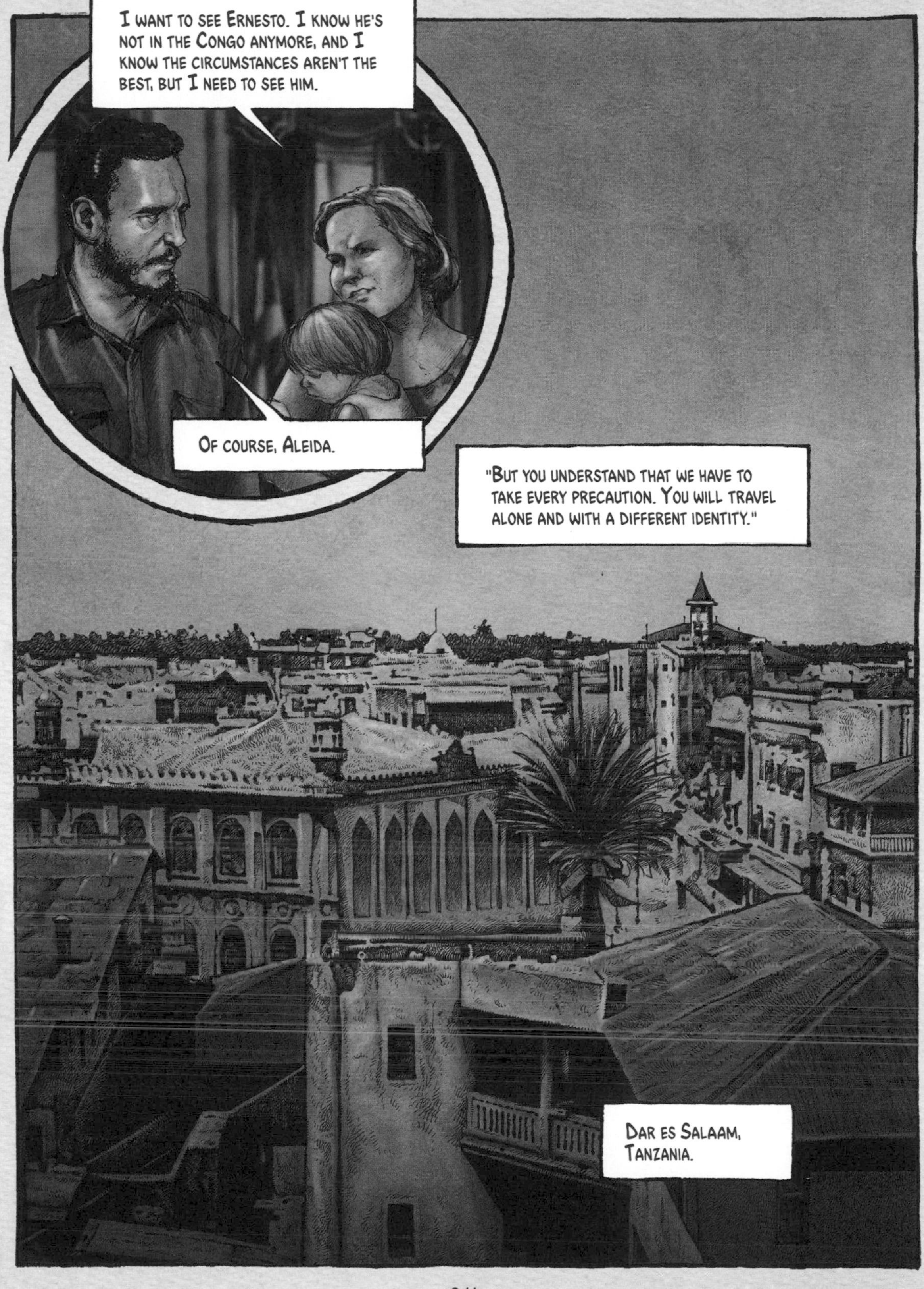
I WANT TO SEE ERNESTO. I KNOW HE'S NOT IN THE CONGO ANYMORE, AND I KNOW THE CIRCUMSTANCES AREN'T THE BEST, BUT I NEED TO SEE HIM.
OF COURSE, ALEIDA.
"BUT YOU UNDERSTAND THAT WE HAVE TO TAKE EVERY PRECAUTION. YOU WILL TRAVEL ALONE AND WITH A DIFFERENT IDENTITY."
DAR ES SALAAM, TANZANIA.

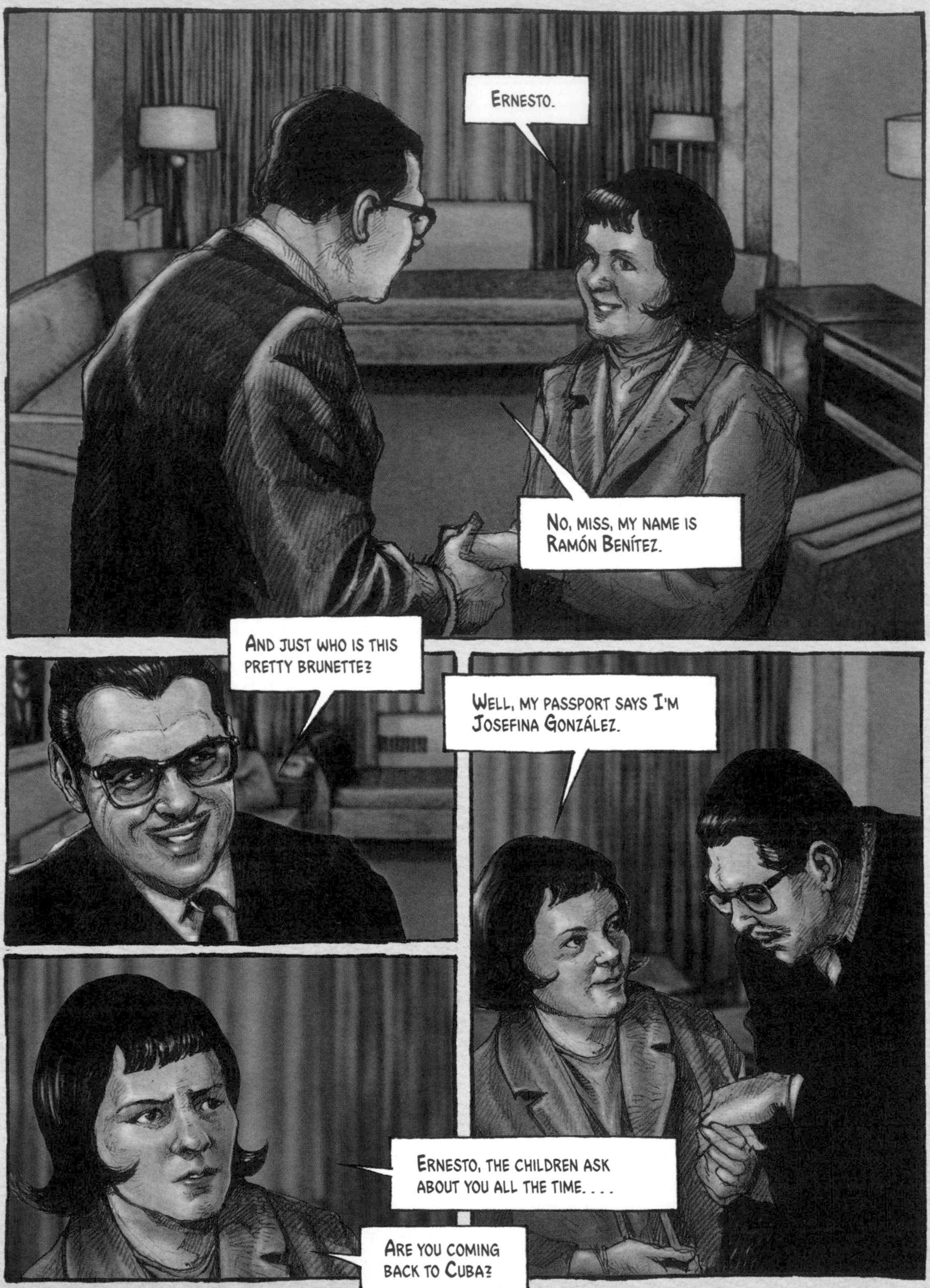
ERNESTO.
NO, MISS, MY NAME IS RAMÓN BENÍTEZ.
AND JUST WHO IS THIS PRETTY BRUNETTE?
WELL, MY PASSPORT SAYS I'M JOSEFINA GONZÁLEZ.
ERNESTO, THE CHILDREN ASK ABOUT YOU ALL THE TIME. . . .
ARE YOU COMING BACK TO CUBA?

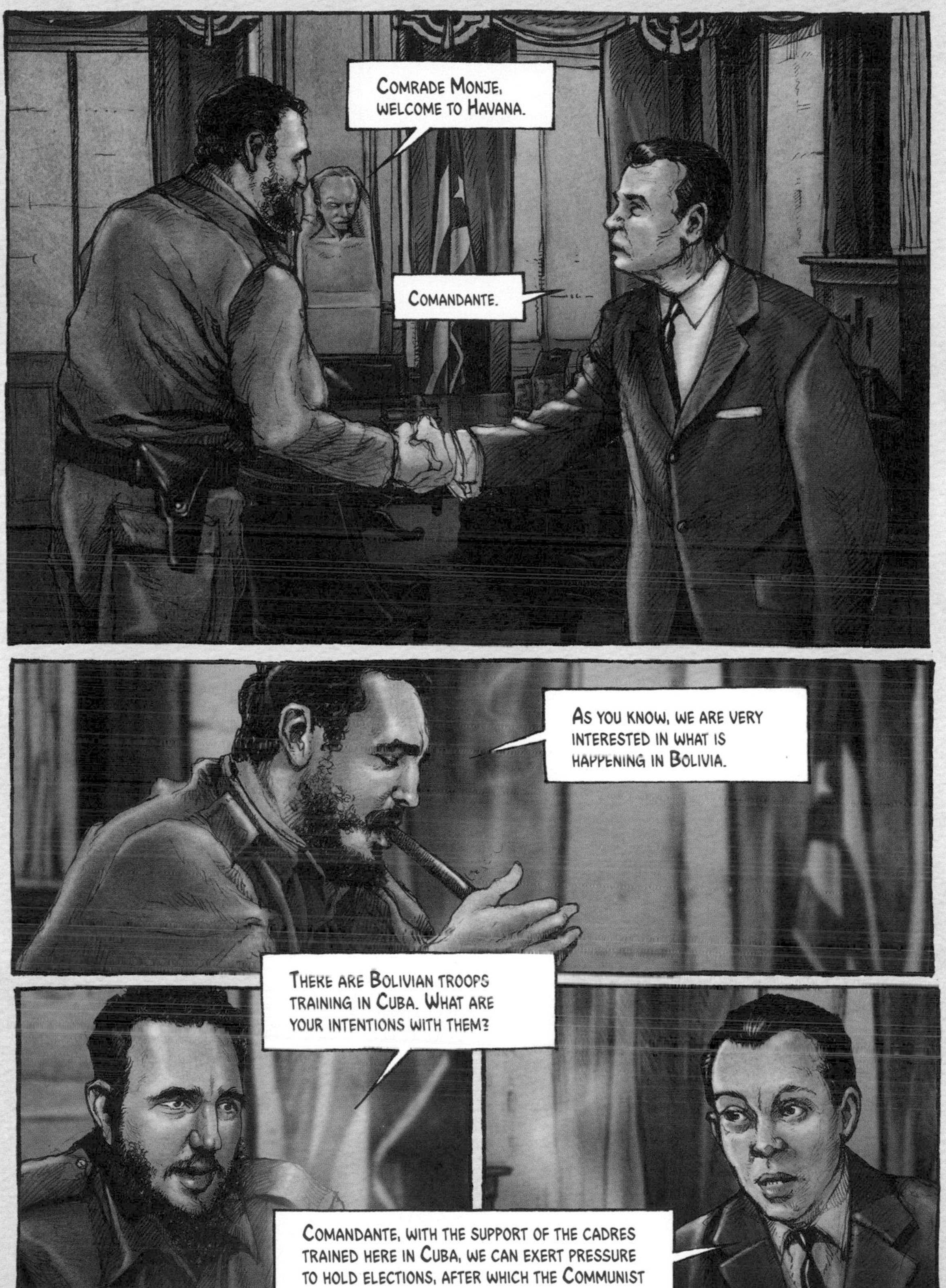
Comrade Monje, welcome to Havana.
Comandante.
As you know, we are very interested in what is happening in Bolivia.
There are Bolivian troops training in Cuba. What are your intentions with them?
Comandante, with the support of the cadres trained here in Cuba, we can exert pressure to hold elections, after which the Communist position will be strengthened.

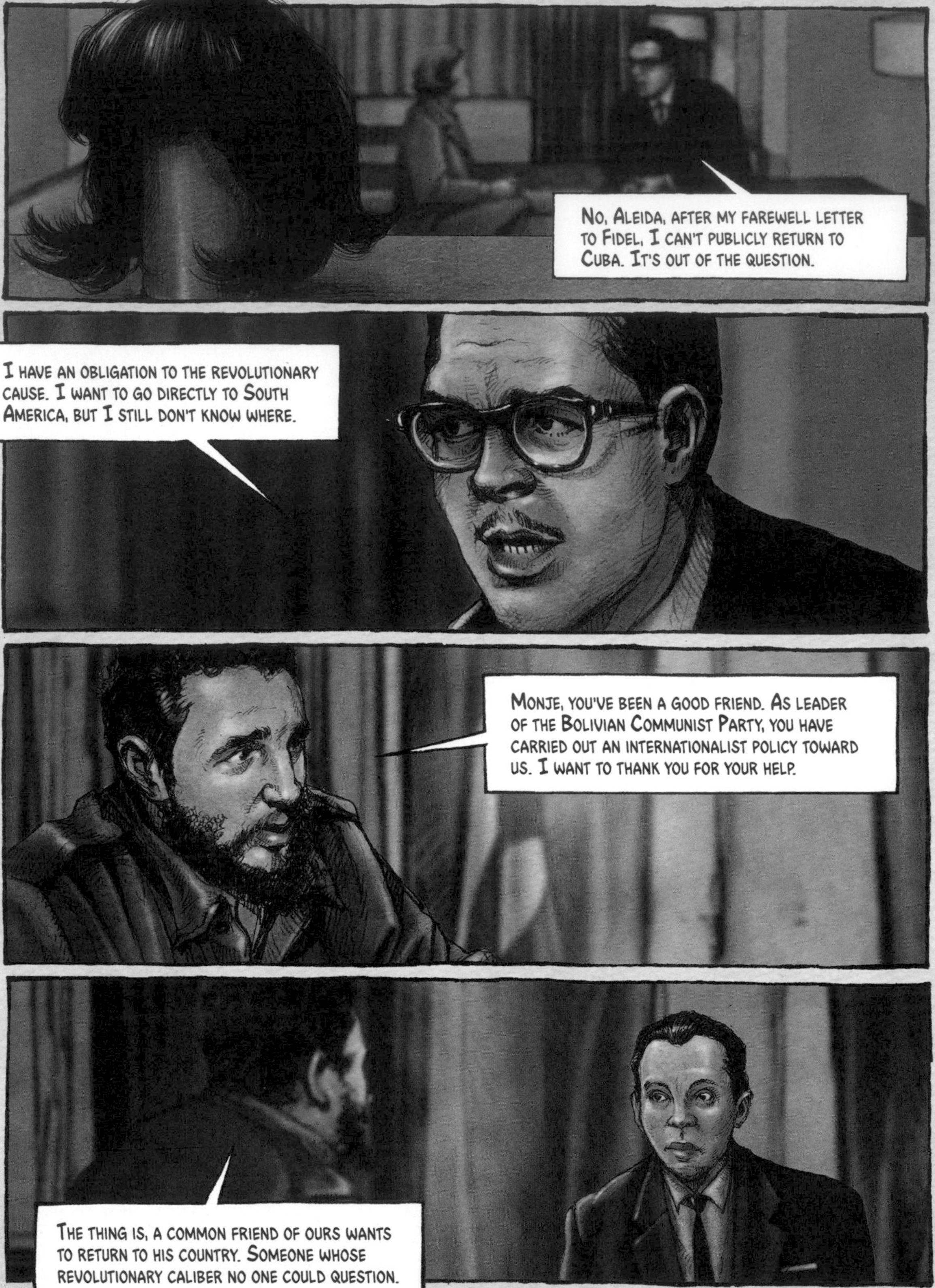
No, Aleida, after my farewell letter to Fidel, I can't publicly return to Cuba. It's out of the question.
I have an obligation to the revolutionary cause. I want to go directly to South America, but I still don't know where.
Monje, you've been a good friend. As leader of the Bolivian Communist Party, you have carried out an internationalist policy toward us. I want to thank you for your help.
The thing is, a common friend of ours wants to return to his country. Someone whose revolutionary caliber no one could question.

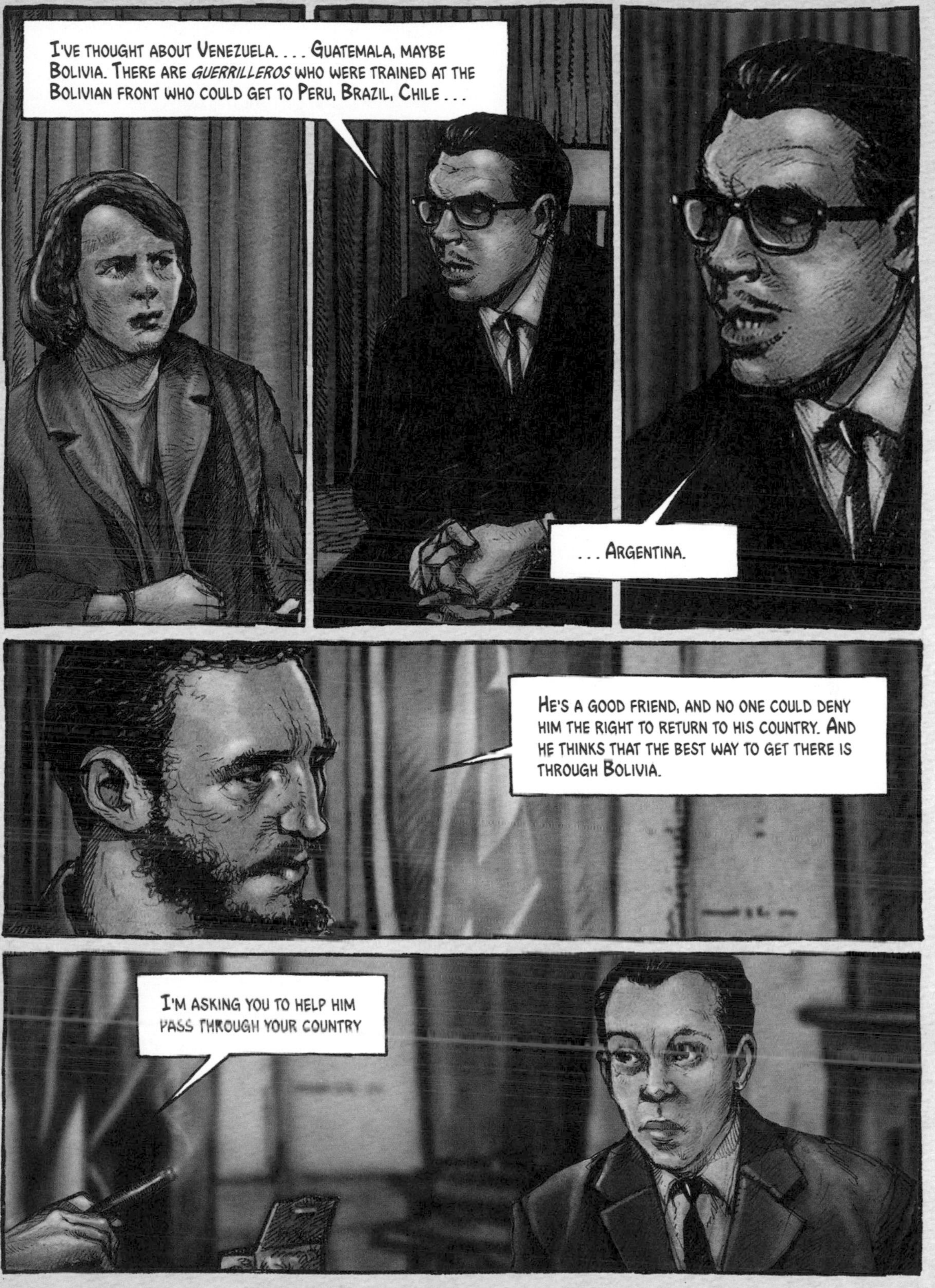
I'VE THOUGHT ABOUT VENEZUELA. . . . GUATEMALA, MAYBE BOLIVIA. THERE ARE *GUERRILLEROS* WHO WERE TRAINED AT THE BOLIVIAN FRONT WHO COULD GET TO PERU, BRAZIL, CHILE . . .
. . . ARGENTINA.
HE'S A GOOD FRIEND, AND NO ONE COULD DENY HIM THE RIGHT TO RETURN TO HIS COUNTRY. AND HE THINKS THAT THE BEST WAY TO GET THERE IS THROUGH BOLIVIA.
I'M ASKING YOU TO HELP HIM PASS THROUGH YOUR COUNTRY

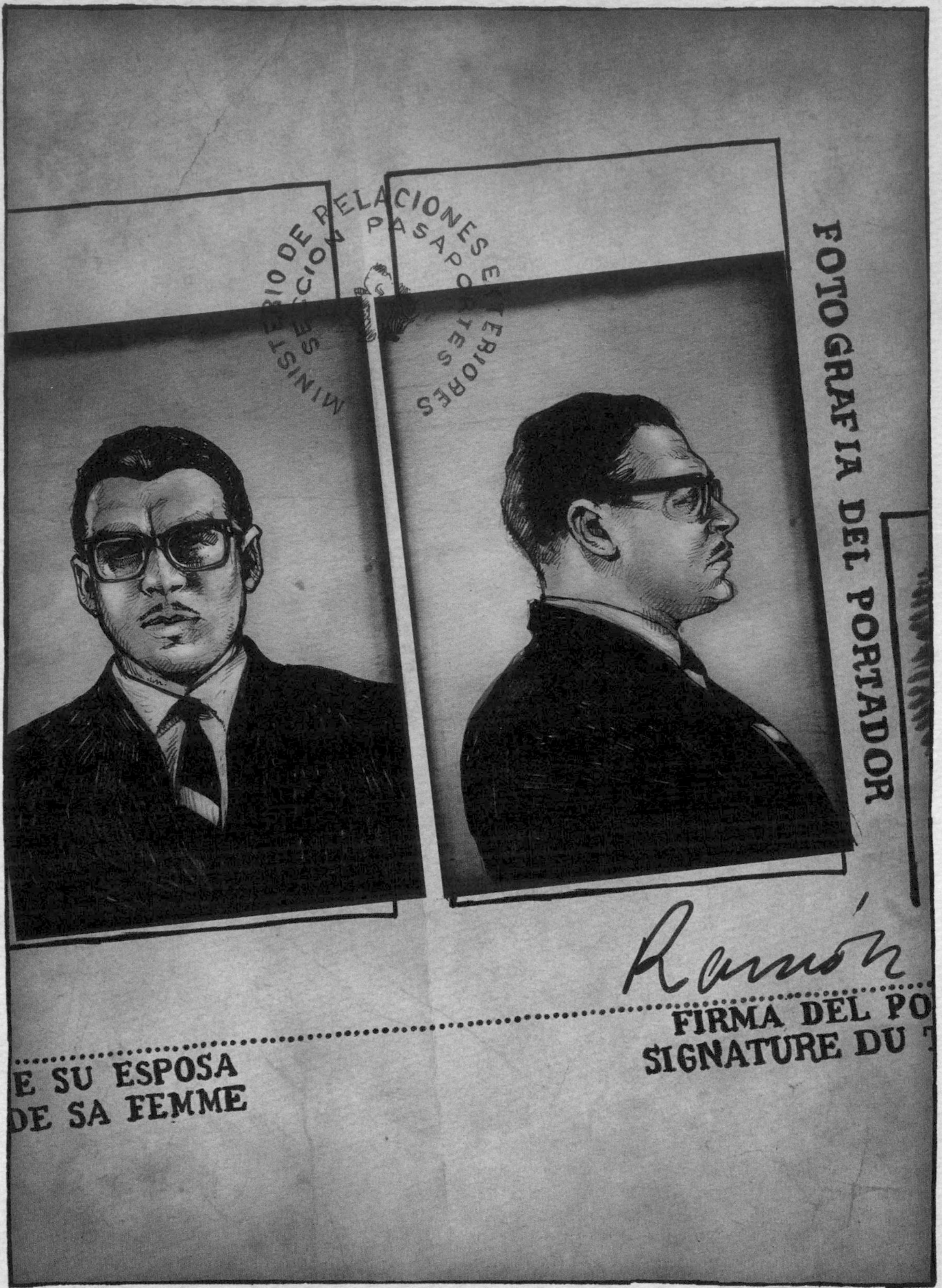
MINISTERIO DE RELACIONES EXTERIORES
SECCION PASAPORTES
FOTOGRAFIA DEL PORTADOR
Ramón
FIRMA DEL PO
SIGNATURE DU
E SU ESPOSA
DE SA FEMME

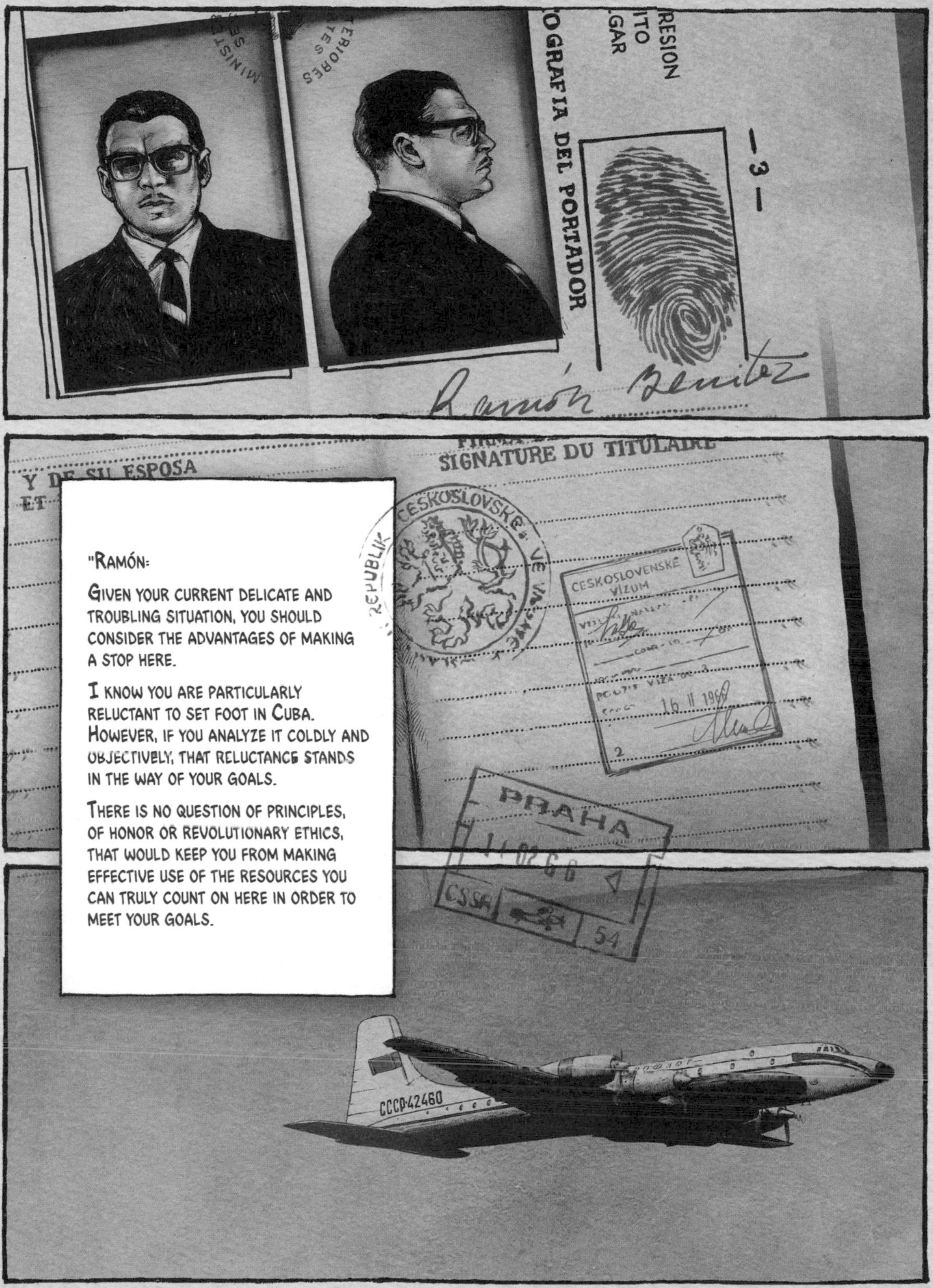
"Ramón:
Given your current delicate and troubling situation, you should consider the advantages of making a stop here.
I know you are particularly reluctant to set foot in Cuba. However, if you analyze it coldly and objectively, that reluctance stands in the way of your goals.
There is no question of principles, of honor or revolutionary ethics, that would keep you from making effective use of the resources you can truly count on here in order to meet your goals.
— 3 —
Ramón Benitez
SIGNATURE DU TITULAIRE
Y DE SU ESPOSA
ČESKOSLOVENSKÉ VÍZUM
PRAHA
CSSR
54
CCCP-42460

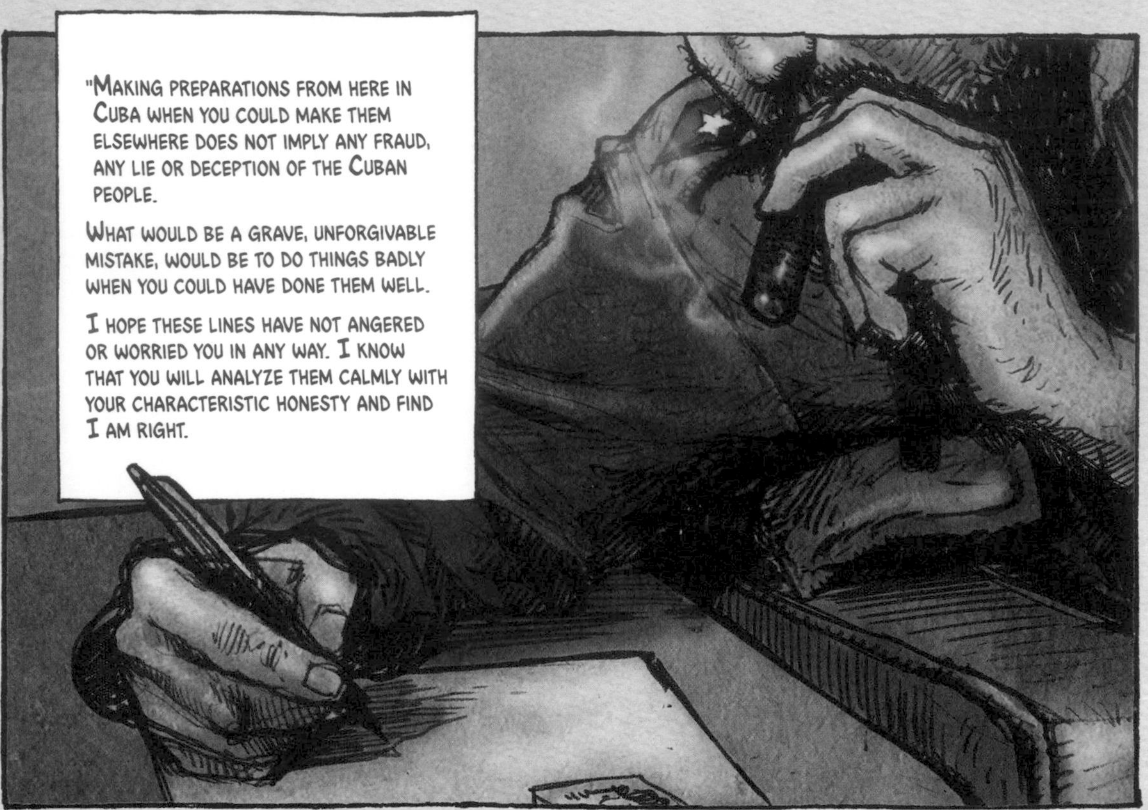
"Making preparations from here in Cuba when you could make them elsewhere does not imply any fraud, any lie or deception of the Cuban people.
What would be a grave, unforgivable mistake, would be to do things badly when you could have done them well.
I hope these lines have not angered or worried you in any way. I know that you will analyze them calmly with your characteristic honesty and find I am right.

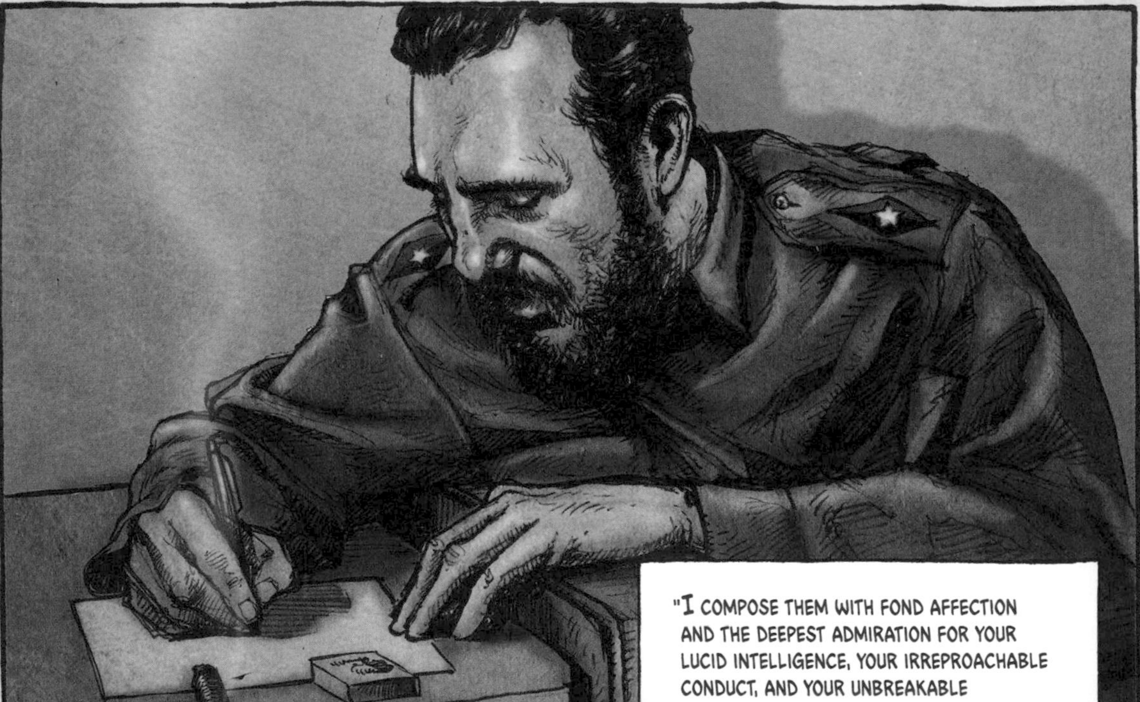
"I compose them with fond affection and the deepest admiration for your lucid intelligence, your irreproachable conduct, and your unbreakable revolutionary character."

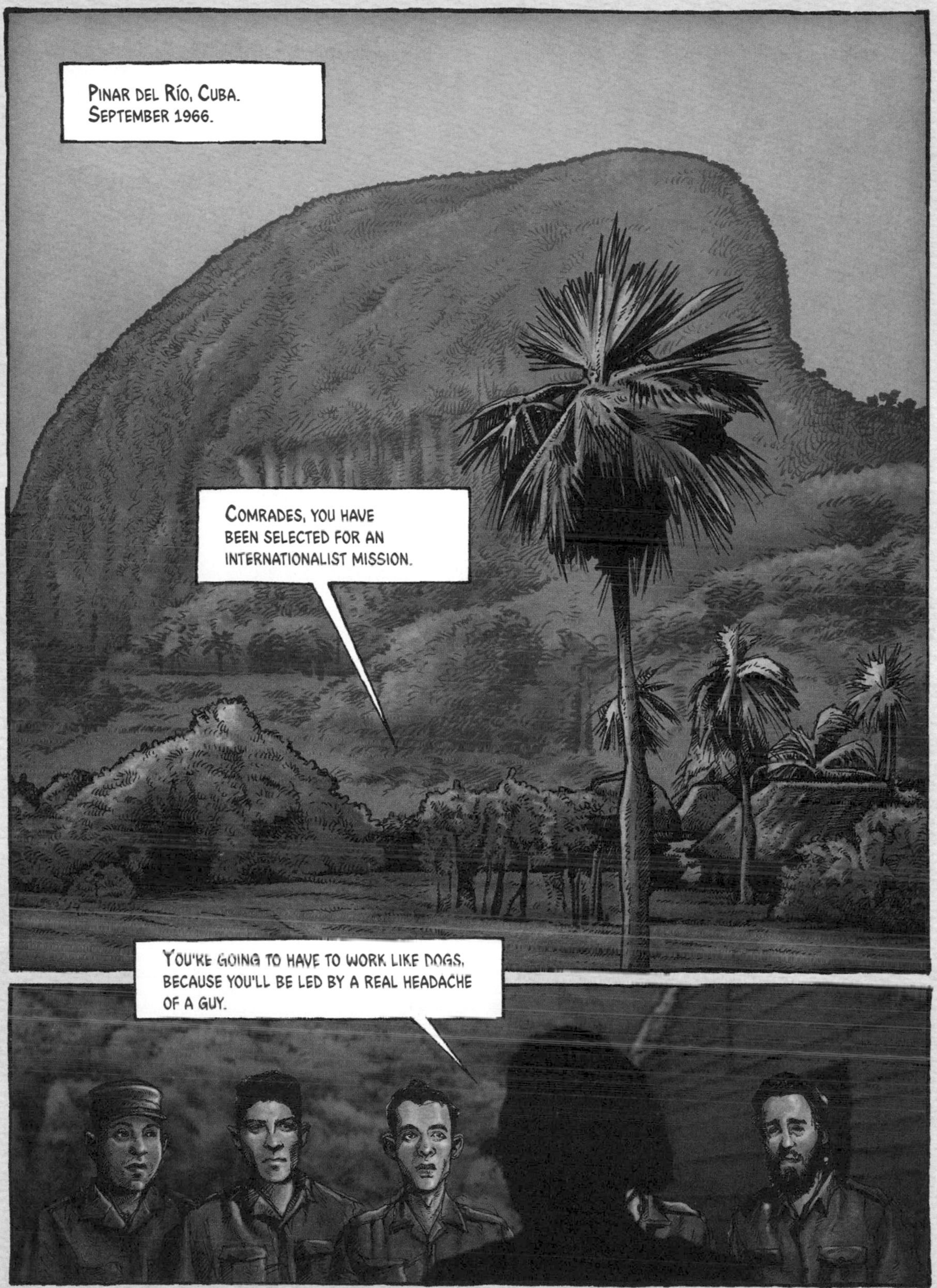
Pinar del Río, Cuba.
September 1966.
Comrades, you have been selected for an internationalist mission.
You're going to have to work like dogs, because you'll be led by a real headache of a guy.

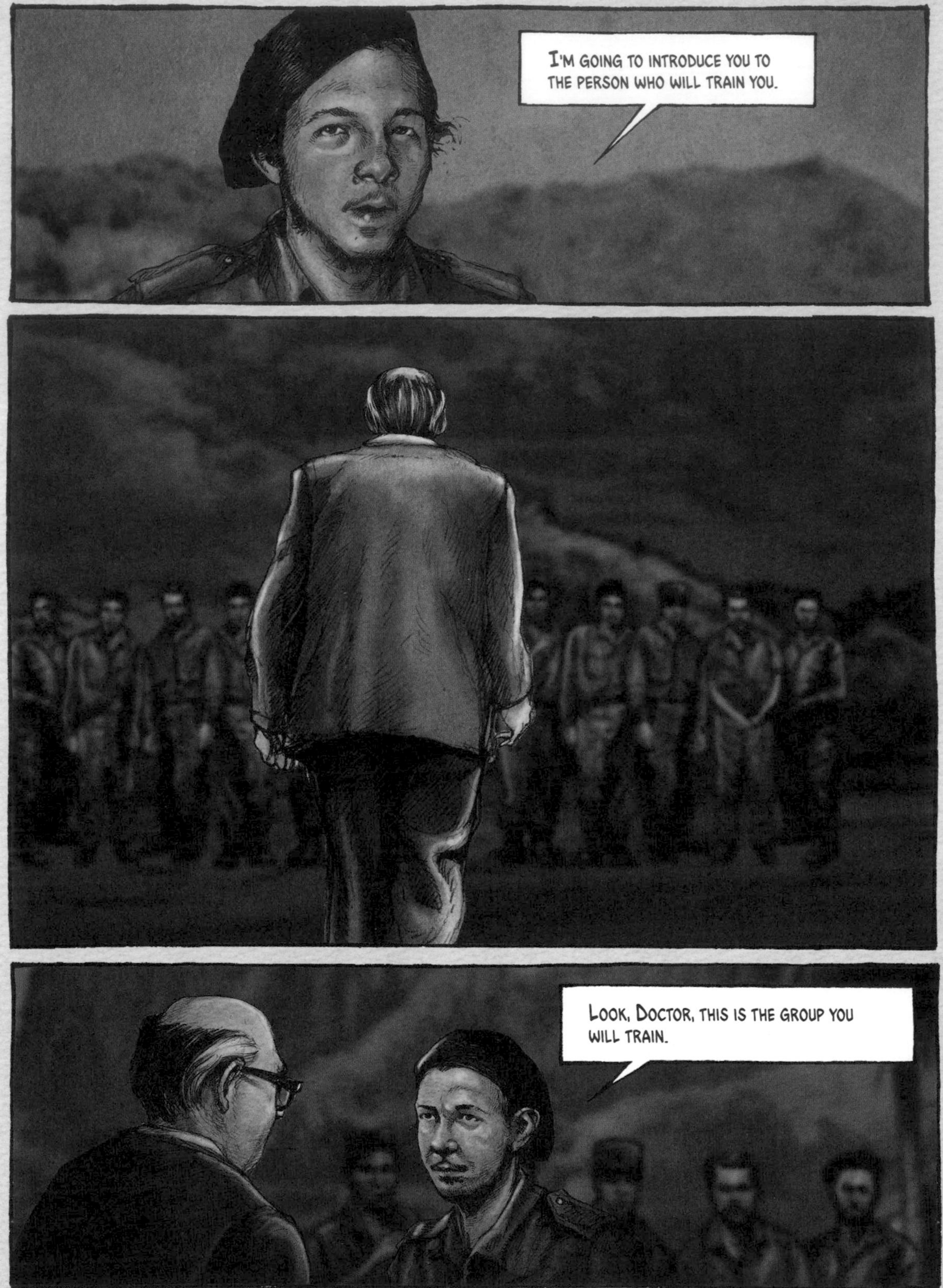
I'M GOING TO INTRODUCE YOU TO THE PERSON WHO WILL TRAIN YOU.
LOOK, DOCTOR, THIS IS THE GROUP YOU WILL TRAIN.

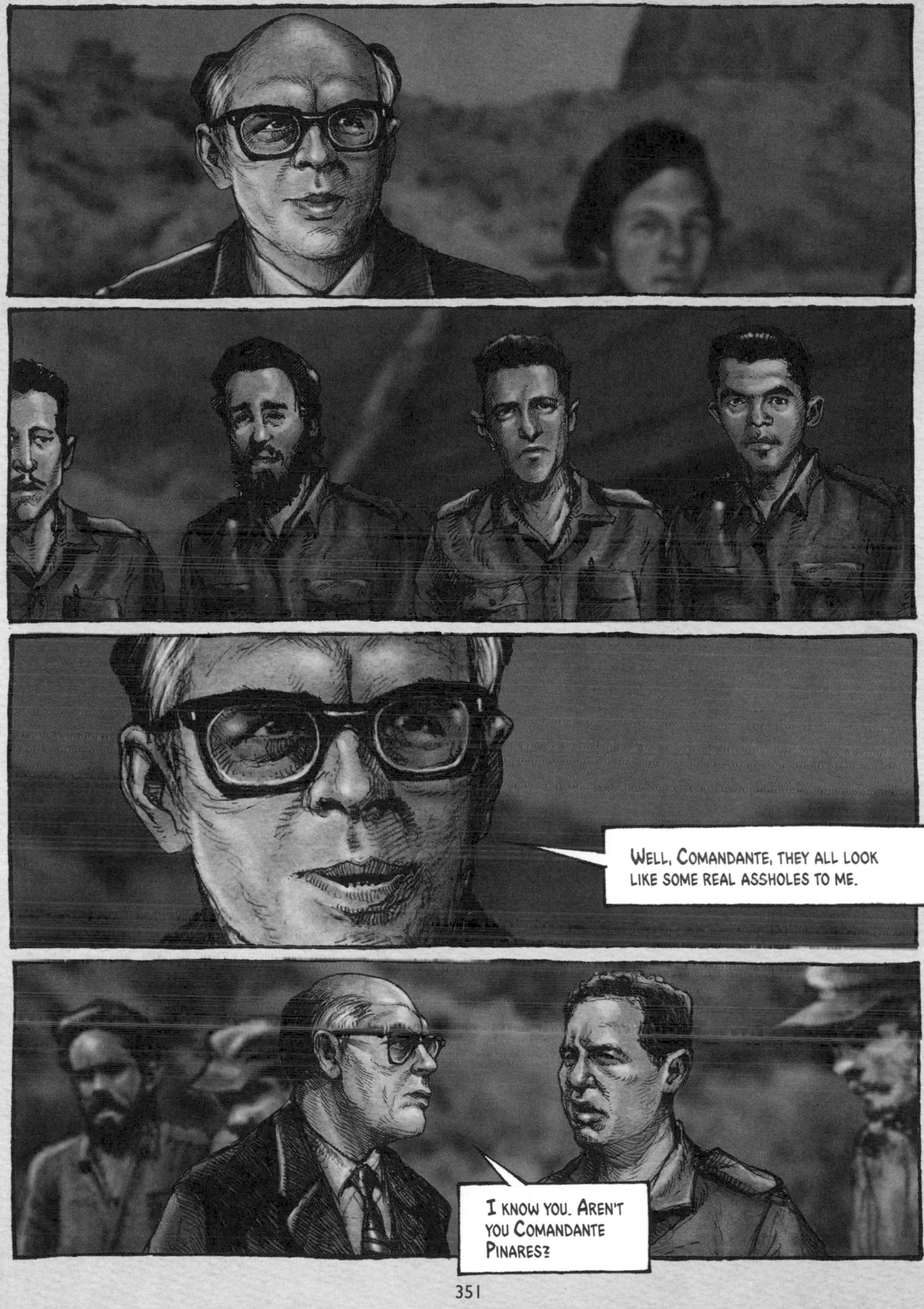

WELL, COMANDANTE, THEY ALL LOOK LIKE SOME REAL ASSHOLES TO ME.
I KNOW YOU. AREN'T YOU COMANDANTE PINARES?

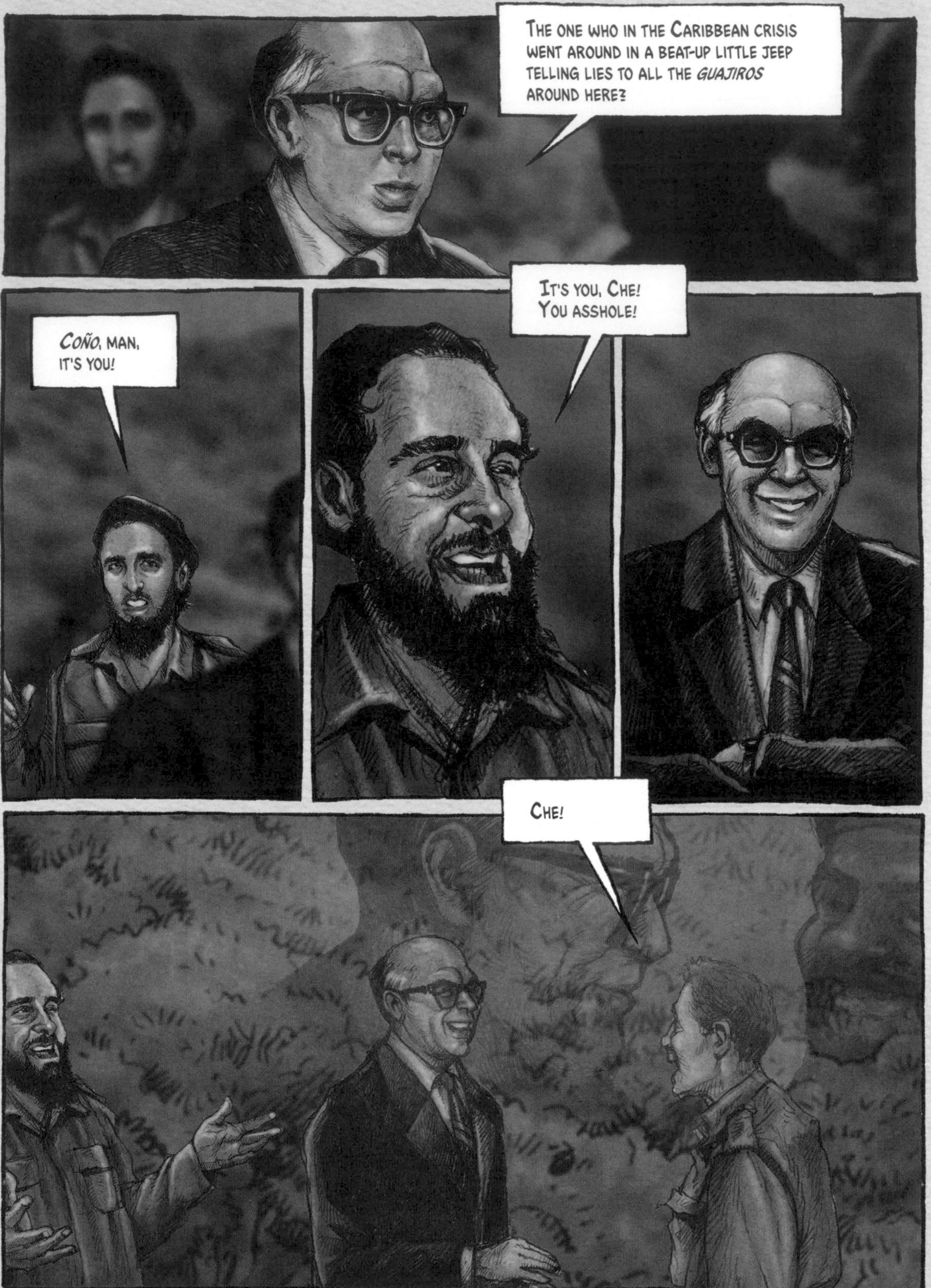
THE ONE WHO IN THE CARIBBEAN CRISIS WENT AROUND IN A BEAT-UP LITTLE JEEP TELLING LIES TO ALL THE *GUAJIROS* AROUND HERE?
COÑO, MAN, IT'S YOU!
IT'S YOU, CHE! YOU ASSHOLE!
CHE!

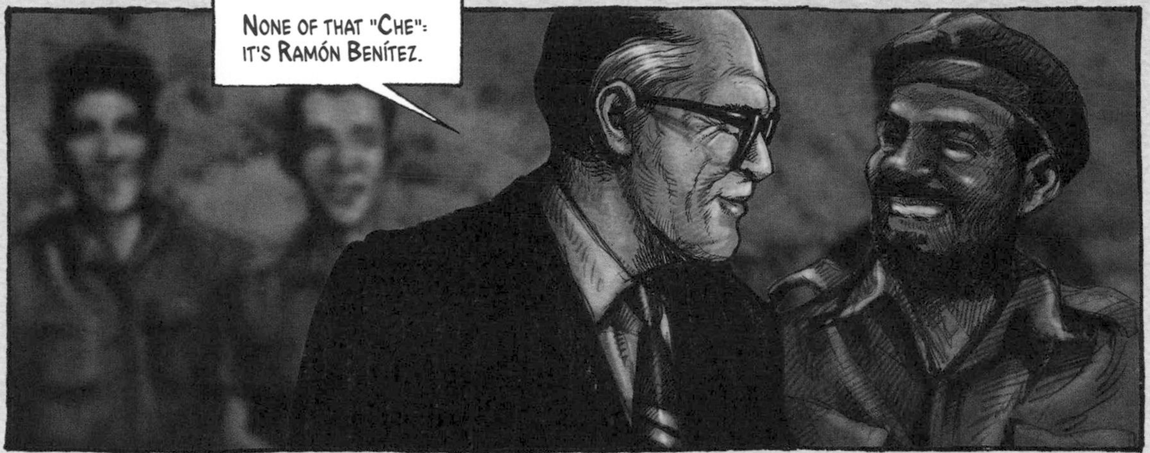
NONE OF THAT "CHE": IT'S RAMÓN BENÍTEZ.

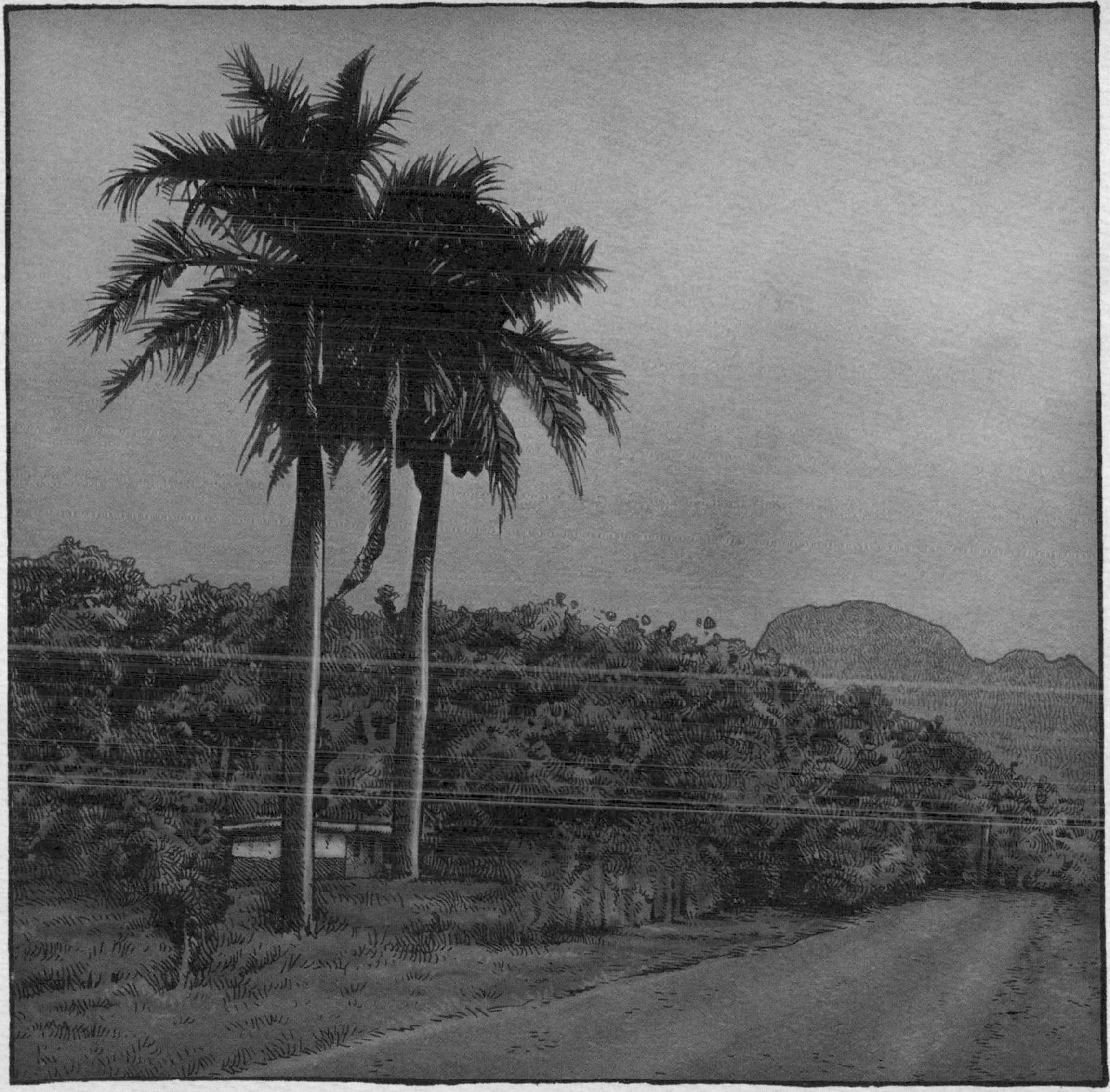

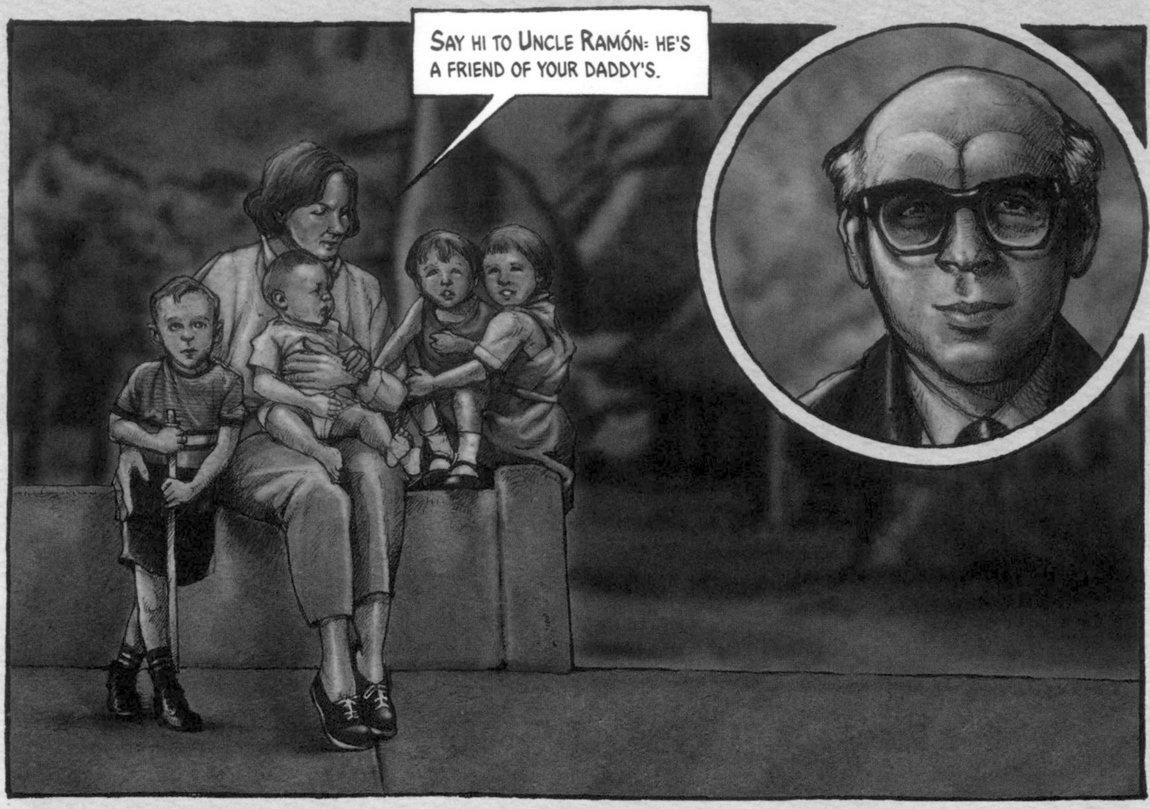
SAY HI TO UNCLE RAMÓN: HE'S A FRIEND OF YOUR DADDY'S.

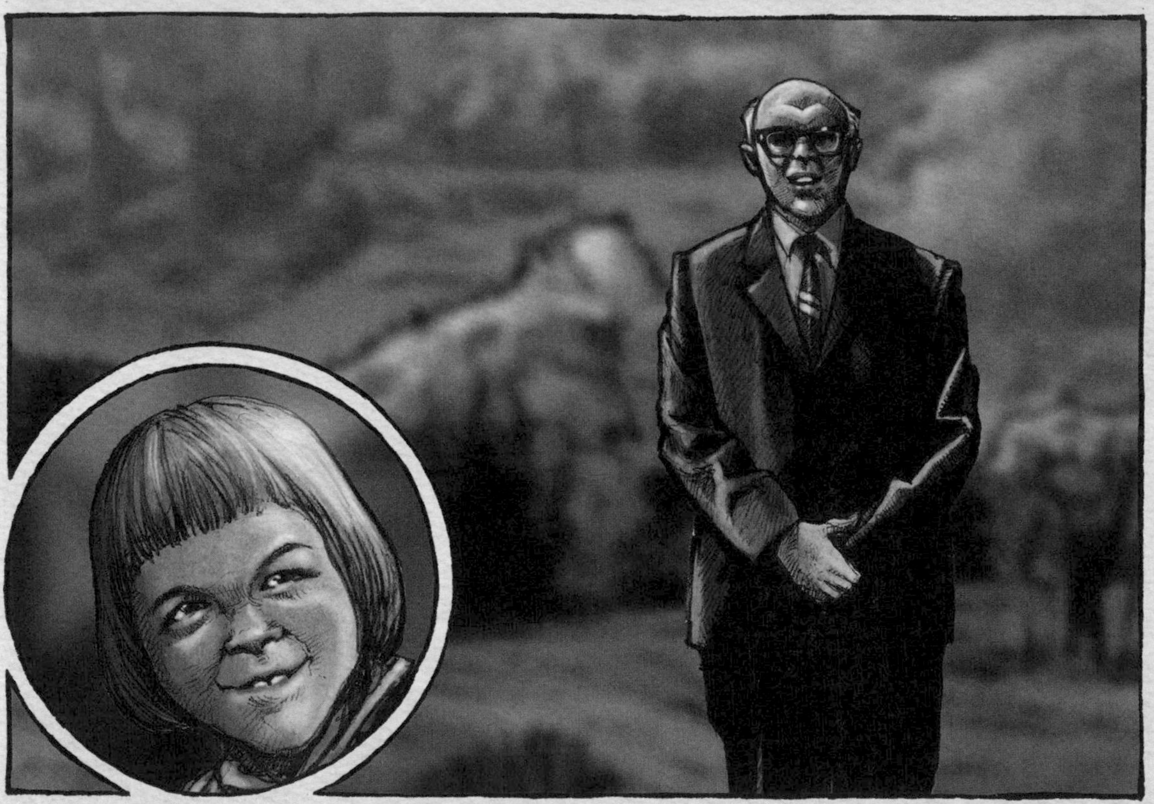

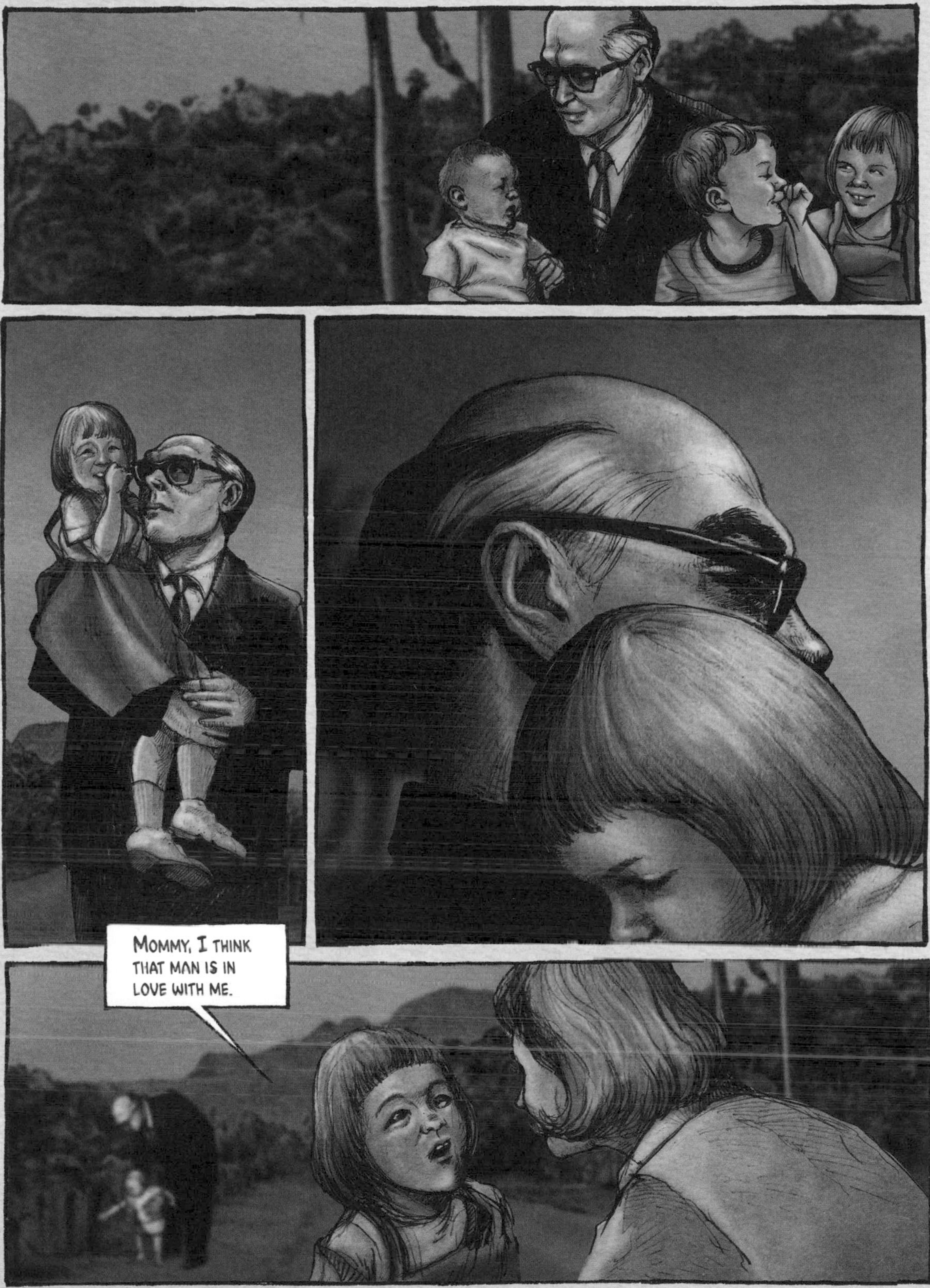
MOMMY, I THINK THAT MAN IS IN LOVE WITH ME.

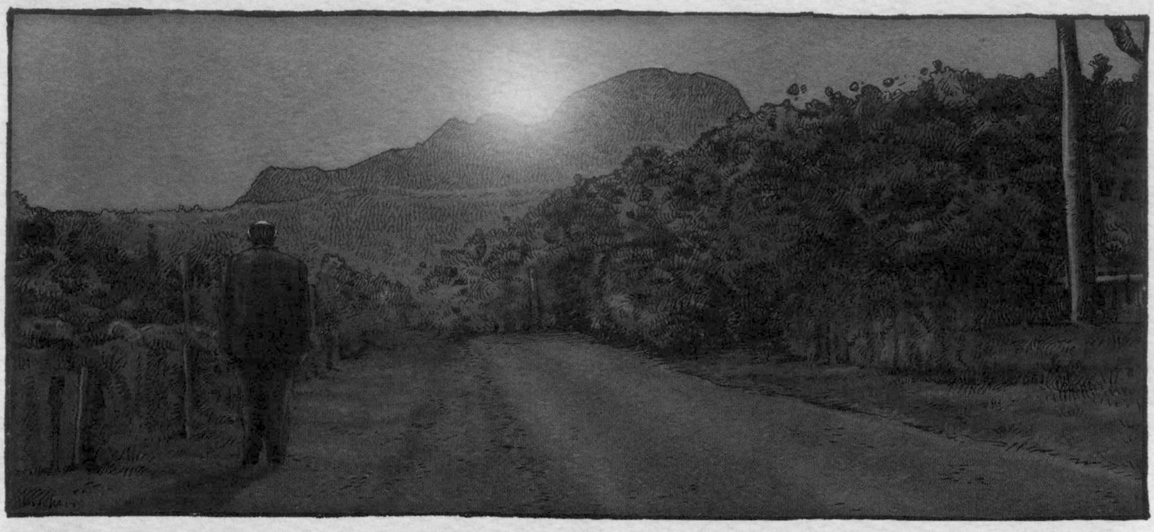

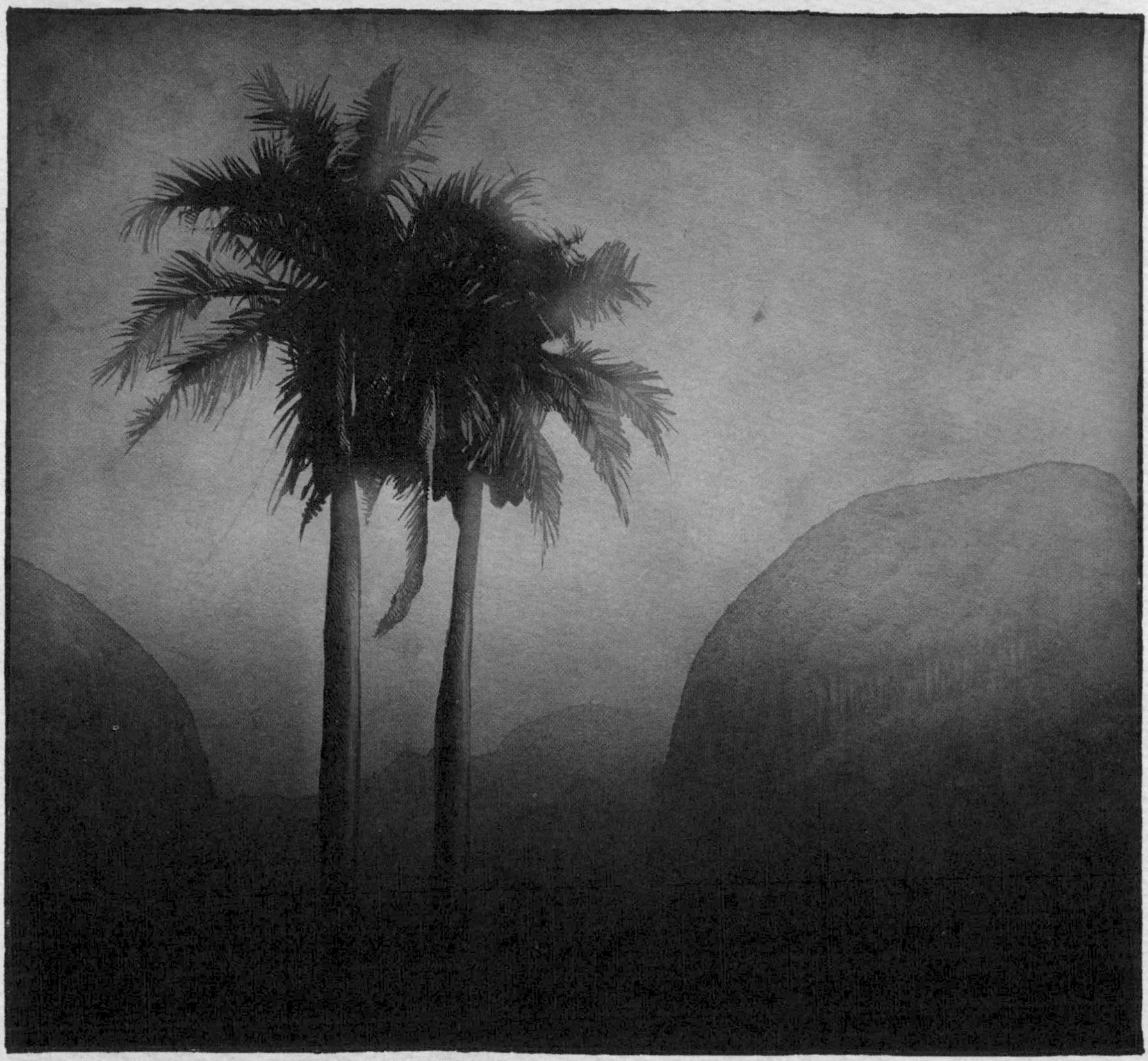

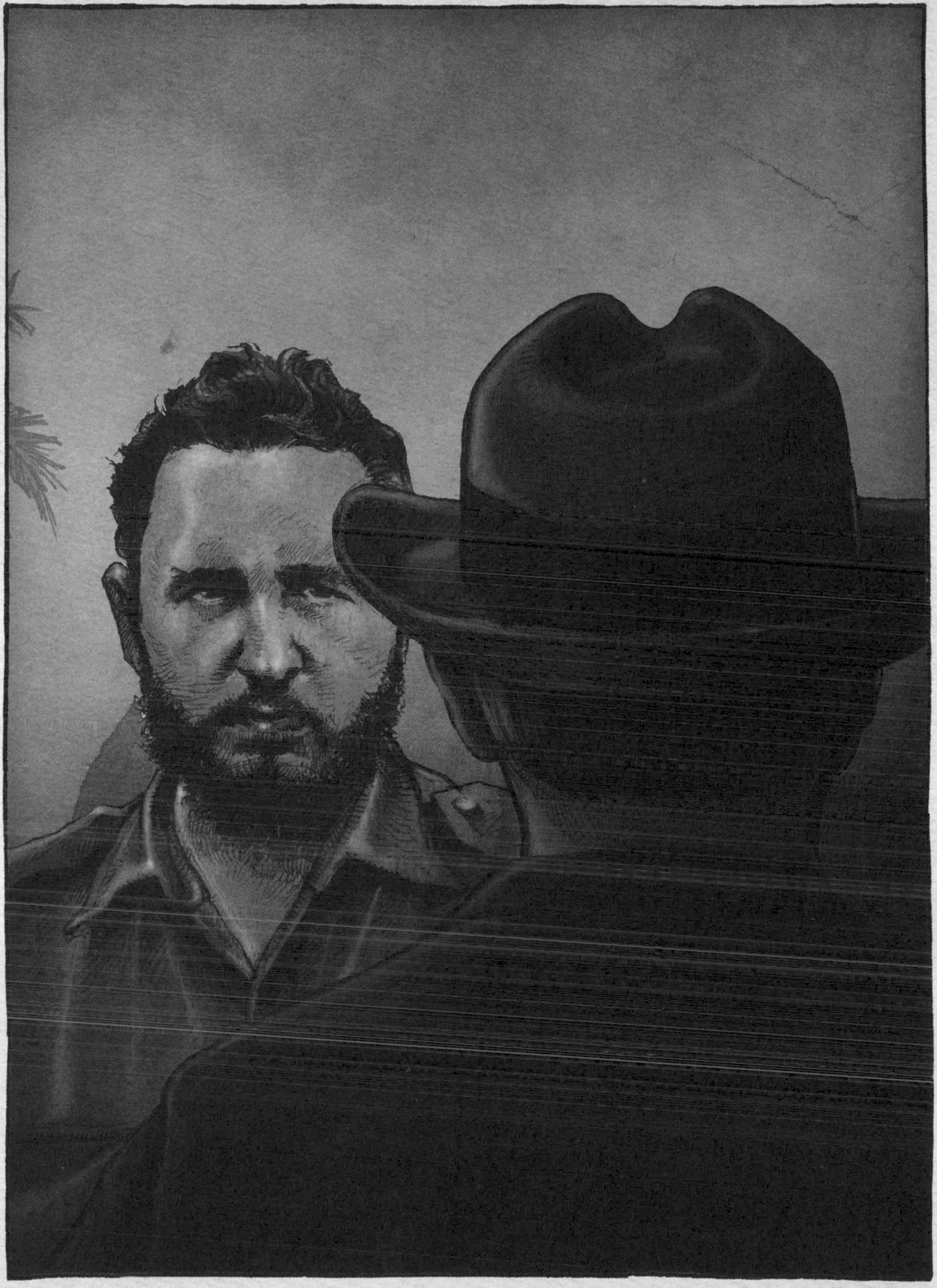

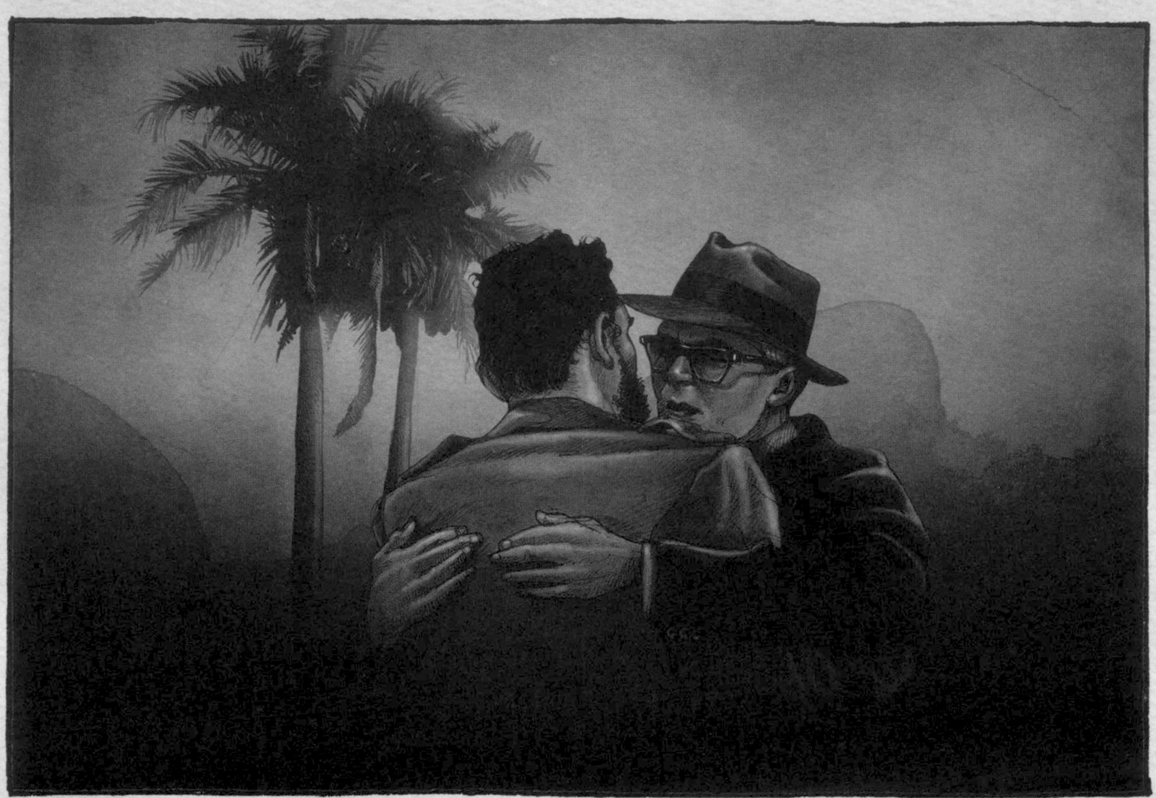

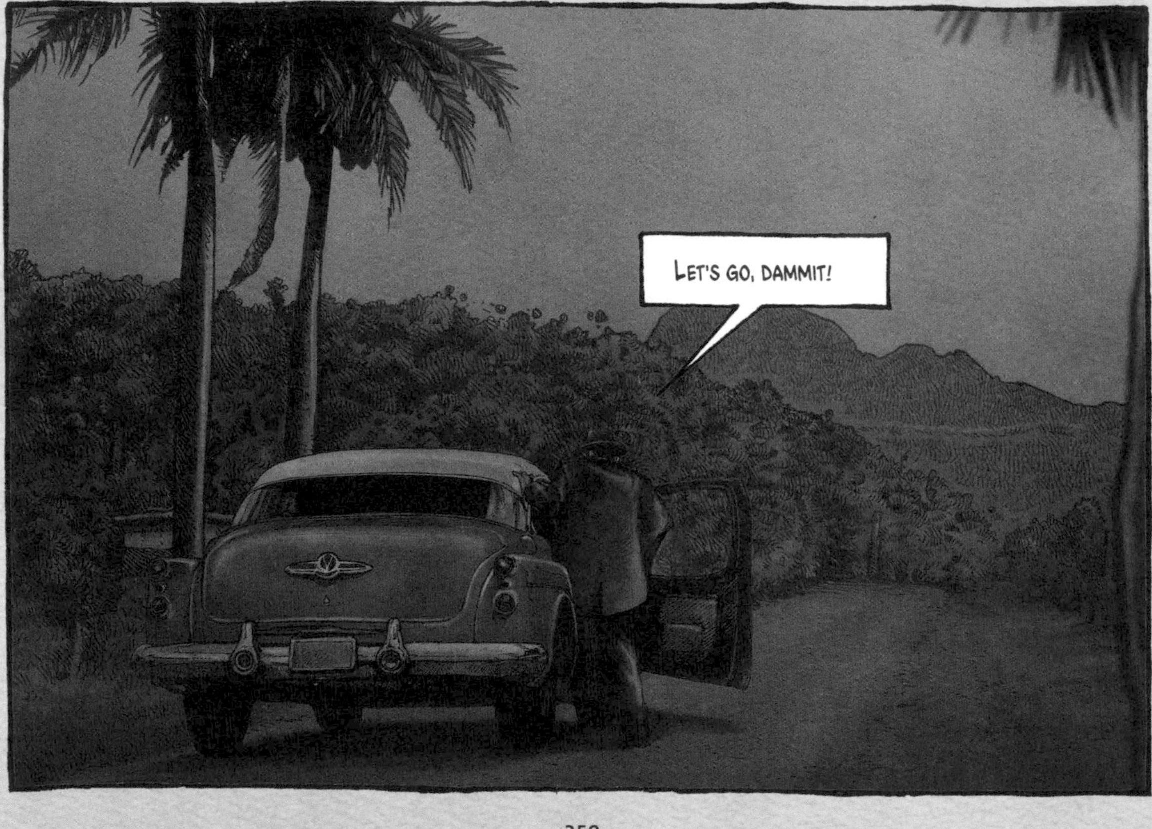

LET'S GO, DAMMIT!

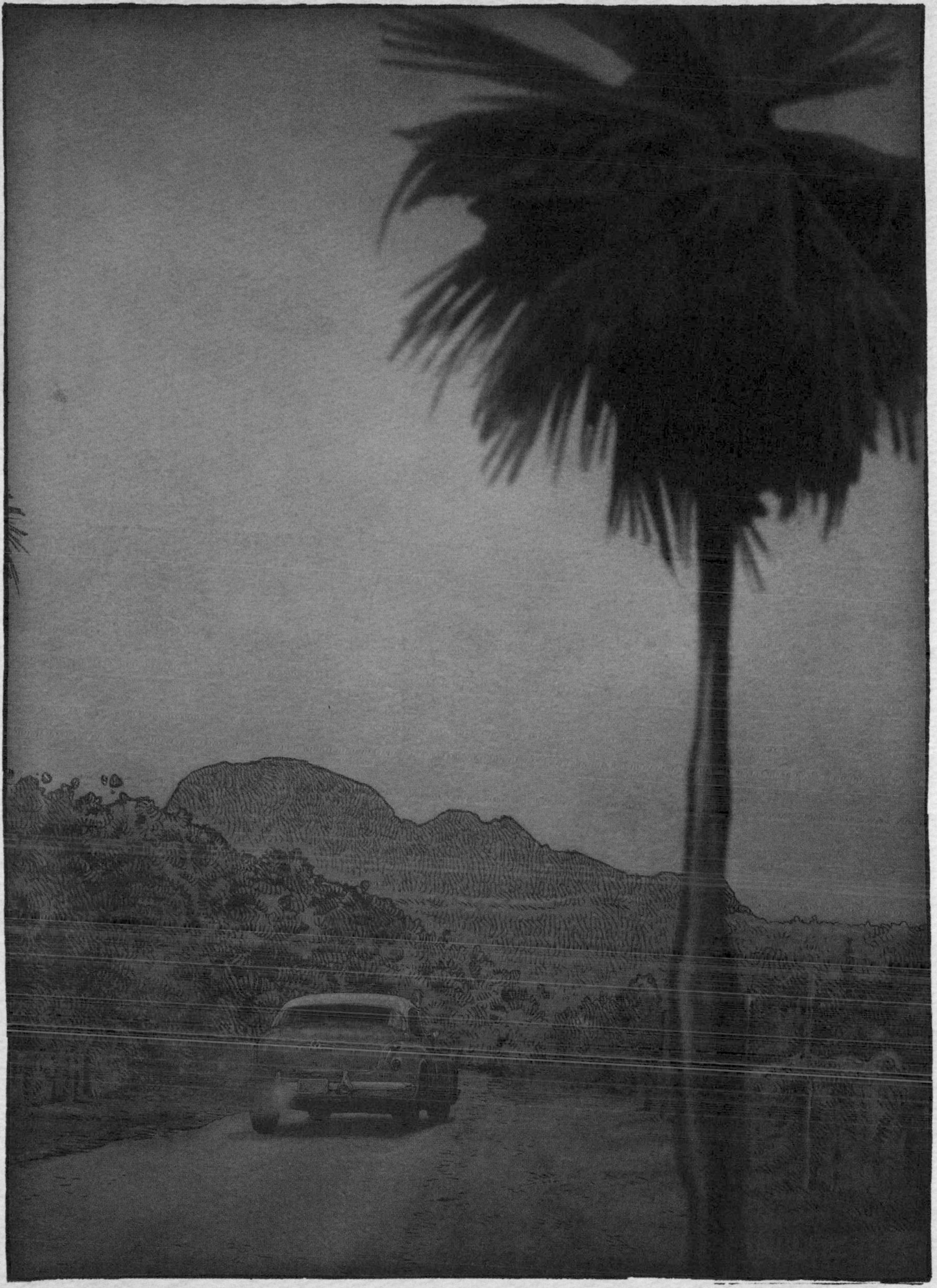

SEÑAS PERSONALES
SIGNALEMENT

Profesión / Profession { *comerciante*

Lugar y fecha del nacimiento / Lieu et date de naissance { *Montevideo*
25- junio - 1921.

Estado Civil / Etat Civil { *casado*

Color de los ojos / Couleur des yeux *castaño*

Color del cabello / cheveux *castaño*

MINISTERIO DE RELACIONES EXTERIORES
SECCIÓN PASAPORTES

FOTOGRAFIA DEL PORTADOR

IMPRESION
DIGITO
PULGAR

Adolfo Mena
FIRMA DEL PORTADOR
SIGNATURE DU TITULAIRE

Y DE SU ESPOSA
ET DE SA FEMME

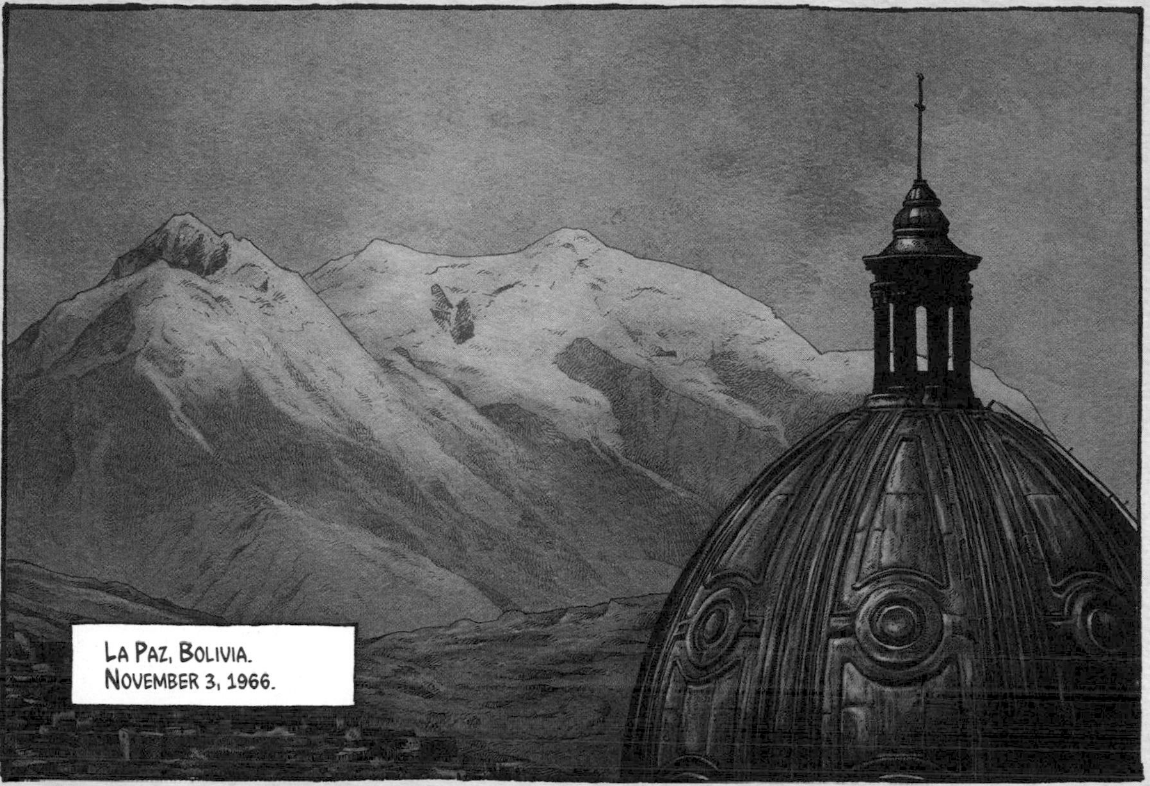
LA PAZ, BOLIVIA.
NOVEMBER 3, 1966.

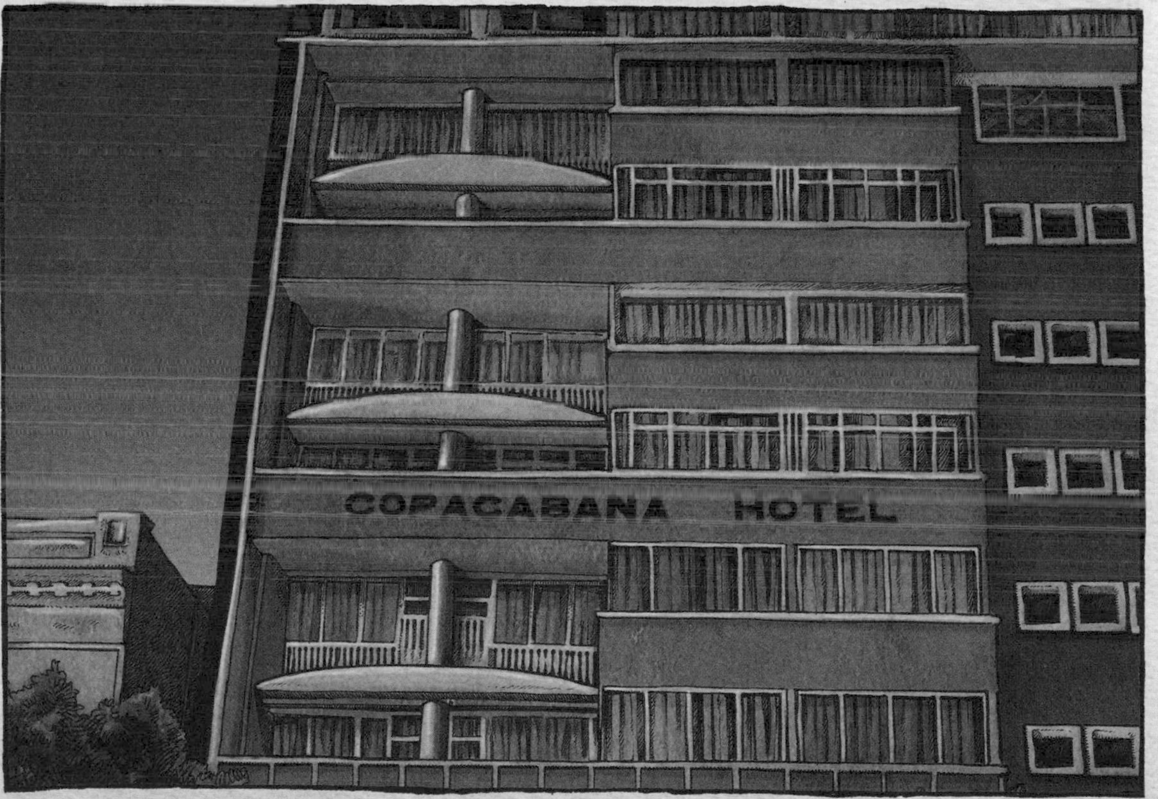
COPACABANA HOTEL

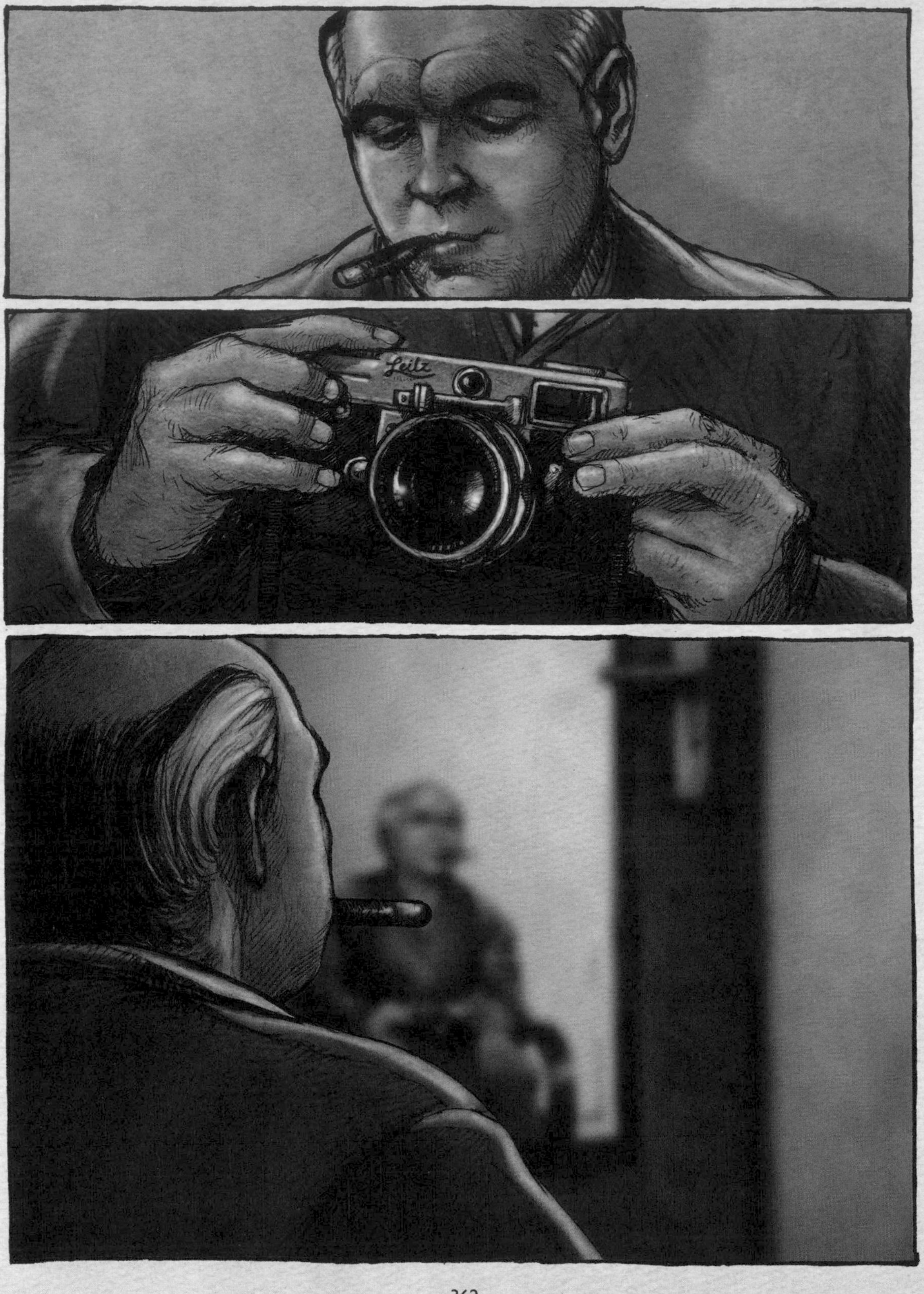
Leitz

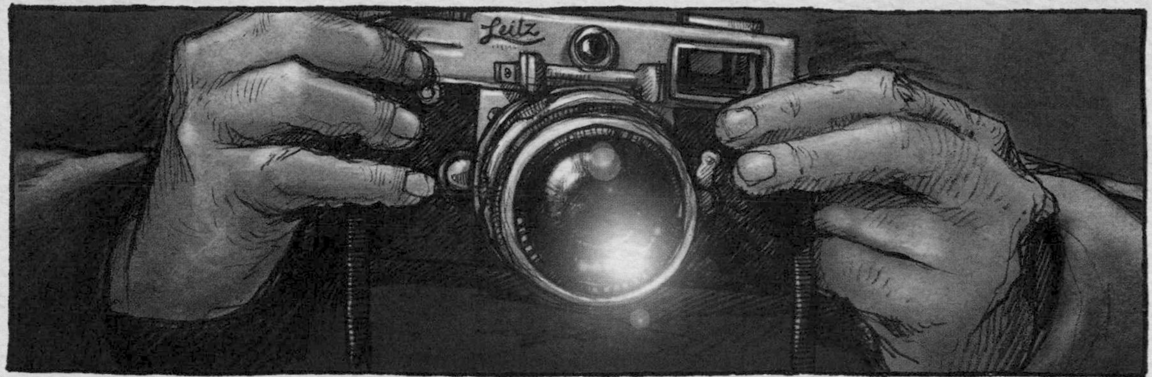
Leitz

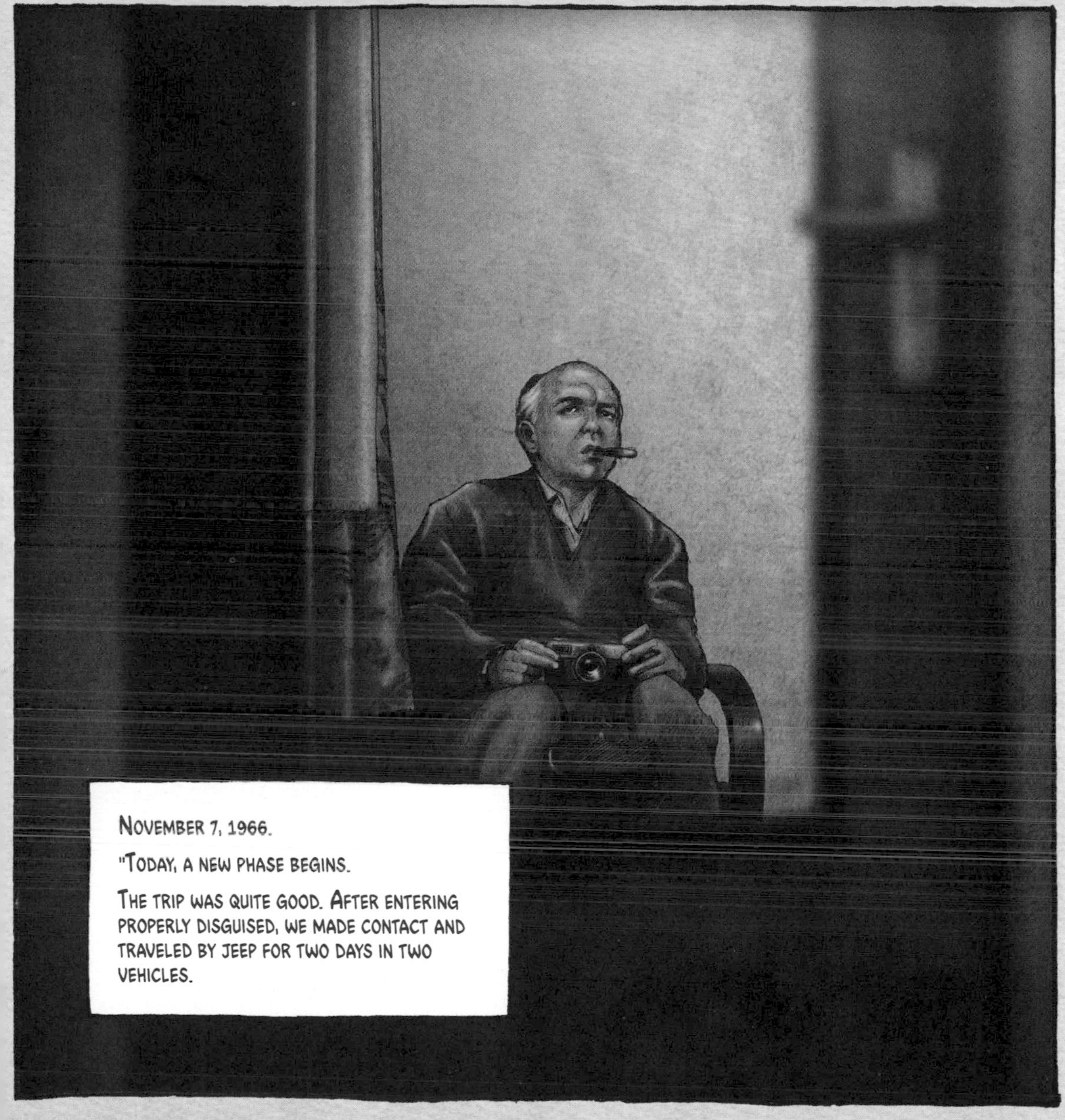
NOVEMBER 7, 1966.
"TODAY, A NEW PHASE BEGINS.
THE TRIP WAS QUITE GOOD. AFTER ENTERING PROPERLY DISGUISED, WE MADE CONTACT AND TRAVELED BY JEEP FOR TWO DAYS IN TWO VEHICLES.

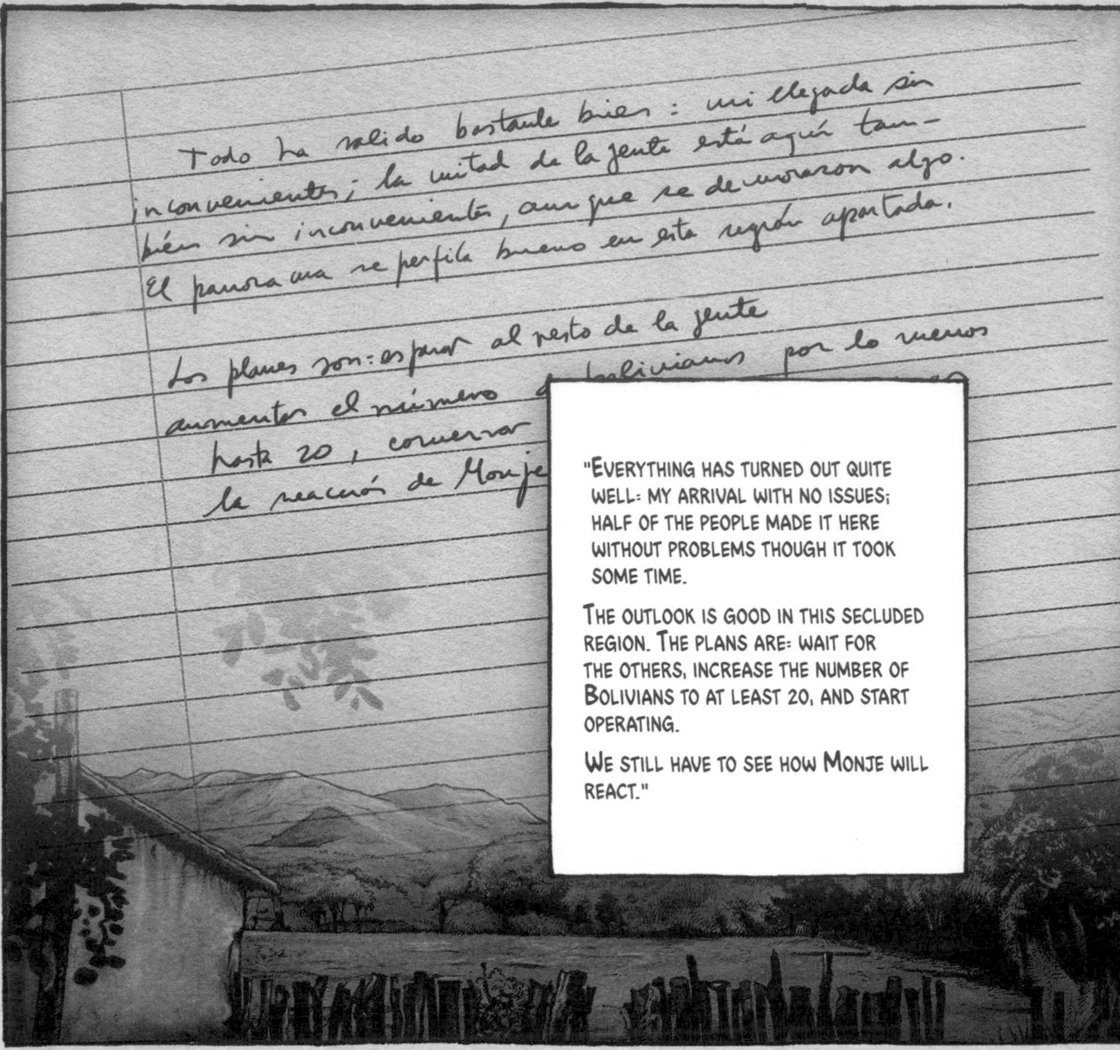
Todo ha salido bastante bien: mi llegada sin
inconvenientes; la mitad de la gente está aquí tam-
bién sin inconvenientes, aunque se demoraron algo.
El panorama se perfila bueno en esta región apartada.
Los planes son: esperar al resto de la gente
aumentar el número
bolivianos por lo menos
hasta 20, comenzar
la reacción de Monje
"EVERYTHING HAS TURNED OUT QUITE WELL: MY ARRIVAL WITH NO ISSUES; HALF OF THE PEOPLE MADE IT HERE WITHOUT PROBLEMS THOUGH IT TOOK SOME TIME.
THE OUTLOOK IS GOOD IN THIS SECLUDED REGION. THE PLANS ARE: WAIT FOR THE OTHERS, INCREASE THE NUMBER OF BOLIVIANS TO AT LEAST 20, AND START OPERATING.
WE STILL HAVE TO SEE HOW MONJE WILL REACT."

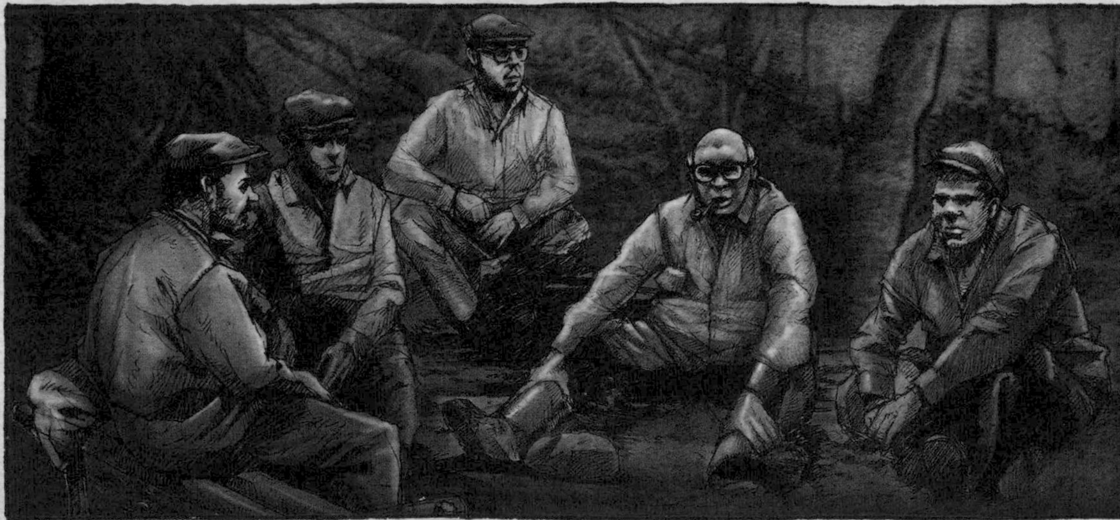

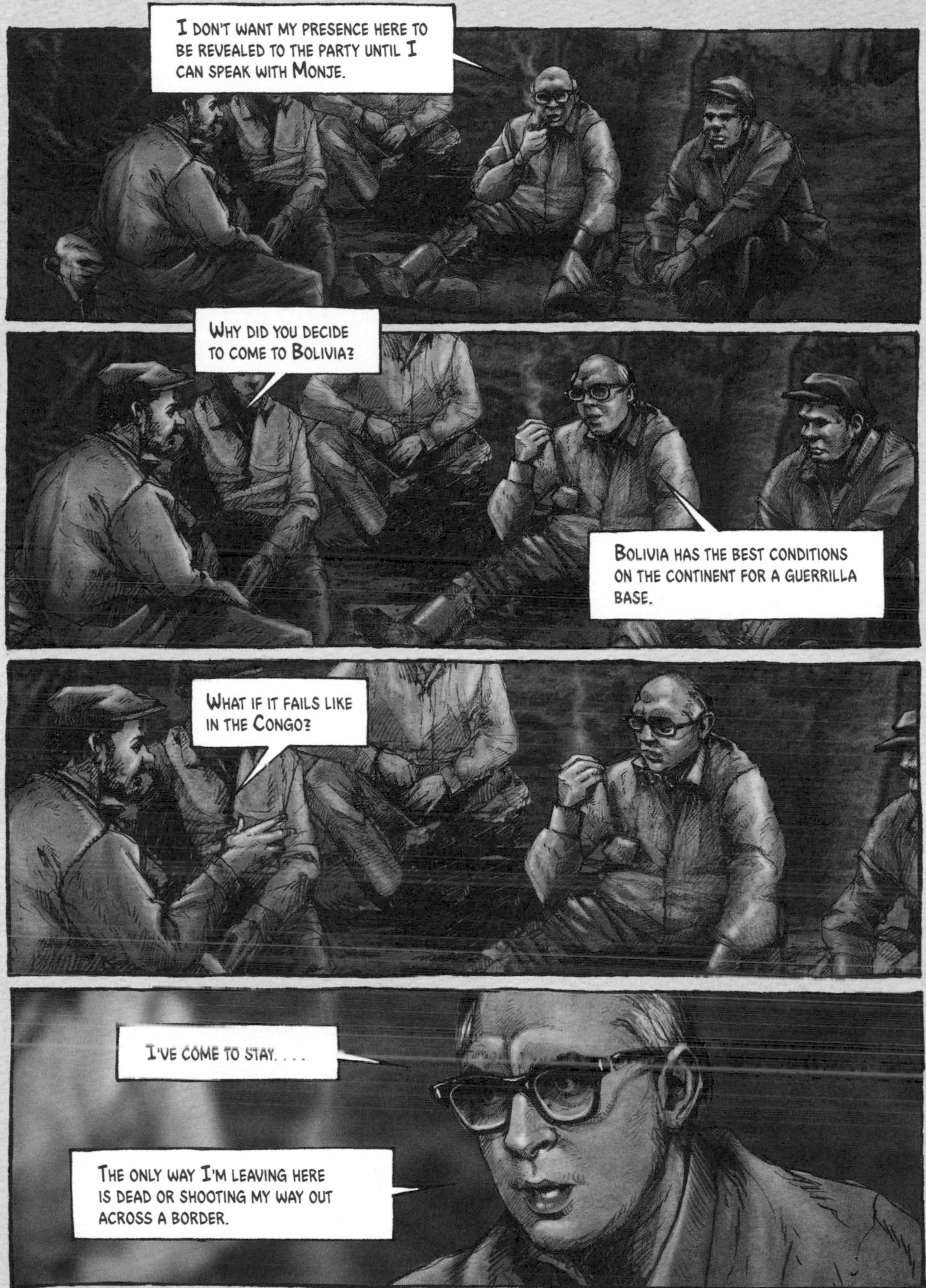
I DON'T WANT MY PRESENCE HERE TO BE REVEALED TO THE PARTY UNTIL I CAN SPEAK WITH MONJE.
WHY DID YOU DECIDE TO COME TO BOLIVIA?
BOLIVIA HAS THE BEST CONDITIONS ON THE CONTINENT FOR A GUERRILLA BASE.
WHAT IF IT FAILS LIKE IN THE CONGO?
I'VE COME TO STAY. . . .
THE ONLY WAY I'M LEAVING HERE IS DEAD OR SHOOTING MY WAY OUT ACROSS A BORDER.

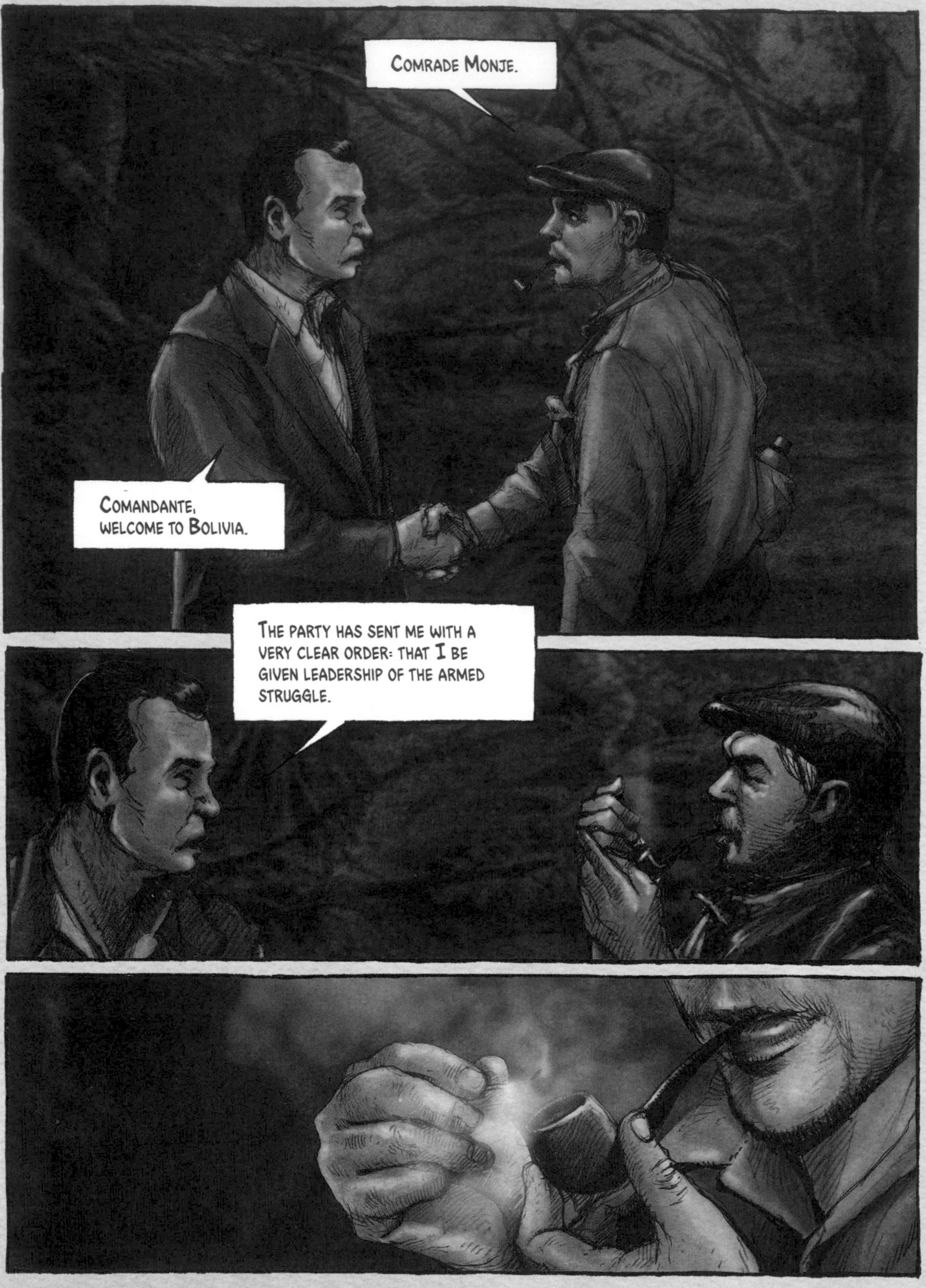
Comrade Monje.
Comandante, welcome to Bolivia.
The party has sent me with a very clear order: that I be given leadership of the armed struggle.

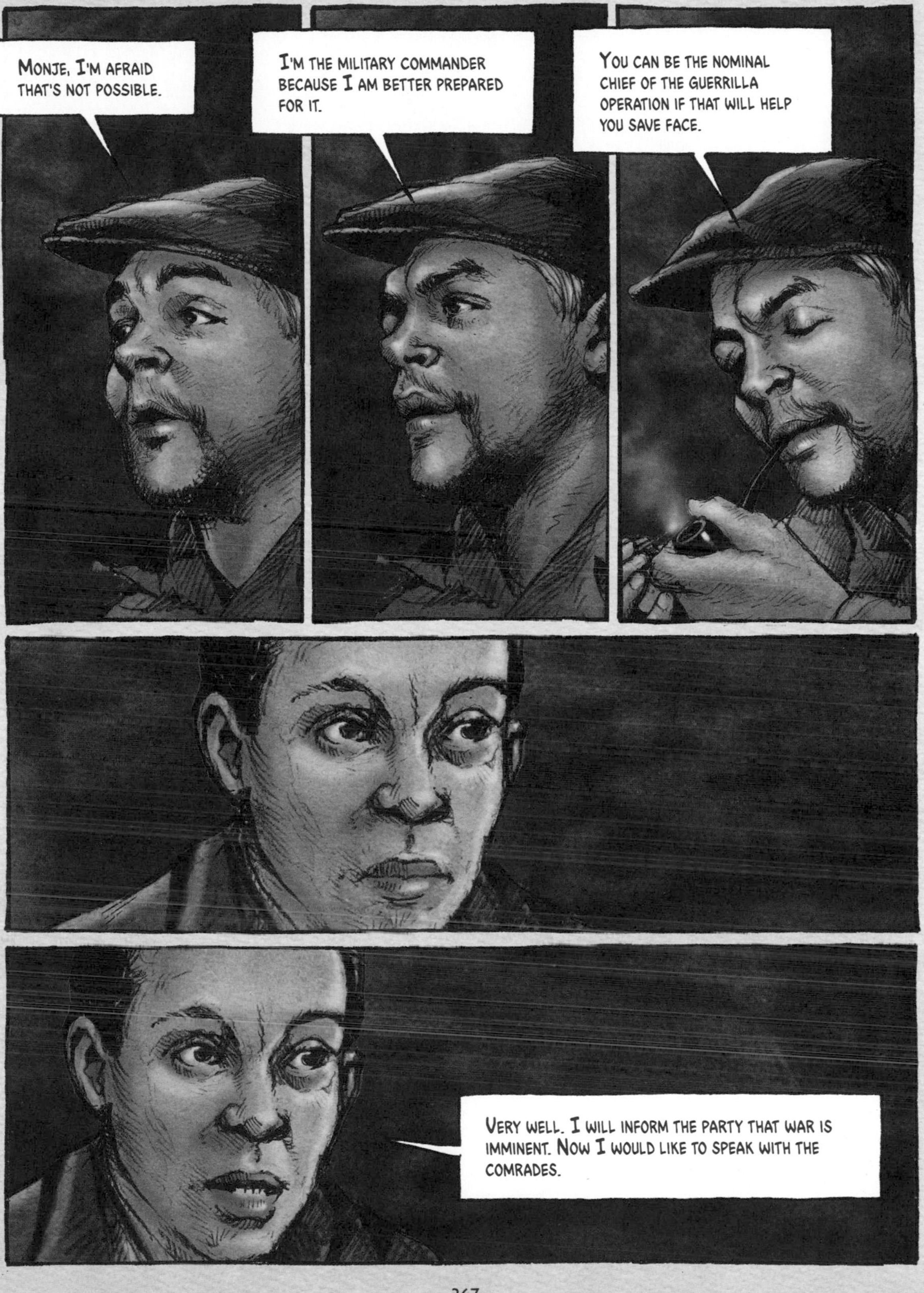
Monje, I'm afraid that's not possible.
I'm the military commander because I am better prepared for it.
You can be the nominal chief of the guerrilla operation if that will help you save face.
Very well. I will inform the party that war is imminent. Now I would like to speak with the comrades.

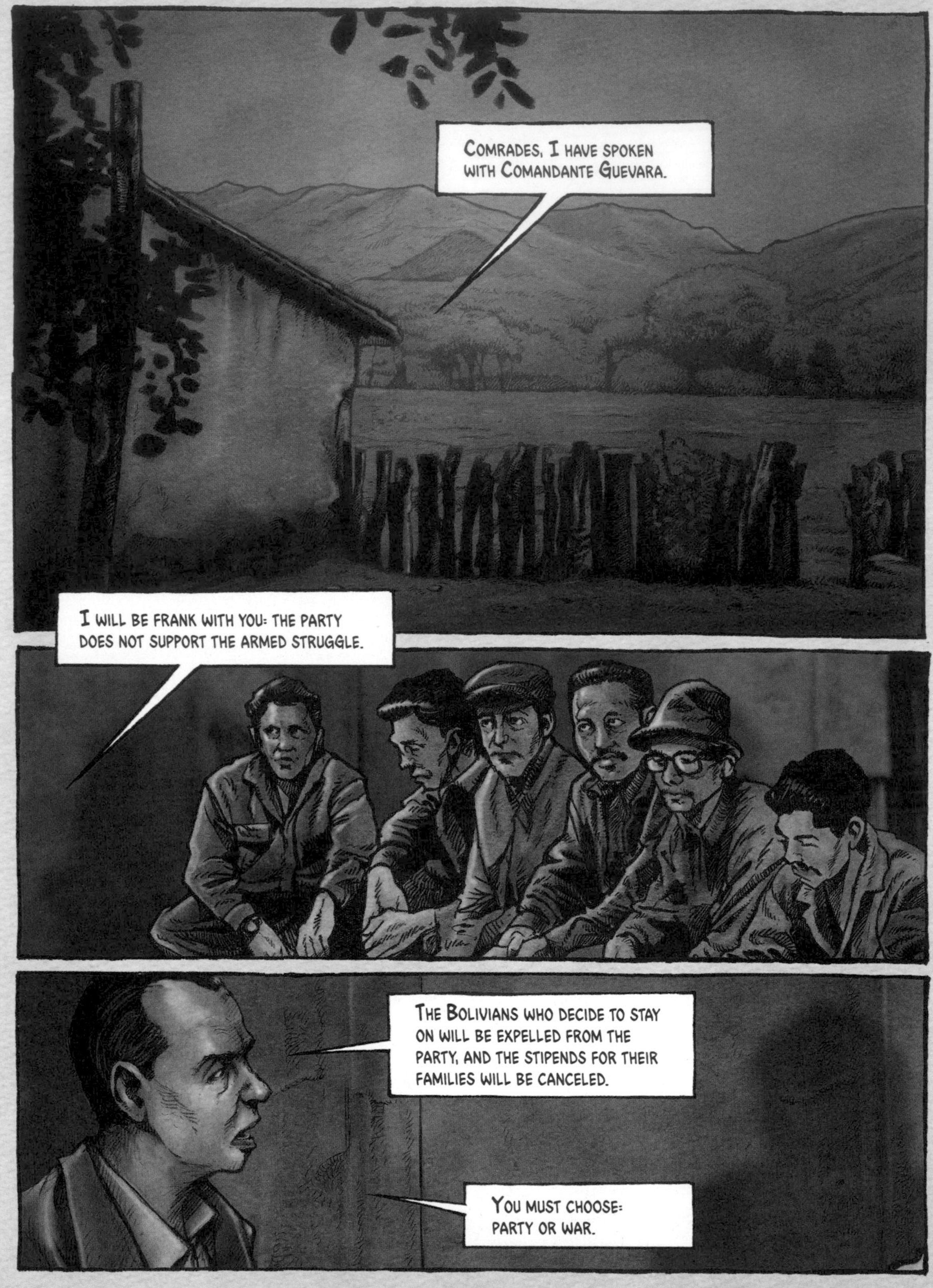
COMRADES, I HAVE SPOKEN WITH COMANDANTE GUEVARA.
I WILL BE FRANK WITH YOU: THE PARTY DOES NOT SUPPORT THE ARMED STRUGGLE.
THE BOLIVIANS WHO DECIDE TO STAY ON WILL BE EXPELLED FROM THE PARTY, AND THE STIPENDS FOR THEIR FAMILIES WILL BE CANCELED.
YOU MUST CHOOSE: PARTY OR WAR.

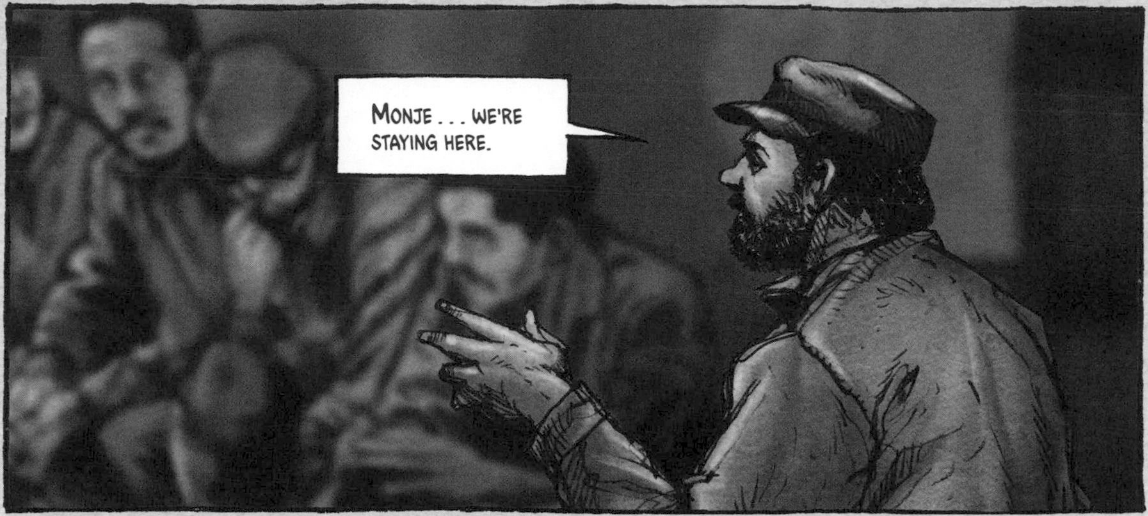
MONJE . . . WE'RE STAYING HERE.

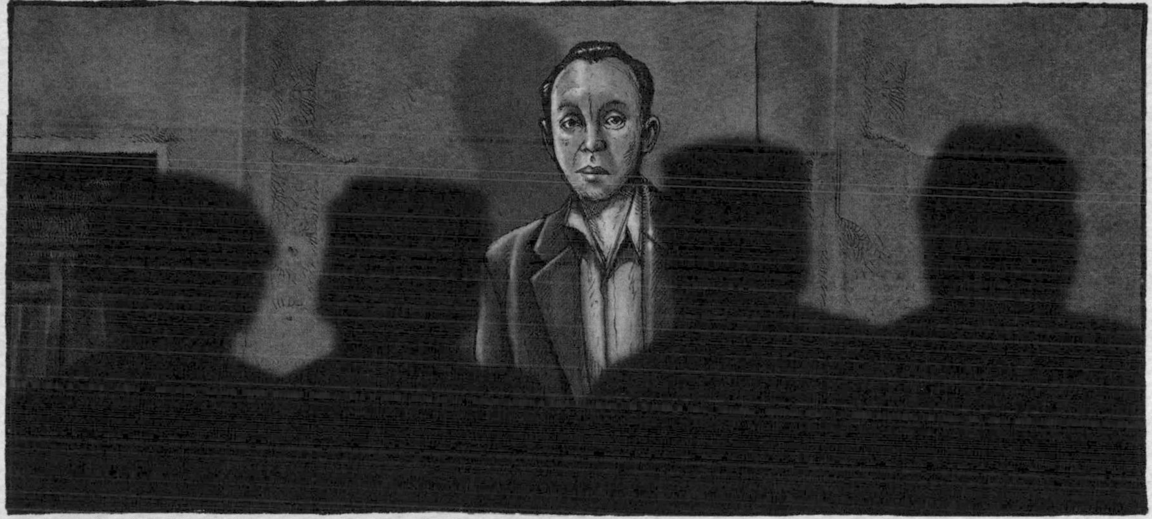

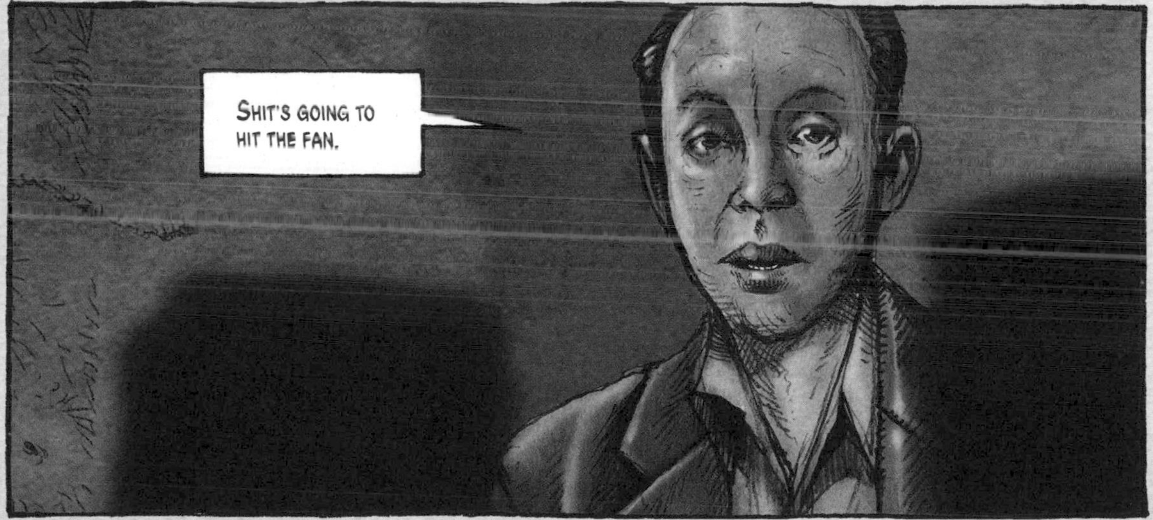
SHIT'S GOING TO HIT THE FAN.

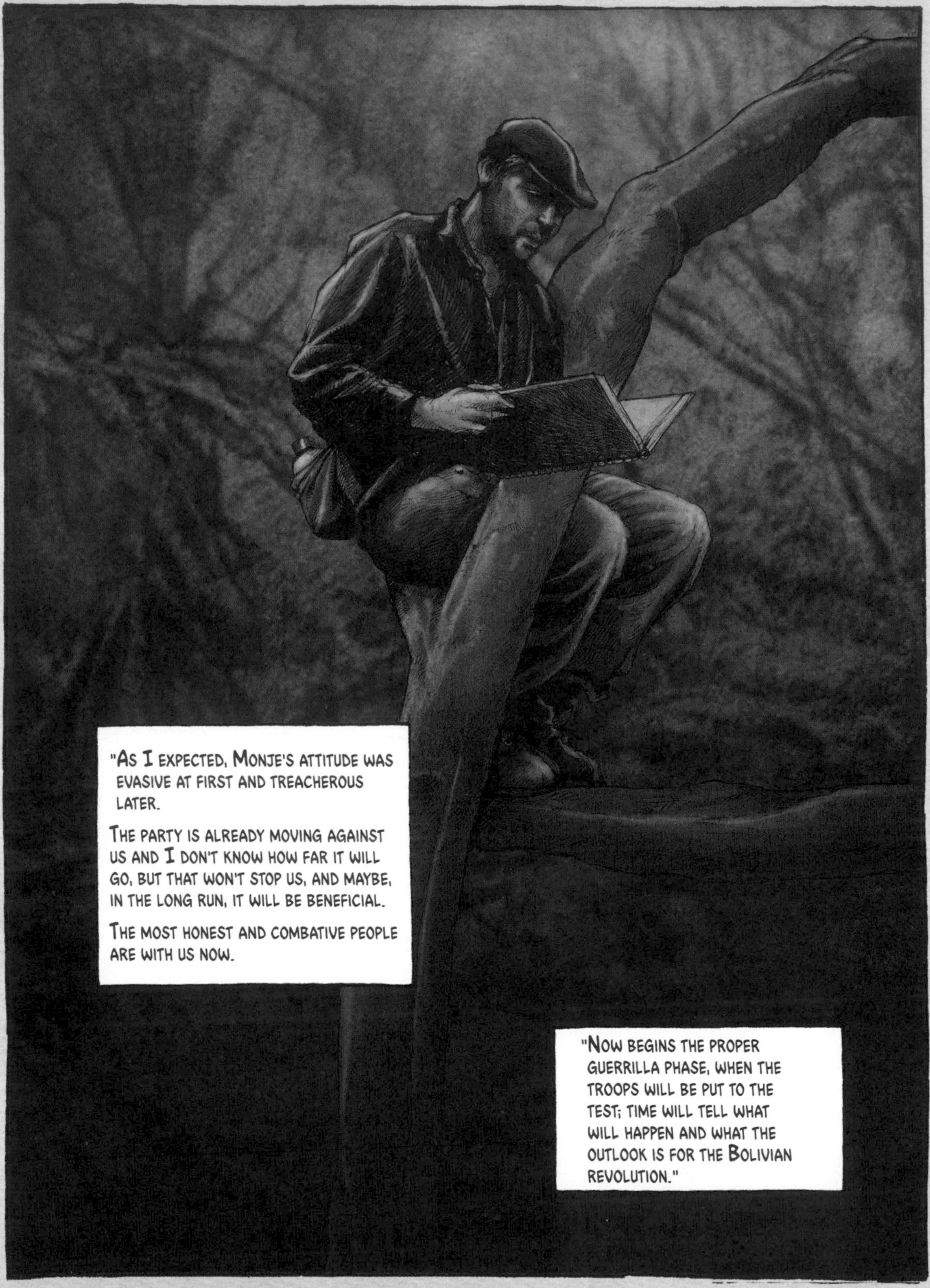
"As I expected, Monje's attitude was evasive at first and treacherous later.
The party is already moving against us and I don't know how far it will go, but that won't stop us, and maybe, in the long run, it will be beneficial.
The most honest and combative people are with us now.
"Now begins the proper guerrilla phase, when the troops will be put to the test; time will tell what will happen and what the outlook is for the Bolivian revolution."

"FEBRUARY 3.

"THE DAY DAWNED RAINY, SO WE PUSHED BACK OUR DEPARTURE UNTIL EIGHT. WE REACHED THE STREAM AT TEN, SOAKED, AND WE RESOLVED NOT TO CONTINUE TODAY. THE STREAM CANNOT BE THE FRÍAS RIVER; IT'S SIMPLY NOT ON THE MAP."

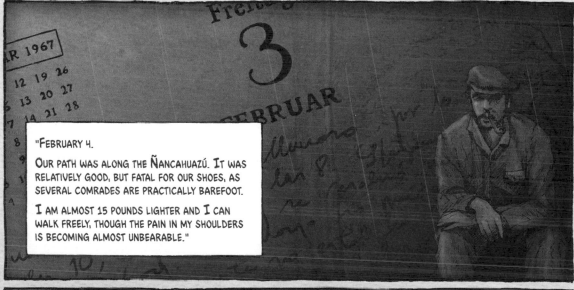

"FEBRUARY 4.

OUR PATH WAS ALONG THE ÑANCAHUAZÚ. IT WAS RELATIVELY GOOD, BUT FATAL FOR OUR SHOES, AS SEVERAL COMRADES ARE PRACTICALLY BAREFOOT.

I AM ALMOST 15 POUNDS LIGHTER AND I CAN WALK FREELY, THOUGH THE PAIN IN MY SHOULDERS IS BECOMING ALMOST UNBEARABLE."

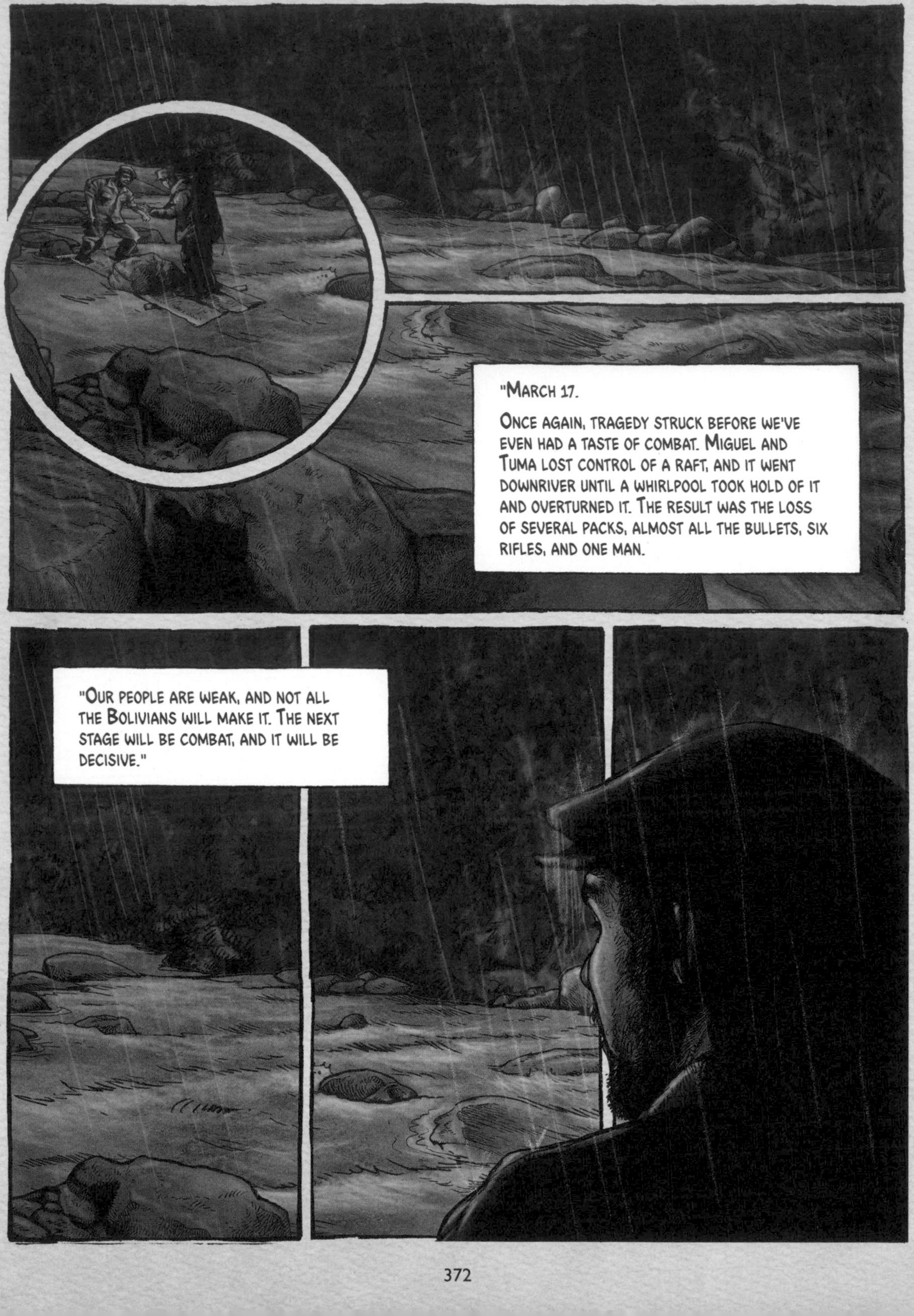
"March 17.
Once again, tragedy struck before we've even had a taste of combat. Miguel and Tuma lost control of a raft, and it went downriver until a whirlpool took hold of it and overturned it. The result was the loss of several packs, almost all the bullets, six rifles, and one man.
"Our people are weak, and not all the Bolivians will make it. The next stage will be combat, and it will be decisive."

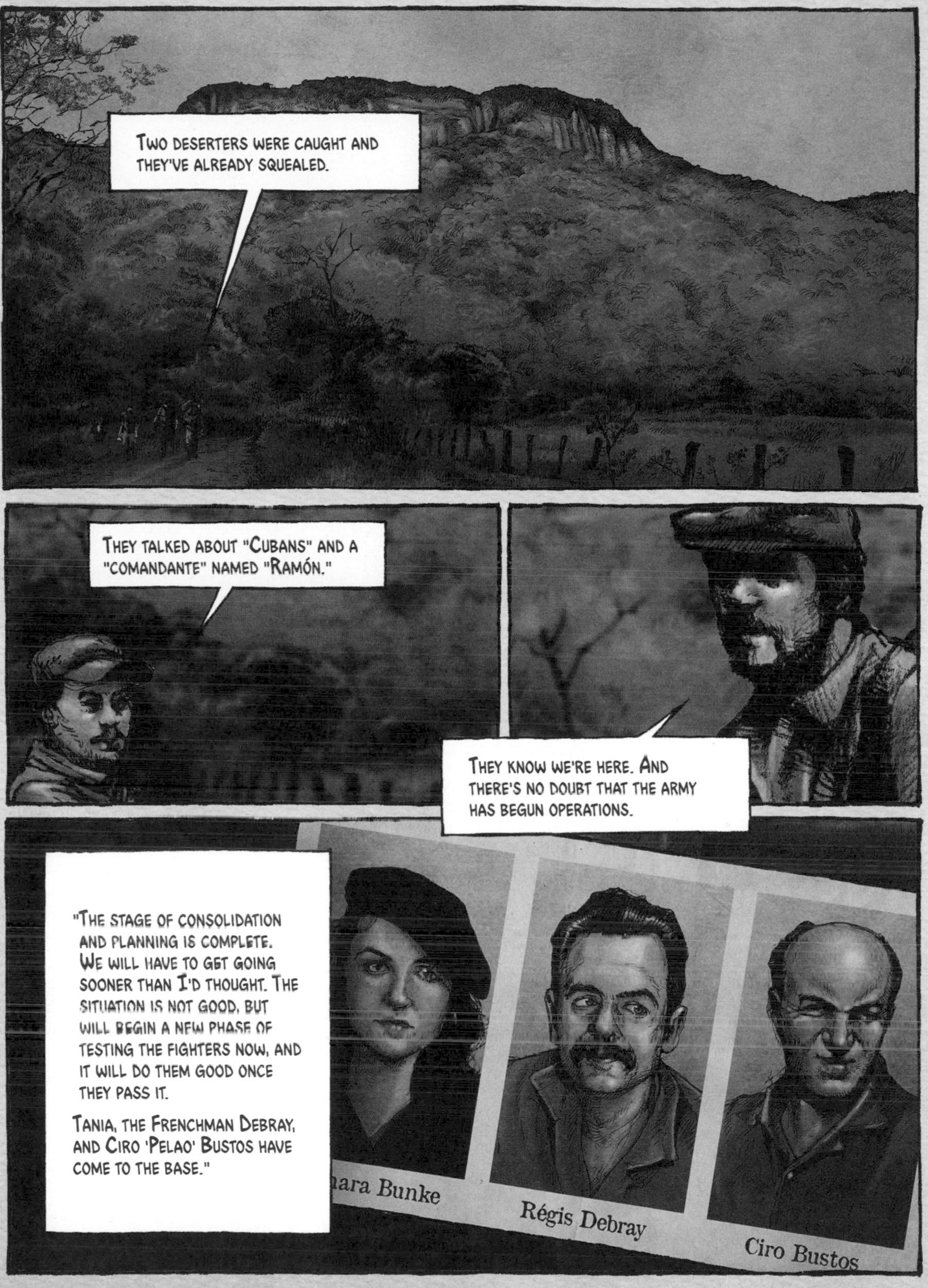
TWO DESERTERS WERE CAUGHT AND THEY'VE ALREADY SQUEALED.
THEY TALKED ABOUT "CUBANS" AND A "COMANDANTE" NAMED "RAMÓN."
THEY KNOW WE'RE HERE. AND THERE'S NO DOUBT THAT THE ARMY HAS BEGUN OPERATIONS.
"THE STAGE OF CONSOLIDATION AND PLANNING IS COMPLETE. WE WILL HAVE TO GET GOING SOONER THAN I'D THOUGHT. THE SITUATION IS NOT GOOD, BUT WILL BEGIN A NEW PHASE OF TESTING THE FIGHTERS NOW, AND IT WILL DO THEM GOOD ONCE THEY PASS IT.
TANIA, THE FRENCHMAN DEBRAY, AND CIRO 'PELAO' BUSTOS HAVE COME TO THE BASE."
ara Bunke
Régis Debray
Ciro Bustos

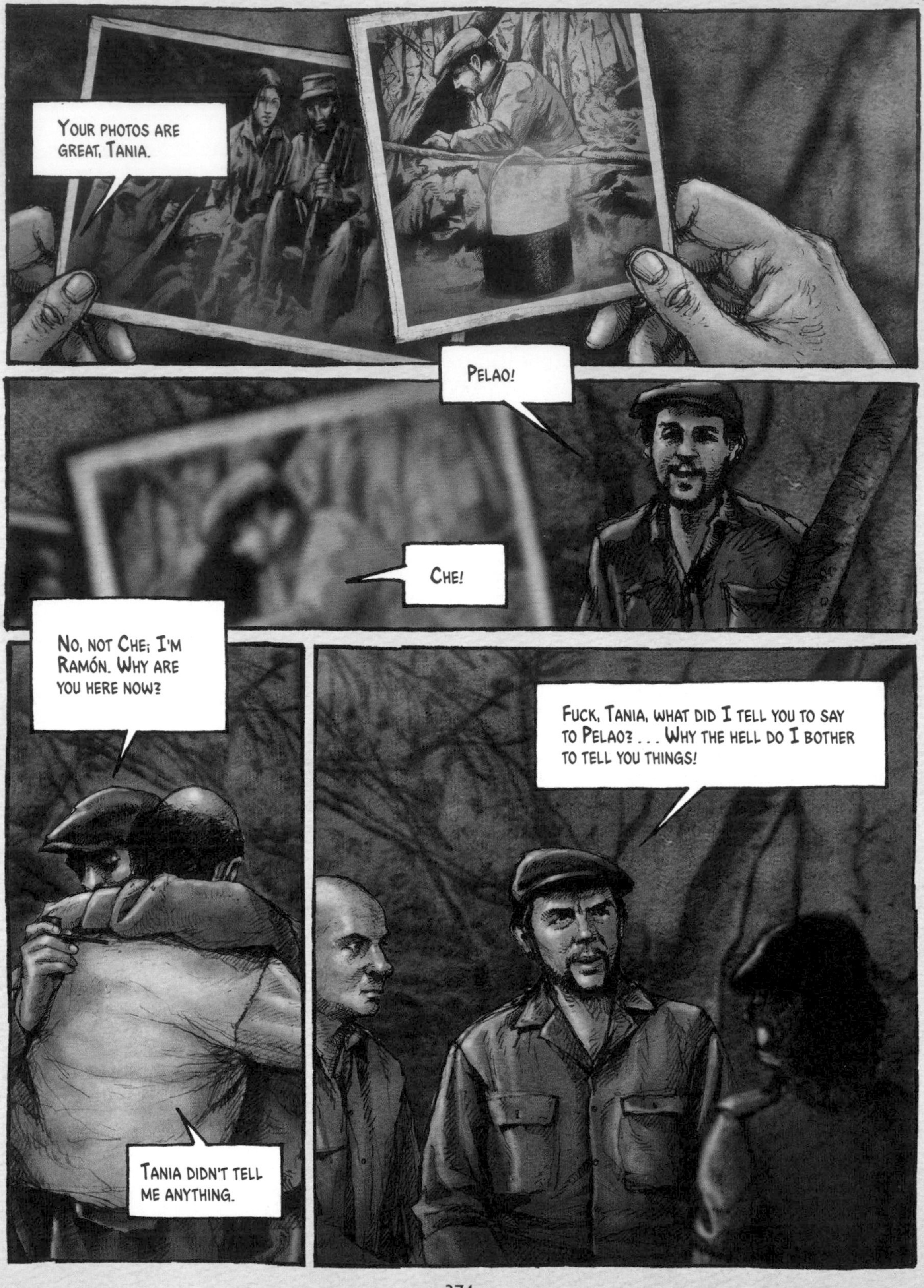
YOUR PHOTOS ARE GREAT, TANIA.
PELAO!
CHE!
NO, NOT CHE; I'M RAMÓN. WHY ARE YOU HERE NOW?
TANIA DIDN'T TELL ME ANYTHING.
FUCK, TANIA, WHAT DID I TELL YOU TO SAY TO PELAO? . . . WHY THE HELL DO I BOTHER TO TELL YOU THINGS!

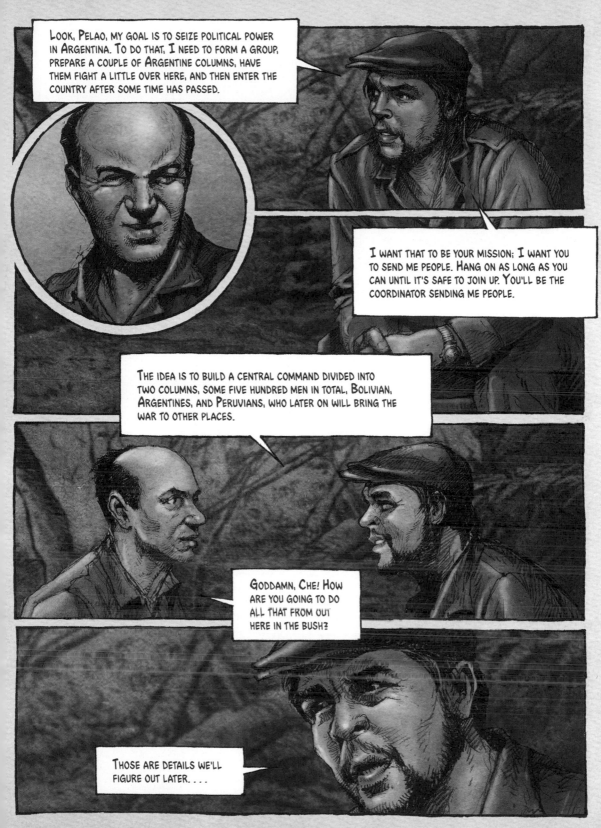

LOOK, PELAO, MY GOAL IS TO SEIZE POLITICAL POWER IN ARGENTINA. TO DO THAT, I NEED TO FORM A GROUP, PREPARE A COUPLE OF ARGENTINE COLUMNS, HAVE THEM FIGHT A LITTLE OVER HERE, AND THEN ENTER THE COUNTRY AFTER SOME TIME HAS PASSED.

I WANT THAT TO BE YOUR MISSION; I WANT YOU TO SEND ME PEOPLE. HANG ON AS LONG AS YOU CAN UNTIL IT'S SAFE TO JOIN UP. YOU'LL BE THE COORDINATOR SENDING ME PEOPLE.

THE IDEA IS TO BUILD A CENTRAL COMMAND DIVIDED INTO TWO COLUMNS, SOME FIVE HUNDRED MEN IN TOTAL, BOLIVIAN, ARGENTINES, AND PERUVIANS, WHO LATER ON WILL BRING THE WAR TO OTHER PLACES.

GODDAMN, CHE! HOW ARE YOU GOING TO DO ALL THAT FROM OUT HERE IN THE BUSH?

THOSE ARE DETAILS WE'LL FIGURE OUT LATER. . . .

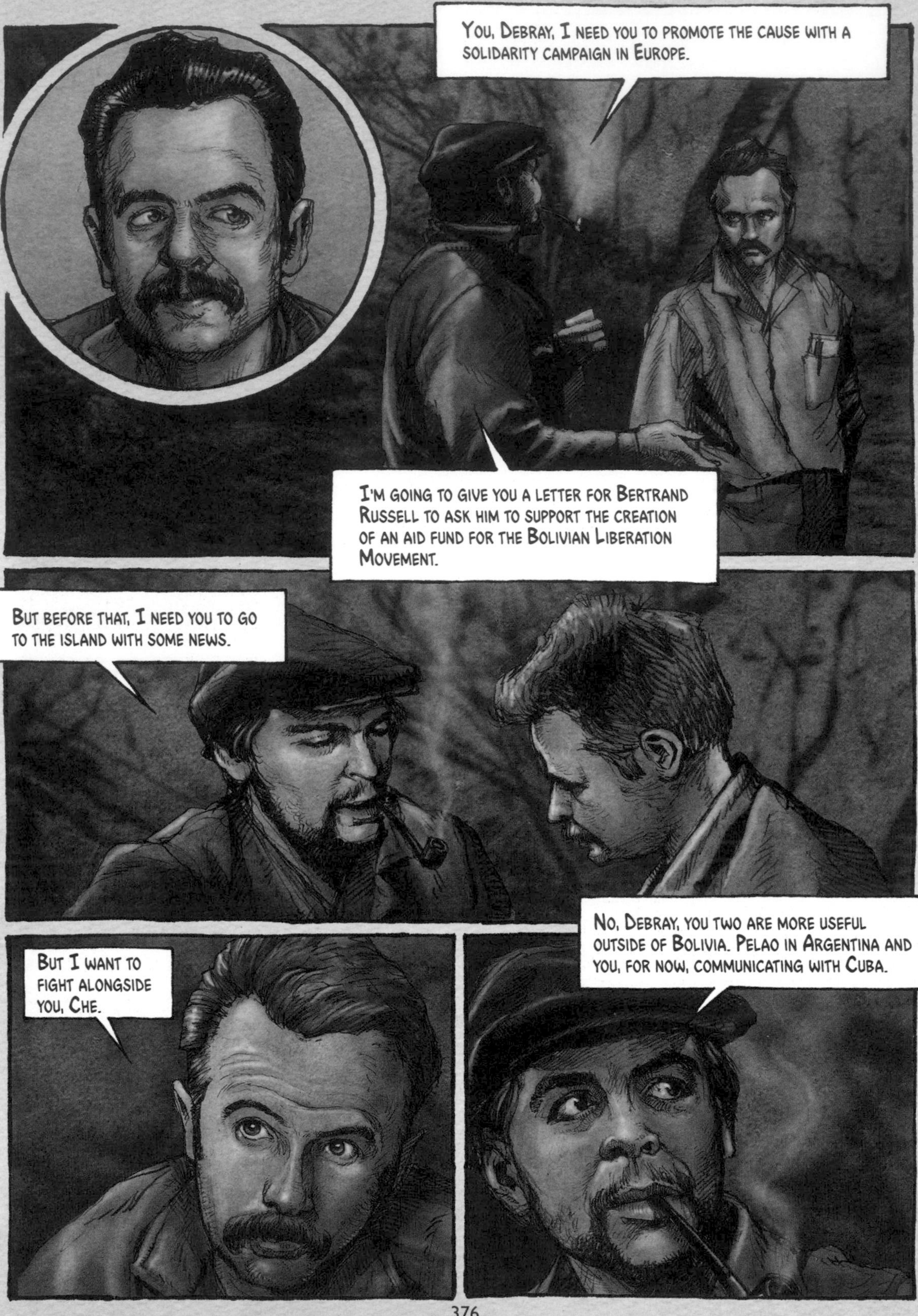
You, Debray, I need you to promote the cause with a solidarity campaign in Europe.
I'm going to give you a letter for Bertrand Russell to ask him to support the creation of an aid fund for the Bolivian Liberation Movement.
But before that, I need you to go to the island with some news.
But I want to fight alongside you, Che.
No, Debray, you two are more useful outside of Bolivia. Pelao in Argentina and you, for now, communicating with Cuba.

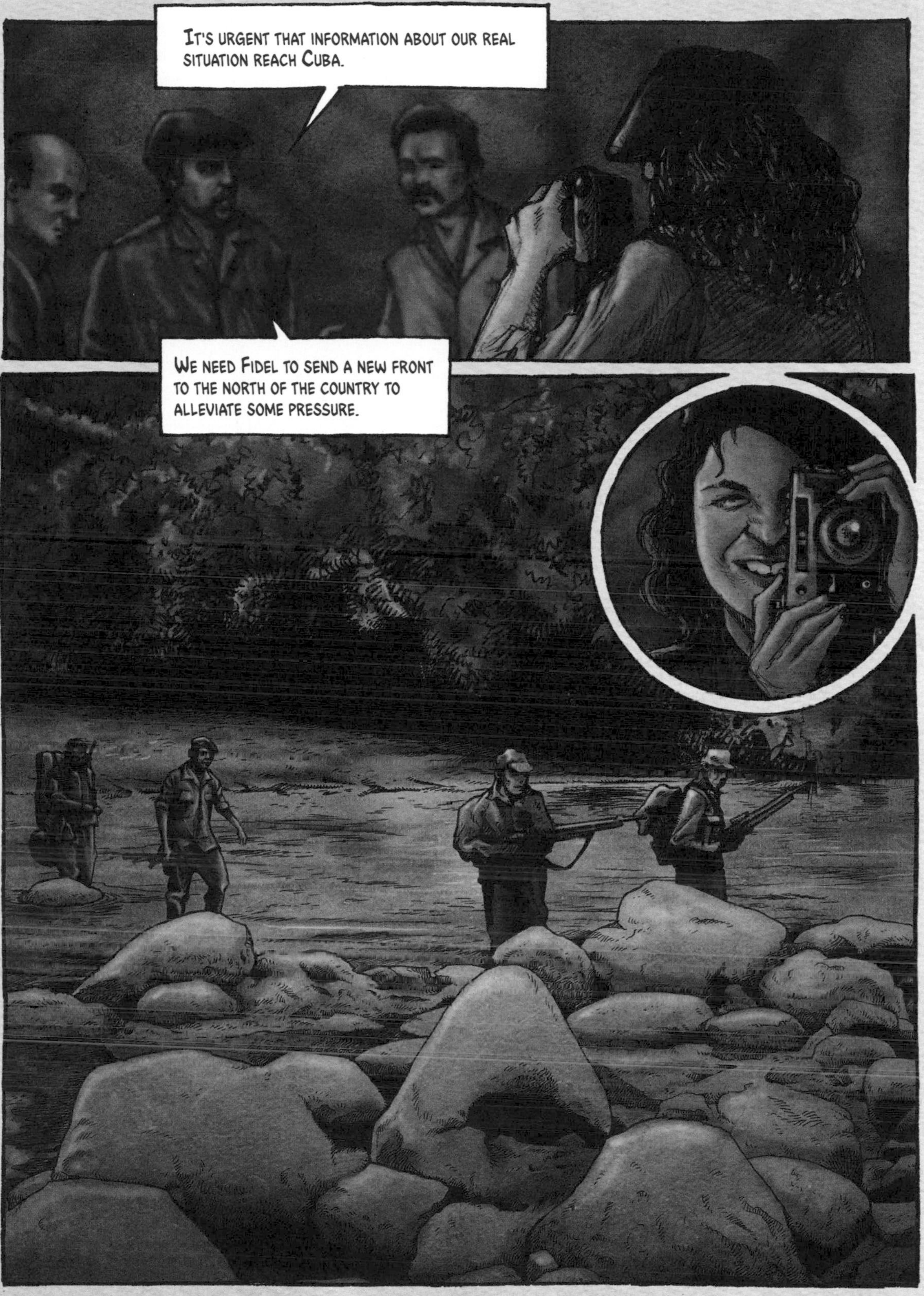
IT'S URGENT THAT INFORMATION ABOUT OUR REAL SITUATION REACH CUBA.
WE NEED FIDEL TO SEND A NEW FRONT TO THE NORTH OF THE COUNTRY TO ALLEVIATE SOME PRESSURE.

APRIL 1967.

"OUR ISOLATION IS COMPLETE: SICKNESS HAS UNDERMINED THE HEALTH OF SOME COMRADES, FORCING US TO DIVIDE INTO TWO COLUMNS, WHICH HAS DIMINISHED OUR EFFECTIVENESS.

"THE PEASANT BASE IS STILL NOT ESTABLISHED, ALTHOUGH IT APPEARS THAT THROUGH PLANNED TERROR WE CAN CONVINCE MOST OF THEM TO REMAIN NEUTRAL; THEIR SUPPORT WILL COME LATER.

NOT ONE BOLIVIAN HAS ENLISTED."

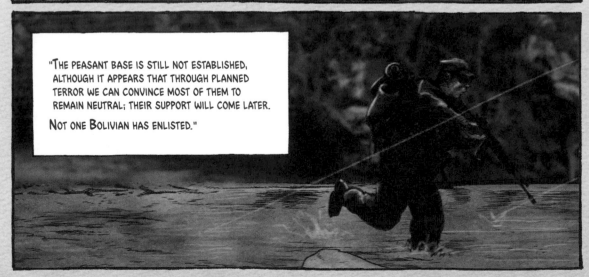

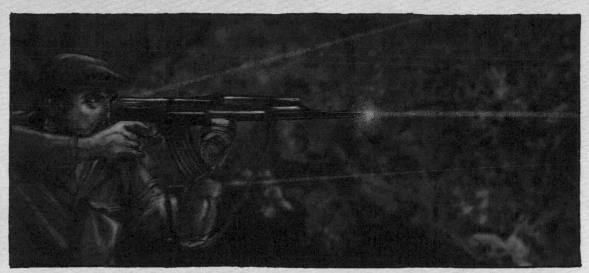

2.000 EFECTIVOS MILITARES EN OPERACION ENVOLVENTE CERCAN A LOS GUERRILLEROS

LA PAZ, BOLIVIA: Un frente de 2.000 efectivos del ejército boliviano... a un grupo de... reunían en...

amaipata y Camiri (mucho más al sur).

El 23 de marzo se produjo el primer choque en el valle de Ñancahuazú, el resultado fue negativo para las fuerzas... cito que fueron embos-... efectivos. El...

Una unidad militar fie embosca... riendo siete soldados, tomó veinti... sioneros y obtuvieron una copia d... del ejército para combatirlos. Al d... ente un avión bombardeó los alre... del campamento y el 27 de marz... bate ganó la primera plana inter...

Las tropas guerrilleras comen... ces a circular por la zona c... ... cerco que estaba...

379

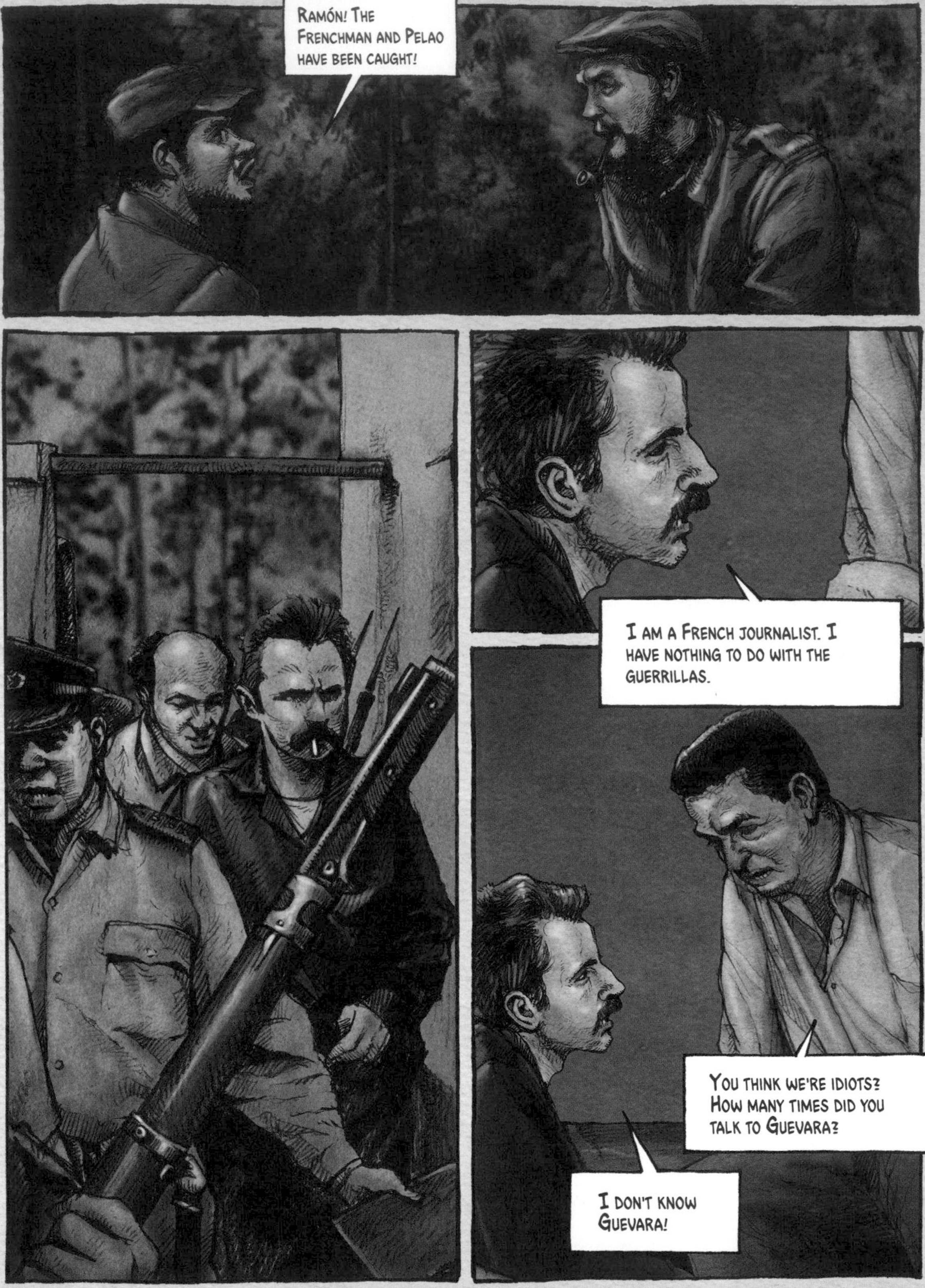
RAMÓN! THE FRENCHMAN AND PELAO HAVE BEEN CAUGHT!
I AM A FRENCH JOURNALIST. I HAVE NOTHING TO DO WITH THE GUERRILLAS.
YOU THINK WE'RE IDIOTS? HOW MANY TIMES DID YOU TALK TO GUEVARA?
I DON'T KNOW GUEVARA!

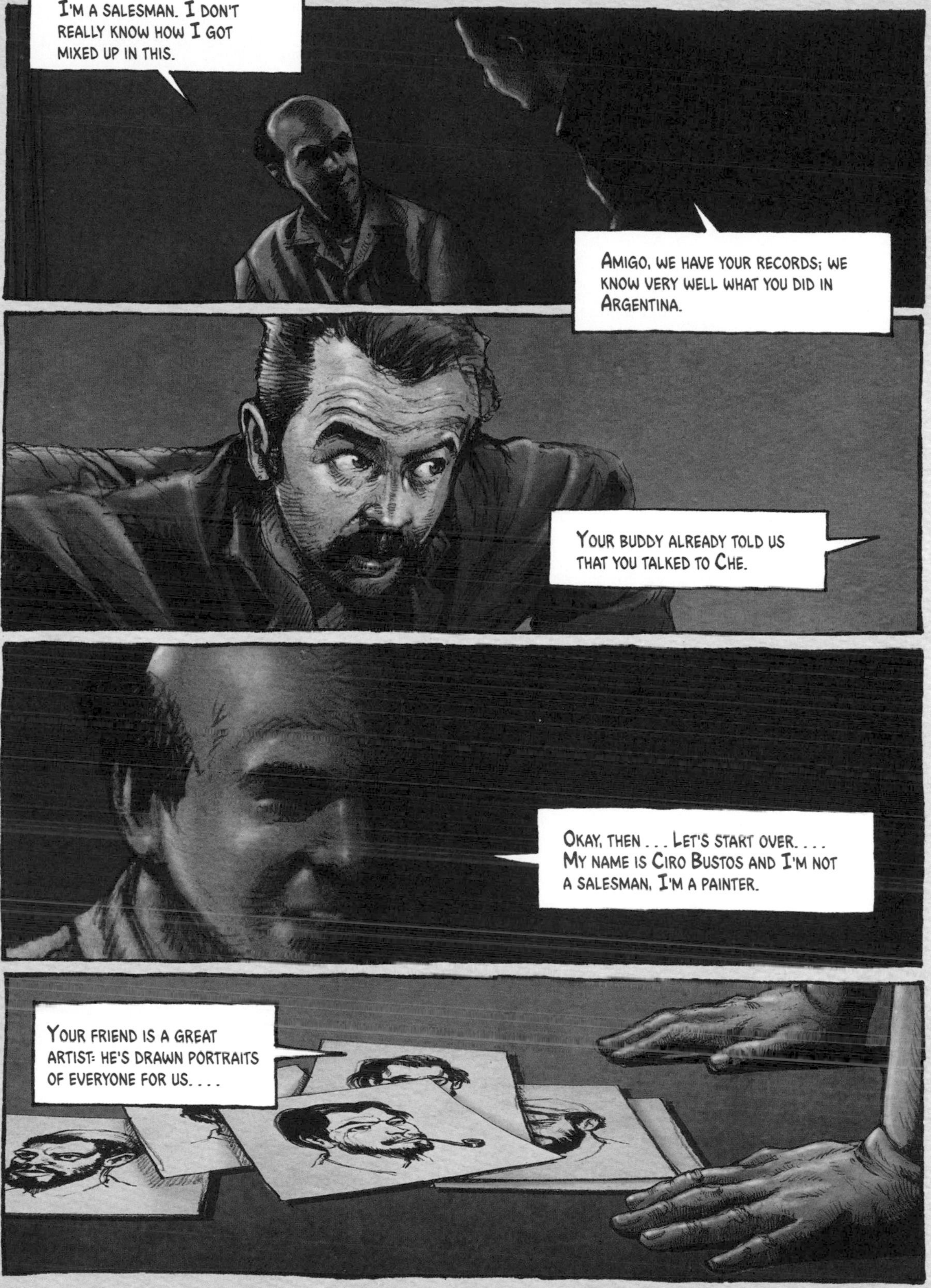
I'M A SALESMAN. I DON'T REALLY KNOW HOW I GOT MIXED UP IN THIS.
AMIGO, WE HAVE YOUR RECORDS; WE KNOW VERY WELL WHAT YOU DID IN ARGENTINA.
YOUR BUDDY ALREADY TOLD US THAT YOU TALKED TO CHE.
OKAY, THEN . . . LET'S START OVER. . . . MY NAME IS CIRO BUSTOS AND I'M NOT A SALESMAN, I'M A PAINTER.
YOUR FRIEND IS A GREAT ARTIST: HE'S DRAWN PORTRAITS OF EVERYONE FOR US. . . .

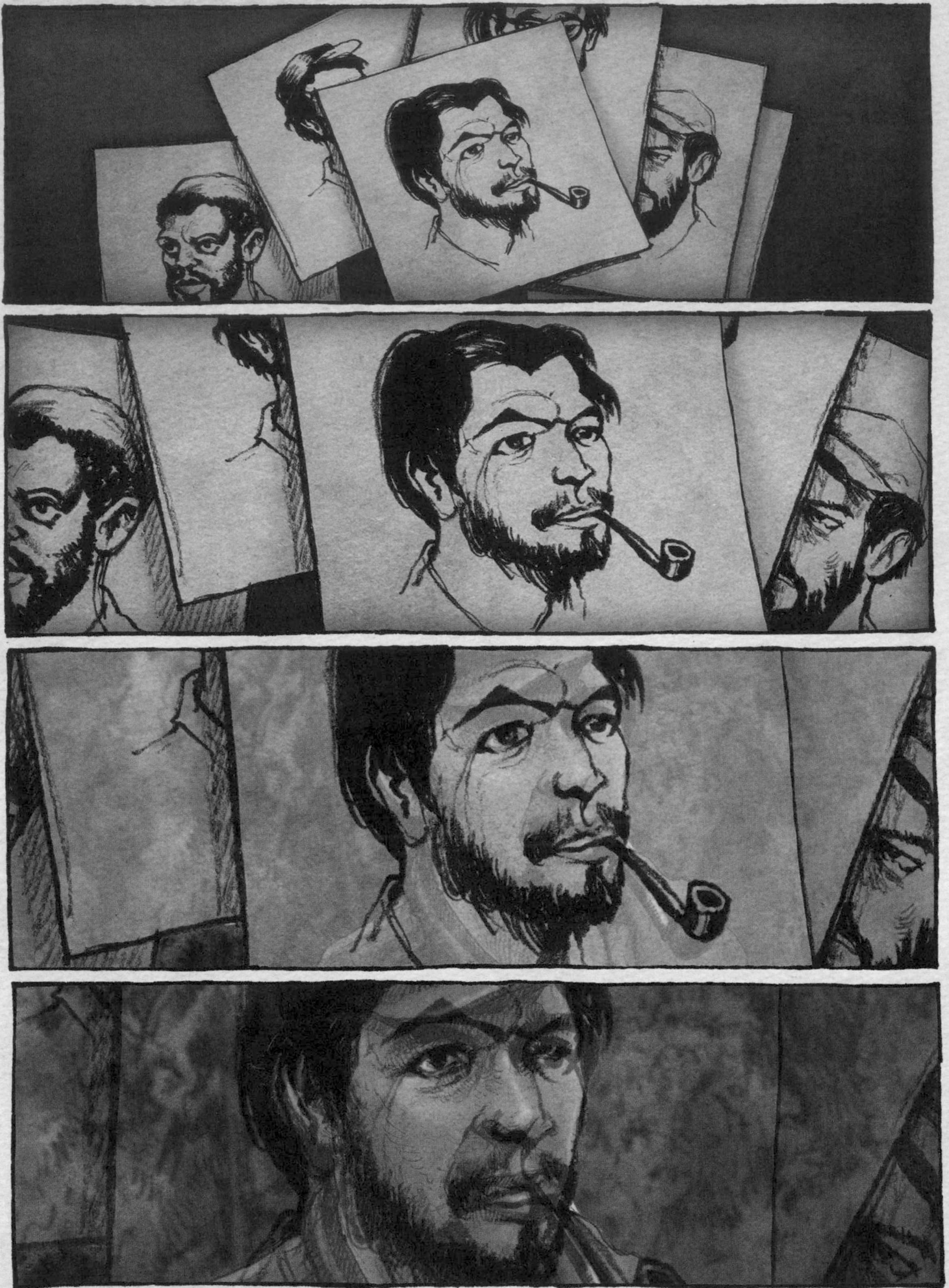

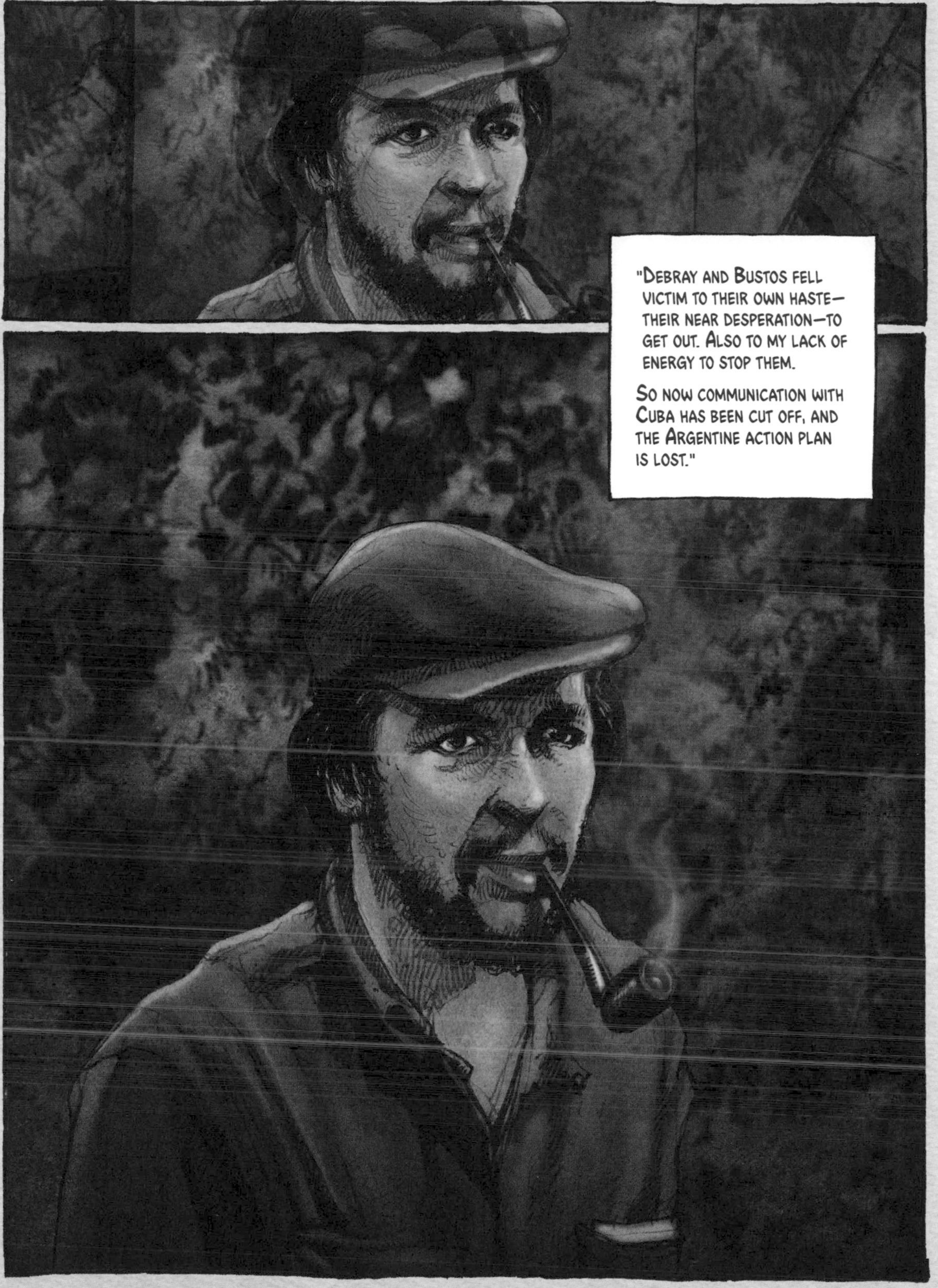
"DEBRAY AND BUSTOS FELL VICTIM TO THEIR OWN HASTE—THEIR NEAR DESPERATION—TO GET OUT. ALSO TO MY LACK OF ENERGY TO STOP THEM.
SO NOW COMMUNICATION WITH CUBA HAS BEEN CUT OFF, AND THE ARGENTINE ACTION PLAN IS LOST."

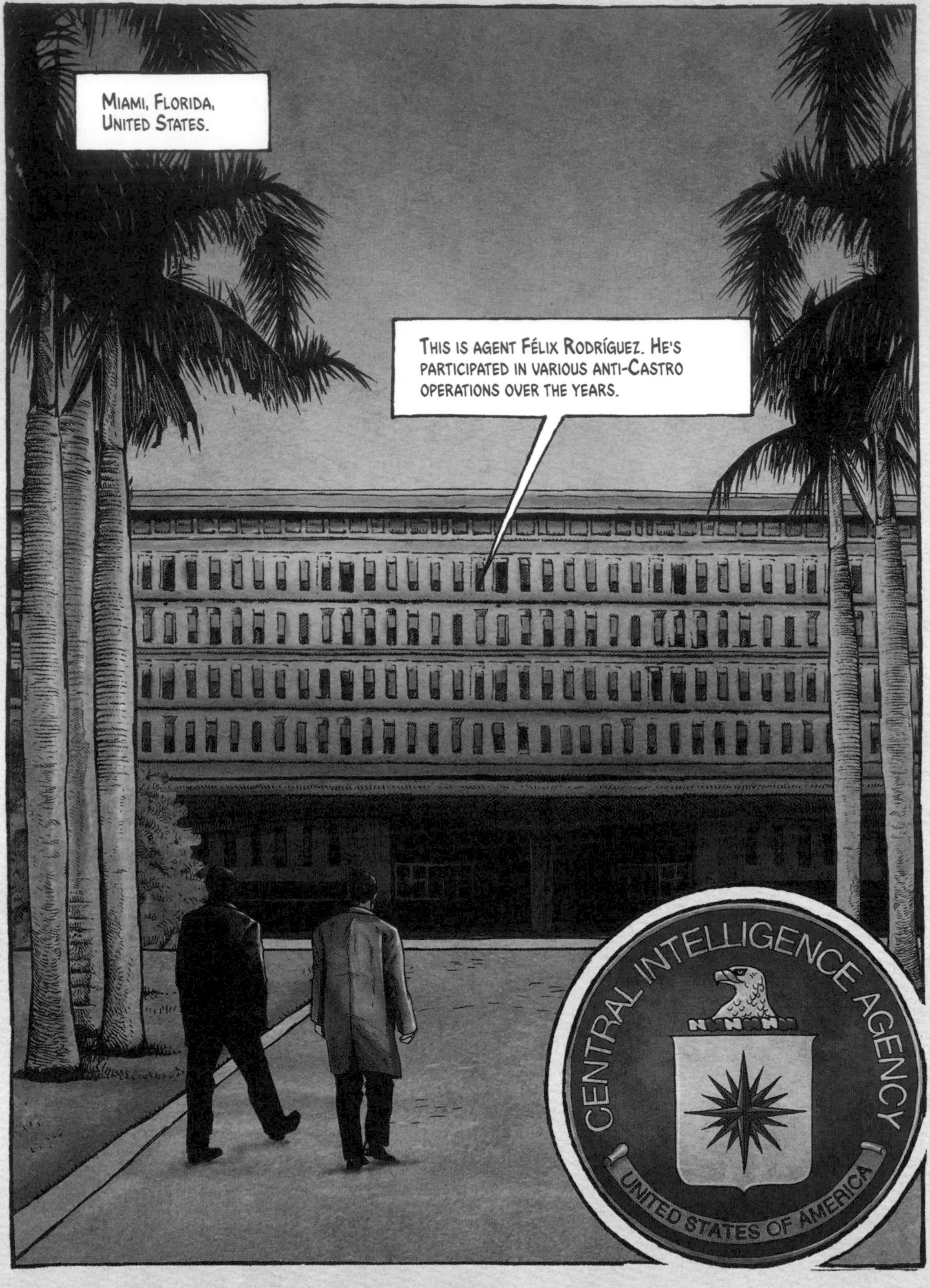

Miami, Florida, United States.
This is agent Félix Rodríguez. He's participated in various anti-Castro operations over the years.
CENTRAL INTELLIGENCE AGENCY
UNITED STATES OF AMERICA

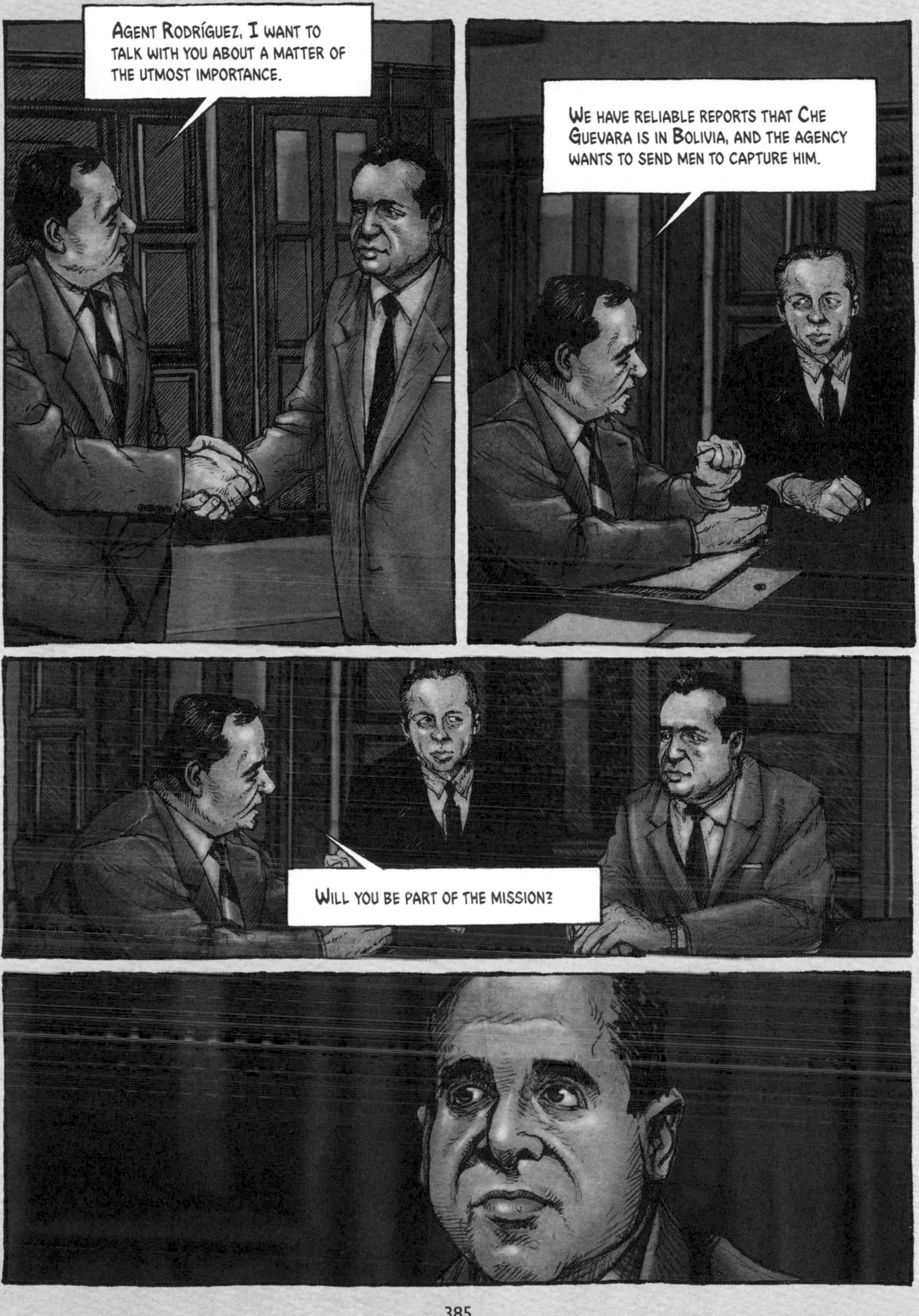
AGENT RODRÍGUEZ, I WANT TO TALK WITH YOU ABOUT A MATTER OF THE UTMOST IMPORTANCE.
WE HAVE RELIABLE REPORTS THAT CHE GUEVARA IS IN BOLIVIA, AND THE AGENCY WANTS TO SEND MEN TO CAPTURE HIM.
WILL YOU BE PART OF THE MISSION?

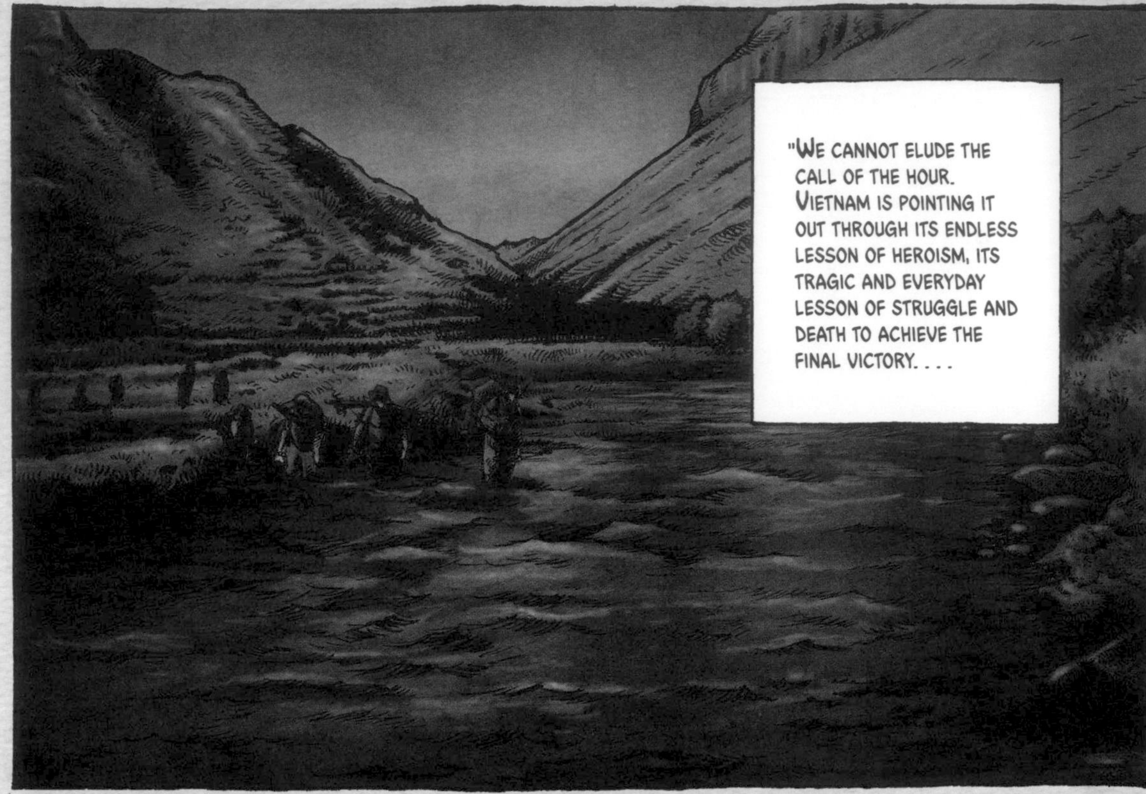
"We cannot elude the call of the hour. Vietnam is pointing it out through its endless lesson of heroism, its tragic and everyday lesson of struggle and death to achieve the final victory. . . .

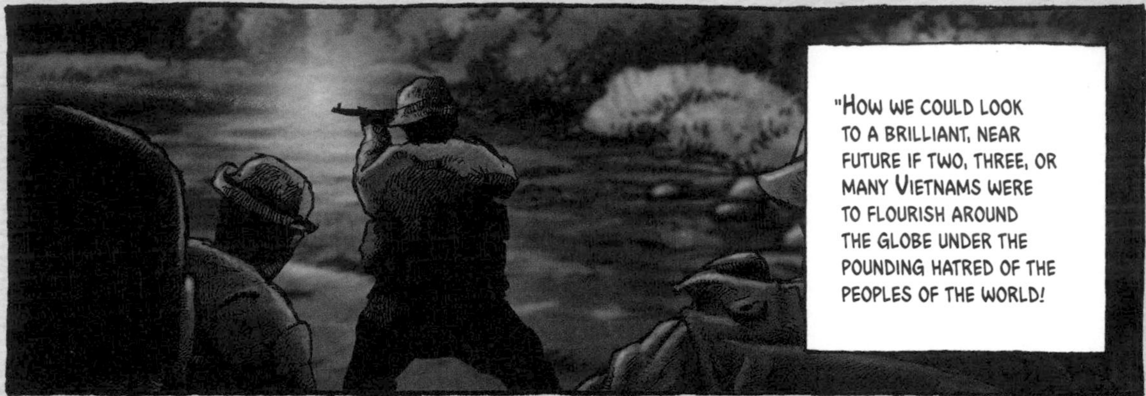
"How we could look to a brilliant, near future if two, three, or many Vietnams were to flourish around the globe under the pounding hatred of the peoples of the world!

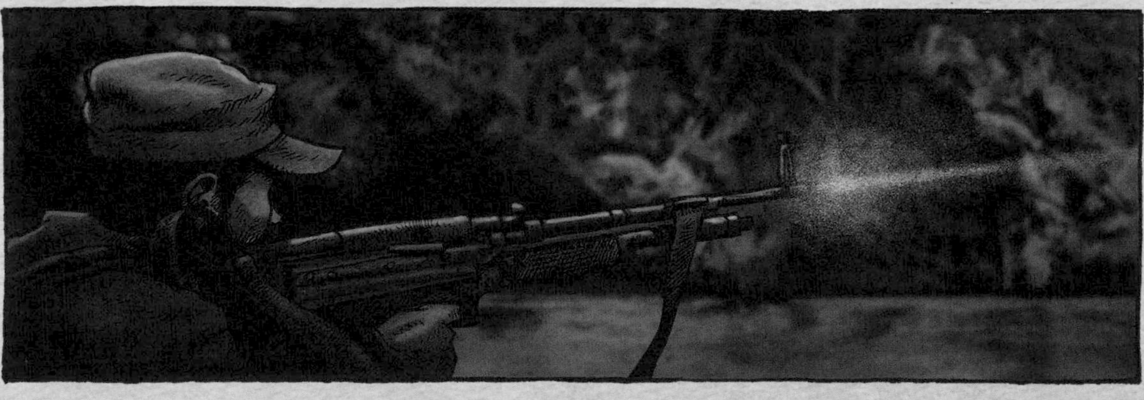

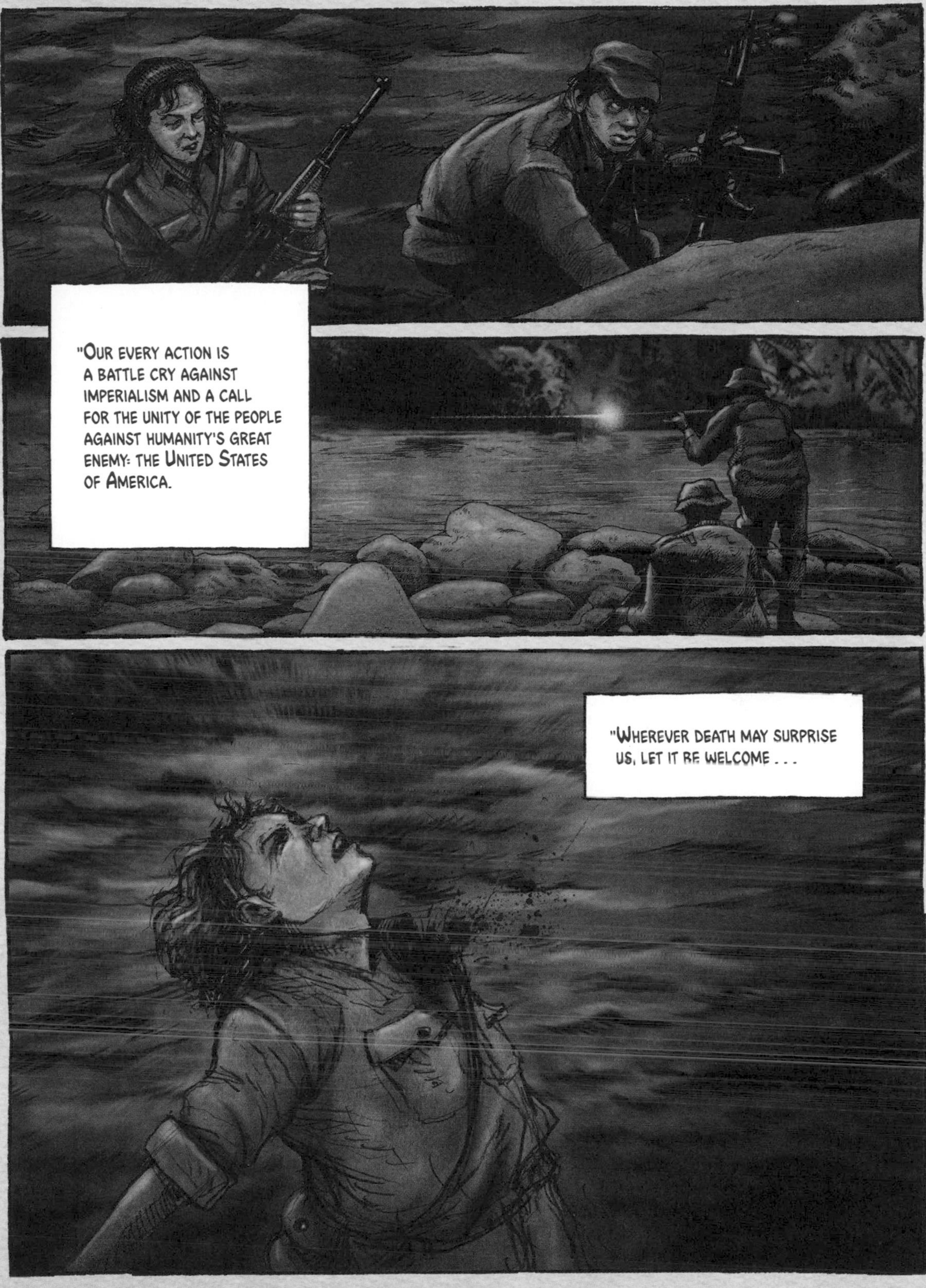
"Our every action is a battle cry against imperialism and a call for the unity of the people against humanity's great enemy: the United States of America.
"Wherever death may surprise us, let it be welcome . . .

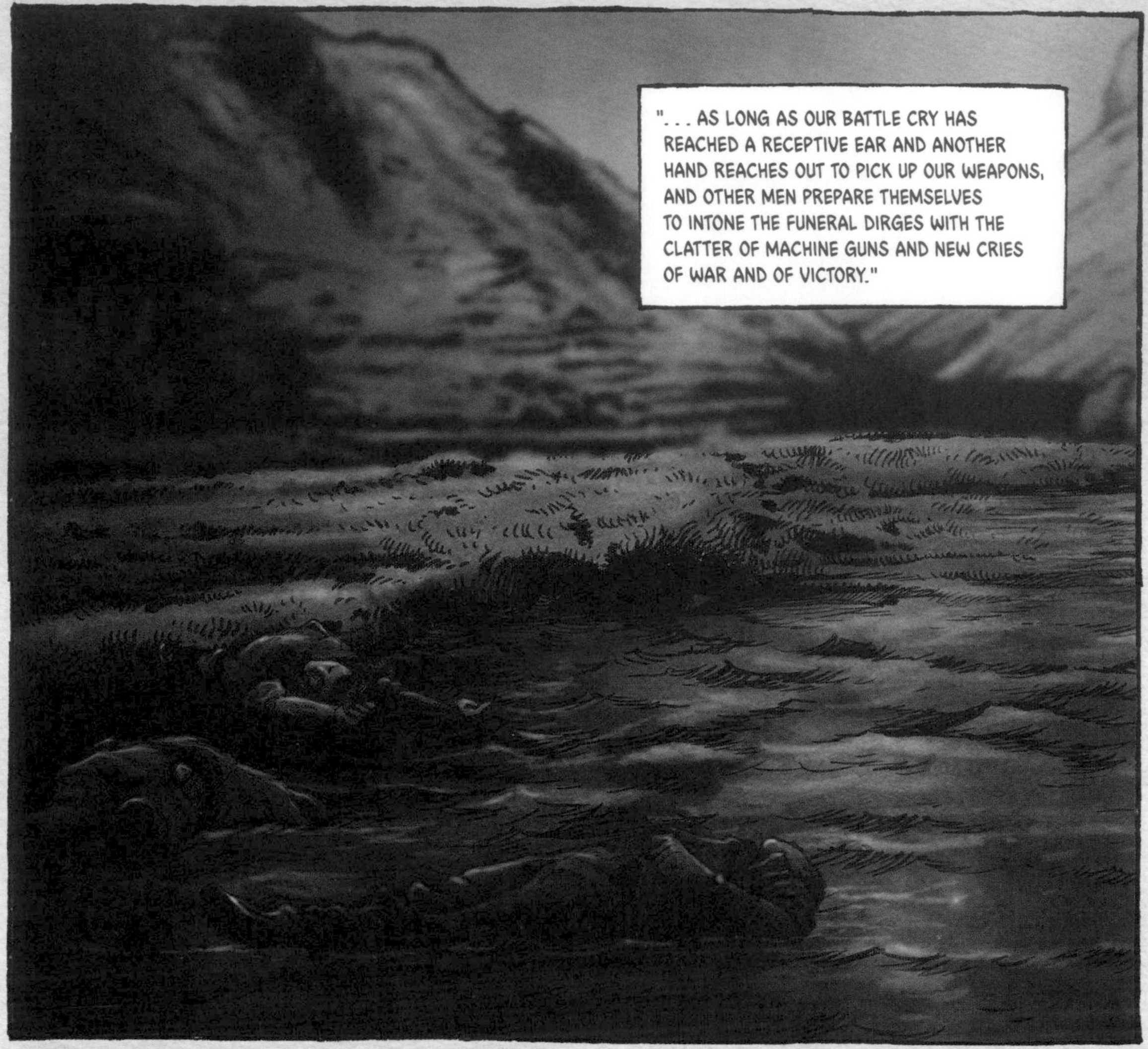
". . . AS LONG AS OUR BATTLE CRY HAS REACHED A RECEPTIVE EAR AND ANOTHER HAND REACHES OUT TO PICK UP OUR WEAPONS, AND OTHER MEN PREPARE THEMSELVES TO INTONE THE FUNERAL DIRGES WITH THE CLATTER OF MACHINE GUNS AND NEW CRIES OF WAR AND OF VICTORY."

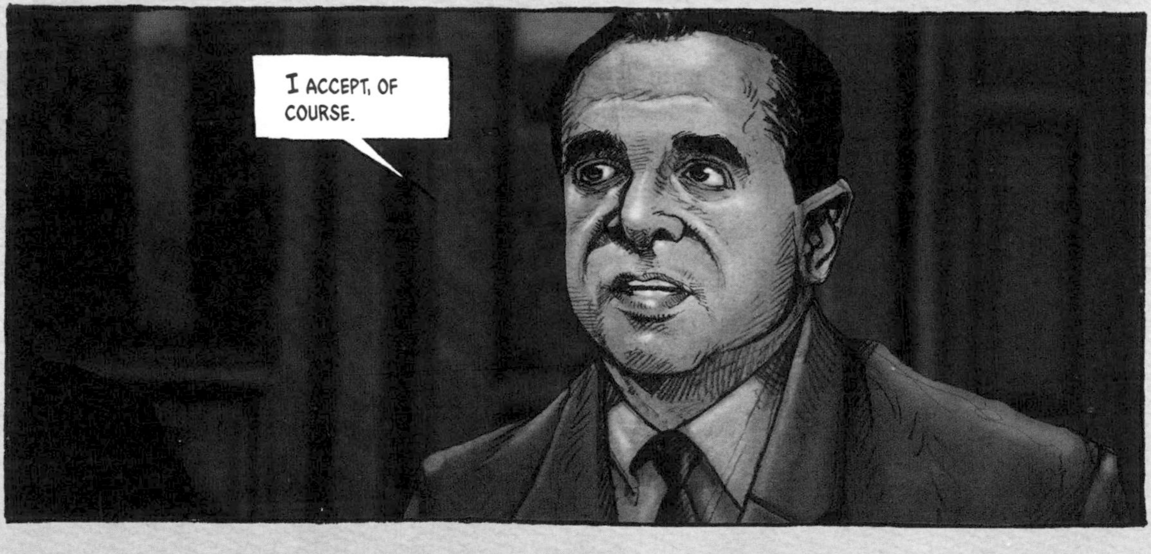
I ACCEPT, OF COURSE.

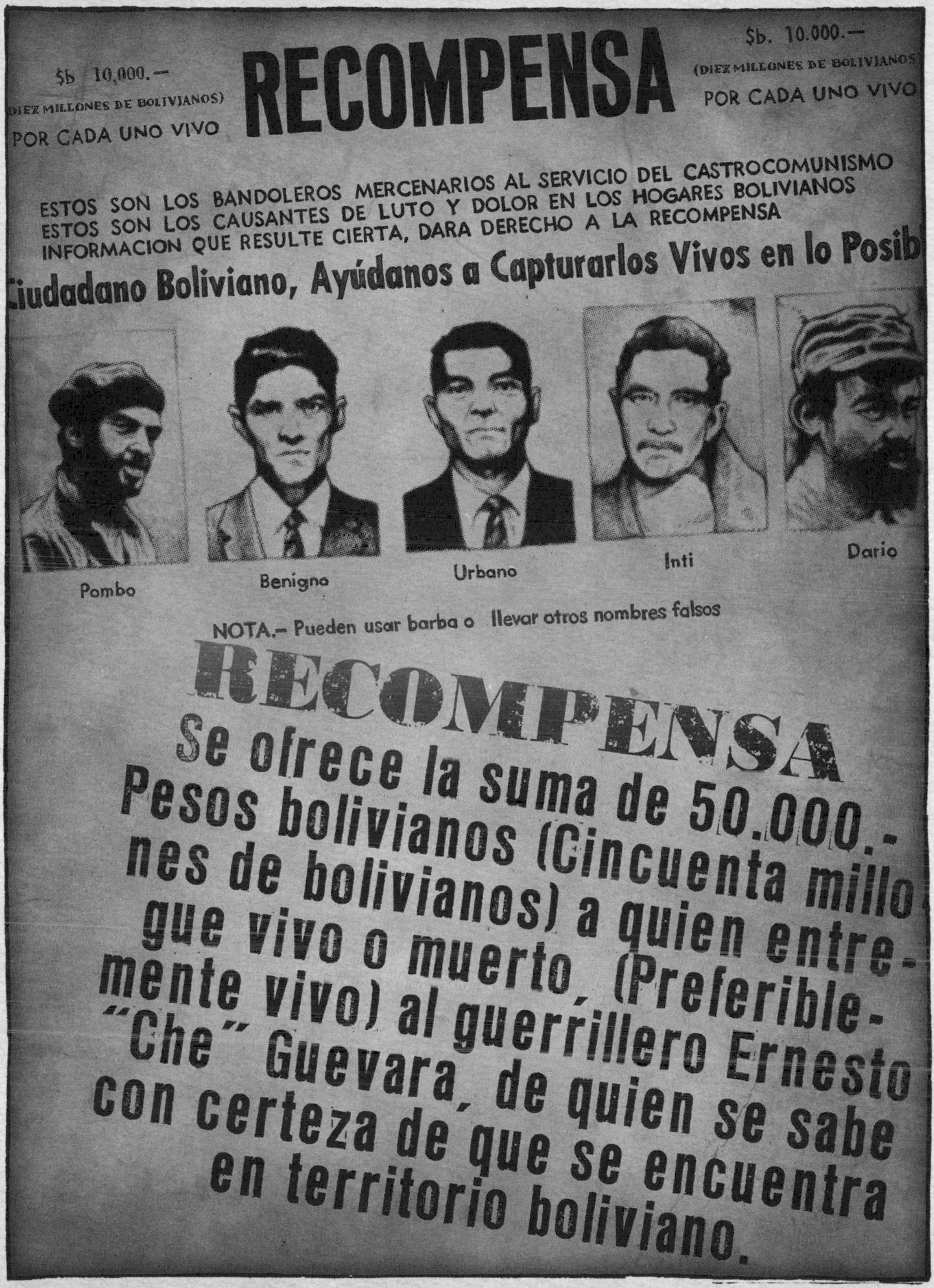
$b 10,000.—
(DIEZ MILLONES DE BOLIVIANOS)
POR CADA UNO VIVO
RECOMPENSA
$b. 10.000.—
(DIEZ MILLONES DE BOLIVIANOS)
POR CADA UNO VIVO
ESTOS SON LOS BANDOLEROS MERCENARIOS AL SERVICIO DEL CASTROCOMUNISMO
ESTOS SON LOS CAUSANTES DE LUTO Y DOLOR EN LOS HOGARES BOLIVIANOS
INFORMACION QUE RESULTE CIERTA, DARA DERECHO A LA RECOMPENSA
Ciudadano Boliviano, Ayúdanos a Capturarlos Vivos en lo Posib
Pombo
Benigno
Urbano
Inti
Dario
NOTA.– Pueden usar barba o llevar otros nombres falsos
RECOMPENSA
Se ofrece la suma de 50.000.-
Pesos bolivianos (Cincuenta millo-
nes de bolivianos) a quien entre-
gue vivo o muerto, (Preferible-
mente vivo) al guerrillero Ernesto
"Che" Guevara, de quien se sabe
con certeza de que se encuentra
en territorio boliviano.

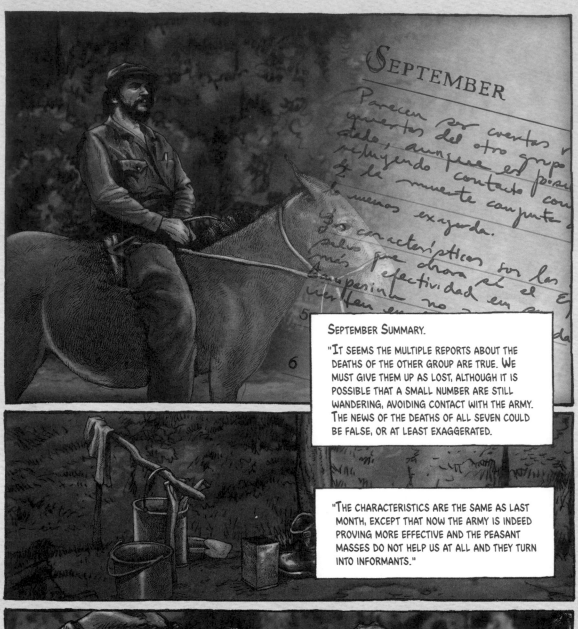

September Summary.

"It seems the multiple reports about the deaths of the other group are true. We must give them up as lost, although it is possible that a small number are still wandering, avoiding contact with the army. The news of the deaths of all seven could be false, or at least exaggerated.

"The characteristics are the same as last month, except that now the army is indeed proving more effective and the peasant masses do not help us at all and they turn into informants."

People are afraid of us. As soon as they see us, they disappear.

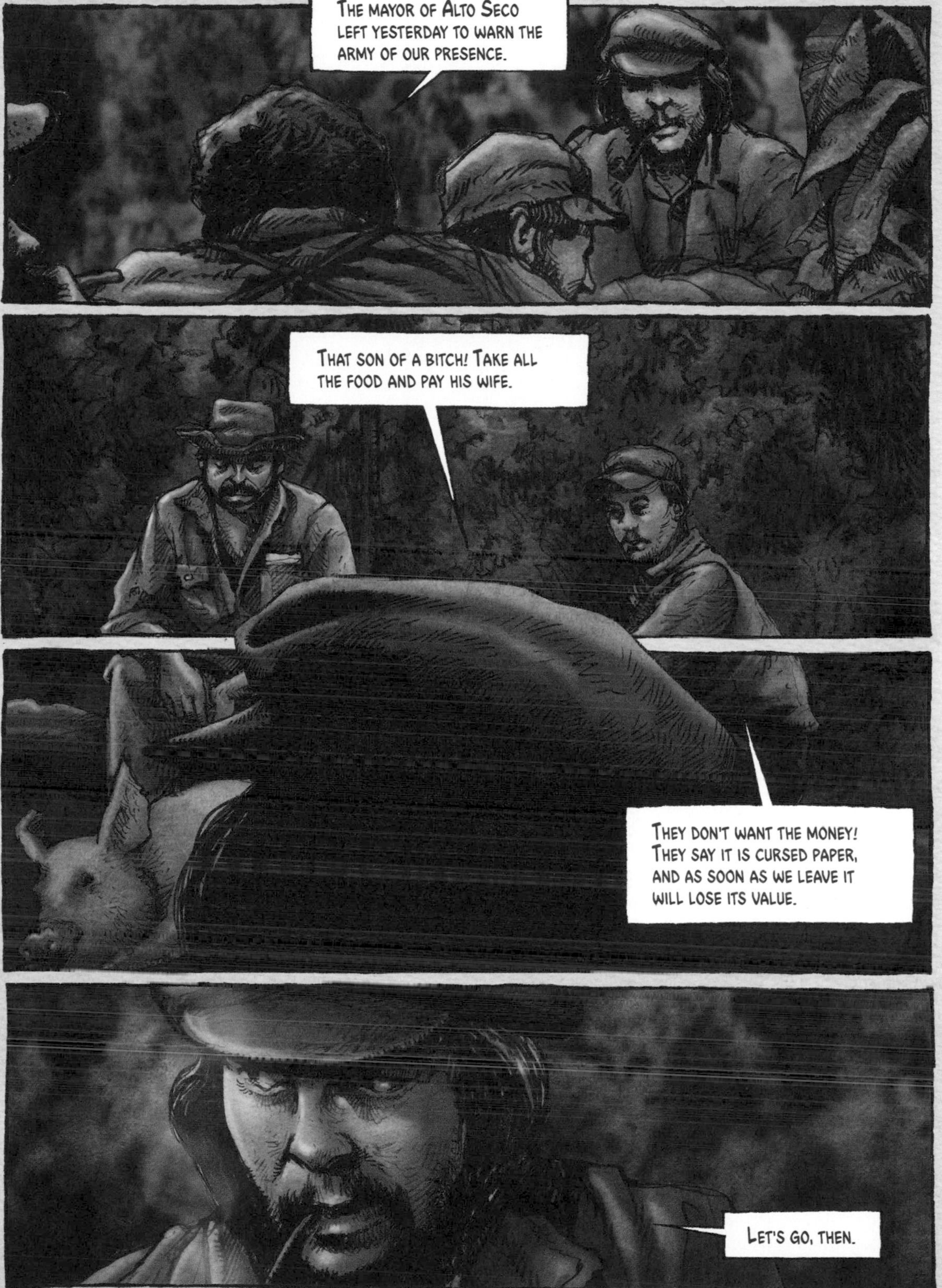
THE MAYOR OF ALTO SECO LEFT YESTERDAY TO WARN THE ARMY OF OUR PRESENCE.
THAT SON OF A BITCH! TAKE ALL THE FOOD AND PAY HIS WIFE.
THEY DON'T WANT THE MONEY! THEY SAY IT IS CURSED PAPER, AND AS SOON AS WE LEAVE IT WILL LOSE ITS VALUE.
LET'S GO, THEN.

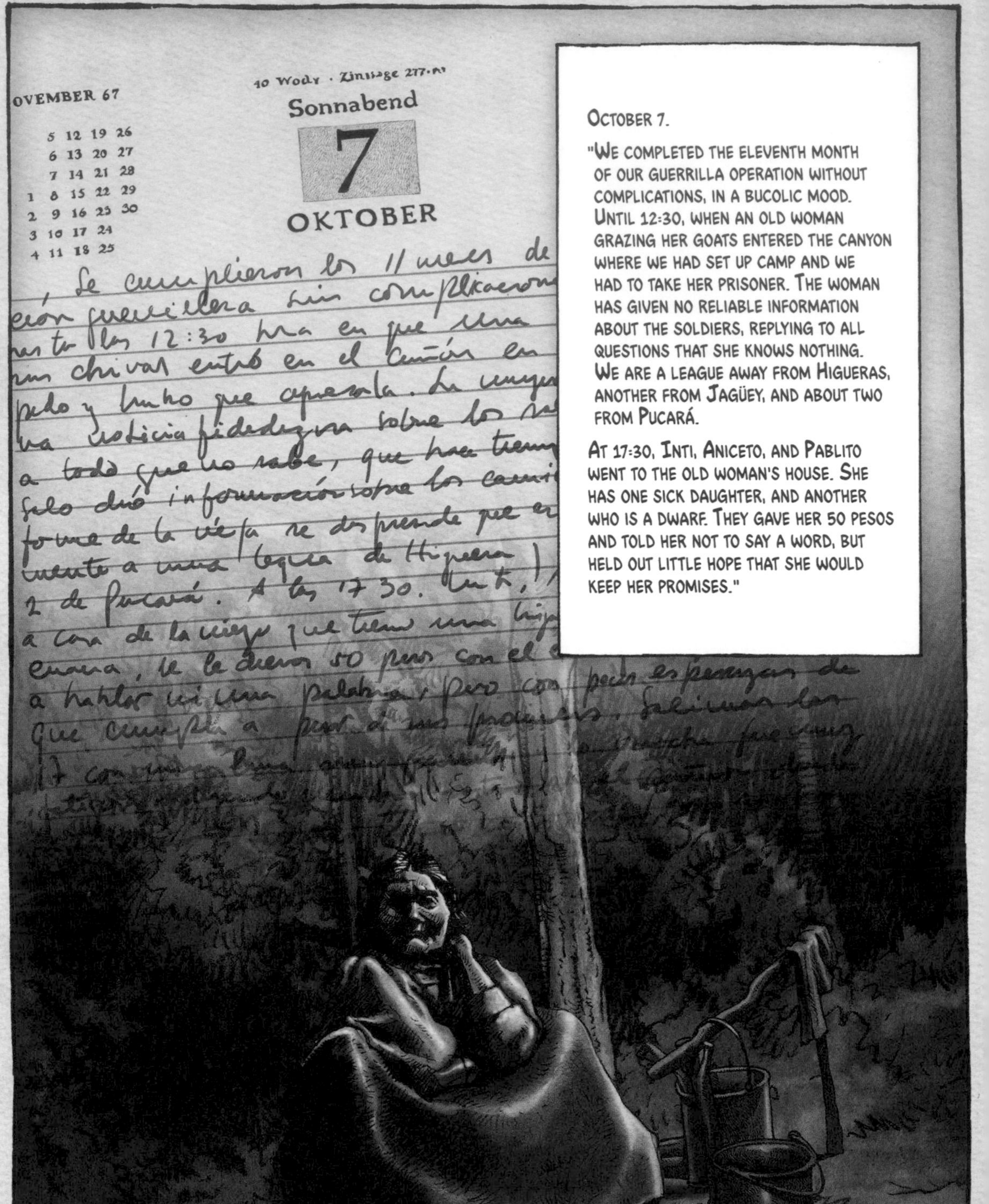
OVEMBER 67
Sonnabend
7
OKTOBER
OCTOBER 7.
"WE COMPLETED THE ELEVENTH MONTH OF OUR GUERRILLA OPERATION WITHOUT COMPLICATIONS, IN A BUCOLIC MOOD. UNTIL 12:30, WHEN AN OLD WOMAN GRAZING HER GOATS ENTERED THE CANYON WHERE WE HAD SET UP CAMP AND WE HAD TO TAKE HER PRISONER. THE WOMAN HAS GIVEN NO RELIABLE INFORMATION ABOUT THE SOLDIERS, REPLYING TO ALL QUESTIONS THAT SHE KNOWS NOTHING. WE ARE A LEAGUE AWAY FROM HIGUERAS, ANOTHER FROM JAGÜEY, AND ABOUT TWO FROM PUCARÁ.
AT 17:30, INTI, ANICETO, AND PABLITO WENT TO THE OLD WOMAN'S HOUSE. SHE HAS ONE SICK DAUGHTER, AND ANOTHER WHO IS A DWARF. THEY GAVE HER 50 PESOS AND TOLD HER NOT TO SAY A WORD, BUT HELD OUT LITTLE HOPE THAT SHE WOULD KEEP HER PROMISES."

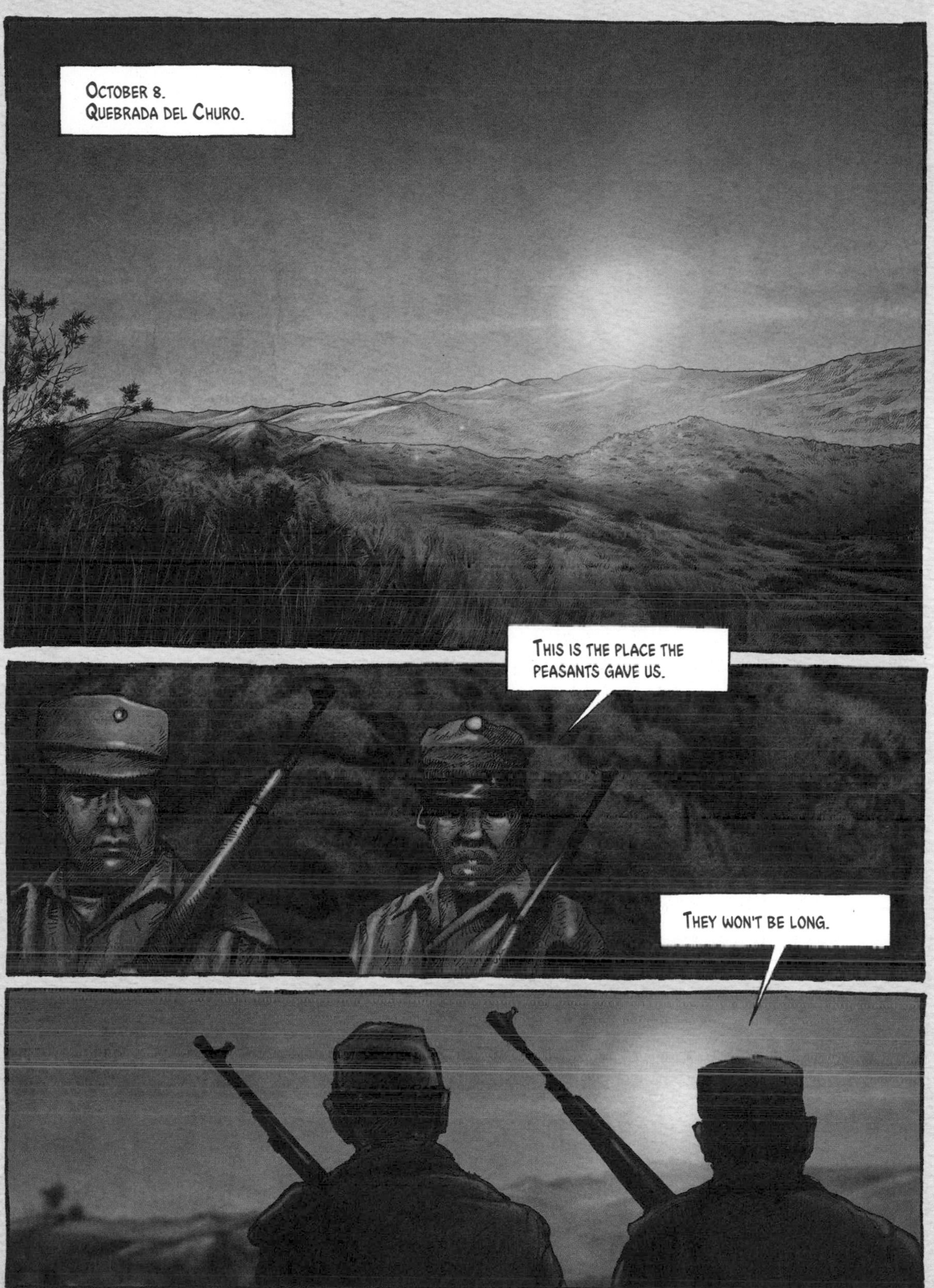
October 8.
Quebrada del Churo.
This is the place the peasants gave us.
They won't be long.

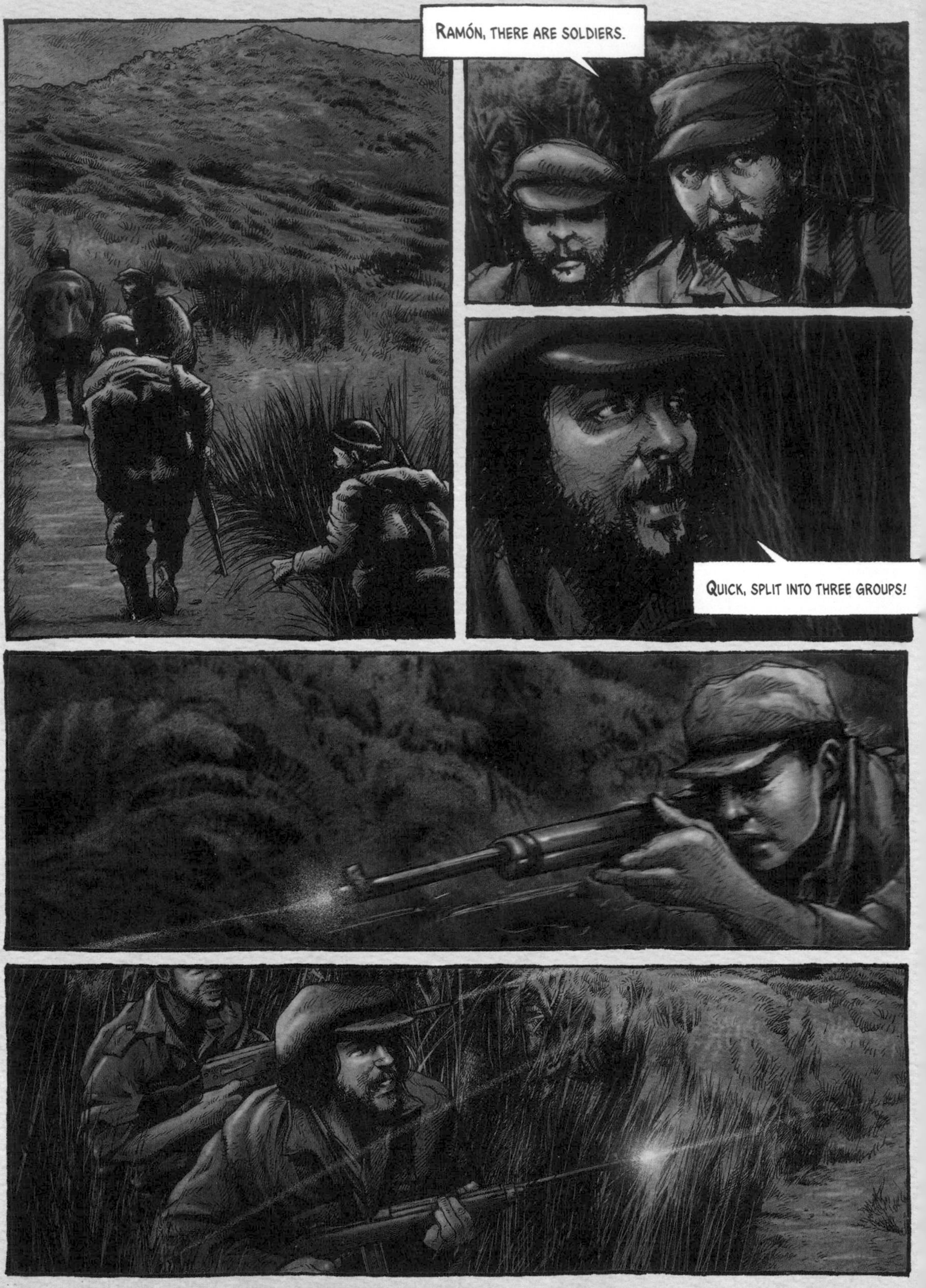
RAMÓN, THERE ARE SOLDIERS.
QUICK, SPLIT INTO THREE GROUPS!

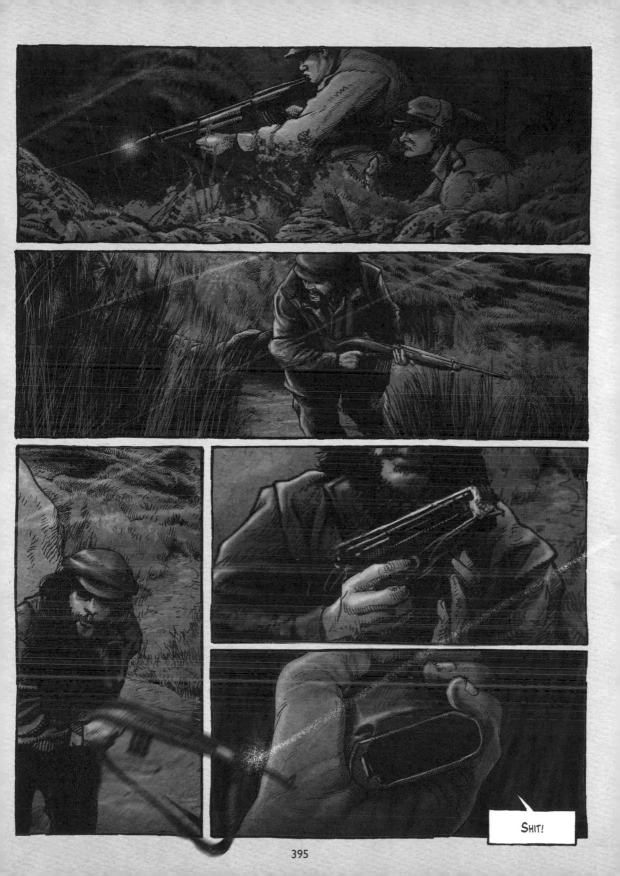

SHIT!

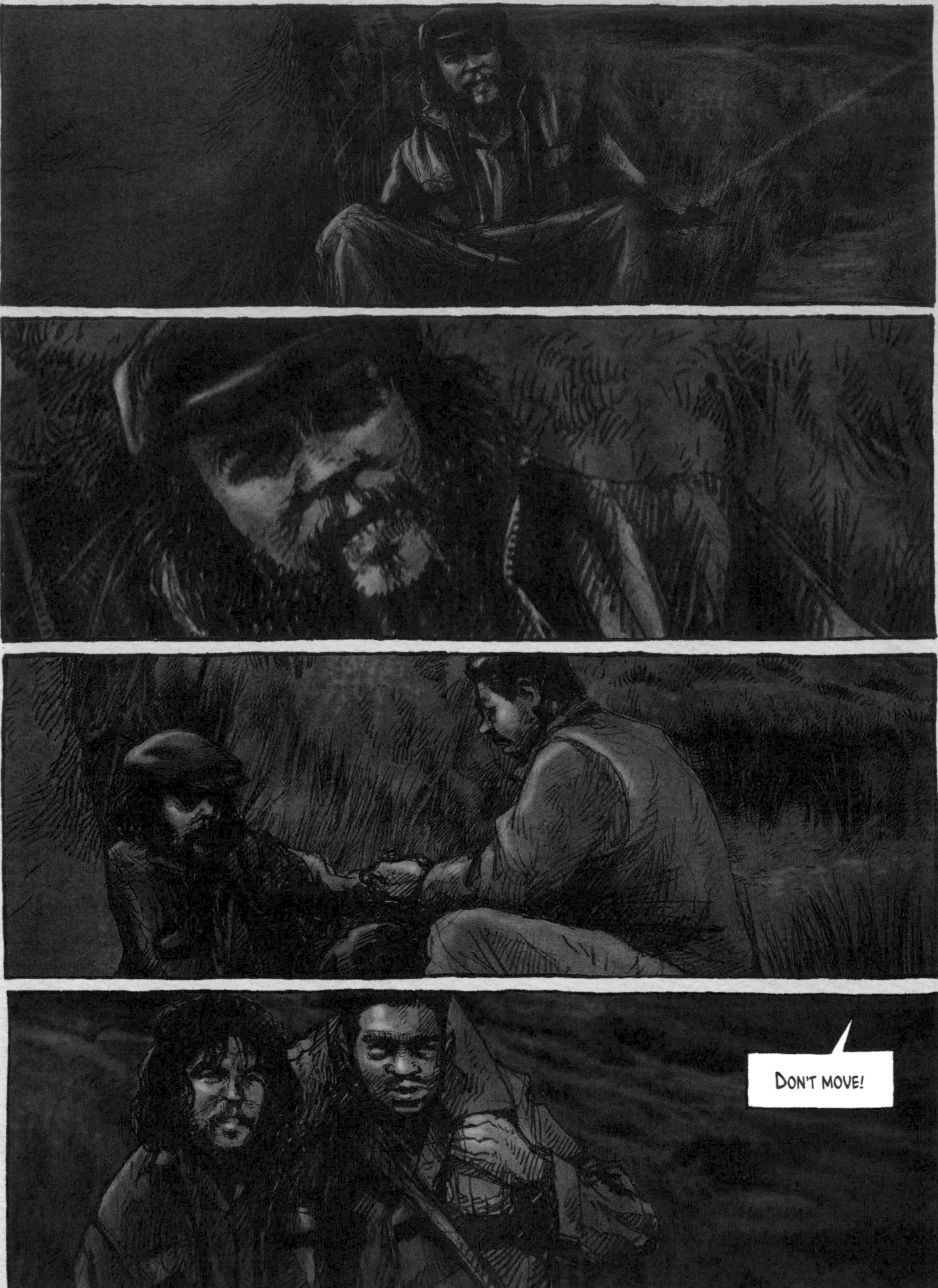
Don't move!

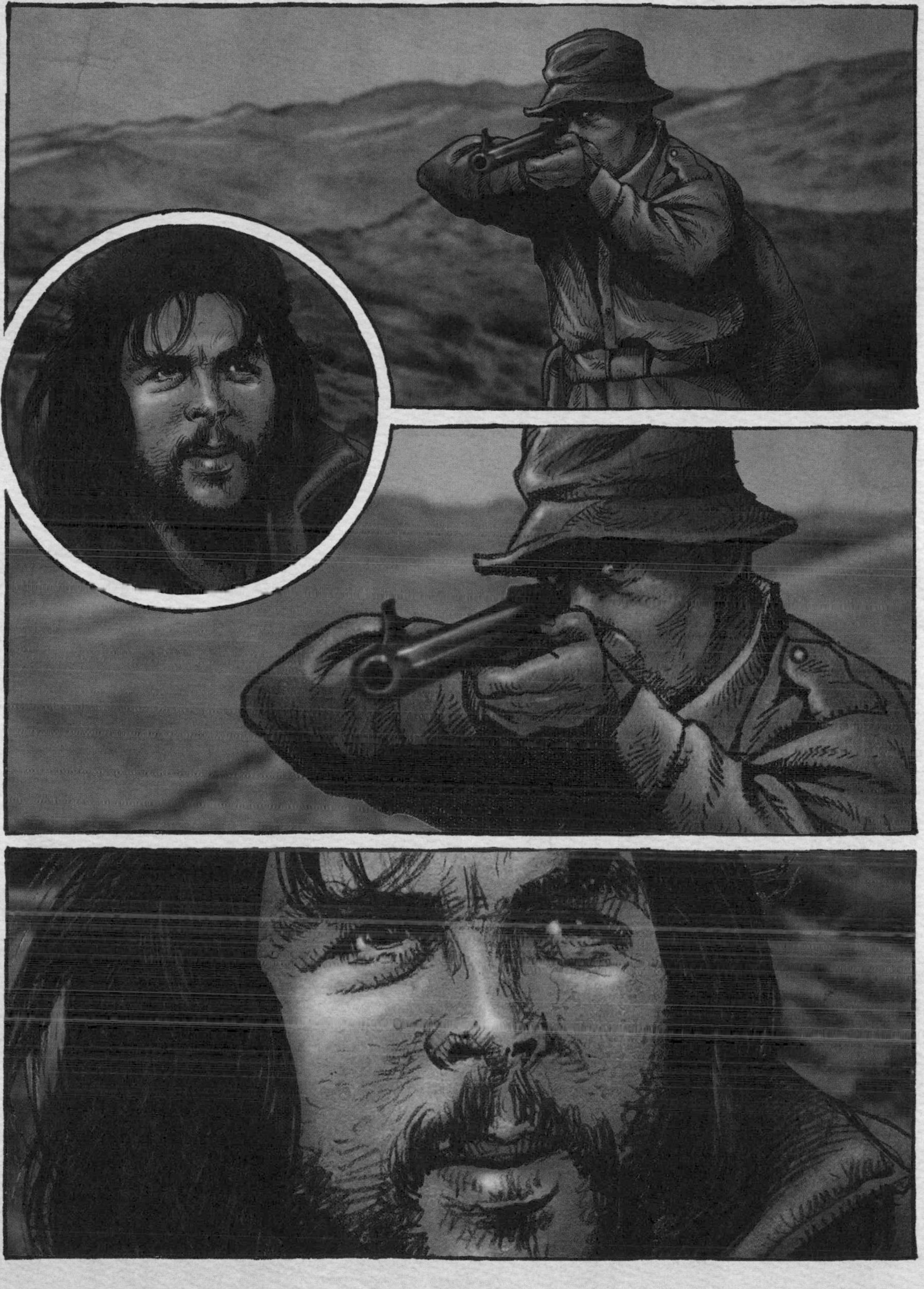

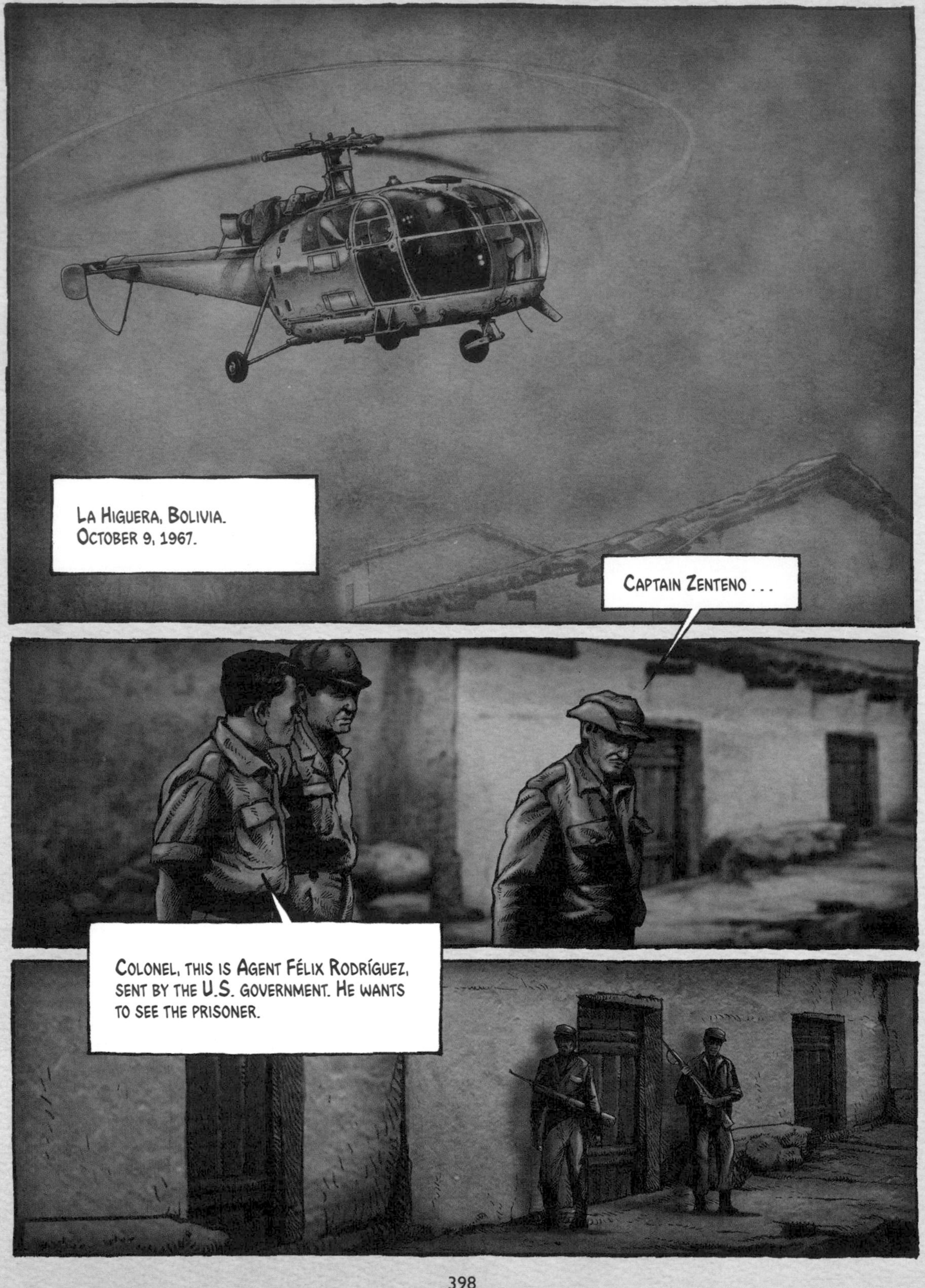
LA HIGUERA, BOLIVIA.
OCTOBER 9, 1967.
CAPTAIN ZENTENO . . .
COLONEL, THIS IS AGENT FÉLIX RODRÍGUEZ, SENT BY THE U.S. GOVERNMENT. HE WANTS TO SEE THE PRISONER.

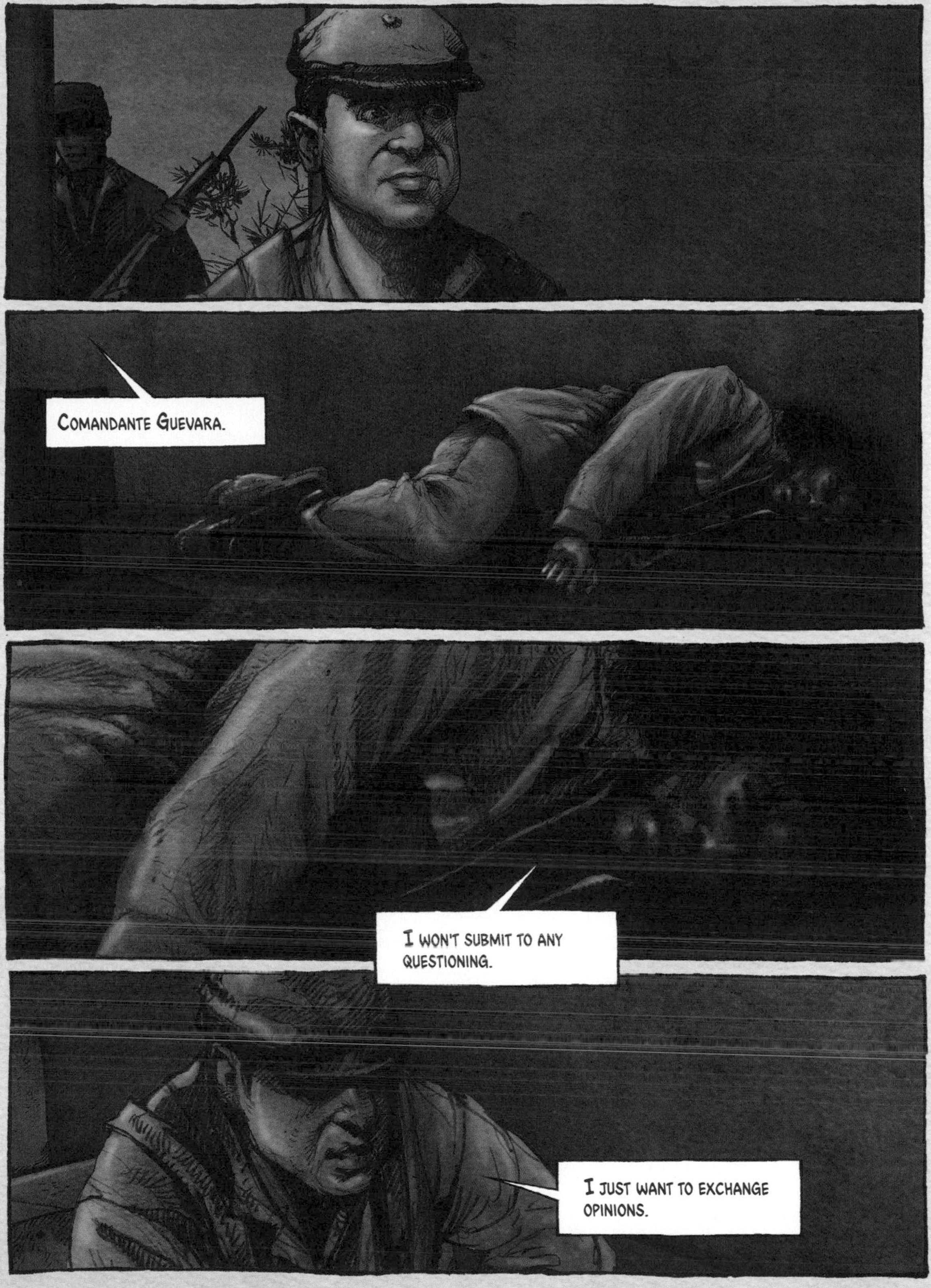
Comandante Guevara.
I won't submit to any questioning.
I just want to exchange opinions.

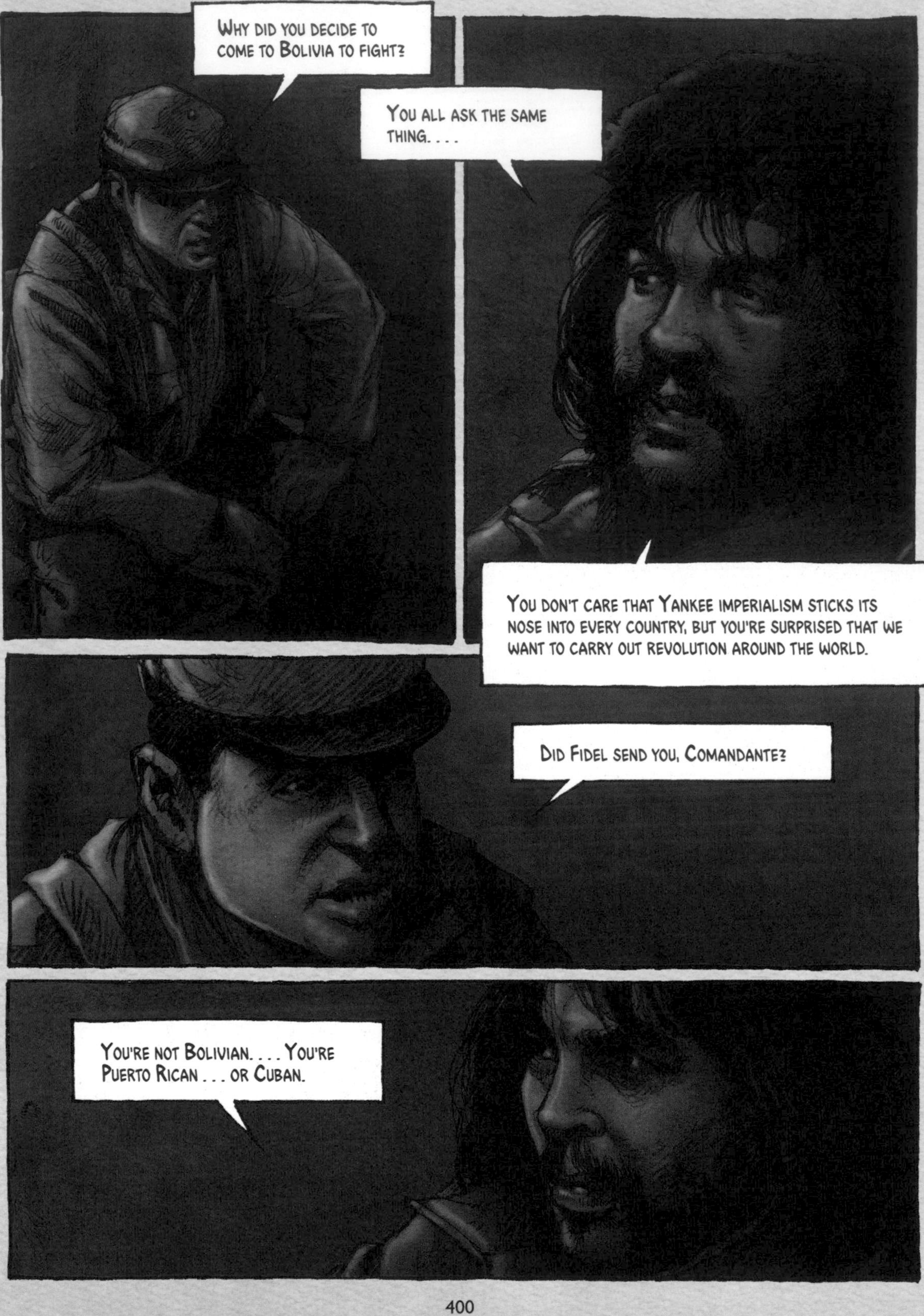
WHY DID YOU DECIDE TO COME TO BOLIVIA TO FIGHT?
YOU ALL ASK THE SAME THING. . . .
YOU DON'T CARE THAT YANKEE IMPERIALISM STICKS ITS NOSE INTO EVERY COUNTRY, BUT YOU'RE SURPRISED THAT WE WANT TO CARRY OUT REVOLUTION AROUND THE WORLD.
DID FIDEL SEND YOU, COMANDANTE?
YOU'RE NOT BOLIVIAN. . . . YOU'RE PUERTO RICAN . . . OR CUBAN.

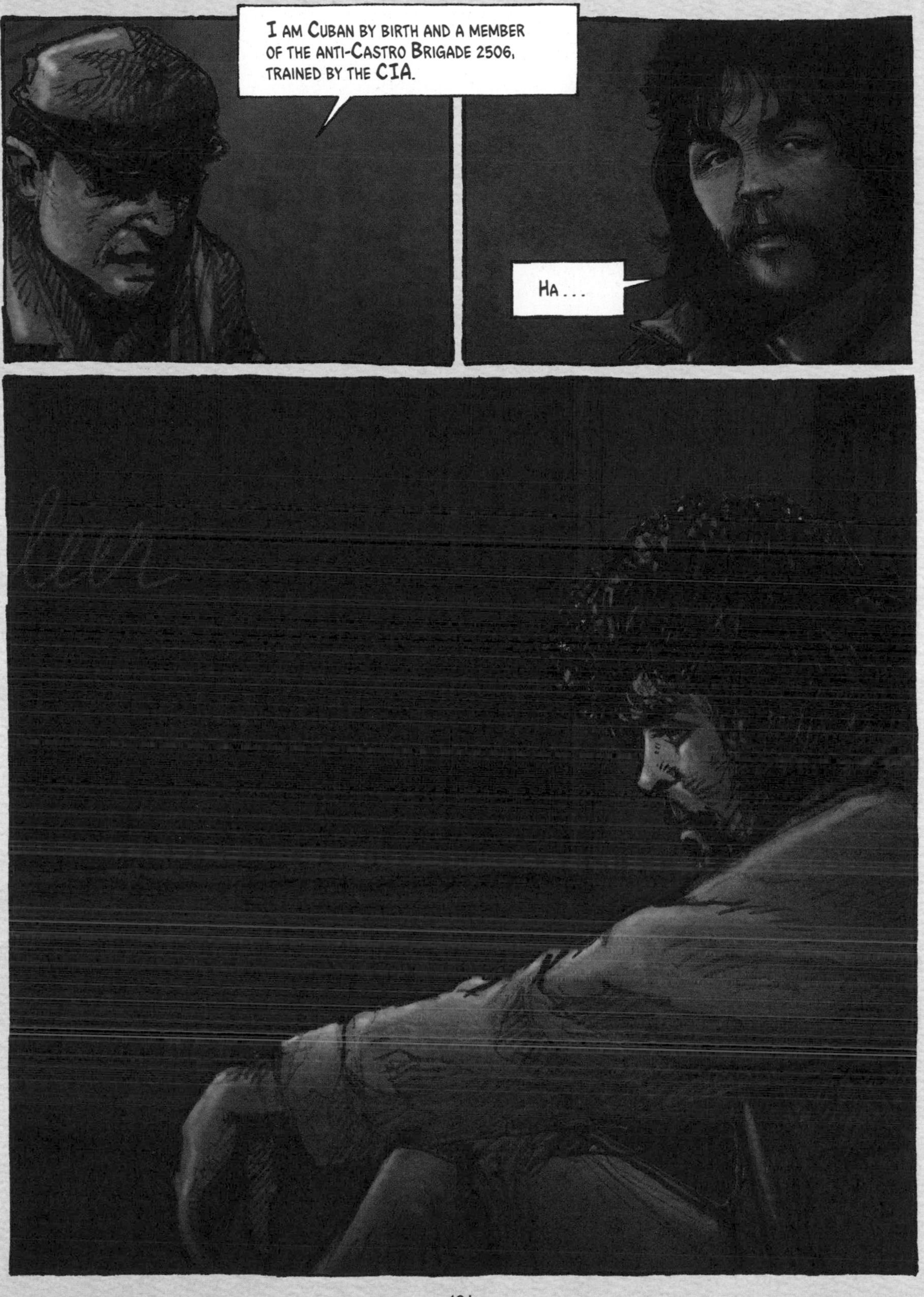
I AM CUBAN BY BIRTH AND A MEMBER OF THE ANTI-CASTRO BRIGADE 2506, TRAINED BY THE CIA.
HA . . .

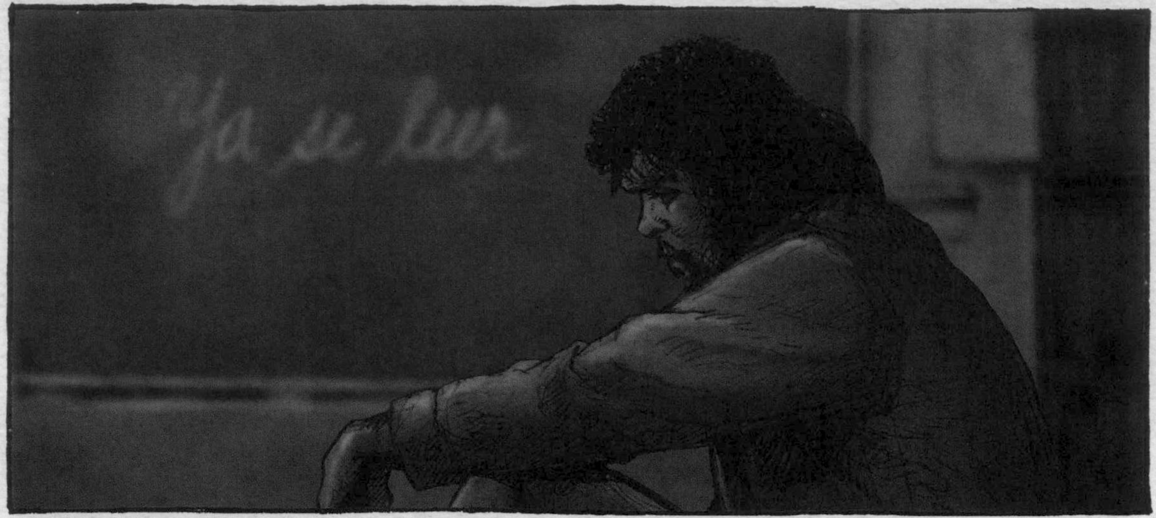
Ya se leer

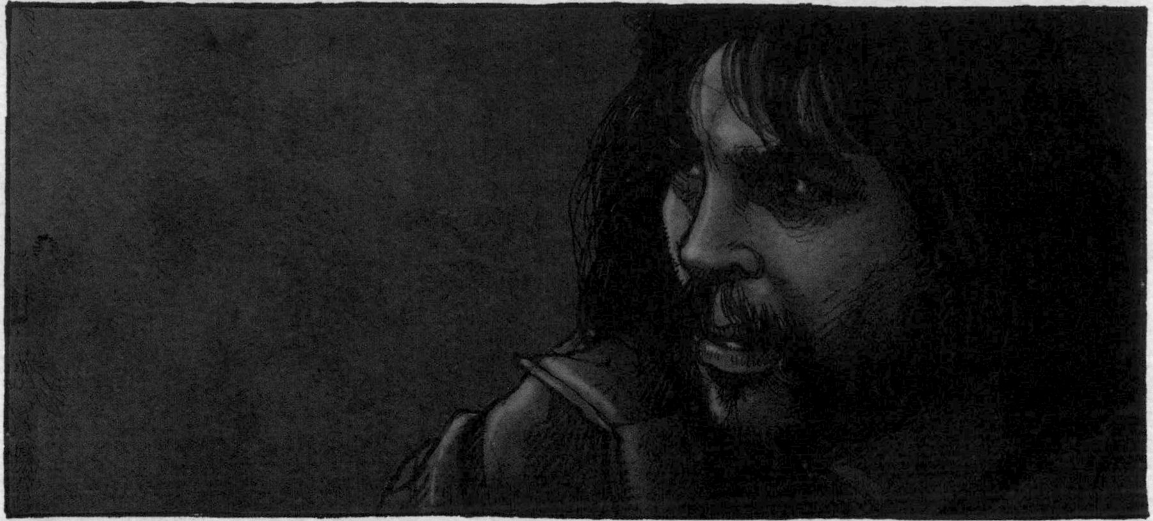

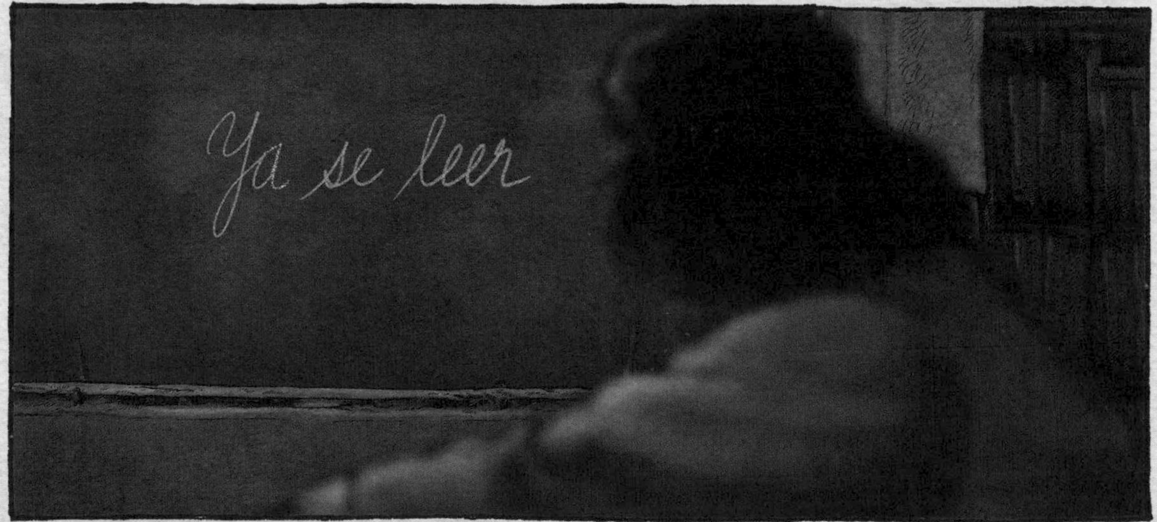
Ya se leer

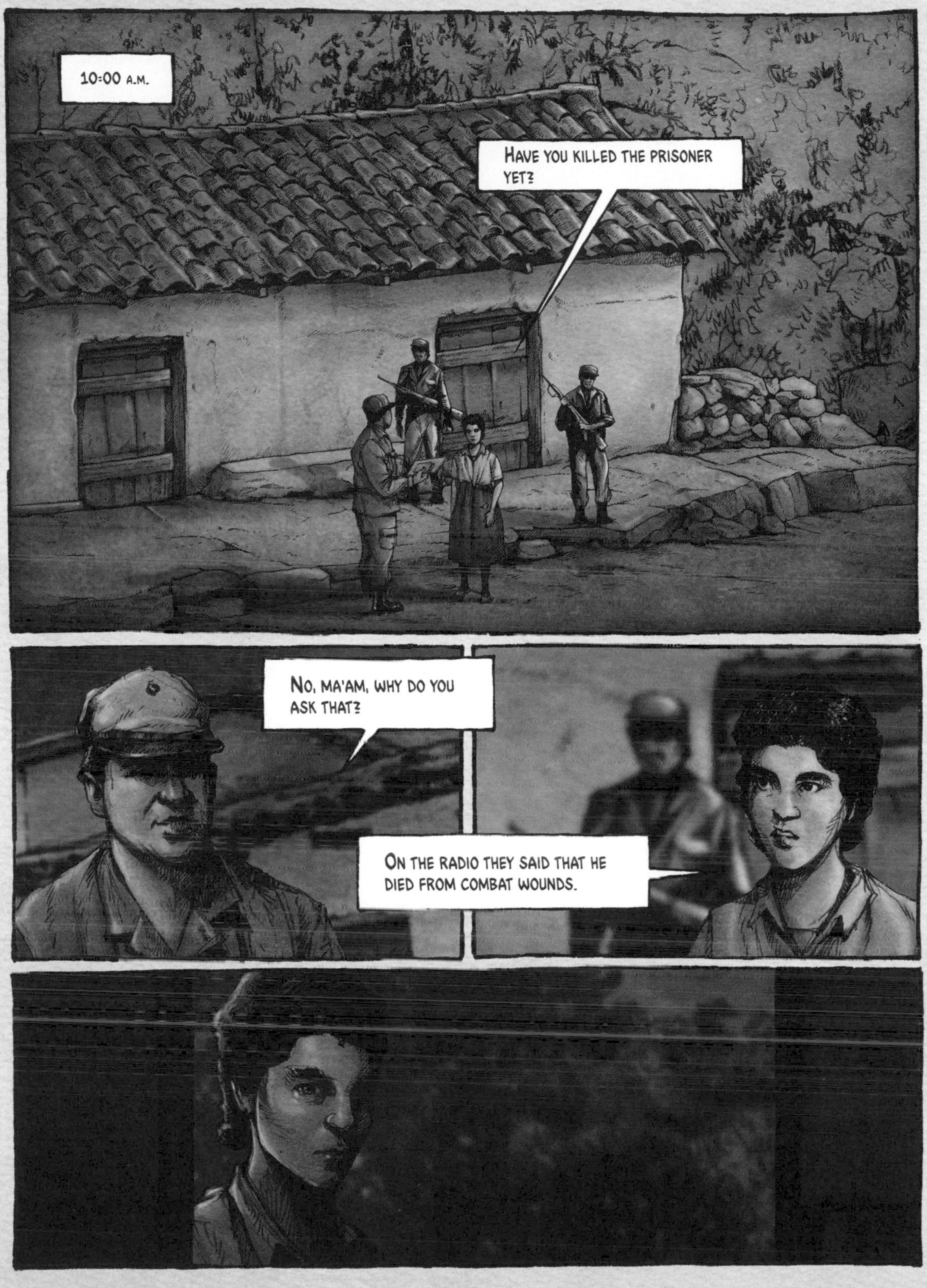
10:00 A.M.
HAVE YOU KILLED THE PRISONER YET?
NO, MA'AM, WHY DO YOU ASK THAT?
ON THE RADIO THEY SAID THAT HE DIED FROM COMBAT WOUNDS.

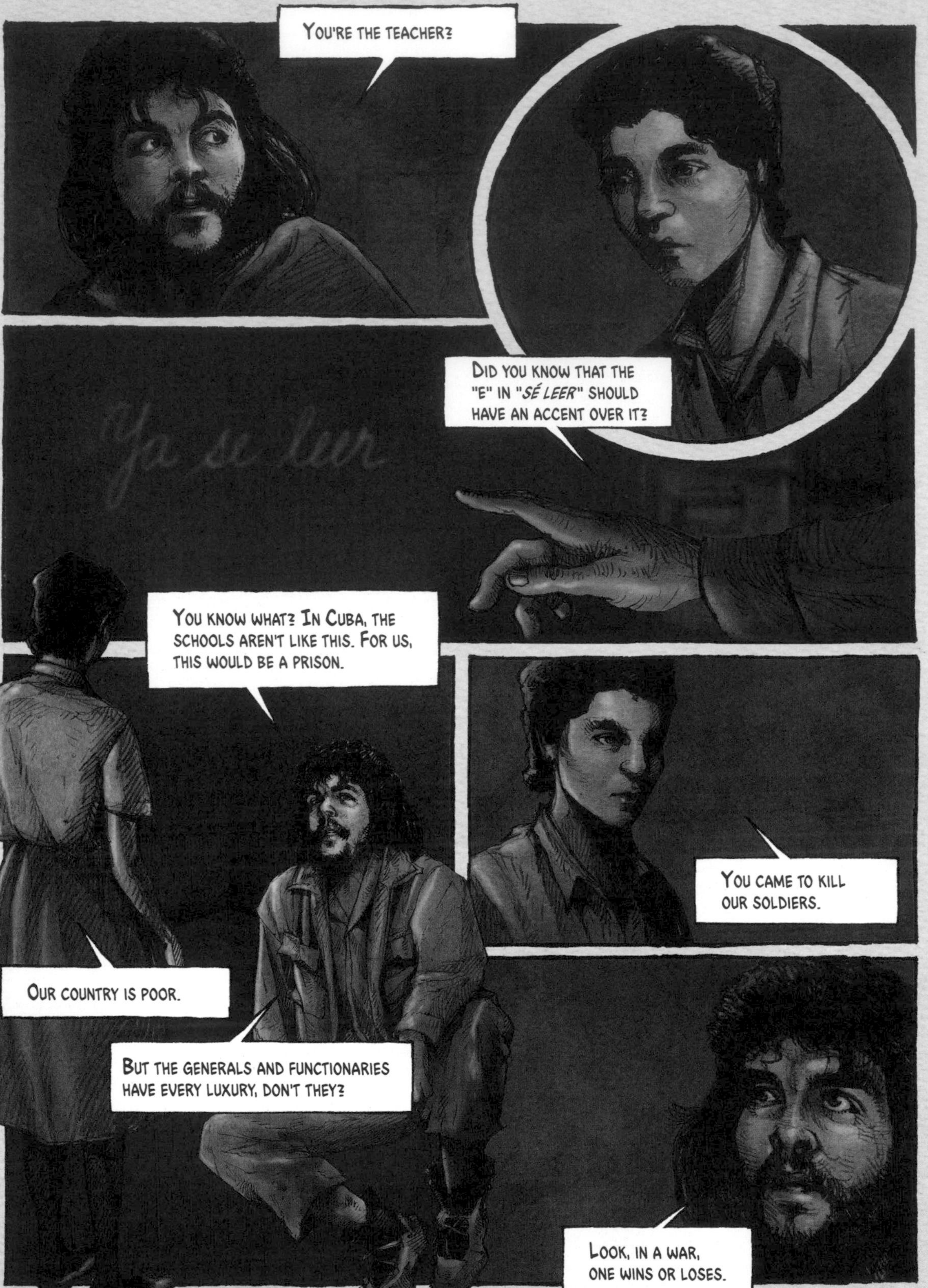
You're the teacher?
Did you know that the "e" in "*sé leer*" should have an accent over it?
Ya se leer
You know what? In Cuba, the schools aren't like this. For us, this would be a prison.
You came to kill our soldiers.
Our country is poor.
But the generals and functionaries have every luxury, don't they?
Look, in a war, one wins or loses.

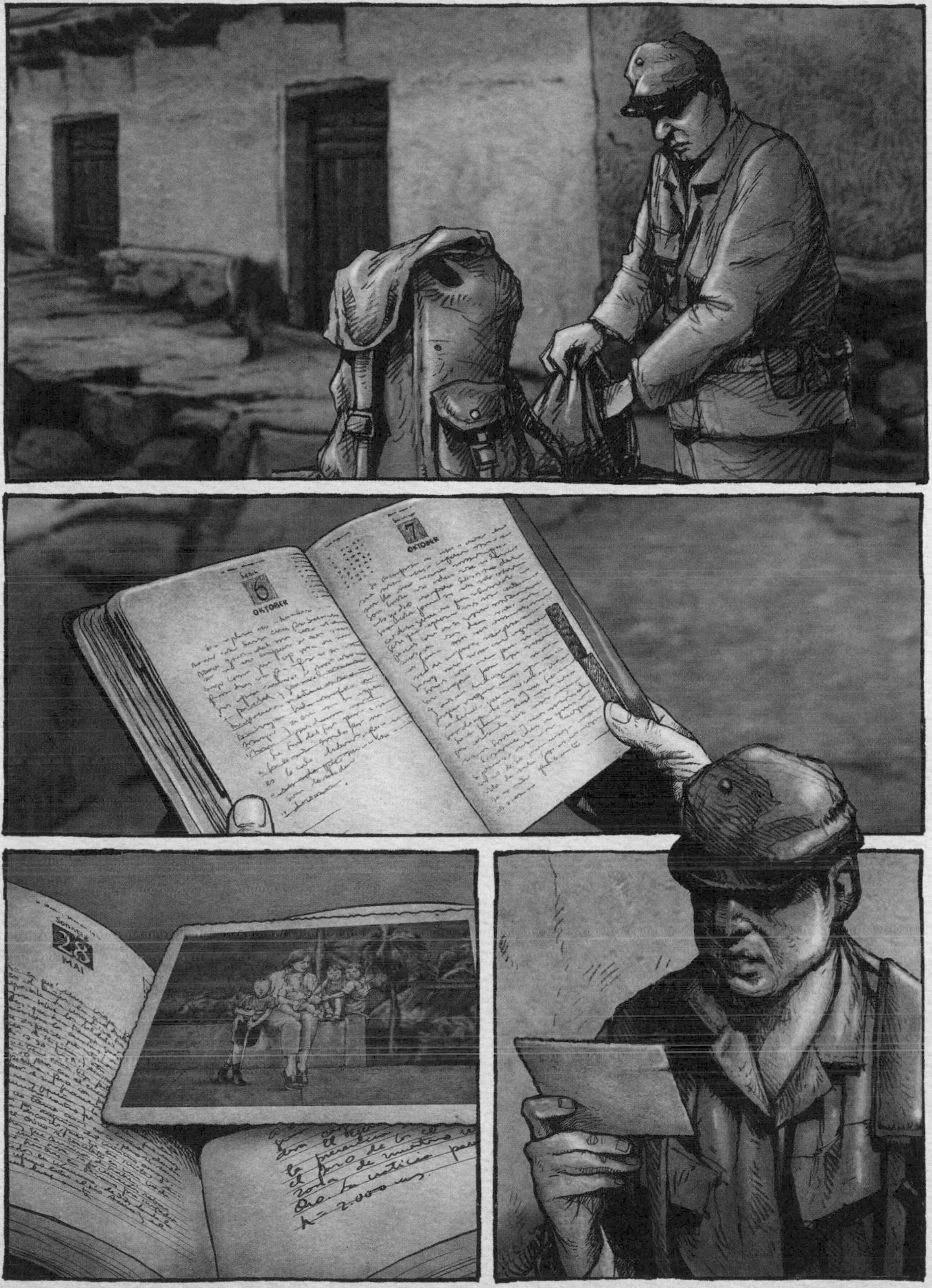
6
OKTOBER
7
OKTOBER
28
MAI

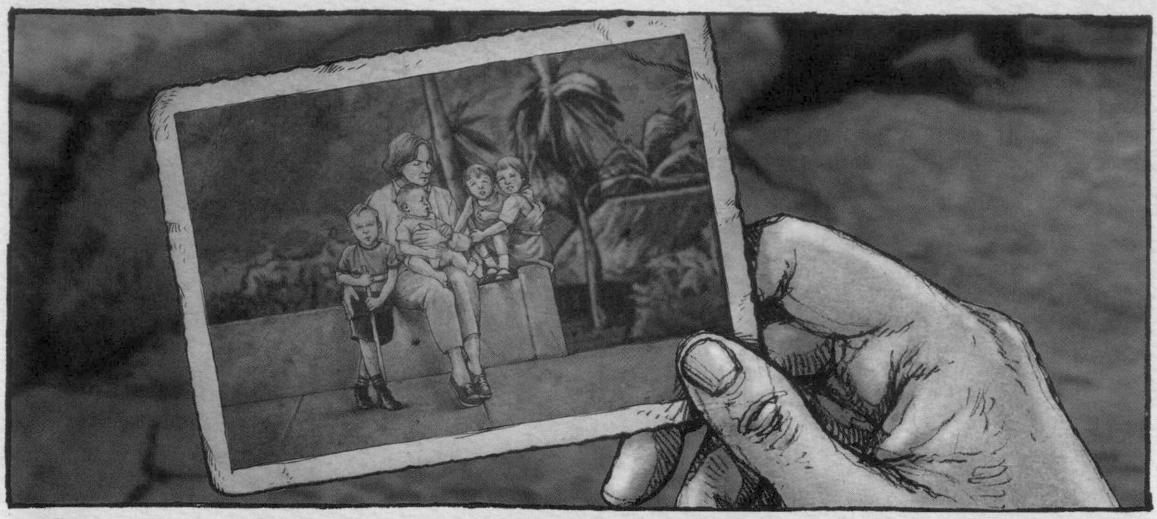

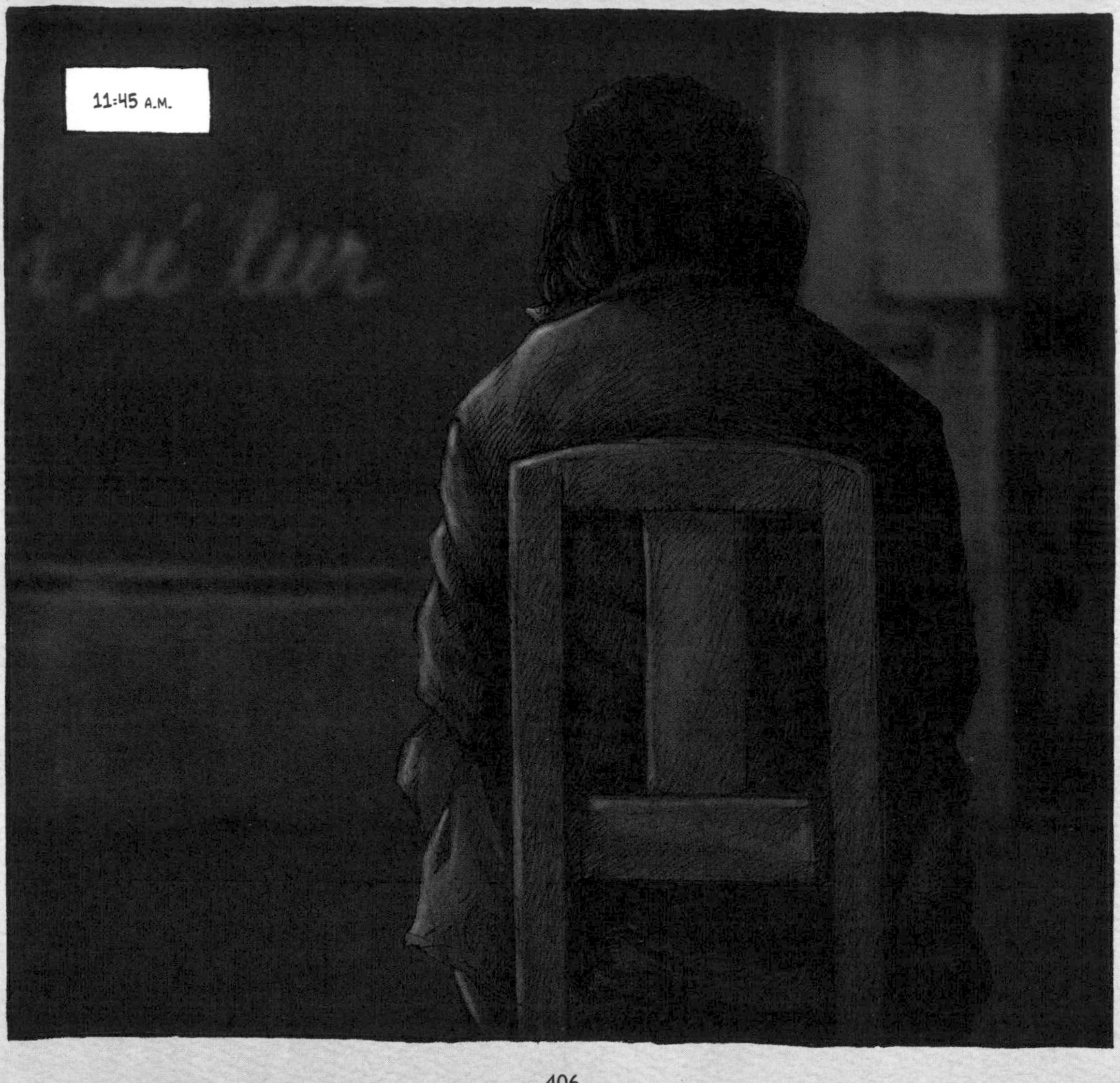
11:45 A.M.

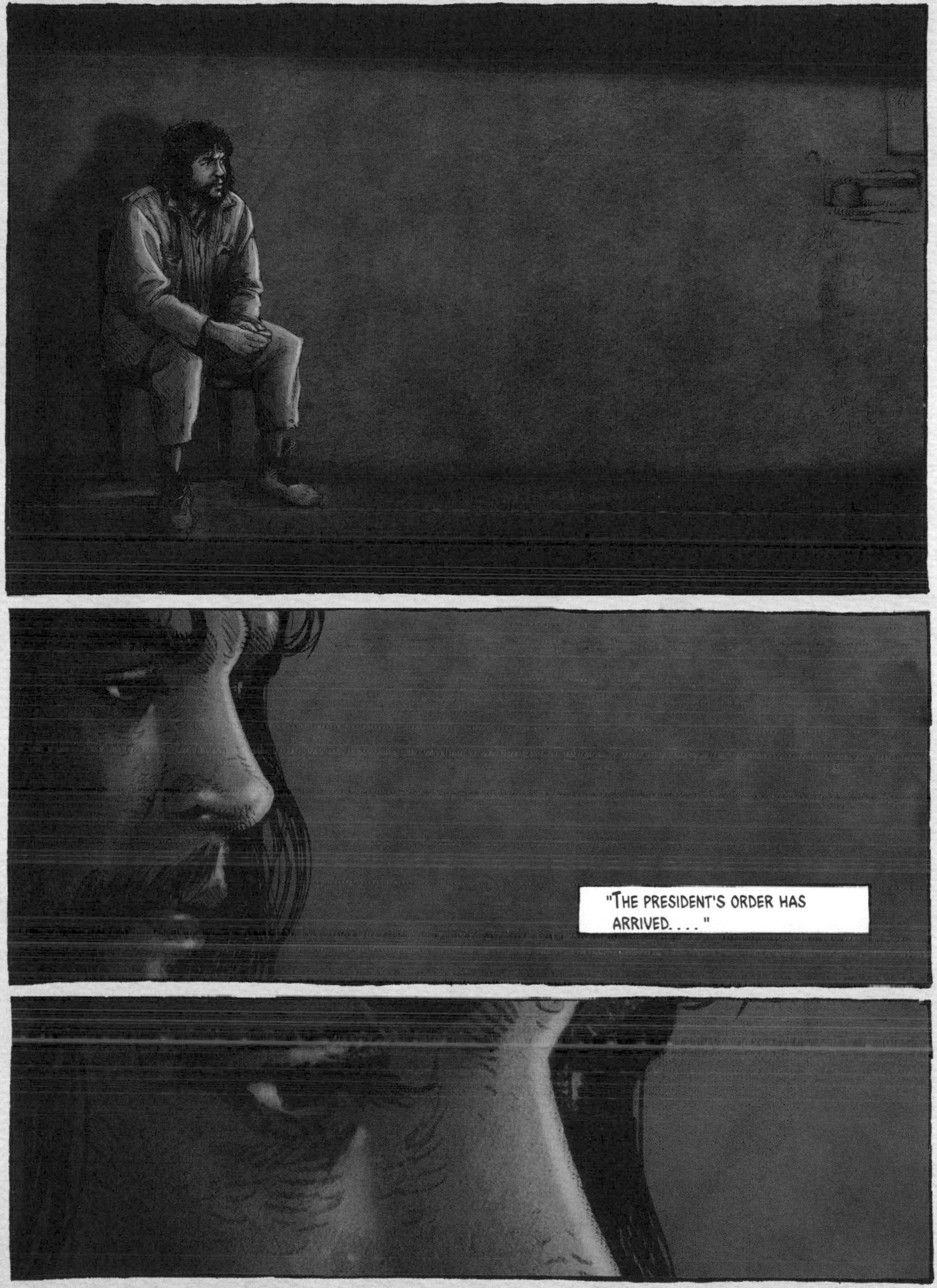
"THE PRESIDENT'S ORDER HAS ARRIVED. . . ."

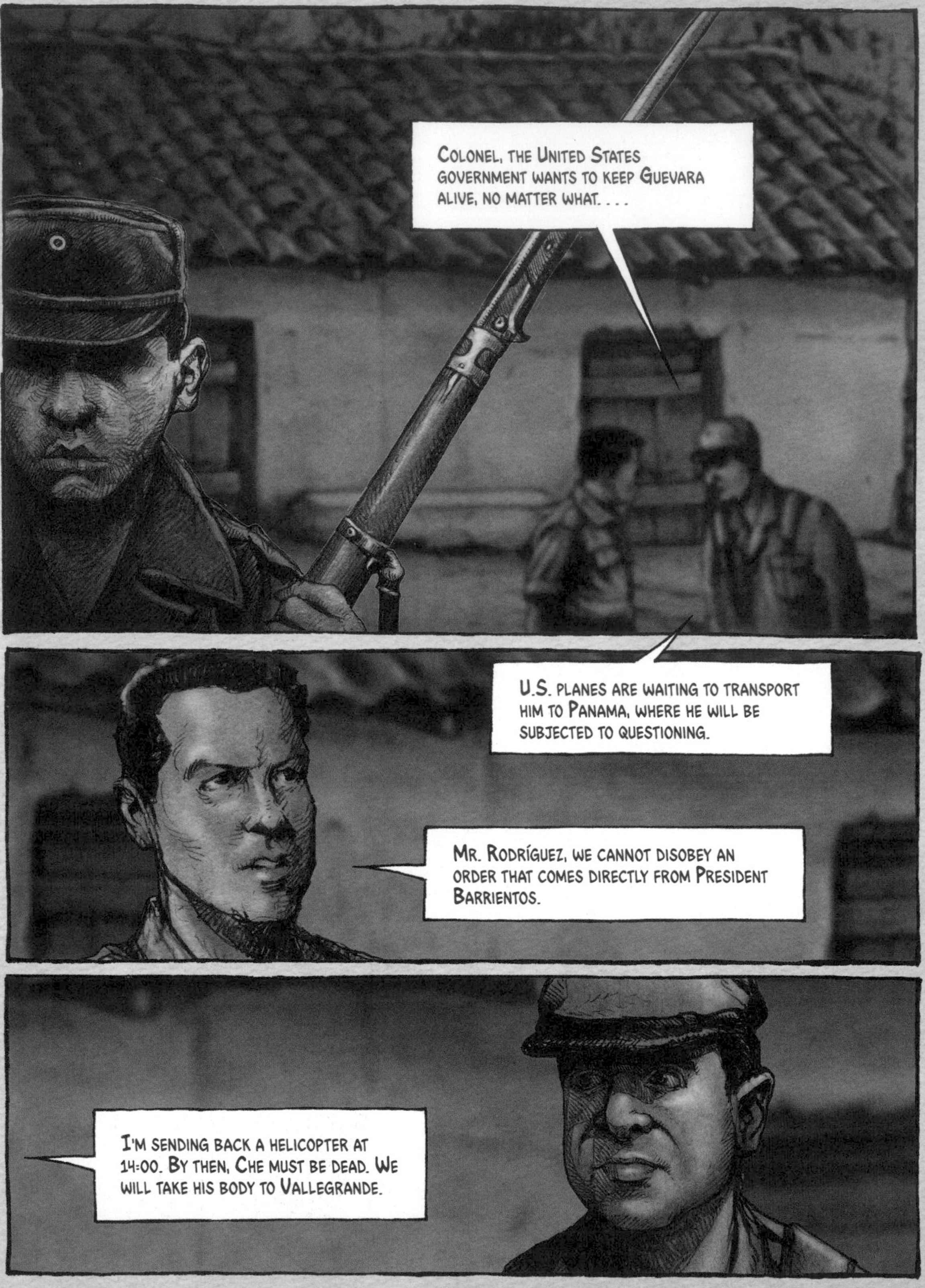
COLONEL, THE UNITED STATES GOVERNMENT WANTS TO KEEP GUEVARA ALIVE, NO MATTER WHAT. . . .
U.S. PLANES ARE WAITING TO TRANSPORT HIM TO PANAMA, WHERE HE WILL BE SUBJECTED TO QUESTIONING.
MR. RODRÍGUEZ, WE CANNOT DISOBEY AN ORDER THAT COMES DIRECTLY FROM PRESIDENT BARRIENTOS.
I'M SENDING BACK A HELICOPTER AT 14:00. BY THEN, CHE MUST BE DEAD. WE WILL TAKE HIS BODY TO VALLEGRANDE.

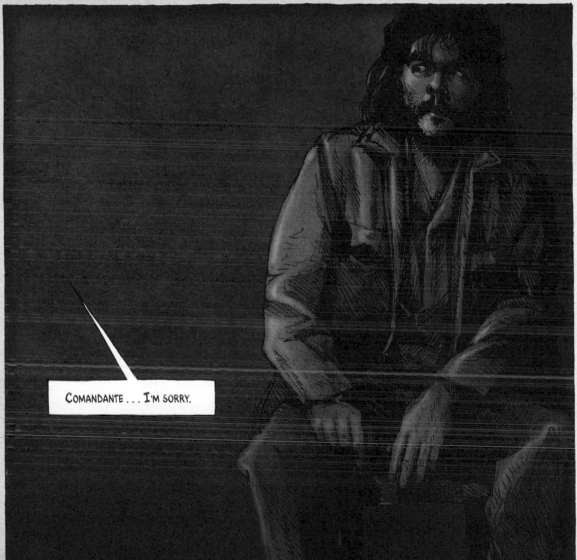

COMANDANTE . . . I'M SORRY.

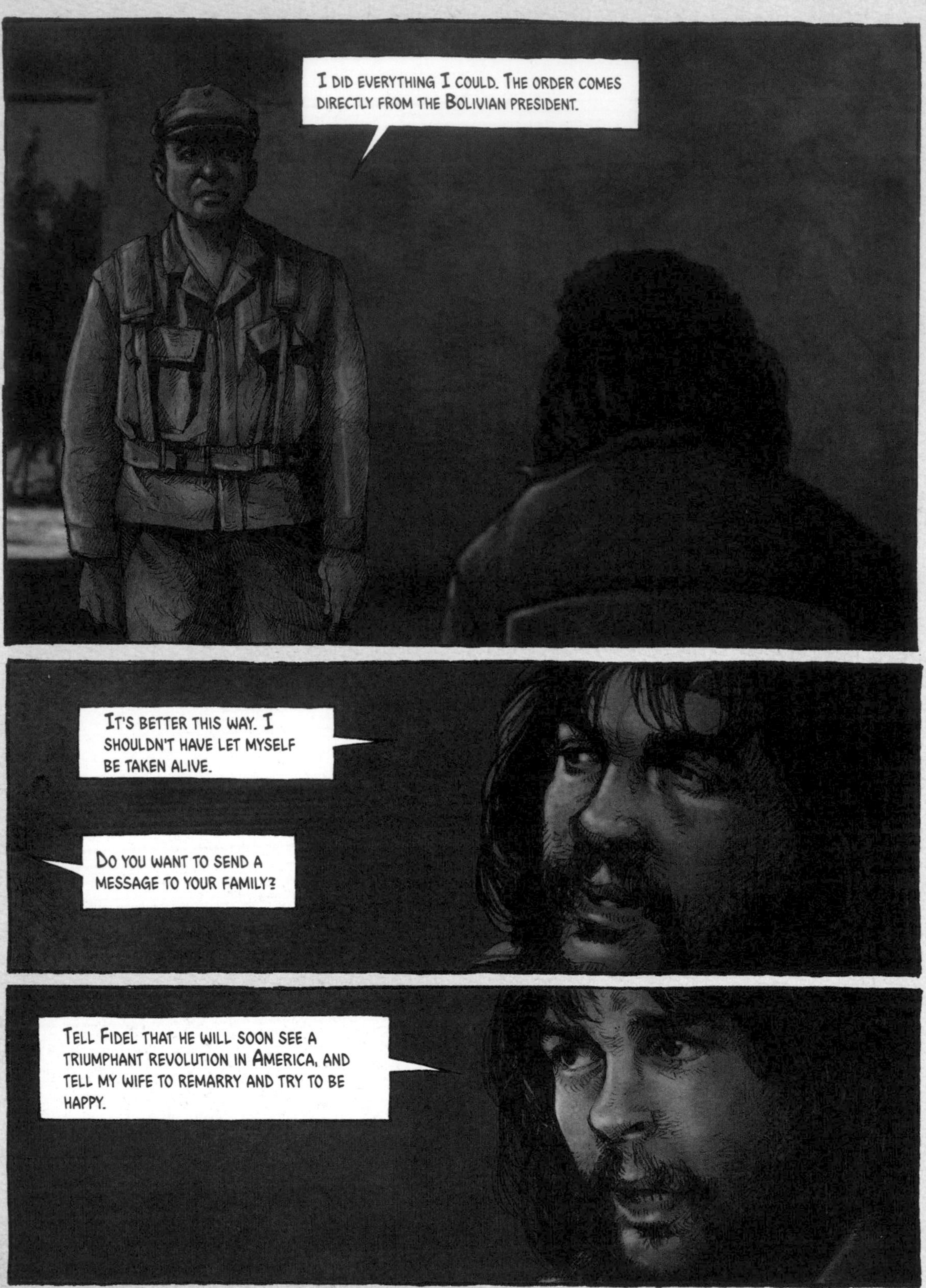
I DID EVERYTHING I COULD. THE ORDER COMES DIRECTLY FROM THE BOLIVIAN PRESIDENT.
IT'S BETTER THIS WAY. I SHOULDN'T HAVE LET MYSELF BE TAKEN ALIVE.
DO YOU WANT TO SEND A MESSAGE TO YOUR FAMILY?
TELL FIDEL THAT HE WILL SOON SEE A TRIUMPHANT REVOLUTION IN AMERICA, AND TELL MY WIFE TO REMARRY AND TRY TO BE HAPPY.

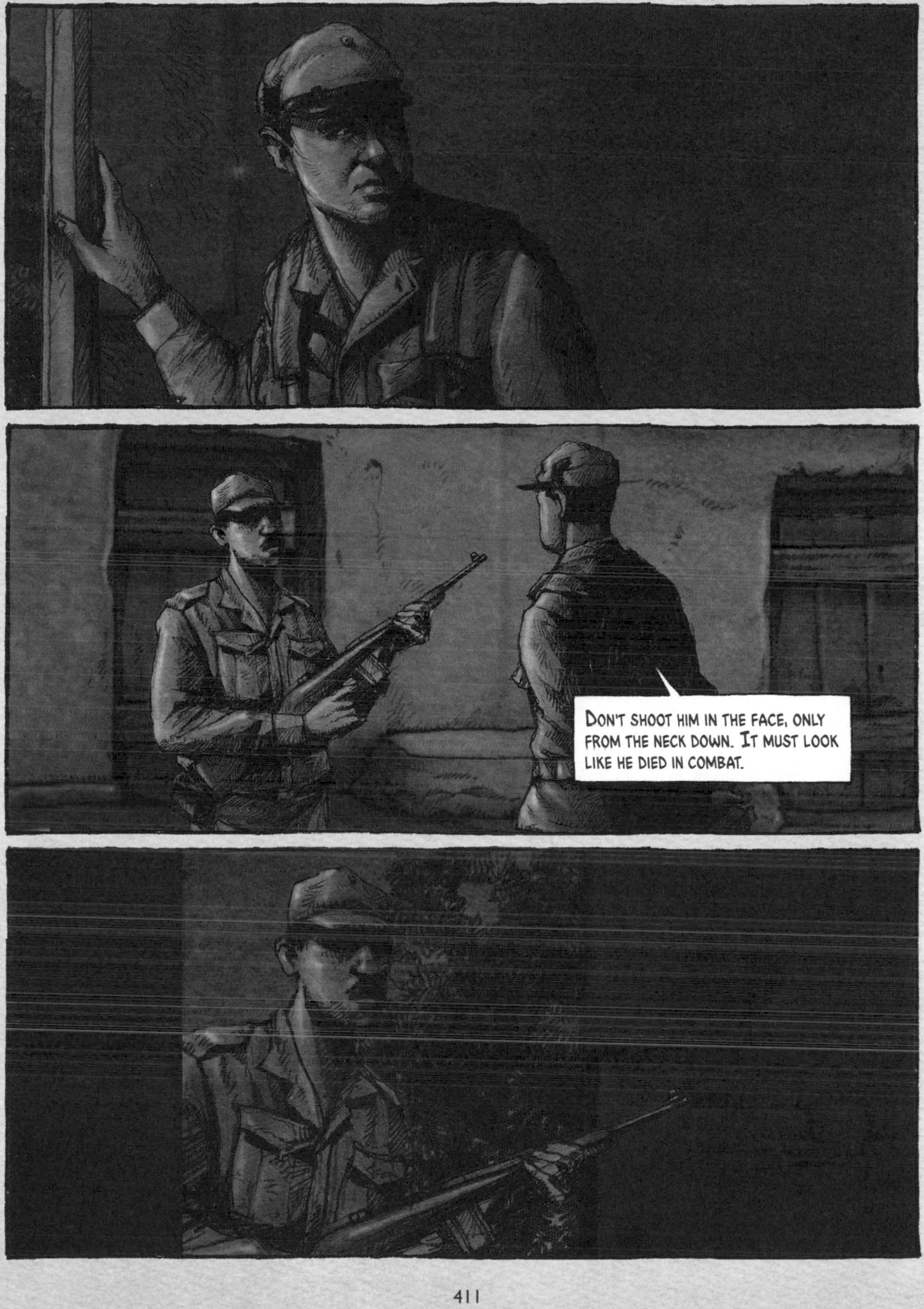
DON'T SHOOT HIM IN THE FACE, ONLY FROM THE NECK DOWN. IT MUST LOOK LIKE HE DIED IN COMBAT.

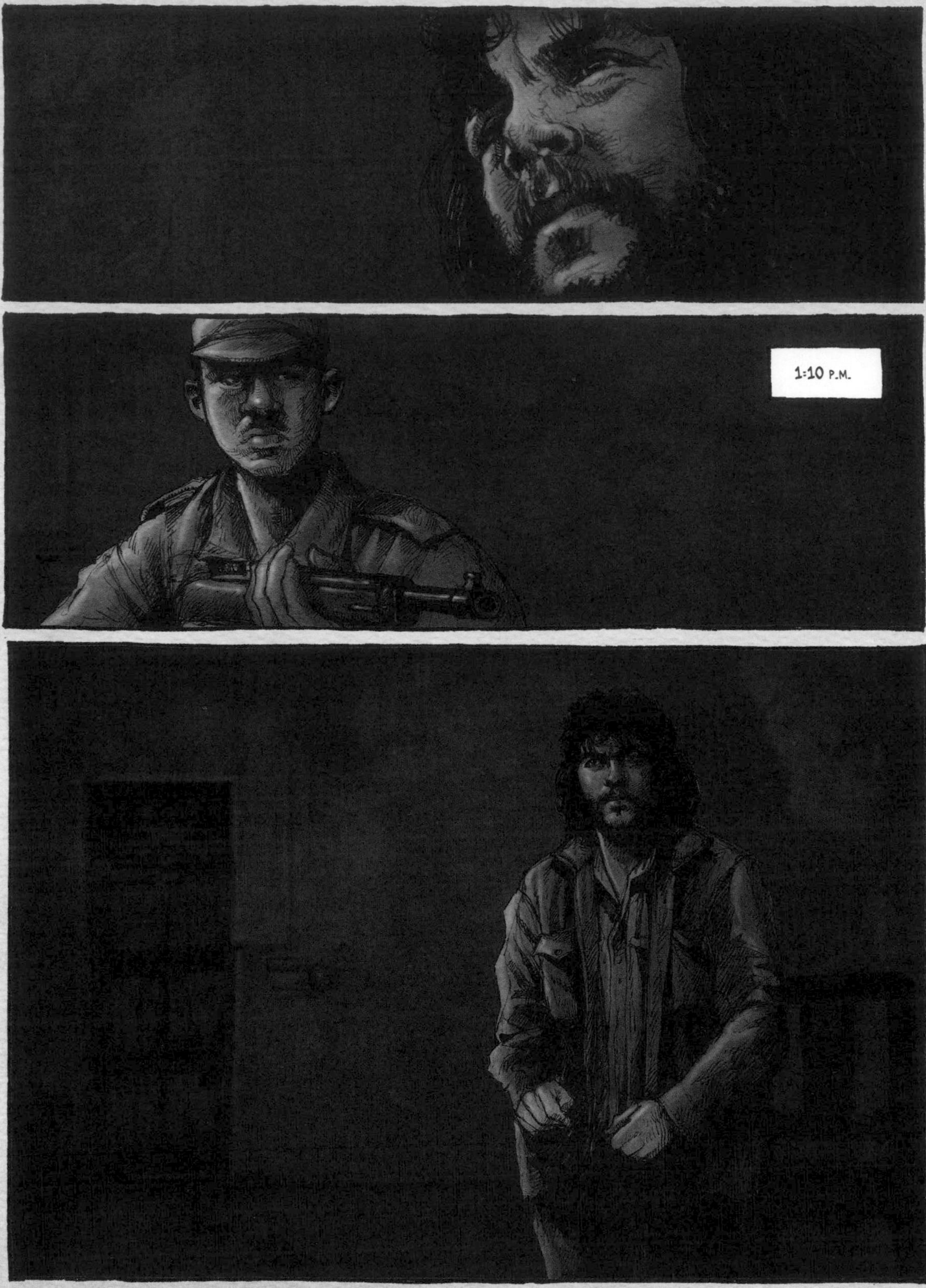
1:10 P.M.

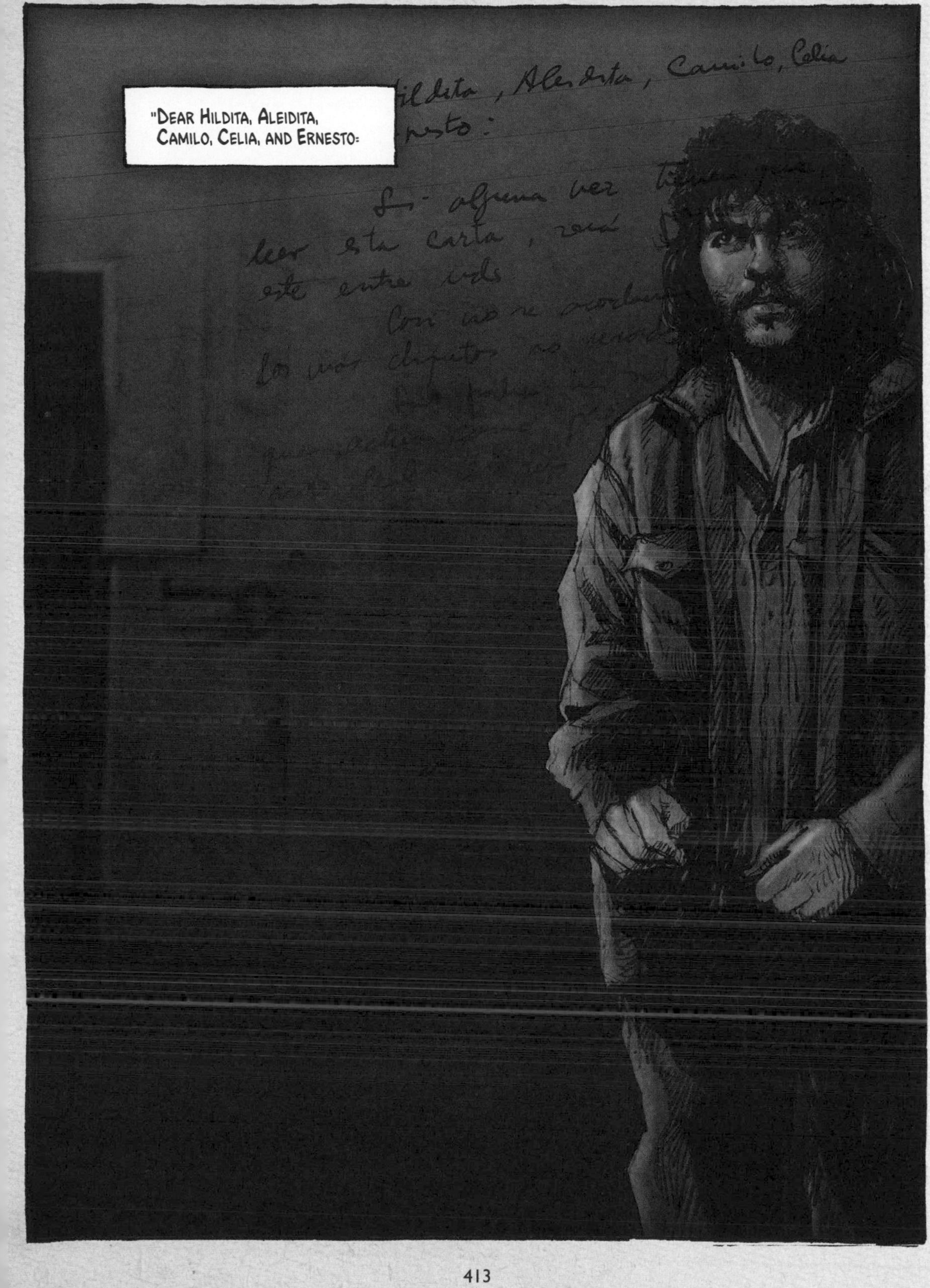
"DEAR HILDITA, ALEIDITA, CAMILO, CELIA, AND ERNESTO:

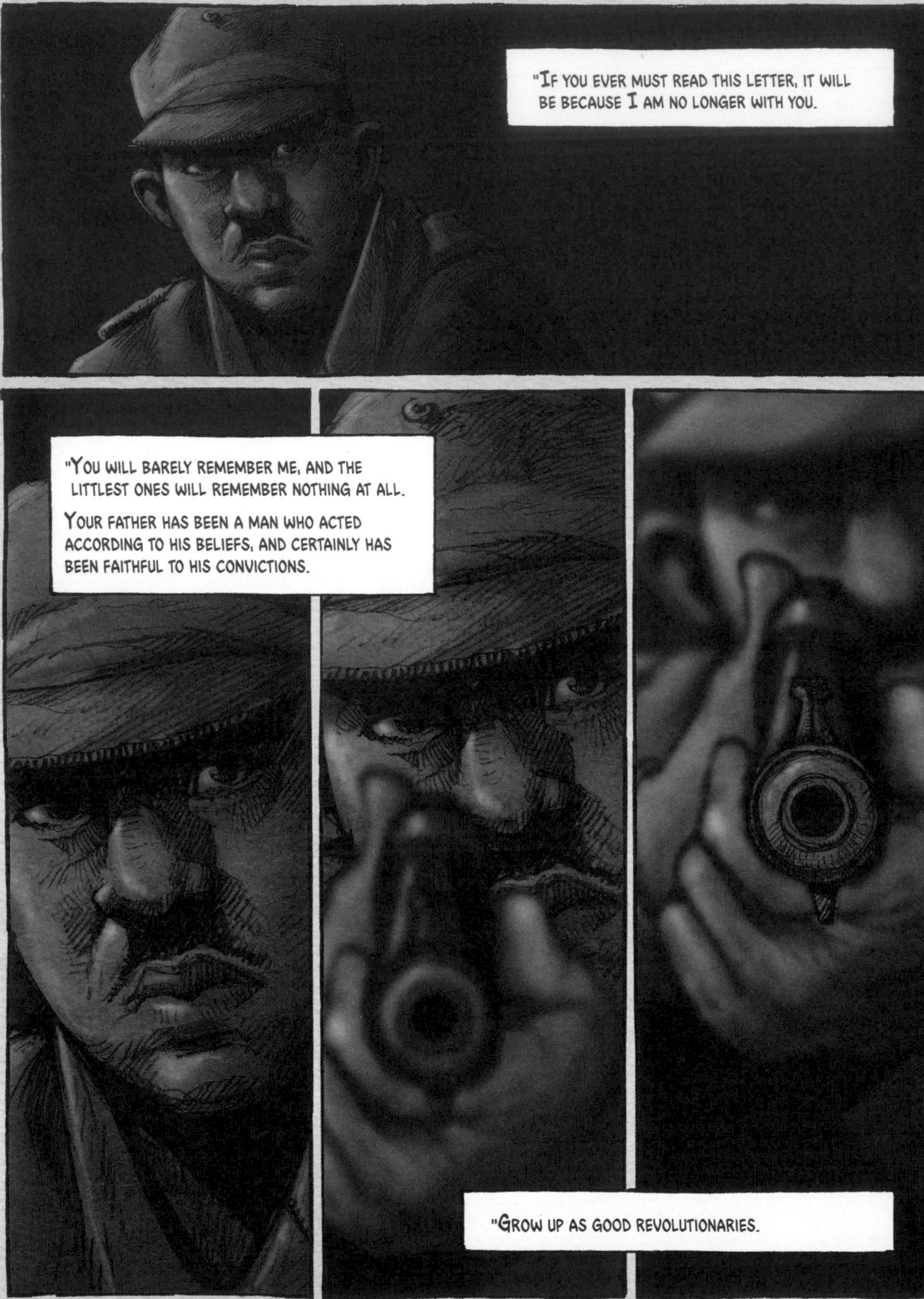
"If you ever must read this letter, it will be because I am no longer with you.
"You will barely remember me, and the littlest ones will remember nothing at all.
Your father has been a man who acted according to his beliefs, and certainly has been faithful to his convictions.
"Grow up as good revolutionaries.

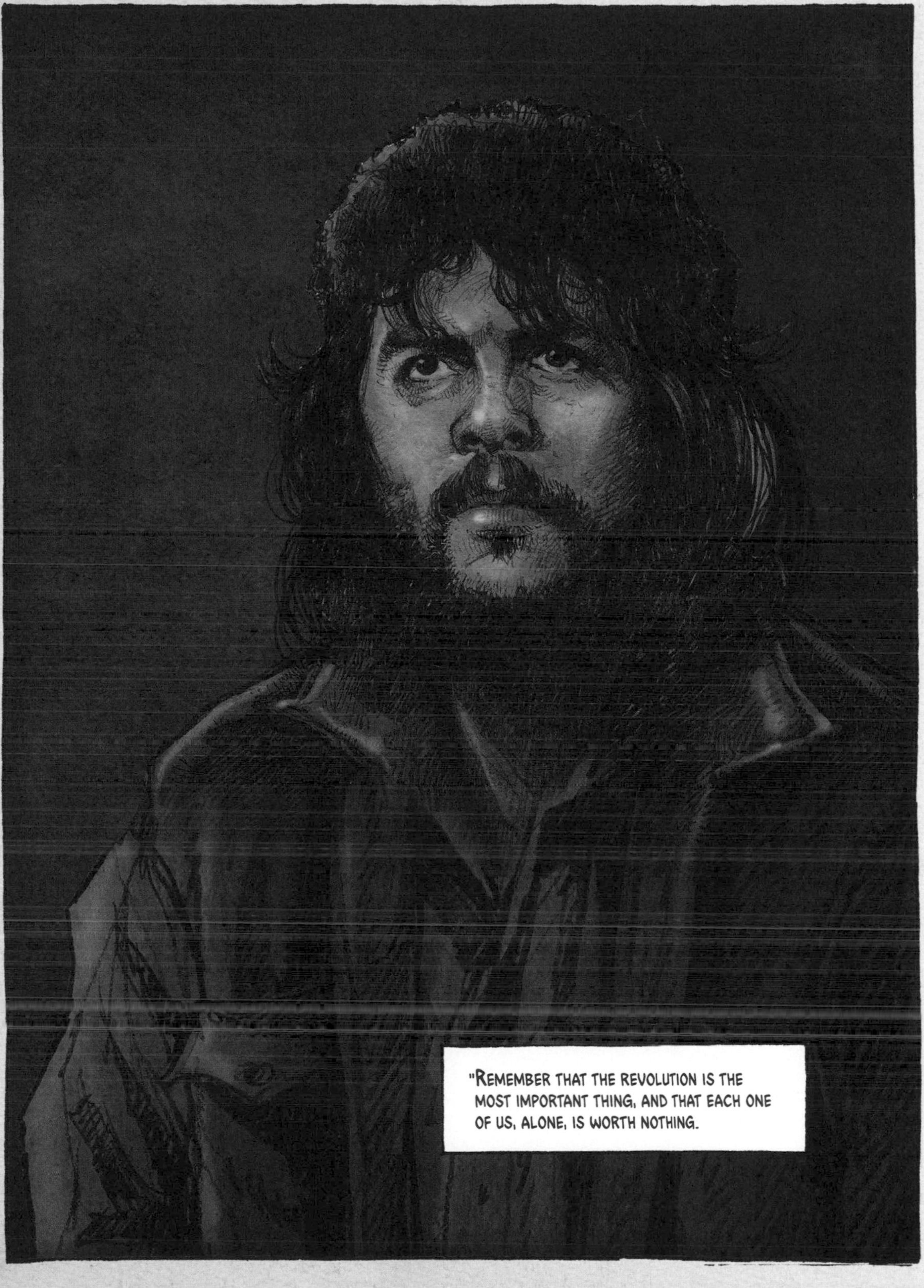
"REMEMBER THAT THE REVOLUTION IS THE MOST IMPORTANT THING, AND THAT EACH ONE OF US, ALONE, IS WORTH NOTHING.

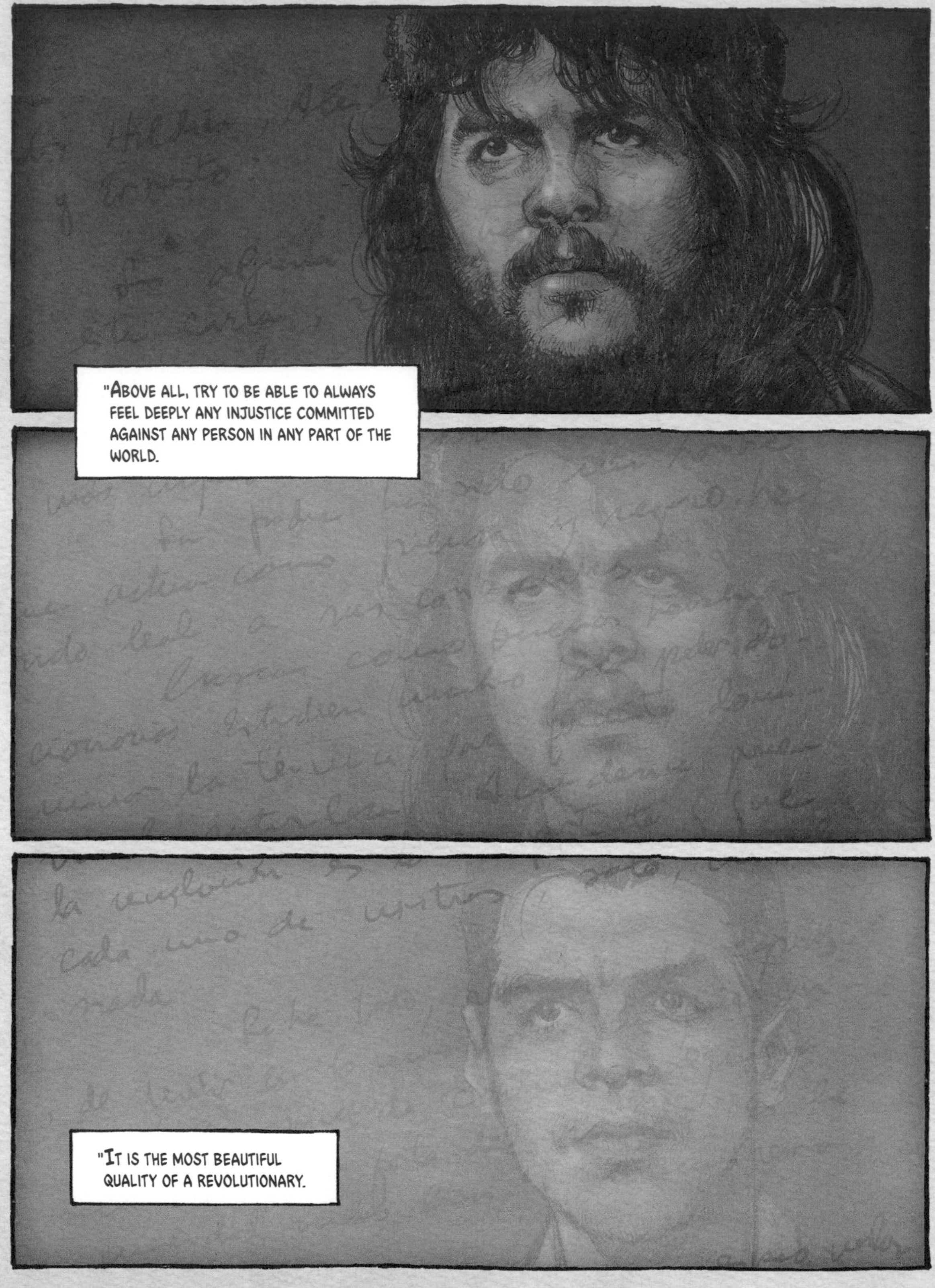
"ABOVE ALL, TRY TO BE ABLE TO ALWAYS FEEL DEEPLY ANY INJUSTICE COMMITTED AGAINST ANY PERSON IN ANY PART OF THE WORLD.
"IT IS THE MOST BEAUTIFUL QUALITY OF A REVOLUTIONARY.

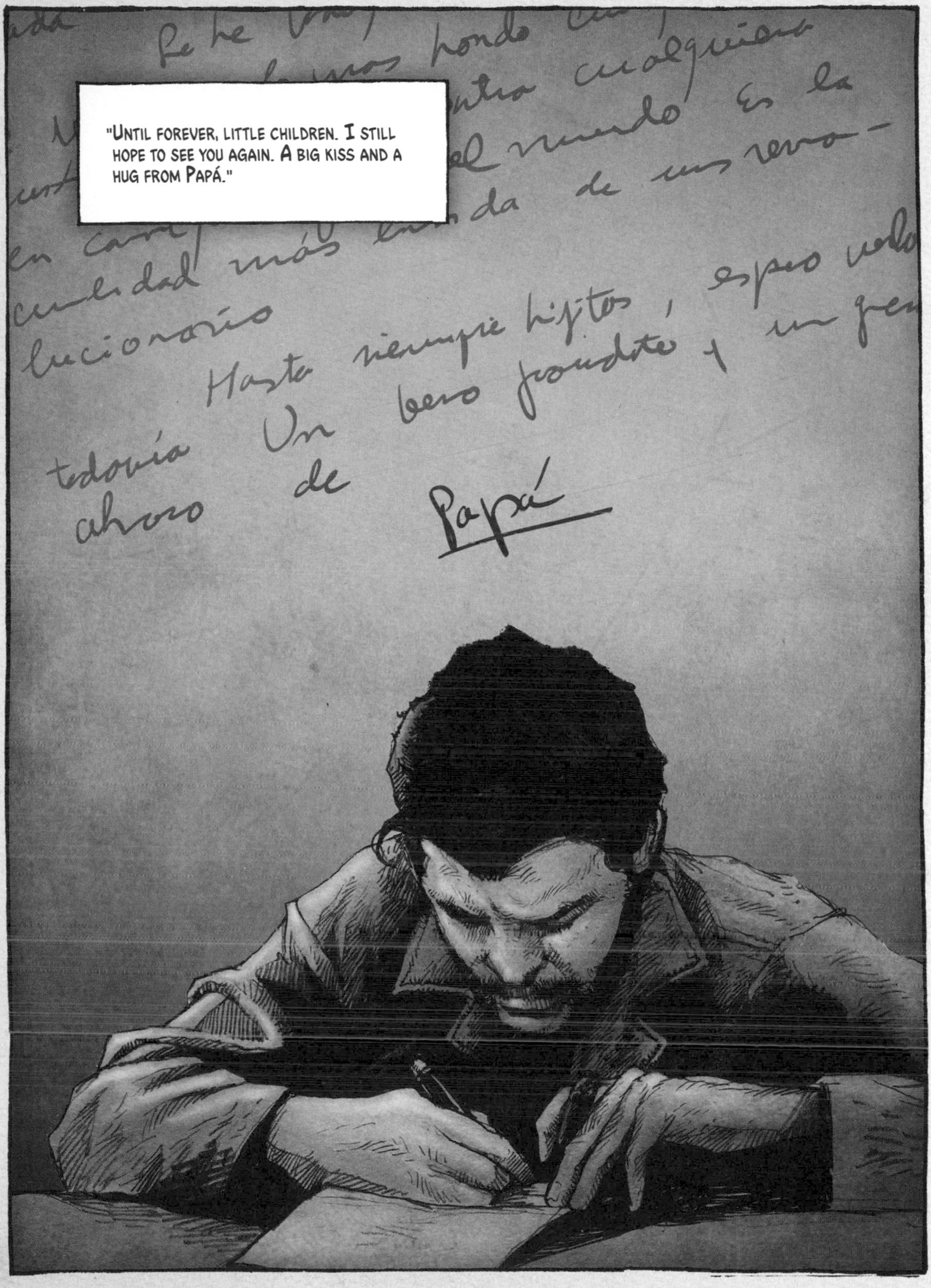
"Until forever, little children. I still hope to see you again. A big kiss and a hug from Papá."

Papá

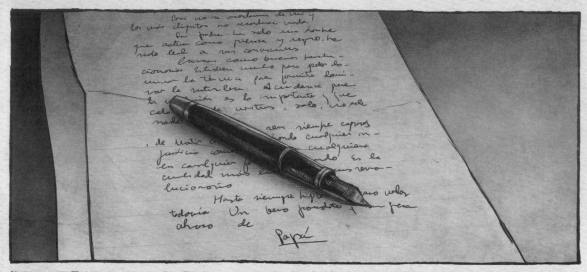

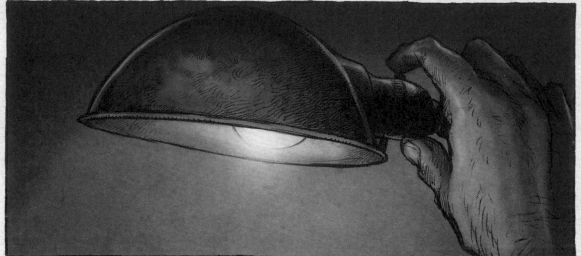

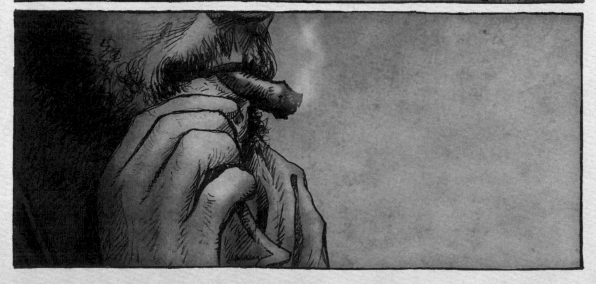

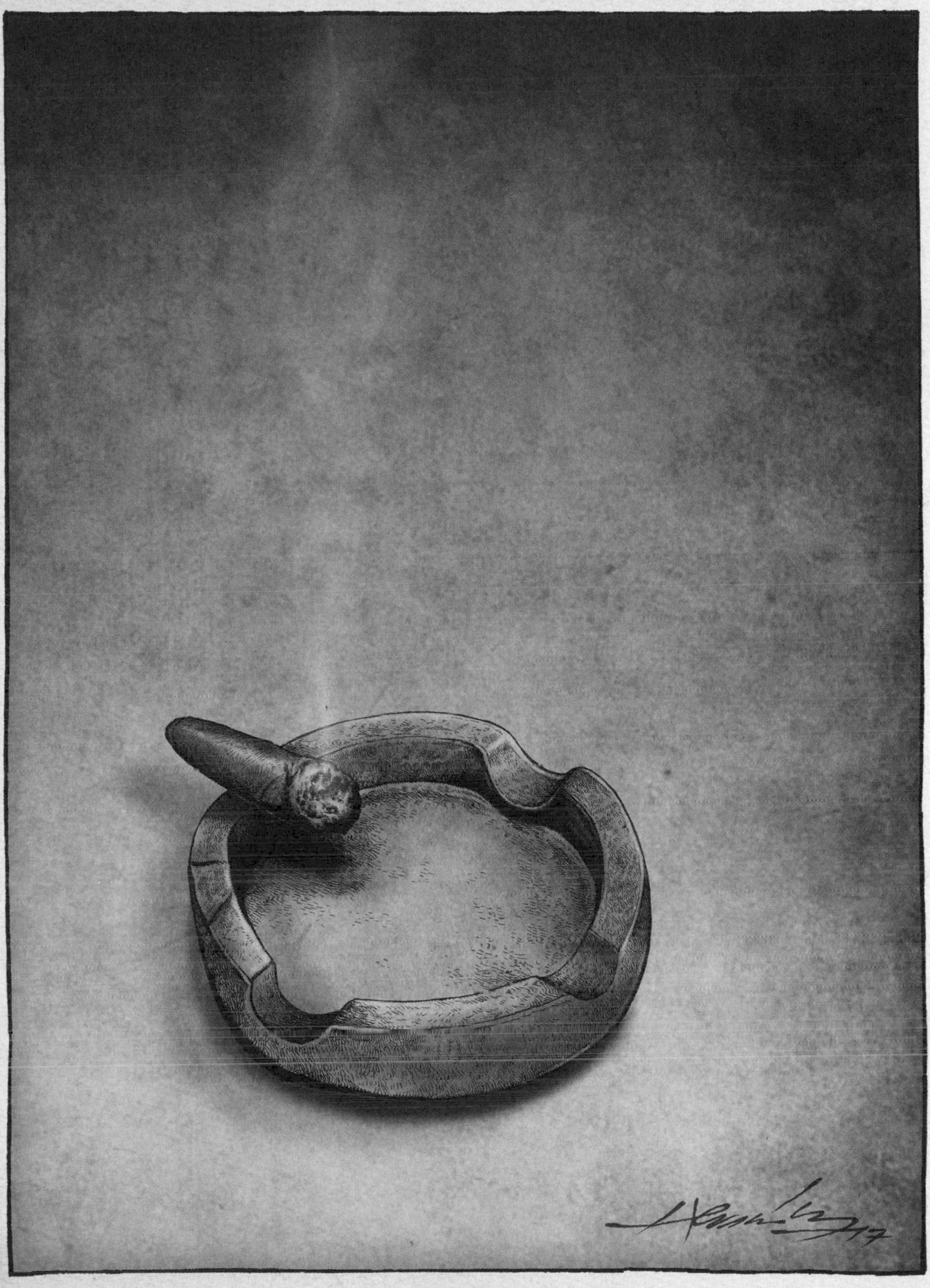

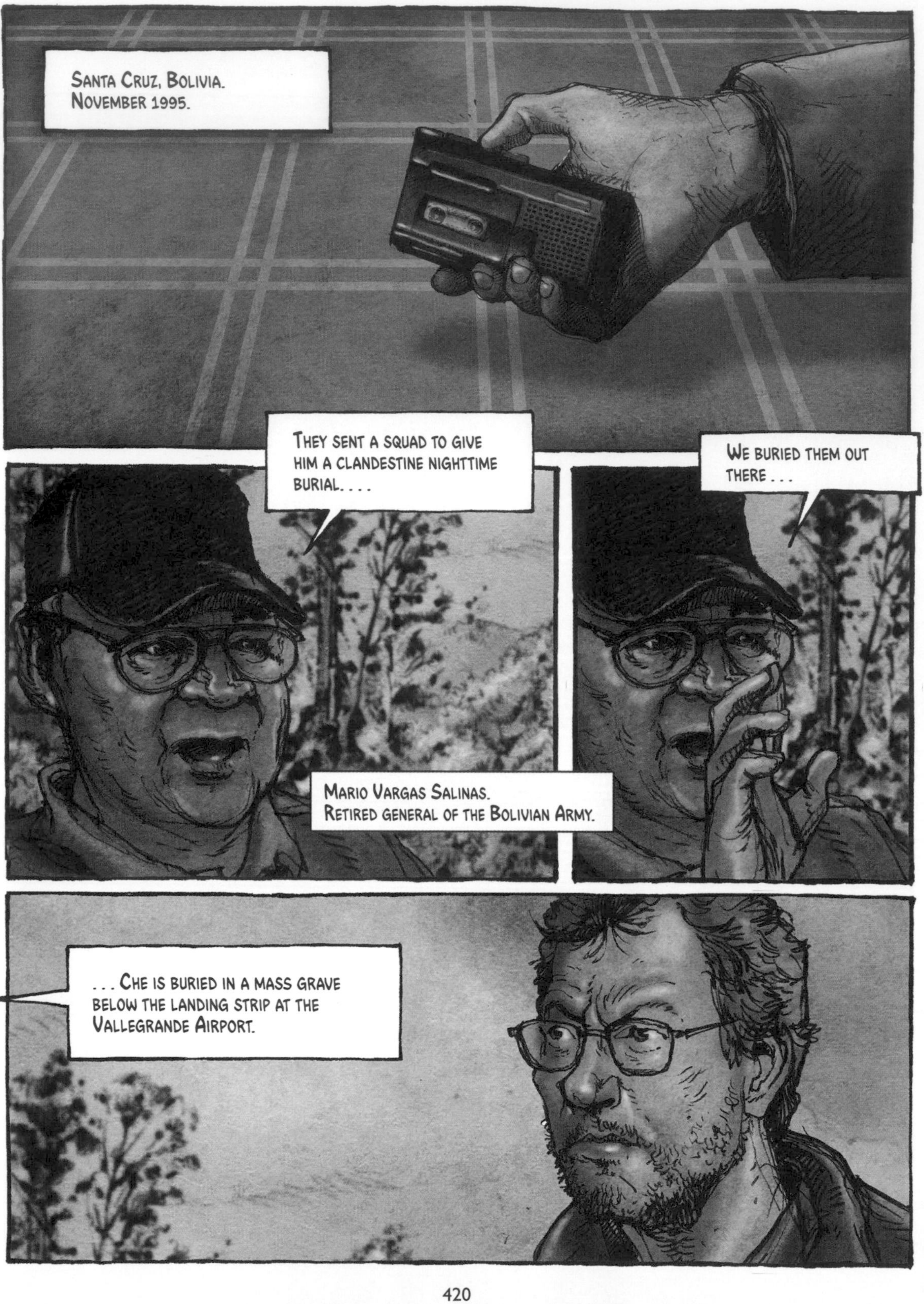
Santa Cruz, Bolivia.
November 1995.
They sent a squad to give him a clandestine nighttime burial. . . .
Mario Vargas Salinas.
Retired general of the Bolivian Army.
We buried them out there . . .
. . . Che is buried in a mass grave below the landing strip at the Vallegrande Airport.

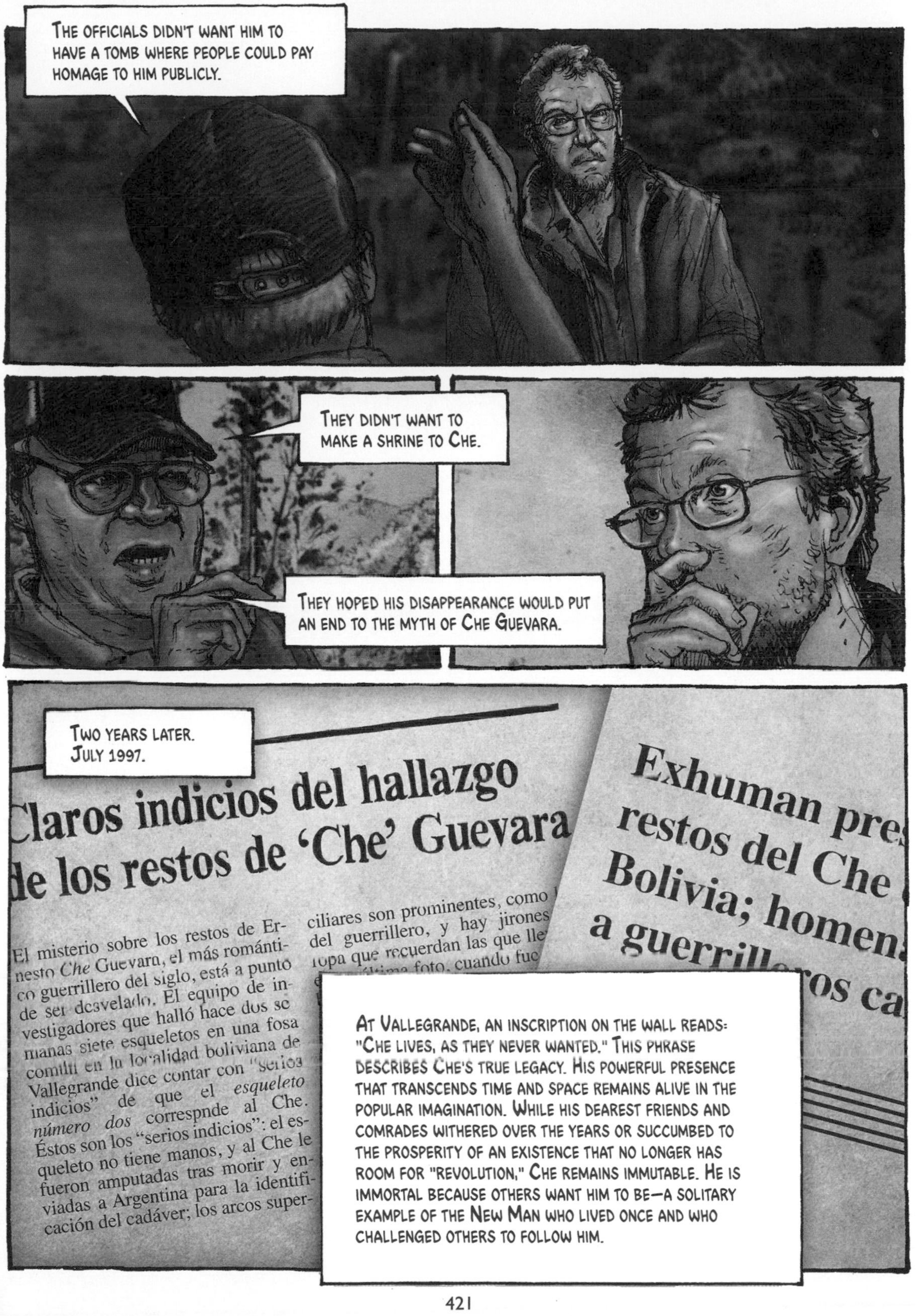
THE OFFICIALS DIDN'T WANT HIM TO HAVE A TOMB WHERE PEOPLE COULD PAY HOMAGE TO HIM PUBLICLY.
THEY DIDN'T WANT TO MAKE A SHRINE TO CHE.
THEY HOPED HIS DISAPPEARANCE WOULD PUT AN END TO THE MYTH OF CHE GUEVARA.
TWO YEARS LATER. JULY 1997.
Claros indicios del hallazgo de los restos de 'Che' Guevara
El misterio sobre los restos de Ernesto Che Guevara, el más romántico guerrillero del siglo, está a punto de ser desvelado. El equipo de investigadores que halló hace dos semanas siete esqueletos en una fosa común en la localidad boliviana de Vallegrande dice contar con "serios indicios" de que el esqueleto número dos correspnde al Che. Éstos son los "serios indicios": el esqueleto no tiene manos, y al Che le fueron amputadas tras morir y enviadas a Argentina para la identificación del cadáver; los arcos super-
ciliares son prominentes, como
del guerrillero, y hay jirones
ropa que recuerdan las que lle
Exhuman pre
restos del Che
Bolivia; homen
a guerrilleros ca
AT VALLEGRANDE, AN INSCRIPTION ON THE WALL READS: "CHE LIVES, AS THEY NEVER WANTED." THIS PHRASE DESCRIBES CHE'S TRUE LEGACY. HIS POWERFUL PRESENCE THAT TRANSCENDS TIME AND SPACE REMAINS ALIVE IN THE POPULAR IMAGINATION. WHILE HIS DEAREST FRIENDS AND COMRADES WITHERED OVER THE YEARS OR SUCCUMBED TO THE PROSPERITY OF AN EXISTENCE THAT NO LONGER HAS ROOM FOR "REVOLUTION," CHE REMAINS IMMUTABLE. HE IS IMMORTAL BECAUSE OTHERS WANT HIM TO BE—A SOLITARY EXAMPLE OF THE NEW MAN WHO LIVED ONCE AND WHO CHALLENGED OTHERS TO FOLLOW HIM.

ILLUSTRATOR'S ACKNOWLEDGMENTS

To José Jorge and Bibiana, for everything and of course.

To Alejandra García, my head editor.

To Liniers, for his help with the Argentine language.

To Ángel Boligán, for his assistance with the Cuban language.

To Julia Santibáñez, for her astute comments.

To Alma Soto, for her observations and her fantastic book trailers.

To Mom and Dad, who lived in this Mexico and, who knows, were maybe photographed by Che.